NEUROPSYCHOLOGY
FOR
PSYCHOLOGISTS,
HEALTH CARE
PROFESSIONALS,
AND
ATTORNEYS

THIRD EDITION

NEUROPSYCHOLOGY
FOR
PSYCHOLOGISTS,
HEALTH CARE
PROFESSIONALS,
AND
ATTORNEYS

THIRD EDITION

ROBERT J. SBORDONE
RONALD E. SAUL
ARNOLD D. PURISCH

CRC Press
Taylor & Francis Group
Boca Raton   London   New York

CRC Press is an imprint of the
Taylor & Francis Group, an informa business

CRC Press
Taylor & Francis Group
6000 Broken Sound Parkway NW, Suite 300
Boca Raton, FL 33487-2742

© 2007 by Taylor & Francis Group, LLC
CRC Press is an imprint of Taylor & Francis Group, an Informa business

No claim to original U.S. Government works
Printed in the United States of America on acid-free paper
10 9 8 7 6 5 4 3 2 1

International Standard Book Number-10: 0-8493-7309-3 (Hardcover)
International Standard Book Number-13: 978-0-8493-7309-1 (Hardcover)

Library of Congress Cataloging-in-Publication Data

Sbordone, Robert J.
   Neuropsychology for psychologists, health care professionals, and attorneys / Robert J. Sbordone, Ronald E. Saul, and Arnold D. Purisch. -- 3rd ed.
      p. ; cm.
   Rev. ed. of: Neuropsychology for health care professionals and attorneys. 2nd ed. c2000.
   Includes bibliographical references and index.
   ISBN-13: 978-0-8493-7309-1 (hardcover : alk. paper)
   ISBN-10: 0-8493-7309-3 (hardcover : alk. paper)
   1. Clinical neuropsychology. 2. Neuropsychological tests. I. Saul, Ronald E. II. Purisch, Arnold D. III. Sbordone, Robert J. Neuropsychology for health care professionals and attorneys. IV. Title.
   [DNLM: 1. Nervous System Diseases--psychology. 2. Neuropsychological Tests. 3. Neuropsychology. WL 140 S276n 2007]

   RC386.6.N48S266 2007
   616.8--dc22
                                      2007002709

Visit the Taylor & Francis Web site at
http://www.taylorandfrancis.com

and the CRC Press Web site at
http://www.crcpress.com

Dedication

———————

This book is dedicated to the memories of D. Frank Benson, M.D., Nelson Butters, Ph.D., and Alexander Luria, M.D., Ph.D., for their achievements in neuropsychology, which have greatly enhanced our understanding of the brain and how it affects behavior.

Contents

Chapter 13

Introduction

Neuropsychology for Psychologists, Health Care Professionals, and Attorneys, Third Edition, has been written for psychologists, physicians, nurses, rehabilitation specialists, and attorneys who have cases involving individuals with memory disorders, cerebral concussion, cerebral contusions, dementia, mild and severe brain damage, and posttraumatic stress disorder. One of the goals of this book is to provide a clear understanding of neuropsychology, its purpose, use, and historical development to individuals whose background and understanding in this area is limited.

This book covers the anatomy of the brain and a number of neurobehavioral and brain disorders in a clear and concise manner, which should be understood by virtually anyone with no prior background or knowledge of this area. It also provides the reader with a clear understanding of disorders such as postconcussion syndrome, posttraumatic stress disorder, frontal lobe disorders, executive dysfunction, mild traumatic brain damage, focal and diffuse brain damage, dementia, seizure disorders, and somatoform disorders. It also covers a number of controversial areas such as deception and malingering, scoring and interpretation of neuropsychological test data, test reliability and validity, the ecological validity of neuropsychological tests, the limitations of neuropsychological testing, and neurodiagnostic testing.

It presents a clear systematic approach to neuropsychological testing and assessment beginning with the patient's chief complaints, interviews with the patient's family and significant others, a history of the patient's symptoms, observations of the patient's behavior and mental status, and the importance of obtaining developmental, educational, family, vocational, legal, military, medical, neurological, and background psychiatric information. It carefully describes the strengths and limitations of different quantitative methods of test scoring and interpretation.

This text describes many of the neuropsychological tests that are currently used to evaluate children, adolescents, and adults with cognitive impairment. It discusses their strengths, limitations, and effectiveness in predicting whether an individual is able to live independently following brain damage, and return to work or school. It also discusses the limitations of our present neuropsychological tests in evaluating patients with specific neurobehavioral disorders.

Numerous case studies are presented throughout the book to illustrate the concepts described in this text. Six sample medicolegal neuropsychological reports are presented that have critically reviewed to demonstrate their inherent strengths and weaknesses. The book contains a glossary of neurological and neuropsychological terms, and list of the widely prescribed medications that are given to patients for a variety of psychiatric and neurological symptoms. The book also contains a summary of the strengths and limitations of neuropsychological tests that are covered in this book.

Because many psychologists, health care professionals, and attorneys frequently have difficulty in understanding many neuropsychological, medical, psychiatric, neurological, and neurobehavioral disorders and their terminology, we have made a concerted effort to present this material as clearly and concisely as possible. We have also included a glossary of neurological and neuropsychological terms to help the reader understand the terminology in this field. We list in Appendix A the various medications that are given to patients with psychological, psychiatric, and neurological disorders.

Robert J. Sbordone, Ph.D.
Ronald E. Saul, M.D.
Arnold D. Purisch, Ph.D.

Authors

Robert J. Sbordone, PhD is internationally recognized for his expertise in clinical neuropsychology, traumatic brain injuries, postconcussion syndromes, posttraumatic stress disorder, and forensic neuropsychology. After receiving his doctorate from the University of California at Los Angeles, he completed his postdoctoral training at the UCLA Neuropsychiatric and Brain Research Institutes. He has been named a diplomate in clinical neuropsychology from both the American Board of Professional Psychology and the American Board of Professional Neuropsychology. He is also a diplomate of the American Board of Assessment Psychology. He is a member of the American Academy of Clinical Neuropsychology, and a Fellow of the National Academy of Neuropsychology and the College of Professional Neuropsychology. Dr. Sbordone has served on the board of directors of the American Board of Professional Neuropsychology and as an examiner for the board. He is a member of numerous professional societies and organizations and has taught at UCLA, California State University at Los Angeles, the University of California at Irvine College of Medicine, and the Fielding Institute. He is the author of over 115 publications, which includes six textbooks and over 30 book chapters. He specializes in evaluating medicolegal cases involving traumatic brain damage, postconcussive disorder, and posttraumatic stress disorder. He has a private practice in Laguna Hills, California.

Ronald E. Saul earned his MD from the University of Pittsburgh. Following residency training in both neurology and psychiatry, he became board certified in both specialties. While serving on the teaching faculty of the University of Southern California School of Medicine, he was director of the Behavioral Neurology Program and the EEG Laboratory at Los Angeles County and Rancho Los Amigos Rehabilitation and Medical Centers. He served as neurological consultant to the Split-Brain Research Program under the direction of Nobel Laureate Roger Sperry at the California Institute of Technology.

Dr. Saul has been elected a fellow of the American Academy of Neurology and is an active member of the Behavioral Neurology Society, the American Neuropsychiatric and American Psychiatric Associations, the American EEG Society, and the Academy of Aphasia. His numerous publications include recent articles on the behavioral consequences of traumatic brain injury and frontal lobe disorders. He is presently a clinical professor of neurology at UCLA and serves as chief of neurological services at the California State Metropolitan Hospital and attending neurologist in the Alzheimer–Memory Disorders and Neuropsychiatry Clinics at UCLA Medical Center.

Arnold D. Purisch, PhD is a clinical and forensic psychologist and neuropsychologist in private practice in Laguna Hills, California, and a faculty member of the Post-Doctoral Neuropsychology Certificate Program of the Fielding Graduate University. He frequently serves as an expert witness and consultant in a wide variety of forensic matters including personal injury, workers compensation, and criminal cases, and he is a Qualified Medical Examiner in the State of California. He is a diplomate in clinical neuropsychology of the American Board of Professional Psychology and the American Board of Professional Neuropsychology. He also holds a diplomate in assessment psychology from the American Board of Assessment Psychology. He has been elected a fellow and is a past vice president of the National Academy of Neuropsychology. He has also been elected a fellow of the American Psychological Association. He is a coauthor of the Luria–Nebraska Neuropsychological Battery, one of major standardized assessment batteries in the field of clinical neuropsychology.

His breadth of interest is reflected in numerous articles and publications, which cover a wide range of topics from neuropsychological assessment methodology, psychiatric disorders, recovery of function after brain injury, rehabilitation, and medicolegal applications of neuropsychological evaluation. His current research pertains to the relationship of brain metabolism and neuropsychological functioning following traumatic brain injury. Dr. Purisch serves on the editorial boards of the *Journal of Forensic Neuropsychology*, the *Archives of Clinical Neuropsychology*, and the *Neuropsychology Review*.

Acknowledgments

We wish to express our gratitude to many health care professionals, whom we have had the privilege of working with in the past, who have taught us the importance of taking detailed clinical histories, observing the patient's behavior, administering appropriate tests, scoring, and interpreting the test data, and recognizing the limitations of the tests we administer. We also express our gratitude to the many attorneys we have worked with in the past who have provided us with an understanding of forensic issues that we never received in graduate school or during our postdoctoral training. We wish to acknowledge the assistance of Chris Benderev, who critically reviewed a number of research publications that were used in this book. We wish to acknowledge the assistance of Mary Smith and Jacki Fucinari. We also wish to acknowledge Carol White who helped to edit each chapter.

1 Clinical Neuropsychology

DEFINITION

Clinical neuropsychology is an applied science that is concerned with the relationship between the brain and behavior. It integrates the fields of clinical psychology and behavioral neurology. It utilizes specialized psychological tests that have been designed to evaluate a wide variety of behavioral, cognitive, and emotional domains that are dependent on the structural and functional integrity of the brain. It can be used to evaluate individuals suspected of having focal or diffuse brain dysfunction by identifying behavioral, cognitive, and emotional problems that require psychological treatment and cognitive rehabilitation. In addition to the patient's test data, it relies on information obtained from significant others and academic, vocational, medical, and psychiatric records to determine the patient's premorbid level of functioning. With this information, the clinical neuropsychologist tries to determine how the individual's behavioral, cognitive, social, and emotional functioning have been altered by a brain insult, particularly the individual's ability to detect and monitor environmental cues and stimuli, recognize their behavioral and cognitive deficits, communicate effectively with others, learn and retain information, perform activities at home and in the community, exercise responsible judgment, maintain relationships with others, make new friends, interact with others in social or work settings, work or maintain employment, achieve specific academic or vocational goals, operate a motor vehicle, live independently, handle finances and stress, and cope with the various demands of their family and environment.

DEFINITION OF A CLINICAL NEUROPSYCHOLOGIST

Division 40 of the American Psychological Association (APA) published a "Definition of a Neuropsychologist" in 1989 (*The Clinical Neuropsychologist*, March, 22, 1989) as a product of a Task Force in Education and Credentialing in Clinical Neuropsychology. At the time of its publication, the definition complied with all APA rules governing public statements and policies. It was adopted by the Division 40 Executive Committee after careful APA appraisal and was reviewed and accepted by the Division again in 1992 and 1996.

A Clinical Neuropsychologist is a professional psychologist who applies principles of assessment and intervention based upon the scientific study of human behavior as it relates to normal and abnormal functioning of the central nervous system. The Clinical Neuropsychologist is a doctoral-level psychology provider of diagnostic and intervention services who has demonstrated competence in the application of such principles for human welfare following:

    A. Successful completion of systematic didactic and experiential training in neuropsychology and neuroscience at a regionally accredited university;

    B. Two or more years of appropriate supervised training applying neuropsychological services in a clinical setting;

    C. Licensing and certification to provide psychological services to the public by laws or the state or province in which he or she practices;

    D. Review by one's peers as a test of these competencies.

Although this definition has stressed that attainment of a diplomate in clinical neuropsychology from the American Board of Clinical Neuropsychology *"is the clearest evidence of competence as a Clinical Neuropsychologist assuring that all of these criteria have been met,"* it has created a great deal of controversy since it makes no mention of a diplomate from the American Board of Professional Neuropsychology. We encourage the reader to review the specific requirements to obtain a diplomate from these boards, which can be found in Chapter 2.

Those interested in the required education and training in clinical neuropsychology, or in consulting an existing definition of a clinical neuropsychologist and description of the practice of clinical neuropsychology, should consult the following sources:

Policy Statement, Houston Conference on Specialty Education and Training in Clinical Neuropsychology (1998) http://www.div40org/pub/Houston_conference.pdf

National Academy of Neuropsychology "Definition of a Neuropsychologist" (2001) http://www.nanonline.org/downloads/paio/Position/NANPositionDef Neuro.pdf

THE PRACTICE OF NEUROPSYCHOLOGY

The practice of neuropsychology can be broken down into five major areas: assessment/diagnosis, treatment/rehabilitation, teaching, consultation, and research.

ASSESSMENT

ASSESSMENT AND DIAGNOSIS

Patients are frequently referred for neuropsychological assessment following a suspected or actual brain insult to determine whether their test scores show evidence of cognitive, behavioral, and emotional problems stemming from a brain injury or insult; the degree of functional overlay of the patient's complaints; the likelihood that this patient's impairments will improve with time and treatment, or have plateaued; the patient's treatment and rehabilitation needs; the likelihood of whether the patient is capable of working, attending school, operating a motor vehicle, living independently, managing his/her finances, exercising proper judgment, and functioning effectively at home, work, and in the community.

Assessment of Brain Damage and the Patient's Behavioral, Cognitive, and Emotional Problems

While computed tomography (CT) and magnetic resonance imaging (MRI) scans and neuropsychological tests are both capable of identifying the presence of brain damage, neuropsychological tests are often superior in identifying brain damage or dysfunction when it is often not detected by CT or MRI scans (e.g., mild traumatic brain damage, memory and executive dysfunction, frontal lobe syndromes, etc.). While neuropsychological tests were designed to assess a patient's behavioral, cognitive, and emotional functioning, CT and MRI scans were never designed to identify or assess these functions. Thus, the neuropsychologist, because of his or her expertise, training, and background, is perhaps the most qualified professional to provide a comprehensive assessment of the cognitive, behavioral, and emotional problems caused by brain injury or dysfunction.

Determination of Cognitive and Behavioral Alterations Caused by Brain Insults

Neuropsychological assessment examines the patient's intellectual functioning, language-processing skills, perceptual skills, higher motor functions, attention and concentration skills, judgment, reasoning, mental flexibility, learning and memory, constructional skills, abstract thinking and conceptualization skills, problem-solving skills, behavioral regulation, executive functions, and emotional functioning. Since the brain is the organ of behavior, an insult to its structural or functional integrity can alter an individual's functioning in one or more of these areas. Thus, the neuro-psychologist's task is to carefully evaluate a patient's functioning in these areas to determine if any significant alterations have occurred and whether such alterations have been caused by a brain insult or are due to nonneurological (e.g., psychological) factors. The neuropsychologist, by virtue of his or her specialized training and expertise, can determine in each of these areas whether a patient is impaired and the severity of these impairments. The neuropsychologist can provide a detailed report of findings to the referral source and offer testimony in medicolegal cases about the causal relationship between a particular brain insult and its effect on the patient's cognitive, behavioral, and emotional functioning. The following case illustrates this.

Case Example

A 27-year-old school teacher was involved in a motor vehicle accident, which was the fault of the other party. He struck his head on the steering wheel and was briefly rendered uncon-scious. When the paramedics arrived, he was awake, but appeared irritable and mildly confused. He was taken to the emergency room of a nearby hospital, where x-rays of his skull were found to be negative. As a consequence, he was discharged later that same day. He stayed out of work for 1 week because of severe aches and pains in his upper back and neck, for which he was prescribed pain medications and muscle relaxants. After returning to his teaching responsibili-ties, his students and fellow teachers noticed a dramatic change in his personality. For example, while he had always been an easygoing and calm individual, he had become impatient, exhib-ited poor frustration tolerance to relatively mild stressors, and began using foul language in his classroom, which upset his students. His students also observed that he often appeared confused and frequently repeated the same material with little or no awareness of doing so. He would often forget his lesson plans or fail to collect his students' homework. On several occasions, he arrived nearly 2 h late at school, appearing unshaven, with poor personal grooming and hygiene. When he was confronted by his principal about these problems, he denied having them or that he had been acting strangely.

Although his principal referred him to a psychiatrist, he failed to keep this appointment. When he was later taken by his wife to see a psychiatrist, his wife informed the psychiatrist that her husband had become irritable, forgetful, and had exhibited poor judgment and inappropriate behavior since his accident. She also pointed out that he was no longer the calm and intelligent man she had once married. She also mentioned that during the past week, her husband had walked outside to fetch the newspaper without wearing any clothes. She pointed out that while he did not appear to be the slightest bit upset or embarrassed by this incident, it embarrassed several of their neighbors who witnessed it.

The psychiatric examination revealed no family history of psychiatric or emotional prob-lems. The patient did not appear depressed and exhibited no clear evidence of psychiatric illness during the psychiatric examination. As a consequence, the psychiatrist diagnosed the patient as having a probable adjustment disorder with features of depression and placed him on anti-depressant medication. This medication had little or no effect on his cognitive or behavioral problems.

Because his wife and principal saw no change in his behavior problems, he was referred to a neurologist whose examination included an electroencephalogram (EEG) study and a CT scan of his brain. Because his neurological examination and neurodiagnostic studies were all within normal limits, he was referred for psychological testing. The psychologist who examined him administered the Wechsler Adult Intelligence Scale–Revised and found that he had a full scale

IQ of 124, which placed him in the superior range of intellectual functioning. The psychologist also administered the Bender–Gestalt Test, which revealed no evidence of "organicity." The patient was also administered the Minnesota Multiphasic Personality Inventory (MMPI), which revealed no evidence of psychopathology.

While the patient continued working as a school teacher, his continued use of foul language within the classroom enraged the parents of his students, who demanded that he resign or be terminated. The principal, bowing to the pressure of the parents, was forced to place the teacher on medical leave. He was later referred to a second neurologist, whose examination of this patient was normal. The neurologist, however, decided to refer this patient for neuropsychological assessment.

Neuropsychological assessment revealed that the patient's judgment, reasoning, problem-solving skills, cognitive flexibility, and memory were impaired. On the basis of an interview with the patient's wife, the neuropsychologist also learned that the patient demonstrated a marked inability to regulate his emotions and behavior. He concluded, on the basis of his clinical interview of the patient, conversations with the patient's wife and significant others, review of the patient's medical and academic records, observations of the patient's behavior, and the patient's neuropsychological test performance, that the patient most likely sustained an injury to his frontal lobes during his motor vehicle accident. As a consequence, he recommended that the patient be placed on medical disability.

PSYCHOLOGICAL TREATMENT/COGNITIVE REHABILITATION

During the last 20 years there has been a growing realization that the emotional and behavioral problems that accompany brain insults are more disabling than the cognitive problems that are produced (Lezak, 1987; Sbordone, 1990). For example, patients who sustain severe traumatic brain injuries often exhibit significant emotional and personality changes including euphoria or apathy, emotional lability, irritability, changes in libido, poor frustration tolerance, impatience, rapid mood swings, impaired social judgment and planning skills, diminished self-control, impulsivity, poor self-evaluation skills, pathological egocentricity and dependency, diminished initiative and motivation, and an inability to regulate their own behavior and emotions. These symptoms typically alienate family members and friends, and create significant interpersonal difficulties such as loss of friends, marital difficulties, and divorce.

Families are frequently under severe psychological stress as a result of coping with the altered cognitive, behavioral, and emotional functioning of a brain-injured family member. Unfortunately, many family members cope with these problems by exhibiting what has been described as a "command performance syndrome" (Sbordone et al., 1984), that is, trying to appear relatively "normal" and denying or concealing their emotional difficulties, which often creates the fallacious impression that they are coping well and are not in need of psychological or psychiatric treatment. As a consequence, many family members require psychological or psychiatric intervention, which is illustrated in the following case.

Case Example

A 16-year-old male was involved in a motor vehicle accident while riding as an unbelted passenger. He was rendered comatose at the scene of the accident. When he was seen in the emergency room, he was noted on CT scan to have an epidural hematoma. He remained comatose for 2 weeks after the epidural hematoma was surgically evacuated. After he returned home, he began using crude and coarse language and began acting inappropriately (e.g., fondling his mother's breasts), which horrified his family. Although his family knew that he had sustained a severe brain injury, they did not understand its behavioral consequences (which had never been explained to them). As a consequence, they tried disciplining him or ignoring his inappropriate behavior, both of which created a great deal of tension in the family. His inappropriate behavior alienated his siblings and friends and caused his parents considerable grief. For example, on one occasion he began masturbating while watching television in the living room in the presence of other family members. Because of their strong religious values, they were very disturbed by their son's behavior and decided to take him to a psychiatrist.

After the psychiatrist had examined their son, he asked them how they were handling their son's difficulties. They indicated that they were both doing well and did not require any psychiatric treatment. The psychiatrist also interviewed the patient's 18-year-old sister, who informed him that her parents had become very depressed about their failure to control their son's behavior and felt helpless and inadequate. Although the parents were initially resistant to any suggestions that they receive any counseling or psychiatric treatment, they discovered that such treatment was actually quite helpful in allowing them to vent their feelings of anger and frustration. As a consequence, they decided to place their son into a brain injury rehabilitation program that specialized in treating brain-injured patients with inappropriate and acting-out behaviors. Their son's disruptive and inappropriate behavior diminished considerably after spending 6 months in this program.

Types of Psychological Treatment

Placing a severely brain-injured patient in a highly structured environment and implementing a strict daily routine frequently will significantly reduce a patient's mental confusion and anxiety (Howard, 1988). As the patient's cognitive functioning improves, cognitive rehabilitation by either a speech pathologist or a neuropsychologist will maximize the patient's ability to function more effectively in his or her environment. Behavior modification techniques have also been utilized with patients who have sustained severe brain injuries. This approach, particularly when used during the post-acute stages of recovery, can reduce the frequency and severity of disruptive social behaviors and significantly improve a patient's motivation and socialization skills. Individual psychotherapy for patients who have sustained severe brain insults may be ineffective or even inappropriate if the patient's self-awareness, memory difficulties, and conceptual and problem-solving abilities are significantly impaired. Psychotherapy appears more appropriate for patients who have sustained a relatively mild brain injury since they often receive benefit from such treatment.

Family therapy is important, particularly if the family has serious misconceptions about a brain injury or if the members are in denial. The patient's neurobehavioral problems can create serious emotional difficulties, particularly feelings of anger and frustration toward the patient and the health care professionals who are treating the patient. Because of their feelings of helplessness, the family may set unrealistic goals for the patient that frequently result in failure and may precipitate serious emotional problems (depression). The importance of providing psychological treatment or counseling to family members of patients who have sustained a severe brain injury has been stressed by Lezak (1978) and is illustrated in the following case.

Case Example

The patient, a 19-year-old right-handed male, sustained a severe traumatic brain injury 3 years earlier when his best friend received a new motorcycle for his birthday and asked him to go for a ride. His friend lost control of the motorcycle, causing it to flip over and land in a ravine. While his friend sustained relatively minor injuries, the patient sustained massive brain damage. Before this accident, the patient had been named valedictorian of his high school class, and had been awarded a full academic scholarship to attend Harvard. His older brother had also been an excellent student in high school and was attending Yale, where he was on the Dean's List. His 12-year-old brother, who was in junior high school was also an excellent student. The patient's mother was a high school principal, while his father was an Air Force career officer and pilot.

When the patient was seen 1-year postinjury for neuropsychological assessment, he exhibited severe cognitive impairment, particularly on tasks involving recent memory; for example, he could not recall what he had done earlier that morning. One year later, the neuropsychologist who previously examined him received a frantic phone call from the patient's mother, requesting psychological help for her oldest son who had dropped out of Yale and had recently been arrested for public intoxication. She also indicated that her youngest son had recently been expelled from school for excessive absences and that she had been asked to resign from her job. The neuropsychologist also learned that the patient's father had recently received a poor performance evaluation and was being pressured to resign his commission.

The neuropsychologist held a meeting with the patient's family which lasted most of the day. During this meeting, each of these individuals blamed themselves for the patient's injury and expressed the need to be harshly punished. As a consequence, they had behaved in a self-defeating manner over the past year and had even given serious thought to committing suicide. The family was subsequently seen on a weekly basis for approximately 1 year. During this period, they began to express considerable animosity toward the patient for having done such a "stupid thing," but admitted that they had previously turned their anger toward themselves because of their pity and sorrow for the patient's condition. As a result of this treatment intervention, the older brother began attending a nearby university, while the younger brother started attending classes on a regular basis and was making good grades. The patient's mother decided to enter the field of rehabilitation so that she could help her son and other children who had sustained brain damage. The patient's father managed to salvage his Air Force career. While the patient continued to live at home, his family no longer felt guilty for his brain injury and accepted his cognitive and behavioral impairments.

TEACHING

Many neuropsychologists hold faculty or clinical teaching appointments at universities or medical schools. As a consequence, they are frequently asked to provide lectures on the neurobehavioral consequences of brain disorders or trauma, neuropsychological assessment, and brain–behavior relationships to medical and graduate students and residents in psychiatry, physical medicine and rehabilitation, neurology, and neurosurgery. Neuropsychologists in these settings are usually abreast of the professional literature and latest developments in their field.

CONSULTATION WITH OTHER PROFESSIONALS

Neuropsychologists are frequently referred patients from physicians, attorneys, insurance carriers, the court, rehabilitation nurses, and other professionals. When this occurs a neuropsychologist is often asked to serve as a consultant to the referral source, which often requires the neuropsychologist to address specific referral questions. For example, a physician may ask the neuropsychologist to "rule out" dementia and cognitive or memory impairments. The neuropsychologist may also be asked to assess the patient's intellectual and cognitive functioning in order to determine whether the patient can return to work, school, or previous household responsibilities. In other cases, the patient may be referred following a neurosurgical procedure (e.g., placement of ventriculoperitoneal shunt) to determine what specific changes have occurred in the patient's functioning as a result of the surgical procedure. The effect of specific medications on a patient's cognitive functioning may be assessed by the neuropsychologist to provide feedback to the treating physician as to how these medications may hinder the patient's ability to function in the workplace or at school.

Referrals from attorneys are typically concerned with the issues of damages and disability (or the absence thereof). The determination of causation, prognosis, the ability of the patient to return to work or school, and the need for any future psychological care or rehabilitation are some of the questions asked of neuropsychologists by the attorneys. In many instances, the neuropsychologist will be asked to review the records of another neuropsychologist to determine if he or she agrees with the opinions or conclusions reached by this individual, while in other cases the neuropsychologist may serve as a consultant and assist in coordinating the patient's treatment and rehabilitation.

The neuropsychologist may serve as an educator/consultant to attorneys who have had minimal experience with brain injury. The role of the neuropsychologist in these cases is typically one of educating the attorney about brain injury and its manifestations, particularly its effect on the patient's life, ability to work and live independently, function in society and lead a rewarding life, and maintain relationships with others. The neuropsychologist may also educate the attorney as to the proper type of medical expert or treatment a patient requires, and the types of behavioral and emotional problems his or her client will most likely have in the future. The neuropsychologist, while serving as an expert witness, can also educate jurors or the trier of fact about the cognitive, behavioral, and emotional consequences of a brain injury, particularly their effects on the patient's ability to engage in competitive employment, return to school, live independently, handle finances, operate a motor vehicle, make responsible decisions, and exercise good judgment.

The neuropsychologist may also serve as a consultant to a number of community agencies that specialize in treating patients with neurological disorders, brain injuries, or developmental disabilities. In this capacity, the neuropsychologist may be asked to provide in-service seminars to the treatment staff as well as to directly consult with the staff on various treatment and rehabilitation issues.

RESEARCH

Many neuropsychologists are actively involved in research studies within their field of expertise or interest. Since neuropsychological tests have often been used to study brain–behavior relationships, they are frequently employed to investigate the particular cognitive and behavioral manifestations of specific brain disorders, learning disabilities, neurological disorders, psychiatric illness, and many medical illnesses. The precision and quantitative nature of many of the commonly used neuropsychological test instruments make them useful for research since many subtle and often clinically unrecognizable changes in the patient's cognitive functioning may be identified by neuropsychological tests. As a consequence, neuropsychologists have significantly contributed to our understanding of the brain's role as the organ of behavior.

HISTORICAL DEVELOPMENT OF CLINICAL NEUROPSYCHOLOGY

Man's interest in the relationship between the brain and behavior extends back at least 2500 years, when Pythagoras argued that the brain was the site of human reasoning. Approximately 100 years later, Hippocrates claimed that the brain was the organ of the intellect and recognized that a depressed skull fracture on the right side of the head could produce motor paralysis on the (contralateral) left side of the body. Galen, in approximately 170 A.D., was able to map out many of the major brain structures and argued that the frontal lobes were the seat of our mental abilities. Galen's hypothesis, however, was later discarded in favor of the belief that reasoning and intelligence were a product of the ventricles of the brain (areas that contain and manufacture the cerebrospinal fluid that cover the brain and spinal cord).

It was not until 15 centuries later that Galen's views of the relationship between the cortex and intelligence were taken seriously, when Vesalius reported an anatomical relationship between the brain and intellectual functioning. He argued that humans are more intelligent than animals, because humans have larger brains.

It was not until the nineteenth century that our present views on brain–behavior relationships began to take form. For example, France Gall, a French neuroanatomist, formulated a theory of phrenology that postulated that each area of the brain was responsible for a specific function or ability. He postulated a phrenological map of the brain, which identified each of these areas. He claimed that a person's character could be determined by examining the skull. However, Gall's views, which at one time were quite popular, were eventually discarded (Boring, 1950). Paul Broca, a neurologist, postulated that the area of the brain responsible for motor (expressive) speech was located in the left posterior frontal lobe. Broca based this on approximately ten patients who had suffered a loss of speech (expressive aphasia) and were found, on postmortem inspection, to have lesions in this region. Approximately 10 years later, another neurologist, Wernicke, found that damage to the posterior portion of the superior temporal lobe produced another type of disturbance in language processing. The patients could speak fluently, but could not understand what was being said. This was described as a receptive aphasia.

During this period of time, Fritsch and Hitzig reported that the posterior region of the frontal lobes controlled the movement of the various muscles located throughout the entire body and that the most anterior (toward the front of the head) portion of the parietal lobes contained the major area of the brain responsible for sensation throughout the entire body. Specific areas of frontal cortex were identified as controlling the behavior of specific muscle groups. Thus, the functions of specific brain regions began to be delineated and the expected effects of injury to specific parts of the brain became more gradually understood (Walsh, 1978).

During the nineteenth century, another school of neurologic thought regarding brain–behavior relationships developed. This school argued that specific behaviors were not entirely controlled by specific parts of the brain, but were, in fact, controlled by the entire brain. The proponents also asserted that loss of a particular behavior or function was determined by the extent or amount of brain damage, not by the location of the specific area damaged. They argued that the entire brain was "equipotential," that is, if one part of the brain is damaged, the remaining brain tissue will take over its functioning. The debate between the conflicting views of the "localiza-tionists" who argued that specific behaviors are controlled by specific parts of the brain and the "equipotentialists" resulted in numerous research studies, which have considerably enhanced our understanding of brain–behavior relationships, specifically the relationship between brain damage and behavior.

Our current understanding today is that while sensory and motor functions are highly localized in specific areas of the brain, more complex behaviors, such as planning, judgment, reasoning, and calculations, involve the conjoint participation of many diverse and interacting areas of the brain (Cummings, 1985; Luria, 1966). This more integrative school of thought arose during the latter half of the nineteenth century and has continued to gain popularity over the past several decades. This school, which does not have a name, has been identified with a number of great neurologists, including the great neurologist and neuropsychologist, Alexander Luria, who argued that while behavior reflects the functioning of the entire brain, each area of the brain plays a specific role in behavior.

Luria was able to analyze what appeared to be relatively simple behaviors, such as catching a ball, into a series of complex behaviors that involved specific areas of the brain working in coordination with each other. For example, the individual must see and identify the object as a ball, which involves the visual cortex and its adjacent association areas also located in the occipital lobes. This information must be relayed to the frontal lobes, which direct the motor activities of the body, thus causing the person to move his or her hands to the area in which the ball would be expected.

As the ball is moving toward the gloved hand, the frontal lobe must make a number of fine adjustments, involving the parietal lobes, which determine the proper spatial coordinates for the placement of the glove in space and time the sequence of movements to mesh with the position of the ball in space. As soon as the ball strikes the glove, this tactile information must be relayed to the parietal lobe to indicate that the ball has been caught and is now secure. This information is sent to the temporal lobes, which store the information in memory for future use. The frontal lobes now discontinue catching activities and redirect the player's attention to the next step in the sequence — throwing. A series of judgments is made. Throw? Yes? No? If so, to whom? This information is then processed by the frontal lobes of the brain, which direct the throwing hand to grasp the ball and also send this information back to the parietal lobes so that the hand can be properly positioned on the basis of the sensory (kinesthetic) feedback from touching the ball. The frontal lobes again must assess information stored in the temporal lobes to recall what action is required on the basis of past experience. This information is then used by the frontal lobes, which direct the occipital lobes to search out where the ball should be thrown.

As you can see from the above example, the relatively simple task of catching a ball involves all four lobes of the brain, with portions of each lobe serving a different purpose in allowing the activity to be successfully completed. Luria emphasized the importance of what he described as functional systems, each responsible for specific behaviors, so that a pattern of interaction between various parts of the brain is necessary for a specific behavioral act to be completed. The disruption of one or more of these functional systems during any stage of the complex act is sufficient to produce any of a variety of alterations of the act. For example, if the individual sustained an injury to his frontal lobes, his ability to direct and coordinate the activities of the different functional areas of his brain would be impaired. He may begin moving toward the ball too late or too soon, which could result in missing or dropping the ball. A lesion in the occipital lobes could prevent him from recognizing that the object traveling toward him is, in fact, a ball, rather than a bird or some other object. Damage in the frontal lobes could also result in his inability to execute the proper sequence of movements, resulting in the ball going past him. A lesion in the parietal lobes could result in the inaccurate positioning of his gloved hand to catch the ball, while a lesion in his temporal lobes might leave him wondering what to do next after he catches the ball, since he may not recall whether he was playing a game of catch or a varsity game. Thus, it is evident that injuries to various specific areas of the brain can influence the performance of the given task of catching a ball.

If you wanted to determine how a brain injury affects a person's performance on a task, such as catching a ball, you would most likely approach this task in several different ways. First, you might want to observe how this person catches a ball. You might note the percentages of errors made, given the number of balls thrown. This would serve as a "quantitative" approach. You might then compare this to his performance prior to brain injury, if that were possible. In the absence of such preexisting data, you might interview people who may have played catch with this person in the past. If each of these persons interviewed described him as a good catcher, then you would expect that he rarely made errors. If you wanted to be more precise, you might pool this group and find that they consistently agreed that he missed catching the ball only 1% of the time. However, now you find that he misses the ball 10% of the time. The issue, of course, that arises is, "Does this really make a difference?" In other words, "Is this difference significant?" This is obviously a difficult question. However, if this individual earned his livelihood from playing baseball, then it might seriously jeopardize his ability to play the game at a professional level. If, on the other hand, this were an activity that he occasionally engaged in with his 10-year-old son, one might not take this very seriously. However, the effects of this brain injury may cause problems in other areas in his life. For example, if he were an artist, surveyor, traffic cop, baseball umpire, or a member of any other profession that placed heavy emphasis on intact visual–perceptual skills, his ability to perform tasks, which required intact visual–perceptual skills prior to his brain injury, would most likely be significantly compromised after a brain injury.

HISTORY OF NEUROPSYCHOLOGICAL ASSESSMENT

Neuropsychological assessment relies heavily on the use of specific tests to investigate brain–behavior relationships. The use of psychological tests to investigate the behavioral consequences of brain damage was first utilized approximately 70 years ago in the United States. For example, a number of publications appeared during the 1930s and 1940s that described the effects of frontal lobe lesions on intelligence and other functions, visual–spatial impairments following right frontal lobe lesions, the effect of brain damage on abstract thinking, and memory impairments following focal brain lesions (Jones and Butters, 1983). In the Soviet Union during this same time, Luria utilized psychological tests to investigate the effects of brain trauma and disease.

The first neuropsychological laboratory in the United States was set up by Ward C. Halstead in 1935. He used neuropsychological tests to study the effects of brain damage on a wide range of cognitive, perceptual, and sensory motor functions. Before using psychological tests, he spent a great deal of time observing brain-damaged patients in a variety of work and social settings to familiarize himself with the types of problems they experienced. He then put together a battery of tests, which he administered to these patients. On the basis of the results of his findings, he assembled a collection of ten psychological tests. In 1951, Halstead collaborated with his former student, Ralph M. Reitan, who had established a neuropsychology laboratory at Indiana University Medical Center. Reitan (1955) modified Halstead's neuropsychological battery and created what is now described as the "Halstead–Reitan Battery." Reitan administered this battery to a number of patients with documented focal and diffuse brain damage, as well as to a group of hospitalized control patients, presumably free of brain disease. Scores obtained by the brain-damaged group were contrasted with scores of the controls to develop a set of test norms. Reitan developed indices of brain damage on the basis of the patients' scores and performance patterns. These indices allowed him to localize which areas of the brain had been damaged, as well as to infer the cause of the neurological injury (e.g., whether it was due to a brain tumor, stroke, or traumatic brain injury) (Wheeler, Burke, and Reitan, 1963).

Reitan and his collaborators have utilized the Halstead–Reitan Battery in numerous studies to identify specific areas of the brain that have been damaged, determine if an acute or chronic condition is present, and predict a specific diagnosis (e.g., type of tumor, cerebrovascular, or hypoxic insult). Reitan has also provided numerous seminars, in which he attempted to teach psychologists how to utilize his comprehensive test battery to evaluate patients who are suspected of having focal or diffuse brain damage. The Halstead–Reitan Battery still remains the most widely used neuropsychological battery in the United States.

Brenda Milner and her colleagues at the Montreal Neurological Institute and at McGill University have utilized neuropsychological assessment techniques to evaluate behavioral changes in patients who have undergone the surgical removal of portions of their temporal lobes, which were believed to cause uncontrollable seizures. Milner and her students studied the behavior of these patients both before and after neurosurgical intervention. She described the relationships between verbal and nonverbal learning following temporal lobe lesions. For example, she found that patients whose surgery involved the left temporal lobe had impaired verbal learning skills, while the patients who underwent right temporal lobe surgery had impaired visual learning skills (Milner, 1970). She also found that bilateral removal of the hippocampi, which is located in the medial temporal lobes of both hemispheres, produced a severe and permanent impairment in the ability to learn new information. On the basis of the research studies of Milner and her colleagues, a number of neuropsychological tests were developed that were particularly sensitive to damage to specific areas of the brain.

Hans-Lukas Teuber, at the Massachusetts Institute of Technology, used neuropsychological tests to study the effects of local brain damage on a variety of visual and spatial skills. He studied World War II veterans who had sustained penetrating missile wounds to the brain. He and his colleagues identified the importance of the parietal lobes in spatial relations and the role of the frontal lobes in problem solving. These studies led to the development of several psychological tests that were found to be highly sensitive to specific brain lesions and the functions served by these regions (Teuber, 1972).

The Boston V.A. Medical Center, under the leadership of Harold Goodglass, Edith Kaplan, and Nelson Butters, was responsible for the development of a number of neuropsychological tests based upon numerous research studies, which were conducted over a period of over 30 years. These investigators focused on an assessment of patients with aphasia (disorders of language processing secondary to brain damage), amnesia (disorders of learning and memory secondary to brain damage), and dementia (a global loss of cognitive functioning secondary to a neurologic disease process). These investigators also developed "qualitative" methods for analyzing the various psychological and behavioral manifestations and damage to specific parts of the brain. They developed a "process" approach to neuropsychological assessment that relied heavily on their behavioral observations of the patient's performance on a particular test or task.

Their approach has provided clinical neuropsychologists with a greater appreciation of the specific effects that brain damage can have on the individual. For example, they found that patients who had sustained damage to the right parietal lobe often lost their ability to draw or place objects together according to their "Gestalt" (overall configuration or shape). Patients who sustained left parietal lobe damage generally maintained this ability, but the internal details of their drawings were severely distorted while the outer shape remained intact. Thus, the Boston group has strongly maintained that without behavioral observations, or the use of a "process" (qualitative) approach during neuropsychological assessment, much important information can be lost that may be crucial in determining whether an individual can return to work or school or remain within a specific profession. As a consequence, neuropsychologists trained in this approach tend to test their own patients rather than rely upon numeric scores generated by testing technicians (Jones and Butters, 1983).

Arthur Benton, at the University of Iowa, developed a number of neuropsychological tests and made a number of important contributions to clinical neuropsychology. He studied a wide variety of cognitive impairments following brain damage utilizing the tests he created. He has also been responsible for training many distinguished neuropsychologists and played a prominent role in the development of this field.

Alexander Luria, who was initially trained as a cognitive psychologist and then later as a physician and neurologist, spent over 40 years studying the behavioral and psychological impairments of head-injured war victims and neurological and neurosurgical patients. He developed numerous neuropsychological tests that could be administered at the patient's bedside. They permitted Luria and his colleagues to understand the relationship between a specific area of the brain and its effect on complex behaviors. Luria formulated a theory of brain–behavior relationships that emphasized that complex behavior could be broken down into their respective components and studied separately to determine which aspects of a "functional system" had been compromised. His evaluation procedure heavily emphasized qualitative methods based upon observation of the types of errors made by the patient. His selection of tests, method of administration, and test interpretation were tailor-made for the individual patient, based upon his extensive clinical experience and on his model of brain–behavior relationships. Luria's work emphasized using the judgment of expert clinicians in deciding whether brain dysfunction was present and, if so, what was the nature of the dysfunction.

Through collaboration with Anna-Lise Christensen, a Danish psychologist, Luria's tests and method of neuropsychological assessment were introduced in the United States in 1975 under the title of Luria's Neuropsychological Investigation. Christensen's test battery emphasized the flexible individualized approach toward specific patients, which had been developed by Luria. Unfortunately, it was generally not well received in the United States since it required the neuropsychologist to have extensive training and a strong background in behavioral neurology. In an attempt to rectify this, Charles Golden, Thomas Hammeke, and Arnold Purisch administered the several hundred test items contained in Luria's Neuropsychological Investigation to normal controls and later to neurological patients. They utilized discriminant function statistical analysis techniques to determine which test items were sensitive to the presence of brain damage. Their research (Golden et al., 1978) resulted in a battery of 269 items, which could be administered to a patient in 2 or 3 h. This test battery was eventually named the Luria–Nebraska Neuropsychological Battery and first introduced in 1978.

Within the past 20 years, neuropsychologists have often been asked to examine patients who had sustained traumatic brain damage in motor vehicle accidents. They were also asked to utilize their test data to predict whether these patients could return to work, school, or their preinjury duties and responsibilities. Unfortunately, the neuropsychological tests they utilized were primarily developed to determine if the patient had brain damage and how it affected the patient's cognitive functioning. They were never designed to make such predictions. This forced neuropsychologists to focus on the ecological validity of the test data and how well are the tests able to predict a patient's ability to function in real-world settings (Sbordone, 1997; Sbordone and Guilmette, 1999).

This approach tries to utilize tests and measures that more closely simulate the demands of the patient's environment rather than utilizing tests that were only designed to detect brain damage. It observes how the patient behaves in unstructured complex and novel environments rather than the highly structured and artificial test environment. It recognizes that many of the neurobehavioral manifestations caused by brain damage such as irritability, an inability to regulate one's behavior and emotions, rapid mood swings, use of crude or coarse language, inappropriate behavior, impulsivity, egocentricity, insensitivity to the needs and welfare of others, poor frustration tolerance, diminished motivation, loss of libido, and apathy are not detected by the neuropsychological tests that are administered to these patients. As a consequence, interviews with significant others are included in the neuropsychological examination to identify any observed change in the patient's neurobehavioral functioning since their brain injury. This information increases the accuracy of any predictions made about the patient's ability to function in real-world settings, live independently, work, and attend school. It can also identify the patient's needs and treatments that can maximize the patient's ability to function more effectively in real-world settings.

REFERENCES

Boring, E. G. 1950. *A History of Experimental Psychology*, 2d ed. New York: Appleton-Century-Crofts.

Cummings, J. L. 1985. *Clinical Neuropsychiatry*. New York: Grune & Stratton.

The Division 40 of APA 1989. Definition of a Neuropsychologist. *The Clinical Neuropsychologist, 3*, 22.

Golden, C. J., Hammeke, T. A., and Purisch, A. D. 1978. Diagnostic Validity of a Standardized Neuropsychological Battery Derived from Luria's Neuropsychological Tests. *Journal of Consulting and Clinical Psychology, 46*, 1258–1265.

Howard, M. E. 1988. Behavior Management in the Acute Care Rehabilitation Setting. *Journal of Head Trauma Rehabilitation, 3*, 14–22.

Jones, B. P. and Butters, N. 1983. Neuropsychological Assessment. In Hersen, M., Kazdin, A. E., and Bellack, A. S. (Eds.) *The Clinical Psychology Handbook*. New York: Pergamon Press, pp. 377–396.

Lezak, M. D. 1978. Living with the Characterologically Altered Brain-Injured Patient. *Journal of Clinical Psychiatry, 39*, 592.

Lezak, M. D. 1987. Relationships between Personality Disorders, Social Disturbances and Physical Disability Following Traumatic Brain Injury. *Journal of Head Trauma Rehabilitation, 2*, 57–69.

Luria, A. R. 1966. *Human Brain and Psychological Processes*. New York: Harper & Row.

Milner, B. 1970. Memory and the Medial Temporal Regions of the Brain. In Pribram, K. H. and Broadbent, D. E. (Eds.) *Biology of Memory*. New York: Academic Press.

Reitan, R. M. 1955. The Distribution According to Age of a Psychological Measure Dependent upon Organic Brain Functions. *Journal of Gerontology, 10*, 338.

Sbordone, R. J. 1990. Psychotherapeutic Treatment of the Client with Traumatic Brain Injury. In Kreutzer, J. S. and Wehman, P. (Eds.) *Community Integration Following Traumatic Brain Injury*. Baltimore: Brookes, pp. 139–156.

Sbordone, R. J. 1997. The Ecological Validity of Neuropsychological Testing. In Horton, A. M., Wedding, D., and Webster, J. (Eds.) *The Neuropsychology Handbook, Vol. 1: Foundations and Assessment*, 2d ed. New York: Springer-Verlag, pp. 365–392.

Sbordone, R. J., Gerard, M. L., Kral, M. J., and Katz, J. 1984. The Command Performance Syndrome: Emotional Behavior of Significant Others of Head Trauma Victims. *Clinical Neuropsychology*, *6*, 183–185.

Sbordone, R. J. and Guilmette, T. J. 1999. Ecological Validity: Prediction of Everyday and Vocational Functioning from Neuropsychological Test Data. In Sweet, J. J. (Ed.) *Forensic Neuropsychology.* Lisse, The Netherlands: Swets & Zeitlinger, pp. 227–254.

Teuber, H. L. 1972. Unity and Diversity of Frontal Lobe Functions. *ACTA Neurobiologica Experimentalis*, *32*, 615–656.

Walsh, K. W. 1978. *Neuropsychology: A Clinical Approach.* New York: Churchill Livingstone.

Wheeler, L., Burke, C. H., and Reitan, R. M. 1963. An Application of Discriminant Functions to the Problems of Predicting Brain Damage Using Behavioral Variables. *Perceptual and Motor Skills*, *16*, 417.

2 The Education and Training of the Neuropsychologist

The clinical neuropsychologist typically holds a doctorate in the field of psychology from an accredited university. By virtue of their background and training, many neuropsychologists have a broad background in the assessment and treatment of patients with various types of emotional, behavioral, and neurological disorders. The neuropsychologist is also grounded in such basic knowledge areas as learning, cognitive and development psychology, psychopathology, the physiological correlates of behavior, perception, learning and memory, personality theory, statistics, and research design. Completion of the doctoral degree (Ph.D. or Psy.D.) indicates that the individual has completed rigorous academic training at the graduate level, which usually takes 4 to 5 years on a full-time basis. This training frequently includes supervision by clinical faculty and neuropsychologists engaged in full-time practice.

While most psychologists have taken courses on the physiological correlates of behavior, which usually include the neuroanatomy and the functional organization of the brain, such courses are generally inadequate to appreciate the complexity of brain–behavior relationships necessary for the practice of clinical neuropsychology. While a number of doctoral programs in psychology offer courses and supervision in neuropsychological assessment, many of these courses are taught by individuals whose clinical experience and expertise in this area is often limited. As a consequence, many students may learn only how to administer, score, and interpret a specific test or neuropsychological test battery without understanding the complexity of underlying brain–behavior relationships.

Although many psychologists supplement the limited training in neuropsychology they have received during graduate school or at the postdoctoral level through continuing education seminars that are frequently offered throughout the year, the content of these seminars is typically focused on learning how to administer, score, and interpret specific neuropsychological tests that have been used on specific patient populations (e.g., those with learning disabilities). While some of these seminars may actually offer some training in understanding complex brain–behavior relationships, this training is often inadequate for what is needed to obtain expertise in clinical neuropsychology. This situation is somewhat analogous to training someone who has never seen a schizophrenic to administer and score Rorschach ink blots in the hope that the trainee will some day be able to diagnose schizophrenia on the basis of the patient's test scores.

Most clinical neuropsychologists obtain their specialty training in the field of neuropsychology at the postdoctoral level. This is often performed in a medical school or hospital setting where they receive training in the basic neurosciences, including courses in neuroanatomy (anatomy of the brain), neuropathology (diseases of the brain), and clinical or behavioral neurology (symptoms and neurobehavioral syndromes resulting from diseases of the brain). In addition, neuropsychologists are taught, under the supervision of a qualified neuropsychologist, to administer a wide variety of neuropsychological tests to patients with well-documented neurological and neuropsychiatric disorders. Neuropsychologists in this setting are taught to write clinical reports. Such training typically lasts 1 or 2 years and would be the functional equivalent of a residency program in a medical specialty.

A variety of ongoing seminars, workshops, and teaching rounds, such as neurobehavioral rounds, neurology rounds, and neuropsychology case conferences, are available to neuropsychologists for continuing education. In addition, the American Psychological Association, the International Neuropsychological Society, and the National Academy of Neuropsychologists offer seminars each year at their respective annual conferences. During these seminars, experts in various areas of neuropsychology and neurology are invited to give a workshop or lecture on specific topics to provide continuing education to clinical neuropsychologists. In addition, many professional journals are published on a monthly or bimonthly basis to keep neuropsychologists abreast of the latest research and clinical findings in this growing field. Included within these journals are the reliability and validity of specific neuropsychological tests, as well as relationships between specific test scores and specific neurological disorders. These journals contain articles on such topics as traumatic brain injuries, carbon monoxide exposure, dementia, frontal lobe syndromes, executive functions, memory disorders, ecological validity, malingering, and specific ethical or practice issues. Topics on neuropsychological issues are often published in the following journals: *Annals of Neurology*; *Applied Neuropsychology*; *Archives of Clinical Neuropsychology*; *Biological Psychiatry*; *Brain and Cognition*; *Brain and Language*; *Brain Injury*; *The Clinical Neuropsychologist*; *Cortex*; *The International Journal of Clinical Neuropsychology*; *Journal of Abnormal Psychology*; *Journal of Clinical Psychology*; *Journal of Clinical and Consulting Psychology*; *Journal of Clinical and Experimental Neuropsychology*; *Journal of Head Trauma Rehabilitation*; *Journal of the International Neuropsychological Society*; *Journal of Neuropsychiatry*; *Journal of Nervous and Mental Diseases*; *Journal of Neurology, Neurosurgery, and Psychiatry*; *Neurology*; *Neurorehabilitation*; *Neuroscience*; *Neuropsychiatry, Neuropsychology, and Behavioral Neurology*; *Neuropsychologia*; *Neuropsychology*; *Neuropsychology Review*; *Perceptual and Motor Skills*; *Psychological Assessment*; and *Rehabilitation Psychology*.

EXPERIENCE IN CLINICAL NEUROPSYCHOLOGY

It should be obvious to health care professionals and attorneys that many psychologists who offer neuropsychological services may, in fact, have very limited experience evaluating and treating patients who have sustained a brain insult or posttraumatic stress disorder. For many psychologists in private practice, limited experience evaluating patients with neurological injuries is the rule rather than the exception. Obviously, there are many reasons for this. A psychologist offering such services may have recently completed a workshop ranging from 1 to 5 days' duration on how to administer, score, and interpret the results of a specific neuropsychological test or battery and now wishes to offer such services to the public. He or she may be operating under the naive assumption, often inadvertently conveyed by the presenters of such workshops, that the results of the neuropsychological tests or batteries can stand alone and that a background in brain–behavior relationships, neuropathology, neurology, and the neurosciences is not necessary to interpret the results of the tests administered to patients suspected of having a brain insult. In other words, the test data are thought to be sufficient to permit the psychologist to offer an opinion regarding damages and causation.

One can usually recognize reports written by these individuals since they are typically brief (two or three pages long), contain little background information about the patient, and do not contain a review of the patient's medical records. These reports typically contain the actual test scores and a set of statements describing the areas of the brain believed to be damaged and the degree of severity of the damage. These reports typically lack any description of the patient's performance during testing and fail to mention or discuss any possible extraneous factors, such as peripheral motor problems, psychiatric illnesses, medications, chronic pain and discomfort, orthopedic problems, or visual difficulties, which might confound test interpretation or mitigate the particular psychologist's opinions.

These psychologists may often receive referrals from physicians (whose understanding of neuropsychological testing is usually quite limited) to rule out "organicity." The vast majority of these psychologists have probably seen fewer than 50 patients who have had some type of neurological disorder. These psychologists are usually unaware of many of the cognitive and behavioral problems that these patients have, because they rely almost entirely on the results of their test scores (which can be confounded by a number of factors) and the information they received from the patient (without trying to determine whether it is accurate or consistent with the patient's medical records).

Many psychologists who offer neuropsychological services receive little or no clinical supervision from competent and board-certified neuropsychologists after they have completed their internship. While many psychologists have taken relatively brief workshops in neuropsychological testing (e.g., how to administer, score, and interpret a particular neuropsychological test or battery), many of these individuals do not receive supervision from a qualified/board-certified neuropsychologist after they have completed the workshops. As a consequence, errors in test scoring or interpretation may go unchecked. The following case illustrates this.

Case Example

A neuropsychological report written by a psychologist with limited training in neuropsychology concluded that the patient showed evidence of rather significant memory deficits, which he attributed to the patient's industrial injury (a slip and fall accident at work). Careful review of the psychologist's report revealed, however, that he had failed to use age-appropriate test norms when interpreting the patient's test data. For example, he compared the patient's performance on a test of recent memory to norms for 25-year-old patients, even though the patient was 63 years old. The psychologist was unaware that test norms for 60-year-old patients were available since after completing the workshop he had never sought or received any supervision and was unaware that it was inappropriate to compare the test performance of a 63-year-old patient with norms for 25-year-old individuals. When this patient's test scores were compared with norms for persons of his age, his scores actually placed him within the normal range.

THEORETICAL ORIENTATION OF THE PSYCHOLOGIST

The theoretical orientation of the psychologist is likely to influence the way in which he or she views the particular complaints of a patient who presents with a history of a neurological disorder or brain injury. For example, Sbordone and Rudd (1986) found that one third of the psychologists practicing within the community failed to recognize rather salient underlying neurological disorders when they were asked to read a clinical vignette that contained a description of the patient's clinical history, symptoms, and complaints. Analysis of this data revealed that psychologists who had a primary psychodynamic or behavior modification treatment orientation were less likely to recognize patients with underlying neurological disorders. Thus, psychologists with limited training, background, and experience in evaluating patients with brain injuries may reach the spurious conclusion that a particular patient's problems may be due to motivational or psychological factors, rather than the consequences of a brain injury. The following case study illustrates this.

Case Example

A clinical psychologist was asked by a patient's physician to administer neuropsychological tests on a patient who had sustained a severe brain injury in a motor vehicle accident 1 year earlier. Although the psychologist was aware that the patient had been rendered unconscious for several days following her injury, had a residual left-sided hemiparesis (weakness and restricted movements of the entire left side of the body), and had been diagnosed as having a cerebral contusion based on the results of computerized tomography, the psychologist, who had a strong psychoanalytic orientation, interpreted the patient's symptoms of irritability, poor frustration tolerance, impulsivity, distractibility, and inappropriate behavior as evidence of "passive–aggressive behavior," which was attributed to a faulty relationship the patient had had with her mother. This psychologist had failed to recognize that the patient's behavior was consistent with damage to the orbital surface of her frontal lobes and resulted in the patient's inability to regulate her emotions or behavior. Thus, this psychologist's particular theoretical orientation, combined with his lack of knowledge of neurobehavioral syndromes, caused him to overlook that the cause of this patient's symptoms was the result of a severe brain injury, a fact clearly documented in this patient's medical records.

THE TRAINING ENVIRONMENT OF THE PSYCHOLOGIST

The type of setting in which patients are seen may contribute to the biases held by the particular psychologist. For example, Sbordone and Rudd (1986) found that psychologists who completed their clinical training in counseling centers were often unlikely to recognize the presence of an underlying neurological disorder when they were asked to read several clinical vignettes carefully and determine which type of treatment or referral would be most appropriate. A high percentage of psychologists with this background felt that such patients had psychological problems that could be treated appropriately through such modalities as individual or group psychotherapy. By way of contrast, psychologists working in the departments of neurology and neurosurgery were likely to view the behavioral problems of patients seen in these settings as a consequence of their underlying brain or neurological disorder. Thus, they tend to ignore motivational, environmental, or psychological factors in determining the cause of the patient's symptoms.

EXPERIENCE IN BRAIN-INJURY REHABILITATION

Many neuropsychologists have had little, if any, experience in the rehabilitation of patients who have sustained brain injuries. As a consequence, their opinions regarding the relative permanency of the patient's cognitive problems and the patient's ability to return to competitive employment, school, or household responsibilities are often inaccurate or inappropriate. Consistent with this is the fact that most psychologists are unfamiliar with cognitive rehabilitation techniques and have had little or no experience teaching brain-injured patients to use compensatory strategies and techniques to maximize their behavioral and cognitive functioning following brain injury. Thus, their opinions are often overly pessimistic, even though through the use of cognitive rehabilitation techniques many of these patients may be able to function reasonably well at work, at home, or in their community. Rehabilitation psychologists may, conversely, be unduly optimistic about a brain-injured patient's cognitive and behavioral potential because these are the services that they "sell."

CONSEQUENCES OF INSUFFICIENT EXPERIENCE WITH BRAIN-DAMAGED PATIENTS

Psychologists who lack the background and experience in working with patients who have sustained brain injuries may base their opinions about the patient's ability to return to work or school or to function in society entirely on the neuropsychological test data, even though such tests were never designed to make such predictions. This often results in a number of erroneous conclusions about the patient. For example, the test items may lack sufficient "ecological validity" and may be insensitive to the patient's cognitive and behavioral impairments that may only be observed or occur in real-world settings. The tests may also fail to assess the patient's ability to generalize his or her newly acquired skills from one setting to another. Because of the psychologist's inexperience and lack of understanding of specific neurobehavioral disorders such as frontal lobe syndromes, the psychologist may only report the test data and fail to gather information from the patient's significant others (Sbordone, 1991; Sbordone and Purisch, 1996; Sbordone and Saul, 2000). As a consequence, the opinions reached by a psychologist may result in spurious conclusions about the patient's ability to return to work or school or to perform household activities. The following case illustrates this.

Case Example

The patient, a 28-year-old right-handed male, had sustained a severe traumatic brain injury after falling approximately 19 feet during an industrial accident and striking his head on the ground. The patient remained comatose for 1 week and was referred to a psychologist for neuropsychological testing approximately 4 months postinjury. While the psychologist reported that the patient denied having any cognitive or behavioral problems, the psychologist failed to interview the patient's family or significant others. The psychologist reported that the patient's IQ had not changed appreciably since his accident and thus concluded that the patient could return to school. However, when the patient's family learned of the psychologist's recommendations, they phoned the psychologist and informed him that the patient's personality had dramatically changed since the accident and he had become extremely irritable, easily frustrated, egocentric, and insensitive to the needs and welfare of others. The psychologist informed them that while he had actually observed some of these behaviors during his examination, he felt that since the patient's IQ had not changed to any appreciable degree, the patient should have little difficulty returning to school. The patient's parents went along with the psychologist's recommendations and permitted the patient to return to school, where he began exhibiting significant academic and conduct/behavioral difficulties (e.g., he swore at several of his teachers, failed to turn in homework assignments, and did not bring his books home at night). As a consequence of these problems, he was referred to a continuation school, which he failed to attend.

LIMITED FORENSIC EXPERIENCE

Many psychologists, particularly those with minimal training and experience in neuropsychology, may also have limited forensic experience. As a consequence, we have a psychologist who not only lacks competence in the area in which he or she has been designated an expert, but also lacks experience on the complicated medicolegal issues involved in the case. The following case study illustrates this.

Case Example

Dr J was asked by an attorney to evaluate a plaintiff who had sustained a relatively mild brain injury. Although the psychologist concluded that the patient had sustained severe brain damage based on the patient's neuropsychological test performance, he admitted during his deposition that the patient had been severely depressed and appeared intoxicated. The psychologist was unable to adequately explain why he had gone forward and tested this patient and also confessed that he had not bothered to administer any tests to see if the patient was malingering. He also admitted that he had never reviewed the patient's academic or medical records and had relied entirely on the history that the patient had provided him, even though he was later informed that it was inaccurate. The case was settled 2 days later for an amount that was substantially lower than the demands of the plaintiff's attorney before the psychologist's deposition.

RISK OF UTILIZING EXPERTS WHO LACK EXPERTISE IN ASSESSING BRAIN DAMAGE

The attorney who utilizes a clinical psychologist, particularly one who is improperly trained or who lacks expertise in assessing brain damage, rather than a neuropsychologist to evaluate a client runs the risk of weakening the damages part of the case if the defense hires a neuropsychologist who points out that the plaintiff's expert lacked the proper training, experience, and expertise to support his or her opinions. If the plaintiff's attorney either loses the case or receives a paltry judgment because of this, the attorney may be sued by his client for malpractice for failing to utilize the services of an appropriate expert. Thus, in the "battle of experts," the testimony of a clinical neuropsychologist would most likely be superior to that of a clinical psychologist, particularly if the discrepancy between the training, background, and experience is substantial.

COMPETENCE IN THE FIELD OF NEUROPSYCHOLOGY

In medicine, specialty boards have existed for a number of years to ensure that a particular medical specialist is competent in the area of his specialty. To qualify for board certification, the medical specialist has to complete residency training in his or her specialty and successfully complete a series of written, practice, and oral examinations. Before 1983, board certification did not exist in the field of clinical neuropsychology, which often resulted in considerable embarrassment to the profession by so-called "instant neuropsychologists" who began sending out business cards notifying legal, medical, and other psychological professionals that they had expertise in clinical neuropsychology as a result of completing only a 2- or 3-day workshop in the administration of a particular neuropsychological test battery.

THE AMERICAN BOARD OF PROFESSIONAL NEUROPSYCHOLOGY

The American Board of Professional Neuropsychology (ABPN) was created by a group of neuro-psychologists in 1982 in response to the growing need to formally evaluate the competence of neuropsychologists practicing in the field in order to protect the consumer. Between 1982 and 1985, the ABPN evaluated the competence of neuropsychologists to practice in the field by reviewing their academic training, background, and professional practice information, as furnished to them by the applicant, and the submission of two work samples that were reviewed by at least three members of the board. In 1991, the ABPN reorganized its credentialing process and only granted diplomate status on the basis of oral competence examinations that included questions about the candidate's knowledge of neuropsychology, work samples, and ethics. All prior ABPN diplomates were offered the opportunity to undergo the newly established oral examination process. Many of these individuals took and passed the oral examination.

    The ABPN requires that the candidates meet the following criteria before submitting an application for diplomate status (1) a doctoral degree in psychology; (2) a minimum of 3 years of professional experience in neuropsychology of which 1 year may be a supervised neuropsycho-logy internship; (3) current licensure/certification to practice psychology in a state, province, or territory; (4) a minimum of 500 hours per year during the last 5 years providing neuropsychological services; and (5) involvement in APA-approved (or equivalent) formal continuing education in neuropsychology. By the end of 2006, over 200 psychologists have been granted diplomate status by the American Board of Professional Neuropsychology based on successful completion of the oral examination and passing of the work samples. Health care professionals and attorneys wishing to obtain further information about this board or a list of ABPN diplomates can contact its website at www.abpn.net.

THE AMERICAN BOARD OF CLINICAL NEUROPSYCHOLOGY

The American Board of Clinical Neuropsychology (ABCN) was incorporated in 1981 and became affiliated with the American Board of Professional Psychology in 1984. The ABCN offers a diplomate in clinical neuropsychology to neuropsychologists who meet its rather stringent criteria (1) a doctoral degree in psychology from a regionally accredited university; (2) licensing or certification to practice independently in their state or province; (3) training or courses in the basic neurosciences, neuroanatomy, neuropathology, clinical neurology, psychological assessment, clinical neuropsychological assessment, psychopathology, and psychological intervention; (4) 5 years of postdoctoral professional experience in psychology; and (5) at least 3 years of experience in clinical neuropsychology, including at least 1 year of full-time supervised clinical neuropsychology experience at the postdoctoral level (6 months may be credited for a documented postdoctoral specialty internship in neuropsychology) and at least 1 year of additional experience as a clinical neuropsychologist, or the equivalent of 3 years of unsupervised postdoctoral experience as a clinical neuropsychologist.

If candidates satisfy these criteria, they must take a written examination consisting of 100 multiple-choice questions that evaluate their knowledge of the neurosciences, neurology, psychiatry, pharmacology, and clinical neuropsychology. Upon passing this examination, candidates must submit two samples of their neuropsychological test reports (including the raw data). Their reports must be supported by a lengthy written statement that justifies their analysis of the cases, their choice of specific neuropsychological tests, and the opinions that they have formulated in their sample reports. These materials are then carefully reviewed by three diplomates of the Board. Candidates whose work samples are found to be acceptable are then permitted to take three oral examinations to assess their clinical competence, professional judgment, ethics, and knowledge of neuropsychology. By the end of 2006, over 700 Diplomates in Neuropsychology had been granted by this board. Health care professionals and attorneys wishing to obtain further information about this board or the listing of its diplomates should contact its website at www.abpp.org/

"VANITY BOARDS" IN CLINICAL NEUROPSYCHOLOGY

Within the past several years, a number of "vanity boards" have made it possible for virtually any psychologist to become "board certified" or obtain a "diplomate in clinical neuropsychology" irrespective of whether they are competent, have a background in neuropsychology, or had ever received any training in neuropsychology, if he or she is willing to pay a rather hefty fee. These boards typically do not require the applicant to meet the rigorous educational and background criteria necessary for competency in this area by the two boards described above. For example, applicants are typically not required to submit work samples, or undergo a comprehensive examination process to evaluate their background, training, knowledge, ethics, and competence in neuropsychology. As a consequence, the competence of any psychologist who holds him or herself out as a diplomate in neuropsychology from these "vanity boards" should be viewed with suspicion.

REFERENCES

Sbordone, R. J. 1991. *Neuropsychology for the Attorney*. Delray Beach, FL: St. Lucie Press.

Sbordone, R. J. and Purisch, A. D. 1996. Hazards of Blind Analysis of Neuropsychological Test Data in Assessing Cognitive Disability: The Role of Confounding Factors. *Neurorehabilitation*, 7, 15–26.

Sbordone, R. J. and Rudd, M. 1986. Can Psychologists Recognize Neurological Disorders? *Journal of Experimental and Clinical Neuropsychology*, 8, 285–291.

Sbordone, R. J. and Saul, R. J. 2000. *Neuropsychology for Health Care Professionals and Attorneys*. Boca Raton, FL: CRC Press.

3 Comparison of Roles and Training of Different Mental Health Specialists

This chapter will compare the roles and training of clinical neuropsychologists with specialists such as clinical psychologists, psychiatrists, and neurologists to allow the reader to better understand their respective roles, particularly their similarities and differences with respect to their background, training, and expertise.

COMPARISON OF CLINICAL NEUROPSYCHOLOGISTS WITH CLINICAL PSYCHOLOGISTS

While both clinical psychologists and clinical neuropsychologists hold a doctorate (Ph.D.) in the field of psychology, the clinical neuropsychologist has received advanced training (usually at the postdoctoral level). Such training typically consists of taking courses and seminars in neuroanatomy, neuropathology, neurology, behavioral neurology, and clinical neuropsychology in order to better understand the brain.

CLINICAL PSYCHOLOGISTS

The clinical psychologist primarily specializes in the assessment and treatment of patients with symptoms such as anxiety and depression usually stemming from divorces, marital difficulties, significant losses (e.g., death, abandonment, job, etc.), work or occupational conflicts, sexual difficulties, child custody or rearing issues, troubled backgrounds, emotional neglect, history or physical and sexual abuse, poor self-esteem, paranoia, traumatic experiences, or rejection.

The clinical psychologist often utilizes psychological tests such as the Wechsler Adult Intelligence Scale–Third Edition (WAIS-III), the Minnesota Multiphasic Personality Inventory-2 (MMPI-2), and the Rorschach to evaluate a patient's intellectual functioning, personality style, and current emotional problems and determine the proper course of treatment. This course typically consists of one or more of the following treatment modalities: individual, marital, family, or group psychotherapy; relaxation therapy; desensitization; or biofeedback.

While there are many different schools of thought regarding the treatment of patients with emotional or psychological problems, most psychologists ascribe to the assumption that most of these problems are the result of maladaptive learning or intrapsychic conflicts stemming from the interaction of one's childhood experiences and current emotional or environmental stressors. However, many of these problems may actually represent psychological manifestations of a medical illness or endocrine, metabolic, or neurological disorder (Jefferson and Marshall, 1981).

Clinical psychologists typically receive little or no training in such areas as neuroanatomy, neurology, or neuropathology. While they may at times be asked to "rule out organicity," this typically has been done in the past by the administration, scoring, and interpretation of the Bender–Gestalt test. Some clinical psychologists who have taken courses in the administration, scoring, and interpretation of either the Halstead–Reitan or Luria–Nebraska Neuropsychological Batteries may utilize these batteries in addition to the WAIS and Bender–Gestalt tests to determine whether a particular patient is brain-damaged or "organic."

The major limitations of clinical psychologists are their relative lack of training or expertise in the neurosciences, neuroanatomy, neuropathology, or neurology and their relative unfamiliarity and lack of experience in assessing patients with neurological disorders. As a consequence, they may overlook factors in the patient's history (e.g., hypothyroidism, medical problems, prior injuries, medications, or motivational or emotional factors), which may confound clinical interpretation of the patient's test results. Consequently, the conclusions of the clinical psychologist may be erroneous regarding causation (Purisch and Sbordone, 1987).

CLINICAL NEUROPSYCHOLOGISTS

The clinical neuropsychologist works primarily with patients who have neurological disorders or brain insults and is trained to recognize the cognitive, emotional, and neurobehavioral manifestations of brain injury or disease. The clinical neuropsychologist typically uses tests or procedures that have been specifically designed to assess cognitive or neurobehavioral impairments caused by brain dysfunction or damage. The neuropsychologist is aware of the relative sensitivity or insensitivity of these tests to detect cognitive or behavioral impairments secondary to focal or diffuse brain damage.

Because of the neuropsychologist's background and understanding of the relationship between neurological and psychiatric disorders, the neuropsychologist has a greater appreciation and understanding of the influence of extraneous factors, such as fatigue, medications, peripheral neuropathies, depression, medical diseases, and medications, on test performance.

The neuropsychologist typically gathers a comprehensive background and clinical history of the patient that chronicles the onset of the patient's symptoms in relationship to the injury, reviews various neurodiagnostic or neurological examinations, and notes changes in the patient's behavioral and cognitive functioning after the patient has undergone rehabilitation and treatment. A standardized highly detailed history-taking methodology to gather this information has been developed by Siegal (1996). The neuropsychologist may also use a wider variety of neuropsychological tests than the clinical psychologist that have greater sensitivity to the patient's cognitive impairments following a brain insult. The neuropsychologist's conclusions regarding the presence or absence of brain impairment or damage are typically based on an understanding of the patient's neurological disease or insult, interviews with significant others, review of the various medical or neurological records, comprehensive history obtained from the patient and significant others, behavioral observations of the patient, and interpretation of test scores and performances.

While the clinical psychologist and clinical neuropsychologist typically are both trained to provide psychotherapy, the primary function of the clinical neuropsychologist is to serve as a consultant to referring physicians, attorneys, and health care professionals. Thus, the clinical neuropsychologist may spend the overwhelming majority of his or her time performing neuropsychological assessments, reviewing records, and writing reports. A clinical neuropsychologist typically treats fewer patients than does the clinical psychologist, since the practice of the clinical neuropsychologist is concerned primarily with assessment and consultation with other professionals. Part of this, however, also reflects the fact that many patients with neurological impairments or brain insults are often relatively poor candidates for psychotherapy, particularly if their cognitive or behavioral problems are severe. In addition, these patients are often highly distractible, relatively unaware of their problems, and are often unable to retain what transpired during therapy because of their cognitive deficits. They may also have difficulty recalling or generalizing what they have "learned" in psychotherapy into the "real world" even if their memory is intact.

Case Example

A 35-year-old woman was referred to a clinical psychologist by her physician in a case of suspected toxic exposure to industrial chemicals during the course of her employment. The patient claimed that she had developed memory and concentration difficulties, dizziness, hair loss, numbness, and tingling in her fingers. A weight gain of approximately 40 pounds was evident. The psychologist, who was unfamiliar with the neuropsychological sequelae resulting from toxic exposure, administered the WAIS, which revealed a 15-point difference between her verbal and performance IQ scores, with her performance IQ being lower. He also administered the Halstead–Reitan and reported that the patient performed poorly on most of the tests within this battery. He also noted that the patient complained of severe memory difficulties, an inability to use her hands, and a variety of somatic and cognitive difficulties. He concluded that the results of neuropsychological testing demonstrated that this woman had sustained brain damage as a result of exposure to industrial solvents during the course of her employment.

The patient was later referred to a clinical neuropsychologist. The neuropsychologist obtained a careful background history from this patient, which revealed that she had a long-standing history of stress-related emotional and physical problems stemming back to her adolescence. He also found that she had a history of hypothyroidism and had been involved in a motor vehicle accident 2 years previously, wherein she had sustained a probable concussion. He noted that she had been involved in a highly distressing relationship with her boyfriend, who lived with her. To cope with these problems, she consumed large amounts of alcohol and street drugs. The neuropsychologist also pointed out that her performance on the WAIS-III was atypical for patients with histories of toxic exposure. He felt that her performance on the Halstead–Reitan was more consistent with patients who had a history of mild traumatic brain injury and hypothyroidism. He administered a number of neuropsychological tests that corroborated this and led him to conclude that her complaints were most likely not due to toxic exposure in the workplace.

COMPARISON OF CLINICAL NEUROPSYCHOLOGISTS WITH CLINICAL PSYCHIATRISTS

PSYCHIATRISTS

Unlike the clinical neuropsychologist, the psychiatrist has a medical degree and has completed medical school and a residency in psychiatry. The psychiatrist is concerned with the diagnosis and treatment of emotional disorders. Psychiatrists generally treat patients with disorders such as schizophrenia, major depression, bipolar depressive disorders (manic–depressive illness), severe neuroses, acting-out adolescents, and paranoia, as well as patients with organic brain syndromes. Psychiatrists have typically received training in neurology (usually consisting of both coursework and a rotation in neurology).

Psychiatrists typically do not administer psychological tests to patients, since they are not qualified to score and interpret such tests. However, psychiatrists frequently utilize the results of psychological and neuropsychological tests (which have been administered, scored, and interpreted by a clinical psychologist or neuropsychologist) in arriving at their conclusions. Psychiatrists typically conduct a clinical interview, history, and mental status examination, which are typically qualitative, nonstandardized, and subjective. It is usually based on the psychiatrist's training, theoretical orientation, and experience. The vast majority of psychiatrists have had little experience in evaluating and treating patients who have sustained traumatic brain injuries. Their treatment of patients typically consists of either psychotherapy and psychopharmacology (prescribing medications that are specifically designed to alleviate a patient's mental confusion, emotional problems, or mood swings). Since there has been increasing evidence that many of the classic psychiatric disorders such as schizophrenia and depression appear to be caused by a combination of genetic, organic, and environmental factors, psychiatrists have become increasingly aware of the relationship between specific psychiatric disorders and the brain's ability to regulate and produce a variety of neurochemical substances.

CLINICAL NEUROPSYCHOLOGISTS

Clinical neuropsychologists, by comparison, typically spend considerably more time evaluating patients than do psychiatrists. For example, most psychiatric evaluations last from 1 to 2 h, while a neuropsychological examination (obtaining a history, interviewing the significant others, and the administration of neuropsychological tests) can take 6 to 8 h. While the histories obtained from psychiatrists and clinical neuropsychologists are often similar, their mental status examinations are dramatically different. For example, the clinical neuropsychologist may administer as many as 30 different neuropsychological tests to evaluate a patient's intellectual, cognitive, behavioral, and emotional functioning, whereas the psychiatrist typically does not administer any formal tests to assess the patient's cognitive or psychiatric functioning, but may rely on the interpretations of psychological tests that may be administered by a clinical psychologist (who may work in the psychiatrist's office) or computerized psychological test interpretative reports (e.g., MMPI). Because the neuropsychologist typically has had more experience with patients with brain impairment, the neuropsychologist's examination is usually more sensitive to the underlying neurological aspects of the patient's complaints and symptoms. For example, it is generally well known that the standard psychiatric examination is generally insensitive to frontal lobe disorders since these patients typically fail to show evidence of language, psychiatric, or cognitive problems when interviewed. On the other hand, these patients will usually demonstrate significant impairments on neuropsychological tests that are sensitive to frontal lobe pathology.

Case Example

A psychiatrist requested neuropsychological testing of a 29-year-old male patient who had recently been admitted to the psychiatric unit of a large hospital. The psychiatrist initially diagnosed the patient as schizophrenic because the patient appeared delusional and exhibited a flat affect. A review of this patient's medical records revealed that he had taken a probable overdose of barbiturates, which had resulted in a cardiac arrest. When this patient was discovered by his mother, he was not breathing and was blue. The paramedics were summoned and they arrived a few minutes later. They started emergency resuscitation procedures, which were eventually successful. The patient, however, spent the next 3 days in a coma, after which he was noted to be apathetic, extremely lethargic, confused, disoriented, and forgetful. During his psychiatric examination, the patient denied having any cognitive or psychiatric symptoms. This patient was seen as being in denial and was diagnosed as schizophrenic because of his flat affect and indifference to his surroundings.

Neuropsychological testing revealed a variety of severe profound cognitive impairments consistent with hypoxic encephalopathy and diffuse brain damage secondary to a lack of oxygen to the brain. The neuropsychologist recommended that the psychiatrist reconsider the use of Haloperidol (an antipsychotic medication that is used for treating patients with schizophrenia) in his treatment of this patient. The neuropsychologist also recommended that the patient be referred to an acute brain injury rehabilitation unit that was highly structured (unlike the psychiatric unit) and had the experience treating such patients in the past. The psychiatrist eventually concurred with the neuropsychologist's recommendations and confessed that he had no experience with such patients.

COMPARISON OF CLINICAL NEUROPSYCHOLOGISTS WITH NEUROLOGISTS

NEUROLOGISTS AND THE NEUROLOGICAL EXAMINATION

A neurologist is a medical school graduate who has completed a 3-year residency in the field of neurology. Neurologists are concerned with the diagnosis and treatment of disorders of the nervous system. They work almost exclusively with patients who have some form of neurological disease or dysfunction. This would include patients who have or have sustained cerebral concussions, mild or severe head trauma, hypoxic encephalopathy, Alzheimer's disease, Parkinson's disease, intracranial neoplasia (brain tumors), cerebrovascular disorders (strokes), obstructive hydrocephalus, infectious diseases of the brain or nervous system, spinal cord injuries, and a variety of other neurological diseases and disorders including peripheral neuropathy and neurological symptoms secondary to a variety of medical illnesses.

In many respects the neurologist's approach, in contrast to that of other medical specialists, is unique. The history of the patient's complaints and the patient's age and sex help the neurologist formulate a hypothesis as to the probable etiology of the patient's symptoms. The neurologist then determines whether the disease affects the central or peripheral nervous system and, if central, as in the brain, for example, whether the involvement is diffuse (Alzheimer's) or in a limited discrete area (stroke and tumor).

Although the site of injury provides some clue as to the cause of the problem, the time course of the patient's illness is of greatest help in identifying the responsible pathology. An illness of sudden onset followed by subsequent gradual recovery is likely due to trauma or vascular disease, whereas one of gradual onset and relentless progression suggests a tumor or degenerative disorder. Brief episodes of neurological disability lasting minutes or hours are typical of epilepsy, migraine, or transient ischemic attacks (mini-strokes caused by brief, reversible interruptions of the blood supply to the brain that can herald a major stroke).

The result of this analysis is a differential diagnosis of the disease or diseases, in order of probability, with which the symptoms, clinical course, signs, and localization are consistent. From this list, a provisional diagnosis is generally made to guide the subsequent diagnostic workup. With many common neurological disorders, for example migraine, no further investigation is needed. Many patients, however, will require special diagnostic studies, for example, electroencephalograms (EEGs) or imaging (computed tomography — CT, magnetic resonance imaging — MRI) to confirm, refute, or refine the provisional clinical diagnosis. The neurologist is then prepared to initiate an appropriate plan of management, including specific treatment, if available.

A primary purpose of the standard neurological examination is to provide conclusive evidence that neurological disease is present or, of even greater importance in forensic cases, absent. Although such evidence is needed for either conclusion, psychologically induced and neurological symptoms and signs must be considered separately at this initial stage of the workup. Unlike a behavioral neurologist, neuropsychologist, or psychiatrist, most neurologists do not rely on a mental status exam to determine that a disorder is psychogenic or neurological. When the findings on physical exam conflict with those of the mental status exam, the former are usually given considerably greater weight. This is particularly the case if they represent hard signs, unequivocally abnormal findings such as an extensor plantar response (positive Babinski) or muscle wasting, as opposed to soft signs, for example, unreliable minor degrees of apparent weakness, imbalance or incoordination, slight reflex asymmetries, or inconsistent sensory changes.

Neurologists also can identify psychogenic disorders when pseudoneurological signs, violating the laws of neuroanatomy and physics, are found on examination. Tunnel vision and sensory deficits that split the midline are classic examples. Others include psychogenic limb paresis (weakness), manifested by a sudden giving way in response to the examiner's steady opposition, and astasia–abasia, a bizarre reeling gait in which the patient exhibits a remarkable capacity to maintain his balance and avoid a fall with injury. Inexperienced neurologists, however, may err in mislabeling unique or relatively uncommon conditions as psychogenic in the suspected presence of such pseudoneurological signs or when hard signs are absent. In a number of disorders, for example, frontal or temporal lobe trauma, psychomotor (complex partial) seizures, small strokes, or multiple sclerosis, objective neurological signs may be subtle, transient, or easily masked by emotional distress.

In clinical practice and the current medicolegal climate, a psychiatric diagnosis is unfortunately often made by the neurologist only after exhaustive and expensive diagnostic tests have excluded both rare and common neurological disorders. The patient is often reassured that the condition is not permanent and offered face-saving placebos, ineffective medication, or physical therapy. These short-term measures are pragmatic, but inappropriate. A concomitant psychiatric and neuropsychological evaluation should preferably be substituted. The resulting findings and recommendations should be given serious consideration in the patient's management. Neither a psychiatric nor neurological etiology should be a diagnosis of exclusion; mutual coexistence is more common than recognized (Kaufman, 1995; Marsden and Fowler, 1998).

CLINICAL NEUROPSYCHOLOGISTS

While neurologists have considerable expertise in evaluating the structural integrity of the nervous system, they may lack an appreciation of the neurobehavioral sequelae of injuries. This would include an examination of what has been referred to as the patient's "higher cortical" or "executive functions." Included within this would be the patient's problem-solving skills, judgment, reasoning, higher-order motor skills, memory (particularly under conditions of interference), insight, higher-level perceptual functioning, cognitive flexibility, and higher-level attentional and concentration skills.

Although the neurologist has expertise in the diagnosis of specific disorders of the central nervous system (brain and spinal cord), the neuropsychologist is usually better able to determine the effects of this disorder on the patient's cognitive and intellectual functioning, including attention, concentration, and memory skills; perception; and language. Higher-order motor skills, problem solving, reasoning, judgment, and abstract thinking are also assessed as is behavior in structured and unstructured settings, emotional functioning, and social interpersonal relationships. As a result of their respective areas of expertise, neurologists frequently refer patients who have sustained various forms of brain insults to neuropsychologists for assessment, since the clinical neuropsychologist spends considerably more time evaluating the patient's mental status through a combination of interview techniques and neuropsychological testing.

ROLE OF BEHAVIORAL NEUROLOGISTS AND NEUROPSYCHIATRISTS

Over the past two decades the overlapping fields of behavioral neurology and neuropsychiatry have emerged. While behavioral neurologists are concerned with disorders of brain function, neuropsychiatrists are concerned with nearly all behavioral abnormalities that can be clustered into a clinically identified syndrome (a syndrome is a group of symptoms that is characteristic of a given disorder and occurs together at a level greater than chance). Behavioral neurology initially emphasized negative deficit syndromes that resulted from lesions of the cerebral cortex or white matter tracts connecting the cortical areas of the brain. Examples of such negative deficit syndromes would include aphasia (a speech and language disorder resulting from a middle cerebral artery territory lesion in the left hemisphere of the brain) and the left-sided inattention and neglect syndrome (due to a lesion in the posterior right hemisphere). Advances in neuroimaging, particularly functional imaging with single photon emission computed tomography (SPECT) and positron emission tomography (PET), have revealed evidence of altered cerebral metabolism in specific areas of the frontal and temporal lobes in psychiatric patients who have depression, mania, schizophrenia, and obsessive–compulsive disorder. As a consequence, the boundaries between these two disciplines, behavioral neurology and neuropsychiatry, have become artificial (Cummings and Hegarty, 1994).

Training in behavioral neurology and neuropsychiatry has become available over the past decade at many university medical centers. After completing a minimum of 3 years of residency training in either neurology or psychiatry, physicians receive an additional year or two of training in behavioral neurology/neuropsychiatry in both inpatient and outpatient settings. They are taught to utilize a more extensive mental status examination, providing the opportunity of examining the higher cognitive functions of the brain and the patient's emotional functioning in much greater depth than the standard neurological or psychiatric examination. This examination typically evaluates a patient's level of arousal, concentration, and performance on cognitive tasks involving attention, memory (learning, recall, and recognition), language (comprehension, naming, reading and writing, repetition, and spontaneous speech), visuospatial skills, arithmetic skills, praxic skills (e.g., motor programming), and frontal lobe skills (executive functions). The examination also assesses the patient's appearance, attitude, behavior, mood and affect (the felt internal and outward display of emotion, respectively), thought content and associative processes, insight, and judgment (Mueller and Fogel, 1996).

A number of clinical rating scales and mental status examinations have been developed to screen patients for cognitive impairments and evaluate their mental status. For example, the Folstein Mini-Mental State Examination, the 3MS (an extended version of the Folstein) (Teng and Chui, 1987), the Neurobehavioral Cognitive Status Examination (Kiernan et al., 1987), and the UCLA Neuropsychiatric Inventory (Cummings et al., 1994) are frequently helpful in identifying the cognitive functioning of patients over time, particularly after medications and treatment interventions.

When a potential area of brain dysfunction or a specific neurobehavioral syndrome (e.g., dementia, amnesia, frontal lobe) is suspected, follow-up with specific diagnostic tests and procedures is often useful in corroborating the clinician's suspicions. For example, if a patient with a history of brain trauma exhibits labile affect, expansive mood, disinhibited behavior, difficulty in changing mental set, motor perseveration, and reduced verbal fluency on mental status examination, the behavioral neurologist/neuropsychiatrist would evaluate for the presence of anosmia (loss of smell from an olfactory nerve injury); inquire about previous episodes of impulsivity, prior head trauma, and deficits in the patient's academic performance; and request for a neuropsychological evaluation and a brain MRI study with special coronal (cross-sectional) views and imaging parameters to detect a frontal lobe contusion (a surface bruise). The neuropsychiatrist may not be able to fit the patient's symptoms into the standard DSM-IV psychiatric syndromes. For example, even though the symptoms may fit the criteria for a recognized psychiatric diagnosis, their expression may be modified by brain trauma or dysfunction. Conversely, the manifestations of a recognized neurobehavioral syndrome (e.g., amnesia) may be modified by psychological defense mechanisms (e.g., denial) or sociocultural/linguistic influences (Mueller and Fogel, 1996).

Although they are somewhat more objective and quantitative, the above neurodiagnostic procedures and clinical mental status evaluations should not be considered a substitute for a more rigorous and comprehensive neuropsychological evaluation. Behavioral neurologists and neuropsychiatrists frequently rely on neuropsychological assessment to clarify diagnostic issues and develop a comprehensive plan of treatment, which may include the use of psychotherapy and behavior modification techniques. In the medicolegal arena, the collaboration of clinical neuropsychologists and behavioral neurologists/neuropsychiatrists in the evaluation of patients who have sustained brain insults or trauma is rapidly becoming the norm.

REFERENCES

Cummings, J. L. and Hegarty, A. 1994. Neurology, Psychiatry, and Neuropsychiatry. *Neurology*, *44*, 209–213.

Cummings, J. L., Mega, M., Gray, K., Rosenberg-Thompson, S., Carusi, D. A., and Gornbein, J. 1994. The Neuropsychiatric Inventory: Comprehensive Assessment of Psychopathology in Dementia. *Neurology*, *44*, 2308–2314.

Jefferson, J. W. and Marshall, J. R. 1981. *Neuropsychiatric Features of Medical Disorders*. New York: Plenum Press.

Kaufman, D. M. 1995. *Clinical Neurology for Psychiatrists*, 4th ed. Philadelphia: W. B. Saunders.

Kiernan, R. J., Mueller, J., Langston, J. W., and Van Dyke, C. 1987. The Neurobehavioral Cognitive Status Examination. *Annals of Internal Medicine*, *107*, 481–485.

Marsden, C. D. and Fowler, T. J. 1998. *Clinical Neurology*, 2d ed. New York: Oxford University Press.

Mueller, J. and Fogel, B. S. 1996. Neuropsychiatric Evaluation. In Fogel, B. S., Schiffee, R. B., and Rao, S. M. (Eds.) *Neuropsychiatry*. Baltimore: Williams & Wilkins, pp. 11–29.

Purisch, A. D. and Sbordone, R. J. 1987. Clinical Neuropsychology: Medicolegal Applications (Part 2). *Trauma*, *6*, 61–94.

Siegal, A. W. 1996. Historical, Phenomenologic, and Observational Data: A Context for Neuropsychological Test Findings. In Sbordone, R. J. and Long, C. J. (Eds.) *Ecological Validity of Neuropsychological Testing*. Delray Beach, FL: GR/St. Lucie Press, pp. 43–74.

Teng, E. L. and Chui, H. C. 1987. The Modified Minimental State (3MS) Examination. *Journal of Clinical Psychiatry*, *48*, 314–318.

4 Neuroanatomy

It is necessary for health professionals and attorneys having cases involving brain trauma to understand a few fundamental facts about neuroanatomy, even though this is one of the most difficult courses offered in medical school. Hence, these individuals will be provided with a simplified overview of the brain, particularly concerning the functional significance of certain areas of the brain and their behavioral and psychological implications.

THE BRAIN

The brain weighs approximately 3 pounds. It is surrounded by a bony chamber or vault known as the skull. Between the skull and the cerebral hemispheres lie three coverings, or membranes, which are termed the meninges. The outermost membrane is known as the dura mater. It is composed of a thick elastic material, which adheres to the inner surface of the skull. Below the dura mater is the arachnoid membrane. The third membrane is known as the pia mater. The outermost covering of the brain, the dura mater, forms what is known as the falx cerebri, which divides the two cerebral hemispheres. The dura mater also provides a protective covering (tentorium cerebelli) that divides the most posterior part of the cerebral hemispheres from the cerebellum. Located between the dura mater and the underlying subarachnoid membrane is the cerebrospinal fluid (CSF), which surrounds the brain and serves as a sort of shock absorber whenever the skull makes contact with an immovable object or the movement of the brain is rapidly accelerated or decelerated.

The right and left cerebral hemispheres appear roughly symmetrical. Close inspection, however, reveals subtle hemispheric asymmetries that reflect differences in their style of information processing. For example, the left hemisphere is a discrete, analytic, and sequential two-dimensional processor that is suited for the expression and comprehension of language and the analysis of linguistically based material. Compared to the right-hemisphere, it has more gray matter and a larger posterior temporal and parietal–occipital region. The right-hemisphere is an intuitive and three-dimensional parallel processor that is designed to handle larger patterns of information and allows us to see the big picture (e.g., gestalt) rather than discrete amounts of information (e.g., the forest instead of the trees). Compared to the left hemisphere, it has relatively more white matter and a larger frontal area. Hemisphere dominance has a rough correlation with hand preference (see Lateral Dominance, Chapter 10). Nearly all right-handers and a majority of left-handers are left hemisphere dominant for language and fine motor skills and right-hemisphere dominant for visuospatial and emotional functions. The remaining left-handers have right or bilateral language representation (Taylor, 1999).

The importance of the cerebral hemispheres within neuropsychology cannot be overemphasized, since they are concerned with such functions as intelligence, language, perception, judgment, memory, problem solving, knowing, thinking, social behavior, executive functions, personality, and emotions. The surface of the cerebral hemispheres is made up of convolutions, causing it to appear to be made of various hills and valleys. The hills are called gyri, while the valleys are known as sulci. The brain's convolutions permit the surface of the brain to be folded into a much smaller area, so that it can be fit into the skull, and 80% of the brain's surface remains hidden from view in its sulci. In this respect, it should be noted that the number of convolutions within the brain increases as one goes up the phylogenetic scale. For example, animals such as rats have considerably fewer convolutions than cats or dogs, while humans have considerably more convolutions than the latter.

THE CEREBRAL LOBES OF THE BRAIN

The cerebral hemispheres can be further divided into four lobes on the basis of four large sulci, which form the lobes' boundaries (see Figures 4.1 and 4.2). For example, the frontal lobe, the largest lobe of the brain, makes up approximately 44% of the total mass of the cerebral hemispheres and lies anterior (toward the front of the head) to the central sulcus. This sulcus divides the frontal from the parietal lobes. Thus, the parietal lobes are located posterior to (behind) the central sulcus. Located directly below the frontal and parietal lobes and separated by a very large sulcus (which is known as the lateral fissure) is the temporal lobe. Thus, the temporal lobe is inferior to (below) the frontal and parietal lobes. The occipital lobe lies at the most posterior aspect (toward the back) of the cerebral hemispheres, separated from the parietal lobe by the parietal–occipital sulcus.

The cerebral hemispheres house a bundle of neural fibers (corpus callosum) deep within the brain, which connect the two cerebral hemispheres and allow information to be transmitted from one side of the brain to the other. Research studies (Gazzaniga, 1998) have demonstrated that surgical severing of the corpus callosum (performed in cases of intractable epilepsy) produces an individual with two brain hemispheres that cannot communicate with each other. For example, a blindfolded individual following this procedure would be unable to verbally identify an object such as an orange if it were placed in his left hand but could later differentiate it, on the basis of weight, size, and texture, from other objects such as an apple or a peach. This is because sensory information coming from the left hand is transmitted to the right side of the brain, which, in the overwhelming majority of individuals, lacks the capacity for anything but the most rudimentary language production. The right side of the brain is better able to analyze this object and determine that it is an orange; however, it cannot send this information to the left side of the brain. The individual cannot verbally name it as "an orange" but can recognize the orange by touch alone, since the right-hemisphere possesses knowledge of the object. Thus, information processed relatively independently by each hemisphere regarding a specific event is synthesized and integrated by the corpus callosum.

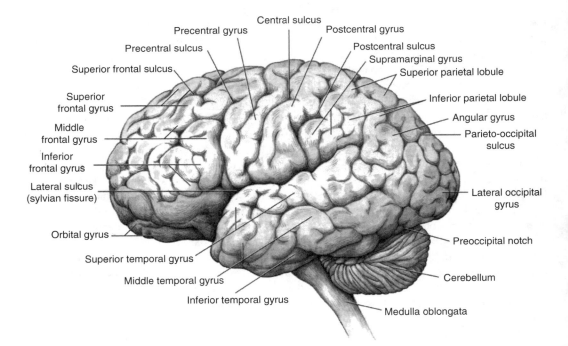

FIGURE 4.1 The human adult brain as seen in lateral view. (*Source:* Devinsky, O. and D'Esposito, M. 2004. *Neurology of Cognitive and Behavioral Disorders.* New York: Oxford University Press, p. 2. With permission.)

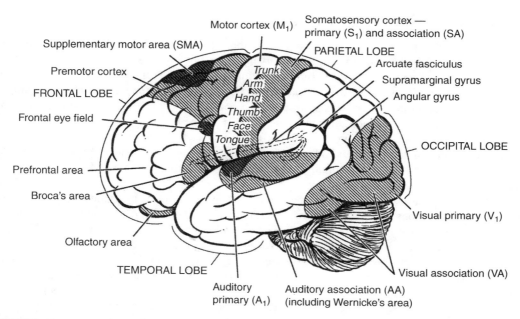

FIGURE 4.2 The cerebral cortex in lateral view showing major functional areas subserving somatosensory, auditory, and visual processing. (*Source:* Devinsky, O., Feldmann, E., and Weinreb, H. J. 1997. *The Resident's Neurology Book*. Philadelphia: F.A. Davis, p. 245. With permission.)

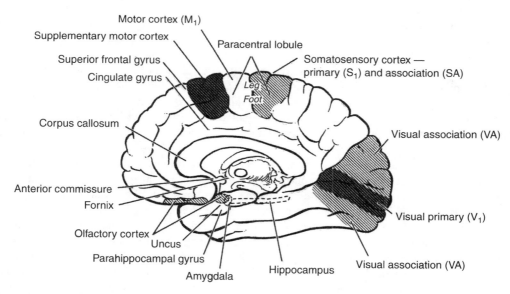

FIGURE 4.3 The cerebral cortex in medial view showing major functional areas subserving somatosensory and visual processing. (*Source:* Devinsky, O., Feldmann, E., and Weinreb, H. J. 1997. *The Resident's Neurology Book*. Philadelphia: F.A. Davis, p. 245. With permission.)

The occipital, parietal, and temporal lobes can each be broken down into cortical zones, according to Luria (Kolb and Whishaw, 2003), to understand how the brain receives, analyzes, and stores sensory information arriving from various parts of the body through the senses (see Figures 4.2 and 4.3).

Primary and Secondary Cortical Zones

According to Luria's model of brain–behavior relationships, each of these lobes contains neurons (nerve cells) that only respond to a specific sensory modality. For example, the primary cortical zones located in the occipital lobe respond to only visual information, while the primary cortical zones in the parietal lobe respond to only tactile (touch) and kinesthetic (movement feedback) information. The primary zone in the temporal zone responds to only auditory information. Thus, damage to any of these primary zones would result in the inability of the brain to process a specific type of information. The areas surrounding the primary cortical zones within each respective lobe are known as secondary cortical zones, because information arriving at the primary cortical zones is transferred to the secondary zones so that the brain can formulate a perception or elaborated image of the raw sensory information that it receives.

When the primary cortical zone in one occipital lobe is damaged, the patient will frequently develop a homonymous hemianopsia (a loss of vision in the half-field opposite the lesion). Bilateral damage results in what has been described as cortical blindness, a total visual loss, of which the patient may be unaware. If the primary cortical zones in the occipital lobes are preserved and damage occurs to the secondary or association area (which frequently occurs in patients who sustain hypoxic encephalopathy), these individuals will develop "visual agnosia" and be unable to recognize the object that they can, in fact, see. For example, such patients may not visually recognize objects such as a watch or a pen by sight alone, but will have little or no difficulty recognizing such objects by touch. The primary sensory cortex is located in the medial posterior area of the occipital lobe; the surrounding area that is anterior and lateral to the primary sensory cortex makes up the secondary cortical zone.

The primary cortical zone within the parietal lobe is situated directly behind (posterior) the central sulcus and is located in the most anterior part of the parietal lobe. It has a point-to-point representation with specific body regions for sensation. When damage occurs to specific parts of this zone, a person will experience a corresponding numbness or loss of sensation in an area of the body that corresponds to this region (see Figures 4.2 and 4.3). When the secondary zones, which are located posterior to the primary zones, are damaged (in the absence of primary lobe damage), the individual might not be able to distinguish a quarter from a dime, which he is holding in the hand directly contralateral (opposite) to the site of brain injury. This condition is known as astereognosis, which is a form of tactile agnosia. It should be noted that patients who sustain strokes would frequently exhibit this condition on the side of their body contralateral (opposite) to the site of their stroke.

The primary cortical zone of the temporal lobe is responsible for the reception of auditory information. When bilateral damage occurs to this region, the patient will exhibit what has been termed cortical deafness. The primary cortical zone in the temporal lobe is buried in the floor of the lateral fissure. The secondary and tertiary cortical zones are located adjacent to the primary cortical zone in superior and posterolateral regions of the temporal lobe. When these specific areas of the brain are damaged in the left hemisphere, the patient's ability to decipher speech sounds or phonemes will be severely compromised. There is also difficulty comprehending word meanings. As a consequence, the patient typically will be unable to follow commands such as "Raise your right hand over your head and touch your stomach with your left hand." A comparable lesion on the right may compromise the patient's ability to comprehend or recognize environmental sounds, such as the singing of birds, music, or the sound of a waterfall. More often, the emotional tone, as opposed to the linguistic content, of a spoken communication is not appreciated, resulting in interpersonal difficulties. When right-handed patients sustain an injury to the secondary cortical language zone in the left hemisphere, they exhibit frequent word substitution (paraphasic) errors. For example, the patient may use the word "spoon" when attempting to say the word "fork." The patient may also use the word "dare" when attempting to say the word "pear." The patient may also speak in a fluent but garbled manner, not making any sense at all. This condition is known as fluent or Wernicke's aphasia.

TERTIARY CORTICAL ZONES

The tertiary cortical zones of the brain integrate information received in their respective sensory modalities from the various secondary cortical zones. The tertiary cortical zones are frequently referred to as association cortices and are found at the borders of the parietal (somatosensory), temporal (auditory), and occipital (visual) secondary cortical zones. They convert concrete perceptions into abstract thoughts or representations. The left hemisphere tertiary zone supports such complex cognitive operations as reading, writing, and calculating; the right-hemisphere plays a primary role in body and spatial awareness. According to Luria, an injury to the tertiary sensory zone, which integrates data from the parietal and occipital secondary cortical zones, may result in a patient who would have considerable difficulty solving the following problem: A father is 45. He is 19 years older than his son. How old are the two of them together?

A comparable but more extensive lesion on the right will produce a striking contralateral inattention and neglect of the left side of the body and of the surrounding environment. Such a patient may neglect to wash or dress the left side of his or her body, ignore food on the left side of his or her tray, and even lack awareness of a left-sided paralysis.

THE FRONTAL LOBES

The frontal lobes of the brain are primarily responsible for the initiation, organization, planning, execution, and regulation of complex motor movements and actions. The primary cortical zone for movement is found in the posterior frontal lobe just anterior to the central sulcus (Rolandic fissure) with a point-to-point relationship with muscles under voluntary control (see Figures 4.2 and 4.3). Injuries to this region impair the ability to perform voluntary movements on the contralateral side of the body. The contralateral limbs become spastic and the reflexes become hyperactive in comparison with the unaffected side. Pathological reflexes such as the Babinski can also be elicited by stroking the sole of the contralateral foot. The neurons in this region give rise to the corticospinal tract, which travels downward through the internal capsule (passageway), and brain stem (midbrain and pons) to the medulla oblongata, where it decussates (crosses over to the opposite side of the brain stem) and continues down the spinal cord as the lateral corticospinal tracts. Connecting nerve fibers eventually exit the spinal cord, passing through the peripheral nervous system (outside of the brain and spinal cord) to innervate (control) the body's musculature.

The primary motor region, the precentral gyrus, contains the sites for the initiation of specific movements of various parts of the body. This region (see Figures 4.2 and 4.3) is distributed like an upside-down homunculus (man). The motor areas for the initiation of movements of the face and hands are located in the inferior aspects (close to the temporal lobe), while the regions for the trunk and lower extremities are more anterior and located dorsally (highest area of the cerebral hemispheres) and medially (near the longitudinal fissure). The secondary cortical zones of the frontal lobe have been termed the premotor region and are located in the adjacent anterior regions of the frontal lobe (see Figure 4.2). They play a prominent role in the organization of movements and control specific complex motor skills. The primary cortical zones, which control the movements of the feet and lower legs, are located in the uppermost part of the frontal lobe on the medial surface. A strong relationship exists between the size of the primary and secondary motor zones and the degree of control over the muscles of the hand and other body parts. Areas of the body that contain numerous muscles, such as the lower face, tongue, and hands, and are involved in complex motor movements tend to have a disproportionately large number of nerve cells located in these motor cortical zones.

When these regions are injured, often the patient can no longer produce organized or complex motor movements.

THE LEFT HEMISPHERE

The gray and white matter structures around the lateral fissure in the left hemisphere constitute the cerebral basis of propositional language. The emotional component of speech and gesture, termed prosody, is mediated by an analogous area of the right-hemisphere. Prosodic changes in pitch and melody reflect sadness, happiness, anger, or surprise in the patient's mood. For example, Broca's area, located in the posterior left inferior frontal gyrus, anterior to the primary motor speech zone, is devoted to the production of language. Broca's nonfluent aphasia, described as halting, effortful, agrammatic speech and writing, typically results from a stroke involving Broca's area and adjacent cortical and subcortical regions. Its proximity to the lower precentral gyrus usually produces an associated weakness of the right face and arm. Since language comprehension is mediated by the posterior speech zone in the temporal lobe, it is largely preserved (see Figure 4.2).

The tertiary zones of the motor cortex are located in the most anterior regions of the frontal lobe. These zones are referred to as the prefrontal cortex. These zones play a prominent role in carrying out executive functions that involve the planning, organization, initiation, execution, and regulation of complex motor skills and actions. Injuries to the tertiary zone will result in impulsive behavior, poor judgment, and repeated mistakes because of the patient's inability to recognize errors and regulate their behavior. Such patients also show deficits in the initiation of spontaneous behavior and motivation. They typically exhibit severe impairments on problem solving and higher-order intellectual tasks, are easily distracted, and have considerable difficulty shifting from one task to another. As a consequence, they are likely to exhibit perseverations (repeating the same action without achieving any objective) and frequently show evidence of confabulation (their recall of recent events is colored either by their imagination or by certain aspects of the material). For example, the patient is asked to perform a task in which he must add 3 to each new number, beginning with the number 1. He begins correctly by stating "1, 4, 7," but then continues with "8, 9, 10." Thus, the patient has lost the set or "motor program" for performing the particular task that is subsequently replaced by a well-learned or stereotyped activity, such as counting. The patient, however, shows no awareness that he has made an error, and when asked what he was asked to do, he replies, "Count by threes." The verbal instruction is retained in memory but cannot continuously guide the patient's motor performance.

Figures 4.2 and 4.3 are schematic drawings showing the major functional areas of the brain, subserving primary and complex motor, somatosensory, visual, auditory, language, visuospatial, and cognitive functions. Right-sided motor and sensory deficits and the aphasias (Broca's and Wernicke's) result from lesions involving the respective functional lateral regions of the left hemisphere. The contralateral neglect syndrome, however, is typically more frequent and severe following right rather than left-hemisphere damage. Left homonymous hemianopsia (left-sided half-field defects in the visual field of each eye) results from a lesion involving the right visual primary and association areas. A corresponding lesion involving the left visual areas will produce a right homonymous hemianopsia.

THE RIGHT HEMISPHERE

Lesions in the posterior right-hemisphere of the brain can produce visual–perceptual difficulties such as being unable to recognize familiar objects, places, and persons, even the faces of family members and friends. Right-hemisphere impairment of visual–spatial and visual memory functions can be detected by asking the patient to copy or draw objects or perform assembly tasks. Patients with left hemiplegia as a result of a stroke involving the right parietal lobe may not only fail to use their paralyzed limbs, but may even deny their paralysis. The ability of such patients to perform basic activities of daily living, such as personal grooming, bathing, dressing, and finding one's way

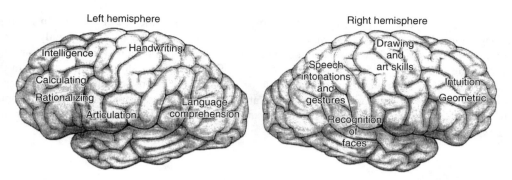

FIGURE 4.4 Contrasting higher mental functions of the left and right-hemispheres. (*Source:* Young, P. A. and Young, P. H. 1997. *Basic Clinical Neuroanatomy*. Baltimore: Williams & Wilkins, p. 198. With permission.)

around the neighborhood is usually severely compromised. The unique role of the right-hemisphere in the production of neuropsychiatric syndromes, involving the regulation of emotions and behavior, is frequently underestimated. Mania, often associated with hypersexuality, may arise from lesions of right orbital (inferior) frontal cortex, caudate nucleus, thalamus, or inferior temporal region, whereas depression is frequently associated with left prefrontal pathology. Although psychosis with delusions may occur with lesions of either hemisphere, marked visual hallucinations are typical of right-hemisphere pathology.

Right-hemisphere patients often fail to comprehend the subtle shades of meaning, conveyed in conversation by connotation, humor, and metaphor. For example, they may not recognize sarcasm or grasp the point of a joke. The patients have difficulty expressing emotion (expressive aprosodia) and understanding emotion (receptive aprosodia) by failing to comprehend speech inflections, melody, and stress. Such disorders and a customary indifference or denial in the face of hemiplegia or other deficit leads to significant disturbances in interpersonal relationships. Their inability to recognize their functional limitations leads to arguments with caregivers and poor cooperation when they are placed in rehabilitation. Hyposexuality, a loss in a person's sexual interest or desire, is also more common after right-hemisphere lesions than left (Cummings and Trimble, 2002; Edwards-Lee and Saul, 1999) (Figure 4.4).

Since Luria's pioneering work in Russia, there have been remarkable advances in our understanding of regional cerebral functions and their corresponding cognitive and behavioral disorders. The diagnosis of lesion lateralization, especially with regard to complex behaviors and cognitive functions such as language, had been limited in the past by standard neurological and psychiatric examinations. However, with the advent of neuroimaging techniques and sophisticated neuropsychological testing, specific lesioned areas of the brain and the patient's specific cognitive and behavioral deficits can be identified. It should not be presumed, however, that these deficits are caused by damage to that specific area. In fact, positive symptoms such as hallucinations and seizures, as opposed to negative symptoms (e.g., aphasia, agnosia), result primarily from preserved or partially dysfunctional brain regions (Devinsky, 1992).

Mesulam (1990) has formulated a network theory of directed attention that provides a useful model for understanding complex cognitive processes that are mediated by the brain. This model stresses that complex behaviors (e.g., language, problem solving) are controlled not by isolated regions of the brain, but by a number of regions distributed throughout the brain that form an integrated functional system, determined in turn by their neural interconnections. Consequently, an injury in a specific region of the brain may produce multiple cognitive and behavioral deficits, because it may disrupt other brain regions through its interconnections with them. Although language is localized to specific regions of the dominant hemisphere, these areas are connected to subcortical regions of the brain that activate and coordinate language and other cortical functions. A lesion in one of these subcortical areas can also disrupt language, but usually only transiently because of the functional compensation by other neuronal structures along the same neural network. In addition, the degree to which specific cognitive and behavioral deficits can be localized frequently depends on numerous factors such as the patient's age, sex, handedness, previous brain insults, and the nature, time course, and etiology of the brain insult. For example, a slow-growing tumor in the frontal lobes of a young adult may cause subtle personality changes over months and even years, whereas damage (e.g., by stroke) to Wernicke's area (the posterior superior region of the temporal lobe in the dominant hemisphere) in an elderly patient can immediately disrupt the comprehension and expression of language (Devinsky, 1992).

THE LIMBIC SYSTEM

Within the temporal lobes lies the limbic system (see Figure 4.5), which is a duplicate set (one in each hemisphere) of anatomically linked structures that extend anteriorly into the orbital frontal lobe and posteriorly into the midbrain (the areas surrounding and including the upper part of the brain stem). There are four principal components: amygdala, hippocampus, septum, and cingulate gyrus (see Figure 4.5). Within the limbic system is the Papez circuit, which plays a vital role in the retention of new information; it includes the following major structures that form a closed loop through their interconnections: hippocampus (lying behind, i.e., medial and posterior to the amygdala), mammillary body (lying in the ventral hypothalamus), anterior thalamus, cingulate gyrus, and parahippocampal gyrus. The fornix, a reversed C-shaped structure connects the hippocampus and mammillary body; the mammillo-thalamic tract connects the mammillary bodies and

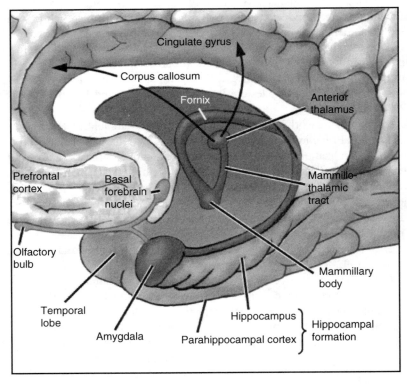

FIGURE 4.5 The limbic system; lateral three-dimensional view of the medial surface of the brain. (*Source:* Kolb, B. and Whishaw, I. Q. 2003. *Fundamentals of Human Neuropsychology*, 5th ed. New York: Worth Publishers, p. 526. With permission.)

anterior thalamus. Other connecting pathways exist but are not shown in the figure. A lesion involving any part of the Papez circuit will interfere with memory formation and new learning.

The memory impairment in such patients is most severe when bilateral damage occurs to these structures. In these cases, the patient will exhibit evidence of profound memory impairment for recent events. These patients are typically unable to recall what they did only a few moments previously or have no recollection of ever having been examined by a particular physician, even though the physician may have spent over 30 min with the patient. For example, the patient may be given a story to recall in which a woman who lives in South Boston and works as a cleaning lady is robbed of $15 on her way home one evening. She has four children who have not eaten for 2 days. She informs the police, who feel sorry for her plight and take up a collection in order to help her feed her children. The patient is then asked to repeat this story. The patient states, "It is about a woman who is robbed," but he cannot recall any of the details of this story. One hour later, the patient is again asked to recall this story but has no recollection that he had ever been given a story to recall.

A number of limbic structures, in particular the amygdala, septum (and other basal forebrain nuclei), anterior cingulate gyrus, and hypothalamus, are vital for the generation and regulation of emotional behavior. Through its strong cortical connection, the limbic system acts as a mediator between the basic and primitive drive-related demands of the hypothalamus (hunger, thirst, aggression, sex, and defense) and the often externally based, more conceptual, and civilized needs of association cortex. Damage to the limbic system can result in a number of emotional or behavioral disorders, arising from neuronal activity that is suppressed (hypolimbic) or increased (hyperlimbic) to an excessive degree. A lesion, focal tissue damage, in the anterior cingulate gyrus above the corpus callosum will produce hypolimbic apathy, defined as a loss of motivation. These patients typically lose their desire to engage in previously enjoyable pastimes. A reduction in their spontaneous speech and movement also occurs.

Bilateral extensive temporal lobe damage, including the amygdala and adjacent cortex, can produce the Kluver–Bucy syndrome with the following components: hypersexuality, emotional placidity, hypermetamorphosis (compulsive exploration of objects in the environment), hyperorality (mouthing inedible items), and dietary changes (carbohydrate craving). Herpes encephalitis, cerebral trauma, Alzheimer's disease, and frontotemporal dementia are frequently reported causes of this syndrome (Devinsky, 1992).

Conversely, patients who develop epilepsy from focal limbic pathology may develop the Gastaut–Geschwind syndrome, a classical hyperlimbic syndrome, with behavioral and personality changes in many respects opposite to those seen in Kluver–Bucy. For example, they typically exhibit symptoms such as hyposexuality (diminished sexual drive), hypergraphia (excessive writing, often reflected in their lengthy letters or numerous diaries), obsessive concerns, social viscosity (inability to terminate conversation or personal contact), and hyperreligiosity (excessive and uncharacteristic interest in religious matters). The observed behaviors are not components of their characteristic seizures, but are enduring personality traits, which are present during their seizure-free intervals. These patients may also display rapid mood swings, irritability, angry outbursts, philosophical preoccupation, delusions, and hallucinations, both visual and auditory (see section on Posttraumatic Epilepsy, Chapter 8).

Frontal-limbic pathology in such neurological disorders as temporal lobe epilepsy, postencephalitic Parkinsonism, Huntington's disease, and Tourette's syndrome may produce altered sexual drive and preferences including paraphilias (sexual aberrations) such as exhibitionism, cross-dressing, fetishism, pedophilia, sexual sadism–masochism, and voyeurism (Cummings and Mega, 2003; Cummings and Trimble, 2002).

The frontal–orbital region (located above the roof of the orbit), the adjacent ventral midline frontal region (VM), and the basal forebrain, located behind VM, have recently been implicated in social cognition and memory. Bilateral VM patients, for example, develop a severe disruption of social conduct with defects in planning, judgment, decision making, empathy, and insight that has been appropriately labeled an acquired sociopathy. Damage to the basal forebrain, composed of the nucleus accumbens and the septum, illustrated in Figure 4.5 produces severe recall and learning deficits, often accompanied by unprompted bizarre confabulation (the production of bizarre, false, and unverifiable verbal responses, usually in association with amnesia). Interruption of the basal forebrain's cholinergic (mediating the neurotransmitter acetylcholine) projections to the hippocampus and posterior temporal–parietal cortex is one of the major reasons for the memory impairment in Alzheimer's disease (Clark et al., 2005).

THE BASAL GANGLIA

The basal ganglia are subcortical neuronal structures, which include the putamen, the globus pallidus, caudate, and the amygdaloid complex. The globus pallidus and putamen collectively form the lentiform nucleus. The putamen is the largest and most lateral neuronal structure of the basal ganglia. It is continuous anteriorly with the head of the caudate nucleus. The globus pallidus makes up the medial portion of the lentiform nucleus. Descending fibers from the motor strip of the frontal lobes and internal capsule form its medial border. The caudate nucleus is a long arched structure that is adjacent to the lateral ventricles throughout its length. Its enlarged anterior head extends into the anterior horn of the lateral ventricles. The body and tail of the caudate lie dorsolateral to the thalamus, near the lateral wall of the ventricle. Its tail follows the inferior or temporal horn of the lateral ventricles and terminates in the temporal lobes near the amygdaloid nucleus and hippocampus. These relationships are illustrated in Figure 4.6, where the cingulate gyrus, caudate nucleus, putamen, thalamus, amygdala, hippocampus and retrosplenial cortex of the left hemisphere are portrayed. The route of the

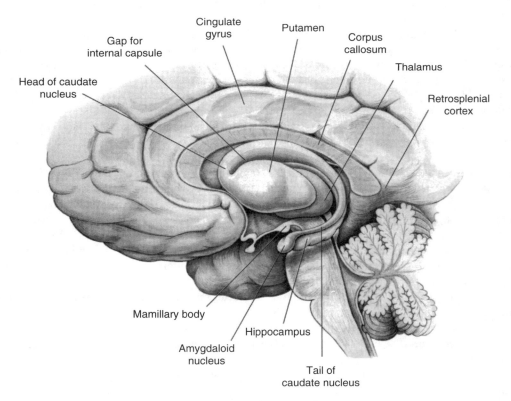

FIGURE 4.6   Three-dimensional view of the principal cortical and subcortical components of the basal ganglia and limbic systems. (*Source:* Devinsky, O. and D'Esposito, M. 2004. *Neurology of Cognitive and Behavioral Disorders*. New York: Oxford University Press, p. 333. With permission.)

descending fibers of the internal capsule originates in the motor cortex and continues laterally to the caudate nucleus and thalamus but medially to the lentiform nucleus (globus pallidus and putamen) on its way to the brain stem and spinal cord (see also Figures 4.3 and 4.7).

The cerebral cortex and many brain stem and thalamic nuclei (groups of neurons) provide massive input to the basal ganglia, whose output goes predominantly into the thalamus and brain stem, with additional secondary connections from these areas going to the cortex and spinal cord. As a consequence, the basal ganglia are uniquely wired to subserve complex integrative motor and behavioral functions. They are a major component of the extrapyramidal system, which is responsible for the automatic execution of learned motor behaviors or programs. For example, in golf a seasoned player adopts a characteristic stance, followed by an efficient and coordinated swing at the ball. The extrapyramidal system is primarily responsible for postural adjustments involving large muscle groups of the trunk and limbs, as in the golfer's stance and swing in teeing off. In contrast, the smaller manual or articulatory muscles, under the control of the corticospinal-pyramidal system, carry out the more precise and refined motor movements, which are required in putting the ball and in speech, writing, or drawing.

Disorders of the extrapyramidal system can produce negative symptoms that are characteristically seen in Parkinson's disease, for example, loss of motor spontaneity and initiative, decreased and slowed movements, and loss of postural reflexes (needed to maintain an upright posture). Positive symptoms would include rigidity (muscle stiffness); tremor and other involuntary movements, including facial grimaces, tics, chorea (fine twitching of the limbs, head, and trunk); dystonia (sustained abnormal postures of the neck, trunk, or limbs); and athetosis (slow, successive and writhing involuntary movements, usually of the hands and forearms).

Lesions of the caudate nucleus and putamen can also produce significant cognitive, affective (mood), and personality changes that accompany motor abnormalities and closely resemble the cognitive and behavioral symptoms commonly seen in frontal lobe syndromes. Negative symptoms typically consist of depression, inertia, lack of drive, apathy, blunted affect, difficulty formulating plans, and impaired attention. Positive symptoms typically include irritability, impulsivity, agitation and aggressiveness, sexual promiscuity, delusions, and hallucinations (Devinsky and D'Esposito, 2004).

THE BRAIN STEM

Contained within the brain stem in ascending order are the medulla oblongata, pons (Figure 4.7), midbrain, and diencephalon. The brain stem serves several functions. It provides a direct link from the spinal cord to the cerebral hemispheres with a descending pathway for information coming directly from the brain to the spinal cord (the cerebrospinal tract) and an ascending pathway for information traveling from the spinal cord to the thalamus (spinothalamic tract), which is then relayed to other parts of the brain. The brain stem contains the 12 cranial nerves that play a major role in all of our special senses (smell, sight, hearing, touch, balance, and taste). Listed in Table 4.1 are the 12 cranial nerves, their principal motor and sensory functions, and the symptoms resulting from impaired function of each cranial nerve. Note that cranial nerves III, IV, and VI are involved in the control of eye movement, while cranial nerves VII, X, and XII innervate the articulatory and phonatory muscles involved in speech.

The brain stem also houses the neural centers for cardiovascular activity, consciousness, and respiration. Lying within the core of the brain stem is the reticular formation, which serves to activate the brain and improve its efficiency. The brain stem also plays a major role in attention and sleep. Damage to the reticular system produces drowsiness, stupor, or even coma. Damage to the lower brain stem, particularly when it is severe, can result in death, since the nerve centers that maintain our life support systems are located within the medulla oblongata.

The pons (which in Latin means bridge) is located in the anterior portion midway up the brain stem. Visually, it resembles a large bulge or pouch and contains fibers, which relay information

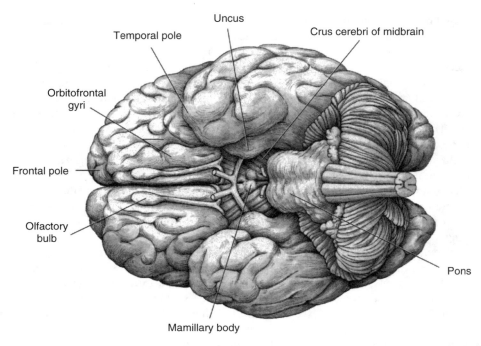

FIGURE 4.7   The human adult brain as seen in inferior view. (*Source:* Devinsky, O. and D'Esposito, M. 2004. *Neurology of Cognitive and Behavioral Disorders*. New York: Oxford University Press, p. 3. With permission.)

TABLE 4.1
The Cranial Nerves

Number/name of nerve	Function	Symptoms of impaired function
I Olfactory	Smell	Loss of sense of smell (anosmia)
II Optic	Vision	Loss of vision (blindness or field cut)
III Oculomotor	Eye movement	Diplopia (double vision), lid droop, dilated pupil, lateral deviation of eye
IV Trochlear	Eye movement	Diplopia, impaired downward gaze
V Trigeminal	Facial sensation, jaw movement	Impairment of pin/light touch sensibility of face, facial pain, difficulty chewing
VI Abducens	Eye movement	Diplopia, inward deviation of eye
VII Facial	Facial movement, taste	Facial paralysis, loss of taste in anterior tongue, slurred speech
VIII Auditory/vestibular hearing	Hearing, maintenance of equilibrium	Deafness, tinnitus, loss of balance and equilibrium
IX Glosso-pharyngeal	Sensation and motor function of tongue/pharynx	Loss of sensation/paralysis of palate, loss of taste in posterior tongue
X Vagus	Sensation and motor function of pharynx, larynx, heart, blood vessels	Hoarseness, palatal/pharyngeal paralysis and sensory loss, slurred speech, visceral symptoms
XI Spinal accessory	Motor function of neck/shoulder muscles	Inability to rotate neck/raise shoulders
XII Hypoglossal	Motor function of tongue muscles	Tongue weakness/wasting, slurred speech

Source: Adapted from Kolb, B. X. and Whishaw, I. Q. 1996. *Fundamentals of Human Neuropsychology*. New York: W. H. Freeman, p. 50.

between the motor cortex of the frontal lobes to the cerebellum for fine motor coordination and balance. Areas within the pons also control the regulation of various stages of sleep. The midbrain, which is located between the pons and the diencephalon, contains a number of major cell groups: motor nuclei that regulate eye movements as well as the red nuclei and the substantia nigra (components of the extra pyramidal system).

Finally, the diencephalon, which is located at the most dorsal (highest) level of the brain stem, contains two very important structures — the thalamus and hypothalamus. The thalamus is an obliquely situated gray matter collection of neurons located on either side of the midline at the rostral (upper) end of the brain stem. These paired masses are separated by the third ventricle and lie medially and more posteriorly in relation to the basal ganglia. The thalamus receives information from the spinal cord (spinothalamic tract) and relays this information to various brain structures. It also serves as a relay center within the brain and allows transfer of information between different brain regions. As a result of its primary function as a relay center for various forms of sensory and motor information, it plays a major role in such areas as attention, orientation, concentration, learning and memory, perception of the environment, language, and emotional functioning. The hypothalamus, although very small, is extremely complex and has been shown to play a major role in activities such as appetite, thirst, fatigue, sexual libido, sleep, temperature regulation, weight control, and the generation of raw emotion, which, as discussed earlier, is modulated by the limbic system in concert with the frontal lobes.

The cerebellum lies directly below the occipital and parietal lobes and directly behind (posterior) the brain stem and adjacent to the pons. The cerebellum plays a major role in coordinating and regulating fine motor control, as it receives information via the pons from the motor cortex, the spinal cord, and vestibular structures located in the inner ear (see Figure 4.1). Damage to the cerebellum is likely to result in ataxia (poorly regulated and jerky movements that produce balance difficulties and limb incoordination).

Schmahmann (1998) has recently described an adult cerebellar cognitive affective syndrome. Based on clinical features and brain MRI findings, this unique cerebellar syndrome arises from pathology principally confined to the cerebellum. Distinctive features include executive function deficits in planning, set shifting (changing attentional focus), verbal fluency, abstract reasoning, and working memory. Symptoms such as visual–spatial deficits, memory impairment, language disorders, personality changes, blunted affect, and disinhibited behavior often accompany this syndrome.

CEREBROVASCULAR SYSTEM

The brain requires a constant and copious supply of blood to fulfill its needs for oxygen. Any blockage of the blood supply to the brain, even for only 5 s, will result in a loss of consciousness. When the brain is deprived of oxygen for 3 min or longer, the cells in specific areas of the brain begin to die. Loss of oxygen for 8 to 10 min or longer will typically produce widespread brain damage (hypoxic encephalopathy). The brain relies exclusively on its cerebrovascular system for its supply of oxygen. The cerebrovascular system can be broken down into the internal carotid artery system and the basilar vertebral artery system.

INTERNAL CAROTID ARTERY SYSTEM

The internal carotid artery system is composed of arteries, which enter the skull from the common carotid artery located in the neck. Shortly after this artery enters the skull, it divides into two anterior cerebral arteries, which travel along the longitudinal fissure, at first anteriorly and superiorly and then posteriorly toward the parietal occipital fissure. These arteries supply blood and oxygen to the medial surface of the cerebral hemispheres. The second branch of the internal carotid artery forms the middle cerebral artery system and supplies blood and oxygen to the lateral areas of the frontal and

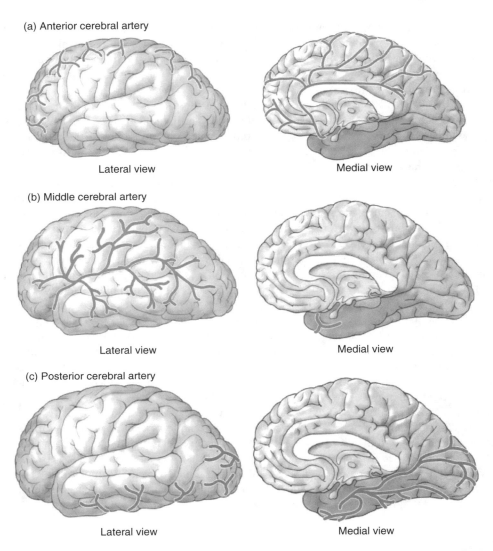

(a) Anterior cerebral artery

Lateral view   Medial view

(b) Middle cerebral artery

Lateral view   Medial view

(c) Posterior cerebral artery

Lateral view   Medial view

FIGURE 4.8   (a–c) Distribution of the major cerebral arteries in the hemispheres. (*Source:* Kolb, B. and Whishaw, I. Q. 2003. *Fundamentals of Human Neuropsychology*, 5th ed. New York: Worth Publishers, p. 321. With permission.)

parietal lobes, as well as the superior and middle temporal lobes. The middle cerebral artery also contains smaller branches (striae), which furnish blood to the internal capsule and basal ganglia (see Figure 4.8).

BASILAR VERTEBRAL ARTERY SYSTEM

The vertebrobasilar artery system supplies blood and oxygen to the thalamus, brain stem, cerebellum, and inferior temporal lobes. It comprises the two vertebral arteries, which enter the cranial cavity from the neck, traverse the foramen magnum (a large opening at the base of the skull), and unite at the upper end of the medulla to form the basilar artery. The basilar artery terminates by dividing into two posterior cerebral arteries and the two posterior communicating arteries (see Figure 4.9).

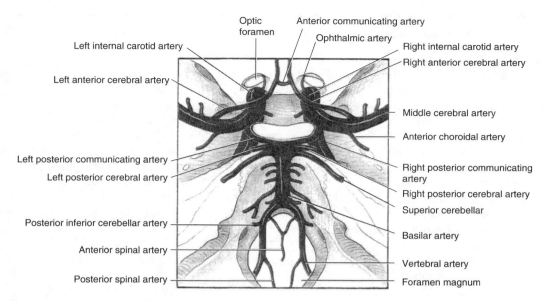

FIGURE 4.9 The cerebral arterial Circle of Willis and other major cerebral arteries on the base of the brain. (*Source:* Young, P. A. 1997. *Basic Clinical Neuroanatomy.* Baltimore: Williams & Wilkins, p. 238. With permission.)

The anterior, middle, and posterior cerebral arteries connect together at the base of the brain and form what is called the Circle of Willis. The anterior communicating artery forms a bridge between the anterior cerebral arteries anteriorly; the posterior communicating artery likewise forms a bridge posteriorly between each posterior cerebral artery and its internal carotid artery mate to complete the circle. This connection allows blood to be critically shunted (transferred) from one hemisphere to the other when a major arterial branch on one side becomes obstructed and cannot provide an adequate amount of blood and oxygen.

DAMAGE TO THE CEREBROVASCULAR SYSTEM

An acute obstruction (thrombosis) of a blood vessel, which restricts blood flow (ischemia) or a significant reduction in the amount of oxygen contained within the blood (hypoxia) can produce damage to specific parts of the brain or more widespread brain damage. For example, a lack of oxygen caused by cardiac arrest frequently causes damage to the hippocampi, temporal lobe structures that play a major role in the learning of new information. If the patient is deprived of oxygen for more than several minutes, neurons (brain cells) located in the watershed zones (areas of the brain that lie between the areas of the brain perfused by the major arterial systems) are likely to be severely damaged. As a consequence, the patient may develop visual agnosia, balance and coordination difficulties, and problems executing hand–eye coordination tasks. When a blockage or interruption of the blood supply occurs in one of the arterial systems, that area of the brain, which is normally supplied blood and oxygen by this system, will die. This is referred to as a stroke.

A transient ischemic attack (TIA), on the other hand, is a reversible vascular neurologic deficit, which can last up to 24 h, but is usually less than 30 min. These attacks were originally thought to be primarily due to obstructing clots (emboli), which had broken off and traveled upstream from the heart or the carotid artery. In many cases, however, a TIA may result from watershed ischemia in areas distal to a stenotic (narrowed by arteriosclerosis) artery when there is a critical drop in blood pressure. Frequently repetitive, they herald a major stroke; such a patient should be immediately referred for a diagnostic workup and therapeutic intervention.

Case Study: False Attribution — Stroke Following a MVA

M.L., a 71-year-old widow, filed suit against an auto manufacturer. She claimed that she lost control of her car when the brakes failed. She veered from side to side on the street and finally crashed into a tree, sustaining what was possibly a very mild concussion. There was no loss of consciousness, and bystanders and police arriving quickly on the scene described her as alert and coherent with no obvious deficits. Six hours after returning home, she developed right-sided weakness. There was no evidence of neck trauma that could have compromised circulation in the carotid artery. A brain CT scan revealed a left parietal hemorrhagic infarction, the apparent cause of her stroke; there was also evidence of an old stroke in the opposite hemisphere. On neurobehavioral examination, she had a right hemiparesis, but no aphasia or cognitive deficits. The biomechanics expert hired by her attorney, however, found the car to be in perfect condition and the suit was dropped. In retrospect, she probably suffered a TIA, which heralded the subsequent stroke and was probably responsible for the loss of control of her vehicle. The contribution of any concussion was negligible. This is a case of false attribution and illustrates the fallacy of assuming events that follow one another in close temporal sequence (MVA and stroke) imply causation.

A major stroke involving the middle cerebral artery territory in the language dominant left hemisphere will most likely produce a fluent or nonfluent aphasia. There are often associated deficits in writing (agraphia), reading (alexia), calculating (acalculia), and programming of skilled motor acts (apraxia). Right-hemisphere strokes will frequently produce a left-sided neglect of body and space, visual–perceptual and constructional disorders, and impaired awareness of disability (anosognosia). With either hemisphere, such a stroke will invariably produce a contralateral hemiparesis and hemisensory deficit (face and arm greater than leg) and a homonymous hemianopsia. Anterior cerebral artery strokes, which are uncommon, will produce a contralateral hemiparesis (leg greater than arm and face), a gait disorder, and frontal lobe deficits. Strokes involving the posterior cerebral artery territory may produce a mild hemiparesis, contralateral visual field cut, memory loss, alexia, topographic (environmental) disorientation, and difficulty recognizing faces (prosopagnosia) or colors.

THE CEREBROVENTRICULAR SYSTEM

The cerebroventricular system (see Figure 4.10) is composed of four ventricles (cavities) within the brain that generate and circulate CSF. CSF serves as a protective liquid cushion or shock absorber for the brain and spinal cord. Each lateral ventricle lies within a cerebral hemisphere. The anterior portion of the lateral ventricles (anterior horns) resides in the frontal lobes, while the major portion of the ventricles (body) lies within the frontal and parietal lobes. The ventricles extend posteriorly into the occipital lobe (posterior horns) and inferiorly into the temporal lobe (inferior horns). Within the lateral ventricles lies the choroid plexus, which manufactures the CSF. CSF flows downward from the lateral ventricles through an opening (the Foramen of Monro) into the third ventricle, which lies within the diencephalon. The third ventricle contains choroid plexus and also produces CSF. After flowing downward and out through the third ventricle, CSF passes through a long, narrow chamber known as the Aqueduct of Sylvius or cerebral aqueduct, into the fourth ventricle, which is located within the brain stem. The fourth ventricle also contains choroid plexus and is capable of producing CSF. After exiting the fourth ventricle, CSF circulates over the surface of the brain in the subarachnoid space located between the arachnoid and the underlying pial membrane. The CSF also travels down the spinal canal, enveloping the spinal cord.

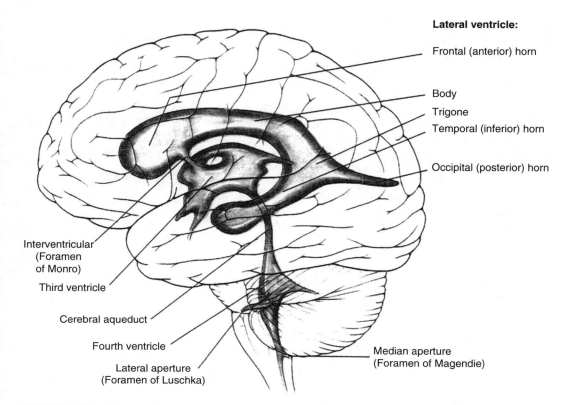

Lateral ventricle:

Frontal (anterior) horn

Body

Trigone

Temporal (inferior) horn

Occipital (posterior) horn

Interventricular
(Foramen
of Monro)

Third ventricle

Cerebral aqueduct

Fourth ventricle

Lateral aperture
(Foramen of Luschka)

Median aperture
(Foramen of Magendie)

FIGURE 4.10 The ventricular system in lateral view. (*Source:* Young, P. A. 1997. *Basic Clinical Neuroanatomy*. Baltimore: Williams & Wilkins, p. 252. With permission.)

BRAIN DAMAGE CAUSED BY HYDROCEPHALUS

When an obstruction occurs within the CSF system or when its drainage system located within the arachnoid villi is blocked, CSF will accumulate and cause an expansion of the ventricular system and compression of the surrounding brain tissue. This condition, known as hydrocephalus, frequently requires neurosurgical intervention, consisting of the placement of a ventriculo–peritoneal shunt, which allows excessive CSF to flow out of the brain and into the patient's abdomen. Hydrocephalus is commonly seen following traumatic brain injuries, particularly if there has been hemorrhage within the brain. Patients who sustain this condition will typically exhibit the progressive development of gait and balance difficulties, memory impairment, lethargy and confusion in the early stage, and bladder and bowel incontinence in late stage.

REFERENCES

Clark, D. L., Boutros, N. N., and Mendez, M. F. 2005. *The Brain and Behavior*. Cambridge, U.K.: Cambridge University Press, chapter 6.
Cummings, J. L. and Mega, M. S. 2003. *Neuropsychiatry and Behavioral Neuroscience*. New York: Oxford University Press.
Cummings, J. L. and Trimble, M. R. 2002. *Neuropsychiatry and Behavioral Neurology*, 2d ed. Washington, D.C.: American Psychiatric Publishing.
D'Esposito, M. 2004. *Neurology of Cognitive and Behavioral Disorders*. New York: Oxford University Press, p. 2.

Devinsky, O. 1992. *Behavioral Neurology*. St. Louis: Mosby.

Devinsky, O. and D'Esposito, M. 2004. *Neurology of Cognitive and Behavioral Disorders*. New York: Oxford University Press.

Edwards-Lee, T. A. and Saul, R. E. 1999. Neuropsychiatry of the Right Frontal Lobe. In Miller, B. L. and Cummings, J. L. (Eds.) *The Human Frontal Lobes, Functions and Disorders*. New York: Guilford Press.

Gazzaniga, M. S. 1998. The Split Brain Revisited. *Scientific American, 279*, 50–55.

Kolb, B. and Whishaw, I. Q. 2003. *Fundamentals of Human Neuropsychology*, 5th ed. New York: Worth Publishers, chapter 8.

Mesulam, M. M. 1990. Large Scale Neurocognitive Networks and Distributed Processes for Attention, Memory and Language. *Annals of Neurology, 28*, 597–613.

Schmahmann, J. D. 1998. The Cerebellar Cognitive Affective Syndrome. *Brain, 121*, 561–579.

Taylor, M. A. 1999. *The Fundamentals of Clinical Neuropsychiatry*. New York: Oxford University Press, chapter 1.

5 Neurobehavioral Disorders

AMNESIA

Amnesia refers to a condition in which the patient's ability to learn new information is impaired despite relatively normal attention and concentration skills. The ability to recall remote information (e.g., the name of the high school attended or names of childhood friends and teachers) may be spared in many forms of amnesia. The vast majority of patients who have been exposed to some form of severe trauma will complain of problems with their recent memory. One must, however, distinguish between complaints of memory difficulties and true impairments of recent memory. For example, patients who have severe amnesia rarely complain of memory difficulties. When asked to describe their memory, they will typically say, "It's fine," even though they cannot recall what they did several minutes earlier, what they ate for breakfast that morning, or what they did the night before the examination. Patients who complain, however, of severe memory problems most likely either have mild amnesia or are neurotic, depressed, or histrionic. Similarly, patients who complain of numerous problems and difficulties typically have an intact memory for recent events. Patients with severe amnesia rarely, if ever, voice such complaints unless they are currently experiencing muscular pain or discomfort in some part of their bodies. Thus, their complaints are typically confined to their current somatic problems. Patients who complain of problems with their remote memory usually are depressed, since such memories are typically preserved following brain trauma.

Immediate or working memory refers to the ability to recall material immediately after it is presented. Short-term (often called recent) memory refers to the ability to remember information after a temporal delay, during which time the individual's attention is focused away from the material. Information in short-term memory can be retained up to a few minutes but will usually be lost or replaced by new information unless a conscious effort is made to retain the information via a process known as rehearsal. Information stored in long-term memory can be held almost indefinitely without any conscious effort to retain it. When amnesia occurs, an individual is unable to transfer the information from short-term to long-term memory. Thus, the information, which is presented, will be lost or forgotten several minutes later. Furthermore, in cases of severe amnesia, if individuals are subsequently asked if they had ever been presented with this information, they will typically say "no" and ironically deny that they have any memory problems.

ANTEROGRADE AMNESIA

Amnesia typically includes an *anterograde* and a *retrograde* component. Anterograde amnesia (AA) is defined as a forward extending learning deficit with onset at the time of neurological insult. Individuals who have sustained a traumatic brain injury (TBI) will be unable to recall or have difficulty recalling the events that occurred after their brain injury. For example, they may report having no recollection of being taken out of their vehicle, speaking to paramedics, or being taken to the hospital in an ambulance. The AA in severe cases may be permanent.

RETROGRADE AMNESIA

Retrograde amnesia (RA) refers to an inability to recall or recognize information or events that occurred before the onset of a brain injury. It extends backwards from the time of the insult for varying times from a few seconds to a number of years. For example, patients who have sustained a TBI will typically report that they have no recollection of the accident or the events that occurred immediately before the accident. In fact, in some cases, particularly if the individual has sustained a severe TBI, the duration of RA may be days, weeks, or even months long. Most amnesiacs exhibit a temporal gradient with the greatest impairment for more recently acquired memories. Information learned before the period of RA is spared and does not extend over the individual's entire life. Patients with RA are usually able to recall factual information about themselves (e.g., date of birth, names of children, marital status, and occupation) and historical facts (e.g., name of high school attended, grades in school, name of the president). When an individual claims not to recall date of birth, names of parents and children, high school attended, or jobs held in the past after receiving a blow to the head or after a motor vehicle accident, it is highly unlikely that the RA is related to a specific injury or accident. In fact, such a claim or one of loss of personal identity suggests a psychogenic form of amnesia or malingering. After functional recovery in typical cases, the period of AA remains relatively permanent, whereas the duration of RA lessens over time.

CONFABULATION

Confabulation is defined as the distortion of recalled information without a deliberate intent to deceive. It tends to occur in the acute phase of amnesia and is rarely seen in chronic amnestic disorders. While it often may be based on an individual's prior experiences, it usually contains an inaccurate synthesis (Cummings and Mega, 2003a).

Confabulations may be spontaneous or provoked. The spontaneous type commonly follows frontal lobe pathology, particularly with involvement of the inferior medial regions, but may occur in acute metabolic or toxic confusional states such as the alcoholic Wernicke–Korsakoff syndrome. Memories may be recalled out of order or attributed to an incorrect source. Typically amnesic patients show provoked or momentary confabulations, defined as fleeting, intrusive errors or distortions in response to a memory test or other challenge. Viewed as a genuine effort to reconstruct a memory from a weak trace, it can be seen in normal individuals and does not necessarily imply a conscious or deliberate attempt to fill in a memory gap.

Delusional memories in psychosis may resemble spontaneous confabulations, but usually revolve around a single pathological theme. For example, the patient may hold the firm belief of an impending attack by Martians. With bilateral and particularly right frontal lobe pathology, symptoms such as reduplicative paramnesia and delusional identification syndromes, such as Capgras, are often reported. The reduplicative disorder is best described as a disorientation syndrome in which the patient claims to be present in two or more locations at the same time, such as his home and the hospital. In the Capgras syndrome, the patient has a firm delusional belief that familiar people have been replaced by identical appearing imposters. These conditions commonly occur in the recovery phase following a posttraumatic encephalopathy or toxic–metabolic disorder. Fantastic confabulation is a rare disorder associated with frontal lobe disease, in which patients describe colorful and adventurous but impossible experiences. For example, they may report that they flew to Mars in their own spaceship (Kopelman, 2002; Cummings and Mega, 2003a).

Case Example

A 48-year-old woman was referred for neuropsychological testing by her physician after she claimed that she had lost the ability to recall any information about her past, following a relatively insignificant motor vehicle accident. She claimed that she had no recollection of her childhood, including her date of birth, where she was born, the names of her parents, where she attended school, what types of work or jobs she had performed, or anything else about her past. Despite these complaints, neuropsychological testing revealed no evidence of any memory or cognitive impairment.

When she returned for a follow-up visit, the neuropsychologist noticed a faded tattoo on her right arm, which appeared to have some numbers on it. When she was asked about the tattoo, she became visibly upset and refused to discuss it. After several follow-up visits, she tearfully admitted that she had spent the first 10 years of her life in a concentration camp at Auschwitz during World War II. She had been physically and sexually abused by her German captors and had witnessed the death of thousands of fellow Jews, including her parents and older siblings.

Several months before her motor vehicle accident, she had gone to see a psychiatrist after she had begun having terrifying nightmares of people being killed and tortured. As therapy proceeded, she began having flashbacks of her early childhood, which she tried to suppress. When the accident occurred, she had been struggling to come to grips with the painful reality of her childhood. Thus, her claim that she had no recollection at all of her childhood most likely represented her unconscious efforts to suppress the painful memories of her childhood.

Memory Is Not a Unitary Phenomenon

Research has shown that memory for acquisition of facts, information about events, and experiences can be retrieved and brought to conscious awareness. This type of memory is known as *declarative memory*, as opposed to nondeclarative memory, which refers to specific skills, habits, and reactions to stimuli that have been developed over a lifetime. Declarative memory can be divided into *episodic* and *semantic memory*. Episodic memory refers to specific information that was learned at a particular time and place in one's life, for example, one's recollection of what was being done and where when first learning that John F. Kennedy had been killed. Semantic memory refers to general knowledge that does not have a particular temporal and spatial context, for example, recalling the names of the last five presidents of the United States or the name of the person who shot Abraham Lincoln. Unfortunately, declarative memory can be unreliable since our episodic and semantic memories may be inaccurate. For example, we may initially recall that we were playing baseball with some friends when we first learned of John F. Kennedy's death, only to later discover that we were actually at home watching a baseball game on television when the announcement was heard. We may inaccurately recall that Andrew Johnson instead of John Wilkes Booth killed Abraham Lincoln (Delis and Lucas, 1996).

Nondeclarative or *procedural memory* can be broken down into habits and memories for specific perceptual motor skills that are learned during the course of a lifetime. Skills such as swimming, riding a bicycle, or driving a car can usually be performed automatically. In other words, the individual does not have to consciously try to recall the specific movements necessary for swimming or riding a bicycle to perform these skills. Habits such as the route taken to work each day or driving to the home of a close friend or reactions to events (e.g., the death of a loved one or seeing specific individuals) are types of nondeclarative memory. In recent years, psychologists have identified another type of memory referred to as working or immediate memory. This is a limited-capacity system, holding about seven items and capable of storing and manipulating information for only 20 or 30 s without rehearsal (mental repetition of stored items).

Amnesic patients typically have severe impairment of *episodic memory*, which may involve primarily stored verbal information with a left hemisphere lesion, stored visual spatial information with a right hemisphere lesion, or both stored verbal and stored visual spatial information with bilateral lesions. Working, semantic, and procedural memory is usually normal in amnestic patients, except in cases of diffuse and progressive dementia (Alzheimer's disease [AD]). The loss or impairment of episodic memory indicates damage to one or more temporal lobe or diencephalic structures comprising the medial limbic or Papez circuit, discussed in Chapter 4.

Damage to the prefrontal cortex can produce working or "scratch pad" memory impairment, which can be distinguished from episodic memory deficits associated with limbic circuit damage. For example, patients with frontal damage can normally store new episodic information but usually have difficulty strategically manipulating and retrieving both old and new episodic memories. In addition, they frequently lose their mental set; for example, when asked to recall a word list, they begin recalling a different list of words or simply repeat the examiner's instructions. Patients with amnestic disorders and with frontal lobe damage will usually not recall previously presented items. Patients with frontal lobe damage, however, show significantly improved recall when tested with a recognition format that places minimal demands on their compromised retrieval processes.

Unlike episodic and working memory, semantic knowledge is stored in widely distributed cortical association areas, particularly in the lateral temporal lobes. Thus, patients with diffuse and progressive degenerative brain disease are likely to have semantic memory (memory for factual information) impairment usually with associated episodic memory deficits. Amnesic patients generally have preserved perceptual motor skills, which indicates procedural memory is not dependent upon the medial limbic circuit. A cortical–subcortical system with reciprocal connections between frontal neocortex, basal ganglia, and the thalamus is the apparent neural substrate supporting procedural memory. The striatum, composed of the caudate and putamen, is the critical link in these parallel circuits. Dementia patients with frontal and striatal pathology, for example, Huntington's or Parkinson's disease, may have selective deficits in working and procedural memory; however, their episodic memory impairment resembles the frontal deficit pattern with impaired recall and relatively preserved recognition (Cummings and Mega, 2003a).

What is important is that a brain injury does not produce amnesia across these different types of memory. For example, an individual who has sustained a significant brain injury may have difficulties in declarative memory but not with nondeclarative memory. Thus, we should not expect patients who have sustained traumatic injuries to complain that they can no longer remember how to drive or perform a particular skill (e.g., bricklaying or typing).

Case Study: Pseudo-Retrograde Amnesia

A 30-year-old mechanic sustained head trauma when several rolls of paper fell on him. He did not lose consciousness but subsequently developed some amnesia for events around the time of the accident, severe headaches, dizziness, and other postconcussive symptoms. He was hospitalized; the initial neurological examination, C-spine films, and an electroencephalogram (EEG) were normal. Because of a questionable aneurysm on brain computed tomography (CT) scan, an angiogram was done and proved negative. Several hours after the study, he suddenly became totally amnesic for past events, the RA extending backward to early childhood. However, his memory for ongoing events from the time of this incident was unaffected. There were no associated deficits on neurological exam. Neuropsychological testing revealed that his cognition, apart from remote memory, was consistent with his previous level of intelligence and education. There was no past history of head trauma, substance abuse, or other medical/emotional disorder. Because of persistent problems with his past memory, he underwent multiple evaluations during the following 2 years.

While several examiners felt that he had sustained a chronic brain syndrome, the majority of them diagnosed psychogenic amnesia related to a hysterical personality or factitious disorder. When seen by one of the authors (R.E.S.), he related his family's description of events that occurred in the early months after the onset of his amnesia. At first, he could not recognize family members. He burned his mouth drinking coffee because he did not know it was hot. He put salt and pepper on all his food, including ice cream. He had to "relearn everything" (e.g., the meaning of words, how to tie his shoes, and how to work the controls on his car). He did not recognize his own tools. When his young nephew played with a windup toy dog in his hospital room, he pet it, mistaking it for a real animal. This information appeared well rehearsed and was presented with a blunted affect.

Testing revealed, with the exception of remote memory, preserved cognition with normal attention, new learning, and recent memory skills. There were no neurological deficits. This patient claimed an isolated severe loss of past memory, including semantic (fact) and procedural memory in addition to episodic (event) memory. New learning and recent ongoing memory were preserved, and there were no other significant cognitive or neurological deficits. Such an extreme loss of past autobiographical memory for specific events, general knowledge, and learned skills, dating back to early childhood, was inconsistent with any recognized pattern of organic amnesia. In typical cases of traumatic amnesia, RA shrinks with time and is invariably associated with impairment of new learning and ongoing memory (AA). In the absence of an associated dementia, semantic and procedural memory should be unaffected. There was no final consensus regarding the psychiatric diagnosis of this patient; conversion disorder and malingering were primary considerations. His amnesia, however, was unequivocally labeled psychogenic.

Transient Global Amnesia

In the clinical syndrome of transient global amnesia (TGA), an individual experiences an acute transient period of amnesia. There is typically ongoing AA of several hours duration and a spotty RA for events during the several weeks prior to the onset of the TGA, which, as in TBI, lessens with recovery. These patients usually do not have difficulty performing their everyday activities, but cannot remember recent events or what they are told by others. They appear bewildered and will repeatedly ask the same questions, a hallmark of the syndrome. They do not lose their personal identity, which distinguishes this disorder from psychogenic dissociative amnesia. There are no other behavioral or neurological symptoms during an attack. Although the etiology remains controversial, interruption of blood supply to the hippocampal region is considered the most likely (Cummings and Mega, 2003a).

A variety of drugs and medications can produce transient and chronic amnesia. For example, alcohol, antiadrenergic agents, anticholinergic medications, anticonvulsants, antihistamines, antihypertensive agents, anti-Parkinsonian medications, benzodiazepines, corticosteroids, neuroleptic medications, and a number of antidepressant medications can produce memory difficulties (Delis and Lucas, 1996).

Causes of Amnesia

Amnesia is often seen in patients who have sustained head trauma, cerebral anoxia, brain tumors, or cerebrovascular accidents (strokes) or have a history of acute cardiopulmonary arrest. Electroconvulsive therapy, insulin overdose, and surgical removal of the temporal lobes may also produce amnesia. Patients who have a history of excessive drinking, which may result in Wernicke–Korsakoff's syndrome, will typically exhibit severe amnesia. Amnesia is most commonly seen in patients who have AD. Any insult to the hippocampus, which is located in the medial temporal lobes, as a result of hypoxia or trauma, is likely to produce a profound impairment in recent memory. Patients who sustain significant frontal lobe injuries are likely to exhibit memory impairments for recent events, which frequently take the form of confabulation, distortions, and intrusion errors. Table 5.1 lists the causes of permanent or progressive amnesia and those disorders associated with transient memory loss. The underlying pathologic mechanism in both cases is disruption of the medial temporal–diencephalic limbic circuit, subserving the initial encoding of memories for subsequent storage and retrieval. Those conditions associated with transient memory loss involve the same circuit to a lesser extent (Cummings and Mega, 2003a).

TABLE 5.1
Differential Diagnosis of Memory Disorders

Causes of permanent or progressive amnesia
    Traumatic brain injury
    Anoxic brain injury
    Wernicke–Korsakoff syndrome secondary to thiamine deficiency in chronic alcoholism
    Alzheimer's disease
    Lewy body dementia — mixed features of amnesia and Parkinsonism
    Herpes encephalitis
    Hippocampal infarction associated with posterior cerebral artery occlusive disease
    Thalamic tumor or stroke
Disorders associated with transient and reversible memory loss
    Head trauma and whiplash
    Migraine
    Epilepsy and electroconvulsive therapy
    Transient ischemic attack (TIA) and Transient global amnesia (TGA)
    Alcoholic blackout
    Normal pressure hydrocephalus
    Hypoglycemia
    Cerebral and coronary angiography
    Dissociative disorder

PSYCHOGENIC AMNESIA AND RELATED DISSOCIATIVE DISORDERS

Neuropsychological assessment is invaluable in assessing patients who are suspected of having amnesia or to rule out amnesia in patients who present with complaints such as, "My biggest problem is my memory. I can't remember anything. My memory is simply terrible. Yesterday my wife told me about my brother-in-law's problems with the IRS, and an hour later I completely forgot what she had said." Neuropsychological testing can also determine whether the patient's memory problems are due to faulty encoding (organization) of new information or impaired storage.

Memory impairments are frequently seen in patients who have poor concentration or attention skills, which may be due to the inability to encode the information at the time it was presented. Encoding difficulties, however, may also be due to high levels of anxiety.

Dissociative Disorders

Dissociative disorders are characterized by a disturbance in the patient's sense of identity, memory, and consciousness. They must be differentiated from dissociative experiences that are common in normal individuals (e.g., an inability to recall part of a conversation or feeling abnormally absorbed in a TV program or movie). In psychogenic or dissociative amnesia, the failure to recall important personal information cannot be explained by normal forgetfulness. An individual, for example, may not remember significant personal life events (e.g., their childhood or the death of a loved one) or may find himself in a particular place or location without recalling how he or she got there (Cummings and Mega, 2003b). Psychogenic amnesia and psychogenic fugue are common dissociative disorders. Patients with these disorders will exhibit intact and integrated behaviors during a particular event that cannot be recalled later.

Psychogenic memory loss

Kopelman (2002) has classified psychogenic memory loss as global or situation specific. In the *global* type, exemplified by a fugue state (physical flight from one's present life situation to a new environment that is less threatening), patients experience a sudden and profound loss of past memories, often including their personal identity. They may exhibit a period of wandering where they will travel from their home or workplace to another location, which they are unable to recall when they are later questioned. In the *specific* form, the memory loss is for a particular incident (e.g., being unable to recall a terrifying event or accident) or portions of the incident (e.g., how they got out of their car after their accident). Fugue states usually last several hours or days; fugue states that are reported to last several weeks or longer should be viewed with suspicion and suggest that the patient is trying to simulate memory loss.

A number of predisposing factors for fugue episodes have been identified. They are always preceded by a severe precipitating wartime or civilian stressor (e.g., witnessing your best friend killed during wartime or people seriously injured or killed), severe emotional or financial problems, bereavement, or a criminal offense. Depressed mood is a common antecedent. The individual may also have a history of a transient organic amnesia resulting from epilepsy, head injury, or an alcoholic blackout. In fact, the fugue state may resemble organic amnesia with fragments of preserved memory within the period of amnesia, in which people or things may seem strange or unfamiliar. In psychogenic amnesia, as illustrated in the above case, verbal learning and semantic and procedural memory skills may remain intact or become impaired to a varying degree.

Situation-specific amnesia

Situation-specific amnesia occurs in such circumstances as committing a crime (e.g., killing one's child or spouse) or being the victim of an offense (e.g., childhood sexual abuse), which often results in posttraumatic stress disorder. Offenders and victims of crimes involving violence commonly claim amnesia. For example, amnesia is reported by 25 to 45% of individuals who commit homicide. A neurological workup is required to exclude possible disorders such as epileptic automatism, postictal confusional state, TBI, hypoglycemia, sleepwalking, and rapid eye movement (REM) disorder (a sleep disorder that is characterized by complex movements such as kicking, punching, and leaping from the bed). REM sleep disorder occurs in older males, patients with Parkinson's disease, and patients who suffer from Lewy body dementia (a dementia seen in older adults that resembles AD and is associated with motor symptoms that mimic Parkinson's disease).

Amnesia for a crime is usually associated with three conditions: (1) a state of extreme emotional arousal in which the unpremeditated homicidal offense involves a lover, wife, or family member. It is often preceded by depression and followed by remorse; (2) alcoholic intoxication, usually seen in individuals with a very high blood alcohol level and a long history of alcohol or general substance abuse; and (3) florid psychosis (Kopelman, 2002).

In addition to psychogenic amnesia and psychogenic fugue, the dissociative disorders include dissociative identity (multiple personality) disorder; depersonalization–derealization disorder (feelings of detachment or estrangement from oneself or from the world); trance, hypnotic, and possession states and Ganser syndrome (a state resembling severe dementia in which the patient repeatedly gives illogical or near miss answers to simple questions, e.g., 1 plus 2 equals 4).

DELIRIUM

Delirium can be defined as a transient, usually reversible, mental disorder, acute or subacute in onset, and is most commonly observed in elderly patients. It is characterized as a global disturbance in cognitive functioning with associated clouding of consciousness, impaired attention, disorientation, increased sympathetic nervous system activity, and altered sleep–wake cycles and psychomotor activity. Individuals who are delirious will typically have difficulty focusing or sustaining their attention, become distracted easily, or exhibit reduced alertness with apathy or enhanced alertness with agitation. Many delirious patients are often worse at night, particularly when they are in relatively unfamiliar settings. Many have insomnia with disturbing nightmares. They also exhibit mood swings with anger or fear in response to threatening visual hallucinations and often experience delusions of persecution. The most common causes of delirium include medical disorders (e.g., infections; system failures, secondary to cardiac, pulmonary, renal, liver disease or metabolic encephalopathy), prescription or over-the-counter medications, and diffuse or focal brain lesions. A thorough medical and neurological workup can frequently identify the cause of the patient's delirium and lead to effective treatment. The EEG is a highly sensitive instrument for detecting the diffuse impairment of brain function, characteristically seen in delirious patients. For example, bilateral slowing of background EEG activity is highly correlated with the severity of the patient's cognitive impairment.

DEMENTIA

Dementia refers to a clinical syndrome in which the patient's cognitive and behavioral functioning is significantly impaired. There is a significant deterioration from the patient's previous intellectual level, which occurs in clear consciousness, that is, in the absence of delirium. Delirium, however, is a common complication of chronic dementia. DSM-IV diagnostic criteria require, in addition to memory impairment, deficits in at least one of the following cognitive domains: language (aphasia), perceptual recognition (agnosia), skilled movements (apraxia), and executive functions (American Psychiatric Association, 2000). Cummings and Benson (Mendez and Cummings, 2003a) offer what many consider more appropriate diagnostic criteria — sustained loss or impairment in at least three of the following: memory, language, perception (especially visuospatial), praxis, calculations, conceptual or semantic knowledge, executive functions, personality or social behavior, and emotional awareness and expression. Regardless of the criteria used, there must be a global and sustained cognitive deterioration with significant impairment of occupational or social functioning. Typically, the term dementia is reserved for cognitive disorders of the elderly and is only occasionally used to characterize acquired mental deterioration in young adults.

EVALUATION OF DEMENTIA

The principal disorders causing the dementia syndrome fall into two categories based on their mode of onset. Acute conditions, such as severe TBI, cerebral anoxia from cardiopulmonary arrest, and major strokes, produce dementia through the inactivation or destruction of a large volume of cerebral tissue. Spontaneous recovery is variable. Chronic disorders, such as the primary dementing degenerative disorders, exemplified by Alzheimer's (the most common form), have an insidious onset and a slowly progressive course. A prolonged but stepwise course is characteristically seen in vascular (multi-infarct) dementia. Prion-slow virus disease, on the other hand, can lead to death within a year (see Table 5.2).

Dementia or delirium can also be produced by a variety of medications that lower levels of acetylcholine and dopamine within the brain, resulting in mental confusion with impaired problem solving and recent memory. A number of over-the-counter nonprescription drugs can further impair brain function in elderly patients with dementia or cerebrovascular disease. It should also be noted that patients who are placed on anticonvulsant medications, such as Dilantin® and especially phenobarbital, typically show a significant reduction in their cognitive functioning, which is alleviated when they are taken off these medications. Exposure to a variety of metals (lead, mercury, manganese, arsenic, and thallium), a variety of organic solvents (trichloroethylene, toluene, carbon tetrachloride, and carbon disulfide), carbon monoxide (CO), and insecticides are likely to produce dementia (Mendez and Cummings, 2003b). In many cases, elimination of exposure to these substances results in a gradual improvement in the patient's condition.

Table 5.3 lists a large group of disorders that can produce either an acute/subacute delirium or a chronic dementia. Since all are potentially reversible with treatment, a comprehensive diagnostic workup is justified to identify a remediable disorder in its early stages. Major categories

TABLE 5.2
Common Causes of Dementia — Classified by Mode of Onset and Clinical Course

Acute onset/spontaneous recovery-variable	Insidious onset/progressive course
TBI	AD
Cerebral anoxia from cardiopulmonary arrest	Frontal–temporal dementia
Stroke	Parkinson's (Lewy body) dementia
	VAD
	AIDS–dementia complex
	Motor neuron disease (amyotrophic lateral sclerosis)
	Huntington's disease
	Prion-slow virus disease (Creutzfeldt–Jakob disease)

TABLE 5.3
Treatable and Potentially Reversible Causes of Delirium or Dementia

Infectious disorders	Bacterial, fungal, and viral meningoencephalitis, brain abscess, AIDS, neurosyphilis
Endocrine vascular and metabolic	Thyroid, parathyroid and pituitary disorder; porphyria, vasculitis, recurrent TIAs, liver and renal failure, congestive heart failure, pulmonic encephalopathy, fluid and electrolyte imbalance, Wilson's disease
Mechanical	Chronic subdural hematoma, boxer's encephalopathy, electrical trauma, hypothermia/hyperthermia, normal pressure hydrocephalus
Tumors	Primary (glioma, meningioma), secondary (metastatic), obstructive hydrocephalus
Other neurological disorders	Epilepsy (partial complex seizures, postictal states), recurrent cephalalgia-headaches (migraine, cluster), multiple sclerosis, Parkinson's disease, sleep apnea
Nutritional	Thiamine (Wernicke–Korsakoff syndrome), vitamin B-12, folate deficiencies
Chemical intoxication	Alcohol, CO, organophosphates, organic solvents, heavy metals
Drugs and drug withdrawal	Sedative hypnotics and narcotics, anticholinergics, cardiac agents, lithium, steroids, antidepressants, anticonvulsants, stimulants, recreational drugs
Pseudodementia	Somatoform disorder, conversion disorder, depression

include infectious, endocrine, vascular, metabolic, and neurological disorders; diseases caused by trauma, physical agents, chemical toxins, deficiency states, drugs, and drug withdrawal; tumors; hydrocephalus; and the emotionally based pseudodementias, which can mimic an organic disorder.

Table 5.4 lists the laboratory tests required for a dementia evaluation. The standard tests, considered mandatory in most major medical centers, are listed in the first column. The second column lists tests that may be indicated by the history and examination findings.

Dementias may be additionally characterized as cortical or frontal–subcortical. Their contrasting features are listed in Table 5.5, grouped by symptom category. Impairment of memory, language, numerical ability, and visual spatial perception occur at an early stage in cortical dementia. In frontal–subcortical dementia, for example, Parkinson's and Huntington's diseases, there is early impairment of executive function and complex attention. Patients can exhibit psychomotor slowing, disturbed social comportment, and signs of basal ganglia dysfunction, including rigidity, abnormal movements, and postural and gait disorders. Such cortical functions as language, visual spatial perception, and memory, impaired early and severely in cortical dementia, are spared until a later stage

TABLE 5.4
Dementia — Laboratory Evaluation

Standard	Indicated by history and examination findings
CBC	Sedimentation rate/ANA
Chemistry panel (serum glucose, BUN, creatinine, electrolytes, calcium)	HIV and Lyme tests
	Chest x-ray and EKG
	Thyroid function tests
Vitamin B-12, folate levels	Urinalysis
Syphilis serology	Neuropsychological evaluation
	Cerebral spinal fluid studies
	Toxicology and heavy metals screen
	EEG
	Brain CT and MRI scans
	PET/SPECT brain scans

TABLE 5.5
Features of Cortical and Frontal–Subcortical Dementia

Cognitive functions	Cortical dementia	Frontal–subcortical dementia
Executive	Unimpaired	Impaired early and late
Complex attention	Unimpaired	Impaired
Psychomotor speed	Unimpaired	Slowed
Memory	Free recall/new learning impaired	Free recall impaired
	Recognition impaired	Recognition intact
	Temporal gradient of memory with oldest memory preserved	No temporal gradient for remote memory
Language	Impaired word finding/naming	Early language intact, limited verbal output
	Aphasia early	Aphasia late
Speech	Articulate	Slurred
Visuospatial	Impaired early	Impaired late
Perception	Impaired during early stages	Not impaired
Calculations	Impaired early	Impaired late
Motor skills	Basic skills preserved	Impaired gait/posture
	Complex, well learned skills impaired	Tremor, rigidity or chorea often present, motor perseveration
Social behavior	Not impaired during early stages	Disinhibited behavior
Mood and affect	Depression early	Depression or apathy early
Lack of concern/denial of illness	Present late	Present early

Source: Modified from Mendez, M. F. and Cummings, J. L. 2003. *Dementia: A Clinical Approach*, 3rd ed. Philadelphia: Butterworth-Heinemann, p. 478. With permission.

TABLE 5.6

Major Causes of Cortical and Frontal–Subcortical Dementia

| | Subcortical diseases | |
Cortical diseases	Frontal–subcortical gray matter	Frontal–subcortical white matter
Alzheimer's	Parkinson's disease	Small vessel vascular disease
Frontal temporal dementia	Lewy body dementia	Multiple sclerosis
TBI	Small vessel vascular disease	TBI
Large vessel multi-infarct dementia	Huntington's disease	Hydrocephalus
		AIDS encephalopathy

of subcortical dementia. Vascular dementia (VAD) often has both cortical and frontal–subcortical features. Common causes of cortical and subcortical dementia are listed in Table 5.6.

Case Study: Progressive Subcortical Dementia Following Emotional Trauma Misdiagnosed as Hysteria

A 39-year-old male suffered emotional trauma in the spring of 1991 when he failed to resuscitate an infant while working as a fireman. Because of depression, daytime somnolence, and unusual eye movements, he underwent a neurological exam, a brain MR scan, and poly-somnography (overnight EEG), none of which revealed specific brain pathology. During the following year, there were two hospitalizations for depression, and he did not respond to conventional treatment measures, including electroconvulsive therapy. By early 1992, he exhibited slurred speech, incoordination, and a drunken gait. VA physicians, on his third hospitalization, considered his problem psychiatric and attributed these findings to a hysterical conversion disorder. A neurobehavioral consultant, however, found cognitive deficits consistent with a frontal–subcortical dementia.

His condition rapidly deteriorated over the next 9 months, and he was admitted to a nursing home for total care. His family had filed suit, claiming that his illness was precipitated by emotional stress on the job. A neurobehavioral assessment by one of the authors (R.E.S.) revealed nystagmus (jerky eye movements), hand tremors, tongue protrusion, limb/gait ataxia, difficulty swallowing, and markedly slurred speech — unmistakable signs of cerebellar and ganglionic pathology. He was also severely depressed.

Using nonverbal response techniques, his dementia was found to be only moderate in degree. His recent verbal memory deficit reflected fluctuating attention and difficulty with retrieval of stored memoranda. Relative preservation of language, calculating, motor programming, and visual perceptual–constructional skills was characteristic of frontal–subcortical dementia. There were also frontal deficits in the form of emotional lability, echopraxia (involuntary mimicking of the examiner's movements), and behavioral disinhibition. A repeat brain magnetic resonance imaging (MRI) scan revealed cerebral, brain stem, and cerebellar atrophy.

In retrospect, his early arousal and unusual eye movements were the earliest objective signs of a degenerative brain disorder. These early cerebellar signs, however, were associated with a significant depression that followed an emotionally stressful event. Although his speech and gait had significantly deteriorated by the time of his second psychiatric hospitalization, his physicians categorized his neurological findings as hysterical and falsely attributed his condition to emotional job stress. The failure of his depression to respond to treatment also suggested an underlying organic process.

Subsequent neurobehavioral evaluations revealed the presence of a cerebral–cerebellar degeneration with associated dementia. The progressive clinical course was inconsistent with cerebral anoxia; clinical and laboratory findings excluded multiple sclerosis (MS) and related disorders. There is no conclusive evidence in the medical literature that emotional stress can precipitate a primary degenerative neurological disorder or significantly accelerate the course of the degenerative process.

THE DEMENTIA SPECTRUM — NORMAL AGING TO DEGENERATIVE DEMENTIA

Normal Aging and Mild Cognitive Impairment

The boundaries between normal forgetfulness and dementia are not fixed. In general, our memory for recent information becomes less efficient after age 67 or so; however, across a range of memory tasks, there is no general or uniform decline in memory ability. Working memory may also be affected in healthy older people. Episodic memory is affected to a much greater degree than procedural or semantic memory, but recognition memory is typically spared. Information retrieval is slower and less efficient, while forgetting is more rapid and extensive in older individuals. Elderly individuals who experience difficulty recalling recent events often benefit from external aids and reminders. Autobiographical memories (ability to recall important life experiences) tend to become less detailed and vague with increasing age (Clare, 2004).

Mild cognitive impairment (MCI) is a relatively broad clinical disorder that consists of a slight memory or cognitive deficit. It represents a transient state between healthy normal aging and dementia, typically caused by either AD or by other common causes (e.g., alcohol use, medications, medical illnesses, psychiatric disorders, etc.) of cognitive decline in the elderly. Individuals who have this condition often fail to exhibit or experience significant impairment in their social, occupational, or everyday functioning. Approximately 10 to 15% of individuals with amnestic MCI will progress to developing AD each year, compared with a 1 to 2% of healthy control subjects. Since it can be caused by a variety of medical or nonmedical conditions and can remain stable or be reversible with medication, it should not be regarded as a precursor to AD (Petersen et al., 2001).

MAJOR CORTICAL DEGENERATIVE DEMENTIAS

Alzheimer's Disease

Alzheimer's disease is the prototype degenerative dementia with insidious onset (it cannot be determined when it exactly began) and gradual progression resulting in death (typically 10 years after it is diagnosed). It is age related and increasingly common after age 65. Early signs of Alzheimer's typically include the following symptoms: impaired recent memory, personality change characterized by indifference to one's surrounding and others, declining interest in previously enjoyed activities, an inability to recognize such changes, language difficulties and visual spatial deficits. As the disease progresses, memory worsens to include both new learning and remote recall. Patients are easily disoriented, cannot accurately copy or draw and become aphasic (their ability to speak and use language becomes impaired). For example, they initially have difficulty naming familiar objects. Impaired comprehension of spoken language usually follows, but their ability to pronounce and repeat words remains preserved. At this stage, their abstraction, arithmetic skills, and executive functions become compromised. As the disease progresses their memory becomes totally lost and their speech becomes incoherent. The patient may also exhibit echolalic speech (uncontrollable repetition of examiner's speech). Symptoms such as anxiety, delusions, and dysphoria can also occur. Since many of these patients exhibit agitation, incontinence, and nocturnal wandering in the late stages of the disease it often creates serious problems for their family, which usually results in the patient being sent to a nursing home.

Although brain CT and MRI studies often reveal nonspecific cerebral atrophy, at the present time there is no specific noninvasive diagnostic test for AD. A definite diagnosis can only be made by a brain biopsy or at the time of autopsy. Clinical assessment, consisting of neurological examination and neuropsychological testing, combined with laboratory studies, for example, blood chemistry and spinal fluid studies, to rule out other possible causes, and brain imaging, CT or MRI, can lead to a probable diagnosis of AD with 85% accuracy. The diagnosis of AD can also be corroborated from functional imaging studies utilizing single photon emission computed tomography (SPECT) or positron emission tomography (PET), which may reveal diminished cerebral blood flow or neuronal hypometabolism in the hippocampus, deep within the temporal lobe, and in the inferior parietal and parietal–temporal cortical junction areas (Chen et al., 1998).

Vascular Dementia

VAD often presents as a mixed cortical and subcortical dementia that is caused by multiple small cerebrovascular infarcts (strokes) within the brain. Individuals with this disorder typically exhibit symptoms such as classical aphasia, amnesia, apraxias (impaired learned motor skills), and agnosias (impaired perceptual recognition). The infarcts are often scattered throughout subcortical regions of the brain such as the thalamus, basal ganglia, and white matter and can produce mixed Parkinson's symptoms and motor weakness. In addition, small strategically located vascular infarcts can disrupt a number of cognitive functions. For example, an infarct in the left angular gyrus can produce alexia or agraphia (impaired reading/writing), anomia (impaired naming skills), or acalculia (impaired calculating skills), right–left confusion, finger agnosia (impaired digit identification), apraxia (inability to perform tasks involving goal directed motor behavior), and verbal memory impairment. An angular gyrus syndrome caused by vascular infarct must be differentiated from posterior cortical atrophy, a focal variant of AD. This can be best determined by examining for clinical signs of a vascular infarct and neuroimaging studies. A history of prior transient ischemic attacks or completed stroke may provide additional support of a vascular infarct.

Patients with VAD frequently suffer from sustained hypertension, cardiac disease, or diabetes. Symptoms such as apathy, irritability, depression, and psychosis have also been frequently reported (Cummings and Trimble, 1995a). Although the incidence of VAD in the elderly has been reported to be 10 to 30%, the lower figure appears to be a better estimate of pure VAD. VAD and AD can both be present in the same individual.

Parkinson's Dementia

Parkinson's disease (PD) is a degenerative movement disorder produced by destruction of neurons with the basal ganglia. This results in the depletion of dopamine and, to a lesser extent, norepinephrine that can significantly disrupt an individual's cognition, mood, motivation, and personality. PD has a mean age of onset between 58 and 62 with an average duration of 13 to 14 years. The major motor features of bradykinesia (decreased movement and spontaneity); rigidity and tremor (involuntary repetitive movements) are followed years later by overt dementia in approximately 40% of patients and subtle features of a mild subcortical dementia in an additional 30% of patients. Dysphoric mood and apathy frequently accompany the patient's cognitive deficits. Mild to moderate cerebral atrophy may be seen on brain CT or MRI. Psychosis with hallucinations and delusions are common and result from treatment with dopaminergic agents, for example, L-dopa, usually in the absence of frank delirium. Older patients who are taking multiple medications or have dementia are most vulnerable to developing psychotic symptoms. A Parkinson syndrome may also be seen in patients who are taking medications that block dopamine receptors to treat psychotic or gastrointestinal symptoms.

Lewy Body Dementia

Lewy body dementia (LBD) is a progressive dementia, characterized by the following symptoms: visual hallucinations, marked cognitive fluctuations on a daily or even hourly basis and Parkinsonian signs (which are usually mild). Other symptoms, such as delusional thinking, depression, and sensitivity to antipsychotic medications, are helpful in diagnosing LBD. The differentiation of LBD from AD and VAD is often difficult. However, functional imaging with SPECT or PET scans may be helpful by revealing abnormalities in both the parietal and occipital lobes (Cummings and Trimble, 1995b).

The Frontal Temporal Comportmental Dementias

The frontotemporal dementias (FTDs) refer to a group of syndromes that are caused by progressive degenerative disease of unknown etiology that produces atrophy (wasting away) of frontal and temporal lobes. FTD is increasingly recognized as an important cause of early onset dementia, which begins between the ages of 50 and 60. This is in contrast to the onset of AD (with the exception of familial forms), which typically occurs after age 65. Individuals with this disorder usually exhibit symptoms such as changes in their personality and behavior. The symptoms of frontotemporal dementias clinically overlap with schizophrenia, depression, sociopathy, and obsessive–compulsive disorder. As a consequence, they are often initially misdiagnosed as a psychiatric disorder. The degenerative dementias as a group are associated with abnormal protein aggregation in the cerebral cortex. While amyloid buildup is usually seen in AD, FTDs are characterized by tau or ubiquitin protein buildup in the frontal or anterior temporal cortex that account for their behavioral, linguistic, and cognitive features.

Frontotemporal Degeneration

Frontotemporal degeneration, the pathological term for the disease process, encompasses three syndromes: the more prevalent frontotemporal dementia (FTD) or so-called frontal variant, the relatively rare semantic dementia (SD), and a primary progressive aphasia (PPA). In FTD, socially inappropriate and disinhibited behavior develops in association with deteriorating insight and social skills. Antisocial behaviors, including indecent exposure, shoplifting, or embezzlement may occur as the disease progresses. Even though these patients are frequently arrested and even incarcerated, they are usually found incompetent to stand trial and are often referred to a psychiatric facility. If the patient has no significant prior history of conduct or related behavioral disorder, it is possible to differentiate the acquired sociopathy symptoms caused by FTD from a long standing antisocial personality disorder.

More subtle deterioration in social skills with loss of tact is common. Patients may become overfriendly and initiate personal conversations with complete strangers. Repetitive and stereotyped behaviors can be seen in the form of obsessive fixed routines or compulsive singing, hoarding, collecting, or counting rituals. Patients with FTD stand out because of odd mannerisms. They may also exhibit sudden changes in their long-standing political or religious beliefs. Symptoms such as apathy or emotional blunting can be seen. Hyperorality, manifested by overeating, excessive smoking or alcohol consumption, and dietary changes including carbohydrate craving or food fads may occur. Loss of insight and personal awareness with neglect of hygiene and grooming has been described. Disinhibition, including inappropriate jocularity (e.g., laughing at a funeral), restless pacing, unrestrained sexuality, and combative behavior, has also been reported.

In the early stages of this disease the patient's memory is usually relatively intact. As the disease progresses, the patient develops a memory retrieval deficit, characterized by difficulty recall recent information unless they are given cues by the examiner. The memory retrieval deficit in FTD stands in contrast to the encoding and storage memory deficits that are characteristic of patients with AD. For example, the AD patient will exhibit poor recall even when provided with cues from the examiner. Unlike patients with AD, the patient's spatial–perceptual and constructional skills are preserved. Unlike AD patients, the speech of FTD patients may be pressured, preservative (filled with repetitive words and phrases), or sparse with a loss of spontaneity. Early in the course of this disorder, neuropsychological testing may not detect the patient's neurobehavioral symptoms. As the disease progress, neuropsychological testing will usually detect deficits in the patient's executive and cognitive functions.

Speech and language impairment are initial symptoms in PPA and SD, the two other subtypes of FTD. PPA patients develop a nonfluent aphasia with word finding and reduced speech output resulting from left posterior frontal degeneration. In SD, a loss of semantic knowledge results in impaired naming and recognition of familiar objects and faces. Although their speech is fluent, verbal and reading comprehension is impaired because of the loss of word meaning. Brain CT or MRI usually reveals asymmetric bilateral temporal lobe atrophy that is greater in the left hemisphere. Behavioral changes characteristic of the FTD subtype can occur when the degenerative process spreads to the amygdala and orbital frontal lobe (Mendez and Perryman, 2002; Mendez and Cummings, 2003b; Hou et al., 2004).

In addition, there are two recognized temporal variants of FTD, a *left* and a *right* form that respectively affect the left and right temporal lobes with relative sparing of the frontal lobes. Right temporal lobe atrophy patients may exhibit remote or bizarre affect, atypical depression, severe irritability, and disinhibited and antisocial behavior. Patients with left temporal lobe atrophy are more likely to have a flat affect, mild or no disinhibition, and infrequent depression or sociopathic behavior. The sociopathic behavior in FTD, however, more closely resembles acquired sociopathic behavior arising from focal traumatic orbitofrontal pathology than the sociopathy associated with a long-standing antisocial personality disorder. While patients in both the FTD and sociopathy groups may share an emotional shallowness and impaired emotional responsivity, FTD patients lack the grandiosity, deliberate deceitfulness, and need for constant stimulation that is typical of sociopaths. In a recent study of antisocial behavior of 16 patients with FTD, Mendez et al. (2005) found that while these patients were aware of their antisocial behavior and its wrongfulness, they were unable to inhibit this behavior. Although they claimed remorse for their actions (unlike patients with a sociopathic personality disorder), they were unable to inhibit their behavior or exhibit concern for the consequences of their actions. SPECT or PET studies done on these patients revealed predominantly right temporal hypoperfusion or hypometabolism. Although standard EEG studies are usually normal with FTD, quantitative EEG changes in the frontal and temporal regions have been reported.

Case Study: Frontotemporal Dementia

A 67-year-old male was hospitalized because of gradual personality changes over a 2-year period. He sold a successful business and acquired large debts on items indiscriminately purchased from a TV shopping network. His bills remained unpaid. He became distractible, hyperactive, disinhibited, and impulsive. He inappropriately fondled his wife in public and made sexual advances towards his daughters. He uttered racial slurs at social events. He exhibited compulsive and oral behaviors such as pulling the hair from his arms and overeating at home and in restaurants. This patient met criteria for a diagnosis of FTD. The presence of dementia in his father and a paternal grandparent suggested a familial basis. His disinhibited behavior and poor judgment were consistent with orbitofrontal cortex pathology. The SPECT scan showed extensive bifrontal hypoperfusion (reduced blood flow), which was greater in the right hemisphere. A PET scan revealed prominent hypometabolism in both frontal lobes (Mendez et al., 1997).

OTHER ACQUIRED NEUROBEHAVIORAL DISORDERS

DEMENTIA OF ACQUIRED IMMUNE DEFICIENCY SYNDROME

Acquired immune deficiency syndrome (AIDS) was first identified in the early 1980s. The putative causal agent, the HIV virus, was isolated in 1984. Most patients infected with the HIV virus are asymptomatic until seroconversion occurs 1 to 4 years after they are infected, following which the disease progresses into full-blown AIDS as a result of their compromised immune system. A wide range of neurological and psychiatric symptoms are associated with HIV. Individuals who are initially diagnosed as having AIDS will usually experience adjustment reactions, disturbances of mood (depression), and even schizophreniform and paranoid disorders which must be distinguished from symptoms caused by an infection of the central nervous system. Confusional states (delirium) are particularly common in patients with AIDS dementia.

AIDS DEMENTIA COMPLEX

The AIDS dementia complex, which is also called HIV encephalitis, is a disorder characterized by neurological, cognitive, and behavioral deficits. Its onset is usually insidious, with early neurological motor symptoms such as problems with balance, clumsiness, and leg weakness. Early cognitive and behavioral symptoms typically include mental slowing, impaired concentration, forgetfulness, difficulty with sequential mental tasks, apathy, reduced emotional responsiveness and withdrawal, malaise, and loss of sexual drive. While neuropsychological test results of patients in the early stages of this disorder can be normal, they often reveal slowed responses and impairment on tasks involving delayed recall, with naming and vocabulary skills largely preserved. However, as the syndrome progresses, global cognitive deterioration occurs characterized by severe psychomotor retardation, word-finding difficulties and slowed speech, which can progress to mutism, loss of insight, apathy, and indifference. The AIDS dementia complex, which is the most prevalent of the frontal–subcortical dementias in young adults, can be differentiated from a primary cortical dementia such as frontotemporal dementia by prominent motor signs in the absence of aphasia, apraxia, and agnosia (Roberts et al., 1993).

MULTIPLE SCLEROSIS

Multiple sclerosis is considered a prototype subcortical white matter dementia (e.g., the brain white matter consists of largely myelinated neuronal axons). In MS, episodes of demyelination (destruction of the myelin coating the axonal sheath) occur at various sites in the nervous system, predominantly in the cerebral peri-ventricular region, optic nerves, brain stem, and spinal cord. The diagnosis requires evidence of multiple white matter lesions distributed in space and time (i.e., widely scattered lesions throughout the central nervous system that develop over many years, often decades). Its onset is usually between 20 and 40 years of age. MS has a highly variable course, which is usually relapsing–remitting, but can be slowly progressive in 20% of patients. Brain MRI studies have demonstrated that the distribution, size, and configuration of cerebral demyelination can be meaningfully correlated with neurobehavioral dysfunction, including frontal dementia, other focal syndromes, depression, and psychosis.

The disease produces a wide variety of physical handicaps including visual loss, limb weakness and clumsiness, ataxia, impaired urinary–sexual dysfunction, and altered sensation. Neurobehavioral impairment can be seen in a substantial number of patients. Cognitive assessment, however, may be difficult because of the depression that often accompanies this disorder even though the patient may paradoxically appear euphoric or exhibit emotional lability. The frequently observed deficits in the patient's motor speed, speed of information processing, and memory retrieval function are usually more severe than their deficits in executive, language, and visuoperceptual functions, which

---

TABLE 5.7

Characteristics of Alzheimer's Dementia and Dementia of Depression

Alzheimer's dementia	Depression
Gradual onset	Rapid onset
Slow progression, months to years	Rapid progression — 2 weeks to months
Typically no prior history of depression	May have history of prior depression
Shallow affect, detached, irritable	Depressed affect
Cognitive complaints are rare	Cognitive and memory symptoms emphasized by patient
Family observes gradual decline in patient's cognitive functioning	Gradual decline in the patient's cognitive functioning not typically observed
Few somatic complaints	Many somatic complaints
Word-finding difficulty, empty speech	Reduced verbal output
Attention preserved until late stages	Attention fluctuates
Impaired recall and recognition	Impaired recall, repetition preserved
Cognitive impairment on testing	Variable and inconsistent test findings

Source: Modified from Mendez, M. F. and Cummings, J. L. 2003a. *Dementia: A Clinical Approach*, 3rd ed. Philadelphia: Butterworth-Heinemann, p. 478. With permission.

---

are usually mild to moderate in severity. Symptoms such as frank dementia and psychosis are rarely seen (Marsh and Willoughby, 2004).

PSEUDODEMENTIA

Patients who have numerous complaints of severe amnesia and cognitive problems, found upon careful neuropsychological testing to be groundless, are often diagnosed as having pseudodementia, particularly if their complaints appear to be caused by depression or if they are expressed in a histrionic fashion and accompanied by displays of anger and tears. These patients tend to have little insight into their emotional problems and continue to complain of severe memory problems, even though they are able to provide their treating or examining doctor with a detailed chronological history of their illness and the development of their symptoms. Table 5.7 lists distinguishing features of dementia and depressive pseudodementia. Helpful differentiating features are the clinical course, prior psychiatric history, exhibited affect, the complaining party, the presence of somatic complaints, and the findings on neurological examination, neuropsychological assessment, and laboratory tests.

Patients with a history of bipolar depression (manic–depressive illness) can appear demented during the depressed phase of their illness. Thus, it is essential to take a careful history, including interviews with significant others and a review of past medical records, to rule out this possibility. Patients with hysterical conversion disorders will often evidence the superficial appearance of a dementia. These patients are typically able to provide a rather detailed chronological history of their illness or symptoms (which contradicts their complaint of memory difficulties) and even though they often describe the degree of their memory problems as "extremely severe," it is usually stated in either a bland or dramatic manner.

Case Example

One of the authors (R.J.S.) was asked to consult on a case in which a 42-year-old woman reported that she had sustained a head injury, when a small piece of insulation material fell from the ceiling and struck her on the head as she was working. She denied a loss of consciousness and was able to easily recall the events that occurred immediately before, during, and following her injury. The patient was able to provide 30 complaints, each of which was very detailed and elaborate. Although she described her recent memory as "profoundly impaired," she was able to provide numerous detailed examples of her memory difficulties. When she was asked questions about her childhood (which she described as "fine"), particularly her relationship with her parents, she was unable to recall anything about it. When she was asked where she spent the first 10 years of her life, she stated, "Somewhere in Europe." However, when she was asked to be more specific, she stated, "I can't remember." When she was asked if there had been any problems in her life or marriage, she denied any problems and described her life and marriage as "perfect."

Her husband, who was later interviewed, reported that she had a history of alcoholism, frequent extramarital affairs, and drug abuse. She had been previously married three times. Each of her husbands had been unfaithful to her and physically and psychologically abused her. When she was asked, how she handled their abuse, she stated, "It really didn't bother me. I took it well." She was also asked about her 15-year-old daughter who had recently run away from home and was now pregnant. She replied, "My daughter is fine. She's doing well." Her 17-year-old son had recently been arrested for selling drugs. She denied that her children's problems had created any psychological difficulties for her or were stressful.

Neuropsychological testing revealed a pattern of atypical responses on memory testing that was characteristic of patients who are repressing long-standing and current feelings of anger and rage consistent with pseudodementia. Testing also indicated that she was most likely converting her emotional problems into a variety of somatic complaints to draw attention to herself, since she apparently had not felt any caring from her family. Later, it was learned that this woman had spent 5 years of her childhood in a Nazi concentration camp where both of her parents had been killed.

Case Study: Pseudodementia from CO Poisoning

A 38-year-old nurse supervisor with a history of migraines was working feverishly in her office, preparing a report due later in the day. She was chain smoking with the door closed, because workmen were doing remodeling about 15 yards down the hall, using gasoline-powered equipment. She suddenly developed a splitting headache, was rushed to the ER, and inhaled oxygen, which provided minimal relief. Hospitalized with a diagnosis of severe CO poisoning, she underwent two largely unsuccessful treatments in the hyperbaric chamber. She subsequently filed suit, complaining of severe memory and cognitive impairment resulting in total disability. She was referred to one of the authors (R.E.S.) for neurobehavioral examination 2 years later.

She appeared to be a bright and loquacious professional woman who reiterated her present illness in minute detail. Yet on testing, she was able to recall only three digits forward and exhibited moderate to severe impairment in orientation, recent verbal and visual memory, and calculating ability. These findings were highly inconsistent with the detailed history she provided and her observed level of cognitive functioning. A review of the nursing notes in the hospital chart revealed that all of the elevated CO levels were obtained during periods when she was caught surreptitiously chain smoking in the bathroom. Her attending physicians at that time, apparently not informed of these incidents, mistakenly diagnosed her condition as acute CO intoxication and ordered inappropriate therapy. On the basis of the findings of her neurobehavioral evaluation, it was felt that her CO exposure was self-induced and that she had no bona fide residual cognitive or neurological deficits.

THE EXECUTIVE FUNCTIONS OF THE BRAIN

DEFINITION

The executive functions of the brain refer to the complex process by which an individual goes about performing a novel problem-solving task from inception to completion. This process begins with the awareness that a particular problem exists, and then proceeds to the evaluation of the problem, including an analysis of the problem's conditions. Following this, the individual formulates specific goals that are necessary to solve the problem, develops a set of plans that in turn determine actions needed to solve the problem, evaluates the potential effectiveness of these plans, and then selects and initiates a particular plan of action to solve the problem. The individual evaluates any progress that is made toward solving the problem, modifies the plan if it has not been effective, disregards ineffective plans and replaces them with more effective plans, and compares the results achieved by the new plan with the conditions of the problem. He or she finally terminates the plan when the conditions of the problem have been satisfied and stores the plan for retrieval if the same or a similar problem appears in the future (Sbordone, 2000).

ANATOMY OF THE EXECUTIVE FUNCTIONS

A complex model of frontal–subcortical circuits has been formulated that holds that the executive functions can become impaired when a circuit or loop involving the brain structures that comprise this circuit is broken. Thus, Cummings argues that patients may exhibit what has been commonly termed "a frontal lobe syndrome," even though their frontal lobes may be neurologically intact, as a result of sustaining an injury to one of the neural mechanisms in the circuit or following an alteration in the metabolic activity of the neural structures, which form the circuit. For example, damage to the dorsolateral prefrontal cortex has been reported to produce a neurobehavioral dysexecutive syndrome (an inability to maintain one's attentional set), dissociation between verbal and motor behavior, deficits in complex or programmed motor activities, concrete thinking, poor mental control, and stimulus-bound behavior (Cummings, 1995). Damage to the parietal, temporal, or occipital association areas; the globus pallidus, ventral anterior (VA) and mediodorsal (MD) thalamic nuclei, or the dorsal caudate nucleus may produce similar symptoms since the dorsolateral prefrontal cortex has direct connections with these regions (Chow and Cummings, 1999).

DISORDERS OF EXECUTIVE FUNCTIONS

Damage to the orbitofrontal cortex has been reported to produce a neurobehavioral syndrome characterized by a lack of social tact, the use of crude or coarse language, an inability to regulate one's behavior or emotions (disinhibition), emotional lability, insensitivity to the needs and welfare of others, and antisocial acts (Mendez and Cummings, 2003b). Similar behaviors, however, can be produced by damage to nonfrontal cortical or subcortical structures within an orbitofrontal–subcortical circuit, including the nucleus accumbens, the globus pallidus, and the VA and MD nuclei of the thalamus (Chow and Cummings, 1999). The nucleus accumbens, one of the basal forebrain nuclei, lies inferior and somewhat medial to the head (anterior portion) of the caudate (see Figure 4.5). As the main crossroad between the limbic (hippocampus and amygdala) and motor systems, the nucleus accumbens and related components of the orbitofrontal circuit are responsible for the integration of motivational and emotional processes into motor behavioral responses (Groenewegen, 1997).

While damage to the *medial frontal cortex* has been shown to produce a neurobehavioral syndrome characterized by apathy, diminished motivation and interest, psychomotor retardation, diminished social involvement, and reduced communication (Cummings, 1995), damage to a variety of nonfrontal cortical and subcortical structures may produce similar behaviors. The *anterior cingulate cortex* forms a mediofrontal–subcortical circuit with the nucleus accumbens, globus pallidus, MD nucleus of the thalamus, and the amygdala. This anterior cingulate–subcortical circuit is required for motivated behavior (Mega and Cummings, 1997).

The *dorsolateral prefrontal cortex* receives information about the external environment, internal milieu, and the emotional state of the individual and serves as the principal organ responsible for integrating information from the above three circuits. These circuits essentially provide the individual with the ability to guide behavior through mental representation of the perceived world (e.g., working memory) and, thus, free the individual from dependency on the environment (Devinsky, 1992).

ELECTRICAL INJURY

Damage to the central nervous system (brain and spinal cord) can result from the thermal and mechanical effects of electrical shock as a result of coagulation necrosis (death of tissue due to clotting of blood vessels), reactive gliosis (increase in nonneural support cells within the central nervous system as a response to injury), demyelination (destruction of the protein that covers many of the nerves), vacuolization (small holes within the brain tissue), and perivascular hemorrhage (small areas of bleeding) (Pliskin et al., 1994). Damage to the central nervous system can also occur as a result of cardiorespiratory arrest, which results in anoxia or ischemic damage resulting from thrombosis (the formation or presence of clotting within a blood vessel, which can cause infarction of the tissues supplied by the vessel). When fatalities occur, the cause of death is generally attributed to ventricular fibrillation with subsequent cardio-respiratory arrest (Petty and Parkin, 1986). Although relatively little research has been done on the neuropsychological changes following electrical injury, many patients report such symptoms as confusion, altered consciousness, visual disturbances, memory loss, psychomotor difficulties, diminished intellectual functioning, and aphasia (Daniel et al., 1985; Troster and Ruff, 1988; Hooshmand et al., 1989).

Pliskin et al. (1994) critically reviewed these studies and found that the conclusions reached by the authors were based on single-case reports or small sample sizes and that no consistent constellation of neuropsychiatric symptoms emerged as a result of the methodological difficulties in these studies. For example, these studies frequently failed to control for the effects of depression or other psychological trauma (e.g., PTSD) on the patient's neuropsychological test performance. Finally, they noted that many of the individuals described in these studies were involved in litigation and that little was known about these individuals before their electrical injury. Furthermore, many of these patients, seen in outpatient clinics with neuropsychological complaints, may not necessarily be representative of patients who sustain electrical injuries. For example, having made a successful adjustment to their injury, a significant number of patients may not seek treatment. In fact, they note that several studies have been reported that found no evidence of neuropsychological impairment or, when such impairments were present, they were only transient.

While some victims of electrical injuries sustain brain damage, many develop an acute or posttraumatic stress disorder. In fact, these individuals often report being haunted by intrusive recollections of the traumatic event, flashbacks, and nightmares of being electrocuted. They will also display avoidance behavior, such as shunning any contact with electrical appliances or devices, and are reluctant to discuss their electrical injury. Since many of these patients experience dissociative episodes, characteristic of an acute stress disorder following their electrical injuries, they are likely to report amnesia, bewilderment, or mental confusion during or immediately following their electrical injury. Unfortunately, they are also frequently diagnosed as having sustained a brain injury, despite negative neurological examinations and neurodiagnostic testing (e.g., EEG, CT, or MRI studies). Being informed that they have sustained brain damage only serves to exacerbate the severity of their posttraumatic stress disorder and may also cause them to develop a generalized anxiety or depressive disorder. Thus, when they present themselves for neuropsychological testing, they are usually very anxious, tense, depressed, and extremely apprehensive that their test data will corroborate the referring doctor's suspicion that they have brain damage. Under such circumstances, their neuropsychological test performances, particularly on measures of attention, concentration, recent memory, and problem solving, are likely to be impaired due to their emotional state at the time of testing.

Pliskin et al. (2006) recently administered neuropsychological tests of 29 electrical injury patients who had been screened and matched according to their premorbid intellectual functioning to a group of 29 "demographically similar" electricians. They found that electrical injury patients performed significantly worse on measures of attention, mental speed, and motor skills. This finding could not be explained by electrical injury parameters, demographic factors, litigation status, or a mood disorder. They did not find any difference in these groups on measures of working memory, or verbal and visual memory. These results suggest that individuals who sustain electrical injury can develop cognitive deficits in specific cognitive domains.

HYPOXIC ENCEPHALOPATHY

Hypoxic encephalopathy refers to a loss of neurons and brain tissue as the result of an insufficient amount of oxygen to the brain. This disorder is frequently seen in patients who have overdosed on drugs, nearly drowned, or been exposed to oxygen-replacing gases, such as CO, for a sufficient length of time. It is also seen in patients who have sustained cardiac arrests or whose brains did not get sufficient oxygenation because of multiple trauma sustained during a severe motor vehicle accident. Patients with hypoxic encephalopathies may exhibit severe, even profound, problems with recent memory and display mental confusion, psychomotor retardation, gait and balance difficulties, ataxic (jerky) movements, and a depressed appearance. These patients may also display poor judgment, as well as a limited ability to process new information, and may become confused when they are required to process more than one event at a time. The clinical course of these patients frequently depends upon the duration of coma following their cerebral insult. Research studies have shown that when patients are in comas for 48 h or longer, they most likely will be left with permanent cognitive and behavioral impairments for the remainder of their lives. Thus, the prognosis for patients who have sustained severe hypoxic encephalopathies is typically poor.

POSTOPERATIVE COGNITIVE DYSFUNCTION

Long-term postoperative cognitive dysfunction (POCD) has become of increasing concern as more middle-age patients undergo coronary artery bypass grafting (CABG). Reversible delirium occurs in up to 40% of older individuals after cardiac and orthopedic surgery. There are many potential causes of POCD including perioperative cerebral hypotension and hypoxia, anesthetic effects, systemic inflammatory response, use of a cardio-pulmonary bypass pump during CABG surgery, and cerebral micro-emboli (clumps of tissue that lodge in a blood vessel) that occur during aortic manipulation and cross-clamping.

Neuropsychological testing has revealed changes in memory, executive function, and motor speed in a subset of POCD patients during the first days to weeks after CABG, which is reversible for most patients within 3 months. Late cognitive deficits between 1 and 5 years postsurgery have been documented, but whether this can be attributed to the bypass itself or to the progression of the underlying cerebrovascular disease or other age-related changes remains unclear (Selnes et al., 2006).

NEUROTOXIC DAMAGE

Damage to the central nervous system can occur as a result of exposure to a variety of neurotoxic agents (e.g., lead, mercury, manganese, organophosphate pesticides, and toluene). Damage to the nervous system may occur over weeks, months, and even years before a medical specialist diagnoses it as a clinical syndrome. Furthermore, in some cases the clinical syndrome may not become apparent until the individual ages and age-related cell reductions deplete their neuronal reserves below what is needed to function effectively. For example, in cases involving neurotoxin-induced Parkinsonism, it has been estimated that loss of approximately 80% of the dopaminergic neurons in the substantia nigra is necessary before individuals exhibit clinical signs of Parkinson's disease (Reuhl, 1991).

Neurotoxic injury to the brain is most likely caused by alterations of the excitable neuronal membrane, interference with neurotransmitter systems, and the destruction of dendrites, axons, or perikaryon (Spencer, 1990). Since the neurons within the brain have a limited ability to regenerate when damaged, neurotoxic damage to the brain is usually permanent. As a consequence, an individual's neurological and neuropsychological functioning may become profoundly disrupted. Neurotoxins can damage specific areas of the brain and leave other areas relatively unaffected. For example, neurotoxins such as cyanide, lead, mercury, and methyl bromide damage primarily the gray matter of the cortex. CO, however, has been shown to damage the hippocampi, while manganese frequently damages the caudate nucleus and putamen (Hartman, 1995).

TOXIC LEUKOENCEPHALOPATHY

Toxic leukoencephalopathy (the structural alteration of cerebral white matter from toxic exposure) is increasingly recognized as a major cause of neurobehavioral dysfunction. Its clinical spectrum generally parallels the severity of white matter damage and its distribution, which is usually diffuse. Mild cases present as a chronic confusional state with symptoms such as inattention, forgetfulness, and personality change suggestive of a psychiatric disorder. Moderate to severe cases are characterized by symptoms such as somnolence, apathy, and dementia which progress to mutism, stupor, and coma in the late stages. In contrast to disorders of cortical gray matter (e.g., AD), these patients' language skills are not primarily affected.

Neuropsychological testing of these patients will usually reveal deficits in attention, memory, visuospatial skills, and executive functions in the absence of aphasia. A firm diagnosis of leukoencephalopathy requires radiological evidence of white matter abnormalities, which can usually be seen on a brain MRI. A normal MRI, in fact, typically suggests the presence of a metabolic disorder such as hypothyroidism, hepatic encephalopathy, or uremia. Toxicological screening can also be helpful since it will detect recent exposure to substances such as alcohol, cocaine, and heavy metals such as lead, arsenic, and mercury.

CAUSES OF TOXIC LEUKOENCEPHALOPATHY

Excessive use of many different substances of abuse can produce selective white matter damage. Toxic levels of toluene may follow prolonged inhalation of volatile fumes from glues and spray paints, resulting in dementia, ataxia, and brain stem dysfunction. Alcoholic dementia increasingly reflects leukotoxicity rather than diencephalic (subcortical midline) damage that produces Korsakoff's amnesia as a result of thiamine deficiency. The frontal white matter is preferentially involved and is manifested by deficits in attention, working memory, and executive functions. Other illicit drugs associated with MRI-confirmed leukoencephalopathy include MDMA or "ecstasy," and heroin (inhaled or administered intravenously). Cocaine abuse can produce vascular spasm, leading to strokes involving nerve fibers in cerebral white matter. After an initial period of recovery, CO poisoning can also produce white matter loss several weeks following exposure (Filley and Kleinschmidt-DeMasters, 2001).

NEUROPSYCHOLOGICAL ASSESSMENT OF NEUROTOXIC EXPOSURE

Neuropsychological assessment of individuals suspected of having been exposed to neurotoxic substances has been handicapped by the fact that relatively few neuropsychologists have received specialized training in the assessment of neurotoxic disorders. Individuals who are suspected of having been exposed to neurotoxins should undergo a comprehensive neuropsychological examination by a neuropsychologist who has expertise in this area so that the test data can be interpreted within the larger context of the particular individual's medical, educational, and psychological background and available demographic or sociological data. Such information should include records that predated the individual's exposure to neurotoxic substances, including his or her developmental history, academic records, premorbid vocational records, medical, and psychiatric history.

While the effects of neurotoxic exposure may not necessarily be reflected in changes on a patient's full-scale IQ score, some of the performance subtests (e.g., Block Design, Digit Span, Digit Symbol, and Similarities) may be useful for screening purposes. In addition, the Finger Tapping and Trail Making Tests of the Halstead–Reitan Neuropsychological Battery may also be helpful (Hartman, 1995). Unfortunately, an evaluation of the complex cognitive, behavioral, and emotional consequences of neurotoxic exposure is often quite difficult since many individuals have preexisting and psychological conditions that can mimic the symptoms of neurotoxic exposure. For example, a variety of medical conditions, drug or alcohol problems, and even stress can mimic neurotoxic symptoms. Neuropsychologists who are unaccustomed in dealing with these complex multifactorial diagnostic questions may find it rather difficult to sort out the relative contributions of each of these complicating factors.

Health care professionals and attorneys wishing to obtain more information on this topic should review *Neuropsychological Toxicology: Identification and Assessment of Human Neurotoxic Syndromes*, 2nd edition (Hartman, 1995).

PREEXISTING NEUROBEHAVIORAL DISORDERS

ATTENTION-DEFICIT HYPERACTIVITY DISORDER

Attention-deficit hyperactivity disorder (ADHD) is a serious neurobehavioral disorder that affects 3 to 9% of children. It is characterized by a triad of symptoms such as attention, impulse control, and hyperactivity (Barkely, 1990). Approximately 40% of these children will continue to exhibit this disorder when they reach adulthood (Klein and Mannuzza, 1991). This disorder can arise from multiple etiologies, including severe early malnutrition, low birth weight, fetal alcohol exposure, and prenatal or postnatal lead exposure. For example, the mothers of ADHD children are more likely to have been exposed to nicotine and alcohol while they were pregnant (Anastopoulos and Barkley, 1988). There also appears to be an underlying genetic basis for the hyperactivity aspect of this disorder based on studies utilizing identical and fraternal twins. Monozygotic (identical) twins showed a higher concordance rate of hyperactivity than dizygotic (fraternal) twins (Willerman, 1973; Goodman and Stevenson, 1989). It also tends to run in families (Comings et al., 2000).

ADHD is four to nine times more prevalent in males than females (Ross and Ross, 1982). This may be due to the fact that females are more likely to exhibit symptoms that reflect their mood, affect, and emotion, while males are more likely to display more salient symptoms such as aggression and antisocial behavior. The biological parents of ADHD children also appear to have an increased prevalence of psychiatric illness including antisocial behavior, neurosis, suicide, alcoholism, sociopathy, and hysteria (Morrison and Stewart, 1971; Wender, 1971). Children with ADHD, in summary, are characterized by an inability to sustain attention and inhibit impulsive responding on tasks or in social situations that require focused, reflective, organized, and self-directed activity (Douglas and Peters, 1979). They also exhibit a shorter attention span when playing with other children (Ullman et al., 1978).

Diagnostic Criteria for ADHD

The Diagnostic and Statistical Manual of Mental Disorders (DSM-IV-TR, 2000), provides the following operational diagnostic criteria to diagnose ADHD:

> inattention for mental age, motor overactivity, impulsivity, the symptoms occur prior to age 7 years and have a duration greater than 6 months; functional impairments that can be seen in 2 or more settings (school, work or home), and in the individual's social, academic or occupational functioning. Six or more of the following symptoms of inattention and six or more of the following hyperactivity–impulsivity symptoms should be present to arrive at the diagnosis of ADHD:
>
> > Inattention: poor attention to details or careless errors, difficulty sustaining attention, does not seem to listen, poor follow through on instructions and work completion, difficulty with organization, avoids tasks that require sustained mental effort, loses necessary items for tasks, easily distracted and forgetful in daily activities.
> >
> > Hyperactivity: fidgets or squirms, runs or climbs excessively (in adolescents or adults, subjective feelings of restlessness), difficulty playing or engaging in leisure activities quietly, is on the go or appears driven, talks excessively.
> >
> > Impulsivity: blurts out answers before questions have been completed, difficulty waiting turn, interrupts or intrudes on others.

Associated Features of ADHD

Associated features of ADHD in children and adolescents includes low frustration tolerance, temper outbursts, mood lability and excessive risk taking, bossiness, stubbornness, and insistence that his or her needs be met; demoralization of family and friends; abnormal mood, poor self-esteem and rejection by peers.

ADHD in Adults

Many children with ADHD do not outgrow their symptoms when they become adults. For example, Borlund and Heckman (1976) found that they are likely to exhibit symptoms of hyperactivity including restlessness, nervousness, impulsivity, and difficulty with their tempers as adults. Furthermore, they are likely to have a lower socioeconomic status and more psychiatric problems, characterized primarily by increased sociopathy, social, and marital difficulties. Although the DSM-IV-TR specifies that a childhood history of hyperactivity–impulsivity before age 7 is required for the diagnosis of adult ADHD, this age criterion was arbitrarily set and remains controversial. Furthermore, it is probably less applicable to women since girls more often have the predominantly affective and inattentive type of symptoms during their childhood. From a diagnostic perspective, the Wender Utah Rating Scale provides a useful screening measure for adult ADHD (Ward et al., 1993).

Psychiatric Disorders in Individuals with ADHD

Other research has found that adults who had been diagnosed as children having ADHD have a significantly higher incidence of psychiatric disorders such as schizophrenia, sociopathy, alcoholism, and drug abuse (Morrison, 1980). In addition, Goodwin et al. (1975) have reported a relationship between alcoholism in adults and ADHD during childhood. In a study by Weiss et al. (1979), many of the children with ADHD were found to have adjustment difficulties when they became young adults, characterized by impulsiveness, a higher incidence of car accidents and residence changes, and complaints of feeling restless. Weiss and her associates also found that the most common personality traits of these individuals were their impulsiveness and immature–dependent personality disorders. Thus, these findings suggest that the symptoms of ADHD do not disappear as these individuals become adults, and that the academic underachievement and low self-esteem of these individuals during adolescence frequently persists into adulthood, resulting in difficulties with law enforcement authorities, alcoholism, and drug-abuse problems.

DIFFERENTIAL DIAGNOSIS OF ADHD

The differential diagnosis of ADHD includes the following: autism/pervasive developmental disorder; anxiety, depressive and bipolar disorders; learning disability, sleep disorder, cognitive and oppositional defiant disorders, developmental mental retardation, and drug effects. ADHD can also be caused by traumatic brain damage, hypoxic-ischemic encephalopathy, encephalitis, stroke, toxins, medications, inborn errors of metabolism, and chromosomal disorders (Wiznitzer, 2006).

TOURETTE'S SYNDROME

Tourette's syndrome is characterized by motor and vocal tics characterized by brief involuntary movements, vocalizations or sensory symptoms that are recurrent, stereotyped, and repetitive. They may be single or multiple tics that can change over time, location, severity, and complexity. Unlike tremors, they are not rhythmic; they are also purposeless and experienced by children as irresistible, although capable at times of voluntary suppression. While distraction typically suppresses tics, when attention is paid to the tics it typically increases their frequency. The urge to perform the motor act is usually followed by a sense of relief.

Tourette's syndrome usually begins at 6 or 7 years of age. It is a chronic lifelong tic disorder that waxes and wanes over the years and can vary from mild to disabling. Motor tics such as eye blinking, facial grimacing, or nose twitching begin around age 7. Vocalizations such as sniffing, throat clearing, coughing, whistling, humming, copropraxia (obscene acts — touching genitals, finger gestures), and coprolalia (obscene swearing) usually start at age 11. The tics tend to become more frequent and complex in adolescence, but may partially abate in adulthood. Most Tourette's patients are able to complete high school and find employment despite their social handicaps.

Tourette's syndrome is associated with multiple neuropsychiatric disorders. Fifty to sixty percent of patients have obsessions and compulsions that include uttering obscenities, imitating the movements of others, counting, cleaning, and self-damaging compulsions such as head banging or body piercing. Coprolalia has been reported in 21 to 37% and copropraxia in 10 to 15% of patients with Tourette's syndrome. Their sexual and at times violent behavior may bring them to the attention of authorities, when the disorder is not recognized. The diagnosis of Tourette's syndrome is made by history and clinical examination since there are no specific diagnostic laboratory or neuroimaging findings for this disorder (Cummings and Mega, 2003c).

LEARNING DISABILITIES

The term learning disabilities refer to significant impairment in a child's ability to listen, speak, read, write, reason, or do math. These disorders, like ADHD, are generally assumed to be due to brain dysfunction, but can also be seen in individuals with mental retardation, sensory impairments, and social and emotional disturbances. Learning disabilities can also occur as a result of environmental influences due to cultural, ethnic, and language factors; insufficient or inappropriate instruction; or psychological factors. Children who are learning disabled constitute up to 15% of the general school population (Gaddes and Edgell, 1993).

DYSLEXIA

The term dyslexia (reading difficulties) has been used to describe children who fail to acquire adequate reading skills. Developmental dyslexia refers to significant difficulties in an individual's ability to read despite conventional instruction, adequate intelligence, and socioeconomic/cultural opportunities. This disorder appears to be due to a variety of unknown factors and does not appear to be the result of a specific lesion in the brain (Critchley and Critchley, 1978). There has been considerable debate, however, about whether dyslexia is a unitary disorder or the result of a variety of brain disorders. For example, dyslexia can be caused by disturbances in the development of visual perception (DeHirsch, 1957), disturbances in eye movement (Rayner, 1983), myopia (Wharry and Kirkpatrick, 1986), and deficits in motor proficiency (Denckla et al., 1985) and neuromotor maturity (Wolff et al., 1985).

Children with dyslexia have been found to have a higher incidence of attention-deficit disorder and behavioral problems (Jorm et al., 1986). There is evidence that dyslexia may be determined by genetic factors (DeFries et al., 1991). There also appears to be evidence that smoking during pregnancy, premature births, and perinatal events may contribute to dyslexia (Spreen et al., 1995). Balow et al. (1976) carefully reviewed the relationship between perinatal events and dyslexia and found that very low birth weight and complications during delivery such as anoxia were related to dyslexia and general learning deficits. For example, perinatal complications were found to be more frequent in children with dyscalculia (arithmetic difficulties) (Austin, 1978). Children with dyslexia have also been found to have abnormal EEGs and soft neurological signs (Smith et al., 1972). There has been anatomical evidence for the relationship between brain asymmetry and dyslexia (Hier et al., 1978). Dyslexia appears to be more common in boys, which may be due to more rapid brain myelination rates in girls (Geschwind and Galaburda, 1987).

DYSCALCULIA

Dyscalculia refers to difficulties performing arithmetic operations such as the reading or writing of numbers or a series of numbers, including recognizing their categorical structure. Dyscalculia should be differentiated from arithmetria (a complete failure of mathematical ability) since the former appears to be due to developmental factors, while the latter occurs after damage to the posterior left hemisphere (Grafman et al., 1982).

DYSGRAPHIA

Dysgraphia is characterized by a disorder in handwriting. An individual may have difficulty tracing shapes, using efficient strokes creating letters, forming letters of appropriate size, or using a comfortable pressure in grasping a writing instrument (De Quiros and Schrager, 1978). In adults, dysgraphia and dyscalculia often occur in conjunction with Gerstmann's syndrome and are usually accompanied by right–left confusion and finger agnosia (an inability to recognize which finger has been touched while blindfolded). This syndrome typically occurs following damage to the left posterior parietal lobe.

NONVERBAL LEARNING DISABILITIES

Nonverbal learning disabilities are characterized by adequate word recognition and spelling, but poor arithmetic skills due to defective visual perception, tactile perception, and impaired psychomotor skills (Rourke and Finlayson, 1978). For example, the arithmetic errors made by individuals with a nonverbal learning disability are usually caused by their inability to read mathematical signs and their faulty alignment of rows and columns due to their perceptual difficulties. Children with this disorder usually have difficulty remembering arithmetic tables or visualizing the steps necessary to solve a particular problem. They tend to have poor social judgment, difficulty recognizing faces and the emotional expressions of other children, and poor adaptation to novel interpersonal situations (Hernadek and Rourke, 1994). These children tend to have a higher incidence of depression, motor clumsiness, and attention–deficit disorder.

LEARNING DISABILITIES IN ADULTS

Individuals who are found to have learning disabilities during their childhood will frequently experience such difficulties as adults. For example, many of these individuals, when they become adults, often do not read for pleasure, including reading daily news reports. They may, however, cover up their deficits by watching television. A significant number of these children (approximately 40%) do not graduate from high school. These individuals tend to have high rates of unemployment and earn lower incomes (Spreen et al., 1995).

REFERENCES

American Psychiatric Association. 2000. *Desk Reference to the Diagnostic Criteria from DSM-IV-TR.* Washington, D.C.: APA.

Anastopoulos, A. D. and Barkley, R. A. 1988. Biological Factors in Attention Deficit-Hyperactivity Disorder. *Behavior Therapist, 11,* 47.

Austin, V. L. 1978. Discriminant and Descriptive Analyses of Neuropsychological Electroencephalographic Perinatal and Developmental History Correlates of Children with Math or Reading Disability. *Dissertation Abstracts International, 38,* 5554.

Balow, B., Rubin, R., and Rosen, M. S. 1976. Prenatal Events as Precursors of Reading Disability. *Reading Research Quarterly, 11,* 36.

Barkley, R. A. 1981. *Hyperactive Children: A Handbook for Diagnosis and Treatment.* New York: Guilford.

Barkley, R. A. 1990. A Critique of Current Diagnostic Criteria for Attention Deficit Hyperactivity Disorder: Clinical and Research Applications. *Journal of Development and Behavioral Pediatrics, 11,* 343–352.

Borlund, B. L. and Heckman, H. K. 1976. Hyperactive Boys and Their Brothers. *Archives of General Psychiatry, 33,* 669.

Chen, S. T., Sultzer, D. L., Hinkin, C. H., Mahler, M. E., and Cummings, J. L. 1998. Executive Dysfunction in Alzheimer's Disease: Association with Neuropsychiatric Symptoms and Functional Impairment. *Journal of Neuropsychiatry and Clinical Neurosciences, 10,* 426–432.

Chow, T. W. and Cummings, J. L. 1999. Frontal–Subcortical Circuits. In Miller, B. L. and Cummings, J. L. (Eds.) *The Human Frontal Lobes: Functions and Disorders.* New York: Guilford, pp. 3–26.

Clare, L. 2004. Assessment and Intervention in Dementia of the Alzheimer Type. In Baddeley, A.D., Kopelman, M. D., and Wilson, B. A. (Eds.) *The Essential Handbook of Memory Disorders for Clinicians.* Chichester, U.K.: John Wiley & Sons.

Comings, D. E., Gade-Andavolu, R., Gonzales, N., et al. 2000. Comparison of the Role of Dopamine, Serotonin, and Noradrenaline Genes in ADHD, ODD and Conduct Disorder: Multivariate Regression Analysis of 20 Genes. *Clinical Genetics, 57,* 178–196.

Critchley, M. and Critchley, E. A. 1978. *Dyslexia Defined.* London: Heinemann.

Cummings, J. L. 1995. Anatomic and Behavioral Aspects of Frontal–Subcortical Circuits. In Grafman, J., Holyoak, K. J., and Boller, F. (Eds.) *Structure and Functions of the Human Prefrontal Cortex,* Vol. 769, New York: New York Academy of Sciences, pp. 1–13.

Cummings, J. L. and Mega, M. S. 2003a. *Neuropsychiatry and Behavioral Neuroscience.* New York: Oxford University Press, chapter 7.

Cummings, J. L. and Mega, M. S. 2003b. *Neuropsychiatry and Behavioral Neuroscience.* New York: Oxford University Press, chapter 22.

Cummings, J. L. and Mega, M. S. 2003c. *Neuropsychiatry and Behavioral Neuroscience.* New York: Oxford University Press, chapter 19.

Cummings, J. L. and Trimble, M. R. 1995a. *Concise Guide to Neuropsychiatry and Behavioral Neurology.* Washington, D.C.: American Psychiatric Press.

Cummings, J. L. and Trimble, M. R. 1995b. *Concise Guide to Neuropsychiaty and Behavioral Neurology.* Washington, D.C.: American Psychiatric Press, chapter 10.

Daniel, M. G., Haban, G. F., Hutcherson, W. J., Bolter, J., and Long, C. 1985. Neuropsychological and Emotional Consequences of Accidental High Voltage Electrical Shock. *International Journal of Clinical Neuropsychology, 7,* 102–106.

DeFries, J. C., Stevenson, J., Gillis, J. J., and Wadsworth, S. J. 1991. Genetic Etiology of Spelling Deficits in the Colorado and London Twin Studies of Reading Disability. *Reading and Writing, 3,* 271.

DeHirsch, K. 1957. Tests Designed to Discover Potential Reading Difficulty. *American Journal of Orthopsychiatry, 27*, 566.

Delis, D. C. and Lucas, J. A. 1996. Memory. In Fogel, B. S., Schiffer, R. B., and Rao, S. M. (Eds.) *Neuropsychiatry*. Baltimore: Williams & Wilkins, pp. 365–400.

Denckla, M. B., Rudel, R. G., Chapman, C., and Kriegee, J. 1985. Motor Proficiency in Dyslexic Children With and Without Attentional Disorders. *Archives of Neurology, 42*, 228.

De Quiros, J. B. and Schrager, O. L. 1978. *Neuropsychological Fundamentals in Learning Disabilities*. San Rafael, CA: Academic Therapy Publications.

Devinsky, O. 1992. *Behavioral Neurology*. St. Louis: Mosby.

Douglas, V. I. and Peters, K. G. 1979. Toward a Clearer Definition of the Attentional Deficit of Hyperactive Children. In Hale, G. A. and Lewis, M. (Eds.) *Attention and Cognitive Development*. New York: Plenum Press.

Filley, C. M. and Kleinschmidt-DeMasters, B. K. 2001. Toxic Leukoencephalopathy. *The New England Journal of Medicine, 345*, 425–432.

Gaddes, W. H. and Edgell, D. 1993. *Learning Disabilities and Brain Function*, 3rd ed. New York: Springer.

Geschwind, N. and Galaburda, A. M. 1987. *Cerebral Lateralization: Biological Mechanisms, Associations and Pathology*. Cambridge, MA: MIT Press.

Goodman, R. and Stevenson, J. A. 1989. Twin Study of Hyperactivity II, The Etiological Role of Genes, Family Relationships and Perinatal Adversity. *Journal of Child Psychology and Psychiatry, 5*, 691.

Goodwin, D. W., Schulsinger, F., Hermauben, L., Guze, S. B., and Winokur, G. 1975. Alcoholism and the Hyperactive Child Syndrome. *Journal of Nervous and Mental Disease, 160*, 349.

Grafman, J., Passafiume, P., Faglioni, P., and Boller, F. 1982. Calculation Disturbances in Adults with Focal Hemispheric Damage. *Cortex, 18*, 37.

Groenewegen, H. J. 1997. Cortical–Subcortical Relationships and the Limbic Forebrain. In Cummings, J. L. and Trimble, M. R. (Eds.) *Contemporary Behavioral Neurology*. Boston: Butterworth-Heinemann, pp. 29–48.

Hartman, D. E. 1995. *Neuropsychological Toxicology: Identification and Assessment of Human Neurotoxic Syndromes*, 2nd ed. New York: Plenum Press.

Hernadek, M. C. S. and Rourke, B. P. 1994. Principal Identifying Features of the Syndrome of Nonverbal Learning Disabilities in Children. *Journal of Learning Disabilities, 27*, 144.

Hier, D., Le May, M., Rosenberger, P., and Perlo, V. 1978. Developmental Dyslexia. *Archives of Neurology, 35*, 90.

Hooshmand, H., Radfar, F., and Beckner, E. 1989. The Neurophysiological Aspects of Electrical Injuries. *Clinical Electroencephalography, 20*, 111–120.

Hou, C. E., Carlin, D., and Miller, B. L. 2004. Non-Alzheimer's Disease Dementias: Anatomic, Clinical and Molecular Correlates. *Canadian Journal of Psychiatry, 49*, 164–171.

Jorm, A. F., Share, D. L., Matthews, R., and MacLean, R. 1986. Behavior Problems in Specific Reading Retarded and General Reading Backward Children: A Longitudinal Study. *Journal of Child Psychology and Psychiatry, 27*, 33.

Klein, R. G. and Mannuzza, S. 1991. *J. Am. Acad Child Adolesc. Psychiatry, 30*, 383.

Kopelman, M. D. 2002. Disorders of Memory. *Brain, 125*, 2152–2190.

Marsh, N. V. and Willoughby, E. W. 2004. Multiple Sclerosis. In Rizzo, M. and Eslinger, P. J. (Eds.) *Principles and Practice of Behavioral Neurology and Neuropsychology*. Philadelphia: Saunders, chapter 35.

Mega, M. S. and Cummings, J. L. 1997. The Limbic System: An Anatomic, Phylogenetic and Clinical Perspective. *Journal of Neuropsychiatry and Clinical Neuroscience, 9*, 315–330.

Mendez, M. F. and Cummings, J. L. 2003a. *Dementia: A Clinical Approach*, 3rd ed. Boston: Butterworth-Heinemann, p. 4.

Mendez, M. F. and Cummings, J. L. 2003b. *Dementia: A Clinical Approach*, 3rd ed. Philadelphia: Butterworth-Heinemann, chapter 3.

Mendez, M. F. and Perryman, K. M. 2002. Neuropsychiatric Features of Frontotemporal Dementia. Evaluation of Consensus Criteria and Review. *Journal of Neuropsychiatry and Clinical Neurosciences, 14*, 424–429.

Mendez, M. F., Bagart, B., and Edwards-Lee, T. 1997. Self-Injurious Behavior in Frontotemporal Dementia. *Neurocase, 3*, 231–236.

Mendez, M. F., Chen, A. K., Shapira, J. S., and Miller, B. L. 2005. Acquired Sociopathy and Frontotemporal Dementia. *Dementia and Geriatric Cognitive Disorders*, *20*, 99–104.

Morrison, J. R. 1980. Childhood Hyperactivity in an Adult Psychiatric Population: Social Factors. *Journal of Clinical Psychiatry*, *41*, 40.

Morrison, J. R. and Stewart, M. A. 1971. A Family Study of the Hyperactive Syndrome. *Biological Psychiatry*, *3*, 189.

Petersen, R. C., Stevens, J. C., Ganguli, M., Tangalos, E. G., Cummings, J. L., and DeKosky, S. T. 2001. Practice Paramenters: Early Detection of Dementia: Mild Cognitive Impairment (An Evidence Based Review). Report of the Quality Standards Subcommittee of the American Academy of Neurology. *Neurology*, *56*, 1133–1142.

Petty, P. G. and Parkin, G. 1986. Electrical Injury to the Central Nervous System. *Neurosurgery*, *19*, 282.

Pliskin, N. H., Ammar, A. N., Fink, J. W., Hill, S. K., Malina, A.C., Ramati, A., Kelley, K. M., Lee, R. C. 2006. Neuropsychological Changes Following Electrical Injury. *J. Int. Neuropsychol. Soc.*, *12*, 17–23.

Pliskin, N. H., Meyer, G. J., Dolske, M. C., Heilbronner, R. L., Kelley, K. M., and Lee, R. C. 1994. Neuropsychiatric Aspects of Electrical Injury: A Review of Neuropsychological Research. In Lee, R. C., Capelli-Schellpfeffer, M., and Kelley, K. M. (Eds.) *Annals of the New York Academy of Sciences*, Vol. 720. New York: New York Academy of Sciences, pp. 219–223.

Rayner, K. 1983. *Eye Movements and Reading: Perceptual and Language Processes*. New York: Academic Press.

Reuhl, K. R. 1991. Delayed Expression of Neurotoxicity: The Problem of Silent Damage. *Neurotoxicology*, *5*, 187–204.

Roberts, G. W., Leigh, P. N., and Weinberger, D. R. (Eds.) 1993. In *Neuropsychiatric Disorders*. London: Wolfe, chap. 6.

Ross, D. M. and Ross, S. A. 1982. *Hyperactivity Current Issues: Research and Theory*. New York: Wiley.

Rourke, B. P. and Finlayson, M. P. J. 1978. Neuropsychological Significance of Variations in Patterns of Academic Performance: Verbal and Visuospatial Abilities. *Journal of Abnormal Child Psychology*, *6*, 121.

Sbordone, R. J. 2000. The Executive Functions of the Brain. In Groth-Marnat, G. (Ed.) *Neuropsychological Assessment in Clinical Practice: A Practical Guide to Test Interpretation and Integration*. New York: Wiley, pp. 437–456.

Selnes, O. A., Mckhann, G. M., Borowicz, L. M. Jr, Gregg, M. A. 2006. Cognitive and Neurobehavioral Function after Cardiac Bypass Procedures. *Neurologic Clinics*, *24*, 133–145.

Smith, A. C., Flick, G. L., Ferris, G. S., and Sellman, A. H. 1972. Prediction of Developmental Outcome at Seven Years from Prenatal, Perinatal, and Postnatal Events. *Child Development*, *43*, 495.

Spencer, P. S. 1990. Environmental Causes of Neurodegenerative Diseases. In Russell, R. W., Flattau, P. E., and Pope, A. M. (Eds.) *Behavioral Measures of Neurotoxicity*. Washington, D.C.: National Academy Press, pp. 268–284.

Spreen, O., Risser, A. H., and Edgell, D. 1995. *Developmental Neuropsychology*. New York: Oxford.

Troster, A. J. and Ruff, R. M. 1988. Accidental High Voltage Electrocution: Neurobehavioral Sequelae in Three Cases. Paper presented at the National Academy of Neuropsychology, Orlando, FL.

Ullman, R. K., Barkley, R. A., and Brown, H. W. 1978. The Behavioral Symptoms of Hyperkinetic Children Who Successfully Responded to Stimulant Drug Treatment. *American Journal of Orthopsychiatry*, *48*, 425.

Ward, M. F., Wender, P. H., and Reimherr, F. 1993. The Wender Utah Rating Scale. *American Journal of Psychiatry*, *150*, 885.

Weiss, G., Hechtman, L., Perlman, T., Hopkins, J., and Wener, A. 1979. Hyperactives as Young Adults: A Controlled Prospective 10-Year Follow-Up of 75 Children. *Archives of General Psychiatry*, *36*, 675.

Wender, P. H. 1971. *Minimal Brain Dysfunction in Children*. New York: Wiley InterScience Series.

Wharry, R. E. and Kirkpatrick, S. W. 1986. Vision and Academic Performance of Learning Disabled Children. *Perception and Motor Skills*, *62*, 323.

Willerman, L. 1973. Activity Level and Hyperactivity in Twins. Child Development, *44*, 288.

Wiznitzer, M. 2006. Attention Deficit-Hyperactivity Disorder. Syllabus 2BS-004-18, 2006 Annual Meeting American Academy of Neurology. Minneapolis, MN: American Academy of Neurology.

Wolff, P. H., Gunnoe, C., and Cohen, C. 1985. Neuromotor Maturation and Psychological Performance: A Developmental Study. *Developmental Medicine and Child Neurology*, *27*, 344.

6 Posttraumatic Stress Disorder

Posttraumatic stress disorder (PTSD) refers to the development of a set of specific symptoms following exposure to traumatic and physical events such as combat, fire, flood, molestation, natural disasters, rape, or witnessing someone badly injured or killed, and so forth. According to the fourth edition of the Diagnostic and Statistical Manual of Mental Disorders (DSM-IV) (American Psychiatric Association, 1994), an individual who develops PTSD must be confronted with an event or events that involve actual or threatened death, or serious injury, or threat to the physical integrity of self or others, which produces intense feelings of fear, helplessness, or terror. The diagnostic criteria for PTSD requires that the traumatic event be persistently reexperienced by either recurrent or intrusive recollections, distressing dreams, flashbacks, or by stimuli that symbolize or resemble some aspect of the traumatic event; conscious efforts to avoid specific thoughts, feelings, people, places, or activities that could trigger recollections of the event; symptoms of emotional arousal (e.g., hypervigilance) and heightened reactivity (e.g., exaggerated startle responses).

ACUTE STRESS DISORDER

The diagnosis of Acute Stress Disorder (ASD) was introduced in the Diagnostic and Statistical Manual of Mental Disorders (DSM-IV) by the American Psychiatric Association in 1994 and was conceptualized as an acute form of PTSD, which occurs within 1 month following exposure to a traumatic event. While ASD has been regarded as a predictor of a PTSD (Bryant and Harvey, 1997), Harvey and Bryant (1998) found that 40% of the individuals who met the diagnostic criteria for ASD did not develop chronic PTSD. The major difference between PTSD and ASD is that the latter requires the presence of significant dissociative symptoms, where the patient reports a subjective sense of numbing, emotional detachment, or absence of emotional responsiveness; a reduction in awareness of his or her surroundings, derealization; depersonalization; or dissociative amnesia. The DSM-IV diagnostic criteria for ASD also place more stringent requirements on intrusive, avoidance and arousal symptoms than PTSD. While numerous structured interviews and self-report inventories currently exist to assess PTSD, only a few inventories have been developed to assess ASD (Bryant et al., 1998; Bryant and Harvey, 2000; Briere, 2001).

ROLE OF DISSOCIATION

One explanation of ASD argues that since dissociation is a primary coping mechanism for managing traumatic experiences, individuals who are exposed to traumatic events are likely to minimize the adverse emotional consequences of the trauma by restricting their awareness of the experience (Van der Kolk and Van der Hart, 1989). Foa and Hearst-Ikeda (1996), however, have argued that following a traumatic event, fear structures develop, which contain the mental representations of the traumatic experience that produce an attentional bias to threat-related material.

These investigators have proposed that the initial dissociative responses following exposure to a traumatic event may impede deactivation of fear structures, which results in impaired emotional functioning that may lead to chronic PTSD. Their theoretical explanation is corroborated by research studies that demonstrate that traumatic individuals frequently display disorganized and fragmented memories (Foa et al., 1995) and often develop overgeneral memories of the traumatic event (McNally et al., 1995). Other investigators (Horowitz, 1986) have argued that dissociative responses are common and serve as adaptive short-term reactions to a traumatic event, which may subsequently produce a resolution of the traumatic experience. Conversely, other research has shown that dissociative reactions at the time of traumatic event are highly predictive of chronic PTSD (McFarlane, 1986; Solomon and Mikulincer, 1992; Shalev et al., 1993, 1996b).

Bryant and Harvey (1997) have stressed that the role of dissociation in ASD is complicated by the ambiguity concerning when the dissociative response occurs. They point out that according to the DSM-IV criteria the dissociative symptoms may occur either during or after experiencing the traumatic event. This time frame, however, contrasts markedly to the requirement that the intrusive avoidance and arousal symptoms need to be experienced as ongoing problems. This also contrasts with the DSM-IV criteria that the symptoms of ASD persist for a minimum of 2 days following the traumatic experience.

COMPLEX PTSD

Although the DSM-IV presents criteria to allow clinicians to differentiate between an acute stress disorder and chronic PTSD (i.e., the duration of the patient's symptoms in the former is more than 1 month but less than 3 months, while the duration of symptoms of the latter is greater than 3 months), it fails to mention complex PTSD, which is a broader and more severe form of PTSD that stems from early and repetitive psychological trauma (Herman, 1993; Symth, 1999). Individuals with complex PTSD are likely to have had a history of sexual or physical abuse throughout their childhood or exposure to chronic trauma as adults (e.g., repeated physical and/or sexual abuse, frequent torture, or exposure to repeated combat trauma).

A number of investigators (Herman, 1993; Ide and Paez, 2000) have stressed that the definition of PTSD contained in the DSM-IV implicitly refers to the development of symptoms following exposure to a single or discreet stressor rather than frequent or numerous exposure to stressors throughout one's life. Smyth (1999) has stressed the prognosis for complex PTSD is substantially worse than for simple PTSD. For example, he points out that individuals with complex PTSD exhibit symptoms such as severe affect regulation dysfunction approaching what is typically seen in individuals with bipolar and/or borderline personality disorders, and frequently exhibit somatic difficulties and dissociative symptoms. Thus, the symptom picture of individuals with complex PTSD, as a result of prolonged victimization, is far more complex than the simple PTSD patient (Ide and Paez, 2000).

Complex PTSD has also been defined as a syndrome with varied and divergent symptoms such as alteration in attention and consciousness, which includes symptoms such as amnesia, transient dissociative episodes, and depersonalization. These dissociative symptoms, however, may cause health professionals to misdiagnose many of these individuals with a closed head injury if they become involved in motor vehicle accidents (MVAs). For example, when these individuals are seen by a physician in the emergency room or later by a neurologist, they frequently claim that they are unable to recall the accident or some of the events surrounding the accident even though they did not strike their head, lose consciousness, or display symptoms such as confusion or disorientation at the time of the accident. Unfortunately, as a result of their complex PTSD, their symptoms can be shaped over time by others, particularly those who are in a position of authority and control (e.g., attorneys, physicians, etc.) (Symth, 1999).

Case Example

A 49-year-old female slipped and fell in the parking lot of a hardware store that was covered with snow and ice and landed on her buttocks. She immediately got up and finished loading her supplies into a car and drove approximately 12 miles home. The next day, she went to see her family physician and complained of stiffness and soreness in her lower back. She remained out of work for a week and returned to work without incident. Several months later, she became very depressed as a result of several tragic personal losses, which triggered a delayed PTSD as a result of a childhood history of repeated sexual molestation, physical abuse, and torture that she had managed to repress. She consulted with an attorney, who suggested to her that she may have sustained a brain injury during her slip and fall accident. The attorney then referred her to a neurologist. When she saw the neurologist, she complained of symptoms that were similar to the information she had received from her attorney about closed head injuries. For example, she informed the neurologist that she had no recollection of the accident, and complained of severe problems with her recent memory, attention, and problem-solving skills, even though she did not report any alteration of consciousness or head trauma when she was examined the day following her accident by her family physician. She was then referred for neuropsychological testing and was found to have moderate to severe neuropsychological impairments (most likely as a result of her extremely high levels of internal anxiety and/or the effects of her complex PTSD).

On the basis of her test scores, the neuropsychologist diagnosed a severe closed head injury. She was then encouraged by her attorney to quit her job since it would result in a larger financial award. Unfortunately, quitting her job created serious financial difficulties, which resulted in frequent arguments with her husband, conflicts with her children, and feelings of worthlessness as a result of her perceived inability to contribute to her family's welfare. These problems exacerbated her delayed PTSD and caused her to develop comorbid psychiatric disorders, which resulted in her being placed in a psychiatric unit for several weeks. All of her symptoms and problems were attributed by her "treating doctors" to the "brain injury" she had sustained as a result of her slip and fall accident.

Individuals with complex PTSD symptoms can exhibit a wide spectrum of psychological impairment. While some of these individuals may exhibit high levels of interpersonal, social, and vocational functioning, many are unable to function in society. Not uncommonly, the explanation given for their disability is "brain damage," rather than their complex PTSD, particularly if the healthcare professionals are unaware of the patient's history of repeated psychological trauma. In other cases, the symptoms of such individuals may be attributed to a borderline personality disorder (Herman, 1993; Briere, 1997; Ide and Paez, 2000).

HISTORICAL BACKGROUND OF PTSD

Psychological distress following exposure to a traumatic event can be found in many early literary works. For example, Samuel Pepy described PTSD symptoms after witnessing the Great London Fire during the seventeenth century (Boudewyns, 1996). Descriptions of PTSD were made by Abercrombie in 1828 and Brodie in 1837 (Millen, 1966). PTSD symptoms were observed by military physicians during the World Wars I and II, and were labeled as "shell shock," "war neurosis," or "combat exhaustion." When similar symptoms were reported by individuals who had filed personal injury lawsuits or workers' compensation claims after they had been involved in motor vehicle or railway accidents, these symptoms were often given pejorative labels such as "posttraumatic neurosis," "accident neurosis," or "railway spine," particularly when physical injuries were not sustained (Sparr, 1995).

Kardiner (1941) and Grinker and Spiegel (1945) described the short- and long-term psychological sequelae of combat veterans. Articles were published in the late 1960s and early 1970s that described the psychiatric symptoms of soldiers who had fought in Vietnam (Goldsmith and Cretekos, 1969; Fox, 1972). PTSD began gaining acceptance after studies continued to appear in prominent medical and psychiatric journals describing the emotional and psychological reactions of survivors to extreme traumas such as fires, explosions, floods, military combat, concentration camps, and rape (Horowitz, 1976). These studies significantly enhanced the understanding of PTSD and resulted in the inclusion of specific criteria for PTSD in the DSM-III and the DSM-III-R (Rahe, 1995).

EPIDEMIOLOGY OF PTSD

EXPOSURE TO A TRAUMATIC EVENT

Because the DSM-II did not contain specific diagnostic criteria for PTSD, little research was done on the prevalence of traumatic events and the incidence and prevalence of PTSD prior to the publication of the DSM-III in 1980. The prevalence of witnessing a traumatic event during one's lifetime was examined by Norris (1992). He interviewed 1000 people living in the southeastern United States and found that 69% of the respondents had experienced at least one traumatic event in their lifetime — 73.6% of the men reported that they had witnessed at least one traumatic event in comparison with 64.8% of the women. Resnick et al. (1993) found that 68.9% of over 4000 women who were interviewed via telephone reported that they had been exposed to at least one traumatic event in their lifetime (e.g., a crime or sexual assault). However, when younger adults between the ages of 21 and 30 who had been employed at a health maintenance organization were interviewed, only 39.1% reported exposure to trauma (Breslau et al., 1991). This relatively low prevalence rate may reflect the fact that the sample interviewed was relatively young, contained relatively few people in low socioeconomic classes, and did not include veterans with combat experience (Breslan et al., 1998).

More recently, Kessler et al. (1995) investigated the lifetime prevalence in the general population of witnessing a traumatic event. They interviewed 5877 people living in the 48 contiguous states between the ages of 15 and 54, using face-to-face interviews with a modified version of the Diagnostic Interview Schedule (DIS). They found that 60.7% of the men and 51.2% of the women had been exposed to at least one traumatic event during their lifetime. Traumatic events such as witnessing a person being badly injured or killed or being involved in a fire, flood, natural disaster, or life-threatening accident were reported by approximately a third of the respondents. Traumatic events such as sexual molestation, rape, combat, physical attack, or physical abuse were reported by fewer than 15% of the respondents. Men were more likely to report traumatic events such as combat, physical attacks, or being kidnapped or threatened with a weapon, while women were more likely to report traumatic events such as rape, sexual molestation, and childhood physical abuse.

INCIDENCE AND PREVALENCE

The incidence of PTSD in Vietnam combat veterans was investigated in a large epidemiological study involving 2493 participants (Helzer et al., 1987). These investigators found that the incidence of PTSD was 6.3% for veterans who were not wounded and 20% for veterans who had been wounded in combat. In a carefully designed study, Kulka et al. (1991) found that the incidence of PTSD was 15.2% in male and 8.5% female Vietnam veterans, while the lifetime prevalence of PTSD in these groups was 30.9 and 26.9%, respectively, with even higher ratios reported for veterans who had sustained physical injuries or had served in high-stress war zones. Helzer et al. (1987) emphasized that one of the limitations of this type of research is that many Vietnam veterans who have PTSD are homeless or have dropped out of society. Thus, the prevalence rates of PTSD in Vietnam veterans may be considerably higher since such veterans were most likely not included in these studies.

Kessler et al. (1995) have estimated that 7.8% of the general population (5% men and 10.4% women) have a lifetime history of PTSD. This estimate is similar to a previous estimate reported by Breslau et al. (1991). The traumatic events most commonly associated with PTSD in women were rape and sexual molestation and were reported by 49% of the women with PTSD.

While children are frequently exposed to a variety of traumatic experiences, very little is known about the prevalence of witnessing traumatic events and PTSD symptoms in children. Nonetheless, Giaconia et al. (1995) found that by age 18 more than 40% of the youths in a community sample reported that they had experienced at least one traumatic event, while more than 6% satisfied the diagnostic criteria for a lifetime diagnosis of PTSD. Although an estimated 69% of the population is exposed to traumatic events during their lifetime (Norris, 1992), the lifetime prevalence of PTSD is only 7.8%. Thus, exposure to a traumatic event does not automatically produce PTSD. It may, however, result in other psychiatric disorders such as major depression or somatic conditions. Thus, there may be multiple factors that determine whether a particular person will develop PTSD after being exposed to a traumatic event.

RISK FACTORS

Factors that have been associated with increased risk for the development of PTSD include the severity of the traumatic events (March, 1993); a preexisting history of abuse, stress, or trauma (Bremner et al., 1993; Zaidi and Foy, 1994); behavioral or psychiatric problems (Helzer et al., 1987); comorbid psychopathology (McFarlane, 1986; 2000); family history of psychiatric illness (Davidson et al., 1985); and subsequent exposure to reactivating environmental stimuli (Kluznick et al., 1986; McFarlane, 1989; Schnurr et al., 1993). In addition to these factors, the most consistently reported risk factors for the development of PTSD are female gender, social disadvantage (e.g., poverty), childhood adversity, genetic predisposition, and substance abuse (Brewin et al., 2000). Women who have been exposed to physical abuse and neglect during their childhood, had parents with psychiatric problems, did not have a close trusting relationship with their mother, have a prior history of affective and anxiety disorders, and have substance abuse were found to be at risk to develop PTSD. Men who had a preexisting history of anxiety disorder, parental substance abuse, and parental divorce were also found to be at risk to develop PTSD (Bromet et al., 1998).

CHRONICITY OF SYMPTOMS

While the DSM-IV claims that approximately 50% of PTSD cases resolve within 3 months, Davidson et al. (1991) found that 47.9% of PTSD patients were still experiencing symptoms more than 1 year after the traumatic event. Helzer et al. (1987) found that a third of PTSD patients were still reporting symptoms 3 years after the traumatic event. Patients with PTSD who received professional treatment reported a shorter duration of their symptoms than patients who did not receive such treatment (Kessler et al., 1995).

COMORBIDITY OF SYMPTOMS

PTSD has a high rate of comorbidity with psychiatric, substance abuse, and somatization disorders. Kessler et al. (1995) found that 88% of men and 79% of women with PTSD had at least one other psychiatric disorder. They found that PTSD patients were almost eight times as likely to have three or more psychiatric disorders than individuals who did not have PTSD. The incidence of somatization disorders in individuals with PTSD was found to be 90 times more frequent than in individuals without PTSD. Although PTSD may significantly increase the likelihood of having other disorders, the onset of a medical illness in persons with PTSD may cause an exacerbation of their PTSD symptoms (Hamner, 1994).

CLINICAL ASSESSMENT OF PTSD

The Structured Clinical Interview (SCID), which utilizes DSM-III-R diagnostic criteria, has been utilized most frequently to evaluate for the presence of PTSD symptoms (Spitzer et al., 1990) because it is easy to administer and score and has good reliability and validity (McFall et al., 1990). The Diagnostic Interview Scale of the National Institute of Mental Health (DIS-NIMH) allows clinicians and technicians to assess for PTSD symptoms using a highly structured interview format. While this scale has been found to correlate well with other PTSD measures in clinical settings, it may not be well suited for nonclinical or community settings (Watson et al., 1991). The Structured Interview for PTSD (SI-PTSD) has excellent test–retest and interrater reliability and contains continuous and dichotomous symptom ratings (Davidson et al., 1989). The Clinician Administered PTSD Scale (CAPS) evaluates not only PTSD symptoms, but also their severity and the patient's social and occupational functioning, as well as the validity of the patient's responses (Blake et al., 1990). None of these tests, however, have built-in measures of validity to determine if some individuals are exaggerating or inaccurately reporting PTSD symptoms. In other words, they were not designed to evaluate the credibility of individuals involved in litigation who are reporting PTSD symptoms to enhance the value of their case. These tests were also not designed to detect individuals whose cognitive difficulties prevent them from understanding the content of the test questions in order to respond in a manner that accurately reflects their symptoms.

PTSD QUESTIONNAIRES

A number of PTSD questionnaires and self-report measures have been widely used in both clinical and research settings. The Mississippi Scale is a 35-item instrument that has both civilian and combat versions (Keane et al., 1987). It can be used in a wide variety of different settings (e.g., clinical, field, community) as well as for research purposes. The Impact of Events Scale (IES) has been widely used to assess the psychological consequences of exposure to traumatic events (Horowitz et al., 1979). While it possesses good internal consistency and high test–retest reliability, it does not appear to measure all of the psychological consequences of PTSD (Sparr, 1995). The Pennsylvania (PENN) Inventory has been used to evaluate the psychological effects of PTSD in combat veterans and nonveterans exposed to trauma (Hammarberg, 1992). Since these scales do not have any built-in measures of validity, some individuals with closed head injuries are likely to be erroneously identified with PTSD as a result of their cognitive impairments and misunderstanding of the test items and questions they are asked (McMillan, 2001). As a consequence clinicians should not rely on these scales to diagnose PTSD without taking a careful history and detailed clinical interview of the patient, particularly when there is good evidence that the patient has sustained a closed head injury.

PTSD FOLLOWING MVAs

Although research on PTSD has focused primarily on traumatic events that involve combat, major catastrophes, or victimization by assault, loss, or rape, relatively few studies have investigated the psychological sequelae of MVAs, even though individuals involved in MVA are often exposed to serious physical harm and the threat of death, as well as serious injuries or the deaths of others (Delahanty et al., 1997). Blanchard et al. (1996) examined 158 victims of MVA who sought medical attention. They found that 39% of these victims met the diagnostic criteria for PTSD. However, they found that factors such as a prior history of major depression, fear of dying during the MVA, extent of the physical injuries sustained, and whether litigation had been initiated accounted for 70% of the MVA victims who went on to develop chronic PTSD. Blanchard et al. (1997) found that

55% of the MVA victims who met the diagnostic criteria for PTSD had either completely or partially remitted at approximately 9 months post-MVA. MVA victims who did not perceive themselves as responsible for their accident were more likely to develop chronic PTSD (Delahanty et al., 1997). Although only 7% of MVA victims developed delayed PTSD during a 1-year prospective follow-up assessment, these particular individuals were found to have significantly lower perceived social support systems and were more likely to be involved in litigation (Buckley et al., 1996).

BIOLOGICAL BASIS OF PTSD

While many healthcare professionals have naively assumed that PTSD is a "psychological" or "mental" condition, their views are at variance with extensive body of research' that demonstrate that PTSD is a physiological, endocrinological, and neurologically mediated disorder.

PHYSIOLOGICAL/ENDOCRINOLOGICAL STUDIES

Research has shown that profound and persistent alterations in physiological reactivity and stress hormone (cortisol) secretion occurs in patients with PTSD. For example, PTSD patients experience heightened physiological arousal in response to stimuli that are related to the traumatic event, characterized by significant increases in heart rate, skin conductance, and blood pressure (Malloy et al., 1983; Blanchard et al., 1986; Pitman et al., 1987; Van der Kolk, 1997). Drugs such as lactate (Rainey et al., 1987) or Yohimbine (Southwick et al., 1993) have been found to trigger panic attacks and flashbacks in PTSD patients by increasing their autonomic arousal levels. Ornitz and Pynoos (1989) found that PTSD patients have abnormalities in their habituation to the acoustic startle response, which suggests that these patients have difficulty evaluating the significance of sensory stimuli while modulating their levels of physiological arousal. These studies suggest that chronic physiological arousal, combined with an inability to regulate their autonomic reaction to internal or external stimuli, can severely hinder patients with PTSD from effectively utilizing their emotions as warning signals and attend to incoming information in order to take necessary adaptive actions. Thus, patients with PTSD tend to immediately begin responding with fight or flight reactions without initially trying to cognitively determine the significance of the stimuli being received (Van der Kolk, 1997).

PTSD patients have been found to have chronically high levels of sympathetic nervous system activity (Kosten et al., 1987) and increased levels of lymphocyte glucocorticoid receptors (Sapolsky, 2000). Yehuda et al. (1990) and Yehuda and Southwick (1991) have proposed that the glucocorticoid system shuts down the body's biological reactions that are activated by acute stress through the release of cortisol, which serves as an antistress hormone. Thus, low levels of glucocorticoids or cortisol would be expected to result in the development of high levels of catecholamine activity that is likely to produce fight or flight reactions, since the glucocorticoids and catecholamines modulate each other's effects.

Low levels of cortisol have been associated with increased vulnerability to PTSD. For example, McFarlane (1996) found that low cortisol levels in MVA victims, when they were seen in the emergency room, were highly correlated with the development of PTSD symptoms 3 months later. Urinary cortisol levels were also found to be lower in inpatient and outpatient combat veterans (Yehuda et al., 1990) and in holocaust survivors (Yehuda et al., 1995a) with PTSD than comparison groups without PTSD.

NEUROLOGICAL/BRAIN IMAGING STUDIES

Bremner et al. (1995) utilized magnetic resonance imaging (MRI) to determine the hippocampal volume of Vietnam combat veterans with PTSD. They found that combat veterans with PTSD had statistically smaller right hippocampal volume than combat veterans without PTSD who were matched for age, sex, race, years of education, socioeconomic status, body size, and years of alcohol use. Since the hippocampus mediates declarative memory, a decrease in hippocampal volume would be expected to produce deficits in short-term memory. In a subsequent study, Bremner (1999) found that hippocampal volume in combat veterans was correlated with deficits in verbal memory on neuropsychological testing. He stressed that PTSD patients demonstrate a variety of memory problems, including deficits in declarative memory (i.e., remembering facts or lists), fragmentation of autobiographic and trauma-related memories, and nondeclarative memory (i.e., types of memory that cannot be willfully brought up into the conscious mind including motor memory such as how to ride a bicycle). He also stressed that since the hippocampus has a rich concentration of receptors for glucocorticoids and modulates glucocorticoid release through inhibitory effects on the hypothalamic–pituitary–adrenal axis it plays a crucial role in the integration of cognitive, neurohormonal, and neurochemical responses to stress. He also points out that studies with normal human subjects have shown that glucocorticoids have direct effects on memory functioning. For example, therapeutic doses of glucocorticoids (dexamethasone or cortisol) have been found to produce impairments in verbal declarative memory functioning in healthy human subjects. He points out that high stress-induced cortisol levels can lead to an exacerbation of memory deficits while an improvement in memory function occurs when stress-induced cortisol levels are reduced. Similarly, adults with PTSD who had histories of childhood physical or sexual abuse were found to have smaller (12%) left hippocampi than nonabused controls (Bremner et al., 1995). Gilbertson et al. (2003) (cited in McNally, 2003) has suggested that hippocampal atrophy may reflect preexisting PTSD risk factors.

Sapolsky et al. (1984) have shown that the chronically high levels of corticoid activity as a result of prolonged stress can either produce reversible dendritic alterations in a neuronal loss, particularly in the hippocampus. They reported that animal studies have shown that exposure to glucocorticoids or to stress over the course of 21 days led to atrophy of dendritic branches in the pyramidal neurons of the rat hippocampus, which was accompanied by impairment of the initial learning of a spatial memory task on an eight-arm radial maze. These investigators stressed that certain levels of glucocorticoids can cause reversible changes in the morphology of hippocampal neurons, and that longer periods of exposure to glucocorticoids produces irreversible hippocampal dysfunction resembling a pattern seen in aging animals at an accelerated rate. They also found that the older the animal, the more vulnerable it is to damage.

Recent studies utilizing MRI to investigate myelination *in vivo* has shown that myelination in the frontal and temporal lobes continues into the mid to late 40s (Bartzokis et al., 2001) to compensate for a reduction in gray matter volume in these areas (Bartzokis et al., 2003). The process of myelination is believed to be crucial for normal adult brain function since it increases neuronal transmission speed and the integration of information across brain regions (Bartzokis, 2002). He has suggested that exposure to stress could interfere with this process and increase the likelihood of excretory amino acid toxicity of the oligodendrocytes which play a crucial role in the myelination process, resulting in a decrease of the speed of information processing and disruptions in the brain's ability to process information.

Research studies have shown that the limbic region of the brain plays a critical role in learning, memory, and emotional regulation. Hamner et al. (1999) have explored the impact of stress on the limbic system. Their findings suggested that the anterior cingulate gyrus may serve as a critical gating function in modulating condition/fear responses and is a key component to neural circuits involved in the pathophysiology of PTSD. For example, they have proposed that the amygdala–locus coeruleus–anterior cingulate circuit may play an important role in chronic noradrenergic activation that has been documented in PTSD patients. According to their model, efferent noradrenergic projections in the locus coeruleus may dampen anterior cingulate function, which in turn would allow the myriad of externally or internally driven stimuli to produce the exaggerated emotional and behavioral responses characteristic of PTSD.

Freedman et al. (1998), using proton magnetic resonance spectroscopy (a noninvasive technique for the *in vivo* measurement of the concentration of various compounds in the human brain to identify neuronal loss or damage), studied 21 veterans with PTSD and eight age-matched control veterans. They found that the *N*-acetyl-L-aspartic acid/creatine ratio was significantly lower for PTSD patients in the right medial temporal lobe in comparison to the left in patients with PTSD and control subjects. Their findings suggest that the neuronal density of right-sided medial temporal structures in patients with combat-related PTSD may have decreased.

Fernandez et al. (2001) studied positron emission tomographic measurements of regional cerebral blood flow in a male patient with war-and torture-related PTSD. They exposed this patient to war-related sounds, which resulted in decreased cerebral blood flow in the insula, and the prefrontal and inferior frontal lobes, while increased blood flow was found in the cerebellum, precuneus, and supplementary motor cortex. They noted that the prefrontal and cingulate cerebral blood flow levels correlated with the patient's heart rate. Mirzaei et al. (2001) examined cerebral regional blood flow using single positron emission computer tomography. They found that cerebral blood flow was markedly more heterogeneous in patients suffering from PTSD than healthy controls. They concluded that severe psychological trauma induced by torture can cause neurobiological alterations, which may contribute to a number of complaints commonly expressed by patients suffering from PTSD even after years following the original trauma.

Positron emission tomography (PET) was used to measure normalized regional cerebral blood flow in 16 women with histories of childhood sexual abuse: eight with current PTSD symptoms and eight without current PTSD symptoms (Shin et al., 1999). In separate script-driven imagery conditions, the subjects recalled and imagined traumatic and neutral autobiographical events. Physiological responses and subjective ratings of their emotional state were measured for each condition. They found that in the traumatic condition vs. the neutral control conditions, both groups exhibited increased regional blood flow in the orbitofrontal cortex and anterior temporal poles; however, these increases were greater in the PTSD group than in the comparison group. The comparison group, on the other hand, exhibited regional blood flow increases in the insular cortex and anterior cingulate gyrus in comparison to the PTSD group. Regional cerebral blood flow decreases in the bilateral anterior frontal regions were greater in the PTSD group than in the comparison group. Only the PTSD group exhibited regional blood flow decreases in the left inferior frontal gyrus. These investigators concluded that the recollection and imagery of traumatic events vs. neutral events was accompanied by regional cerebral blood flow increases in the anterior paralimbic regions of the brain in trauma-exposed individuals with and without PTSD. However, the PTSD group had greater increases in the orbitofrontal cortex and the anterior temporal pole, while the comparison group had greater increases in the anterior cingulate gyrus.

Zubieta et al. (1999) examined the regional blood flow responses to a combat stress-related auditory stimulus in Vietnam veterans diagnosed with PTSD and age-matched combat-exposed subjects without PTSD in twelve healthy control subjects. The subjects were studied twice while listening to combat sounds or white noise. They found significant increases in the blood flow to the medial prefrontal cortex in the PTSD patients, but not in the controls, which correlated with physiological measures of the stress response. Their data support the involvement of the medial prefrontal cortex in the pathophysiology of PTSD, which, they argue, may mediate some of the symptoms of PTSD.

PTSD patients have also been found to have significantly lower P300 amplitudes in comparison to matched control subjects without PTSD (Charles et al., 1995; Gerard, et al., 1995). This finding suggests that patients with PTSD have defective information processing capabilities and are impaired with respect to their ability to discriminate between relevant and irrelevant information.

NEUROPSYCHOLOGICAL INVESTIGATIONS OF PTSD PATIENTS

While relatively few studies have examined the performance of PTSD patients on standardized neuropsychological tests, these studies have found that PTSD patients are unlikely to have memory impairments on standardized neuropsychological measures of memory (e.g., WAIS-R) in the absence of a prior history of neurological disorders, learning disabilities, or closed head trauma (Wolfe and Schlesinger, 1997). While many PTSD patients complain of memory difficulties, such complaints may reflect a comorbid psychiatric disorder (e.g., major depression). In addition, a high proportion of these patients have preexisting backgrounds of learning disability, head trauma, and organic brain dysfunction (Wolfe and Charney, 1991; McCranie et al., 1992; Gurvits et al., 1996).

One of the major problems in evaluating these studies is that the standardized neuropsychological tests that were used to evaluate these patients' memory (e.g., WMS-R) may lack sensitivity to the memory impairments that these patients have. For example, Yehuda et al. (1995b) found that although PTSD patients performed within the normal range on standardized neuropsychological measures of attention, immediate memory, and learning, they tested in the mildly impaired range when their memory was assessed under conditions of interference. When male veterans with PTSD were administered more sensitive neuropsychological measures of learning and memory (e.g., California Verbal Learning Test), their ability to learn verbal material over trials was found to be impaired (Uddo et al., 1993). Thus, the assessment of the memory and cognitive functioning of PTSD patients may depend, to a large degree, on the sensitivity of the particular neuropsychological measures administered to these patients and whether they have a preexisting history of learning disabilities, head trauma, and/or neurological disorders.

Detailed studies of other patient populations have shown that the frontal lobes play a crucial role in a patient's ability to sustain attention, concentration, executive functions, judgment, and encode and retrieve information from memory (Keane and Wolfe, 1987; Oscar-Berman and Bardenhagen, 1998). The frontal lobes also play a major role in the regulation of impulses, affect, mood stability and disinhibition (Stuss and Benson, 1986; Fuster, 1997). Since these functions are often problematic for patients with PTSD, Wolfe (1994) suggested that patients with PTSD may have abnormalities in their frontal brain systems. To test this hypothesis, Koenen et al. (2001) administered neuropsychological tests and measures that had been shown by prior research (Oscar-Berman and Bardenhagen, 1998) to be sensitive to frontal lobe dysfunction as well as standard neuropsychological tests, to identify abnormalities in prefrontal brain systems in PTSD patients. They found that while PTSD subjects were unimpaired on standard neuropsychological tests and measures they exhibited deficits on tests of frontal lobe functioning and on measures that were sensitive to different aspects of prefrontal damage. Their findings demonstrate that PTSD patients have overlapping dysfunction in both the dorsolateral and ventral prefrontal brain systems, which implicated frontal system involvement. They also noted that their findings would explain the memory difficulties that PTSD patients exhibit that are mediated by the prefrontal cortex such as deficits in working memory (e.g., the ability to hold information in a temporary short-term store).

Sachinvala et al. (2000) examined the range and degree of compromised cognitive and functional capacities and the mood state of Vietnam veterans with PTSD in comparison to control subjects for age, sex, and level of education. They found that PTSD subjects performed significantly less well on the cognitive evaluation protocol, a touch screen computer assessment instrument that was self-administered by the subjects twice, 1 month apart, for the cognitive domains of attention, memory, and functional capability.

In a review of the efficacy of neuropsychological tests to assess memory in PTSD patients, Wolfe and Schlesinger (1997) indicated that there was a growing body of evidence that suggests that cognitive alterations occur in PTSD patients. Specifically, they noted that PTSD patients may demonstrate enhanced learning and retention of some trauma-specific stimuli as well as decreased memory functioning on stimuli or information that is nontrauma related. They concluded that the research literature suggests that the memory functioning of PTSD patients range from intact to mildly impaired on general tests of visual or verbal memory. However, at the same time, memory tests involving trauma-specific stimuli point to alterations in cognitive information processing, specifically an attentional bias manifested by changes in speed, accuracy and depth of processing (Brewerton et al., 1999).

CAN PTSD DEVELOP IF THE PATIENT IS AMNESTIC FOR THE TRAUMATIC EVENT OR SUSTAINS A TRAUMATIC BRAIN INJURY?

Within the past decade, there has been considerable controversy as to whether an individual who has suffered an accident-related brain injury can develop PTSD. One school of thought (Sbordone and Liter, 1995) has argued that if the brain injury results in a loss of consciousness, the individual is unable to develop vivid memories of the traumatic event necessary to generate intrusive recollections of the trauma, which are essential in the development of PTSD. This argument receives support from several investigators. For example, Mayou et al. (1993) reported that none of the 51 patients who had sustained mild traumatic brain injury (MTBI) as a result of an MVA and reported loss of consciousness for more than 5 min developed PTSD. Similarly, Warden et al. (1997) found that none of the 47 patients they examined who sustained a closed head injury developed PTSD if they were unable to recall the traumatic event. Although Malhi and Bartlett (1998) reported that only 5 individuals out of a total of 196 adults they examined who sustained closed head injuries as defined by a Glasgow Coma Scale Score of 14 or less, documented loss of consciousness, or posttraumatic amnesia developed PTSD, all five of these individuals had either no or minimal loss of consciousness and were able to clearly recall the traumatic event. Middelboe et al. (1992) reported that only 1 out of a total of 51 patients who had been admitted to the hospital after a "minor head injury" was diagnosed with PTSD. Max et al. (1998) examined 50 children ranging in age from 6 to 14 utilizing psychiatric assessments that were repeated, 3, 6, 12, and 24 months following the TBI. They found that only two (4%) of the subjects were found to have PTSD on at least one of the follow-up assessments. These investigators, however, did not preclude children with preexisting PTSD in their study even though it is generally well known that "minor head injuries" may reactivate symptoms related to previous traumatic experiences. Thus, the diagnosis of PTSD that was given to these children may have reflected reactivation of preexisting childhood trauma (Berthier et al., 1998).

Sbordone and Liter (1995) examined 70 patients who had been previously diagnosed with either MTBI or PTSD. Each patient was interviewed by a board-certified neuropsychologist and was asked to provide a detailed recollection of the events that preceded, occurred during, or followed the traumatic event to determine the extent of their recall, particularly whether they had amnesia for the traumatic event. They found that while all 42 PTSD patients were able to provide a detailed and emotionally charged recollection of these events, none of the 28 MTBI patients were able to recall the event or were observed to become emotionally upset when they were asked to discuss it. Virtually, none of the MTBI patients in this study reported PTSD symptoms such as nightmares, flashbacks, intrusive recollections, hypervigilance, phobic or startle reactions, or became emotionally upset whenever they were exposed to stimuli associated with the traumatic event. Both MTBI and PTSD patients, however, complained of similar cognitive and behavioral problems such as memory, word finding, problem-solving difficulties, distractibility, photophobia, fatigue, diminished libido, and interpersonal difficulties.

These investigators stressed that if the traumatic event occurred prior to the onset of retrograde amnesia (e.g., becoming terrified while riding as a passenger in an automobile that was being driven in a reckless manner for several minutes prior to colliding with another vehicle) or after the cessation of anterograde amnesia (e.g., witnessing the death of a family member who sustained massive injuries several minutes after regaining consciousness following an MVA), an MTBI patient could develop PTSD in response to these events rather than to their brain injury.

Since individuals with acute stress disorders frequently develop dissociative amnesia for some or all of the events surrounding a traumatic event, they are often diagnosed with a cerebral concussion rather than PTSD since they are unable to provide a detailed recollection of the traumatic event (e.g., MVA). Similarly, Sbordone and Liter (1995) found that many patients who developed PTSD initially claimed that they had no recollection of the traumatic event and showed evidence of physiological arousal and anxiety when they were asked to provide a chronological history of events leading up to the accident. For example, when these individuals were asked during the interview "what was going on in your head during the accident itself?" they typically replied, "I thought I was going to die."

Since the clinical interviews of these patients lasted between 2 and 3 hours, it is doubtful that these individuals would have had sufficient time to adequately recall the events leading up to the traumatic event if they were interviewed in a busy emergency room by a physician or later by a neurologist. These investigators have argued the initial claim of amnesia in the PTSD group most likely represented their conscious attempt to avoid discussing the emotionally charged traumatic event. In other words, their initial claim of having no memory of the traumatic event typically meant "I don't want to recall it."

The opposing viewpoint argues that PTSD can be developed following a closed head injury even if the trauma itself cannot be recalled (McMillan, 1991, 1996). For example, Bryant and Harvey (1997) studied the occurrence of acute stress disorder following MTBI to determine its utility in predicting PTSD. Utilizing a questionnaire (e.g., acute stress disorder inventory) and a structured clinical interview based on DSM-IV criteria, they found that acute stress disorder was diagnosed in 14% of adult patients who had sustained MTBI following a MVA. In a follow-up study (Bryant and Harvey, 1998), 24% of these patients satisfied the criteria for PTSD. They also reported that 82% who had been initially diagnosed with an acute stress disorder went on to develop chronic PTSD. These investigators utilized the diagnostic criteria for MTBI that was defined as posttraumatic amnesia of less than 24 hours. They reported that the average duration of estimated posttraumatic amnesia in their subjects (222 patients between the ages of 16 and 65 years of age) was 9.4 hours with a range of 5 minutes to 24 hours. However, they appeared to have relied on the diagnosis of MTBI that had been initially given to these patients by physicians in a major trauma center, and did not exclude patients who may have had PTSD.

Case studies of patients who developed PTSD after they sustained a closed head injury have also been utilized to corroborate the development of PTSD in MVAs. For example, King (1997) described a 21-year-old unemployed man who had been struck from behind by an automobile while hitchhiking. He reported that this patient developed PTSD after his accident, even though he had been given the diagnosis of a "mild head injury" at the time he was admitted to the hospital. This patient, however, was able to recall lying in the road shortly after the accident after being thrown out of his vehicle and seeing the car that hit his vehicle turn around and head directly at him as he lay on the ground. As a result of this patient's orthopedic injuries, he was unable to transport himself to the side of the road and believed that the driver was intentionally trying to kill him in order to "finish him off." McMillan (1996) reported on ten cases that had developed PTSD symptoms from a total of 312 patients who had sustained closed head injuries ranging in severity from mild to severe. These patients, however, were able to recall being trapped in their vehicle, experiencing severe pain as a result of their physically injuries, and/or the witnessing their passengers getting killed or sustain serious injuries. Four of these patients complained of survivor guilt as a result of witnessing two deaths (a child and a passenger), and severe injuries to their passengers. Thus, it would appear that in these case studies, these patients recalled the traumatic event that produced their PTSD symptoms after their anterograde amnesia ended.

Bryant and Harvey (1998) investigated the relationship between PTSD and postconcussion syndromes following an MTBI in survivors of MVAs who had either sustained an MTBI or no traumatic brain injury at 6 months posttrauma for PTSD and postconcussive symptoms. They found that postconcussive symptoms were more evident in MTBI patients with PTSD than those without PTSD and in MTBI patients than non-MTBI patients. Utilizing an administered PTSD module from the Composite International Diagnostic Interview and a postconcussive symptom checklist, they concluded that their findings suggested that postconcussive symptoms may be mediated by an interaction of neurological and psychological factors following MTBI. Although their findings suggest that the presence of a MTBI may facilitate the development of PTSD symptoms, Warden et al. (1997) studied the frequency of PTSD in 47 active duty service members who had sustained moderate traumatic brain injury and had neurogenic amnesia for the events surrounding the traumatic event. They found that when they evaluated these patients with a modified present state examination and other questions at various points during a 24-month follow-up, none of these patients met the full criteria for PTSD. They concluded that posttraumatic amnesia following moderate head injury may protect against recurrent memories of the traumatic event and development of PTSD.

Bryant (2001) examined the relationship between PTSD and mild brain injury through a review of the research literature. He noted that while a number of studies had investigated the initial PTSD in patients who had sustained MTBI, one of the difficulties in evaluating the findings of different studies was that these studies utilized variable definitions of MTBI and different methods of patient recruitment (e.g., many of these studies included individuals who were currently involved in litigation). For example, his research studies relied on the definition of MTBI as put forth by the American Congress of Rehabilitation Medicine (1993). While this definition utilizes as one of its criteria any loss of consciousness or posttraumatic amnesia of less than 24 h, Sbordone and Saul (2000) have pointed out that these criteria could include individuals who had posttraumatic amnesia of less than 1 second, or many individuals with acute stress disorder (without brain injury) since these individuals frequently report dissociative amnesia for the accident. While Bryant (2001) cites a number of studies that demonstrate that patients can develop PTSD following an MTBI, a review of these studies reveals that these investigators in the studies relied heavily on PTSD questionnaires and structured PTSD interviews to arrive at the diagnosis of PTSD in patients who had sustained traumatic brain injuries.

McMillan (2001) has pointed out that the use of structured PTSD interviews and PTSD questionnaires may result in the misdiagnosis of PTSD in individuals with traumatic brain injuries. He cited the example of a 21-year-old male who had sustained a severe closed head injury that had disrupted his cognitive functioning, ability to return to work, and his life. He noted that when this patient was assessed 5 months postinjury on the IES (Horowitz et al., 1979), the patient's score on this test was consistent with individuals who have been diagnosed with PTSD and satisfied the DSM-IV criteria for PTSD. He also noted that on the Posttraumatic Diagnostic Scale (Foa et al., 1993) this patient's severity score also qualified him for a diagnosis of PTSD. Despite these findings, he noted that a clinical interview did not support the diagnosis of PTSD. For example, he pointed out that the patient's responses to the questionnaires were significantly colored by the general disruption to his life that the brain injury had caused, his cognitive deficits, and the fact that many of the symptoms he endorsed were common symptoms of traumatic brain injury. He stressed that this case study demonstrates that PTSD can be easily misdiagnosed in TBI cases since the cognitively impaired patients may not follow the questionnaire instructions consistently and were likely to have physical disabilities and other injuries that were likely to interfere with their day-to-day life functioning. He stressed that this case study suggests that even sophisticated questionnaire measures can be misleading when evaluating TBI cases for the presence of PTSD.

McMillan's (2001) findings suggest that the different findings in the literature on the relationship between traumatic brain injury and PTSD may be, at least in part, due to the different methodologies utilized in these studies. For example, the studies that reported the relative absence of PTSD following a traumatic brain injury appear to have relied heavily on psychiatric interviews with these patients. The studies that reported that patients who sustained traumatic brain injuries also developed PTSD appear to have heavily relied on PTSD questionnaires and structured PTSD interviews.

Another explanation of the endorsement of PTSD symptoms in TBI patients could be due to pending litigation or secondary gain since it may increase the value of their case (Bryant, 2001). For example, Lees-Haley and Dunn (1994) have shown that 85% of the individuals with no history of PTSD were able to accurately endorse PTSD symptoms and experiences to satisfy the DSM-IV diagnostic criteria of PTSD. These authors have argued that lay persons may have some basic knowledge of PTSD through books, magazines, newspapers, television news programs, televisions talk shows, and radio call-in programs hosted by psychologists and psychiatrists. Thus, an individual's scores on a PTSD questionnaire or structured interview could simply reflect their motivation to appear more disabled, particularly if litigation is pending.

DISABILITY FOLLOWING PTSD

There is evidence that PTSD is associated with long-term functional disability in some individuals. For example, Grunert et al. (1992) reported relatively high levels of moderate to severe psychiatric symptoms that included flashbacks, avoidance, marital distress, irritability, fear of reinjury, and preoccupation with the appearance of the effected limb of burn survivors during an 18-month follow-up evaluation of patients who had suffered traumatic work-related burn injuries. Michaels et al. (2000) evaluated 35 adults prospectively, who were returned to functional employment after injury, using demographic data, validated psychological and health measures, and the Michigan Critical Events Perception Scale. They found that approximately 10% of the variance of these individuals returning to work was accounted for by poor psychological outcome, which was largely attributed to PTSD symptoms. Similarly, Green et al. (1993) examined the influence on PTSD on subsequent levels of disability in MVA victims. They found that individuals with PTSD had higher levels of disability utilizing the Sickness Impact Profile Scale, particularly in the domain of social functioning. They concluded that PTSD was associated with work-related dysfunction equal to that of individuals who had severe physical handicaps. Zatzick et al. (1997) examined female Vietnam veterans to determine whether their current PTSD symptoms were associated with impaired functioning. They found that PTSD was associated with a significantly higher risk of poor functioning in five of the six outcome domains. They also found that PTSD was associated with significantly higher levels of bed days, poor physical health, and unemployment.

Amir et al. (1997) studied the prevalence of fibromyalgia syndrome-related symptoms, quality of life, and functional impairment among PTSD patients in comparison to controls. They found that 21% of the PTSD patients showed evidence of a fibromyalgia syndrome in comparison to none of the control subjects. They also noted that the subjects in the PTSD group were more physically tender than controls and reported more pain and a lower quality of life, higher functional impairment, and suffered more from psychological distress than PTSD patients who were not experiencing fibromyalgia syndrome.

Davis and Kutter (1998) examined the independent living skills, traumatic experiences, and symptoms of PTSD in women residing in a supportive housing program for women and in families who were homeless. These subjects' independent living skills were evaluated by the Kohlman Evaluation of Living Skills Scale and a structured interview format to determine whether they had met the diagnostic criteria for PTSD. They found that traumatic experiences and PTSD were more prevalent among women who were homeless than among women in the general population. Michaels et al. (2000) evaluated 247 patients without severe neurotrauma at the time of admission and at 6 and 12 months posttrauma. They found that at 12 months the work status, general health, and overall satisfaction of recovery were heavily dependent on these patient's mental health functioning. More specifically, they found that individuals who had developed symptoms of PTSD were at higher risk to be unemployed, have poor general health, and be unsatisfied with their recovery. Similarly, Kimerling and Calhoun (1994) found that individuals with PTSD were at elevated risk for health problems and were disproportionate users of the healthcare system. Finally, Leserman et al. (1996) found that women with PTSD attending a clinic specializing in gastrointestinal problems tended to be sicker, have had more surgery, and have more disabling symptoms than women without a history of PTSD.

The healthcare costs associated with a diagnosis of PTSD appears to be extremely costly (Mackenzie et al., 1988; Solomon and Davidson, 1997). For example, Miller et al. (1996) estimated that the true cost of trauma to PTSD victims was 450 billion dollars a year, which included medical costs, lost earnings, public program costs related to victim assistance, pain and suffering, loss of quality of life, and jury awarded compensation. They also noted that very little of the mental health costs were spent on professional mental health treatment since many people who seek mental health professionals fail to realize that their symptoms could result from a traumatic experience; therefore, they fail to mention the trauma. They also noted that individuals with PTSD were more reluctant than others with emotional problems to seek professional help even if they know they need it.

Prigerson et al. (2001) examined 587 persons ranging in age from 15 to 44 to determine the risk and course of PTSD associated with combat trauma relative to other traumas. They found that men who reported combat as their worst trauma were more likely to have lifetime PTSD, delayed PTSD symptom onset, be unemployed, divorced, and physically abusive to their spouses. Gregurek et al. (2001) examined 42 disabled Croatian war veterans ranging in age from 19 to 44 who were receiving long-term physical rehabilitation in a hospital setting. They found that patients with PTSD symptoms had significantly higher anxiety levels than patients without PTSD symptoms. However, they noted that the percentage of patients manifesting PTSD symptoms increased from 19 to 41% 5 years later, while the anxiety levels decreased in patients with PTSD who were not receiving long-term physical rehabilitation. They concluded that staying in the same homogeneous group for a substantial period of time, in combination with inadequate social support and deficient psychological care, contributed to the development of PTSD-related disability. There is evidence that PTSD is associated with long-term functional disability in some individuals. For example, Grunert et al. (1992) reported relatively high levels of moderate to severe psychiatric symptoms that included flashbacks, avoidance, marital distress, irritability, fear of reinjury, and preoccupation with the appearance of the effected limb of burn survivors during an 18-month follow-up evaluation of patients who had suffered traumatic work-related burn injuries. Michaels et al. (1998) evaluated 35 adults prospectively, who were returned to functional employment after injury, using demographic data, validated psychological and health measures, and the Michigan Critical Events Perception Scale. They found that approximately 10% of the variance of these individuals returning to work was accounted for by poor psychological outcome, which was largely attributed to PTSD symptoms. Similarly, Green et al. (1993) examined the influence on PTSD on subsequent levels of disability in MVA victims. They found that individuals with PTSD had higher levels of disability utilizing the Sickness Impact Profile Scale, particularly in the domain of social functioning. They concluded that PTSD was associated with work-related dysfunction equal to that of individuals who had severe physical handicaps. Zatzick et al. (1997) examined female Vietnam veterans to determine whether their current PTSD symptoms were associated with impaired functioning. They found that PTSD was associated with a significantly higher risk of poor functioning in five of the six outcome domains. They also found that PTSD was associated with significantly higher levels of bed days, poor physical health, and unemployment.

Amir et al. (1997) studied the prevalence of fibromyalgia syndrome-related symptoms, quality of life, and functional impairment among PTSD patients in comparison to controls. They found 21% of the PTSD patients showed evidence of a fibromyalgia syndrome in comparison to none of the control subjects. They also noted that the subjects in the PTSD group were more physically tender than controls and reported more pain and a lower quality of life, higher functional impairment, and suffered more from psychological distress than PTSD patients who were not experiencing fibromyalgia syndrome.

PSYCHOLOGICAL TREATMENT OF PTSD

Although an exhaustive review of the efficacy of the various psychological treatments that have been utilized to treat patients with PTSD is beyond the scope of this chapter, treatments such as crisis intervention, hypnosis, psychodynamic treatment, cognitive treatment, behavioral treatment, and eye movement desensitization have been frequently utilized to treat patients with PTSD (Foa et al., 1997). While crisis intervention has been used to treat female assault and rape victims with some success, there is little empirical evidence that crisis intervention is effective in preventing the development of chronic PTSD (Foa and Meadows, 1997). Furthermore, if such interventions are made by inexperienced clinicians, their interventions may be harmful (McFarlane, 1989). Although hypnotic techniques have been widely used to treat PTSD patients, one of the major problems with using hypnosis is that some patients with PTSD appear to be resistant to hypnosis since they fear losing control, while others may respond by developing severe dissociative states (Shalev et al., 1996a). Psychodynamic treatment utilizing concepts such as denial, abreaction, and catharsis in dealing with PTSD patients has been reported to be helpful; however, many of the studies that have demonstrated improvement are confounded by methodological problems such as lack of inappropriate controls, inadequate assessment of outcome, and so forth. (Foa and Meadows, 1997).

Cognitive treatment approaches have also been utilized relying on the basic assumptions about the belief systems of individuals regarding personal safety, control, and survival. This form of treatment views the patient's PTSD symptoms as a set of self-protective strategies that are utilized to survive in a seemingly dangerous world (Horowitz, 1976). Cognitive treatment approaches have been found to be effective in reducing symptoms of stress, depression, avoidance, intrusion of traumatic memories, and also appear to improve the patient's self-concept (Shalev et al., 1996a).

Behavioral treatments using classic operant conditioning have been utilized to understand and treat patients with PTSD by focusing on extinguishing the conditioned responses of these patient to the conditioned stimuli through the use of techniques such as gradual desensitization or massive flooding which involves reexposure to the conditioned stimuli, either using a live object or a situation related to trauma (*in vivo*), or mental imagery of the trauma (*in vivo*). Research (Shalev et al., 1996a) has shown that behavioral treatments such as flooding can not only reduce the patient's PTSD symptoms, but can also exacerbate them.

Eye movement desensitization consists of eliciting saccadic eye movements while the patient mentally focuses on the traumatic event and describes his or her feelings about the event (Shapiro, 1989). Despite reports of excellent treatment results, more control studies are needed to determine its effectiveness since there is no convincing theoretical basis to explain its rapid effect in reducing PTSD symptoms (McCulloch and Feldman, 1996).

SUMMARY

Approximately seven out of ten people are exposed to traumatic events such as assault, combat, fire, flood, sexual molestation, physical abuse, rape, or witnessing someone being badly injured or killed during their lifetime. While exposure to a traumatic event appears necessary for the development of PTSD, it is not sufficient to cause PTSD since the vast majority of individuals who are exposed to a traumatic event do not develop PTSD. Multiple risk factors including, but not limited to, female gender, social disadvantage, education, childhood adversity, genetic predisposition, childhood physical or sexual abuse, prior head trauma, psychiatric illness, and substance abuse appear to significantly increase the likelihood of whether an individual will develop PTSD. Patients with PTSD are almost eight times more likely to have three or more comorbid psychiatric disorders and ninety times more likely to have a comorbid somatization disorder than individuals without PTSD.

PTSD produces profound and long-lasting alterations in physiological reactivity characterized by significant increases in heart rate, skin conductance, and blood pressure. This chronic state of physiological arousal, combined with an inability to regulate the autonomic nervous system, severely handicaps PTSD patients from effectively utilizing their emotions as warning signals and results in the development of fight or flight reactions without attempting to cognitively determine the significance of the information received. PTSD also produces chronically high levels of sympathetic nervous system activity and lower glucocorticoid levels in response to acute stress, which leads to high levels of catecholamine release that can be neurotoxic. This has been shown to reduce the volume of the hippocampus and produce deficits in short-term memory. Neurodiagnostic testing, using PET, cerebral blood flow, and other measures, has shown that alterations in functioning of cortical structures are commonly seen in patients with chronic PTSD. Neuropsychological testing has shown that patients with PTSD frequently demonstrate cognitive impairments on neuropsychological tests of attention, concentration, recent memory, and executive functions.

Although considerable controversy exists at the present time as to whether patients can develop PTSD if they have sustained a closed head injury, the inconsistent results obtained by investigators may reflect the different methodologies that were utilized in these studies. For example, studies that have reported little or no PTSD following closed head injuries have relied heavily on psychiatric interviews, while studies that reported the development of PTSD following closed head injuries have relied heavily on PTSD questionnaires and structured PTSD interviews. This later technique may have produced a high false positive rate in the diagnosis of PTSD in patients with closed head injuries.

PTSD has been found to produce significant psychiatric disability that, in some individuals, can last their entire lifetime. Patients with chronic or complex PTSD are at higher risk of being unemployed and having disabling medical symptoms such as pain and discomfort, and abuse alcohol, drugs, and their spouses. While a variety of psychological treatment modalities have been utilized on PTSD patients, some of these treatments may actually exacerbate the patient's negative symptoms, while others may only be of limited value.

REFERENCES

American Psychiatric Association. 1984. *Diagnostic and Statistical Mental Disorders*, 3rd ed. Washington, D.C.: APA.

American Psychiatric Association. 1994. *Diagnostic and Statistical Mental Disorders*, 4th ed. Washington, D.C.: APA.

Amir, M., Kaplan, Z., Neuman, L., Sharabani, R., Shani, N., and Buskila, D. 1997. Posttraumatic Stress Disorder Tenderness, and Fibromyalgia. *Journal of Psychosomatic Research*, 42, 607–613.

Bartzokis, G. 2002. Schizophrenia: Breakdown in the Well Regulated Lifelong Process of Brain Development and Maturation. *Neuropharmacology*, 27, 672–683.

Bartzokis, G., Beckson, M., Lu, P. H., Nuechterlein, K., Edwards, N., and Mintz, J. 2001. Age Related Changes in Frontal and Temporal Lobe Volumes in Men: A Magnetic Resonance Imaging Study. *Archives of General Psychiatry*, 58, 461–465; *Neuropsychopharmacology*, 27, 672–683.

Bartzokis, G., Nuechterlein, K. H., Lu, P. H., Gitlin, M., Rodgers, S., and Mintz, J. 2003. Dysregulated Brain Development in Adult Men with Schizophrenia: A Magnetic Resonance Imaging Study. *Society of Biological Psychiatry*, 53, 412–421.

Berthier, M. L., Kulisevsky, J., Fernandez-Benitz, J. A., and Gironell, A. 1998. Reactivation of Posttraumatic Stress Disorder after Minor Head Injury. *Depression and Anxiety*, 8, 43–47.

Blake, D. D., Weathers, F. W., and Nagy, F. N. 1990. A Clinical Rating Scale for Assessing Current and Lifetime PTSD: The CAPS-1. *Behavior Therapist*, 18, 187–188.

Blanchard, E. B., Hickling, E. J., Forneris, C. A., Taylor, A. E., Buckley, T. C., Loos, W. R., and Jaccard, J. 1997. Prediction of Remission of Accurate Posttraumatic Stress Disorder in Motor Vehicle Accident Victims. *Journal of Traumatic Stress*, 10, 215–234.

Blanchard, E. B., Hickling, E. J., Taylor, A. E., Loos, W. R., and Gerardi, R. J. 1996. Psychological Morbidity Associated with Motor Accidents. *Behavior Research and Therapy*, 32, 283–290.

Blanchard, E. B., Kolb, L. C., and Gerardi, R. J. 1986. Cardiac Response to Relevant Stimuli as an Adjunct-ive Tool for Diagnosing Posttraumatic Stress Disorder in Vietnam Veterans. *Behavior Therapy*, *17*, 592–606.

Boudewyns, P. A. 1996. Posttraumatic Stress Disorder: Conceptualization and Treatment. In Hersen, M., Eisler, K. M., and Miller, P. (Eds.) *Progress in Behavior Modification*, Vol. 3C. New York: Brooks Cole, pp. 165–189.

Bremner, J. D. 1999. Does Stress Damage the Brain? *Society of Biological Psychiatry*, *45*, 797–805.

Bremner, J. D., Randall, P., Scott, T. M., Bronen, R. A., Shelby, J. P., Southwick, S. M., Delany, R. C., McCarthy, G., Charney, D. S., and Innis, R. B. 1995. MRI-Based Measurement of Hippocampal Volume in Patients with Combat-Related Posttraumatic Stress Disorder. *American Journal of Psychiatry*, *152*, 973–981.

Bremner, J. D., Southwick, S. M., and Johnson, D. R. 1993. Childhood Physical Abuse and Combat-Related Post-Traumatic Stress Disorder. *American Journal of Psychiatry*, *150*, 234–239.

Breslau, N., Davis, G. C., Andreski, P., and Peterson, E. 1991. Traumatic Events and Posttraumatic Stress Disorder in an Urban Population of Young Adults. *Archives of General Psychiatry*, *48*, 216–316.

Breslau, N., Davis, G. C., Peterson, E. L., and Schultz, L. R. 1998. A Second Look at Comorbidity in Victims of Trauma: The Posttraumatic Stress Disorder–Major Depression Connection. *Biological Psychiatry*, *48*, 902–909.

Brewerton, T., Dansky, B., and Kilpatrick, D. 1999. Bulimia Nervosa, PTSD and "Forgetting." Results from the National Women's Study. In Williams, L. M. and Banyard, V. L. (Eds.) *Trauma and Memory*. Thousand Oaks, CA: Sage Press, pp. 127–138.

Brewin, C. R., Andrews, B., and Valentine, J. D. 2000. Meta-Analysis of Risk Factors for Posttraumatic Stress Disorders in Trauma-Exposed Adults. *Journal of Consulting and Clinical Psychology*, *68*, 748–766.

Briere, J. 1997. Psychological Assessment of Child Abuse Effects in Adults. In Wilson, J. P. and Keane, T. M. (Eds.) *Assessing Psychological Trauma and PTSD*. New York: Guilford Press, pp. 43–68.

Briere, J. 2001. *Detailed Assessment of Posttraumatic Stress*. Odessa, FL: PAR.

Bromet, E., Sonnega, A., and Kesler, R. C. 1998. Risk Factors for DSM-III-R Posttraumatic Stress Disorders: Findings from the National Comorbidity Survey. *American Journal of Epidemiology*, *147*, 353–361.

Bryant, R. A. 2001. Posttraumatic Stress Disorders and Traumatic Brain Injury: Can They Co-Exist? *Clinical Psychology Review*, *21*, 931–948.

Bryant, R. A. and Harvey, A. G. 1997. Acute Stress Disorder: A Critical Review of Diagnostic Issues. *Clinical Psychology Review*, *17*, 753–757.

Bryant, R. A. and Harvey, A. G. 1998. Relationship Between Acute Stress Disorder and Posttraumatic Stress Disorder Following Mild Traumatic Brain Injury. *American Journal of Psychiatry*, *155*, 625–629.

Bryant, R. A., Harvey, A. G., Dang, S. T., and Sakerville, T. 1998. Assessing Acute Stress Disorder: Psychometric Prospective of a Structured Clinical Interview. *Psychological Assessment*, *10*, 215–220.

Bryant, R. A., Marosskeky, J. E., Crooks, J., Baguley, J., and Gurka, J. 2000. Coping Style and Posttraumatic Stress Disorder Following Severe Traumatic Brain Injury. *Brain Injury*, *14*, 175–180.

Buckley, T. C., Blanchard, E. B., and Hickling, E. J. 1996. A Prospective Examination of Delayed Onset PTSD Secondary to Motor Vehicle Accidents. *Journal of Abnormal Psychology*, *105*, 617–625.

Charles, G., Hunsenne, M., Ansseau, M., Pitchot, W., Machowski, R., Schittecatte, M., and Wilmotte, J. 1995. P300 in Post-Traumatic Stress Disorder. *Neuropsychobiology*, *32*, 72–74.

Davidson, J., Swartz, M., and Storck, M. 1985. A Diagnostic and Family Study of Posttraumatic Stress Disorder. *American Journal of Psychiatry*, *142*, 90–93.

Davidson, J. R. T., Huges, D., Blazer, D., and George, L. K. 1991. Posttraumatic Stress Disorder in the Community: An Epidemiological Study. *Psychological Medicine*, *21*, 1–19.

Davidson, J. R. T., Smith, R. D., and Kuder, H. S. 1989. Validity and Reliability of the DSM-III Criteria for Posttraumatic Stress Disorder: Experience with a Structured Interview. *Journal of Nervous and Mental Diseases*, *177*, 336–341.

Davis, J. and Kutter, C. J. 1998. Independent Living Skills an Posttraumatic Stress Disorder in Women Who are Homeless: Implications for Future Practice. *The American Journal of Occupational Therapy*, *52*, 39–44.

Delahanty, D. L., Herberman, H. B., Craig, K. J., Hayward, M. C., Fullerton, C. S., Ursano, R. J., and Baum, A. 1997. Acute and Chronic Distress and Posttraumatic Stress Disorder as a Function of

Responsibility for Serious Motor Vehicle Accidents. *Journal of Consulting and Clinical Psychology*, *65*, 560–567.

Fernandez, M., Pissiota, A., Frans, O., Von Knorring, Fischer, H., and Fredrikson, M. 2001. Brain Function in a Patient with Torture Related Post-Traumatic Stress Disorder before and after Fluoxetine Treatment: A Positron Emission Tomography Provocation Emission Tomography Study. *Neuroscience Letters*, *297*, 101–104.

Foa, E., Riggs, D., Dancu, C., and Rothbaum, B. 1993. Reliability and Validity of a Brief Instrument for Assessing Post-Traumatic Stress Disorder. *Journal of Traumatic Stress*, *6*, 459–474.

Foa, E. B. and Hearst-Ikeda, D. 1996. Emotional Dissociation in Response to Trauma: An Information-Processing Approach. In Michelson, L. K. and Ray, W. J. (Eds.) *Handbook of Dissociation: Theoretical and Clinical Perspectives*. New York: Plenum Press, pp. 207–222.

Foa, E. B. and Meadows, E. A. 1997. Psychosocial Treatments for Post-Traumatic Stress Disorder: A Critical Review. *Annual Review of Psychology*, *48*, 449–480.

Foa, E. B., Cashman, L., Jaycox, L., and Perry, K. 1997. The Validation of a Self-Report Measure of Post-Traumatic Stress Disorder: The Post-Traumatic Diagnostic Scale. *Psychological Assessment*, *9*, 445–451.

Foa, E. B., Molnar, C., and Cushman, L. 1995. Changes in Rape Narratives During Exposure Therapy for Post-Traumatic Stress Disorder. *Journal of Tramatic Stress*, *8*, 675–690.

Fox, R. P. 1972. Postcombat Adaptation Problems. *Comprehensive Psychiatry*, *13*, 435–443.

Freedman, T. W., Cardwell, D., Karson, C. N., and Komoroski, R. A. 1998. *In Vivo* Proton Magnetic Resonance Spectroscopy of the Medial Temporal Lobes of Subjects with Combat-Related Post-Traumatic Stress Disorder. *Magnetic Resonance in Medicine*, *40*, 66–71.

Fuster, J. M. 1997. *The Prefrontal Cortex*, 3rd ed. New York: Lippincott-Raven.

Gerard, G., Hansenne, M., Ansseau, M., Pitchot, W., Machowski, R., Shittecatte, M., and Wilmotte, J. 1995. P300 in Post-Traumatic Stress Disorder. *Neuropsychology*, *32*, 72–74.

Giaconia, R. M., Reinherz, H. Z., Silverman, A. B., Pakiz, B., Frost, A. K., and Cohen, E. 1995. Traumas and Post-Traumatic Stress Disorder in a Community Population of Older Adolescents. *Journal of the American Academy of Child and Adolescent Psychiatry*, *34*, 1369–1380.

Gilbertson, M. W., Shenton, M. E., Ciszewski, A., Kasai, K., and Kasko, N. B. 2003. Hippocampal Volume as a Vulnerability Factor for Chronic Post-Traumatic Stress Disorder: MRI Evidence from Monozygotic Twins Discordant for Combat Exposure. Cited in McNally, R. J. Progress and Controversy in the Study of Post-Traumatic Stress Disorder. *Annual Review of Psychology*, *54*, 229–252.

Goldsmith, W. and Cretekos, C. 1969. Unhappy Odysseys: Psychiatric Hospitalizations Among Vietnam Returnees. *Archives of General Psychiatry*, *20*, 78–83.

Green, M. M., McFarlane, A. C., Hunter, C. E., and Griggs, W. M. 1993. Undiagnosed Post-Traumatic Stress Disorder Following Motor Vehicle Accidents. *Medical Journal of Australia*, *159*, 529–534.

Gregurek, R., Pavic, L., Vuger-Kovacic, D., Vukusic, H., Potrebica, S., Bitar, Z., Kovacic, D., Danic, S., and Klain, E. 2001. Increase of Frequency of Post-Traumatic Stress Disorder in Disabled War Veterans During Prolonged Stay in a Rehabilitation Hospital. *Croation Medical Journal*, *42*, 161–164.

Grinker, R. R. and Spiegel, R. R. 1945. *Men Under Stress*. Philadelphia: Blackston.

Grunert, B. K., Devine, C. A., Matloub, H. S., Sanger, J. H., Yousif, N. J., Anderson, R. C., and Roell, S. M. 1992. Psychological Adjustment Following Work-Related Hand Injury: 18-month Follow-Up. *Annals of Plastic Surgery*, *29*, 537–542.

Gurvits, T. V., Gilbertson, M. W., Lasko, N. B., Orr, S. P., and Pitman, R. K. 1996. Neurological Status of Combat Veterans and Adult Survivors of Sexual Abuse PTSD. In Yehuda, R. and McFarlane, A. C. (Eds.) *Psychobiology of Posttraumatic Stress Disorder Annals of the New York Academy of Sciences*, Vol. 821. New York: New York Academy of Sciences, pp. 468–471.

Hammarberg, M. 1992. PENN Inventory for Posttraumatic Stress Disorder: Psychometric Properties. *Psychological Assessment*, *4*, 67–76.

Hamner, M. B. 1994. Exacerbation of Posttraumatic Stress Disorder Symptoms with Medical Illness. *General Hospital Psychiatry*, *16*, 135–137.

Hamner, M. B., Lorberbaum, J. P., and George, M. S. 1999. Potential Role of the Anterior Cingulate Cortex in PTSD: Review and Hypothesis. *Depression and Anxiety*, *9*, 1–14.

Harvey, A. G. and Bryant, R. A. 1998. The Relationship between Acute Stress Disorder and Posttraumatic Stress Disorder: A Prospective Evaluation of Motor Vehicle Accident Survivors. *Journal of Consulting and Clinical Psychology*, 66, 507–512.

Helzer, J. E., Robins, L. N., and McEvoy, L. 1987. Posttraumatic Stress Disorder in the General Population. *New England Journal of Medicine*, 317, 1630–1634.

Herman, J. 1993. Sequelae of Prolonged and Repeated Trauma: Evidence for a Complex Posttraumatic Syndrome. In Davidson, J. and Foa, E. (Eds.) *PTSD: DSM-IV and Beyond*. Washington, D.C.: American Psychiatric Association Press.

Horowitz, M. J. 1976. *Stress Response Syndrome*. New York: Jason Aronson.

Horowitz, M. J. 1986. *Stress Response Syndromes*, 2nd ed. New York: Jason Aronson.

Horowitz, M. J., Wilner, W. R., and Alvarez, W. 1979. Impact of Event Scales: A Measure of Subjective Stress. *Psychosomatic Medicine*, 41, 209–218.

Ide, M. S. and Paez, A. 2000. Complex PTSD: A Review of Current Issues. *International Journal of Emergency Mental Health*, 2, 43–51.

Kardiner, A. 1941. *The Traumatic Neuroses of War*. New York: Hoeber.

Keane, T. M., Wolfe, J., and Taylor, K. L. 1987. Posttraumatic Stress Disorder: Evidence for Diagnostic Validity and Methods of Psychological Assessment. *Journal of Clinical Psychology*, 43, 32–43.

Kessler, R., Sonnega, A., and Bromet, E. 1995. Posttraumatic Stress Disorder in the National Comorbidity Survey. *Archives of General Psychiatry*, 52, 1048–1060.

Kimerling, R. and Calhoun, K. S. 1994. Somatic Symptoms, Social Support, and Treatment Seeking Among Sexual Assault Victims. *Journal of Consulting and Clinical Psychology*, 62, 333–340.

King, N. 1997. Posttraumatic Stress Disorder and Head Injury as a Dual Diagnosis: "Islands" of Memory as a Mechanism. *Journal of Neurology, Neurosurgery, and Psychiatry*, 62, 82–84.

Kluznick, J. C., Speed, N., and Van Valkenberg, C. 1986. Forty Year Follow Up of United States Prisoners of War. *American Journal of Psychiatry*, 43, 1443–1446.

Koenen, K. C., Driver, K. L., Oscar-Berman, M., Wolfe, J., Folsom, S., Huang, M. T., and Schlesinger, L. 2001. Measures of Prefrontal System Dysfunction in Posttraumatic Stress Disorder. *Brain and Cognition*, 45, 64–78.

Kosten, T. R., Mason, J. W., and Giller, E. L. 1987. Sustained Urinary Norepinephrine and Epinephrine Elevation in PTSD. *Psychoneuroendocrinology*, 12, 13–20.

Kulka, R. A., Schlenger, W. E., and Fairbank, J. A. 1991. Assessment of Posttraumatic Stress Disorder in the Community: Prospects and Pitfalls from Recent Studies of Vietnam Veterans: Psychological Assessment. *Journal of Consulting and Clinical Psychology*, 3, 547–560.

Lees-Haley, P. and Dunn, J. T. 1994. The Ability of Naïve Subjects to Report Symptoms of Mild Brain Injury, Post-Traumatic Stress Disorder, Major Depression, and Generalized Anxiety Disorder. *Journal of Clinical Psychology*, 50, 252–256.

Leserman, J., Drossman, D. A., and Li, Z. 1996. Sexual and Physical Abuse History in Gastroenterology Practice: How Types of Abuse Impact Health Status. *Psychosomatic Medicine*, 58, 538–547.

MacKenzie, E. J., Siegel, J. H., Shapiro, S., Moody, M., and Smith, R. T. 1988. Functional Recovery and Medical Costs of Trauma: An Analysis by Type and Severity of Injury. *Journal of Trauma*, 28, 281–297.

Malhi, G. S. and Bartlett, J. R. 1998. Loss of Consciousness and Posttraumatic Stress Disorder. *British Journal of Psychiatry*, 173, 537.

Malloy, P. F., Fairbanks, J. A., and Keane, T. M. 1983. Validation of a Multi Method Assessment of Posttraumatic Stress Disorders in Vietnam Veterans. *Journal of Clinical and Consulting Psychology*, 51, 488–494.

March, J. S. 1993. The Stress Criterion in DSM-IV Posttraumatic Stress Disorder. In Davidson, J. R. and Foa, E. B. (Eds.) *Posttraumatic Stress Disorder: DSM-IV and Beyond*. Washington, D.C.: American Psychiatric Press, pp. 37–54.

Max, J. E., Castillo, C. S., Robin, D. A., Lindgren, S. D., Smith, W. L., Sato, Y., and Arndt, S. 1998. Posttraumatic Stress Symptomology after Childhood Traumatic Brain Injury. *Journal of Nervous and Mental Disease*, 186, 589–596.

Mayou, R., Bryant, B., and Duthie, R. 1993. Psychiatric Consequences of Road Traffic Accidents. *British Medical Journal*, 307, 647–651.

McCranie, E. W., Hyer, L. A., Boudewyns, P. A., and Woods, M. G. 1992. Negative Parenting Behavior, Combat Exposure and PTSD Symptom Severity: Test of a Person–Event Interaction Model. *Journal of Nervous and Mental Diseases*, 180, 431–438.

McCulloch, M. J. and Feldman, P. 1996. Eye Movement Desensitization Utilizes Positive Visceral Element of the investigatory Reflex to Inhibit the Memories of Posttraumatic Stress Disorder: A Theoretical Analysis. *British Journal of Psychiatry, 169*, 571–579.

McFall, M. E., Smith, D. E., and Roszell, D. K. 1990. Convergent Validity of Measures of PTSD in Vietnam Combat Veterans. *American Journal of Psychiatry, 147*, 645–648.

McFarlane, A. C. 1986. Posttraumatic Morbidity of a Disaster. *Journal of Nervous and Mental Disease, 174*, 4–14.

McFarlane, A. C. 1989. The Treatment of Posttraumatic Stress Disorder. *British Journal of Psychiatry, 62*, 81–90.

McFarlane, A. C. 1996. *Control Response as a Predictor of the Development of PTSD Following Motor Vehicle Accidents.* Paper presented at the New York Academy of Sciences, September, New York.

McFarlane, A. C. 2000. Posttraumatic Stress Disorder: A Model of the Longitudinal Course and the Role of Risk Factors. *Journal of Clinical Psychiatry, 61*, 15–23.

McMillan, T. M. 1991. Posttraumatic Stress Disorder and Severe Head Injury. *Psychiatry, 159*, 431–433.

McMillan, T. M. 1996. Post-Traumatic Stress Disorder Following Minor and Severe Closed Head Injury: 10 Single Cases. *Brain Injury, 40*, 749–758.

McMillan, T. M. 2001. Errors in Diagnosing Posttraumatic Stress Disorders after Traumatic Brain Injury. *Brain Injury, 15*, 39–46.

McNally, R. J. 2003. Progress and Controversy in the Study of Posttraumatic Stress Disorder. *Annual Review of Psychology, 54*, 229–252.

McNally, R. J., Lasko, N. B., Machlin, M. L., and Pitman, R. K. 1995. Autobiographical Memory Disturbances in Combat-Related Posttraumatic Stress Disorder. *Behavioral Research Therapy, 33*, 619–630.

Michaels, A. J., Michaels, C. E., Smith, J. S., Moon, C. H., Peterson, C., and Long, W. B. 2000. Outcome from Injury: General Health, Work Status, and Satisfaction 12 months after Trauma. *Journal of Traumatic Injury, Infection, and Critical Care, 48*, 841–850.

Mild Traumatic Brain Injury Committee of the Head Injury Interdisciplinary Special Interest Group of the American Congress of Rehabilitation Medicine. 1993. Definition of Mild Traumatic Brain Injury. *Journal of Head Trauma Rehabilitation, 8*, 86–87.

Millen, F. J. 1966. Post-Traumatic Neurosis in Industry. *Industrial Medical Surgery, 35*, 929–935.

Miller, T. R., Cohen, M. A., and Wiersma, B. 1996. *Victim Costs and Consequences: A New Look.* National Institute of Justice Research Report, Washington, D.C.: U.S. Department of Justice.

Mirzaei, S., Knoll, P., Keck, A., Priether, B., Gutierrez, E., and Umek, H. 2001. Regional Cerebral Blood Flow in Patients Suffering from Posttraumatic Stress Disorder. *Neuropsychobiology, 43*, 260–264.

Norris, F. H. 1992. Epidemiology of Trauma: Frequency and Impact of Different Potentially Traumatic Events on Different Demographic Groups. *Journal Consulting and Clinical Psychology, 60*, 409–418.

Ornitz, E. M. and Pynoos, R. S. 1989. Startle Modulation in Children with Posttraumatic Stress Disorder. *American Journal of Psychiatry, 146*, 866–870.

Oscar-Berman, M. and Bardenhagen, F. 1998. Nonhuman Primate Models of Memory Dysfunction in Neurodegenerative Disease: Contributions from Comparative Neuropyschology. In Troster, A. (Ed.) *Memory in Neurodegenerative Disease.* New York: Cambridge University Press, pp. 3–20.

Pitman, R. K., Orr, S. P., and Forgue, D. F. 1987. Psychological Assessment of Posttraumatic Stress Disorder Imagery in Vietnam Combat Veterans. *Archives of General Psychiatry, 44*, 970–975.

Prigerson, H. G., Maciejewski, P. K., and Rosenheck, R. A. 2001. Combat Trauma: Trauma with Highest Risk of Delayed Onset and Unresolved Posttraumatic Stress Disorder Symptoms, Unemployment, and Abuse Among Men. *Journal of Mental Disease, 189*, 99–108.

Rahe, R. H. 1995. Stress and Psychiatry. In Kaplan, H. I. and Sadock, B. J. (Eds.) *Comprehensive Textbook of Psychiatry,* 6th ed. Baltimore: Williams & Wilkins, pp. 1545–1559.

Rainey, J. M., Aleem, A., and Ortiz, A. 1987. Laboratory Procedure for the Inducement of Flashbacks. *American Journal of Psychiatry, 144*, 1317–1319.

Reinherz, H. Z., Giaconia, R. M., Lefkowitz, E. S., Pakiz, B., Frost, A. K. 1993. Prevalence of Psychiatric Disorders in a Community Population of Older Adolescents. *Journal of the American Academy of Child and Adolescent Psychiatry, 32*, 369–377.

Resnick, H., Kilpatrick, D. G., Danksy, B. 1993. Prevalence of Civilian Trauma and Posttraumatic Stress Disorder in a Representative National Sample of Women. *Journal of Clinical and Consulting Psychiatry, 61*, 984–991.

Sachinvala, N., Von Scotti, H., McGuire, M., Fairbanks, L., Bakst, K., McGuire, M., and Brown, N. 2000. Memory, Attention, Function, and Mood Among Patients with Chronic Posttraumatic Stress Disorder. *Journal of Nervous and Mental Disease, 188*, 818–823.

Sapolsky, R. M. 2000. Glucocorticoids and Hippocampal Atrophy in Neuropsychiatric Disorders. *Archives of General Psychiatry, 57*, 925–935.

Sbordone, R. J. and Liter, J. C. 1995. Mild Traumatic Brain Injury Does Not Produce Post-Traumatic Stress Disorder. *Brain Injury, 9*, 405–412.

Sbordone, R. J. and Saul, R. E. 2000. *Neuropsychology for Health Care Professionals and Attorneys*, 2nd ed. Boca Raton, FL: CRC Press.

Schnurr, P. P., Friedman, M. J., and Rosenberg, S. D. 1993. Preliminary MMPI Scores as Predictors of Combat-Related PTSD Symptoms. *American Journal of Psychiatry, 150*, 479–483.

Shalev, A. Y. 1999. Psychophysiological Expression of Risk Factors for PTSD. In Yehuda, R. (Ed.) *Risk Factors for Posttraumatic Stress Disorder*. Washington, D.C.: American Psychiatric Press, pp. 143–161.

Shalev, A. Y., Orr, S. P., and Peri, T. 1992. Physiological Response to Loud Tones in Israeli Patients with Post-Traumatic Stress Disorder. *Archives of General Psychiatry, 49*, 870–875.

Shalev, A. Y., Orr, S. P., and Pitman, R. K. 1993. Psychophysiologic Assessment of Traumatic Imagery in Israeli Civilian Patients with Posttraumatic Stress Disorder. *American Journal of Psychiatry, 150*, 620–624.

Shalev, A. Y., Bonne, O., and Eth, S. 1996a. Treatment of Posttraumatic Stress Disorder: A Review. *Psychosomatic Medicine, 58*, 165–182.

Shalev, A. Y., Peri, T., Canetti, L., and Schreiber, S. 1996b. Predictors of PTSD in Injured Trauma Survivors: A Prospective Study. *American Journal of Psychiatry, 153*, 219–255.

Shapiro, F. 1989. Eye Movement Desensitization: A New Treatment for Posttraumatic Stress Disorder. *Journal of Behavioral and Experimental Psychiatry, 20*, 211–217.

Shin, L. M., McNally, R. J., Kosslyn, S. M., Thomson, W. L., Rauch, S. L., Alpert, N. M., Metzger, L. J. 1999. Regional Cerebral Blood Flow During Script-Imagery in Childhood Sexual Abuse-Related PTSD: A PET Investigation. *American Journal of Psychiatry, 156*, 575–584.

Solomon, S. D. and Davidson, J. R. T. 1997. Trauma: Prevalence, Impairment, Service Use, and Cost. *Journal of Clinical Psychiatry, 58 (suppl 9)*, 5–11.

Solomon, Z. and Mikulincer, M. 1992. Aftermaths of Combat Stress Reactions: A Three-Year Study. *British Journal of Clinical Psychology, 31*, 21–32.

Southwick, S. M., Krystal, J. H., and Morgan, A. 1993. Abnormal Noradrenergic Function in Posttraumatic Stress Disorder. *Archives of General Psychiatry, 50*, 266–274.

Sparr, L. F. 1995. Post-Traumatic Stress Disorder: Does It Exist? *Neurologic Clinics, 13*, 413–429.

Spitzer, R. L., Williams, J. B., Gibbon, M., and First, M. B. 1990. *Structured Clinical Interview for DSM-III-R*. Washington, D.C.: American Psychiatric Press.

Stuss, D. T. and Benson, D. F. 1986. *The Frontal Lobes*. New York: Raven Press.

Symth, L. D. 1999. *Clinicians Manual for The Cognitive-Behavioral Treatment of Post Traumatic Stress Disorder and Other Anxiety Disorders*, 2nd ed. Baltimore, MD: RTR.

Uddo, M. J., Vasterling, J. J., Bailey, K., and Sutker, P. B. 1993. Memory and Attention in Combat-Related Post-Traumatic Stress Disorder (PTSD). *Journal of Psychopathology and Behavioral Assessment, 15*, 43–52.

Van der Kolk, B. A. 1997. The Psychobiology of Posttraumatic Stress Disorder. *Journal of Clinical Psychiatry, 58*, 16–24.

Van der Kolk, B. A. and Van der Hart, O. 1989. Pierce Janet and the Breakdown of Adaptation in Psychological Trauma. *American Journal of Psychiatry, 146*, 1530–1540.

Warden, D. L., Labbate, L. A., Salazar, A. M., Nelson, R., Sheley, E., Staudenmeier, J., and Martin, E. 1997. Post-Traumatic Stress Disorder in Patients with Traumatic Brain Injury with Amnesia for the Event. *The Journal Neuropsychiatry and Clinical Neurosciences, 9*, 18–22.

Watson, C. G., Juba, M. P., and Manifold, V. 1991. The PTSD Interview: Rationale, Description, Reliability and Concurrent Validity of a DSM-III Based Technique. *Journal of Clinical Psychology, 47*, 179–188.

Wolfe, J. 1994. Applying the Neuropsychology of Memory Disorder. In Cermak, L. S. (Ed.) *Neuropsychological Explorations of Memory and Cognition: Essays in Honor of Nelson Butters*. New York: Plenum Press, pp. 285–293.

Wolfe, J. and Charney, D. S. 1991. Use of Neuropsychological Assessment in Posttraumatic Stress Disorder. *Psychological Assessment, 3*, 573–580.

Wolfe, J. and Schlesinger, L. K. 1997. Performance of PTSD Patients on Standard Tests of Memory: Implications for Trauma. In Yehuda, R. and McFarlane, A. C. (Eds.) *Annals of the New York Academy of Sciences, Vol. 821, Psychobiology of Posttraumatic Stress Disorder.* New York: New York Academy of Sciences, pp. 208–218.

Yehuda, R. and Southwick, E. L. 1991. Hypothalamic Pituitary–Adrenal Dysfunction in Posttraumatic Stress Disorder. *Biological Psychiatry, 30,* 1031–1048.

Yehuda, R., Kahana, B., and Binder-Byrnes, K. 1995a. Cortisol Excretion in Holocaust Survivors with Post-Traumatic Stress Disorder. *American Journal of Psychiatry, J52,* 982–986.

Yehuda, R., Keefe, R. S. E., Harvey, P. D., Levengood, R. A., Gerber, D. K., Geni, J., and Slever, L. J. 1995b. Learning and Memory in Combat Veterans with Posttraumatic Stress Disorder. *American Journal of Psychiatry, 152,* 137–139.

Yehuda, R., Southwick, S. M., and Mason, J. W. 1990. Interactions of the Hypothalamic-Pituitary Adrenal Axis and the Catecholaminergic System of the Stress Disorder. In Giller, E. L. (Ed.) *Biological Assessment and Treatment of PTSD.* Washington, D.C.: American Psychiatric Press.

Zaidi, L. Y. and Foy, D. W. 1994. Childhood Abuse and Combat-Related PTSD. *Journal of Traumatic Stress, 7,* 33–42.

Zatzick, D. F., Weiss, D. S., Marmar, C. R., Metzher, T. J., Wells, K., Golding, J. M., Stewart, A., Schlenger, W. E., and Browner, W. S. 1997. Posttraumatic Stress Disorder and Functioning and Quality of Life Outcomes in Female Vietnam Veterans. *Military Medicine, 162,* 661–665.

Zubieta, J., Chinitz, J. A., Lombardi, V., Fig, L. M., Cameron, O. G., and Leberzon, I. 1999. Medial Frontal Cortex Involvement in PTSD Symptoms: A SPECT Study. *Journal of Psychiatric Research, 68,* 259–264.

7 Mild Traumatic Brain Injury

INCIDENCE AND RISK FACTORS

It has been estimated that over 7 million Americans sustain traumatic brain injury (TBI) each year (Caveness, 1977; Frankowski, 1986). TBI is the leading cause of death and disability in young adults. In 1991, approximately 300,000 people died from TBIs (Rimel et al., 1981). Sosen et al. (1996) reported that 23 to 44% of all deaths due to injury involved significant brain injuries. At highest risk for sustaining a TBI are individuals between the ages of 15 and 24 with a history of alcoholism and low socioeconomic status. Transportation devices (automobiles, bicycles, motorcycles, aircraft, watercraft, and farm equipment) are the most common causes of TBIs. Falls are the second leading cause and are more frequently seen in older adults.

ASSESSING THE SEVERITY OF A TBI

The Glasgow Coma Scale (GCS), which was developed by Teasdale and Jennett (1974), is based on the patient's best motor, verbal, and eye-opening responses following a head trauma. Scores on this test can range from as low as 3 to as high as 15 (normal). A patient's GCS score can be determined by a paramedic at the scene of the accident or later by an emergency room physician. A GCS score of 8 or less indicates that the patient is in coma and has sustained a severe TBI. GCS scores ranging from 9 to 12 are indicative of a moderate brain injury, while scores of 13 to 14 are indicative of a mild brain injury (Rimel et al., 1981).

DURATION OF POSTTRAUMATIC AMNESIA

The duration of a patient's posttraumatic or anterograde amnesia is also frequently used to determine the severity of a patient's initial brain injury. Posttraumatic amnesia (PTA) refers to the period of time before an individual's memory of ongoing events becomes continuous following a brain injury. Thus, when a patient initially begins to recall ongoing events in chronological order, the duration of PTA has ended.

Considerable clinical skill, however, is required when assessing the duration of PTA, since a number of patients who sustain brain injuries will often have difficulty differentiating between isolated (islands of) memory and continuous memory processing. Thus, the unskilled examiner may underestimate the duration of a patient's PTA. In general, the longer the duration of PTA, the more severe the initial TBI and the greater the likelihood of prolonged disability (Figure 7.1).

DEFINITION OF MILD TRAUMATIC BRAIN INJURY

The Mild Traumatic Brain Injury Committee of the Head Injury Interdisciplinary Special Interest Group of the American Congress of Rehabilitation Medicine (1993) has defined mild traumatic brain injury (MTBI) as an "injury to the brain caused by acceleration–deceleration forces with or without physical trauma to the head that produces physiological disruption of brain function manifested by

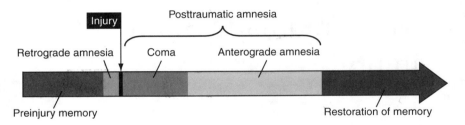

FIGURE 7.1   Acute alterations in memory after closed head injury. (*Source:* Kolb, B. and Whishaw, I. Q. 2003. *Fundamentals of Human Neuropsychology*, 5th ed. New York: Worth Publishers, p. 705. With permission.)

at least one of the following criteria: any loss of memory for events immediately before or after the accident, any alteration in mental state at the time of the accident (e.g., feeling dazed, disoriented, or confused), focal neurological deficits which may or may not be transient, a loss of consciousness of approximately 30 minutes or less, an initial GCS score of 13 to 15, and PTA of less than 24 hours."

The vast majority (80 to 90%) of TBIs can be classified as "mild" on the basis of the patient's GCS score or duration of PTA. The causes of MTBI are essentially the same as with severe TBI, except that there appears to be a proportionately higher incidence of physical assaults in mild TBI cases.

PROBLEMS WITH THIS DEFINITION

Individuals who sustain an acute stress disorder following exposure to an emotionally traumatic event (e.g., rape, natural disasters, or witnessing someone being killed or injured) will frequently experience dissociative symptoms, either during or after the traumatic event, which can alter their recollection of the event. For example, they may report that they are unable to recall part or the entire traumatic event (dissociative amnesia) or that they had gone to heaven or were floating on a cloud looking down at themselves (dissociative reaction).

Since they may meet one or more of the MTBI criteria (difficulty recalling the traumatic event, feel dazed or stunned, or feel confused), they may be inaccurately diagnosed as having sustained an MTBI, particularly if they were involved in a motor vehicle accident and have minor physical trauma to their head (e.g., a scalp abrasion or hematoma). Malec (1999) has emphasized that it is essential for physicians and neuropsychologists to determine that the change in a patient's mental state is due to an MTBI and is not due to a psychological etiology or other physical injuries. For example, many individuals report feeling "stunned" after witnessing a catastrophic event or sustaining physical trauma to other parts of their body other than to their head.

The MTBI criteria do not have any clearly defined lower limits. For example, an individual who reports a loss of consciousness or amnesia of 1 s or less will satisfy the MTBI criteria (Kibby and Long, 1997), even though this cannot be objectively verified. Alexander (1995) has also pointed out that these criteria may misclassify individuals who sustain more severe brain injuries such as a cerebral contusion (a bruise on the surface of the brain), because these individuals may not report a loss of consciousness or amnesia. Thus, these criteria may result in individuals who did not sustain a brain injury being misdiagnosed as brain-damaged or individuals who sustained a more severe brain injury being diagnosed as having a mild brain injury.

RELIABILITY OF THE PATIENT'S ESTIMATE OF THE DURATION OF THEIR LOSS OF CONSCIOUSNESS

A person who has sustained a TBI cannot accurately determine how long they were unconscious following a TBI without an external reference (e.g., observations of others present at the scene of the accident). Individuals who state that they were unconscious for a specific duration of time (e.g., 8 min) because they looked at their watch or a clock immediately after they awoke should be suspected of malingering. Patients may, however, confuse the duration of their loss of consciousness with the duration of their PTA. Even when this occurs they are never able to state exactly how long they were rendered unconscious. For example, they often assume that they must have been unconscious if they are unable to recall the events that occurred during their posttraumatic amnesia. As a consequence, they may report that they were unconscious for several hours or days even though they may not have actually been rendered unconscious or had only been unconscious for few minutes. Thus, a patient's estimate of the duration of loss of consciousness should never be assumed to be reliable unless it is corroborated by witnesses who were present at the scene of the accident and observed the patient to be unconscious, the paramedic report, and the emergency room records on the day of the accident.

NEUROLOGICAL EXAMINATION OF MTBI

While the neurological examination of the MTBI patient is typically normal, it may reveal a number of "soft" neurological signs such as motor incoordination, impaired balance, or exaggerated reflexes. While the electroencephalography (EEG) and magnetic resonance imaging (MRI) are typically normal in MTBI cases, dysrhythmias may occasionally be seen on the EEG and tiny lucencies or hyperintensities on the brain MRI. It should be emphasized, however, that these findings are *nonspecific and are rarely, if ever, diagnostic of an MTBI*. Furthermore, mental status tests that are administered in the emergency room to assess a patient's attention and memory (e.g., digits forward and backward, and memory for four words) are usually *too insensitive to detect the subtle cognitive deficits of MTBI patients*.

PATHOLOGY OF MTBIs

The underlying pathology of MTBI appears to be a diffuse axonal injury (DAI) to the parasagittal (adjacent to the midline) deep white matter structures, extending from the cortex to the brain stem as a result of acceleration–deceleration forces. More simply put, when the brain is rapidly accelerated and decelerated during a collision with another vehicle or object (e.g., tree), damage can occur to the white matter fibers of the brain as a result of shearing forces within the brain, in the absence of physical trauma to the skull (Ommaya and Gennarelli, 1974; Gennarelli et al., 1982). Nevertheless, the issue of what constitutes sufficient force to produce MTBI remains relatively speculative at the present time and is complicated by the fact that neuroimaging studies are typically, but not always, normal (Levin et al., 1992).

CAN WHIPLASH INJURY PRODUCE AN MTBI?

There has been a great deal of controversy as to whether a whiplash injury (i.e., traumatic stretching of the longitudinal cervical vertebral facets, ligaments, and paraspinous muscles and compression of the facet joints) can produce a brain injury. This controversy has been prolonged by studies that have reported cognitive abnormalities in whiplash victims (Yarnell and Rossi, 1988) and studies that have found no demonstrable cognitive deficits (DiStefano and Radanov, 1995). Although many individuals who sustain whiplash injuries will complain of cognitive and behavioral symptoms similar to those reported by individuals who sustain MTBI, these symptoms can be caused by a variety of factors besides a brain injury (e.g., pain and discomfort, orthopedic problems, medications, depression). Although Gennarelli (1986) has reported that monkeys who sustained whiplash injuries were found to have microscopic hemorrhages in their upper brain stem (when their brains were later removed), as a result of repeated rapid mechanically induced acceleration–deceleration forces within the brain in the absence of physical trauma to their skulls, these findings may not generalize to humans (Cullum and Thompson, 1997).

CEREBRAL CONCUSSION AND THE "POSTCONCUSSIVE SYNDROME"

The most common form of MTBI is referred to as a *cerebral concussion*, which may involve a brief loss of consciousness following a rapid acceleration–deceleration injury. Such injuries commonly occur in motor vehicle accidents, boxing matches, or falls.

Individuals who sustain a cerebral concussion are typically unable to recall the event that produced their concussion. While some individuals may not report a loss of consciousness, they will typically report amnesia for the events immediately before (retrograde amnesia) and following (anterograde amnesia) the accident. Although amnesia can last up to 30 min, this does not mean that the individual was unconscious during this period of time. It simply means that this individual was not registering and processing ongoing events, even though they were conscious at that time. Unfortunately, many individuals who sustain a concussion may report that they were unconscious for several minutes, even though they may have been unconscious for only a few seconds, and have misclassified their PTA as unconsciousness.

Individuals who sustain cerebral concussions typically appear confused or bewildered immediately after their accident. This is often reflected in the paramedic report taken at the scene of the accident, which documents the confusion. As a consequence, their GCS score will usually be less than 15. The length of time taken by the paramedics to arrive at the scene of the accident is an important factor. If the paramedics arrive within a few minutes of the accident and observe that the individual appears confused or bewildered, this individual will probably receive a GCS score of less than 15 (usually 13 or 14). However, if the paramedics do not arrive for some time after the accident (30 min or longer), the individual may no longer be confused, even though he or she has no recollection of the accident or the events surrounding it. As a consequence, these individuals may be given a GCS score of 15 (normal). A number of factors, however, can confound the assessment of an individual's GCS score. For example, if the individual is under the influence of alcohol or drugs when the paramedics arrive, he or she is likely to be given a score of less than 15, even without having sustained a brain injury. Severe pain secondary to physical injuries sustained during the accident may cause the individual to appear confused and disoriented. Individuals with language difficulties, who are deaf, or have a medical condition that impairs their awareness of their surroundings (e.g., epilepsy, diabetes), may also receive lower GCS scores.

Information obtained from reliable informants who were present at the scene of an accident can be helpful in determining whether the individual appeared confused. However, identifying an individual as confused following a traumatic event can be difficult, since individuals who are in a state of shock following exposure to a traumatic event may appear confused even though no brain injury was sustained.

CEREBRAL CONTUSIONS

Blows to a stationary head, which occur during an assault, or as a result of striking the head on the ground (particularly when the person is struck by a motor vehicle when crossing the street or is thrown from a moving motor vehicle) are more likely to produce a focal brain injury such as a cerebral contusion (bruising on the surface of the brain) than a DAI (Margulies, 2000). In many cases, these individuals report no loss of consciousness or amnesia for the events surrounding the accident in which they were injured. However, they will frequently exhibit combative behavior at the scene of the accident or an inability to regulate their behavior and emotions when they are seen in the emergency room (see Chapter 8).

THE DSM-IV CRITERIA FOR A POSTCONCUSSIVE DISORDER

Although the term mild traumatic brain injury is frequently used interchangeably with a cerebral concussion, the diagnostic criteria for a postconcussional disorder specified by the DSM-IV (American Psychiatric Association, 1994) are considerably more stringent than the MTBI committee's criteria. For example, while the MTBI criteria only require any period of loss of consciousness, the DSM-IV requires a duration of unconsciousness of more than 5 min. Instead of "any loss of memory" for events immediately after the accident, the DSM-IV requires a minimum of 12 h of posttraumatic (anterograde) amnesia. In addition, while the MTBI criteria make no mention of the duration of a patient's cognitive or behavioral symptoms following a brain injury, the DSM-IV specifically requires that the symptoms persist for at least 3 months and be documented by neuropsychological testing. Thus, one can easily see that the vast majority of individuals who satisfy the MTBI criteria would not meet the DSM-IV criteria for a postconcussive disorder, even if all of the individuals who meet the MTBI criteria are later diagnosed as having a postconcussion syndrome.

COGNITIVE AND BEHAVIORAL SYMPTOMS OF A POSTCONCUSSIVE SYNDROME

Many individuals who sustain a concussion will also develop what has been termed as postconcussive syndrome (PCS) (Alves et al., 1993). Although the most common symptoms of a PCS are headaches, photosensitivity, dizziness, fatigue, irritability, and problems with attention and concentration, as well as a variety of cognitive and physical symptoms (see Table 7.1), many individuals who sustain a concussion may not complain of any cognitive or behavioral

---

TABLE 7.1
Symptoms of PCS

Somatic
  Headache
  Dizziness or vertigo
  Blurred vision, difficulty focusing
  Tinnitus
  Impaired smell and taste perception
  Slurred speech
  Impaired balance and fine motor coordination
  Intolerance of bright lights and loud noises
  Sleep disturbance
  Easy fatigability
  Slowed movement
Cognitive
  Impaired attention and concentration
  Impaired recent and remote memory
  Slowed information processing
  Impaired thinking and planning
  Decreased cognitive flexibility
Emotional and behavioral
  Irritability
  Anxiety and depressed mood
  Disproportionate increase in emotionality
  Reduced frustration tolerance
  Rapid mood swings

---

difficulties or may minimize them (Sbordone et al., 1998). As a consequence, the spouse and family of an individual suspected as having a PCS need to be interviewed to determine if they have observed any cognitive, behavioral, or emotional changes in the patient since his or her injury.

One of the confounding issues when interviewing significant others is denial; that is, some family members may deny that they have observed any changes in the patient's behavior, even though this view may not be shared by other family members. Another issue is whether the information, obtained from significant others, accurately describes the patient's behavior. For example, the family may exaggerate the patient's cognitive and behavioral symptoms following a questionable MTBI, particularly after filing a lawsuit.

NONSPECIFICITY OF POSTCONCUSSIVE SYMPTOMS

The subjective complaints of individuals who are often diagnosed with "a postconcussion syndrome" are not specific to a brain injury (Binder, 1997). For example, approximately 50% of the individuals who are involved in litigation and have no history of head trauma or brain injury will report symptoms such as confusion, concentration difficulties, dizziness, and word-finding problems that most likely reflect the stress of litigation (Lees-Haley and Brown, 1993). Approximately one third of relatively healthy college students reported "postconcussive" symptoms that were even corroborated by their significant others, even though none of these students had a history of closed head injury or neurological disease (Gouvier et al., 1988). The majority of individuals who have psychiatric disorders such as a major depression or generalized anxiety or panic disorders will also complain of these symptoms (Binder, 1997). Finally, Sbordone and Liter (1995) found that the cognitive and behavioral symptoms reported by patients with chronic posttraumatic stress disorder were nearly identical to patients with PCS. For example, they complained of symptoms such as memory and concentration problems, dizziness, tinnitus (ringing in the ears), and hypersensitivity to light and noise. Thus, the subjective complaints of individuals cannot be solely used to diagnose a PCS, since these symptoms are nonspecific and can be seen in normal individuals who are involved in litigation, who experience chronic pain, and who have a psychiatric and a posttraumatic stress disorder.

PERSISTENCE OF PCSs

While recovery, following PCS, usually occurs within 3 months in the vast majority of individuals who sustain a concussion, a relatively small percentage of individuals (10 to 25%) will report, after 3 months, persistent symptoms, which are often worse than their initial symptoms (Bohnen et al., 1991). Some investigators (Gronwall and Wrightson, 1974; Dikmen et al., 1983; Dacey et al., 1991) have even suggested that persistent postconcussive symptoms are the result of a combination of organic and psychological factors.

Individuals with persistent PCS symptoms tend to be older, have a history of prior brain injury or preexisting psychiatric difficulties, and complain of predominantly physical symptoms (e.g., headache, neck pain) following their accidents. Research, however, has not yet identified the specific factors that will reliably predict which individuals will develop persistent postconcussive symptoms (Malec, 1999). One of the issues that have complicated our understanding of persistent postconcussive symptoms is the high base rate of symptoms in individuals who have not sustained brain injuries (Gouvier et al., 1988, 1992), particularly individuals with chronic pain (Uomoto and Esselman, 1993) and psychiatric disorders (Binder, 1997).

INFLUENCE OF PREMORBID FACTORS ON THE PERSISTENCE OF POSTCONCUSSIVE SYMPTOMS

Premorbid factors such as age, education, occupation, alcohol abuse, personality, emotional adjustment, and neuropsychiatric history can influence the duration of postconcussive symptoms and a person's adjustment to such symptoms. For example, Denker (1944) found that individuals over the age of 40 were twice as likely to have persistent postconcussive symptoms as individuals under the age of 40. Similarly, Russell and Smith (1961) found that the duration of postconcussive symptoms tended to be longer in older patients. Individuals, who were older, less educated, and had lower occupational status, tended to report more postconcussive symptoms (Dikmen et al., 1989).

Preexisting personality traits such as dependency, hysteria, or perfectionism may exacerbate the extent and duration of an individual's postconcussive symptoms (Ruff et al., 1986). Individuals with premorbid personality disorders and psychosocial adjustment difficulties are more likely to have difficulty coping with their postconcussive symptoms than are individuals without such backgrounds. Personality traits such as denial, defensiveness, dependency, aggression, or anger may adversely affect recovery following a concussion. For example, such personality traits may cause individuals with postconcussive symptoms to become depressed and anxious, as well as produce a variety of somatic symptoms that may delay recovery. Since there is some evidence that repeated brain trauma may produce a cumulative effect (Gronwall and Wrightson, 1975; Levin et al., 1992), an individual's persistent postconcussive symptoms could reflect the cumulative effect of prior brain trauma.

POSTTRAUMATIC FACTORS THAT INFLUENCE THE PERSISTENCE OF POSTCONCUSSIVE SYMPTOMS

Individuals with postconcussive symptoms frequently experience high levels of stress if they try to return quickly to their preinjury activities. For example, many of these individuals have considerable difficulty handling the cognitive demands of their jobs after they return to work and frequently become anxious and depressed (Long, 1991). Some of these individuals were never informed by their treating physicians to expect such difficulties when they returned to work. As a consequence, they often feel as if they are going "crazy" or "losing their mind" when they begin experiencing such symptoms at work. Other individuals may be given unrealistic expectations of how quickly their symptoms should resolve. When their symptoms persist longer than expected, they often become anxious and depressed and may fear that they have sustained a more serious brain injury than was initially believed.

Individuals with concussions may also sustain whiplash injuries, which produce neck stiffness as well as pain and discomfort in the upper back. The combination of these symptoms may disrupt their ability to work and enjoy life. When these individuals are placed on pain or psychiatric medications, their medications may exacerbate or prolong their cognitive difficulties. In trying to cope with postconcussive symptoms, some individuals may abuse alcohol or drugs, which may also exacerbate or prolong their symptoms (Levine, 1988).

The expectations of the families of MTBI patients can be quite problematic during the early stages of recovery (Long, 1991). For example, if a patient fails to meet the expectations of their family, he or she may feel like a failure and develop secondary psychological symptoms (e.g., anger, aggression, depression), which may seriously undermine their coping skills (Ruff et al., 1986). In other instances, where the patient is the "breadwinner" of the family, the injury may affect the patient's ability to work, which may lead to financial difficulties that can be quite stressful for the patient and his or her family (Stambrook et al., 1990).

Gualtieri (1995) has concluded that patients with persistent PCS fall into four major categories: patients whose initial TBI was misclassified as mild rather than moderate or severe; patients

TABLE 7.2
Unusual Sequalae of MTBI

These symptoms should serve as a red flag to exclude the possibility of MTBI:
   Late symptom onset
   Posttraumatic stress disorder — controversial
   Complex partial and nonepileptic seizures
   Chronic fatigue syndrome
   Rage attacks, episodic explosive disorder
   Directed violence or planned crime
   Chronic pain syndrome
   Selective memory loss (dense amnesia with islands of recall)
   Retrograde without anterograde amnesia

Source: Modified from Tranel, D. and Rizzo, M. 1996. In Tranel, D. and Rizzo, M. (Eds.) *Head Injury and Postconcussive Syndrome.* New York: Churchill-Livingston, p. 13.

with significant premorbid psychiatric or neurological conditions (e.g., attention-deficit or learning disorder); patients who develop posttraumatic depression, headache, and related somatic symptoms that are treated poorly or not at all; and patients with somatoform disorders, hysteria, or malingering. Table 7.2 lists the unusual sequalae of MTBI. These sequalae should heighten suspicion that the observed symptoms attributed to an MTBI most likely reflect preexisting or more serious neuropathology or an undiagnosed medical or psychiatric disorder.

Individuals who sustain a concussion are more susceptible to the effects of a subsequent concussion or brain injury. Gualtieri (1995) has stressed that while the redundancy in the brain neural networks allows it compensate after the initial trauma, its capacity to compensate following subsequent or even repeated trauma is diminished.

BOXER'S ENCEPHALOPATHY

Professional boxers, especially those who have sustained cumulative rotational subconcussive head blows during multiple bouts, may develop a chronic traumatic encephalopathy (CTE). This disorder usually begins with symptoms such as tremor, dysarthria, incoordination, decreased complex attention and impulse control, euphoria, and emotional lability. These symptoms are often referred to as a "punch drunk syndrome." In a small percentage of cases, this condition progresses from Parkinson symptoms (as exhibited by heavyweight champion Mohammed Ali) and various psychiatric syndromes, notably paranoia, to an advanced state of severe cognitive impairment, which is termed *dementia pugilistica.* Its prominent symptoms include slowed thought and speech, impaired executive function, cheerful or silly affect, and uninhibited belligerence. Dementia pugilistica usually has its onset near the end of a boxing career or after retirement, but may develop anywhere from 7 to 35 years after the boxer's first bout. CTE may be differentiated from other dementias, especially the Parkinson group, by its characteristic course and combination of motor, cognitive, and psychiatric symptoms. It should be pointed out that amateur boxers, in contrast to professionals, typically show mild or no cognitive changes (Mendez and Cummings, 2003).

CONCUSSIONS IN SPORTING EVENTS

The American Academy of Neurology has recognized the potentially deleterious cumulative effects of repeated mild concussive injuries in sporting events such as football and soccer. They have recommended that individuals who sustain a concussion with a loss of consciousness be immediately removed from the game and undergo a mental status and neurological examination. This policy will hopefully minimize the possibility of another concussion while the individual is still symptomatic from the first, and the subsequent development of the so-called "second impact syndrome" (Kelly and Rosenberg, 1997).

USE OF NEUROPSYCHOLOGICAL TESTS TO CORROBORATE POSTCONCUSSIVE SYMPTOMS

Neuropsychological tests are frequently utilized to corroborate a patient's postconcussive symptoms. However, in forensic cases, an individual may not be referred for neuropsychological testing until their postconcussive symptoms have resolved. In other cases, neuropsychologists, evaluating individuals reporting postconcussive symptoms, may base their opinions solely on the patient's complaints and their neuropsychological test data, even though these factors are under the individual's control and can be easily manipulated. In such cases, neuropsychologists may neglect to review the patient's academic, vocational, and medical records and naively assume that the information furnished by the patient is accurate. This information, however, may be inaccurate for a variety of reasons and may fail to include a history of confounding factors that can significantly affect an individual's neuropsychological test performance. In other cases, the neuropsychologist may not interview collateral sources such as the individual's spouse, parents, or significant others to determine their premorbid level of functioning and corroborate the individual's subjective complaints.

Because many individuals will report that their cognitive and somatic symptoms began immediately after their injury or accident, many health care professionals and attorneys often assume that their symptoms are of neurological origin. Too often, however, support for this assumption comes from psychologists who find impaired cognitive performances on neuropsychological tests. An individual's neuropsychological test performance has no diagnostic specificity because poor test performance can be caused by a variety of extraneous factors. In fact, Stuss (1995) has urged psychologists not to rely solely on the results of neuropsychological testing to determine the etiology of a patient's injury, but rather to work forward from the event to determine if there is a neuropsychological profile that fits with the facts of the case. Often the patient with persistent PCS has had negative CT, MRI, and EEG studies and has shown no or minimal improvement with analgesics and antidepressants. Currently, there is no single neurological test or measure that can unequivocally diagnose MTBI, even including newer neurodiagnostic techniques such as SPECT, PET, and brain mapping, which have yet to demonstrate their clinical value in even more severe brain injury cases (Alexander, 1995).

PSYCHIATRIC DISORDERS THAT CAN MIMIC A PCS

The neuropathophysiology of MTBI includes changes and disturbances in brain neurotransmitters and neuromodulators that can result in a significant mood disorder. For example, depression, if severe, can affect a patient's cognitive and behavioral functioning (see Table 7.3). Table 7.4 lists the clinical features of major mood disorders — depression and mania. Cognitive deficits can also result from an unrecognized adult form of a childhood developmental disorder (e.g., attention-deficit hyperactivity disorder or dyslexia) that can mimic the symptoms of a PCS (Gualtieri, 1995). Individuals who exhibit persistent and disabling symptoms, which cannot be explained by their clinical history, medical records, neurological examinations, neurodiagnostic or neuroimaging studies, or even the results of neuropsychological testing, may have a conversion or somatoform disorder.

CONVERSION DISORDER

In a conversion disorder, anxiety from a repressed unconscious emotional conflict is converted into pseudo-neurological symptoms, such as loss of memory, paralysis, loss of speech, or pseudoseizures.

TABLE 7.3
Disorders that Can Mimic Persistent Postconcussive (Posttraumatic Head) Syndrome

Medical
  Viral illness — hepatitis, AIDS, Lyme disease
  Drug toxicity — prescription, over-the-counter, illicit drugs
  Fibromyalgia, chronic fatigue syndrome
  Early organ failure — cardiopulmonary, hepatic, renal
  Hematologic and autoimmune disorders — anemia, blood dyscrasia, lupus

Neurological

Adolescents/young and middle-aged adults	*Elderly*
Attention-deficit and learning disorder	Alzheimer's disease
Limbic seizures	Vascular dementia — early stages
Migraine	Recurrent TIAs and nonparalytic strokes
Multiple sclerosis	Parkinson's — early stages
Myasthenia gravis	
Sleep disorders — narcolepsy, sleep apnea	

Psychiatric
  Depression — major, dysthymia (mild chronic form)
  Anxiety and panic disorder
  Somatoform disorder — conversion and dissociative forms
  Chronic pain disorder
  Factitious disorder and malingering

TABLE 7.4
Clinical Features of a Mood Disorder

Depression
  Depressed mood ranging from mild sadness to intense feelings of worthlessness, hopelessness, and
    inappropriate guilt
  Fatigue or loss of energy
  Cognitive symptoms (difficulty thinking and concentrating, indecisiveness)
  Loss of interest and pleasure in usual activities
  Somatic symptoms (increased or decreased appetite, insomnia or hypersomnia, decreased sex
    drive)
  Significant weight loss
  Social withdrawal
  Suicidal ideation or attempt
  Psychomotor agitation or retardation
  Hypochondriacal and persecutory delusions in severe cases

Mania
  Spectrum of mood changes — expansive, elevated, irritable
  Racing thoughts, flight of ideas
  Hyperactivity, inappropriate reckless behavior (e.g., reckless driving, buying sprees, promiscuity)
  Loquaciousness
  Reduced need for sleep
  Grandiose delusions in severe cases

Conversion disorder is more common in women and in poorly educated individuals from rural and lower socioeconomic backgrounds.

SOMATOFORM DISORDER

Individuals who develop a somatoform disorder will complain of numerous problems (e.g., pain, fatigue, memory difficulties) that cannot be fully explained by any known medical condition or the side effects of their medications. Pain is one of the most common complaints of individuals with somatoform disorders. It is more commonly seen in females and is frequently associated with depression. Although in some cases, an individual may have a physical condition that produces pain, psychological factors usually play a prominent role in the onset, exaggeration, and duration of complaints.

ANXIETY DISORDER

Individuals with anxiety disorders will complain of attention, concentration, or memory difficulties, but ironically are able to provide rather detailed examples of these difficulties. They may also complain of seizure-like symptoms, headaches, faintness, fatigue, and interpersonal and social difficulties.

PANIC DISORDER

Panic disorder is characterized by brief, recurrent, unpredictable episodes of intense anxiety, frequent agoraphobia (fear of open spaces), dyspnea (shortness of breath), tachycardia (rapid heartbeats), palpitations, headaches, dizziness, paresthesias (sensations of numbness or tingling), choking, feelings of being smothered, nausea, or feelings of impending doom.

DISSOCIATIVE SYMPTOMS

The most common dissociative symptoms are sleepwalking, fugue (sudden unexpected travel from home or work with an associated loss of personal identity), depersonalization (altered perception of self and a sense of detachment from one's surroundings), and an inability to recall emotionally traumatic events. Dissociative symptoms may also mimic the symptoms of patients who have temporal lobe epilepsy (Eisendrath, 1998).

FACTITIOUS DISORDER

Patients with factitious disorders may also complain of symptoms that mimic postconcussive symptoms. These individuals will consciously feign their symptoms to adopt a dependent role and develop a child–parent relationship with their treating doctors, which symbolize their long-standing but unsatisfied dependency needs. They frequently are medically sophisticated and manipulative with a history of alcohol and substance abuse. They may also exhibit neurological impairments as a result of having sustained prior brain trauma, which may have occurred as a result of deliberately falling down a flight of stairs or as a consequence of drug or alcohol abuse. Since many of these individuals are bright, they often read medical and neuropsychological textbooks on TBI to become familiar with the diagnostic criteria set forth in these texts. They may also become familiar with the neuropsychological tests that are likely to be administered and will frequently perform poorly on these tests to "prove" that they have brain damage. These individuals are often difficult to detect, unless the neuropsychologist has had the opportunity to review their extensive and often voluminous medical records, which can sometimes fill several large boxes or filing cabinets.

DETECTION OF MALINGERING BY A MENTAL STATUS EXAMINATION

The use of the mental status examination to detect malingered symptoms following TBI can be a formidable task. Resnick (1994) provides an excellent description of simulated psychiatric symptomatology and the techniques to detect malingering. For example, individuals feigning auditory hallucinations such as voices usually deny that they can make them go away by getting involved in activities, even though this is commonly reported by psychiatric patients. Simulators can be questioned about the nature and circumstances of their hallucinations. For example, true hallucinations do not change if the eyes are closed or open; visual hallucinations appear suddenly and more often occur in low light conditions. Finally, reports of very dramatic and atypical hallucinations should raise suspicions of malingering.

CLINICAL CHARACTERISTICS OF CONVERSION DISORDER AND MALINGERING

Clinical characteristics that may be helpful in differential diagnosis of conversion disorder and malingering are as follows: malingerers are often ill at ease, sullen, suspicious, secretive, aloof, and unfriendly; conversion patients are usually cooperative, appealing, and dependent. Malingerers often try to avoid examinations unless legally required and may refuse to undergo diagnostic procedures or recommended treatment; conversion patients eagerly seek an organic basis for their symptoms. Malingerers in comparison to conversion patients more often refuse employment if offered and frequently give a highly detailed account of their accident and its sequalae, whereas the history and subjective symptoms provided by conversion patients are usually vague and often contain gaps and inaccuracies (Granacher, 2003).

MEDICATIONS THAT CAN MIMIC MTBI SYMPTOMS

A variety of medications can produce cognitive deficits that can mimic the symptoms of MTBI or even more severe TBIs. The medications most commonly implicated are anticholinergics, benzodiazepines, neuroleptics, narcotics, and sedative hypnotics. Although cognitive functions such as vigilance and speed of cognitive processing are usually impaired when these medications are taken, the cognitive deficits produced by these medications can range from toxic delirium or dementia to subtle mood alterations. Factors that increase the risk of developing cognitive impairment with the use of these medications include advanced age, preexisting dementia or prior head trauma, polypharmacy (multiple drug use), and hepatic or renal dysfunction, which interferes with drug metabolism and elimination, respectively. Sedating, low-potency, dopamine-blocking neuroleptics, such as thorazine and thioridazine, are more likely to produce cognitive dysfunction than more potent agents such as haloperidol.

Newer neuroleptic agents such as clozapine, risperidone, olanzepine, and quetiapine have been reported to produce significantly less cognitive impairment. Although most of the tricyclic antidepressants, as well as trazodone, tend to deplete brain acetylcholine (a neurochemical transmitter that plays a prominent role in attention and memory) and can frequently produce attention and concentration difficulties, confusion, and recent memory difficulties, selective serotonin reuptake inhibitors such as fluoxetine, sertraline, paroxetine, buspirone, and a number of reversible monoamine oxidase (MAO) inhibitors produce relatively few adverse cognitive effects. Anti-Parkinson drugs such as trihexyphenidyl and benztropine, as well as many over-the-counter medications, particularly sleep aids, eye drops, and cold preparations, which are anticholinergic and contain antihistamines, can interfere with cognitive functioning. Dopaminergic agents used in the treatment of Parkinson's disease, such as L-dopa, carbidopa, and bromocriptine, are well known to produce nocturnal confusion.

TABLE 7.5

Common Medications Causing Cognitive and Psychiatric Disorders

Analgesics	Opiates, salicylates, nonsteroidals
Antihistamines	Over-the-counter cold medications
Antipsychotic agents	Phenothiazines, haloperidol, thiothixene, risperidone, olanzepine, quetiapine
Antidepressants	Imipramine, desipramine, amitriptyline, trazadone, fluoxetine, sertraline, paroxetine
Antianxiety agents	Benzodiazepines, buspirone
Antihypertensives	Propranolol, reserpine, clonidine, methyldopa, hydralazine, hydrochlorothiazide
Anticonvulsants — mood stabilizers	Phenytoin, phenobarbital, lithium, valproate, primidone, carbamazepine, oxcarbazepine, topirimate, levetiracetam, gabapentin
Antiinfectious and antiinflammatory agent	Corticosteroids, penicillin, sulfa compounds
Cardiovascular drugs	Digoxin, quinidine
Anti-Parkinson agents	Benztropine, trihexiphenidyl, levodopa, carbidopa, bromocriptine
Stimulants and weight reduction agents	Amphetamines, methylphenidate, phenylephrine, and phenylpropanolamine (nose drops/spray)
Sedative–hypnotic agents	Atropine, scopolamine
Others	Oral contraceptives, cimetidine, thyroxine

A variety of antiseizure medications such as phenytoin, valproate, carbamezapine, primidone, phenobarbital, and topirimate frequently produce cognitive impairments on tasks involving attention, speed of cognitive processing, recent memory, and problem solving. The adverse effects of these medications can be enhanced when they are given in combination with other medications or anticonvulsant drugs or used in high doses. Although these medications can significantly affect a patient's cognitive functioning, the adverse effects produced can often be justified by the beneficial effects of seizure control. Several new anticonvulsant medications such as gabapentin have few, if any, adverse effects on cognitive functioning. In fact, one of the newer anticonvulsants, lamotrigine, may have a somewhat beneficial effect on cognitive functioning as it appears to produce positive CNS alerting effects.

Other medications such as antihypertensive agents, particularly beta-blockers and reserpine, are well known to produce deleterious cognitive effects. Cardiac medications such as digoxin have also been found to produce delirium and even dementia when they are given at high levels. Significant cognitive deficits can be produced when digoxin and antiarrhythmic medications such as quinidine are given to patients within the therapeutic range. Antiinflammatory medications, in particular steroids, can also produce cognitive impairments including delirium and psychosis. Finally, antibiotics, antineoplastic agents, amphetamines, cimetidine, lithium, and neosynephrine (a nasal spray) can impair cognitive functioning (see Table 7.5) (Meador, 1998). (See Appendix A for a table of generic and proprietary drug names.)

CONSEQUENCES OF INACCURATE DIAGNOSIS OF A CONCUSSION OR MTBI

The misdiagnosis of patients as having sustained a concussion or MTBI, when in fact they have not, poses a potential danger to their psychological and emotional welfare. For example, being told they are brain-injured may exacerbate their long-standing emotional problems (e.g., feelings of inadequacy and insecurity, poor self-esteem, paranoia, unhappiness), which may not even be recognized by these patients. It may also justify acts of irresponsibility, such as aggressive behavior toward others, and may be used to avoid seeking out psychological or psychiatric treatment for their emotional difficulties. Furthermore, if these individuals are later referred for controversial neurodiagnostic procedures such as SPECT or PET scans that may show evidence of "brain damage," the results of such studies may reinforce the patient's despair and cause significant depression. Referring these patients to a brain injury program or for cognitive rehabilitation may reinforce their belief that they have a serious brain injury, which may cause them to become even more anxious and depressed (Alexander, 1995).

REFERENCES

Alexander, M. P. 1995. Mild Traumatic Brain Injury Pathophysiology, Natural History and Clinical Management. *Neurology, 45*, 1253–1260.

Alves, W. M., Macciocchi, S. N., and Barth, J. T. 1993. Postconcussive Symptoms after Uncomplicated Mild Head Injury. *Journal of Head Trauma Rehabilitation, 8*, 48–59.

American Psychiatric Association. 1994. *Diagnostic and Statistical Manual of Mental Disorders*, 4th ed. Washington, D.C.: American Psychiatric Association, pp. 704–706.

Binder, L. R. 1997. A Review of Mild Head Trauma, Part II: Clinical Implications. *Journal of Clinical and Experimental Neuropsychology, 19*, 432–457.

Bohnen, N., Twijnstra, A., and Jolles, J. 1991. Tolerance for Light and Sound of Patients with Persistent Post-Concussional Symptoms Six Months after Mild Head Injury. *Journal of Neurology, 238*, 443–446.

Caveness, W. 1977. Incidence of Craniocerebral Trauma in the United States. *Transactions of the American Neurological Association, 102*, 136–138.

Cullum, C. M. and Thompson, L. L. 1997. Neurological Diagnosis and Outcome in Mild Traumatic Brain Injury. *Applied Neuropsychology, 4*, 6–15.

Dacey, R., Dikmen, S., Temkin, N., McLean, A., Armsden, G., and Winn, H. R. 1991. Relative Effects of Brain and Non-Brain Injuries on Neuropsychological and Psychosocial Outcome. *Journal of Trauma, 31*, 217–222.

Denker, P. G. 1944. Post-Concussion Syndrome: Prognosis and Evaluation of the Organic Factors. *New York State Journal of Medicine, 15*, 379–384.

Dikmen, S., Reitan, R. M., and Temkin, N. R. 1983. Neuropsychological Recovery in Head Injury. *Archives of Neurology, 40*, 333–338.

Dikmen, S., Temkin, N., and Armsden, G. 1989. Neuropsychological Recovery: Relationship to Psychosocial Functioning and Postconcussional Complaints. In Levin, H. S., Eisenberg, H. M., and Benton, A. L. (Eds.) *Mild Head Injury*. New York: Oxford University Press, pp. 229–241.

DiStefano, G. and Radanov, B. P. 1995. Course of Attention and Memory after Common Whiplash: A Two-Years Perspective Study with Age, Education and Gender Pair-Matched Patients. *ACTA Neurologica Scandinavica, 91*, 346–352.

Eisendrath, S. J. 1998. Psychiatric Disorders. In Tierney, Jr., L. M., McPhee, S. J., and Papadakis, M. A. (Eds.) *Current Medical Diagnosis and Treatment*. Stamford, CT: Appleton-Lange, pp. 973–1030.

Frankowski, R. F. 1986. Descriptive and Epidemiological Studies of Head Injury in the United States: 1974–1984. *Advances in Psychosomatic Medicine, 16*, 153–172.

Gennarelli, T. A. 1986. Mechanisms and Pathophysiology of Cerebral Concussion. *Journal of Head Trauma Rehabilitation, 1*, 23–30.

Gennarelli, T. A., Thibault, L. B., Adams, J. H., Graham, D. L., Thompson, C. J., and Marcincin, R. P. 1982. Diffuse Axonal Injury and Traumatic Coma in the Primate. *Annals of Neurology, 12*, 564–574.

Gouvier, W. D., Cubic, B., Jones, G., Brantley, P., and Cutlip, Q. 1992. Post-Concussion Symptoms and Daily Stress in Normal and Head-Injured College Populations. *Archives of Clinical Neuropsychology, 7*, 193–211.

Gouvier, W. D., Uddo-Crane, M., and Brown, L. M. 1988. Base Rates of Post-Concussional Symptoms. *Archives of Clinical Neuropsychology, 3*, 273–278.

Granacher, R. P. 2003. *Traumatic Brain Injury: Methods for Clinical and Forensic Neuropsychiatric Assessment*. Boca Rotan: CRC Press, pp. 327–336.

Gronwall, D. and Wrightson, P. 1974. Delayed Recovery of Intellectual Function after Minor Head Injury. *Lancet, ii*, 605–609.

Gronwall, D. and Wrightson, P. 1975. Cumulative Effect of Concussion. *Lancet, ii*, 995–997.

Gualtieri, C. T. 1995. The Problem of Mild Brain Injury. *Neuropsychiatry, Neuropsychology and Behavioral Neurology*, 8, 127–136.

Kelly, J. P. and Rosenberg, J. H. 1997. Diagnosis and Management of Concussion in Sports. *Neurology*, 48, 575–580.

Kibby, M. Y. and Long, C. J. 1997. Effective Treatment of Minor Head Injury and Understanding its Neurological Consequences. *Applied Neuropsychology*, 4, 34–42.

Lees-Haley, P. R. and Brown, R. S. 1993. Neuropsychological Complaint Base Rates of 170 Personal Injury Claimants. *Archives of Clinical Neuropsychology*, 8, 203–209.

Levin, H. S., Williams, D. H., Eisenberg, H. M., High, W. M., and Guinto, F. C. 1992. Serial MRI and Neurobehavioral Findings after Mild to Moderate Closed Head Injury. *Journal of Neurology, Neurosurgery and Psychiatry*, 55, 255–262.

Levine, M. J. 1988. Issues in Neurobehavioral Assessment of Mild Head Injury. *Cognitive Rehabilitation*, 6, 14–20.

Long, C. J. 1991. A Model of Recovery to Maximize the Rehabilitation of Individuals with Head Trauma. *The Journal of Head Injury*, 2, 18–28.

Malec, J. F. 1999. Mild Traumatic Brain Injury: Scope of Problem. In Varney, N. R. and Roberts, R. J. (Eds.) *The Evaluation and Treatment of Mild Traumatic Brain Injury*. Mahwah, NJ: Lawrence Erlbaum, pp. 15–38.

Margulies, S. 2000. The Postconcussion Syndrome after Mild Head Trauma: Is Brain Damage Overdiagnosed? Part 1. *Journal of Clinical Neuroscience*, 7, 400–408.

Meador, K. J. 1998. Cognitive Side Effects of Medications. *Neurologic Clinics North America*, 16, 141–155.

Mendez, M. F. and Cummings, J. L. 2003. *Dementia — A Clinical Approach*, 3rd ed. Philadelphia: Butterworth-Heinemann, pp. 513–521.

Mild Traumatic Brain Injury Committee of the Head Injury Interdisciplinary Special Interest Group of the American Congress of Rehabilitation Medicine. 1993. Definition of Mild Traumatic Brain Injury. *Journal of Head Trauma Rehabilitation*, 8, 86–87.

Ommaya, A. K. and Gennarelli, T. A. 1974. Cerebral Concussion and Traumatic Unconsciousness: Correlation of Experimental and Clinical Observations on Blunt Head Injuries. *Brain*, 97, 633–654.

Resnick, P. J. 1994. Malingering. In Rosner, R. (Ed.) *Principles and Practice of Forensic Psychiatry*. New York: Chapman & Hall, p. 417.

Rimel, R. W., Giordani, B., Barth, J. T., Boll, T. J., and Jane, J. A. 1981. Disability Caused by Minor Head Injury. *Neurosurgery*, 9, 221–228.

Ruff, R. M., Levin, H. S., and Marshall, L. F. 1986. Neurobehavioral Methods of Assessment and the Study of Outcome in Minor Head Injury. *Journal of Head Trauma Rehabilitation*, 1, 43–52.

Russell, W. R. and Smith, A. 1961. PTA in Closed-Head Injury. *Archives of Neurology*, 5, 16–29.

Sbordone, R. J. and Liter, J. C. 1995. Mild Traumatic Brain Injury Does Not Produce Post-Traumatic Stress Disorder. *Brain Injury*, 9, 405–412.

Sbordone, R. J., Seyranian, G., and Ruff, R. M. 1998. Are the Subjective Complaints of Traumatically Brain Injured Patients Reliable? *Brain Injury*, 12, 505–515.

Sosen, D. M., Sniezek, J. E., and Thurman, D. J. 1996. Incidence of Mild and Moderate Brain Injury in the United States, 1991. *Brain Injury*, 10, 47–54.

Stambrook, M., Moore, A. D., Peters, L. C., Deviaene, C., and Hawyrluk, G. A. 1990. Effects of Mild, Moderate and Severe Closed Head Injury on Long-Term Vocational Status. *Brain Injury*, 4, 183–190.

Stuss, D. T. 1995. A Sensible Approach to Mild Traumatic Brain Injury. *Neurology*, 45, 1251–1252.

Teasdale, G. and Jennett, B. 1974. Assessment of Coma and Impaired Consciousness: A Practical Scale. *Lancet*, ii, 81–84.

Uomoto, J. M. and Esselman, P. C. 1993. Traumatic Brain Injury and Chronic Pain: Differential Types and Rates by Head Injury Severity. *Archives of Physical Medicine and Rehabilitation*, 74, 61–64.

Yarnell, P. R. and Rossi, G. V. 1988. Minor Whiplash Injury with Major Debilitation. *Brain Injury*, 2, 255–258.

8 Severe Traumatic Brain Injuries and Seizures

FOCAL BRAIN INJURY

Focal brain injury usually refers to a contusion or damage to the surface of the brain that contains the brain cells that regulate our behavior, cognition, and emotions. Contusions frequently occur after an individual sustains a blow to the head, which causes the skull to bend inward and strike the surface of the brain beneath the point of impact (coup contusion), whereas contusions to the brain opposite the site of impact are known as contrecoup contusions. Blows to the front of the head will typically produce coup contusions, while blows to the back of the head will typically produce contrecoup contusions to the anterior frontal and temporal lobes.

Irrespective of the site of head impact, postmortem computed tomography (CT) studies of cerebral contusions have shown that the prefrontal and anterior temporal lobes of the brain are most likely to be damaged as a result of anomalies within the skull (i.e., the bony surfaces on the anterior portions of the skull base tend to be rough and jagged in contrast to the relatively smooth bony surfaces on the posterior skull base). In general, when the area of the brain that has been contused becomes swollen and hemorrhagic, this damage can often be seen on a CT scan. After the brain has been contused, the brain cells, which have been damaged, begin to die, a process known as necrosis that may continue for up to a week. After a few months, a scar will often develop on the surface of the brain, which can result in the development of seizure disorder (see Figure 8.1).

THE EFFECTS OF DAMAGE CAUSED BY CONTUSIONS TO THE PREFRONTAL CORTEX

Individuals who sustain extensive prefrontal lobe damage frequently exhibit the following neuro-behavioral symptoms: a dramatic change in their personality; an inability to regulate their behavior and emotions; loss of initiative, curiosity, exploratory behavior, motivation, creativity, and sex drive; an inability to organize their thoughts, plan, remain on task, monitor their actions, solve problems, recognize their mistakes, or rectify them when they are made aware of them; impaired social behavior; inflexible thinking; poor judgment; impulsivity; egocentricity; apathy; an inability to show affection or feel compassion toward others; use of crude and coarse language in inappropriate circumstances; lack of plans or concern for future events; an inability to profit from experience; confabulation when they are asked to recall recent information; perseverative behavior (Stuss and Benson, 1986).

UNDERSTANDING THE ROLE OF THE PREFRONTAL CORTEX ON BEHAVIOR

The prefrontal cortex is not homogenous since different areas serve different behavioral and cognitive functions. This occurs as the result of the connections these different areas have with specific cortical and subcortical structures in the brain that modulate these functions. The prefrontal lobes can be divided into three functionally specialized regions: orbitofrontal, dorsolateral, and medial. The cognitive and neurobehavioral effects of contusions to these surfaces of the brain are discussed below (Figure 8.2).

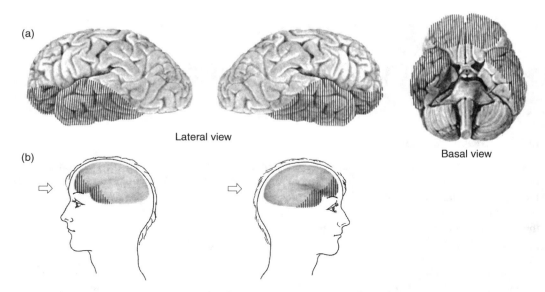

FIGURE 8.1 (a) Regions (shaded) of the cerebral hemispheres most often damaged when cerebral contusions occur. (b) Demonstration of how a blow (arrow) to the forehead or occiput can produce a cerebral contusion of the frontal and temporal lobes. Left: The blow directly damages the brain (coup injury). Right: The blow causes the brain to be compressed forward, producing a contrecoup injury. (*Source:* Kolb, B. and Whishaw, I. Q. 1996. *Fundamentals of Human Neuropsychology*. New York: W. H. Freeman and Company, p. 572. With permission.)

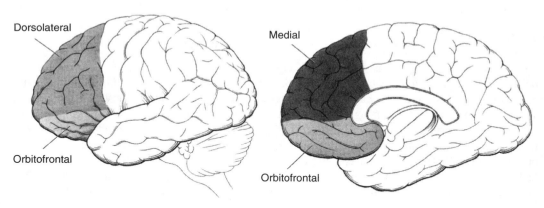

FIGURE 8.2 Location of lesions in the three classical frontal lobe syndromes — dorsolateral, medial, and orbitofrontal. (*Source:* Devinsky, O. and D'Esposito, M. 2004. *Neurology of Cognitive and Behavioral Disorders*. New York: Oxford, p. 314. With permission.)

CONTUSIONS OF THE LATERAL ORBITAL FRONTAL LOBES

Contusions to the lateral orbital frontal lobes produce the following neurobehavioral symptoms: a dramatic change in personality (which is reported by significant others but not by the patient); an inability to control their behavior and regulate their emotions; poor anger management; rapid mood swings; poor judgment; antisocial behavior; loss of social tact; an inability to empathize with others; marked egocentricity; frequent use of crude and course language; inappropriate social comments; poor frustration tolerance; insensitivity to the needs and welfare of others; impulsivity.

Individuals who have sustained such injuries typically have a poor awareness of these symptoms, particularly the effect that their symptoms have on others. They usually will only complain of their physical symptoms (e.g., headache, orthopedic problems). Their performance on standardized neuropsychological tests is often normal, particularly on IQ tests since this region of the brain primarily regulates our behavior and emotions, and only plays a minimal role in our intellectual and cognitive functioning.

While individuals who sustain lateral orbital frontal lobe contusions may create significant problems at home, school, or at work, the etiology of their symptoms may not be recognized by health care professionals. For example, these individuals are unlikely to complain of any cognitive or psychological difficulties or exhibit many of the above neurobehavioral symptoms when they are seen in highly structured settings such as in a physician's or attorney's office. Because of their poor neurobehavioral symptom awareness, they are unlikely to seek out psychological or psychiatric treatment or the services of an attorney. They are usually unwilling to attend brain rehabilitation programs even when it has been established that the etiology of their symptoms is the result of a brain injury since they fail to recognize their symptoms and do not see themselves in need of such services.

When these individuals return to work or school, their neurobehavioral symptoms typically create problems for their coworkers, supervisors, teachers, or other students, which often results in job termination, or suspension from school. If they are married, their neurobehavioral symptoms usually create significant marital problems, which often result in separation and divorce. Mental health professionals may not recognize the relationship between the patient's orbitofrontal lobe injury and neurobehavioral symptoms, particularly if the patient's mental status examination and neuropsychological test scores are normal. Neurologists may also not recognize the etiology of these patient's symptoms if the patient's neuroimaging studies and neurological examinations are normal.

Many neuropsychologists are unaware of the specific role that the lateral orbitofrontal lobes play in the regulation of our emotions and behavior. For example, they typically administer standardized neuropsychological tests to these patients in highly structured settings, which often do not reveal any abnormalities. On the basis of their test results, neuropsychologists often conclude that either the patient has not sustained a brain injury, or no longer has residual cognitive deficits from their brain injury, even though the patient's significant others and family (who are often not interviewed) continue to observe and remain troubled by the patient's neurobehavioral symptoms.

Case Example

A college professor, who had gone to school at an Ivy League University, arrived on time for his scheduled appointment. He had sustained a closed head injury a year ago as a result of striking his head on the asphalt after falling 12 ft from a ladder. He had been referred for neuropsychological testing because of marked changes in his behavior after this accident. When he arrived for his appointment, he denied any cognitive difficulties or emotional problems. His wife who accompanied him described him as having "completely changed" since the accident. Specifically, she observed that he got irritated very easily, cursed a great deal around others including their young children, exhibited rapid mood swings, seemed insensitive to her needs and the needs of their children, was no longer interested in having sex with her, was no longer affectionate toward her or their children, acted inappropriately in social settings, and had become very egocentric. Neuropsychological testing revealed no evidence of any cognitive deficits or psychological problems. The neuropsychologist failed to recognize the cause of the patient's symptoms and instead suspected that this patient had a bipolar disorder and referred the patient to a psychiatrist, who placed this patient on a variety of psychiatric medications that did not improve the patient's symptoms.

EFFECTS OF MEDIAL FRONTAL CONTUSIONS

The medial surfaces of the frontal lobes (the area between the cerebral hemispheres) receive inputs from the ascending reticular activating system in the brain stem. This system prepares the brain for emergencies and plays a major role in arousing and alerting the cerebral cortex of the arrival of important information about events that are occurring in the environment. Contusions of the medial frontal lobes can produce the following neurobehavioral symptoms: apathy; lack of drive or motivation; indifference to their surroundings; loss of initiative; loss of pleasure from the environment (anhedonia); pseudodepression (they may appear depressed even though they are not depressed); diminished social involvement; reduced communications; psychomotor retardation; changes in eating habits and food preferences; loss of sex drive; loss of curiosity; obsessive–compulsive behavior characterized by a compulsive need to clean their room or home and keep everthing in its designated place.

These individuals are often misdiagnosed as lazy or depressed and may even be placed on antidepressant medications. More extensive damage to the medial frontal lobes can produce akinetic mutism, a mute state characterized by a lack of spontaneous movement, sparse verbalizations, and a lack of responsiveness to the environment (Cummings and Mega, 2003).

EFFECTS OF DORSOLATERAL FRONTAL LOBE CONTUSIONS

Individuals who sustain contusions to the dorsolateral frontal lobes frequently exhibit the following neurobehavioral symptoms: executive dysfunction (they are unable to plan, organize, initiate, regulate, or monitor their behavior); easy distractibility; difficulty completing tasks even though they recognize the importance of completing such tasks; circumstantial and tangential thinking; significant deficits in their abstract thinking, conceptual, and problem-solving skills; an inability to attend to more than one activity at a time; perseverative behavior; poor judgment; inability to learn from experience; confabulated recall of recent or remote events.

These symptoms often may not be apparent when these individuals are observed in highly structured and familiar settings. They often perform well on IQ and many standardized neuropsychological tests and measures. When they are given tasks to perform that adequately challenge their executive functions they often perform poorly. Regardless of the tests they are administered, the best way to evaluate their cognitive functioning is to interview their significant others and observe how they function in complex, unstructured, and novel settings.

EFFECTS OF CONTUSIONS OF THE SURFACE OF THE TEMPORAL LOBES

Contusions of the surface of the temporal lobes can produce the following neurobehavioral symptoms: sudden outbursts of anger following relatively mild provocations or stress; memory difficulties for recent events; psychiatric disturbances such as depression and hallucinations; rapid mood swings; epileptic seizures (Saul, 1993).

PENETRATING BRAIN INJURIES

Bullets fired from rifles or handguns at high velocities can penetrate the skull and produce extensive tissue damage for a considerable distance around the missile tract. If the missile penetrates the lower levels of the brain stem, death is usually spontaneous since this region plays a major role in controlling respiration and cardiac activity. In many cases, intracranial bleeding and rising pressure within the skull occur as a result of traumatized brain tissue swelling. The majority of patients who sustain penetrating missile wounds become comatose (see case history below for a notable exception). The mortality rate caused by missile injuries to the brain (approximately 88%) is more than twice the mortality rate that occurs following blunt head trauma (Adams et al., 1997).

If the patient does not die, he or she is likely to pass through an initial stage of stupor, followed by confusion with amnesia. Patients who sustain penetrating missile wounds typically exhibit the following neurobehavioral symptoms: significant cognitive impairments; difficulty with recent memory; slow thinking; indifference; concentration difficulties; poor judgment; emotional lability; rapid fatigue; focal neurological deficits (similar to those seen following a stroke); focal seizures.

Case History: A Classic Case of Penetrating Frontal Lobe Injury

In 1848, Phineas Gage, a 25-year-old railroad construction foreman, was the victim of a bizarre accident. In order to lay new rail tracks, it was necessary to level the ground by controlled blasting. Gage was in charge of the detonations. Holes were drilled in the stone and partially filled with explosive powder. The powder was covered with sand. A fuse and tamping iron were used to trigger an explosion into the rock. On the day of the accident, Gage began tamping directly over the powder before his assistant could cover it with sand. There was a powerful explosion that hurled the fine pointed 3 cm thick and 109 cm long tamping iron through his face, frontal skull and lobe and into the sky. Gage, was momentarily stunned, but was not rendered unconscious. He was able to talk and walked away with assistance from his crew.

Gage survived but underwent a profound personality change. He had been a responsible, intelligent, church-going family man. Months after the accident, Gage was as intelligent as before his injury, and there was no impairment of movement or speech. Memory and new learning were intact. On the other hand, he had become capricious and irreverent with no respect for social conventions. His employer dismissed him because he could not be trusted and had lost his sense of responsibility. His profanity was particularly offensive. His friends stated that he was no longer Gage.

Damasio et al. (1994) reported that they were able to reconstruct the trajectory of the tamping iron by measuring Gage's surviving skull and using neuroimaging techniques. They found that the motor cortex, Broca's speech area, and the dorsolateral frontal regions were spared. They found that the damage primarily involved the medial orbital (inferior) regions of both frontal lobes. These areas are part of a neuronal circuit with reciprocal connections to subcortical structures such as the amygdala and hypothalamus, which control emotional regulation, social cognition, and behavior. In addition to confirming the important functional role of the orbital frontal region in emotion and social comportment, this classic case shows that it is possible for an individual to sustain a severe penetrating anterior frontal contusional injury with no significant loss of consciousness or residual motor and speech deficits.

DIFFUSE AXONAL BRAIN INJURIES

Diffuse axonal brain damage (damage to nerve fibers in the brain white matter) usually occurs when the head and brain of an individual is subjected to rapid acceleration–deceleration forces following a high-speed motor vehicle accident. This damage is more likely to occur if the vehicle strikes an immovable object or the individual is ejected from the vehicle. It can also occur with a fall from a significant height. These acceleration–deceleration forces, particularly when they are rotational rather than linear, cause a shearing of nerve fibers and adjacent small blood vessels in the midbrain, corpus callosum, and deep hemispheric white matter, which results in multiple microhemorrhages throughout the brain. Shearing forces can also produce widespread damage to subcortical brain structures.

Diffuse axonal injury (DAI) typically results in acute and chronic disturbances of consciousness (e.g., coma), vestibular dysfunction, and a variety of motor impairments. Because of the diffuse damage, various and widespread regions of the brain are no longer able to function or communicate with each other. As a result, patients who sustain DAI may remain in a prolonged coma or in a vegetative state. Ironically, this is most likely to occur when the patient does not sustain a skull fracture (Joseph, 1996). Brain CT scans are often unable to detect DAI; however, newer brain magnetic resonance imaging (MRI) techniques can frequently visualize the resulting blood breakdown products as areas of altered signal intensity, even up to a year or more after a severe injury (Saul, 1993). Patients who sustain severe diffuse axonal brain damage typically exhibit the following neurobehavioral symptoms that can often be recognized by nonmedical personnel: significant attention and concentration deficits; language deficits (particularly word-finding difficulties); impaired problem-solving skills; deficits on tasks that assess learning and recent memory; impaired speed of cognitive processing.

These impairments will frequently compromise the patient's ability to return to the job he or she held at the time of their injury, engage in competitive employment, continue with their academic studies, or perform household activities.

SECONDARY BRAIN DAMAGE

The more severe the initial brain injury, the greater the likelihood that the patient will develop secondary brain damage, which develops over a period of hours, days, or weeks after the initial brain insult. Among the major causes of secondary brain injury are neurochemical changes that alter cerebral metabolism and blood flow. These include the release of excitatory amino acids, endogenous opioids, acetylcholine, and monoamine neurotransmitters. Ionic changes, such as the intracellular influx of calcium and magnesium with a corresponding efflux of potassium, and the release of oxygen-free radicals further accelerate this process and lead to cellular damage and even death. Future research is likely to focus on the early identification of these auto-destructive agents and the development of neuroprotective compounds to prevent or attenuate this neurochemical pathologic cascade after a brain injury (Marion, 1998). See Table 8.1 for further mechanisms of traumatic brain injury (TBI).

INTRACRANIAL HEMATOMA

Regardless of the severity of the initial brain injury, the likelihood of a patient's sustaining an intracranial hematoma is considerable. The classic course of an intracranial hematoma is a short period of unconsciousness, regaining consciousness, and then a secondary loss of consciousness due to pressure on the brain by an expanding hematoma within the space enclosed by the skull. If this hematoma remains undetected and untreated (by neurosurgical intervention or medications), the patient is likely to exhibit a progressive deterioration of neurological functioning, followed by decreased respiratory cardiovascular function and death.

An *intracranial hematoma* causes a displacement and distortion of the brain away from the expanding hematoma. This results in neurological impairment of contralateral motor and sensory function. As this process continues, herniation of the brain through the dura (the outer covering membrane) can occur. In some cases, an intracranial hematoma in the medial portion of the temporal lobe will produce a herniation of the lobe against the tentorium cerebelli (a rigid dural membrane separating the middle and posterior fossa of the skull), compressing the descending motor fibers in the midbrain and resulting in progressive motor dysfunction. As the process of herniation and brain stem compression continues, the reticular activating system in the upper stem (which

TABLE 8.1
Mechanisms of TBI

Primary damage
   Diffuse axonal shearing injury (DAI), maximal gray–white matter junction, midbrain reticular formation, and
     corpus callosum
   Multiple microscopic hemorrhages
   Subarachnoid hemorrhage
   Cortical contusions — coup injury at site of trauma; most common sites of contrecoup injury — orbitofrontal
     region, frontal and temporal polar areas
   Depressed skull fracture
Primary or secondary damage
   Subdural hematoma
   Epidural hematoma
   Intracerebral hemorrhage (lobar or basal ganglia)
Secondary damage
   Release excitatory neurotransmitters and free radicals, cellular calcium influx, activation of destructive
     enzymes with resulting cell death
   Cerebral hypoxia and ischemia, hypotension, resulting in cerebral infarction, frequently in posterior cerebral
     artery distribution
   Increased intracranial pressure from cerebral edema or expanding hematoma with resulting brain stem
     herniation
   Hydrocephalus — primarily obstructive
   Seizures — generalized and partial (simple or complex) type
   Infection — complication of skull fracture or surgery
   Metabolic encephalopathy — hypoglycemia, hyponatremia (low sodium)
   Endocrinopathy — pituitary or hypothalamic injury

keeps us alert and awake) becomes dysfunctional, resulting in a loss of consciousness. Invariably, the oculomotor nerve also becomes compressed, resulting in a third-nerve palsy. The pupil on the same side of the lesion becomes fixed, dilated, and unresponsive to a bright beam of light. With further herniation, there is greater compression of the lower part of the brain stem, resulting in changes in the patient's respiration and blood pressure, leading to death. Although such severe consequences may be averted through neurosurgical intervention, the patient may often be left with a severe amnestic (memory) disorder as a result of tentorial compression of the posterior cerebral artery and hippocampal infarction (Miller, 1983; Long, 1989).

There are several types of intracranial hematomas. A hematoma within the brain substance is referred to as an *intracerebral hematoma*. The force of the impact following TBI can also cause a rupture of the veins traversing the space between the dural membrane lining the skull and the pia-arachnoid membranes covering the brain surface. This venous bleeding produces a *subdural hematoma*. A blow, forceful enough to cause a skull fracture, often causes arterial shearing and an *epidural hematoma* (a clot within the potential space external to the dura). As arterial bleeding is faster and more forceful than venous, an epidural hematoma expands rapidly and is of greater danger to the patient. All three varieties of hematoma, however, can cause a potentially fatal mass effect with compression of the gyri, shift of midline structures, and herniation as outlined above. The subarachnoid space between the arachnoid and the underlying brain normally contains cerebrospinal fluid (CSF). Cranial trauma frequently produces subarachnoid hemorrhage, turning the CSF bloody. Meningitis, an infection predominantly in the subarachnoid space, which produces cloudy, purulent CSF, can also occur.

Occasionally, the hematoma may not be initially recognized by the emergency room physician, particularly if there was no loss of consciousness and the patient's behavior in the emergency room appears relatively normal. As a consequence, patients may be sent home from the emergency room without being given head injury precautions. These precautions include initial monitoring of the patient's behavior on an hourly basis, and checking for nausea, vomiting, or changes in the patient's neurological functioning. These patients should also be awakened every hour to ensure that their neurological status has not changed. If the patient cannot be aroused, his or her neurological status may have been compromised as a result of secondary brain damage due to brain-stem compression, mandating an immediate return to the hospital for reevaluation.

BRAIN SWELLING

Brain swelling, also known as cerebral edema, is a common occurrence following severe brain trauma and can be complicated by such factors as secondary ischemia or hypoxia. Two causal mechanisms have been postulated: dilatation of the cerebral vasculature, which increases the brain blood volume, and an increase in the brain's water content following cerebral contusions and related focal injuries. Diffuse swelling of the brain with a global increase in blood volume is two to five times more common in children than in adults and places them at increased risk for secondary intracranial hypertension and herniation.

ELEVATED INTRACRANIAL PRESSURE

As a result of intracranial hemorrhaging and brain swelling within the skull, the patient's intracranial pressure is typically elevated. Many neurosurgeons will insert an intracranial pressure monitor into the brain of the comatose, brain-injured patient to monitor intracranial pressure, because significant elevations in intracranial pressure will significantly reduce cerebral blood flow, leading to hypoxia and death. In a normal adult, the intracranial pressure should be between 0 and 10 mmHg while the patient is lying supine. A pressure greater than 20 mmHg falls into the abnormal range. When the intracranial pressure reaches 40 mmHg, the patient's neurological functioning has been seriously compromised and the likely result is death (Miller, 1983). Medical treatment, including the use of medications, may be used to reduce swelling. Acute care records should be reviewed for symptoms of increased intracranial pressure.

CEREBRAL HYPOXIA

The vast majority of patients who sustain severe TBIs are likely to experience hypoxic brain damage as a result of cerebral ischemia (a reduction in the amount of blood perfusing the brain). This frequently occurs as a result of brain swelling and elevated intracranial pressure. It is exceedingly common and, in postmortem examination, was found to be widespread in 91% of 151 patients who had died from severe head injuries (Graham et al., 1978). Other causes of ischemia include arterial hypotension and hypoxemia (a reduction in the oxygen-carrying capacity of the brain following injury), cerebral vasospasm, and disruption of cerebrovascular autoregulation. While ischemic damage is widespread, it occurs most commonly in the hippocampi, basal ganglia, and the watershed zones, which are located between the major cerebral arteries (Miller, 1983).

ARTERIAL HYPOXEMIA

Arterial hypoxemia is the most common insult seen in severely head-injured patients upon their arrival in the emergency room. Whenever the level of arterial partial oxygen pressure (pO_2) falls below 60 mmHg, the amount of oxygen that can be carried in the blood falls dramatically. While the brain attempts to compensate for this by cerebral vasodilatation, this mechanism is frequently impaired as a result of the TBI. The subsequent marked reduction in oxygen to the most severely damaged parts of the brain results in hypoxic injury and necrosis (tissue death) in these areas (Miller, 1983). Patients who sustain severe TBIs are also vulnerable to arterial hypotension, a reduction of systemic blood pressure, which in turn typically produces a reduction in cerebral blood flow.

HYDROCEPHALUS

Hydrocephalus (an abnormal dilation of the cerebral ventricles) frequently occurs following intra-cranial and subarachnoid hemorrhage, which tends to clog up the arachnoid villi and prevent cerebrospinal fluid from exiting the brain. When this occurs, the brain continues to produce cerebrospinal fluid, which causes the cerebral ventricles to dilate and compress the brain. The result-ing pattern of neurological dysfunction is initially characterized by mental confusion, memory loss, and gait and balance impairment with frequent falls. Bladder and bowel incontinence occurs at a later stage. Neurosurgical intervention to place a ventriculo-peritoneal shunt is often required. In many cases, particularly 6 to 12 months postinjury, the ventricles of the brain will become dilated as a result of a loss of brain white matter following a TBI. Thus, the presence of dilated ventricles posttrauma provides strong evidence that the patient had sustained a severe brain injury. This dilatation usually will be even more evident after a year has passed.

INTRACRANIAL INFECTIONS

Intracranial infections are not uncommon and frequently arise following skull fractures, particu-larly when the dural membrane has been torn or injured. This frequently results in a leakage of cerebrospinal fluid through the nasal septum (rhinorrhea) or ear canal (otorrhea). If this condi-tion is not recognized and treated, the patient is likely to develop an intracranial infection such as meningitis or encephalitis or brain abscess, severe complications that can result in further brain damage and increased morbidity.

POSTTRAUMATIC EPILEPSY

Epilepsy can be divided into two major categories: idiopathic and symptomatic. In idiopathic epilepsy, some form of inherited mechanism is believed to produce a propensity for low seizure thresholds in the brain. In the symptomatic type, the seizures result from some type of injury or disease that occurs after birth, for example, head trauma, brain tumors, meningitis, vascular lesions, or cerebral hypoxia. Some patients may have a predisposition to develop seizures following a brain insult. Seizures can be classified as generalized or partial (see Table 8.2).

GENERALIZED SEIZURES

Generalized seizures are accompanied by a loss of consciousness or a transient lapse of conscious-ness. They include attacks characterized by convulsive movements: myoclonic and clonic seizures (sudden jerks of limbs or body), tonic attacks (stiffening of limbs or trunk), and tonic–clonic seizures (often referred to as grand mal seizures). Also included in this category are petit mal or absence seizures, which consist of frequent and brief lapses of conscious awareness, usually taking the form of staring spells, which may be unnoticed by observers. If accompanied by jerks or other involuntary movements, they are termed atypical absence seizures.

PARTIAL SEIZURES

Partial seizures can be further subdivided into seizures with no impairment of consciousness (partial seizures with elementary symptomatology) and seizures that are accompanied by alterations of

TABLE 8.2
Classification of Seizures

Generalized seizures
  Tonic–clonic (grand mal)
  Absence (petit mal)
  Atypical absence
  Myoclonic
Partial (focal) seizures
  Simple partial (consciousness unimpaired)
  Complex partial (consciousness impaired)
  Temporal lobe origin (psychomotor)
  Nontemporal origin — frontal, parietal, occipital
  Partial seizures with secondary generalization — expressed as tonic–clonic seizures

TABLE 8.3
Clinical Features of Temporal Lobe Complex Partial Seizures

I. An aura (warning) often precedes the seizure. Common auras include the following types of sensory or cognitive experiences:
   a. Autonomic — epigastric distress
   b. Sensory illusions and hallucinations — unpleasant smell, metallic taste, altered object size or shape, distorted sounds and tactile sensations, altered perception of time and movement
   c. Psychic or cognitive — *deja* and *jamais vu* (flashback feeling of familiarity or unfamiliarity), depersonalization and derealization (body and environmental feeling of unreality), repetitive thoughts
II. The seizure — an altered state of consciousness, usually 60 to 90 s in total duration. One or more of the following may be observed:
   a. Motionless stare
   b. Oral motor automatisms — chewing, lip smacking
   c. More complex motor automatisms — verbalizations, repetitive hand movements, unbuttoning clothes, abnormal posturing of upper limbs, looking around, whole body movements
III. Postictal confusion with gradual recovery; amnesia for above events, except for the aura that can often be recalled

consciousness (partial seizures with complex symptomatology). A partial or focal seizure may spread from a discrete cortical region to the brain stem, resulting in a generalized convulsion.

Partial complex seizures of temporal origin frequently begin with a warning or aura, only a few seconds in duration. Temporal auras include a subjective feeling of overwhelming fear, forced thinking, and complex visual, auditory, or olfactory hallucinations. Following the aura, changes can be observed in the patient's facial expression (e.g., a blank stare) and complex motor automatisms (stereotypic motor behaviors such as lip smacking, chewing, or gestures). The seizures rarely last more than a minute or two and are followed by a variable period of mental confusion and lethargy (see Table 8.3). Except for the aura, patients are amnestic for these episodes. Although patients generally do not lose consciousness during partial seizures, they are typically unable to respond to their environment in a fully purposeful and meaningful fashion. For example, during a partial seizure, the patient may be unable to respond when called by name, to a red light, or even to a pedestrian crossing the street in front of an automobile driven by the patient.

Seizures of frontal origin exhibit complex motor activity such as kicking, thrashing, vocalizations, genital manipulation, head–eye deviation and unilateral upper extremity posturing. They are usually brief and frequently occur in clusters. Frontal seizures can be easily confused with psychogenic seizures, which typically are precipitated by stress or occur in specific settings, tend to have a more gradual onset, and are more prolonged (Kotagal, 1993).

INCIDENCE OF POSTTRAUMATIC EPILEPSY

Posttraumatic epilepsy can occur at any time following a head injury. While the overall incidence of posttraumatic epilepsy has been reported to be 5%, patients who sustain skull fractures, prominent parietal and temporal lobe damage, intracranial hematoma, intracranial infections, or penetrating injuries to the brain tend to have a much higher incidence (over 40%) of posttraumatic epilepsy (Long, 1989). The likelihood of a patient's developing late-onset posttraumatic epilepsy can be calculated on the basis of three major factors: sustaining an acute intracranial hematoma, having epilepsy during the first week postinjury and sustaining a depressed skull fracture. For patients who had developed an intracranial hematoma within 2 weeks of their accident, the risk of posttraumatic epilepsy was found to be approximately 35% over the subsequent 4 years. Approximately 25% of the patients who develop seizures during the first week after an accident are likely to develop seizures in the future. Depending on these factors, the risk of posttraumatic epilepsy can range from less than 3% to greater than 60% (Jennett, 1975).

Posttraumatic epilepsy can occur in any of the forms described above. Approximately half of the patients develop classic grand mal or generalized seizures, which are potentially hazardous, particularly if the patient is engaged in driving a motor vehicle or working at heights. These highly salient events will typically be noticed by others, who frequently call for medical assistance. Approximately 20% of the patients with posttraumatic partial complex seizures of temporal origin may exhibit subtle behavioral changes that may not be recognizable to an external observer. For example, they may stare off into space, develop a sudden fear or feel detached from their surroundings. Other patients may develop *deja vu* experiences (feeling that an experience has happened before) or olfactory hallucinations (experiencing the smell of rotten eggs or another specific odor). Patients may exhibit complex automatisms, such as saluting, crossing a room, or repeating certain phrases. These behaviors may last from a few seconds to 90 s or so and are typically not recognized as being manifestations of a seizure disorder. Some patients, during the confusional state following one or more temporal lobe seizures, may execute a longer series of more complex activities, such as ending up in a restaurant they never intended to go to without any recollection of how they got there (epileptic fugue). Many of these individuals may be seen as neurotic and, in some cases, even psychotic because of the relative bizarreness of the behavioral manifestations of their seizure disorder (Jennett, 1975).

DIAGNOSIS OF SEIZURES

It should be recognized that all epileptic seizures, regardless of type, originate in the brain. The diagnosis of a seizure disorder is typically made by a neurologist. It is ideally based on an actually observed seizure, but far more commonly the clinical diagnosis depends on the description of a typical episode by family members or other witnesses, if they are considered to be reliable informants. An impairment of consciousness, or seizure-like activity, can also be produced by a variety of causes that lie outside of the brain such as vasovagal syncopal episodes, cardiac arrhythmias, transient ischemic attacks (TIAs), migraine headaches, hypoglycemia, and dissociative psychological or emotional states (pseudoseizures). To rule out seizures of noncerebral origin, it is essential that the patient undergoes a careful neurological examination, including serial electroencephalograms (EEGs). These EEGs should be performed during sleep, or preferably in the morning following a night of sleep deprivation.

A normal interictal (between seizures) EEG is not uncommon in patients with epilepsy. Even the presence of interictal epileptiform activity does not confirm the diagnosis, since it occurs in 1 to 2% of the normal population. Furthermore, patients with psychogenic seizures may have true epileptic seizures, so that the presence of abnormal EEG discharges does not prove that all seizures are epileptic. Effective differentiation in such cases often requires simultaneous video–EEG monitoring. A single seizure episode, furthermore, could be due to such factors as sleep deprivation, fasting, or drug or alcohol withdrawal. If any of these factors is present, if there is no evidence of neurological disease, and if the EEGs reveal no evidence of epileptiform activity, the diagnosis of epilepsy should be seriously questioned. A patient's response to antiepileptic drug treatment can also be helpful in establishing the diagnosis of epilepsy, although this could be due to "placebo" or the mild antidepressant effects of the medication (e.g., Tegretol®) in patients with pseudoseizures of psychogenic etiology (Pedley and Emerson, 1991).

One difficulty in evaluating patients suspected of having epilepsy is that the EEG is a relatively crude neurophysiological instrument, which records the electrical activity of the brain through the thick insulating tissues of the head (hair, scalp, bones, blood vessels, etc.) (Kligman and Goldberg, 1975). It is also handicapped by often being unable to detect electrical potentials that are located more than a few millimeters from the most superficial layers of the brain. An additional problem is that EEG recordings are usually made for 30 min or less. Thus, the EEG only samples a relatively small portion of the electrical activity of a 24-h day (Dodrill, 1981). To increase the likelihood of obtaining epileptiform activity, multiple and more prolonged EEG recordings should be obtained. They should also include activating procedures such as hyperventilation, photic stimulation, sleep deprivation, and, in some cases, special electrode placements for improved detection of deep temporal and frontal lobe discharges.

BEHAVIORAL AND PSYCHOLOGICAL MANIFESTATIONS OF TEMPORAL AND FRONTAL LOBE SEIZURES

Patients who develop temporal lobe seizures (partial complex seizures that originate in one of the temporal lobes) are likely to exhibit a wide range of psychiatric and psychological problems. Research studies (Bear et al., 1982) have shown that patients with temporal lobe epilepsy, in contrast to patients with functional psychiatric disorders, tend to exhibit a significantly greater frequency of behaviors such as excessive interpersonal clinging (viscosity), repetitive preoccupation with peripheral details (circumstantiality), religious and philosophical preoccupations, humorless sobriety, a tendency toward paranoid overinterpretation, and excessive moralistic concerns. They have a predilection for interictal aggressive behavior and for acts of violence. Unlike patients with character or antisocial personality disorders, they are likely to accept responsibility for their violent outbursts and will often exhibit severe remorse and guilt following these outbursts. Nevertheless, most epileptic patients are not violent. Directed violence as a manifestation of a seizure itself is extremely rare and interictal violence may not be related to epilepsy but to other factors, including structural brain damage, anticonvulsant medications, and social variables (Devinsky, 1992).

EPILEPTIC SPECTRUM DISORDER

During the past decade, some neuropsychiatrists and neuropsychologists have described a new clinical syndrome, which has been termed *epileptic spectrum disorder* (ESD). It consists of multiple episodes of cognitive, affective, and sensory symptoms resembling partial seizures, which occur in the context of marked affective lability and dysthymia (chronic depression). Roberts (1999) contends that ESD occurs after mild to moderate TBIs and may account for the unexpected clinically poor outcome in cases of persistent postconcussive syndrome. Individuals with ESD have been found to exhibit multiple spells that may alternate with periods of relative normality or with intense episodic mood swings, episodic psychosensory hallucinations and cognitive dysfunction, unusual nocturnal phenomena, and frequent suicidal ideation or attempts. Nearly all of these patients had abnormal but not clearly epileptiform discharges on their EEGs, suggesting that ESD may be a variant of complex partial seizures.

Intermittent Explosive Disorder

Another related syndrome, previously termed episodic dyscontrol and more recently labeled intermittent explosive disorder (IED), has been reported to have the following characteristics: discrete episodes of loss of control of aggressive impulses resulting in serious assault or property damage, behavior grossly disproportionate to any precipitating stressor, absence of impulsivity or aggressiveness between episodes, and absence of any contributing antisocial personality disorder or psychosis. This poorly defined syndrome groups together episodically violent behaviors that result from numerous disorders, including TBIs. EEG abnormalities, including epileptiform discharges, have been found in such patients. As with ESD, these patients often improve when placed on anticonvulsant medication. Most neurologists, however, have generally rejected claims that ESD and IED represent forms of partial epilepsy. The mood-elevating properties of the anticonvulsants, which have been used to treat these patients, might explain their observed improvement. Engel (1989) contends that directed aggressive behavior in clear consciousness cannot be considered an epileptic seizure, even in a patient with chronic epilepsy, and that epilepsy is not a valid defense for premeditated or directed acts of violence.

Table 8.4 lists the categories of major neuropsychiatric disorders associated with aggression. Included are focal disorders that involve frontal–limbic circuits and may precipitate partial complex seizures with interictal or postictal aggression. Violent behavior can occur with delirium, dementia, mental retardation, or psychosis. Aggression associated with intermittent explosive disorder and with borderline or antisocial personality disorder must also be considered in the differential diagnosis.

TABLE 8.4
Neuropsychiatric Disorders Associated with Aggression

I. Focal disorders involving orbitofrontal lobe, anterior temporal lobe and hypothalamus resulting from cerebral trauma, stroke, tumors, abscess, or encephalitis
Aggressive behavior may appear in a postictal state with altered consciousness, reflecting an associated partial complex seizure disorder

II. Dementing disorders
Alzheimer's disease, Frontal-temporal dementia, Huntington's chorea, and other subcortical dementias
Frontal involvement may result in explosive rage; aggression occurs in context of general personality change

III. Delirium
May be associated with transitory ill-formed delusions and misperceptions

IV. Disorders associated with mental retardation
Self-mutilation seen in 15% of institutionalized mentally retarded

V. Psychotic disorders
More common in mania and paranoid syndromes; usually arises from delusional beliefs

VI. Substance abuse
Aggression may result from acute intoxication (alcohol, stimulants, PCP, and other recreational drugs) or chronic toxic encephalopathy

VII. Intermittent explosive disorders
Discrete episodes of unrestrained violence occurring in clear consciousness

VIII. Personality disorders
Antisocial. Associated with deceitfulness, irresponsibility, and lack of remorse
Borderline. Self-mutilation and deliberate self-harm associated with affective instability and chaotic interpersonal relationships

Source: Modified from Moriarty, J. 1997. In Trimble, M. and Cummings, J. L. (Eds.) *Contemporary Behavioral Neurology*. Boston: Butterworth-Heinemann, p. 154.

TBI IN CHILDREN

TBI is the primary cause of death in children and adolescents (Fenichel, 1988). Mild brain injury occurs in approximately nine out of ten children and adolescents (Kraus et al., 1987) who sustain a TBI. TBIs tend to occur in early childhood as a result of falls (e.g., from furniture, down flights of stairs, or out of windows). Older children are likely to sustain brain injuries as a result of falling from bicycles or playing sports. However, a significant but often unrecognized cause of brain injury in children is abuse. In adolescents, the most common causes are automobile and motorcycle accidents.

The infant's brain is less prone to sustaining cerebral contusions or lacerations than are the brains of older children and adults. This difference appears to be due to the relative immaturity of the infant skull and its smoother surfaces. However, as a result of its thinness and relatively unfused suture lines, it is more easily fractured and deformed (Shapiro and Smith, 1993). Furthermore, infants and young children may be less likely to develop diffuse axonal injuries since these injuries are seen more often in motor vehicle accidents than in falls. Damage to infants can also occur at birth as a result of physical forces on the head that occur as the neonate passes through the birth canal during the final stages of labor and the final extraction from the mother, particularly if the neonate is premature and the birth canal is not physiologically prepared for delivery. It can also occur if the baby is large and the birth canal is small. The use of forceps to extract the neonate during the final stages of delivery may occasionally fracture the skull and damage the underlying brain tissue.

NEUROPSYCHOLOGICAL STUDIES OF INFANTS AND CHILDREN

Neuropsychological studies that have evaluated infants and children who sustained brain trauma have noted that the IQ scores of these children were generally lower if they had been rendered comatose for at least 24 h (Levin and Eisenberg, 1979). Other investigators (e.g., Brink et al., 1970) found that children who were in coma for longer than a week had significantly lower IQ scores. Approximately two thirds of these children had IQs below 80. However, progressive improvement in IQ test performance has been noted to occur up to 5 years postinjury in children who sustained mild to moderately severe brain trauma. The most common cognitive difficulty following pediatric brain trauma appears to be with memory. Levin and Eisenberg (1979) found that verbal memory was particularly impaired in children who had sustained closed head injuries, particularly when the injuries affected primarily the left hemisphere. However, when the damage was restricted to the child's right hemisphere, these children performed poorly only on nonverbal tasks. Levin et al. (1994) found that children and adolescents who had sustained significant TBIs had deficits in their executive functions, which were highly correlated to the severity of their initial brain trauma. The incidence of psychiatric disorders in children who have sustained closed head injuries is twice as high as for children who have only physical handicaps (Seidel et al., 1975). Other investigators (e.g., Eide and Tysnes, 1992) have found that the behavioral functioning of children was most impaired if they had sustained multifocal bilateral lesions.

NEURODIAGNOSTIC STUDIES OF PATIENTS WITH TBIs

The EEG is a highly sensitive, but relatively nonspecific technique for detecting impairments in the functioning of the brain. It will reliably reflect normal changes in a patient's brain state that occur with relaxed wakefulness, heightened arousal, drowsiness, and sleep. However, it should be noted that any abnormal physiological insult to the brain, such as a drop in blood sugar following a missed meal, could alter the EEG. While the most distinctive EEG patterns occur in certain forms of epilepsy, abnormalities can be seen in individuals who are taking barbiturates or benzodiazepines, or have a prior history of encephalitis or hepatic encephalopathy. EEG abnormalities are most pronounced following acute and rapidly evolving injury to the surfaces of the brain, that is, the cerebral cortex. Damage to the deep brain structures may not be detected. The effectiveness of the EEG in evaluating patients who have sustained TBIs depends on an accurate interpretation of their recordings by a competent, experienced electroencephalographer, preferably a neurologist with EEG board certification.

Individuals who lack this experience may misinterpret eye movements or electrode artifacts as epileptiform discharges (seizure activity). Furthermore, a competent technician can identify and minimize such artifacts and make technical recording modifications, which can improve the accuracy of EEG interpretations. The EEG in patients who have sustained mild TBIs can neither support nor exclude the presence of brain dysfunction. For example, EEG abnormalities in patients who sustain mild TBIs, or who have a postconcussive syndrome, may not be related to the brain injury. Conversely, a normal EEG cannot rule out a significant brain injury. However, in severe TBIs, serial EEG recordings can be helpful during the acute stages to determine the extent and duration of abnormal brain functioning and the potential for recovery, allowing more accurate prediction of outcome (Tippin and Yamada, 1996).

EVOKED POTENTIALS

Evoked potentials (EPs) are generated in response to repetitive visual, auditory, or somatosensory (usually a low intensity pain) stimulus. Background activity and artifacts are suppressed and the desired signal is enhanced by computer-assisted averaging. Alterations in the normal timing and locations of these signals can indicate dysfunction in a specific sensory pathway, which can frequently identify the site of a causative focal lesion. The P300 EP is a positive wave appearing approximately 300 ms after the presentation of a rare target stimulus, interspersed with frequent nontarget stimuli. It is generated by multiple neuronal sources, including the frontal cortex and hippocampus. P300 abnormalities can reflect localized brain pathology. In general, however, the P300 should be regarded as a nonspecific measure of the speed and magnitude of cerebral information processing, which can be abnormal following a TBI, with a variety of acquired brain disorders, and in patients who are diagnosed with schizophrenia. Although EPs are helpful at times in predicting outcome during the acute stages of a severe TBI, they rarely provide useful information in patients with uncomplicated mild TBIs and postconcussive syndromes.

QUANTITATIVE EEG AND TOPOGRAPHICAL BRAIN MAPPING

Quantitative electroencephalography (QEEG) refers to a technique involving the display or analysis of EEG activity following computer conversion of the raw EEG signal into a series of numerical values. The summated digitized EEG activity over a number of short time periods (usually 48 s) can be displayed as a topographical map. Different colors are often used to show the voltage ranges (quantities) and scalp distributions of the various frequency bands making up the recorded EEG. The maps, in addition, offer the potential advantage of displaying statistical values, derived from the various and often numerous quantitative comparisons. There has been, however, no general consensus regarding the normal limits for any of the mapped values. Furthermore, QEEG recordings must be interpreted along with the routine EEG to detect artifacts and transient abnormalities, such as epileptic spikes that are not obvious on brain maps. At the present time, this technique should be used only by highly experienced electroencephalographers to provide additional information that can be correlated with the conventional EEG or EP records (Pedley and Emerson, 1991).

The American Academy of Neurology has discouraged the forensic use of QEEG as evidence of cerebral dysfunction in individuals suspected of having mild brain injury or a postconcussive syndrome. There are many reported examples of QEEG studies that have been flawed by poor technique, misinterpretation of sleep and medication effects as abnormalities and misapplication of statistical techniques (Tippin and Yamada, 1996).

In a recent review, Nuwer et al. (2005) found no evidence of any EEG or QEEG features that are unique to mild head injury. They also found that months and years after brain trauma, the relationship between the electrophysiologic findings of the EEG and QEEG and the patient's clinical symptoms is poor. Based on their review of the EEG and QEEG literature, they did not find any reliable diagnostic EEG signatures implicating brain damage as the cause of late signs and symptoms after blunt cranial trauma.

COMPUTED TOMOGRAPHY

In CT, a thin x-ray beam is attenuated by its transmission through the body tissue, reflecting the tissue's density, and is recorded. From different angles, the process is repeated with computer-assisted techniques until sufficient information is obtained to build up a series of images, which are cross-sectional representations of the scanned organ. For the brain, at least twelve 8-mm-thick sections are obtained in the horizontal plane. Images in other planes can also be reconstructed.

MAGNETIC RESONANCE IMAGING

MRI, unlike the CT, is an emission rather than a transmission technique. Instead of recording x-ray tissue transmission as occurs in the CT scan, the MRI detects the concentration and magnetic characteristics of certain atoms, usually hydrogen, in the scanned body region. The patient's body is enclosed in a strong magnetic field and intermittently subjected to radio signals. These radio signals are, in turn, emitted, recorded, and converted into images that reflect the atomic density of the tissue and its rate of decay. Table 8.5 lists the relative advantages of CT and MRI brain scans. CT is the preferred procedure in the ER with acutely ill and uncooperative patients, but MRI, despite its drawbacks, usually furnishes more information of diagnostic value (Wolpert, 1991).

CT and MRI studies of mild TBI patients usually do not demonstrate any major abnormalities or structural defects (Alexander, 1995). Individuals who sustain more severe brain injuries will usually exhibit abnormalities in the form of intracranial hemorrhages or cerebral contusions, edema, midline shifting of the intracranial contents, or herniation (Bigler, 1999). Acute neuroimaging studies can provide a baseline to monitor changes in the brain over time (Bigler, 1996). Individuals who have sustained severe TBIs are likely to exhibit a pattern of pathological changes after 6 months postinjury, usually manifested by increased width of the sulci that represents cortical atrophy, ventricular dilation, and the presence of white matter abnormalities, particularly near the gray–white matter interface. These findings are usually indicators of diffuse axonal injuries (Bigler, 1999). Bigler et al. (1997)

TABLE 8.5
Comparison of MRI and CT Brain Scans

Advantages of MRI over CT
  Finer resolution of brain structures with horizontal, sagittal, and coronal brain cuts
  Detecting pathology missed on CT (e.g., subcortical infarcts from small vessel disease, white
    matter plaques of multiple sclerosis, and lesions adjacent to bone, at base of brain, and in
    posterior fossa)
  Patient not exposed to radiation
Advantages of CT over MRI
  Shorter exposure time
  Simpler operation and maintenance
  Larger enclosure avoiding claustrophobia
  Procedure of choice with restless, uncooperative, and critically ill patients
  Detecting bone pathology and calcifications missed with MRI

have investigated pathological changes following TBI by quantifying the MRI. They have found that following moderate to severe brain injuries, there is a substantial volume loss of total brain parenchyma (tissue), which begins during the first few weeks postinjury and may continue for over 3 years.

Newer more sensitive MRI techniques allow better detection of focal damage resulting from TBI, vascular diseases, and multiple sclerosis. More powerful systems with 1.5 or greater Tesla (measure of magnetic field strength) improve the resolution of generated images with thinner contiguous sections. Hemosiderin (a blood breakdown product) deposits, resulting from small cerebral hemorrhages, can be detected a year or more after TBI. The addition of fluid-attenuated inversion recovery (FLAIR) sequences on the MRI permits the detection of lesions adjacent to the ventricles and other CSF spaces. Diffusion tensor imaging (DTI) uses the speed of water diffusion to detect the direction and integrity of cerebral white matter fiber tracts. MRI spectroscopy can detect and measure the concentration of important neurometabolites such as choline, creatine, NAA, and myoinositol, which can be formatted into a metabolic map or image. Since different brain disorders produce unique chemical changes within the brain, specific brain disorders can be detected with this technique.

THE USE OF PET AND SPECT IN THE EVALUATION OF TBIs

Both positron emission tomography (PET) and single photon emission computed tomography (SPECT) are complementary to anatomic imaging and provide additional information about cerebral functioning by using radioactive tracers (isotopes). PET scans provide functional brain maps of regional glucose metabolism and cerebral blood flow. SPECT scans similarly provide brain maps with measures of both absolute and relative regional cerebral blood perfusion. SPECT resolution has improved with the use of triple and quadruple head cameras. While the SPECT scan is cheaper and easier to use, the PET offers quantification and greater resolution.

PET and SPECT scan studies can reveal areas of hypoperfusion (reduced blood flow) and PET, specifically, can identify areas of hypometabolism that are not detectable by MRI or CT scans. PET and SPECT scans can detect more lesions than CT scans, although whether they can detect more lesions than an MRI scan is unclear at the present time, since the MRI, with its high contrast resolution, is able to pick up very small lesions. While PET and CT scans have limited resolution, their ability to measure brain function makes them even more useful in evaluating TBIs since their findings frequently correlate better with the patient's neuropsychological test scores. Furthermore, they can identify dysfunctional areas within the brain, which may not be detected by neuropsychological tests and can determine whether the abnormal regions in the brain improve over time.

PET imaging, however, has major forensic limitations as a technique for confirming the presence of brain damage. For example, it frequently cannot distinguish between abnormalities caused by structural permanent brain injury and abnormalities reflecting a potentially reversible and treatable alteration of brain function, seen in epilepsy, depression, and other psychiatric disorders (Mamelak, 2000; Granacher, 2003). In addition, there has been variable success in correlating SPECT or PET scan findings of impaired regional perfusion or metabolism with expected neuropsychological deficits in controlled studies with large groups of patients. As with QEEG, "the use of PET or SPECT findings, in patients with suspected mild TBI, as primary evidence of a physiological basis for the patient's sustained cognitive impairments must be considered premature at the present time." In addition, Newberg and Alavi (1996) have stressed that "the use of functional brain imaging in criminal cases has not yet reached the level of sophistication to predict any neurological or psychiatric deficits."

FUNCTIONAL MRI

Functional MRI (fMRI) can produce functional cerebral images by determining the amount of hemoglobin that is converted to oxyhemoglobin, a measure of neuronal activity in selected brain regions during specified cognitive tasks. Both physiological and pathological information can be obtained from studies based on this blood oxygenation level-dependent contrast. Currently considered research instruments, QEEG, DTI, MRI spectroscopy, and FMRI are expected to have widespread clinical applicability in the future in the diagnosis of neurological diseases and monitoring of their progression or resolution (Granacher, 2003; Devinsky and D'Esposito, 2004).

REFERENCES

Adams, R. D., Victor, M., and Ropper, A. H. 1997. *Principles of Neurology*, 6th ed. New York: McGraw-Hill.

Alexander, M. P. 1995. Mild Traumatic Brain Injury: Pathophysiology, Natural History, and Clinical Management. *Neurology*, *45*, 1253–1260.

Bear, D., Levin, K., Blumer, D., Chetham, D., and Ryder, R. 1982. Interictal Behavior in Hospitalized Temporal Lobe Epileptics: Relationship to Idiopathic Psychiatric Syndromes. *Journal of Neurology, Neurosurgery and Psychiatry*, *45*, 481–488.

Bigler, E. D. 1996. Neuroimaging and Traumatic Brain Injury. In Bigler, E. D. (Ed.) *Neuroimaging II: Clinical Applications*. New York: Plenum Press, pp. 261–278.

Bigler, E. D. 1999. Neuroimaging and Mild TBI. In Varney, N. R. and Roberts, R. J. (Eds.) *The Evaluation and Treatment of Mild Traumatic Brain Injury*. Mahwah, NJ: Lawrence Erlbaum, pp. 63–80.

Bigler, E. D., Blatter, D. D., Anderson, C. V., Johnson, S. C., Hopkins, R. O., and Burnett, B. 1997. Hippocampal Volume in Normal Aging and Traumatic Brain Injury. *American Journal of Neuroradiology*, *18*, 11–23.

Brink, J., Garrett, A., Hale, W., Woo-Sam, J., and Nickel, V. 1970. Recovery of Motor and Intellectual Function in Children Sustaining Severe Head Injuries. *Developmental Medicine and Child Neurology*, *15*, 823.

Cummings, J. L. and Mega, M. S. 2003. *Neuropsychiatry and Behavioral Neuroscience*. New York: Oxford University Press, pp. 128–138.

Damasio, H., Grabowski, T., Frank, R., Galaburda, A. M., and Damasio, A. R. 1994. The Return of Phineas Gage: Clues about the Brain from the Skull of a Famous Patient. *Science*, *264*, 1102–1105.

Devinsky, O. 1992. *Behavioral Neurology: 100 Maxims in Neurology*. St. Louis: Mosby Year Book, pp. 293–295.

Devinsky, O. and D'Esposito, M. D. 2004. *Neurology of Cognitive and Behavioral Disorders*. New York: Oxford, pp. 52–54.

Dodrill, C. B. 1981. Neuropsychology of Epilepsy. In Filskov, S. B. and Boll, T. J. (Eds.) *Handbook of Clinical Neuropsychology*. New York: Wiley, pp. 366–395.

Eide, P. K. and Tysnes, O. B. 1992. Early and Late Outcome in Head Injury Patients with Radiological Evidence of Brain Damage. *ACTA Neurologica Scandinavica*, *86*, 194.

Engel, Jr., J. 1989. *Seizures and Epilepsy*. Philadelphia: F.A. Davis, pp. 352–253.

Fenichel, G. M. 1988. *Clinical Pediatric Neurology*. Philadelphia: W. B. Saunders.

Graham, D. I., Adams, J. H., and Doyle, D. 1978. Ischemic Brain Damage in Fatal Non-Missile Head Injuries. *Journal of Neurological Science*, *39*, 213.

Granacher, R. P. 2003. *Traumatic Brain Injury: Methods for Clinical and Forensic Neuropsychiatric Assessment*. Boca Raton: CRC Press, pp. 153–162.

Jennett, W. B. 1975. *Epilepsy after Blunt Head Injuries*, 2nd ed. London: Heinemann.

Joseph, R. 1996. *Neuropsychiatry, Neuropsychology, and Clinical Neuroscience*, 2nd ed. Baltimore: Williams & Wilkins.

Kligman, D. and Goldberg, D. A. 1975. Temporal Lobe Epilepsy and Aggression. *The Journal of Nervous and Mental Disease*, *100*, 324–341.

Kotagal, P. 1993. Psychomotor Seizures: Clinical and EEG Findings. In Wyllie, E. (Ed.) *The Treatment of Epilepsy: Principles and Practice*. Philadelphia: Lea & Febiger, chapter 26.

Kraus, J. F., Fife, D., and Conroy, C. 1987. Pediatric Head Injuries: The Nature, Clinical Course, and Early Outcomes in a Defined United States Population. *Pediatrics*, *79*, 501.

Levin, H. S. and Eisenberg, H. 1979. Neuropsychological Impairment after Closed Head Injury in Children and Adolescents. *Journal of Pediatric Psychology*, *4*, 389.

Levin, H. S., Mendelson, D., Lilly, M. A., Fletcher, J. A., Culhane, K. A., Chapman, S. B., Harward, H., Kusnerik, L., Bruce, D., and Eisenberg, H. M. 1994. Tower of London Performance in Relation to Magnetic Resonance Imaging Following Closed Head Injury in Children. *Neuropsychology*, *8*, 171.

Long, D. F. 1989. Issues in Behavioral Neurology. In Ellis, D. W. and Christensen, A. (Eds.) *Neuropsychological Treatment after Brain Injury*. Boston: Kluwer, pp. 39–90.

Mamelak, M. 2000. The Motor Vehicle Collision Injury Syndrome. *Neuropsychiatry, Neuropsychology and Behavioral Neurology*, *13*, 125–135.

Marion, D. W. 1998. Head and Spinal Cord Injury. *Neurologic Clinics of North America*, *6*, 485–502.

Miller, J. D. 1983. Early Evaluation and Management. In Rosenthal, M., Griffith, E. R., Bond, M. R., and Miller, J. D. (Eds.) *Rehabilitation of the Head Injured Adult*. Philadelphia: F.A. Davis, pp. 37–58.

Newberg, A. B. and Alavi, A. 1996. Neuroimaging in Patients with Traumatic Brain Injury. *Journal of Head Trauma Rehabilitation*, *11*, 65–79.

Nuwer, M. R., Hovda, D. A., Schrader, L. M., and Vespa, P. M. 2005. Routine and Quantitative EEG in Mild Traumatic Brain Injuries. *Clinical Neurophysiology*, *116*, 2001–2025.

Pedley, T. A. and Emerson, R. G. 1991. Clinical Neurophysiology: Electroencephalography and Evoked Potentials. In Bradley, W. G., Daroff, R. B., Fenichel, G. M., and Marsden, C. D. (Eds.) *Neurology in Clinical Practice*. Boston: Butterworth-Heinemann, pp. 429–451.

Roberts, R. J. 1999. Epilepsy Spectrum Disorder in the Context of Mild Traumatic Brain Injury. In Varney, N. R. and Roberts, R. J. (Eds.) *The Evaluation and Treatment of Mild Traumatic Brain Injury*. Mahwah, NJ: Lawrence Erlbaum, pp. 209–248.

Saul, R. E. 1993. Neurobehavioral Disorders Following Traumatic Brain Injury, Part I — Neurobehavioral Sequelae in the Early Stages of Recovery. In Hanley, J. R. and Belfus, M. (Eds.) *Physical Medicine and Rehabilitation: State of the Art Reviews*. Philadelphia: Hanley and Belfus, pp. 581–591.

Seidel, V. P., Chapwick, O., and Rutter, M. 1975. Psychological Disorders in Crippled Children: A Comparative Study of Children With and Without Brain Damage. *Developmental Medicine and Child Neurology*, *17*, 563.

Shapiro, K. and Smith, L. P. 1993. Special Considerations for the Pediatric Age Group. In Cooper, P. R. (Ed.) *Head Injury*, 3rd ed. Baltimore: Williams & Wilkins, p. 247.

Stuss, D. T. and Benson, D. F. 1986. *The Frontal Lobes*. New York: Raven Press, pp. 217–229.

Tippin, J. and Yamada, T. 1996. The Electrophysiological Evaluation of Head Injured Patients: Value and Limitations. In Rizzo, M. and Tranel, D. (Eds.) *Head Injury and Post-Concussive Syndrome*. New York: Livingstone, pp. 119–138.

Wolpert, S. M. 1991. Neuroimaging. In Bradley, W. G., Daroff, R. B., Fenichel, G. M., and Marsden, D. D. (Eds.) *Neurology in Clinical Practice*. Boston: Butterworth-Heinemann, pp. 493–541.

9 Reliability and Validity

Health care professionals and attorneys should become familiar with the *reliability* and *validity* of the psychological and neuropsychological tests psychologists frequently administer to individuals with known or suspected brain dysfunction. Tests that have marginal or poor reliability should not be administered since there is a strong possibility that similar test scores will not be obtained when the same test or tests are later readministered by the same psychologist or by a different psychologist. It also makes the issue of determining whether the patient's cognitive functioning has improved or deteriorated over time very difficult if not impossible. A good example of this would be using a scale that is designed to measure a person's weight. For example, if you weighed yourself on a scale you recently purchased and your weight varied as much as 20% each time you weighed yourself, you would be unable to determine whether you were losing or gaining weight. You would probably return the scale to the store where you purchased because of its poor reliability and begin using a different scale. The issue of validity is perhaps even more important since tests that do not measure what they state they are measuring are likely to produce inaccurate and misleading data even though they may have high reliability. For example, if you began using a new scale to weigh yourself each morning and found that each time you weighed 28 lbs, you would probably stop using the scale because of its poor validity irrespective of its high reliability. These concepts and their respective issues are discussed below.

RELIABILITY

Reliability should be viewed as the degree of consistency between two tests and within a particular test. *Internal reliability* or consistency refers to the extent to which the items within a particular test measure the same cognitive domain (e.g., intelligence, memory, etc.). It is usually determined by examining the correlations between different forms of a particular test, as well as the correlations between the actual test scores and true scores. Since a detailed discussion of this particular topic is beyond the scope of this book, readers wishing additional information should review Cronbach (1984).

The *test–retest reliability* of a particular neuropsychological test or battery refers to the consistency with which a particular test or battery achieves the same score or scores when used on two or more occasions, for example, when a particular psychological test is given to a group of patients suspected of having brain damage and then given again to the same group 1 week later. If 90% of these patients obtain the same or similar scores both times, the reliability coefficient of this test will be 0.90. However, if only half of the individuals obtain the same or similar scores 1 week later, the reliability coefficient will only be 0.50. Test–retest reliability can be affected by a variety of factors, such as the duration of time between test administrations.

Tests that rely heavily on well-learned information acquired over a person's lifetime are likely to have high test–retest reliability. For example, the Wechsler Adult Intelligence Scale (WAIS), which appears to be heavily dependent on what has been termed "crystallized intelligence" (well-learned intellectual abilities), has high test–retest reliability. Thus, if adults who sustain brain injuries are tested 1 to 2 years postinjury, they may show little change from their premorbid IQ scores. This, however, may not be true for children who typically show more variability in their IQ test scores than adults. Although the test–retest reliability of their IQ scores of adults on the WAIS may be high, the validity of this test in terms of identifying them as brain-damaged is usually low.

Sattler (2001) has stressed that psychological tests that are utilized for individual assessment should have reliability coefficients of 0.80 or higher. If a particular test is going to be used for making important decisions (e.g., determining whether a child should be placed in a gifted or special education program) the reliability coefficient should be at least 0.9. Sattler has also stressed that tests with reliability coefficients of less than 0.6 should be considered unreliable, coefficients between 0.6 and 0.7 should be considered marginally reliable, while coefficients above 0.7, but lower than 0.9, should be viewed as relatively reliable.

Acceptable reliability coefficients tend to be lower for neuropsychological tests since the cognitive functioning of individuals who have sustained a brain insult tends to vary both as a function of time since insult or prior testing, and the conditions under which testing is performed. For example, it is not uncommon for the same neuropsychologist or different neuropsychologists to report test scores that vary considerably from initial testing, if the individual who sustained a traumatic brain injury is later reexamined. When this occurs, it most likely reflects one or more of the following factors: the time interval between initial and follow-up testing; the test norms utilized; feedback given to the patient during the examination about a specific test (e.g., the patient is given the correct answers by the examiner on initial testing); practice effects as a result of prior experience with a particular test or battery; the patient's motivation and level of effort during testing; the expectations of the patient or the examiner during initial and follow-up testing; errors made during test administration, scoring, or interpretation; the patient's mood and attitude at the time of testing (e.g., some individuals resent having to be retested); medications taken at time of initial testing that are known for producing deleterious effects on cognitive functioning (e.g., anticonvulsant or psychiatric medications) that were taken when the patient was initially tested or was later repeated; changes in the patient's psychological or neurological functioning since previous testing; or factors that are present at the time of follow-up testing that were not present on initial testing (e.g., patient's spouse has recently asked for a divorce, financial difficulties, job termination, etc.).

Case Example

A 24-year-old Hispanic male was referred for neuropsychological testing after he sustained a cerebral concussion during an industrial accident. The applicant's attorney had previously referred his client to a psychologist who administered the Halstead–Reitan Neuropsychological Battery, which took over 8 hours. After testing was completed, the psychologist reported that the applicant obtained a Halstead impairment index of 1.0, which he stated was indicative of severe brain impairment. Six weeks later, this applicant was referred to another psychologist who specialized in evaluating individuals who had sustained traumatic brain injuries. When the applicant arrived for his scheduled appointment, he appeared extremely tense and angry. The psychologist asked him why he seemed so tense and angry. The applicant said that 2 months earlier he discovered that his wife had been having an affair with his best friend. Since that time, he had been unable to sleep and had felt extremely tense and angry. The psychologist then asked if this had affected him when he underwent neuropsychological testing 6 weeks earlier. The applicant admitted that he had not been unable to sleep the night before he was previously tested, had been feeling very tense and angry, and had become upset with the psychologist who did not appear interested in his marital problems. He also recalled that the psychologist had informed him shortly after testing had begun that he had most likely sustained a severe brain injury. When the applicant asked the psychologist what he meant, the psychologist indicated "Your test scores mean your brain got wiped out and that you'll probably never be normal or work again." The applicant felt so emotionally devastated after hearing this that his motivation to perform to the best of his ability on the remaining tests markedly diminished.

INTERRATER RELIABILITY

The reliability of two or more examiners can also be determined. This is known as interrater reliability and refers to the consistency between the measurements or ratings of two or more observers when they are asked to evaluate a specific patient or problem. High interrater reliability scores indicate a high agreement or concordance between two or more examiners using a particular battery or test. Low interrater reliability indicates low agreement or concordance between examiners. Tests that rely on the examiner's subjective judgment or scoring of a patient's responses tend to have lower reliability ratings. When low interrater reliability is suspected because of this issue, the consistency of the ratings of the different examiners should be carefully evaluated.

THE GENERALIZABILITY OF NORMATIVE TEST DATA

The normative data that are typically utilized by neuropsychologists in determining whether a particular individual is cognitively impaired or brain-damaged is usually obtained when the test subjects are tested in quiet environments that are usually free of any distractions. The furniture and temperature of the room are usually comfortable. The examiners who administered the tests were most likely polite, courteous, kind, and professional. They most likely spoke in a calm manner, provided clear instructions and often gave examples when they were necessary or required. The subjects in these studies were most likely told that their test performances were going to be used for research purposes and that their identities and test scores would remain confidential.

Unfortunately, not all neuropsychological testing is conducted in such artificial settings. For example, when individuals are tested in jails or prisons, many of these settings require the examinee to sit in a small booth behind a thick wire-mesh screen after the examiner and examinee are located in different booths that are electronically locked. The examiner has no control of the lighting (which is often poor), the temperature of the room (which is often too cold or hot), or the background ambient noise (which is often considerable). The examiner and examinee are often required to sit on a small uncomfortable round metal seat that is attached to the floor. Testing in this environment is often interrupted by guards who may stand only several feet away yelling at other prisoners or talking loudly. Testing is also interrupted by loud announcements that are broadcast over the PA system. The guards may stare at the examiner and examinee during the examination. Besides the guards, other prisoners who are often nearby can overhear the patient, which eliminates any confidentiality or privacy.

If the examinee wears glasses or a hearing aid, they may not be brought to the examination. If the examinee needs to retrieve them, he or she must notify a guard who must take them back to their cell. It is not uncommon for this process to take 1 or 2 hours. If the examination is timed around the inmates' feeding and counting schedules, the examinee often must leave the room during these times and may not return until the following day.

Since the tests that are administered to the examinee must be small enough to fit under the wire-mesh screen, tests such as the Block Design, Halstead Category, Tactual Performance, Finger Tapping, Grip Strength, Picture Arrangement, and the Wisconsin Card Sorting cannot be administered in this setting. The background noise (which is often quite distracting) in this setting typically compromises the patient's test performance when they are given tests to assess their attention, concentration, and verbal memory tests. Visual stimuli that assess the examinee's visual perceptual and visual memory skills must be viewed through a thick wire-mesh screen in a dimly lit room. Finally, the examinee may also be forced to wear uncomfortable restraining devices throughout the entire examination, which restrict the movements of his or her arms and legs.

Testing an individual in this environment is not only quite challenging and difficult, but is dramatically different from the standard clinical environment in which the test norms were obtained. Since there are no norms available for individuals who are tested in such environments (Sbordone et al., 2000b), use of standard clinical norms for tests that are administered under these circumstances is likely to lead to a high rate of false-positive errors (e.g., determine that the individual is cognitively impaired or brain-damaged on the basis of the test data when he or she is not). It is also very difficult and nearly impossible to determine if there has been any change in the examinee's cognitive functioning if they were previously tested in a standard clinical environment or had previously been tested in another jail or even the same prison since the conditions in which they were previously tested may have been quite different.

VALIDITY OF NEUROPSYCHOLOGICAL TESTS

Neuropsychological tests can be conceptually viewed as a series of instruments that measure a patient's cognitive and behavioral functioning. Since numerous tests presently exist to evaluate specific cognitive functions, the neuropsychologist's choice of a particular test or battery to administer may reflect the test's *validity* (the likelihood that this particular test is able to measure what it purports to measure), and/or its ability to predict how a patient will function in real-world settings (*ecological validity*). There are several different types of validity that will be discussed below.

Content validity refers to the extent to which a particular test contains items or tasks that are actually related to the underlying trait or ability that is being measured. For example, a test that contains words that the individual must learn over several trials and later recall is likely to have high content validity as a test of verbal learning and memory. Within the context of content validity, the test items may possess high face validity if they can be perceived by the test taker as measuring a particular trait or ability. Unfortunately, the content of tests that have high face validity can be easily recognized by individuals who are malingering. As a consequence, they are likely to perform poorly on tests that have high face validity, but perform well on tests measuring the same trait or ability that have low face validity.

Construct validity refers to a positive relationship between a particular test and other tests that measure a specific trait or ability. It is usually reported as a statistical correlation coefficient that can range from -1.0 to $+1.0$. The higher the positive correlation coefficient, the higher the construct validity between two tests. If the correlation coefficient between two tests is high, both tests are likely measuring the same underlying trait or ability. However, if the correlation coefficient between the tests is low, then there is a high probability that the tests are not measuring the same underlying trait or ability.

Concurrent validity refers to a positive relationship between a particular test and other tests that purport to measure a specific trait or ability.

Predictive validity refers to the ability of a particular test to predict a person's score on another test on the basis of their concurrent validity.

Discriminant validity refers to the ability of a particular test to predict the scores of a particular group of individuals who are administered this test. For example, if test X is given to 100 persons consisting of 50 healthy normals and 50 individuals with a history of brain damage, the predictive validity of this test would be its ability to predict the scores of either the brain-damaged patients or the normal controls.

Criterion validity refers to the degree to which a particular test is able to predict or correlate with specific external criteria (e.g., ability to live independently, graduate from high school or college, or successfully return to work).

Ecological validity refers to the functional and predictive relationship between an individual's performance on a particular test or battery and their behavior and ability to function at home, work, school, or in the community (Sbordone, 1996; Sbordone and Guilmette, 1999). Neuropsychologists have utilized two major approaches to enhance the ecological validity of their neuropsychogical test data. The first approach involves utilizing tests that mimic the demands of the patient's every-day functioning. The second approach involves using neuropsychological tests that have been empirically shown to predict an individual's everyday behavior, ability to work or function in the community, or attend school.

The first approach is known as *verisimilitude* and refers to the degree to which the tests and measures utilized mimic the cognitive demands of the patient's environment (Franzen and Wilhelm, 1996). This definition assumes that the neuropsychologists' choice of tests should be determined by the cognitive demands of the settings the patient currently functions within, or will function within in the future. Several tests have been developed for this purpose. For example, The Rivermead Behavioural Memory Test (Wilson et al., 1985) tries to mimic the demands that are made on a patient's memory in everyday life.

The primary focus of this approach is to avoid using tests that were primarily designed to diagnose brain damage, but rather to utilize tests that simulate the cognitive demands of the patient's everyday environment. This approach, however, often overlooks whether the data obtained from such tests, often under highly artificial conditions (e.g., the testing laboratory), irrespective of their apparent verisimilitude, accurately reflect the demands of the patient's environment. Neuropsychologists frequently ignore this issue and use tests that were primarily designed to detect brain damage rather than mimic the demands of the patient's environment. They often do not interview significant others who are familiar with the demands of these environments and routinely observe how the patient functions in these environments. They rarely leave their laboratories or offices to determine whether the tests and the environment in which the tests were administered accurately represent the demands of the patient's environment, and whether the test data obtained under such conditions corroborates the observations of significant others.

The second approach is the degree to which the administered tests are empirically related to measures of everyday functioning (Franzen and Wilhelm, 1996). This approach has been labeled *veridicality* and typically involves the use of statistical techniques to relate a patient's performance on traditional neuropsychological tests to measures of real-world functioning, such as work performance evaluations, questionnaires completed by significant others, or clinician ratings. One issue that confounds the validity of this approach is whether the chosen outcome measure accurately reflects the patient's real-world functioning since the use of inappropriate outcome measures could lead to inaccurate predictions of the ecological validity of a particular neuropsychological test or battery.

ECOLOGICAL VALIDITY: CRITICAL ISSUES

THE ECOLOGICAL VALIDITY OF THE BRAIN-INJURED PATIENT'S SUBJECTIVE COMPLAINTS

Neuropsychologists often rely on questionnaires that are completed by the patient while seated in the waiting room to determine their behavioral and cognitive symptoms rather than directly interview the patient. This is typically done to save time and reduce the costs of the examination, particularly when it is being paid for by an insurance company. This policy, unfortunately, ignores the fact that the vast majority of brain-injured patients have a limited or poor awareness of their symptoms and typically fail to recognize their behavioral and cognitive symptoms that are readily observed by their significant others even when their symptoms are pointed out to them (Sbordone et al., 1998).

When patients are interviewed, they will often only exhibit cognitive deficits when they are asked broad open-ended questions. In such circumstances, these patients may exhibit circumstantial and tangential thinking, confusion, memory difficulties (e.g., being unable to recall the question), a loss of their train of thought, or confabulation, even though they did not identify such symptoms on the questionnaires they completed.

Although some neuropsychologists have assumed that the patient's test performances should be consistent with their subjective complaints, nothing could be further from the truth since the neuropsychological test results typically are inconsistent with the patient's subjective complaints. When the patient's subjective complaints are consistent with the patient's neuropsychological test data, malingering should be suspected (Sbordone et al., 2000a).

The presence of family members or significant others during such interviews can shed considerable light on the patient's symptoms and improve the ecological validity of the psychologist's opinions about the patient's ability to return to school or work, live independently, or function in the community. When neuropsychologists rely on the brain-injured reported assessment of their ability to function at work, they are apt to make predictions about the patient's ability to return to work or school that are frequently inaccurate and potentially harmful to the patient's economic and psychological welfare.

Case Example

A 37-year-old male laborer had fallen 12 feet from a ladder at work. He was rendered unconscious for less than a minute. A CT scan did not identify any evidence of intracranial abnormalities. He was placed on medical leave and was referred by his physician for neuropsychological testing to determine if he could return to work. This patient denied any behavioral or cognitive deficits when he was interviewed. He tested in the normal range on all of the cognitive tests that were administered to him. When the psychologist asked him if he felt that he was ready to return to work, he said he did not see any reason why he could not return to work. On the basis of this, the psychologist recommended that this patient return to work. After this patient had returned to work, he became fatigued easily, yelled at his coworkers and supervisors, and made serious mistakes that jeopardized his and their safety. He was terminated and had considerable difficulty finding a similar job.

DEMAND CHARACTERISTICS OF THE PATIENT'S ENVIRONMENT

The demand characteristics of a patient's environments (e.g., work, school, home, etc.) can vary considerably. For example, the demand characteristics within a particular patient's workplace may fluctuate considerably as a result of factors such as economic pressures, absenteeism, sickness, organizational or administrative changes, competition from other companies, changes in the market place, changes in equipment, marketing goals, and so forth. Depending on the interface between a patient's cognitive strengths and deficits, and the demand characteristics of the particular work setting that this patient finds herself or himself within, the setting may either compensate or exacerbate the patient's cognitive and behavioral impairments. When the former occurs, persons in this setting often serve as the patient's ancillary frontal lobes by structuring the environment to compensate for the patient's cognitive impairments. When the latter occurs, the patient's functioning often declines on the basis of the principle of a conditional neurological lesion (Sbordone, 1996, 1997; Sbordone and Guillmette, 1999). This principle argues that factors such as stress, fatigue, lack of sleep, and so forth can have a deleterious effect on the patient's behavioral, cognitive, and emotional functioning. When this occurs, patients can develop secondary psychiatric disorders (e.g., generalized anxiety disorder, adjustment reaction with a depressed or anxious mood, or major depression), which frequently exacerbate their behavioral and cognitive impairments.

Because the demand characteristics of each setting are unique, it is essential that neuropsychologists obtain as much information as possible about the behavioral and cognitive demands that a particular environment places on a patient. This information should be obtained not only from the patient, but also from the patient's family, friends, coworkers, and supervisors, not to mention specialists in the fields of vocational and occupational rehabilitation. This information helps us understand how these environments interact with the patient's behavioral problems (e.g., disinhibition, mood swings, irritability, etc.), cognitive strengths and impairments, goals and objectives, premorbid skills and abilities, attitudes, awareness of their impairments, and biological systems (e.g., medical conditions, general health, etc.). Unfortunately, such information is rarely obtained by neuropsychologists.

In the absence of a clear understanding of the demand characteristics of the patient's environments, predictions about the patient's ability to function at work, school, in the community, or live independently, solely on the basis of neuropsychological test data, are likely to be inaccurate or misleading. Such predictions may also be viewed as "sheer speculation" when they are presented in the courtroom, where such issues are of major importance in determining the extent of the patient's damages and needs (Sbordone and Guilmette, 1999).

Although the vast majority of our widely used neuropsychological tests were never specifically designed to assess the patient's functioning in real-world settings, within the past decade, some effort has been made to determine whether many of our widely used neuropsychological tests and measures possessed ecological validity in predicting real-world functions, such as job performance, activities of daily living, academic performance, work behavior, shopping, everyday life problems, executive functions, adaptive decision making, functional status, and driving and work-related skills (Chaytor and Schmitter-Edgecombe, 2003).

The major problem inherent in such studies is that the environments in which these patients were tested typically had little or no resemblance to real-world settings. For example, individuals who undergo neuropsychological testing are usually tested in quiet and highly structured settings that are relatively free of extraneous or distracting stimuli to optimize their test performance. This type of environment has been a standard in the field for the expressed purpose of reducing extraneous negative influences during the evaluation process and allows different psychologists to compare the patient's test data (Cronbach, 1984). Unfortunately, while these particular conditions may optimize the patient's performance, particularly on tests that require a high level of attention and concentration, the real issue is whether the test results obtained under such artificial conditions can generalize to patient's environment, which is often unstructured, chaotic, noisy, contains numerous extraneous and distracting stimuli, and is highly dissimilar to the conditions under which the test data were obtained.

Testing brain-injured patients in such quiet, structured, and artificial settings, combined with the gentle and calm manner of the examiner, not to mention the examiner's patience and concerted efforts to prevent the patient from becoming fatigued or emotionally upset, frequently mask many of the patient's behavioral and cognitive symptoms that may only appear when the patient is placed in unstructured, complex, noisy, stressful, and cognitively demanding situations, particularly when they are fatigued. Under such conditions, a patient's cognitive and behavioral functioning is often highly discrepant from any predictions of how they will function in real-world situations on the basis of their quantitative test data.

Case Example

A 27-year-old female was referred for neuropsychological testing after she had sustained a severe closed head injury during a bicycle vs. motor vehicle accident. She was rendered comatose for 2 weeks. CT and MRI studies revealed bilateral contusions to her frontal and temporal lobes. Before the accident, she worked as TV news broadcaster, spoke several languages, and had earned a master's degree in economics. During testing, she appeared articulate, demure, and cooperative. Testing revealed a Wechsler full scale IQ of 138 that was consistent with her academic and vocational achievements. She was only found to have relatively mild cognitive impairments on tests that assessed her divided attention skills. Testing revealed no evidence of impairment on neuropsychological tests that assessed her intellectual functioning, memory, language, perceptual, judgment, executive functions, motor, problem solving, and cognitive processing skills.

To assess how this patient functioned in a highly unstructured, complex, and noisy environment with numerous distracting stimuli, she was taken to a large crowed nearby mall on a Saturday afternoon. Before being taken to the mall, she was given a total of $100 by her husband, who instructed her to purchase five specific items. Her behavior in this setting was videotaped using a concealed camera that was hidden in the jacket of a male professional investigator. Another investigator (a strikingly attractive woman in her late 20s) covertly recorded whatever she said. Both investigators were never introduced to her, but remained at her side throughout the entire time (4 hours) that she spent at the mall. At no time was either investigator more than 3 ft away from her. Despite the fact that these individuals were constantly at her side the entire time she spent at the mall, she never recognized their presence, or questioned why they were following her so closely. Their presence, however, was often noted by other shoppers and a security guard who came over and asked what was going on.

As soon as she entered into the mall, she walked up to a large directory trying to locate the kitchen utensils that her husband had asked her to purchase. Although the directory listed where the household items were located, she indicated that she could not find where the kitchen utensils were located. She walked aimlessly throughout the mall without any apparent goal or plan even though her husband had written down on a sheet of paper the items he had asked her to purchase. At no time did she ever pull out this list from her purse to examine its contents or check to see if any of the items she had purchased were on the list. She walked throughout the mall with little or no regard to other shoppers, which resulted in her walking into three shoppers. At no time did she apologize or seem to be the least bit concerned about what had occurred. On several occasions, she walked to the front of a long line of shoppers and demanded the immediate attention of the salesperson. When she was told by the salesperson that she was waiting on another shopper and to please stand in line, she would begin cursing very loudly at the salesperson. She also appeared to have little or no regard for the rights of other shoppers.

When she went into a department store, she walked around one of the floors several times without realizing that she had done this. She would often pick up items and walk away with them rather than take them to the checkout line. She was taken to a restaurant at the mall where she was seated only a few feet away from several young children. When the waitress would not immediately wait on her, she began uttering explicatives in a very loud manner, which created a scene in the restaurant that resulted in her being asked to leave by the manager. Although she had spent the $100 that had been given to her by her husband, she did not purchase any of the items he had requested.

This case example demonstrates the discrepancies that can occur between the patient's neuropsychological test results when they are tested in a very quiet and highly structured artificial setting and their behavior in a highly unstructured, complex, novel, noisy, and crowded setting. This patient's behavior in this latter setting would have not been predicted by observing her behavior in the quiet and highly structured artificial test setting or by a review of her neuropsychological test data. In fact, the neuropsychologist who examined her had recommended that she could return to work.

CONDITIONALITY

If most people were asked if they could fly a 747 passenger jet, they would probably emphatically state that they were unable to do this. The truth is that the most people are capable of flying a 747 without ever going to flight school if the pilot, who was sitting next to them in the cockpit, instructed them how to fly the plane after the plane had reached cruising altitude in a gentle and reassuring manner. If the pilot passed out or died, the individual who had been following the instructions of the pilot would no longer be able to continue to fly and land the aircraft. In other words, under the right set of conditions many individuals would be capable of performing a complex task, such as piloting an aircraft without ever attending flight school. If these conditions changed, the person would be unable to fly the aircraft or continue performing a complex task.

This principle was initially described by the philosopher Plato in one of his dialogues, Meno, when he demonstrated how Socrates was able to cleverly convince Meno that a simple slave boy knew all the principles of geometry by asking him leading questions to demonstrate that all knowledge was innate (Plato, 1952).

This phenomenon, with respect to the ecological validity of our test data, has been termed conditionality (Sbordone, 1996, 1997; Sbordone and Guilmette, 1999). It refers to specific modifications of the test protocol or instructions during testing and the use of compensatory techniques during testing that allow the individual to ignore extraneous or distracting stimuli, attend to the examiner and the task, comprehend and recall the test instructions, perform according to the test requirements, utilize cues and prompts to minimize their problems of initiation and organization, and foster a positive emotional, and psychological state and attitude during the examination to compensate for the individual's cognitive deficits to allow this individual to perform at an optimal level of cognitive efficiency throughout the entire test or battery.

Many neuropsychologists consciously or unconsciously modify standard test instructions or procedures when they are evaluating patients with cognitive impairments. For example, the examiner may repeat the test instructions several times or permit the patient to spend more time warming up before administering a test to them. The examiner may also provide frequent cues and prompts throughout testing to minimize the patient's problems of initiation and the effects of fatigue, frequently redirect the patient back to the task, and keep the patient as motivated as possible to facilitate their performance (e.g., using praise or rewards). Unfortunately, these modifications are often not recorded since the traditional focus in testing has been placed on the patient's quantitative test performance rather than their behavior during testing. If the examiner follows strict test guidelines and does not provide any cues, prompts, or any more rehearsal or practice time that is specified by the test manual, the patient's test scores will most likely be significantly impaired, which will often cause the neuropsychologist to report that the patient has significant cognitive deficits, which render them unable from returning to the job they held before their brain injury. However, if such patients are placed in a highly structured and familiar work setting that provides them with frequent cues, prompts, and contains caring and patient individuals who compensate for the patient's deficits, brain-injured patients can often function reasonably well at their job even though their neuropsychological test scores are impaired.

Case Example

A 35-year-old attorney who had sustained a traumatic brain injury in a motor vehicle accident was referred for neuropsychological testing. Review of his medical records revealed that he had sustained bilateral contusions to the anterior frontal and temporal lobes, a subdural hematoma, and a subarachnoid hemorrhage. The damage to his right temporal lobe was so severe that 6 cm had to be removed surgically. The neuropsychologist who tested him at 1 year postinjury strongly felt that this patient was incapable of ever practicing law based on his poor neuropsychological test scores. When he was later seen by another neuropsychologist after he had returned to work, he denied that he was having any problems performing his job duties.

When the staff at his law firm was interviewed, they admitted they had liked him and felt sorry for him after he returned to work following his brain injury. They admitted that they had been providing him with extensive structure, cues, prompts, feedback, guidance, organization, and reminders to help him function effectively. For example, although the other attorneys in the firm had shared a secretary with one or two other attorneys, he needed three full-time secretaries and two legal assistants to help him perform his job even though he was billing considerable less than any of the other attorneys in the firm. He compensated for his cognitive impairments by putting in long hours each day (usually 11 to 12 hours a day) and working weekends in comparison to working only 6 or 7 hours a day only 4 days a week before his accident.

At home, his wife, who had once practiced law with husband, was no longer practicing law since she had decided to become a full-time homemaker to care for their two young children. She was now making all of the decisions at home even though her husband had made these decisions before his accident. She had also taken over their finances and would assist her husband perform his legal work.

This case illustrates that when a brain-injured patient is placed in a highly structured work environment in the presence of individuals who serve as their "ancillary frontal lobes," who provide frequent reminders, cues, prompts, guidance, structure, feedback, and take over many of their responsibilities to compensate for their cognitive impairments, they can often return to work and create the superficial appearance that they have made an excellent recovery. If this is not provided to them they will typically get terminated or asked to resign.

Neuropsychologists should recognize the issue of conditionality when they are asked to predict whether a patient can return to work, and maintain their job. Unfortunately, neuropsychologists often fail to interview the patient's family, coworkers, employers, friends, or spouses to determine how the patient is performing at work and determine the conditions that allow the patient to perform his or her job duties and household responsibilities.

PREDICTING EVERYDAY FUNCTIONING FROM NEUROPSYCHOLOGICAL TESTS

Prediction of everyday functioning based on the patient's neuropsychological test data to a large degree depends on the type of neurobehavioral disorder that the brain injury has generated. For example, the nature of the aphasia examination itself lends to greater ecological validity than many "laboratory" measures of cognitive functioning. In this case, the examiner is directly assessing the skills that the patient will need to demonstrate outside of the testing environment (e.g., comprehension, fluency, and naming) to allow them to communicate effectively. Thus, the better a clinician can test skills that approximate specific "real-world" ability, the greater the likelihood of accurate prediction of real-world functioning.

When neuropsychological tests are utilized to predict the patient's ability to perform everyday skills, more often than not patients who perform very poorly and who are not malingering would have considerable difficulty at home and function at any job. The ecological validity of neuropsychological test is poorest when evaluating traumatic brain injury cases that test in the normal to mildly impaired range. For example, Williams (1996) stressed that such predictions of these patients are often no better than guesses. Individuals who test with severely impaired test scores who are not malingering and putting forth good effort frequently have impaired functional skills. Their test performance is more likely to have better ecological validity than patients who test in the normal or mildly impaired range. Consequently, it is important to supplement standardized test procedures with observations and descriptions of the patient during testing and from others who observe the patient under more varied and frequent circumstances. It is also important to obtain a careful history of the patient's planning and organizational skills and initiative prior to his or her injury to accurately gauge the effects, if any, the injury has had on these abilities.

Most studies have shown that the overall relationship between neuropsychological measures and everyday skills ranges from low to moderate, with Pearson correlations ranging from

0.2 to as high as 0.5 (Chaytor and Schmitte-Edgecombe, 2003). The modest ability of neuropsychological test to predict everyday functioning suggests that although some test measures may provide some beneficial information under some circumstances, they should not be used in isolation. Clinicians should acknowledge the limitations of their measures in this domain. More importantly, neuropsychologists need to determine whether a test is being used as a diagnostic measure of some clinical syndrome or cognitive deficit vs. the test being used to predict everyday skills.

While neuropsychological tests and measures are used routinely and are usually quite helpful in identifying differences between clinical groups and normal subjects, predicting a patient's performance outside of an office or laboratory setting is an entirely different matter. Thus, while a neuropsychological test or measure may be diagnostically useful, it may not be useful in predicting a patient's everyday functioning (Sbordone and Guilmette, 1999; Chaytor and Schmitte-Edgecombe, 2003) since the behavioral domains are too complex and our understanding of everyday skills too elementary. As a consequence, neuropsychologists need to seek convergent and consistent sources of information to increase our ability to predict an individual's everyday functioning. This is particularly true in a forensic context where all of the neuropsychologists' assumptions and the information upon which they based their opinions can be challenged in the courtroom (Sbordone and Guilmette, 1999).

Research has shown that no one specific neuropsychological test or measure can accurately predict the patient's everyday functioning or skills for all persons. Thus, neuropsychologists should combine information gathered from neuropsychological tests with information gathered from behavioral observations, interviews, rating scales, self-report measures, and other assessment procedures. In short, it is not enough to rely solely on the patient's neuropsychological test performance when predicting everyday competence (Wilson, 1993) since it is important that psychologists seek convergent and consistent sources of information to increase our understanding and ability to predict the individual patient's everyday competencies. Research has suggested that neuropsychological assessment may be more predictive if the tests used closely match or simulate everyday abilities (Sbordone and Guilmette, 1999).

OUTCOME MEASURES OF EVERYDAY FUNCTIONING

Chaytor and Schmitter-Edgecombe (2003) found, in a careful review of 17 empirical studies of the ecological validity of neuropsychological tests and outcome measures of everyday functioning, that there was considerable variability in the choices of neuropsychogical tests and outcome measures that were utilized, even within the same cognitive domain. They found that these studies frequently ignored the issue of specificity between the tests and the outcome measures that were utilized. For example, many of these studies did not specify a priori which neuropsychological tests should be expected to be related to specific measures of everyday functioning and which should not. Irrespective of these methodological issues, tests of memory had the best ecological validity, while tests of executive functions had the poorest. They noted that in these studies that many clinicians seemed perplexed that patients whose test scores on neuropsychological tests were within normal limits had impaired executive functions when their everyday functioning was observed.

PREDICTING VOCATIONAL FUNCTIONING FROM NEUROPSYCHOLOGICAL TESTS

The use of neuropsychological test data to predict the patient's vocational functioning is difficult. Although research studies have shown that neuropsychological tests and measures can be helpful in identifying brain-injured patients who may or may not be successful in the workplace, the predicted relationship between the test data and the patient's vocational skills and functioning is far from perfect (Sbordone and Guilmette, 1999). Unfortunately, many neuropsychologists in forensic settings are often pressured to utilize their neuropsychological test data to predict a patient's work potential even though the empirical relationship between the test data that were utilized in the patient's work potential has not been empirically demonstrated.

Neuropsychologists should be aware of such variables as specific jobs skills, skills necessary for success at the patient's workplace, routine vs. unpredictability of the patient's work day, availability of supervision, the amount of interaction with coworkers and/or the public, degree to which the job matches the patient's behavioral and cognitive strengths, degree to which demands of the job and workplace will have on the patient's behavioral and cognitive weaknesses, level of distraction in the job environment, whether the job duties require multitasking, the patient to recall novel information, the degree to which the workplace contains coworkers or supervisors who are tolerant or intolerant of the patient's behavioral and cognitive problems, the availability of part-time or less cognitively demanding work, the likelihood of integrating the patient slowly back into the work environment, and job coaching. A formal work site evaluation by a vocational specialist or occupational therapist may be helpful in some cases.

Interviewing family members to assess their observations of the patient's organizational skills, initiation, motivation, behavioral controls, emotional lability, social skills and functioning, concentration, persistence, fatigability, and executive functions can also provide useful information about patient's ability to function in real-world settings. This information can help us determine whether there has been a change in the patient's functioning and whether they feel that the patient can and is willing to work. While obtaining this information is quite labor intensive, it is crucial in helping us determine the patient's vocational potential.

While research has shown that no single variable or test can predict all vocational outcomes, Dikmen and Machamer (1995) found that patients who had sustained mild traumatic brain injuries based on their Glasgow Coma Scale (GCS) scores had an 80% chance of returning to work at 1 year postinjury, which was identical with a trauma control group. These investigators found, however, that if the individual had a preexisting unstable work history, low educational background, was over the age of 50, and had sustained severe injuries to other parts of his or her body, the likelihood of returning to work dropped to 15%. They also found that individuals over the age of 60 were less likely to return to work than younger persons. Individuals who failed to graduate from high school were less likely to return to work at 1 year postinjury than those who had completed high school (Greenspan et al., 1996). Sbordone and Guilmette (1999) found in their review of the research literature that an individual patient's preexisting history of dependability on the job, absenteeism, ability to manage frustration at work, and length of employment were important factors in predicting future job success, particularly following a mild traumatic brain injury.

A Vector Analysis Approach to Determine the Ecological Validity of the Test Data

Sbordone (1997), Sbordone and Guilmette (1999), and Sbordone and Purisch (1996) have recommended that neuropsychologists utilize a *vector analysis approach* to evaluate the ecological validity of a patient's neuropsychological test data. They have argued that if the information about the patient's behavior obtained from different sources (e.g., significant others, medical, academic, and vocational records) is consistent or forms a vector with the patient's neuropsychological test data, there is a high probability that the test data is ecologically valid. On the other hand, if the test data is inconsistent with this information (e.g., the test data indicate that the patient is severely impaired 3 years post-motor vehicle accident in the face of medical records indicating no loss of consciousness, amnesia, disorientation, or brain or head trauma combined with academic and vocational records that document appreciable educational and vocational attainments subsequent to the accident), there is a high probability that the ecological validity of the test data is poor. When the latter occurs, these authors recommend that neuropsychologists explore alternative explanations of the test data and avoid at arriving at premature diagnoses, opinions, or predictions about the patient's functioning in real-world situations.

CURRENT USES OF NEUROPSYCHOLOGICAL TESTING

Most psychologists who are practicing today use neuropsychological tests to identify a patient's cognitive strengths and deficits, rather than determine whether the patient has brain damage, since this is typically determined by the patient's medical history and neuroimaging studies. Neuropsychological testing is primarily used today to determine whether a patient has sustained brain damage when the neurological examination is normal, and the neuroimaging studies are negative. However, with the advent of increasing sophistication in neuroimaging, it is unlikely that neuropsychological testing will be utilized in the future to determine whether a patient is brain damaged if the presence of the damage can be accurately identified, localized, and quantified by a functional neuroimaging study. On the positive side, this is likely to place more emphasis on the development of innovative methods of assessing how the brain injury or dysfunction effects the patient's functioning in real-world situations.

USE OF PSYCHOLOGICAL ASSISTANTS OR TECHNICIANS

Many neuropsychologists employ psychological assistants or technicians to administer their psychological and neuropsychological tests. As a consequence, neuropsychologists may spend only a limited amount of time with patients who have been referred for testing. They typically base their evaluations on a neuropsychological questionnaire that is completed by the patient while he or she is sitting in the waiting room, the patient's raw test data, and the observations of their assistant or technician as the patient is tested. Unfortunately, the use of assistants or technicians not only minimizes the time the neuropsychologist actually spends with the patient, but forces the neuropsychologist to rely almost entirely on the written information provided by the patient (which may be inaccurate for a variety of reasons), the patient's quantitative test scores, and the observations of an assistant or technician, whose understanding of the neurobehavioral symptoms of a closed head injury is frequently quite limited. This practice not only weakens the ecological validity of the test results, but limits our ability to recognize many of the patient's cognitive deficits and neurobehavioral symptoms, not to mention predict how this patient will function in real-world settings.

REFERENCES

Chaytor, N. and Schmitter-Edgecombe. 2003. The Ecological Validity of Neuropsychological Tests: A Review of the Literature on Everyday Cognitive Skills. *Neuropsychological Review*, *13*, 181–197.

Cronbach, L. J. 1984. *Essentials of Psychological Testing*, 4th ed. New York: Harper and Row.

Dikmen, S. and Machamer, J. E. 1995. Neurobehavioral Outcomes and Their Determinants. *Journal of Head Trauma Rehabilitation*, *10*, 48–67.

Franzen, M. D. and Wilhelm, K. L. 1996. Conceptual Foundations of Ecological Validity in Neuropsychology. In Sbordone, R. J. and Long, C. J. (Eds.) *The Ecological Validity of Neuropsychological Testing*. Orlando: GR/St. Lucie Press, pp. 51–69.

Halstead, W. C. 1950. Frontal Lobe Functions and Intelligence. *Bulletin of the Los Angeles Neurological Society*, *15*, 205–212.

Greenspan, A. I., Wrigley, J. M., Kresnow, M., Branche-Dorsey, C. M., and Fine, P. R. 1996. Factors Influencing Failure to Return to Work Due to Traumatic Brain Injury. *Brain Injury*, *10*, 207–218.

Plato. 1952. The Dialogues of Plato (Translated by B. Jowett). In Hutchins, R. M. (Ed.) *Great Books of the Western World*, *Volume 7*. Chicago: Encyclopedia Britannica.

Sattler, J. M. 2001. *Assessment of Children; Cognitive Applications*, 4th ed. San Diego: Jerome M. Sattler Publisher, Inc.

Sbordone, R. J. 1996. Ecological Validity: Some Critical Issues for the Neuropsychologist. In Sbordone, R. J. and Long, C. J. (Eds.) *The Ecological Validity of Neuropsychological Testing*. Orlando: GR/St Lucie Press, pp. 15–41.

Sbordone, R. J. 1997. The Ecological Validity of Neuropsychological Testing. In Horton, A. M., Wedding, D., and Webster, J. (Eds.) *The Neuropsychology Handbook, Vol. 1: Foundations and Assessment*, 2nd ed. New York: Springer, pp. 365–392.

Sbordone, R. J. and Guilmette, T. J. 1999. Ecological Validity: Prediction of Everyday and Vocational Functioning from Neuropsychological Test Data. In Sweet, J. J. (Ed.) *Forensic Neuropsychology*. Lisse, The Netherlands: Swets & Zeitlinger, pp. 227–254.

Sbordone, R. J., Seyranian, G. D., and Ruff, R. M. 1998. Are the Subjective Complaints of Brain-Injured Patients Reliable? *Brain Injury*, *12*, 505–515.

Sbordone, R. J., Seyranian, G. D., and Ruff, R. M. 2000a. The Use of Significant Others to Enhance the Detection of Malingers from Traumatic Brain-Injured Patients. *Archives of Clinical Neuropsychology*, *15*, 465–477.

Sbordone, R. J., Strickland, T. L., and Purisch, A. D. 2000b. Neuropsychological Assessment of the Criminal Defendant: The Significance of Cultural Factors. In Fletcher-Jansen, E., Strickland, T. L., and Reynolds, C. R. (Eds.) *Handbook of Cross-Cultural Neuropsychology*. New York: Klewer/Plenum, pp. 335–344.

Williams, J. M. 1996. A Practical Model of Everyday Memory Assessment. In Sbordone, R. J. and Long, C. (Eds.) *Ecological Validity of Neuropsychogical Testing*. Delray Beach, FL: GR Press/St. Lucie Press, pp. 129–146.

Wilson, B. A. 1993. Ecological Validity of Neuropsychological Assessment: Do Neuropsychological Indexes Predict Performance in Everyday Activities? *Applied and Preventive Psychology*, *2*, 209–215.

Wilson, B. A., Cockburn, J., and Baddeley, A. D. 1985. *The Rivermead Behavioural Test Manual*. Bury St. Edmunds: Thames Valley Test Company.

10 Neuropsychological Assessment

DEFINITION

Neuropsychological assessment refers to the complex process that the neuropsychologist goes through to reach opinions regarding the effect of a specific injury on the patient's cognitive and emotional functioning and on the patient's quality of life and ability to work, attend school, and perform activities of daily living, including shopping, cooking, cleaning, handling finances, paying bills, and dealing with family. This assessment process typically includes identifying specific areas of the brain, that have been damaged and demonstrating the relative severity of the patient's cognitive and emotional impairments.

Psychologists unfamiliar with medicolegal reports may often exclude any relationship between a specific injury and a patient's neuropsychological impairments. One of the reasons for this is that neuropsychologists are typically asked by physicians or other psychologists to identify the patient's impairments and how they impact upon the patient's life. For example, referral questions frequently address such issues as "Can this specific patient return to school or work? If he or she returns to work or school, what kinds of problems can be expected to arise?" Thus, neuropsychologists without medicolegal experience may be relatively insensitive to causation issues, unless their importance is carefully emphasized by the referring attorney. Since this issue is so important to attorneys, and should be so to neuropsychologists involved in medicolegal cases, it is essential that a variety of confounding or extraneous factors be ruled out so that the relationship between a specific event (e.g., accident, trauma, or fall) and the patient's neuropsychological impairments may be made as unequivocally clear as possible. This is best done by a careful and systematic neuropsychological assessment, which includes a variety of data bases:

1. A detailed, chronological history of the patient's injury that includes information acquired directly from the patient and significant others, as well as from available medical records.
2. An extensive background history obtained from the patient which includes the patient's developmental, linguistic, educational, family, military, occupational, legal, cultural, religious, marital, sexual, medical, and psychiatric history.
3. Observations of the patient's behavior during the interview, breaks, and testing in both structured and unstructured settings, including interviews with significant others and family members to learn their observations of the patient's behavior in unstructured and familiar settings.
4. A careful review of the patient's academic, vocational, medical, psychiatric/psychological, legal, and military records to supplement patient and family interview data.
5. The administration of a wide variety of specialized tests that have been designed to evaluate the patient's cognitive, emotional, and behavioral functioning.
6. Careful analysis of the test results, using both quantitative and qualitative scoring methods based upon the neuropsychologist's experience, expertise, and training in neuropsychology.

7. Conclusions regarding the patient's impairments, or lack of, based upon an integration of all of the above databases, while ruling out other probable causes of the patient's impairments and determining the relative contributions of these factors on the patient's present condition.
8. Determination of the patient's prognosis and long-term cognitive, behavioral, and emotional difficulties.
9. Determination of the types of treatments that are needed, such as rehabilitation, psychiatric treatment, or cognitive rehabilitation, to improve the patient's quality of life and alleviate or minimize the effects the patient's neuropsychological impairments may have upon daily functioning.
10. Determination of the effect that the patient's impairments have upon the family and significant others.
11. Description of any potential problems, such as epilepsy, depression, or psychiatric conditions, that may arise in the future and create a need for medical, psychological, or other services.

Each of these databases will be covered in greater detail in this chapter and in subsequent chapters.

CLINICAL INTERVIEW WITH PATIENT AND SIGNIFICANT OTHERS

An individual with a suspected or known brain insult should be carefully interviewed by a qualified neuropsychologist prior to the administration of neuropsychological tests. Although the reasons for this may seem obvious to many health care professionals and defense attorneys, they may not be as obvious to plaintiff attorneys. For example, if an individual has sustained a suspected traumatic brain injury during a motor vehicle accident, the neuropsychologist should determine if this individual can provide a chronological history of the events immediately preceding, during, and following the accident. If the individual is able to provide a clear and continuous recollection of these events and it can be established that this individual suffered no loss of consciousness, head trauma, confusion, bewilderment, or deterioration of neurological functioning, it is highly unlikely that this individual sustained a brain injury during the accident.

Case Study

A neuropsychologist was referred a 27-year-old woman for testing after she had been suspected of having a traumatic brain injury as the result of a motor vehicle accident. During her examination, she was asked "What was going on in your head during this accident?" She replied, "I was just frightened out of my mind. I thought I was going to die." She then began sobbing and recalled, "I smelled smoke and thought the car was going to catch on fire and explode." She then tearfully recalled how she tried to get out of her car, but the driver's side door had jammed. She feared she would be trapped in the car and engulfed in flames. Although she was eventually able to exit her car through the passenger side door, she experienced numerous flashbacks of this incident, had frequent nightmares, and would become extremely anxious whenever she was exposed to any stimuli or events that reminded her of the accident. She also indicated that she had never told any of her examining doctors this story (because none of them had ever asked her what had been going on in her head at the time the accident occurred).

She recalled that her doctor seemed particularly interested in the fact that she had sustained a head injury (a scalp hematoma and laceration above her right eye) and that she complained of attention and concentration difficulties after her accident. As a consequence, she had been diagnosed with a cerebral concussion and probable brain injury. Her family corroborated her symptoms, particularly her reluctance to discuss the incident and how, since her accident, she felt terrified whenever she rode in a motor vehicle. Thus, a clinical interview with this patient and her family was helpful in ruling out a brain injury. This information was also consistent with her neuropsychological test performance, which was generally inconsistent with a traumatic brain injury.

PATIENT'S DESCRIPTION OF THE ACCIDENT

Patients who have sustained closed head injuries are usually unable to recall the accident and the events surrounding the accident. When they are asked to describe their accident or the events that occurred immediately before or after the accident, they will usually say, "I don't remember" and do not appear anxious or emotionally upset. When they are asked to describe the first event they recall after the accident, they are likely to say something like, "I remember being on a table in the emergency room and talking to a doctor." When they are asked, "What do you recall this doctor saying to you, or you saying to him?" they are likely to say something like, "I remember him saying something about my head. That's all I can remember." When they are asked, "What's the next thing you remember?" they will typically say something similar to, "I remember my aunt driving me home from the emergency room that evening and being greeted by my dog as I walked in the front door." Thus, one can easily see that the chronology of events provided by an individual who has sustained a traumatic brain injury of mild to moderate severity is dramatically different from that provided by an individual who sustains a posttraumatic stress disorder (PTSD) and is able to provide a highly detailed and emotionally charged recollection of events surrounding the accident (see Chapter 6).

SUBJECTIVE COMPLAINTS OF PATIENT DURING INTERVIEW

The subjective complaints of the patient during the clinical interview are of considerable importance. There is frequently an inverse relationship between the number of subjective complaints provided by the patient and the severity of the brain injury in cases where the patient has actually sustained a traumatic brain injury (Sbordone et al., 1998). For example, individuals who sustain traumatic brain injuries, regardless of their initial severity (mild, moderate, or severe), are likely to minimize or deny their cognitive, behavioral, and emotional difficulties when they are interviewed many weeks, months, or years after their accident.

Case Study

A 17-year-old female was rendered comatose for approximately 3 days following a motor vehicle accident. She was examined by her family physician at 5 months postinjury. At that time, she complained of only mild shoulder and back pain. She did not complain of any cognitive, emotional, or behavioral difficulties. When her attorney asked her if she had any memory or cognitive difficulties, she replied, "No." He referred her to a neurologist who reported back to the attorney that his client's neurological examination, which included an electroencephalogram (EEG) and computed tomography (CT) scan, was normal. On the basis of this information, her attorney considered settling her case for $100,000, even though the defendant was a well-known Hollywood actor. A colleague, however, suggested that prior to settling the case he should have his client undergo neuropsychological testing. When he phoned the neuropsychologist recommended to him and discussed the facts of the case, the neuropsychologist informed him that severely brain-injured patients during this stage of recovery are likely to deny their cognitive, behavioral, or emotional difficulties.

After the neuropsychological examination had been completed, the neuropsychologist informed the attorney that his client appeared to have sustained significant damage to her frontal lobes as a result of the motor vehicle accident. He also reported that his client also had a variety of neuropsychological impairments ranging from mild to marked severity. On the basis of the test results, the neuropsychologist advised the attorney not to settle the case at that time because he felt that patients with similar neuropsychological impairments were at high risk to develop serious psychiatric and behavioral problems. On the basis of the neuropsychologist's advice, the attorney turned down the settlement offer of $100,000.

One month later, his client became very depressed and began acting bizarrely. As a consequence, she was placed in an inpatient psychiatric unit where she spent the next 3 months (at a cost of approximately $1000 a day). During this time, her treating psychiatrist felt that his client had developed an organic mood disorder as a result of her brain injury. It was his opinion that this disorder would most likely require psychiatric treatment for the remainder of her life.

PATIENTS WITH NUMEROUS SUBJECTIVE COMPLAINTS

Some individuals who claim they have sustained a brain injury may provide as many as 30 or 40 subjective complaints. The most frequent of these complaints tends to be memory difficulties, often expressed as: "My biggest problem is my recent memory. I can't remember anything. If someone tells me anything, 5 minutes later I can't even remember it. For example, yesterday my wife told me to buy some groceries at the store. When I went to the store, I completely forgot what she had told me to buy. After I got home, I remembered that she had told me to buy some whipped cream." When these individuals are asked to rate the severity of their memory difficulties, they will usually rate it between 8 and 10 on a 10-point scale of severity. They will also complain of numerous somatic problems (e.g., severe pain and discomfort in various locations throughout their entire bodies).

When they are asked to describe their pain and discomfort and rate its severity, they will typically complain "My pain is horrible. My head and neck hurt constantly. On a scale of 1 to 10, my neck pain is $9\frac{1}{2}$ and my head pain is 10." Ironically, their complaints are usually described with a bland affect (e.g., *la belle* indifference), while they exhibit no physical evidence of pain and discomfort and may even be smiling at the examiner.

An overwhelming number of these individuals have had traumatic childhoods, frequently consisting of physical and sexual abuse, parental neglect, loss of one or both parents, and so forth. They also tend to have a history of abusive marriages and traumatic life experiences (e.g., prior accidents, rape, or serious medical problems). However, they will usually deny ever having any of these problems in the past or any history of emotional difficulties prior to their accident or injury. When they are asked to describe their childhoods, they will usually describe them in an idealistic manner, as if looking through "rose-colored glasses." They will frequently describe their childhoods as "great" or "perfect" and will even deny that they were ever sick or missed school as a child or had ever gotten into an argument with any of their siblings or parents during childhood.

Case Study

A 48-year-old female was referred for numerous complaints of cognitive and somatic difficulties following a relatively minor motor vehicle accident. During the interview, she claimed that her childhood was "great." She denied that she had ever gotten into an argument with her parents or siblings throughout her childhood or adolescence. She denied having any of the usual childhood diseases and claimed that she had never been sick a day in her life until her accident.

When she was asked to describe the unhappiest memory of her childhood, she stated, "I never had any; my childhood was perfect." She denied that she had ever missed a day of school or had ever seen a doctor prior to her accident. However, after a lengthy clinical interview that lasted nearly 4 hours, she mentioned that she had been abandoned by her biological mother when she was four and was raised by her aunt, whose husband sexually molested her between the ages of 5 and 12. She also admitted that she had been physically abused by her aunt throughout her childhood. For example, whenever she would become upset or angry in response to the behavior of her aunt or uncle, she would be severely punished, sent to her room, and forced to go for as long as 2 or 3 days without eating.

As with many children who have been abused throughout their childhood, she had repressed her emotional pain at these incidents and had tried to keep a smile on her face and pretend she was happy. To get away from home, she got pregnant and was married at 16. However, her husband physically abused her and drank heavily. He also had numerous extramarital affairs which he attributed to her sexual frigidity. She married another man, hoping to find someone to take care of her and treat her well. Unfortunately, her second husband was irresponsible and selfish, had a drinking problem, and psychologically and physically abused her. She admitted that she had never previously confided this information to anyone and had tried to suppress her memories of these events.

ROLE OF CONFOUNDING FACTORS ON PATIENT'S NEUROPSYCHOLOGICAL TEST PERFORMANCE

Individuals are referred for neuropsychological testing for a variety of purposes: diagnostic (e.g., does the patient have an organic vs. functional disorder?), descriptive (e.g., what are the cognitive and behavioral manifestations of the brain insult?), evaluative (e.g., how much improvement or deterioration has occurred?), treatment/rehabilitation (e.g., what type of treatment or rehabilitation services are needed?), or forensic (e.g., are the individual's cognitive and behavioral deficits the result of a specific accident or injury?) (Lezak, 1995). While many psychologists rely heavily on the individual's neuropsychological test data to answer these questions, such data is frequently confounded by a variety of factors that necessitates that the psychologist proceed with caution to avoid prematurely arriving at any diagnostic, descriptive, evaluative, treatment, or forensic opinions without a full appreciation of the impact of these factors (Sbordone and Purisch, 1996). The following case study illustrates this.

Case Study

A 35-year-old male was referred for neuropsychological testing by his treating physician 6 months after he had been involved in a motor vehicle accident. The physician wanted to know if his patient's symptoms were organic or functional since there was no clear evidence that his patient had ever been rendered unconscious or sustained a concussion in his motor vehicle accident. When the patient was seen for neuropsychological testing, he complained of numerous cognitive problems, severe low back pain, constant headaches, insomnia, and significant psychiatric difficulties. He underwent an 8 hour battery of neuropsychological tests. After reviewing the test data, the neuropsychologist concluded that this patient had severe cognitive impairments, which were caused by a previously unrecognized head injury this patient had sustained during his motor vehicle accident.

The referring physician was not happy with the neuropsychologist's opinion and referred the patient to another neuropsychologist. A lengthy clinical and background history revealed that this patient had a preexisting history of severe cluster headaches, chronic low back pain, prior head trauma, attention-deficit hyperactivity disorder, and severe learning difficulties (which resulted in this patient's having been placed in special education classes throughout elementary school). The patient also had an extensive drug and alcohol abuse history, had only worked a total of 3 years during the past 10, had been arrested and convicted of two felonies (grand theft and fraud), and had served a total of 5 years in prison. The neuropsychologist also learned that this patient had a preexisting history of psychiatric illness and had received treatment during his late adolescence for bipolar disorder and was currently taking Haldol, Vicodin, Klonopin, Desyrel, Lithium, and Imitrex. The patient had had a rebellious childhood which included gang involvement, reckless disregard for the welfare of others, frequent arrests and fights, repeated lying, poor judgment, impulsivity, and consistent irresponsibility. When the patient arrived for his scheduled appointment, he appeared to be in considerable pain and discomfort and admitted that he had injured his lower back as a result of falling down a flight of stairs yesterday while intoxicated. He also appeared upset since he had had a verbal altercation with his wife that morning, after she informed him that she was leaving him for another man.

This case example illustrates the numerous confounding factors present at the time the patient arrived for neuropsychological testing, any one of which alone, or in combination, would have negatively impacted on his neuropsychological test performance, regardless of whether he had sustained a brain injury in his motor vehicle accident. Given these factors, this patient would have most likely performed poorly on many, if not all, of the neuropsychological tests that were administered to him. Thus, while his neuropsychological test data would be considered technically valid, the presence of the numerous confounding factors described above would have rendered the first neuropsychologist's interpretation of the etiology of this patient's neuropsychological deficits inaccurate.

Sbordone and Purisch (1996) have listed a number of factors that can produce poor performance on neuropsychological tests (see Table 10.1). This list is not meant to be exhaustive, nor is a discussion of some of these factors meant to be more than cursory.

PRIOR BRAIN INJURIES AND CONGENITAL NEUROLOGICAL CONDITIONS

It is generally well known that a number of congenital and preexisting disorders, such as attention-deficit hyperactivity disorder, anoxia, febrile illnesses, mental retardation, epilepsy, learning disability, cerebral palsy, and neurological disorders, can produce poor performance on neuropsychological tests (Boucagnani and Jones, 1989; McCaffrey et al., 1993). Unless the neuropsychologist is aware of these preexisting disorders, the patient's neuropsychological impairments are likely to be attributed to a recent brain injury.

PAIN AND PHYSICAL CONDITIONS

Patients, who have severe headaches or who are sleep deprived, excessively fatigued, or in acute pain at the time of testing, will most likely exhibit deficits on tests of attention, concentration, and recent memory. Unless the neuropsychologist is aware of these conditions at the time of testing (which is frequently done by a technician rather than a neuropsychologist), the patient's neuropsychological impairments may be inaccurately attributed to a recent brain injury. Similarly, if the patient has sustained any musculoskeletal injuries that affect the peripheral nervous system, the psychologist may erroneously conclude that the patient has sustained a brain injury. For example, if the psychologist

---

TABLE 10.1
Factors That Can Significantly Affect a Patient's Neuropsychological Test Performance

Prior brain injury or insult
Congenital or preexisting neurological conditions
Absences (seizures)
Acute pain
Symptoms and impairment secondary to physical injuries
Peripheral sensory impairment
Peripheral motor impairment
Current and chronic medical illness
Sleep deprivation/excessive fatigue
Alcohol/drug abuse
Medication use
Psychiatric illness
Recent psychosocial stressors
Suboptimal motivation and malingering
Negative patient/examiner interaction
Cultural/linguistic discrepancies
Vocational and avocational background
Test sophistication and practice effects

Source: Sbordone, R. J. and Purisch, A. D. 1996. *Neurorehabilitation,*
7, 17. With permission.

---

is unaware that the patient sustained a crush injury to his or her left arm, the psychologist might erroneously conclude that the patient had a right hemisphere brain injury.

MEDICAL ILLNESSES

The neuropsychological test performance of patients with medical illnesses is often impaired. This does not mean that these individuals are brain injured, rather that their illnesses have adversely affected the metabolic functioning of their brains or simply their test performance. A variety of systemic medical disorders, as well as specific medical conditions and treatments, has been shown to produce neuropsychological impairments. For example, patients with hyponatremia (Atchinson et al., 1993), hypoxemia (Guttierrez et al., 1993), multiple sclerosis (Grant, 1987), renal dialysis (Guttierrez et al., 1993), cancer treatment (Adams et al., 1984), HIV infection (Dalakas et al., 1989), thyroid disorder (Trzepacz et al., 1988), cardiac problems (Garcia et al., 1984), cortisol deficits (Basavaraju and Phillips, 1989), porphyria (Grabowski and Yeragani, 1987), Wilson's disease (Goldstein et al., 1968), epilepsy (Homan et al., 1989), systemic lupus erythematosus (Adelman et al., 1986), B12 deficiency (Hector and Burton, 1988), and folate deficiency (Martin, 1988) have been found to be impaired in their performance on a variety of neuropsychological tests.

ALCOHOL/DRUG ABUSE AND MEDICATION USE

Acute alcohol use can produce mild neuropsychological impairments, particularly on tasks involving short-term memory, concept formation, and mental flexibility (Rourke and Loberg, 1996). Chronic alcohol abuse has been shown to produce significant impairments on tasks involving learning, recent memory, mental flexibility, and problem-solving and executive functions (Ryan and Butters, 1980).

Although the chronic neuropsychological effects of street drugs are confounded by a variety of methodological issues, the adverse cognitive effects of chronic polysubstance use is generally well accepted (Sweeney et al., 1989). While specific studies are currently ongoing to assess the chronic effects of street drugs on cognitive functioning, Strickland et al. (1993) have reported that casual cocaine use can produce neuropsychological impairments and abnormal single photon emission computed tomography scans.

A number of medications have been reported to produce cognitive impairments. For example, anticonvulsants such as phenytoin (Dilantin), phenobarbital, and Primidone have been found to produce impairments on tests of attention, concentration, recent memory, perception, and psychomotor performance (Wroblewski et al., 1989). Psychiatric medications, particularly antidepressants such as amitriptyline (Elavil) have been shown to produce impairments on neuropsychological measures of reaction time, vigilance, psychomotor performance, learning, and memory (Thompson and Trimble, 1982; La Rue et al., 1986). Lithium (Glenn and Joseph, 1987) and a variety of antipsychotic medications (Cardenas, 1987) have also been shown to adversely affect a patient's neuropsychological test performance. Stein and Strickland (1998) recently reviewed the neuropsychological effects of commonly used prescription medications and found that psychomotor functioning, concentration, and memory are commonly affected by such medications.

PSYCHIATRIC DISORDERS

Patients with psychiatric disorders have been found to display a wide range of cognitive impairments on neuropsychological tests. For example, patients with depression (Goulet et al., 1986; Newman and Silverstein, 1987; Veiel, 1997; Rosenstein, 1998) or schizophrenia (Walker et al., 1992) frequently exhibit a wide range of cognitive impairments when they are administered neuropsychological tests.

RECENT PSYCHOSOCIAL STRESSORS

A variety of significant psychosocial stressors such as divorce, marital conflicts, financial difficulties, recent arrest, serious illness, physical altercations, physical abuse or assault, rape, or significant emotional losses can affect a patient's performance on neuropsychological tests, particularly tests of attention, concentration, vigilance, and short-term and recent memory. As a result of these stressors, patients are likely to experience high levels of anxiety and depression, as well as significant sleep difficulties, which may cause them to increase their consumption of alcohol and drugs or their doses of medication, which can also adversely affect their neuropsychological test performance (Stein and Strickland, 1998).

SUBOPTIMAL MOTIVATION AND MALINGERING

Suboptimal motivation can occur when individuals are depressed or in pain or become seriously fatigued during testing. These individuals may perform poorly on the neuropsychological tests they are administered, without any voluntary intention to do so. On the other hand, individuals who are seeking financial compensation for their alleged injuries following an accident may be motivated to intentionally perform poorly when they are administered neuropsychological tests. When this is done in an obvious or exaggerated manner, it constitutes malingering. Although nearly anyone can engage in malingering when financial issues or external incentives are present, malingering does not preclude the possibility that the individual has genuine neuropsychological deficits. Finally, the nature of the interaction between the patient and the examiner may create feelings of anger, anxiety, or passive–aggressive behavior toward the examiner, which can significantly lower the patient's motivation to perform optimally and, consequently, the level of test performance.

DEMOGRAPHIC DISCREPANCIES

Individuals with limited intellectual and low educational levels typically perform more poorly on neuropsychological tests than do individuals with normal intelligence or higher educational levels. Thus, if the neuropsychologist uses normative data derived from a population where the individuals were of average or above average intelligence and all high school graduates, individuals with limited education and low premorbid IQs are likely to be erroneously diagnosed as brain damaged. Conversely, since individuals with superior intellectual functioning typically perform better on neuropsychological tests than individuals with average intelligence, the neuropsychologist may fail to identify individuals with high premorbid intellectual functioning (e.g., IQ of 125 or higher) as cognitively impaired if their test performances fall within the expected range for persons of average intellectual functioning.

PRIOR EXPERIENCE AND PRACTICE

A person's performance on neuropsychological tests can be influenced by prior life experiences or familiarity with these tests. For example, well-developed mechanical or visuoconstructional skills that are acquired as a result of vocation or avocation may enhance an individual's performance on assembly/constructional tests and may mask any true visuoconstructional deficits. Similarly, prior testing with identical or similar neuropsychological tests can result in "practice effects," which may artificially enhance an individual's test performance (Lezak, 1995) and may be erroneously interpreted as evidence of recovery to premorbid or baseline cognitive levels of functioning.

USE OF CLINICAL HISTORY TO DETECT MALINGERING

Clinical history can be helpful in ferreting out malingering since malingerers may provide the interviewer with a textbook-like presentation of their symptoms, while avoiding specific questions about the accident or personal background, and may appear guarded and suspicious. A more detailed discussion of malingering can be found in Chapter 11.

Case Study

A 38-year-old male arrived for his scheduled appointment approximately 1 hour late without any excuse or apology. He appeared guarded and suspicious. When he was asked questions about his accident, he stated, "Well, haven't you read the records? Why haven't you read the records so that you can find out what happened to me. I don't think I need to tell you about the accident since you have the records." After the neuropsychologist had stressed how essential it was that he provide him with his subjective recollections of the accident, he stated, "I have a severe brain injury and I can't work."

Later, when he was asked questions about his injuries he stated, "You guys are all alike. All you do is work for the insurance companies. You really don't care what happens to us; all you're interested in is making money." He then added, "I don't see why you are asking me all these questions; you've already made up your mind anyway. It's a waste of my time coming here. You're asking me these questions so that you can prove that I don't have a brain injury." When he was asked which doctors he had seen and what treatments he had received since his accident, he stated, "I don't know. It's in my records."

When he was asked if he had ever had any problems in the past, he said, "What difference does that make? It doesn't make any difference. The fact is I have a brain injury and I can't work." When he was asked to describe his employment history, he stated, "I can't remember anything because I have a brain injury." When he was asked if he had ever been fired from any job in the past, he stated, "What do you want to know that for? That's not important. What really is important is that I can't work because I have a brain injury."

DIFFERENT SCHOOLS OF THOUGHT ABOUT THE IMPORTANCE OF OBTAINING CLINICAL HISTORY

The clinical interview can reveal information about the type of injury sustained, its severity, and a great deal of information about the interviewee. The clinical history can also provide an opportunity to gain insight into the interviewee's motives for filing a lawsuit or workers' compensation claim. Unfortunately, some neuropsychologists do not feel that this information is necessary for them to make a diagnosis or to determine the individual's neuropsychological impairments or whether the individual has sustained a brain injury. One school of thought has emphasized that all the information a neuropsychologist needs to interpret the significance of an individual's neuropsychological test data is the patient's age, sex, handedness, highest grade completed, and occupation. Proponents of this particular school have stressed that taking a clinical history can confound the interpretation of the test data; therefore, the diagnosis of brain dysfunction or damage should only be made on the basis of the test data. There are a number of neuropsychologists who adhere to this philosophy.

Another school of thought has stressed that obtaining a careful and detailed clinical and background history allows the neuropsychologist to formulate hypotheses about the patient's impairments, information that is vital in assessing brain dysfunction or damage. Then, through neuropsychological testing, these hypotheses can be corroborated or refuted. While both schools of thought have their respective merits, health care professionals and attorneys should be aware of the particular philosophy held by the neuropsychologist, particularly the relative importance the neuropsychologist places on the clinical interview and history in arriving at opinions about whether an individual has sustained brain damage.

NECESSITY OF INTERVIEWING SIGNIFICANT OTHERS

The neuropsychologist should attempt to obtain a chronological history of the individual's injury, including all treatments received and the relative effectiveness of these treatments in alleviating medical, cognitive, and behavioral impairments. Since individuals who sustain severe brain damage are usually poor historians, particularly for the events that have occurred since their injuries, the examiner must rely on family and significant others to provide this information. Information obtained from these individuals is likely to reveal the kinds of problems and difficulties the brain-injured patient has exhibited since the accident. For example, family members will frequently describe observing cognitive and behavioral problems, such as dramatic change in personality, memory difficulties for recent events, confusion, irritability, temper outbursts, and rapid mood swings. Family members are also likely to report problems such as poor judgment, disinhibited behavior, impulsivity, impaired problem-solving skills, loss of initiative and motivation, decreased frustration tolerance, impaired interpersonal and social skills, strained relationships with others, loss of friendships, marked egocentricity, and a loss of sensitivity to the needs and welfare of others.

Family members and significant others, as a result of having known the brain-injured individual prior to the injury or accident, are usually able to detect relatively subtle cognitive and behavioral changes that may not be detected by neuropsychologists or medically trained professionals. This also may reflect the environment in which the brain-injured individual is observed. For example, brain-injured individuals are more likely to exhibit their cognitive and behavioral impairments in unstructured rather than structured environments. Since most professional settings are fairly structured, a brain-injured individual may not exhibit his or her cognitive and behavioral impairments in such settings. However, such behaviors may be frequently observed at home, particularly if the home environment is unstructured.

Neuropsychologists face two potential problems if they rely on the information that is furnished to them by the brain-injured individual's family and significant others: its accuracy and the psychological state of the informants at the time they are interviewed. Family members may exaggerate his or her cognitive and behavioral impairments for purposes of financial gain, or minimize the individual's problems as a result of denial. For example, many family members cope with catastrophic events such as a severe brain injury by trying to deny that their loved one has actually been brain injured, even though they had been given this information by their loved one's treating doctors. Families frequently repress this information and will often say something like, "I don't think anyone has ever told us that our son had a brain injury." Unfortunately, their use of denial and repression to cope with the devastating injuries sustained will often sap and drain away their emotional resources and may result in psychiatric difficulties and treatment for one or more family members.

The discrepancy between the number of spontaneous subjective complaints offered by the brain-injured patient and the patient's cognitive, emotional, and behavioral problems as observed by family or significant others (assuming that they are not in denial and are reliable informants) appears to be a fairly reliable indicator of the presence and perhaps even severity of traumatic brain injury (Sbordone et al., 1998). This information can be easily obtained by a health care professional or the plaintiff's attorney, particularly if a brain injury is suspected. When the ratio of the family and significant others' observed problems is considerably greater than the patient's spontaneous subjective complaints, there is a strong possibility that this patient has sustained a brain injury. For example, the patient may complain of only two or three problems, while the family and significant others report that they have observed considerably more problems and of greater severity than the patient reports. It should also be recognized that the converse is also true. If the individual's spontaneous subjective complaints are in excess of the cognitive, behavioral, and emotional problems observed by the significant others (excluding denial), there is a strong likelihood that this individual may not have sustained a brain injury and could actually be malingering, or may have a psychiatric disorder that is unrelated to the accident (Sbordone et al., 2000).

THE IMPORTANCE OF OBTAINING A CAREFUL AND COMPREHENSIVE BACKGROUND HISTORY

One of the critical problems faced by the neuropsychologist when determining whether an individual has sustained brain damage as a result of an accident or injury is the accuracy and comprehensiveness of the background history obtained from the individual. Thus, an individual who is suspected of having sustained a significant brain trauma should arrive for the scheduled neuropsychological examination with at least one family member or significant other who is well known and can rectify any faulty recollections of recent events and furnish details about the individual's childhood (e.g., birth weight, childhood illnesses, or a preexisting history of learning, medical, or neurological disorders) or history of significant traumatic events (physical or sexual abuse), which many individuals may deny or repress. These accompanying individuals may also clarify the accuracy of the information furnished by the patient.

The information from family members and significant others should help the neuropsychologist gather a careful background history that not uncommonly may reveal a preexisting history of neurological disorders (e.g., epilepsy), medical illnesses (e.g., asthma, diabetes), psychological trauma (e.g., loss of or abandonment by a parent during childhood), prior head trauma, attention-deficit disorder, hyperactivity, dyslexia, language difficulties, learning difficulties, or substance abuse.

Knowledge of these factors can assist the neuropsychologist in correctly interpreting the patient's neuropsychological test data, particularly with respect to determining whether the test data reflect preexisting cognitive, behavioral, or emotional difficulties or a recently acquired brain injury. The following example illustrates the importance of obtaining a comprehensive background history to assess the contribution of previous neurological disorders to an individual's claim of brain damage.

Case Report

A 52-year-old electrician was referred for neuropsychological testing. He had fallen approximately 20 ft from a telephone pole while installing new equipment. He fractured both legs and was briefly rendered unconscious. The neuropsychologist who initially evaluated him examined the test data and concluded that he had sustained a severe brain injury as a result of his fall. When this individual was later examined by another neuropsychologist, a careful background history revealed that he had been struck by an automobile when he was ten and rendered comatose for 1 week. The individual had also been a professional boxer and had been knocked out in the ring on at least ten occasions.

Six months prior to his accident, he had noticed that he was dropping objects and experiencing balance problems. He was seen by a neurologist who diagnosed his symptoms as vertebrobasilar artery insufficiency syndrome (the blood supply to his brain stem, inferior temporal lobes, and cerebellum had become occluded as a result of cerebrovascular disease). He was prescribed Persantine, a vasodilator, to treat this condition, which he quit taking after only a week because it interfered with his 30-year history of consuming between 12 and 18 beers a day. On the day of his accident, he had consumed 12 beers over lunch. After lunch, he climbed up a telephone pole and erroneously cut the wire that held the telephone pole in place. Three days after he was hospitalized, he began seeing little green men under his bed and was diagnosed as having delirium tremens (a toxic delirium that follows alcohol withdrawal). When his neuropsychological test data were later reviewed in light of his background history, they were consistent with his 30-year history of chronic alcoholism and prior brain insults.

Table 10.2 refers to areas of information that should be obtained during a neuropsychological examination. Each of the general areas of background history is discussed below.

BACKGROUND INFORMATION TO BE OBTAINED

DEVELOPMENTAL

The presence of low birth weight or prematurity suggests that the individual's mother may have smoked, consumed alcohol, or been ill during her pregnancy. Individuals with low birth weight often have histories of attention-deficit disorder and hyperactivity, learning difficulties, antisocial behavior, and academic and vocational difficulties. Forceps, which might have been used to remove the infant from the birth canal, can damage the brain. A significant number of individuals who sustain traumatic brain injuries have a preexisting history of prior head trauma, developmental delay, hyperactivity, attention-deficit disorder, learning problems, psychiatric/emotional difficulties, or chronic health problems. Individuals with such backgrounds appear to be slower to recover from a mild traumatic brain injury (Kibby and Long, 1997) and appear to be at higher risk to develop chronic PTSD (Gurvits et al., 1996). The following example illustrates the importance of obtaining a careful developmental history.

Case Study

A 24-year-old male was referred for neuropsychological testing by his treating psychiatrist. This patient had been involved in a motorcycle accident 3 years earlier and had been diagnosed with a mild concussion. Shortly after his accident, however, he began experiencing homicidal urges, which caused him to seek psychiatric treatment. He had been placed on Mellaril, an antipsychotic medication, and had been diagnosed as "paranoid schizophrenic." His psychiatrist had heard a neuropsychologist lecture on traumatic brain injuries and thought that it might be helpful for his patient to undergo neuropsychological assessment since he suspected that his patient might have sustained a brain injury during his accident.

While taking the developmental history, the neuropsychologist noted that this patient had a history of severe abdominal cramps during his childhood, which resulted in his being hospitalized on several different occasions. When the patient was asked what this condition had been diagnosed as, he stated, "I can't remember, but I think it starts with the letter P." The neuropsychologist asked, "Porphyria?" The patient said, "Yes, that's it." This patient indicated that he had never drunk, smoked, or used drugs because he had wanted to become a professional football player.

At the time of his injury, he had been scheduled to try out for a professional football team. However, during his accident, he fractured his right arm and dislocated his right shoulder. These injuries not only ended his chances of trying out for a professional football team, but caused severe pain and discomfort. As a consequence of his symptoms, he had been prescribed narcotic pain medications, which alleviated his pain but caused him to develop homicidal impulses, which terrified him and prompted him to seek psychiatric treatment. He also became depressed by his psychiatric problems and at the prospect that he might never be able to play professional football. As a way of coping with his depression, he began consuming alcoholic beverages. This, unfortunately, aggravated his homicidal impulses (porphyria is an inborn metabolic disorder that produces a homicidal psychosis when barbiturates and alcohol are ingested).

This patient's homicidal impulses and psychosis were not directly caused by his accident, but by the pain medications and alcohol he took following his head injury as a result of a pre-existing metabolic disorder that had not been recognized by his treating psychiatrist. When his psychiatrist was later informed that his patient had porphyria, he cursed himself for not taking a more careful medical history. He advised his patient to stop using barbiturates and alcohol, which resulted in a dramatic improvement in the patient's psychiatric problems.

EDUCATIONAL BACKGROUND

A careful history of an individual's educational achievements, grades, courses repeated, remedial training, expulsions, or reasons for leaving school can be important. Poor grades in school can be due to a variety of factors such as poor motivation, physical or psychological abuse, limited intelligence, boredom, attentional difficulties, learning problems, hyperactivity, antisocial or rebellious behavior, frequent moving due to family crises or economic factors, divorce, emotional deprivation, molestation, or frequent medical illnesses. Many individuals, however, may not provide accurate information about their academic background. For example, an individual might report graduating from high school with As and Bs when poor grades had been received or he or she had even dropped out of high school prior to graduation. Therefore, review of an individual's academic transcripts and interviews with teachers or other informants may be necessary to corroborate the accuracy of the information furnished by an individual with an alleged or suspected brain injury. A review of this individual's academic transcripts can also provide the neuropsychologist with valuable insights into the preexisting level of intellectual functioning, motivation, and conduct in the classroom.

TABLE 10.2
Background Information to Be Obtained

Clinical history

Complaints of patient and significant others	Current residual problems
History of injury or illness	Change in patient's functioning during past year
Onset and duration of symptoms	Effect of injury on patient and significant others
Neurological findings	Expectations of the patient and significant others
Hospitalization history	History of medication use/abuse
Treatment/rehabilitation history	Behavioral, psychiatric, or emotional problems since injury

Background history and factors

Developmental
  Problems or drug use during pregnancy
  Place of birth
  Birth order
  Birth weight
  Problems during delivery
  Developmental milestones
  Childhood diseases
  Emotional problems in childhood/adolescence
  History of learning disabilities
  History of health problems
  History of attention-deficit disorder
  History of hyperactivity
  History of physical or emotional trauma
  History of head trauma
  History of neurological diseases
Educational
  Highest level completed
  Grades attained
  Best/preferred courses
  Worse/least preferred courses
  Extracurricular activities
  Awards and achievements
  Courses completed
  History of remedial training
  History of conduct disturbances or expulsions
  Reasons for leaving school
  Additional schooling or nonacademic training
Language
  First language spoken
  Other languages spoken
  Preferred language
  History of speaking or language difficulties
    and treatment
Cultural
  Country of birth
  Ethnic background of patient and family
  History of discrimination
Religion
  Religious background
  Recent changes in religious beliefs
  Church attendance
  History of religious discrimination
  Religious customs observed, beliefs

Medical
  History of major hospitalizations
  Prior health or medical problems
  Previous surgery
History of any of the following
  Alcoholism
  Anoxia/hypoxia
  Arteriosclerosis
  Cancer
  Cancer treatment
  Cerebrovascular disease
  Coronary dysfunction
  Cortisol deficiency
  Diabetes
  Dietary deficiency (e.g., folate, B12)
  Gastrointestinal disorders
  Genitourinary problems
  Headaches
  Head trauma
  HIV
  Hypertension
  Hypoglycemia
  Hyponatremia
  Hypoxemia
  Liver disease
  Motor difficulties
  Pernicious anemia
  Porphyria
  Renal dialysis
  Respiratory problems
  Seizures
  Sleep apnea
  Substance abuse
  Syncope
  Systemic lupus erythematosus
  Toxic or heavy metal exposure
  Vascular disease
  Vertigo
Occupational
  Present occupation
  Job duties
  Salary
  Job aspirations
  Last job held

TABLE 10.2
Continued

Current stressors
    Death or loss of spouse or family member
    Divorce or marital separation
    Marital difficulties
    Job difficulties or termination
    Financial difficulties
    Sexual difficulties
    Loss of friends
    Conflicts with others
    Academic difficulties
    Business difficulties
    Recent accidents
    Recent injuries or illnesses
    Recent relocation of self or family
    Recent travel
    Recent problems with law enforcement authorities
    History of incarceration, probation, or parole
    Pending litigation
    Recent problems of family members or
      significant others
    Recent problems with IRS
Marital status and history
    Marital status
    Number of years married
    History of previous marriages
    Age, education, and occupation of spouse
    Spouse's expectations
    Previous and current marital difficulties
    Current marital stability and conflicts
    Number and ages of children
    Physical and emotional health of children
    Living status of children
    Effects of children on patient
    Current support system
Sexual
    Sexual preference
    Changes in sexual preference
    History of sexual problems
    Changes in libido
    History of extramarital affairs
    History of venereal disease
Psychiatric
    Previous emotional or psychiatric difficulties
    History of suicidal ideation or behavior
    Psychiatric treatment history
    Psychiatric hospitalization history
    History of psychiatric medications
    Family history of psychiatric illness or treatment

Family history
    Parents
    Age and education
    Occupation
    Personality
    Marital status and history
    Alcohol and substance abuse history
    Psychiatric history
    Criminal history
    Health history
    Relationship with patient
    History of neurological disorders
    Stability of patient's marriage
    History of divorce and separation
    Siblings
    Number and ages
    Education and occupation
    Personality
    Marital status and history
    Alcohol and substance abuse history
    Psychiatric history
    Criminal history
    Health history
    History of neurological disorders
    Divorce and separation history
    Relationship with patient
Legal
    Arrest history
    Types of criminal offenses
    Time served in jail
    Current legal problems
    Prior history of litigation
    Prior history of disability claims
    Current court cases
Lateral dominance
    Initial preference
    Changes in preference
    Familial history of sinistrality
    Tasks performed with dominant and
      nondominant hands
Military service
    Branch and dates of service
    Jobs held within service
    Training received while in service
    Combat history
    Rank at discharge
    Type of discharge
    Service connected disabilities

Source: Sbordone, R. J. 2000. In Groth-Marnat, G. (Ed.) *Neuropsychological Assessment in Clinical Practice: A Practical Guide to Test Interpretation and Integration.* New York: Wiley, pp. 100–102. With permission.

Case Study

A 19-year-old individual was referred for neuropsychological testing after he was struck on the left side of his head by a policeman's night stick during a physical altercation, which resulted in his arrest. He was not rendered unconscious and was able to recall the incident in considerable detail. He claimed that the head injury he sustained during this altercation had significantly affected his ability to learn new information, which was essential at his job as a parts supplier (his position actually required him to review parts catalogues). He claimed that he could no longer retain this information after the injury and as a consequence was unable to work.

Neuropsychological testing revealed that he performed poorly on tests that assessed his reading skills, vocabulary, verbal fluency, and verbal memory. A review of his academic transcripts indicated a history of severe dyslexia and learning difficulties, which were identified in elementary school and resulted in his being placed in special education classes throughout elementary and junior high school. After he was forced to repeat the fourth and eighth grades, he dropped out of school during the ninth grade. While this individual might have possibly sustained a brain injury during his altercation with the police officer, his academic records revealed that his preexisting history of dyslexia and learning difficulties could have accounted for his poor neuropsychological test performance.

Language

Most of the clinical neuropsychologists in North America are of Euro-American/Anglo-American descent and grew up speaking English as their primary language. However, a significant number of individuals who are seen by these neuropsychologists either do not speak English or have considerable difficulty communicating in English. If the neuropsychologist lacks linguistic competence in the individual's primary language, this may create serious communication difficulties. The neuropsychologist may not detect some of the individual's symptoms such as abnormal prosody, grammatical errors, and paraphasic errors, and may be limited with respect to evaluating this individual's mood, affect, thought processes, and psychiatric symptoms (Artiola et al., 1998), even though a certified interpreter is used (Marcos, 1979). More importantly, translating a standardized neuropsychological test or battery from English into another language may distort or even violate the assumptions upon which the particular test was normed.

Gathering information about the history of languages spoken, or preferred languages, allows the neuropsychologist to weigh the possible contribution of linguistic and cultural factors when interpreting an individual's neuropsychological test data. Unfortunately, this factor is often ignored by many neuropsychologists. Individuals who are raised in a different culture or speak a different language often perform worse than expected on standardized IQ tests based on their educational and vocational achievements. Unfortunately, some neuropsychologists may interpret the spuriously low IQ scores of these individuals as evidence of a substantial reduction in their intellectual functioning following a relatively mild traumatic brain injury.

Case Study

A Samoan-born 28-year-old male was seen for neuropsychological testing to evaluate his intellectual and cognitive functioning following a concussion. He had lived in Samoa until he was 12 and then migrated to the United States with his family. While his command of English seemed acceptable, his full-scale IQ, as measured by the Wechsler Adult Intelligence Scale, was only 78, even though he had graduated from high school with above-average grades, had completed 1 year of junior college with a 3.1-grade average, and had been working as a journeyman carpenter at the time of his accident. The psychologist argued that the patient's brain injury had reduced his IQ by approximately 30 points, on the basis of her review of academic and occupational achievements.

Three weeks later, this patient was seen by another neuropsychologist who administered a nonverbal and relatively culture-free test of intellectual functioning, which did not penalize the patient as a result of his linguistic and cultural background. He obtained an IQ score of 112 on this test, which suggested that the prior psychologist's choice of intelligence tests reflected her failure to consider this patient's prior linguistic and cultural background.

CULTURAL BACKGROUND

Culture refers to shared behaviors, beliefs, values, and experiences that are common to a group of people (Taussig and Ponton, 1996). While culture is a complex entity, it is often erroneously linked to ethnicity or race, and at times language, which can impair our understanding of this factor. The cultural background of an individual will frequently color the manner in which his or her symptoms are described, as well as the manner in which the family is likely to cope with his or her neurological or psychiatric difficulties. The families of these individuals may not divulge specific details or complain of specific problems for fear of violating the norms of their culture. Cultural factors may also result in the neuropsychologist overpathologizing the patient's behavior and misdiagnosing the etiology of the patient's disorder (e.g., diagnosing some brain-injured patients as hysterics). Cultural factors can also reduce an individual's insight into his or her cognitive and behavioral functioning (Prigatano et al., 1997). Finally, because most of the psychometric tests that are used today by neuropsychologists were designed to evaluate individuals from a Euro-American background, they may not accurately assess individuals from different cultural backgrounds.

Case Study

A 17-year-old East Indian female was referred by her attorney for neuropsychological assessment 7 months after she had sustained a severe traumatic brain injury. Her parents denied observing any cognitive, emotional, or behavioral problems since their daughter's accident. The neuropsychologist was puzzled after hearing this since this patient had sustained a severe traumatic brain injury. The neuropsychologist decided to investigate the validity of their statements and discovered that it was considered taboo for family members of this particular culture to discuss their children's problems with individuals who were not part of that culture. As a consequence, he enlisted the services of a psychiatrist who had been raised in a nearby province to interview this patient and her family in their native language.

After her interview, she reported that the patient's parents had actually observed a dramatic change in their daughter's behavior, which included violent outbursts toward family members. Although the patient had been a very demure individual prior to her accident, she began using crude and coarse language after the accident and, during a verbal altercation, had tried to stab her older brother with a knife. Her family had also observed that her memory for recent events was poor and that she showed little concern for the feelings or welfare of others.

Neuropsychological assessment revealed evidence of executive dysfunction characterized by her inability to regulate her emotions or behavior, impulsivity, pathological egocentricity, and poor awareness of the effect that her behavior had on others. Her test results were consistent with the cognitive and behavioral problems that her parents had described to the psychiatrist. However, as a result of their cultural background they had not felt it proper to admit such problems to anyone who was outside their culture.

Individuals who grow up in a particular culture are often exposed to harassment, cruel jokes, and insensitive treatment from persons of different cultural groups. This can produce feelings of resentment and suspicion toward individuals from other cultures. Changes in an individual's perceptions of others as a result of altered cognitive functioning and diminished coping skills following a brain injury can cause the development of a paranoid disorder that can significantly jeopardize the ability to socially interact or work.

Case Study

A 47-year-old male was referred for neuropsychological testing after he was chronically exposed to industrial solvents during his work in a chemical factory. As an African-American, growing up in the South, he had been exposed to a great deal of injustice and prejudice. He had learned, however, to live with these feelings and was generally able to work with his white coworkers and superiors as long as he consciously kept a lid on his feelings and avoided reacting to occasional racial slights and insults.

After 3 years of work, he became increasingly paranoid and felt that his white coworkers and supervisors were actually plotting to kill him. He refused to join them for lunch or eat at the cafeteria at work. He also feared that they might infect him with a lethal virus or disease if he came into physical contact with them. As a result of his paranoid disorder, he was referred to an industrial medical clinic.

The physician who examined him referred him for neuropsychological testing because he suspected that this individual may have been exposed to industrial solvents. Neuropsychological testing identified recent memory, concentration, perceptual, and problem-solving deficits consistent with neurotoxic exposure. Tests of personality corroborated this individual's paranoid disorder. The neuropsychologist phoned the company physician and informed her that he felt that probable neurotoxic exposure had markedly diminished this individual's ability to cope with his longstanding feelings of animosity and suspiciousness toward whites and had contributed to the development of a paranoid disorder.

ETHNICITY

Ethnicity refers to common social beliefs and behaviors that are shared among people who reflect the composition of a particular group in which its members share a common descent, physical characteristics, and heritage (Ardilla et al., 1994). Ethnic groups living in America can usually be divided into five distinct categories: Caucasian (Euro-American/Anglo-American), African-American, Hispanic/Latin American, native American Indian/Alaska native, and Asia/Pacific Islander Americans. Failing to recognize the importance of ethnic factors during a neuropsychological examination may result in poor rapport between the examiner and the individual being examined, difficulty appreciating the significance of the individual's subjective complaints, a negative attitude toward testing, and a tendency to overpathologize the individual's behavior or complaints and misdiagnose this individual's condition. There are very few norms currently available to compare an individual's test performance to his or her ethnic group, particularly if the individuals are native American Indian/Alaska natives or from an Asian ethnic group.

RELIGION

While an individual's particular religious views may not seem important, they may help the neuropsychologist understand how the individual may cope with his or her cognitive deficits secondary to a traumatic brain injury. Individuals who are raised in strict or fundamentalist religions appear to be at higher risk of developing psychiatric symptoms following brain damage or psychological trauma.

Case Study

A 36-year-old female was referred for neuropsychological testing by her neurologist after she had become depressed and paranoid following a cerebral contusion sustained during a motor vehicle accident 3 years earlier. She had been raised in a fundamentalist religious sect that stressed the importance of keeping one's feelings under rigid control and that failure to control one's feelings and emotions was sinful. After her brain injury, she exhibited frequent temper tantrums in which she swore and cursed at her family. Her family told her she was a sinner and needed to pray to God for the strength to resist these sinful temptations. Unfortunately, her prayers were not enough because she had no control over her emotions and behavior. Her family continued to call her a sinner and told her that the devil was controlling her mind and that she was going straight to hell when she died. As a consequence, she became very depressed and extremely paranoid.

Neuropsychological assessment identified her cognitive impairments, particularly her inability to regulate her emotions and behavior. The neuropsychologist gently informed her that her problems were not the work of the devil but were the result of the cerebral contusion she had sustained in her accident. He also assured her that her behavioral outbursts would gradually diminish over time. Upon hearing this, she felt somewhat relieved and asked the neuropsychologist to explain the findings to her family. Although her family members were initially reluctant to meet with the neuropsychologist, they were more accepting of her behavior after they discovered that her behavioral outbursts were the result of a brain injury and not the work of the devil.

MEDICAL

Since a number of medical disorders can affect cerebral functioning and produce cognitive, behavioral, and psychiatric problems, it is essential that the individual's medical history be carefully reviewed. This should include childhood and adult medical problems, their treatment, and any recurrent medical conditions. Unfortunately, some individuals may provide an inaccurate or incomplete medical history. A variety of medical conditions such as cerebrovascular disorders, coronary difficulties, hypoglycemia, anoxia/hypoxia, near drowning, toxic or heavy metal exposure, hypertension, diabetes, gastrointestinal disorders, respiratory problems, cancer, and endocrine disorders can impair an individual's neuropsychological test performance. The presence of two or more of the above medical conditions often makes it difficult to differentiate cognitive impairments caused by a mild traumatic brain injury and those caused by medical problems on the basis of the individual's neuropsychological test data.

The neuropsychologist should determine how the individual coped with his or her medical problems in the past and what effects such problems may have had on cognitive, emotional, and behavioral functioning. Individuals who develop conversion disorders frequently have a rather lengthy medical history, even though they may actually deny that they were ever sick or saw any doctors on a regular basis prior to their accident.

Case Study

A 48-year-old woman had been referred for neuropsychological testing after she complained of numerous cognitive and somatic difficulties after her vehicle had been rear-ended by another vehicle traveling approximately ten miles an hour. During her interview, she claimed that she had not seen any physicians for the past 10 years. She even denied that she had ever undergone any routine medical examinations, PAP smears, or had made any visits to any health professionals. When her medical records were later obtained and reviewed, they revealed that she had actually been seen by over 200 physicians during the 10 years prior to her accident. In fact, these records revealed overwhelming evidence that for many years she had had each of the problems she claimed she had developed following her motor vehicle accident.

Some neuropsychologists, partially because of their lack of medical training, may fail to inquire into an individual's prior medical history or may not fully appreciate the significance of an individual's medical history or symptoms.

Case Study

A 28-year-old obese woman was referred for neuropsychological assessment by her husband, a clinical psychologist in private practice. He complained that his wife had gained considerable weight; had become depressed, irritable, and anxious; and had been exhibiting memory difficulties during the past year. He wondered whether her symptoms were related to a fall she had had 2 years earlier in which she struck her head on the floor, even though she had not been rendered unconscious and exhibited no amnesia for the events surrounding the fall.

She arrived for her scheduled appointment and indicated that she weighed approximately 280 pounds. She complained of fatigue, sleep difficulties, hypersomnia (excessive sleeping), nervousness, excessive sweating, and tachycardia and stated that she had gained over 80 pounds during the past 6 months. When she was asked if she had ever had a history of endocrine disorders, she indicated that she had been diagnosed with hypothyroidism approximately 5 years ago and was placed on Synthroid at that time. She stated, however, that she had stopped taking this medication several months ago, without bothering to consult with her physician, because of her health and religious convictions, that is, she felt that this medication was not a natural substance and therefore should not be taken since it violated the sanctity of her body. She also mentioned that she had been seeing a clinical psychologist for the past 3 months for her symptoms of anxiety and depression. While she enjoyed her therapy sessions, she reported that her emotional and cognitive problems had actually increased and that she had gained 40 pounds since entering treatment. As a consequence, her self-esteem had become extremely poor and she had seriously contemplated committing suicide.

Neuropsychological assessment revealed cognitive impairments that were generally consistent with a metabolic disorder such as hypothyroidism. The neuropsychologist advised her husband to take his wife to an internist. The internist diagnosed her as having hypothyroidism and placed her back on Synthroid. After 3 weeks, she stopped complaining of cognitive and emotional difficulties. She also began exercising and lost 20 pounds. Her energy level improved considerably, which was accompanied by a marked improvement in her self-esteem.

OCCUPATIONAL

Many individuals who sustain brain injuries have poor prior work histories. While some of these individuals may have had difficulty holding down a job prior to their brain injury as a result of their personality, intellectual limitations, or motivational problems, their ability to hold down a job after a brain injury may be virtually nonexistent as a result of a combination of their preexisting vocational difficulties and the acquired brain injury.

An individual's occupational background, including jobs held, job duties, salary, and history of job promotions and terminations allows the estimation of an individual's level of cognitive and behavioral functioning prior to a specific injury or accident. When combined with the neuropsychological data, this information can also be helpful in assessing whether the individual can return to the job held at the time of injury or become competitively employed in the future (Sbordone and Guilmette, 1999).

Case Study

A 27-year-old female stockbroker had sustained a concussion during an automobile accident 3 months previously. She was unconscious for approximately 20 minutes. When she returned to work a few days later, she found herself having considerable difficulties performing her duties as a commodities broker. Her clients soon began to sense that her ability to provide them with the market's activities was flawed. As a consequence, she began losing clients and became anxious and depressed. After she resigned from her job under pressure from her company, she contemplated committing suicide. She then sought out and received psychiatric treatment.

After 2 months, she tried working for another company as a stockbroker, was still unable to handle the cognitive demands of this new job, and continued to feel like a failure, becoming more depressed. She was referred for neuropsychological testing. While she was found to have an IQ of 127, testing revealed mild to moderate impairments on tasks involving divided attention, recent memory, speed of cognitive processing, and problem solving. On the basis of her test results, the neuropsychologist encouraged her to seek out a less cognitively demanding job. She then found a job at a credit union managing the retirement accounts of its customers. Even though she continued to experience relatively mild impairments in selective cognitive domains on follow-up testing, she had relatively little difficulty handling the cognitive demands of her new job. As a consequence, her mood improved dramatically and she no longer required psychiatric treatment or felt suicidal.

The type of work a particular patient has done prior to his or her brain injury, irrespective of the number of years of education completed or grades received, can serve as a crude index of preexisting cognitive skills and abilities.

Case Study

A 27-year-old male was referred by his physician for neuropsychological assessment after having been involved in a motorcycle accident in which he sustained a moderately severe traumatic brain injury. Even though he had only completed ninth grade and had done poorly in school as a result of a history of dyslexia, he had been employed as an automobile mechanic and specialized in working on exotic foreign cars. His visuospatial and motor skills had been superb. He had been an outstanding athlete who excelled in several sports and had always been able to take anything apart and quickly put it back together again. He began working on cars when he was 14. By the time he was 19, he was considered one of the top foreign car mechanics in the city.

When he returned to work shortly after his accident, he began making a number of costly mistakes at work, which eventually resulted in his termination. However, as a result of the excellent reputation he had had prior to his accident, he was able to find work as a mechanic in another garage. After he had been working there for a few weeks, his supervisor complained that he took twice as long to repair cars as other mechanics and had not been doing a good job.

His physician referred him to a psychologist, who administered the Wechsler Adult Intelligence Scale — Revised to assess his cognitive functioning. This psychologist found that his visuospatial and psychomotor skills were intact on the basis of his performance IQ of 122 and saw no reason why he was having difficulties at work. The psychologist referred him to a neuropsychologist who specialized in assessing closed head injuries.

The neuropsychologist interviewed this individual's employers and coworkers, who, while attesting to his excellent visuospatial and motor skills prior to his accident, indicated that he was no longer the same mechanic he had been prior to the accident and that since his accident he frequently made a lot of "dumb" mistakes while working on cars. Neuropsychological testing revealed that this patient's executive functions were significantly impaired as a result of his traumatic brain injury. As a consequence, the neuropsychologist concluded that this individual's problems at work were due to his impaired planning, organizational, and problem-solving skills and an inability to recognize his errors and rectify them.

CURRENT STRESSORS

Many individuals who are referred for neuropsychological testing to evaluate their cognitive, behavioral, and emotional functioning following an accident or injury may be exposed to a number of stressors that are unrelated to their accident or injury. Such stressors may be of sufficient magnitude to create a number of disabling psychological symptoms and may cloud the assessment of any cognitive and behavioral symptoms created by an accident or injury. Stresses such as the death or loss of a family member, divorce, marital difficulties, job difficulties or termination, financial difficulties, loss of significant relationships, and health or sexual problems can create psychological symptoms that can mimic a brain injury or PTSD.

Case Study

A 36-year-old male was referred by his physician for neuropsychological assessment to evaluate his cognitive functioning after having slipped and fallen at work. While he claimed that he had struck his head on the ground, he denied a loss of consciousness or amnesia. Nonetheless, he reported that he had developed severe headaches and memory difficulties since his accident. He arrived for his scheduled appointment, appearing extremely fatigued and nervous. When the neuropsychologist inquired why he appeared fatigued, he indicated that he had not slept much during the past week as a result of the untimely death of his mother. He also indicated that he was over $30,000 in debt, that his wife had recently asked him for a divorce, and that their two sons had recently been arrested for possession of heroin and drug paraphernalia. He was so fatigued and physically exhausted that he actually dozed off several times during the interview. He had dark circles under his eyes, appeared disheveled, and seemed preoccupied with the numerous stressors in his life. As a consequence, neuropsychological testing was put off until these stressors were resolved.

Approximately 3 months later, he phoned the neuropsychologist and scheduled an appointment. He indicated at that time that his wife had agreed to remain with him and that his sons had been placed on probation. He admitted that he felt much more relaxed and had been sleeping better. This was corroborated by physical observations of his behavior in which he seemed relaxed and rested. He confessed that if he had been tested 3 months earlier, he would have performed poorly because he was so preoccupied with the numerous stressors that were going on in his life.

Individuals who sustain brain injuries may develop a secondary depression if they are exposed to stressors that exacerbate their cognitive, emotional, and behavioral symptoms. Unfortunately, many health professionals may either ignore or fail to recognize the various stressors that are present in the patient's life and may erroneously inform the patient that his or her brain injury is worse than originally believed. This only serves to take away any hope that this patient might have had for a successful recovery and adds additional stress, which results in an increase in the patient's symptoms.

MARITAL STATUS AND HISTORY

The marital status and history of an individual who complains of a variety of cognitive and somatic problems following a suspected or actual brain injury may be important because marital stresses are well known to produce significant psychological problems. A brain injury can aggravate preexisting marital conflicts and contribute to problems such as extramarital affairs, alcoholism, drug abuse, incest, child abuse, problems with in-laws, and financial difficulties.

Case Study

A 30-year-old female had been employed at a film studio where she was occasionally exposed to industrial solvents. For the past year, she complained of concentration difficulties and severe memory problems. She claimed that she could no longer work because of these difficulties and filed a workers' compensation claim that she had developed brain damage as a result of being exposed to industrial solvents at work. Her attorney sent her to a psychologist, who administered a standardized neuropsychological battery and reported that she had sustained "brain damage." The psychologist felt that the claimant was no longer capable of competitive employment and was totally disabled.

The claimant was later seen by a neuropsychologist who took a careful history. During this interview, the claimant stated that she was currently on her third marriage and suspected that her husband was sexually molesting her two daughters. She first suspected this approximately one and a half years earlier (1 month prior to the onset of her symptoms). She admitted that she feared confronting her husband about this issue because she believed that he might leave her. She also admitted that after her two previous husbands had left her, she had become extremely depressed and felt suicidal. Because she saw herself as an overweight and unattractive woman, she feared that if her husband left her, she would never find another man. She had been having considerable difficulty sleeping at night and found herself feeling very tense. In addition, her relationship with her two daughters had become strained. Her daughters had begun to have academic and emotional problems, which she feared were the result of their being sexually abused, which caused her to feel guilty and helpless.

Neuropsychological testing revealed mild cognitive problems that appeared to be the result of her severely depressed mood, psychological conflicts, and high levels of anxiety. Because of her fear of losing her husband and her guilt feelings about her children, she had attributed her cognitive and emotional problems to the chemicals that she was occasionally exposed to at work, after she had read a newspaper article claiming that chronic exposure to chemicals in the workplace could cause brain damage.

SEXUAL

Sexual difficulties are common following brain damage. Individuals who sustain traumatic brain injuries, hypoxic encephalopathy, strokes, or progressive neurological disorder (e.g., Alzheimer's or Pick's disease) typically show a marked reduction in their libido (sexual desire or activity). Individuals who become severely depressed or psychotic or who develop a PTSD may also exhibit a loss of libido. To complicate matters even further, many of the medications that are commonly prescribed for individuals who are depressed will frequently cause sexual dysfunction. A diminished sex drive may be experienced by individuals with temporal lobe epilepsy. Significant frontal lobe damage may cause diminished libido or hypersexuality characterized by excessive sexual activity including frequent masturbation. Thus, alterations in libido or sexual functioning are the rule rather than the exception following a significant brain injury, psychiatric disorder, or PTSD.

When individuals deny any changes in their sexual functioning after sustaining a brain injury or being exposed to severe psychological trauma, the neuropsychologist should interview the spouse or significant other to corroborate the statement. Because normal sexual functioning following a brain injury tends to be rare, the neuropsychologist should question whether the individual has actually sustained a brain injury or PTSD, particularly if this individual's medical records reveal no loss of consciousness or amnesia.

Case Study

A 35-year-old woman was referred by an attorney for neuropsychological testing after she had sustained an injury at work. She maintained that she was struck on the head at work when part of the ceiling directly above her head collapsed during a rainstorm. While she was unclear as to whether she had lost consciousness, she was able to provide the neuropsychologist with a detailed history of the events surrounding the incident. Although she did not report any complaints about her work performance during the first month following her accident, she began experiencing severe problems with her attention and recent memory after this time. She also began to experience severe headaches, which she claimed were present 24 hours a day. When she was asked if there had been any change or decrease in her sexual functioning since her accident, she denied any difficulties and claimed that she and her husband had always enjoyed a satisfying sexual relationship throughout their entire marriage.

Her husband was also interviewed and denied any changes in his wife's sexual behavior or functioning. Although she had undergone extensive neurodiagnostic testing that included several CT scans, magnetic resonance imagings, EEGs, electromyograms, and topographical brain-mapping studies, each of these studies had been interpreted as negative. When she appeared for neuropsychological testing, she exhibited no physical evidence of pain or discomfort and showed no evidence of sleep deprivation, despite her claim that she had not slept for the past 3 months as a result of pain or discomfort. The neuropsychologist also noted that her affect was bland and that she exhibited prominent *la belle* indifference while describing her symptoms. Her complaints and observed behaviors were consistent with a conversion disorder which was corroborated by psychological testing and by further observations of her behavior during the examination.

PSYCHIATRIC

Some individuals have a preexisting history of psychiatric disorders, which may include hallucinations, suicidal ideation or attempts, hospitalization, or being placed on psychiatric medications.
Because many individuals are often reluctant to disclose a history of psychiatric illness or treatment,
the help and cooperation of the individual's family may be necessary in obtaining this information.
However, it should be noted that many culturally unsophisticated individuals or families with limited
educational backgrounds may not know what constitutes a mental or psychiatric disorder or illness.

Case Study

A 53-year-old Hispanic female complained of memory difficulties and attentional problems,
sleeplessness, nervousness, headaches, and a variety of aches and pains throughout her entire
body, after she had been involved in an automobile accident 2 years previously. She had been
wearing a seatbelt at the time of the accident and did not sustain any visible physical injuries
or report any loss of consciousness or amnesia. However, her symptoms had steadily increased
since her accident and had become disabling.

During her neuropsychological examination, it was discovered that she had only completed
3 years of formal education, rarely watched the news, and could not read. Although she had
been seen by a number of psychiatrists and physicians who disagreed about the etiology of her
symptoms, a careful review of their records revealed that she consistently denied a history of
depression or psychiatric illness, even though she appeared quite depressed and anxious. When
she was asked during the interview if she knew what the words depression and psychiatric illness meant, she admitted that she had no idea what they meant. However, when she was asked
if she had ever been given any medicines for her nerves in the past, she pulled an old bottle
of tranquilizers from her purse. When she was asked if she had ever felt sad for long periods
of time or had ever lost or gained any weight during this time, she replied, "Yes." When she
was asked to elaborate on this, she indicated that she had felt terrible 5 years earlier, after she
learned that her son had been killed by an unknown assailant. She admitted that she could not
function for nearly 2 years following his death. She also admitted that 10 years earlier she had
felt the same way, after her husband had abandoned her and their children.

Neuropsychological assessment, using a relatively culture-free test of intellectual functioning, which required very little verbalization or language, revealed that she had an IQ of 75.
Her score on this test was consistent with her occupational achievements as a nurse's aide in a
nursing home. When her neuropsychological test performance was corrected for her age, low
intelligence, and limited educational background, it actually placed her within the expected
range. However, she admitted that during the past 3 years she felt rejected by her children, who
had moved out and rarely visited or phoned her. She also complained that she lived in a neighborhood in which drive-by shootings and muggings were common. Her next door neighbor had
been beaten and robbed at gunpoint 2 years earlier. Following this incident, she often awoke
during the night whenever she heard even the slightest noise in her house at night and would
immediately begin breathing rapidly because she feared that someone was breaking into her
house. To exacerbate matters, her older son had been arrested and convicted of murdering his
girlfriend during the past year. As a consequence, her grandchildren were being raised by his
brother's ex-wife who worked as a prostitute to support her cocaine addiction.

FAMILY

An individual's background can often shed considerable light on his or her current psychological
or even medical problems. Therefore, the neuropsychologist should obtain a detailed family history

that includes the following information: the ages of both parents or stepparents; their educational backgrounds, occupations, health status, history of drug or substance use, and personalities; and a description of how they interacted with this individual during his or her formative years, adolescence, and adulthood. This history should also include similar information about this individual's siblings and children. The family should also be questioned about any past history of psychiatric or neurological disorders.

Since a number of individuals who have cognitive, somatic, and behavioral problems grow up in dysfunctional families characterized by parental neglect, physical abuse, sexual molestation, abandonment, divorce, alcoholism, substance abuse, significant health problems, and psychiatric illness, this information can be useful in evaluating the brain-injured patient's family because individuals who sustain severe brain injuries may be forced to reside with their families. This can be very stressful and cause their symptoms to worsen.

Case Study

A 36-year-old male was referred for neuropsychological assessment after he had fallen at work and struck his head on a chair. He admitted that he had not lost consciousness, but had felt dizzy after the accident. He denied any nausea or vomiting, as well as any amnesia for the events surrounding the accident. He complained of severe headaches, severe upper and lower back pain, severe memory difficulties, sleep problems, and hyperventilation. During a lengthy interview, he admitted that his father had abandoned his family prior to his birth and that his mother had deserted him when he was a child. He was raised by his maternal grandparents, whom he described as "mean and cruel." He vividly recalled being repeatedly beaten with a thick belt during his childhood whenever he broke any of their rules. He never felt any love or caring from them. His grandfather would often call him a "sissy" whenever he cried. His grandmother hated him because he reminded her of her despised father. His friends were not allowed to visit him. He was not allowed to participate in any sports and was forced to read the Bible for 2 hours every evening. His grandparents forced him to leave school prior to graduation in order to work at his grandfather's garage as a mechanic's helper. At work his grandfather constantly criticized him and often referred to him as a "bastard."

When he left home at age 21, his grandparents never forgave him and blamed him for all of their problems. This made him feel extremely guilty. He began drinking to cope with his guilt and feelings of poor self-esteem. One day he found out where his biological father lived and decided to pay him a surprise visit. His father denied that he had ever fathered him and told him that he never wanted to see him again. He also tried visiting his mother, who he discovered had been living in a nearby town. When he located her, he learned that she was a heroin addict and worked as a prostitute. Rather than appearing happy and pleased to see her son, she blamed him for her drug addiction and told him, "I wish I had gotten an abortion."

Although neuropsychological testing revealed no evidence of cognitive impairment, psychological tests revealed that he had been chronically depressed since his childhood and exhibited strong tendencies to somatacize his emotional problems. He admitted that he had found his treating doctors to be accepting, understanding, and compassionate individuals, with whom he enjoyed talking. Although his symptoms had not improved, even though he had been treated by eight different physicians, he did not appear sad or upset by his symptoms. As a consequence, the neuropsychologist phoned his treating physician and indicated that this individual's preexisting emotional needs, as a result of having been deprived of understanding, acceptance, and dignity as a child, had actually been met by his treating doctors and had provided him with considerable secondary gains. The neuropsychologist recommended that he be referred to a psychiatrist to deal with these issues.

An individual's siblings can also provide a rough estimate of his or her preexisting intellectual or cognitive functioning, if the individual and his or her siblings were roughly comparable in terms of their academic achievements, skills, and abilities prior to the injury.

Case Study

A 25-year-old male had sustained a depressed skull fracture and brain injury when he was hit by a wrench at work that had fallen approximately 50 ft. He was immediately rendered unconscious and developed an epidural hematoma, which was surgically evacuated. He was eventually referred for neuropsychological testing. He arrived for his scheduled examination accompanied by his identical twin brother. When the psychologist learned that he had an identical twin brother, he asked his brother's permission to undergo neuropsychological testing so that he could compare the patient's performance to his brother's to determine the extent and severity of the patient's brain injury.

While neuropsychological testing revealed only mild impairments in comparison to normative data, when the patient's test scores were compared to those of his identical twin brother, significant differences were found in their performance, which suggested that this patient had moderate impairments in his problem-solving skills, recent memory, perceptual skills, and intellectual functioning that were caused by his accident. Later, when the neuropsychologist reviewed their academic records, he noted that the patient and his brother had virtually identical IQ scores (123 and 124) and had obtained virtually identical grades in both high school and college. They were also identical in their physical characteristics.

LEGAL

The prior litigation history or criminal activities of an individual who complains of severe and disabling pain and discomfort can be important in trying to determine whether this individual's complaints are reliable. A surprising number of individuals who claim brain damage or have sustained traumatic brain injuries have been arrested and convicted in the past for crimes such as burglary, embezzlement, grand theft, attempted murder, selling drugs, or assault and battery. Although some individuals may have never actually been convicted of a felony, they have what has been termed an "antisocial personality disorder" characterized by incorrigibility, frequent fighting, lying, irresponsible behavior, criminal activities, and truancy. Individuals with this personality disorder are also very manipulative, have poorly developed consciences, and have little regard for the welfare of others. Because malingering involves deceit and dishonesty, knowledge of an individual's legal background may shed light on the reliability of any statements made by these individuals during litigation.

Case Study

A 35-year-old woman, the wife of an auto mechanic, sustained a concussion during a single car accident which her attorney argued had occurred as a result of the installation of defective brakes by an auto dealer. Her husband claimed that he had inspected the brakes of her vehicle immediately after he arrived at the scene of the accident. On the basis of his expertise as an auto mechanic specializing in brake repair, it was his opinion that the auto dealer had improperly installed the brakes on his wife's automobile. Neuropsychological assessment was requested by the defendant's attorney to assess this woman's neuropsychological damages.

The neuropsychologist interviewed her husband during his examination to obtain information about his wife's cognitive and behavioral symptoms. While interviewing her husband, the neuropsychologist discovered that he had been arrested and convicted in the past for crimes such as embezzlement, writing bad checks, and grand theft auto. His testimony that the brakes in his wife's car had been improperly installed was later viewed with considerable skepticism during trial after the jury learned of his prior criminal background.

It is also important to determine whether an individual referred for neuropsychological testing has been previously involved in personal injury litigation or has ever previously filed a workers' compensation claim or whether any members of the individual's family have ever been involved in litigation.

Case Study

A 45-year-old Vietnamese male was seen for neuropsychological assessment after he had been involved in a motor vehicle accident while traveling with his family. He claimed that he had been briefly rendered unconscious during the accident and complained of numerous cognitive and behavioral difficulties during his neuropsychological examination. When he was asked during the examination about his work history, he appeared very reluctant to discuss the jobs he had held since coming to the United States.

When his wife was interviewed to obtain information about her husband's cognitive and behavioral functioning, she indicated that she had also filed a lawsuit as a result of sustaining injury to her lower back during their motor vehicle accident. Asked about her vocational history, she also appeared reluctant to discuss the jobs she had held since coming to the United States 14 years earlier.

Further questioning revealed that neither of these individuals had worked since coming to the United States and that they had been involved in several automobile accidents in the past that resulted in litigation. While neuropsychological testing revealed no evidence of cognitive abnormalities, personality testing revealed antisocial personality traits.

While they had never been employed since coming to the United States, they lived in a nice neighborhood and drove expensive cars on the settlements they had received from their prior lawsuits.

LATERAL DOMINANCE

The preferred use of a particular hand, foot, or eye when performing motor tasks is known as lateral dominance. Approximately 85% of the population is right-handed. Virtually all of these individuals have their centers for language located in the left hemisphere. Approximately two thirds of left-handed individuals also have their language center located in the left hemisphere. What this means is that individuals who are left-handed or have a family history of left-handedness (known as sinistrality) are expected to make a better recovery of their language skills following a brain injury or stroke.

Any changes in an individual's hand preference during childhood could reflect considerable pressure by family members or teachers to force the individual to use the right rather than the left hand. When change in hand preference occurs after a brain injury, it frequently reflects the compensatory use of the nondominant hand following an ipsilateral (same hemisphere as the impaired hand or leg) injury. In other words, knowledge of lateral dominance and its history can help the neuropsychologist better appreciate the patient's neuropsychological test data and improve the neuropsychologist's ability to predict recovery of aphasic or word-finding difficulties following a prominent left hemisphere brain injury.

MILITARY SERVICE

Many individuals have served in the armed forces. Some of these individuals may have been wounded or witnessed friends being killed or wounded during combat. As a consequence, these individuals may have developed a PTSD. This history may be particularly relevant if these individuals are now claiming PTSDs as a result of being terminated from their jobs or following motor vehicle accidents. If an individual received a medical discharge as a result of psychiatric difficulties, such information could shed light on current symptoms and complaints.

Case Study

An individual was referred for neuropsychological testing several months after he had been involved in a motor vehicle accident. While he believed that he may have struck his head on the windshield, he denied any loss of consciousness or amnesia. A few weeks after his accident, he began experiencing nightmares, along with concentration and memory difficulties. He was referred to a neurologist who diagnosed him as having a postconcussive syndrome.

A lengthy interview with the individual, however, revealed that he had been discharged from the army 4 years earlier, after experiencing anxiety attacks, nightmares, sleep difficulties, headaches, and gastrointestinal problems following the abrupt termination of a 3-month relationship with a woman. He was seen by an army psychiatrist who diagnosed him as having an adjustment disorder with anxious and depressive features.

Although he returned to his work duties, he was unable to tolerate the stresses and demands of his job. The army decided that he was unfit for military duty and gave him a medical discharge under honorable conditions.

The neurologist who had diagnosed him as having a concussion was unaware of his prior psychiatric history. When this individual began receiving treatment from a psychiatrist, he admitted that he had wrecked his girlfriend's car a few days prior to his own automobile accident. When his girlfriend learned of this, she had abruptly terminated their relationship.

Knowing an individual's rank at the time of discharge from the armed forces may be helpful in determining whether any punitive actions such as a court martial or demotions have been received. This information may provide the neuropsychologist with valuable insight into the person's character, as well as shed light on the motivation for pursuing litigation.

Case Study

A 35-year-old male had been involved in a motor vehicle accident in which his car was rear-ended by another vehicle that was traveling approximately 15 mph. After the accident, he complained of severe low back pain and problems with his recent memory. He claimed that because of these problems, he could no longer work. He said that he had served in the army and had obtained the rank of Captain. When he was asked about his military career, he indicated that he had served in the army for 8 years and then promptly resigned his commission. When he was asked why he had resigned his commission, he stated that he wanted to return to civilian life.

Because his story seemed implausible, the neuropsychologist probed further and discovered that this individual had been given the choice of resigning his commission or being court-martialed for suspected illegal activities (selling military supplies). When he was later asked if he had ever been arrested after being discharged from the army, he bragged that although he had been arrested three times for embezzlement, he was able to hire "smart attorneys" who got him acquitted. An interview with his wife suggested that he was still involved in a number of illegal activities, including drug smuggling.

His neuropsychological test data was consistent with malingering. The neuropsychologist then contacted the man's attorney and informed him that there were strong indications that his client was malingering. His attorney admitted that he had suspected this because of a number of inconsistencies in his client's description of the accident. He also admitted that he had been unaware of his client's military background and past history of criminal activities. As a consequence, he recommended to his client that he settle his case or seek the services of another attorney.

THE MENTAL STATUS EXAMINATION

The mental status examination is an integral part of the neuropsychological assessment process (Strub and Black, 1977; Rogers, 1995). It consists of observing the patient's behavior in a highly subjective manner and gathering information from the patient and significant others about the patient's symptoms — their onset, duration, frequency, and severity — and their impact on the patient and significant others. During the mental status examination, the clinician should listen carefully to what is and is not being said, as well as to discrepancies between the patient's description of symptoms and the symptoms observed by significant others. The clinician should also strive to form a therapeutic alliance with the patient and significant others so that these individuals can feel comfortable in expressing themselves and sharing personal information (Trzepacz and Baker, 1993).

The skilled clinician will usually attend to both the content (overtly communicated material) and the process (how the material is being communicated) of the descriptions of the patient's symptoms. For example, many histrionic patients will complain of numerous and extremely severe cognitive difficulties without appearing troubled by their symptoms. Given this observation, the clinician should inquire into such discrepancies in a gentle and nonthreatening manner without alienating the patient. In addition, open-ended questions permit the clinician to observe the patient's comprehension, language, memory, organizational, and verbal problem-solving skills. The clinician should also strive to phrase his or her observations of the patient's behavior in as objective a manner as possible, using terminology that is nonprejudicial and nonjudgmental. Such terminology will also help communicate to other professionals how the patient appeared and behaved during the examination. Table 10.3 presents the behavioral factors the psychologist should observe during the clinical interview. These factors will be discussed below.

BEHAVIORAL OBSERVATIONS

Behavioral observations refer to direct observation of the patient's behavior in the doctor's office, during the interview and testing, and in relatively structured and unstructured settings. Many patients who complain of severe problems with their memory will demonstrate a superb memory outside of the formal testing situation, for example, providing the examiner with an excellent chronological history of the events that have occurred to them, including the dates of their examinations by treating doctors, conversations with these doctors, and their work experiences. They will often describe numerous incidents that have occurred since their injury that are used to "document" their complaints of severe memory problems.

TABLE 10.3
Behavioral Observations

Appearance	Mental status
Attire and grooming	Arousal level
Facial expression	Attention
Physical characteristics	Orientation to surroundings
Movements	Speech
Posture	Comprehension
Eye contact	Memory
Mannerisms	Cognition
Disabilities	Self-regulation
Attitude toward assessment	Ability to recognize and self-correct errors
Cooperation	Judgment
Motivation	Problem-solving skills
Affect and mood	Executive functions
Anxiety	Insight/coping mechanisms
Depression	Awareness/denial of problems/illnesses
Hostility	Reactions to errors/mistakes
Euphoria	Psychiatric
Suicidal/homicidal ideation	Hallucinations
Irritability	Delusions
Poor frustration tolerance	Paranoia
Paranoia/suspiciousness	Bizarre thinking
Personality traits	Schizophrenia
Eccentric	Viscosity
Dramatic	Concrete thinking
Labile	Circumstantial
Erratic	Perseveration
Demanding	Flight of ideas
Manipulative	Manic–depressive illness
Anxious	Depression
Compulsive	Loose associations
Histrionic	Tangential thinking
Grandiose	Speech and language
Perfectionistic	Voice
Paranoid	Articulation
Narcissistic	Prosody
Antisocial	Rhythm
Avoidant	Rate
Obsessional	Anomia
Suspicious	Circumlocution
Intellectual	Paraphasic errors
Oppositional	Neologisms
Dependent	Echolalia
Controlling	Paucity or empty speech
Detached/withdrawn	Comprehension

Source: Sbordone, R. J. 2000. In Groth-Marnat, G. (Ed.) *Neuropsychological Assessment in Clinical Practice: A Practical Guide to Test Interpretation and Integration.* New York: Wiley, pp. 100–102. With permission.

These patients often arrive for their scheduled appointments precisely on time or even a few minutes early. When these patients are asked if they had any problems getting to the appointment on time, they will often state something like, "No, actually traffic on the way here was pretty good, although I had to take the exit on Harbor Boulevard to avoid a traffic accident up ahead." When asked if they had witnessed the accident on the side of the road, they might state, "Yes, I saw two fire trucks on the freeway and there were three ambulances and two people lying on the ground receiving cardiopulmonary resuscitation." These patients remember where they parked their car during the lunch break and are able to remember precisely how to return to the doctor's office after lunch. They also recall what they had informed the doctor during the morning and often correct the doctor's errors of memory, such as, "I don't believe you asked me about my uncle when we were talking this morning. You only asked me about my father."

Many of these patients indicate that they had taken a particular test before and can even recall many of the questions and how they answered when they were administered the test several months previously. They can also describe the doctors' offices in which they were examined, as well as several unique characteristics of the doctor that distinguish him or her from other doctors they have seen in the past. They also recall, without any prompting, other appointments during the day or later that evening. They are able to describe the family events that have gone on earlier in the day in fairly precise detail. However, when these same individuals are given a formal test of memory, they often perform quite poorly, frequently complaining during testing, "I can't remember anything. My mind is a blank."

The question which arises is, "What should the neuropsychologist focus on?" If the neuropsychologist focuses attention on the patient's performance on formal tests of memory, then the patient is seen as having a severe, possibly profound, memory disorder. However, if the neuropsychologist examines the behavior of the patient outside of the formal testing situation, as well as the patient's qualitative behavior during testing, such as histrionic complaints, then the neuropsychologist will recognize that this patient's memory is intact.

In evaluating the patient's behavior, the neuropsychologist should use what can best be described as a "vector approach," in which each observation, formal or informal, of the patient's behavior constitutes a data vector. Each of these vectors should be consistent with the others. The presence of inconsistent vectors, such as the discrepancy between the patient's behavior during informal settings and formal testing, should cause the neuropsychologist to carefully evaluate the patient's motivation or behavior during both settings. When both vectors are consistent, the patient's behavior during informal and formal settings is basically the same.

Many patients who have sustained severe brain damage will deny that they have a problem with their recent memory, yet they are unable to provide a chronological history of the events that occurred following their accident. They will often appear confused and request that the instructions be repeated several times. They typically have no recollection of having seen other doctors since their injury and have usually forgotten that their family has been sitting in the waiting room for several hours. They will usually not know why they are being examined and cannot recall the name of the doctor who referred them for the examination. They will frequently get lost when they go to the restroom and can be found wandering up and down the hallway, appearing confused. They are usually taken by their spouses or significant others to their medical appointments, because they cannot be trusted to recall their appointments or keep them because of their severe recent memory problems. More importantly, these patients rarely, if ever, complain of having memory difficulties and appear to be trying to perform to the best of their ability on each of the tests they are administered. When asked to recall events or information witnessed or experienced 20 or 30 minutes earlier, they are frequently unable to do so, but do not appear upset for having this problem. They are usually pleasant and do not appear frustrated or draw attention to their memory difficulties.

During the clinical interview, the examiner should note the patient's physical appearance (grooming, facial expressions, physical characteristics, etc.), the patient's attitude toward the assessment process (cooperative, suspicious, guarded, etc.), mental status (level of arousal, attention, orientation to surroundings, etc.), affect and mood (anxiety, depression, hostility, etc.), speech and language (articulation, comprehension, grammar, prosody, rhythm, rate, etc.), personality traits (eccentric, dramatic, labile, etc.), insight and coping mechanisms (awareness vs. denial of problems or illness, reactions to errors or mistakes), and psychiatric disorder (hallucinations, delusions, paranoia, etc.).

ATTENTION

The clinician should observe whether the patient is oriented in all spheres (person, place, time, and purpose), appears bored, disinterested, distractible (unable to screen out irrelevant stimuli such as noise), or exhibits delirium (marked, rapid alterations in cognitive functioning ranging from lucidity to confusion), internally preoccupied thoughts (hallucinations, ruminative thinking), or autism (the patient displays a lack of interest in communicating with the examiner and plays with inanimate objects).

AGE AND POSTURE

The clinician should determine to what extent the patient appears his or her age. Patients who are manic, immature, narcissistic, or who have undergone cosmetic surgery, frequently appear younger than their stated age. On the other hand, patients who appear older than their stated age often have a history of alcohol or drug abuse, excessive psychological and financial hardships, or poor health. The patient's posture can often provide valuable insights into emotional and neurological functioning. For example, patients with Parkinson's disease frequently appear stiff and rigid. Patients who are wheelchair-bound frequently have a history of central nervous system (CNS) injury or disease. Patients who appear to be slumped over or slouch during the interview are often depressed, whereas patients who present as cross-legged are likely to be anxious.

ATTIRE AND GROOMING

The patient's attire and grooming can reflect socioeconomic status, medical condition, psychiatric status, or a brain insult. Poor personal hygiene is frequently seen in patients who have organic brain syndromes, have dementia, or are psychotic. Individuals with antisocial personality traits or psychiatric illness often dress in rather bizarre attire. Individuals who shave only one side of the face may have a neglect syndrome. Individuals, who are fastidiously groomed, in the face of numerous cognitive and somatic complaints are frequently histrionic.

EYE CONTACT AND PHYSICAL CHARACTERISTICS

The degree or lack of eye contact is likely to reflect the patient's current psychiatric or neurological functioning. For example, patients who are depressed, anxious, or psychotic frequently have difficulty maintaining eye contact. Patients who have a history of attention-deficit disorder or hyperactivity are frequently observed to rapidly scan the environment, whereas patients with frontal lobe pathology may exhibit scanning difficulties or have difficulty maintaining eye contact because of their propensity to become distracted easily.

The physical characteristics of the individual may shed light on the patient's medical condition, personality, psychiatric illness, or neurologic status. Individuals who have tattoos and needle marks frequently have a history of antisocial behavior and drug abuse. Individuals who exhibit obesity and excessive sweating often have a history of thyroid disease. The patient's skin color is often a reflection of medical condition, nutritional status, and personal hygiene. For example, unpleasant body odor can be caused by a variety of medical illnesses, alcohol abuse, poor hygiene, psychiatric illness, anosmia, or organic brain syndrome.

LEVEL OF CONSCIOUSNESS

The patient's level of consciousness should be carefully observed. In contrast to individuals who are awake and alert, patients who appear hypervigilant or hyperaroused may have a history of mania, anxiety, or cocaine and amphetamine abuse or may have a medical condition such as hyperthyroidism. Individuals who seem hypoaroused (e.g., lethargic, drowsy, obtunded, stuporous, or comatose) may have a history of sleep deprivation, drug intoxication, cerebral edema, epilepsy, concussion, CNS infection, or intracranial hematoma.

ATTITUDE

The patient's attitude (e.g., friendly, trusting, suspicious, or childlike) may provide the clinician with insight into the patient's medical condition, as well as neurologic and psychiatric functioning. Patients with frontal lobe pathology frequently appear immature and childlike and often make facetious remarks or inappropriate statements. The presence of hostility, suspicion, guardedness, and vigilance suggests that the information being provided to the clinician may be unreliable or incomplete.

ACTIVITY LEVEL

The patient's activity level (hyperactive, active, bradykinesic, psychomotor retardant, catatonic, or comatose) is often pathognomic of neurological or psychiatric functioning. For example, individuals who have a history of attention-deficit disorder, hyperthyroidism, or drug abuse will frequently appear hyperactive and restless. Bradykinesia (a decrease of spontaneity in movement) is a frequent manifestation of subcortical diseases such as Parkinson's. Individuals who seem catatonic frequently have a history of psychiatric illness.

MOVEMENTS

The patient's movements can also reflect neurologic or psychiatric illnesses. For example, individuals who demonstrate weakness of one or both limbs or facial muscles (paresis) are likely to have peripheral CNS disease. Individuals who exhibit motor paralysis are likely to have a history of CNS disease or injury. Individuals who display a lack of motion despite intact motor strength (akinesia) frequently have a history of psychiatric illness. Hypokinesia can be due to the side effects of a variety of medications, depression, diffuse axonal brain injury, catatonia, or subcortical brain diseases.

Clinicians should note whether the patient exhibits any tremors (oscillating movements which have a fairly consistent rhythm). For example, Parkinsonian patients typically exhibit a resting tremor of 3 to 8 cps. This tremor disappears whenever the body part that is exhibiting the tremor is used. Individuals who present with action tremors, which are frequently caused by hyperthyroidism, drug toxicity, alcohol abuse, withdrawal from sedative–hypnotic medications, neurosyphilis, or anxiety, typically exhibit a tremor when a particular body part is used or is held in a fixed posture. However, this tremor disappears when the body part is not in use or is relaxed. Intentional tremors (made when the patient is asked to perform specific fine motor movements such as touching the nose with the finger) are typically caused by diseases of the cerebellum or its connections to the brain, multiple sclerosis, Wilson's disease, drug or alcohol abuse, or anticonvulsant medication toxicity.

Dystonias represent involuntary increases in muscle tone, which produce sustained contractions of the patient's posture or physical movements. Dystonias often reflect the side effects of anti-psychotic medications for a variety of neurological diseases, such as Huntington's, Parkinson's, or Wilson's disease or hypoxic brain damage. Simple or complex involuntary movements that seem purposeless or bizarre (e.g., lip smacking, walking from one room to another, saluting, or undressing) may be the result of simple complex partial seizures or fugue states.

Individuals who exhibit involuntary movements or vocalizations, which they are unable to resist except with considerable effort, such as blinking, facial grimacing, neck jerks, throat clearing, and vocalization of profanities and obscenities (coprolalia), may be exhibiting manifestations of Tourette's syndrome, excessive caffeine use, or obsessive–compulsive disorder.

REVIEW OF RECORDS

The patient's academic, vocational, medical, military, and psychiatric/psychological records should be carefully reviewed. These records frequently contain important information that helps the neuropsychologist interpret neuropsychological test data.

ACADEMIC RECORDS

Academic records frequently contain the patient's grades, IQ score, scholastic rating, and scores on specific achievement and aptitude tests. Grades reflect a combination of intelligence, diligence, motivation, peer competition, and the grading system used by a particular teacher or school. Good grades typically indicate that the individual had been an intelligent and well-motivated individual. Poor grades, on the other hand, can reflect either low intelligence, poor motivation, emotional problems, a history of drug or alcohol abuse, or overinvolvement in extracurricular activities. Working while attending school, pregnancy, emotional trauma, divorce, and a dysfunctional family system may also produce poor grades. It is difficult to determine which of these factors is responsible for a patient's poor academic performance. This can be determined only by interviewing the patient; reviewing other academic records, including the progress notes of the patient's teachers, IQ and test scores of the patient; and querying the patient's family and significant others.

An individual with an IQ of 82 would not be expected to perform well academically, nor would an individual who had a history of dyslexia (impaired reading skills) or hyperactivity who has an IQ of 105. Bright individuals, with IQs of 125 or higher, may not do well in school because they often find their teachers and assignments boring, particularly if they are not placed in classes for brighter or gifted students. Individuals with character disorders, such as an antisocial personality, generally do poorly in school because of excessive absences and negative attitudes toward school and their teachers. These individuals may also be under the influence of alcohol and drugs during class and be too irresponsible to complete homework assignments or prepare for tests. Individuals whose parents are going through severe marital conflicts or divorce may be so preoccupied with the emotional turmoil in the family that they are unable to study or concentrate on their homework. Women who become pregnant out of wedlock or who are sexually molested are prone to develop serious emotional problems, which are likely to significantly compromise their academic performances. Thus, it is much easier to draw conclusions about the causes of good grades than about the causes of poor grades.

VOCATIONAL RECORDS

Vocational records can help the neuropsychologist understand the various cognitive, social, and behavioral demands that the work environment has placed on the patient prior to injury. Such information is also valuable in helping the neuropsychologist decide if the patient requires vocational rehabilitation or is ready to return to work following brain injury. Vocational records can also help identify patients with preexisting characterological difficulties such as paranoia, rebelliousness, hostility, irresponsibility, manipulativeness, or undependability. It should be noted that many individuals who sustain traumatic brain injuries often have a preexisting history of vocational problems as a result of characterological difficulties. This information can help the neuropsychologist determine the degree to which the injury has aggravated the patient's preexisting vocational problems.

MEDICAL RECORDS

A patient's medical records, particularly those that existed before the patient's injury, will frequently contain illnesses, problems, and treatments that the patient may either not recall or have denied at the time of examination. In certain cases, the sheer volume of the patient's medical records that existed before a specific accident or injury are often sufficient to allow the psychologist to raise hypotheses regarding the patient's psychiatric condition.

Case Study

A patient was referred for neuropsychological assessment for toxic exposure to cleaning solvents while working as a pulmonary therapist in a large hospital. The patient arrived for her scheduled appointment nearly 2 hours late, and stated to the doctor's secretary, "I don't want him giving me any of those psychological tests. There is nothing wrong with me psychologically." Within a minute or two, the patient began hyperventilating and fell to the floor. While gasping for air, she demanded that the paramedics be called to take her to the hospital. The paramedics were summoned. The patient was taken to a nearby hospital where she was released several hours later with instructions to return to the psychologist's office.

When the patient returned, she did not wish to be interviewed and wanted to go home, claiming that, "I could have another attack at any time." The psychologist asked her if she had ever had a prior history of breathing difficulties. The patient adamantly denied a prior history and became angry at the doctor for even asking the question. The patient then indicated that she had been hospitalized 30 times during the past 2 years for respiratory problems after her claim that she had accidentally inhaled a cleaning solution while working. The patient refused to take any psychological tests and stated that she had to get home because she feared she would have another attack.

The psychologist phoned the referring source, an attorney representing the insurance carrier, and recommended that every effort be made to obtain this patient's past medical records. The attorney indicated that he was not aware that this patient had ever seen a physician prior to her industrial accident and did not believe there were any records available. The psychologist indicated that from his experience, he felt that the patient showed symptoms and behavioral characteristics consistent with Munchausen's syndrome, a factitious disorder that is deliberately maintained by the patient to avoid work and other responsibilities.

The attorney hired an investigator to check hospitals within a 50-mile geographic area of the patient's home. The attorney was amazed when he discovered that for the 10 years prior to the patient's industrial injury, she had spent an average of 32 weeks per year hospitalized. These hospital records indicated that whenever her treating doctors suggested that there might be a psychological or psychiatric basis for her problems, she became extremely angry and left the hospital against medical advice. These records also indicated that the patient had been hospitalized and had received treatment at over 40 different hospitals, even though none of these hospitals was aware that she had been treated elsewhere. She denied that she had ever had these problems before or had ever been hospitalized. The records corroborated the psychologist's impression that the patient had Munchausen's syndrome.

MILITARY RECORDS

The patient's military records, if applicable and available, can provide valuable insights into how the patient had handled stress, discipline, and authority and interacted with others. These records may also contain information about the patient's medical problems while serving in the military, as well as any disciplinary or punitive actions he or she may have received. Contained within these records are the armed forces qualifying test scores, which can often be utilized to provide an estimate of the patient's prior intellectual functioning. These records may also contain information about the types of duties and responsibilities the patient performed while serving in the military and the type of discharge received.

PSYCHIATRIC/PSYCHOLOGICAL RECORDS

The patient's psychiatric and psychological records prior to and following an injury or accident can alert the psychologist to any preexisting emotional problems and treatments. This information will frequently disclose the patient's background history, as well as identify any external stressors that are unrelated to a specific injury or accident. These records frequently contain psychological and occasionally neuropsychological test data, including narrative computerized reports of tests such as the MMPI-2.

REFERENCES

Adams, F., Quesada, J. R., and Gutterman, J. V. 1984. Neuropsychiatric Manifestations of Human Leukocyte Interferon Therapy in Patients with Cancer. *Journal of The American Medical Association, 252,* 938–941.

Adelman, D. C., Saltiel, E., and Klinenbert, J. R. 1986. The Neuropsychiatric Manifestations of Systemic Lupus Erythematosus: An Overview. *Seminars in Arthritis and Rheumatology, 15,* 185–199.

Ardilla, A., Rosselli, M., and Puente, A. 1994. *Neuropsychological Evaluation of the Spanish-Speaker.* New York: Plenum Press.

Artiola, I., Fortuny, L., and Mullaney, H. 1998. Assessing Patients Whose Language You Do Not Know: Can the Absurd be Ethical? *The Clinical Neuropsychologist, 12,* 113–126.

Atchinson, J. W., Wachendorf, J., Haddock, D., Mysiw, J., Gribble, M., and Corrigan, J. D. 1993. Hyponatremia Associated Cognitive Impairment in Traumatic Brain Injury. *Brain Injury, 7,* 347–352.

Basavaraju, J. and Phillips, S. L. 1989. Cortisol Deficit State: A State of Reversible Cognitive Impairment and Delirium in the Elderly. *Journal of The American Geriatric Society, 37,* 49–51.

Boucagnani, L. L. and Jones, R. W. 1989. Behaviors Analogous to Frontal Lobe Dysfunction in Children with Attention Deficit Hyperactivity Disorder. *Journal of Clinical Neuropsychology, 4,* 161–173.

Cardenas, D. 1987. Antipsychotics and Their Use after Traumatic Brain Injury. *Journal of Head Trauma Rehabilitation, 2,* 43–49.

Dalakas, M., Wichman, A., and Sever, J. 1989. AIDS and the Nervous System. *Journal of The American Medical Association, 261,* 2396–2399.

Garcia, C. A., Tweedy, J. R., and Blass, J. P. 1984. Underdiagnosis of Cognitive Impairment in a Rehabilitation Setting. *Journal of The American Geriatric Society, 32,* 339–342.

Glenn, M. B. and Joseph, A. B. 1987. The Use of Lithium for Behavioral and Affective Disorders after Traumatic Brain Injury. *Journal of Head Trauma, 2,* 68–76.

Goldstein, N. P., Ewert, J. C., and Randall, R. V. 1968. Psychiatric Aspects of Wilson's Disease (Hepatolenticular Degeneration): Results of Psychiatric Tests during Long Term Therapy. *American Journal of Psychiatry, 124,* 113–119.

Goulet, J., Fisher, D., Sweet, J., and Smith, E. A. 1986. Depression and Neuropsychological Impairment. *International Journal of Clinical Neuropsychology, 8,* 14–18.

Grabowski, J. and Yeragani, V. K. 1987. Porphyria and Psychosis: A Case Report. *Canadian Journal of Psychiatry, 32,* 393–394.

Grant, I. 1987. Alcohol and the Brain: Neuropsychological Correlates. *Journal of Clinical Psychology*, *55*, 310–324.

Gurvits, T. V., Gilbertson, M. W., Lasko, N. B., Orr, S. P., and Pitman, R. K. 1996. Neurological Status of Combat Veterans and Adult Survivors of Sexual Abuse. In Yehuda, R. and McFarlane, A. C. (Eds.) *Psychobiology of Posttraumatic Stress Disorder*. New York: New York Academy of Sciences, pp. 468–471.

Guttierez, R., Atkinson, J. H., and Grant, I. 1993. Mild Neurocognitive Disorder: Nosology of Cognitive Impairment (Organic Mental) Disorders. *Journal of Neuropsychiatry*, *5*, 161–177.

Hector, M. and Burton, J. R. 1988. What Are the Psychiatric Manifestations of Vitamin B-12 deficiency? *Journal of Geriatric Society*, *36*, 1105–1112.

Homan, R. W., Paulman, R. G., and Devous, M. D. 1989. Cognitive Function and Regional Cerebral Blood Flow in Partial Seizures. *Archives of Neurology*, *46*, 964–970.

Kibby, M. Y. and Long, C. J. 1997. Effective Treatment of Minor Head Injury and Understanding its Neurological Consequences. *Applied Neuropsychology*, *4*, 34–42.

La Rue, A., D'Elia, L. F., Clark, E. O., Spar, J. E., and Jarvik, L. F. 1986. Clinical Tests of Memory in Dementia, Depression, and Healthy Aging. *Psychological Aging*, *1*, 69–77.

Lezak, M. D. 1995. *Neuropsychological Assessment*, 3rd ed. New York: Oxford Press.

Marcos, L. R. 1979. Effects of Interpreters on the Evaluation of Psychopathology in Non-English Patients. *American Journal of Psychiatry*, *136*, 171–174.

Martin, D. C. 1988. B12 and Folate Deficiency Dementia. *Clinical Geriatric Medicine*, *4*, 841–851.

McCaffrey, R. J., Williams, A. D., Fisher, J. M., and Laing, L. C. 1993. Forensic Issues in Mild Head Trauma. *Journal of Head Trauma Rehabilitation*, *8*, 38–47.

Newman, P. J. and Silverstein, M. L. 1987. Neuropsychological Test Performance among Major Clinical Subtypes of Depression. *Archives of Clinical Neuropsychology*, *2*, 115–125.

Prigatano, G. P., Ogano, M., and Amakusa, B. 1997. A Cross-Cultural Study of Impaired Self-Awareness in Japanese Patients with Brain Dysfunction. *Neuropsychiatry, Neuropsychology, and Behavioral Neurology*, *10*, 135–143.

Rogers, R. 1995. *Diagnostic and Structured Interviewing: A Handbook for Psychologists*. Odessa, FL: Psychological Assessment Resources.

Rosenstein, L. D. 1998. Differential Diagnosis of the Major Progressive Dementias and Depression in Middle and Late Adulthood: A Summary of the Literature of the Early 1900s. *Neuropsychology Review*, *8*, 109–168.

Rourke, S. B. and Loberg, T. 1996. Neurobehavioral Correlates of Alcoholism. In Grant, I. and Adams, K. M. (Eds.) *Neuropsychiatric Assessment of Neuropsychiatric Disorders*. New York: Oxford, pp. 423–485.

Ryan, C. and Butters, N. 1980. Learning and Memory Impairments in Young and Old Alcoholics: Evidence for the Premature Aging Hypothesis. *Alcoholism: Clinical Experimental Research*, *4*, 288–293.

Sbordone, R. J. and Guilmette, T. J. 1999. Ecological Validity: Prediction of Everyday and Vocational Functioning from Neuropsychological Test Data. In Sweet, J. J. (Ed.) *Forensic Neuropsychology, Fundamentals and Practice*. Lisse, The Netherlands: Swets and Zeitlinger, pp. 227–254.

Sbordone, R. J. and Purisch, A. D. 1996. Hazards of Blind Analysis of Neuropsychological Test Data in Assessing Cognitive Disability: The Role of Confounding Factors. *Neurorehabilitation*, *7*, 15–26.

Sbordone, R. J., Seyranian, G. D., and Ruff, R. M. 1998. Are the Subjective Complaints of Traumatically Brain Injured Patients Reliable? *Brain Injury*, *12*, 505–515.

Sbordone, R. J., Seyranian, G. D., and Ruff, R. M. 2000. The Use of Significant Others to Enhance the Detection of Malingerers from Traumatically Brain Injured Patients. *Archives of Clinical Neuropsychology*, *15*, 465–477.

Stein, R. A. and Strickland, T. L. 1998. A Review of the Neuropsychological Effects of Commonly Used Prescription Medications. *Archives of Clinical Neuropsychology*, *13*, 259–284.

Strickland, T. L., Mena, I., Villanueva-Meyer, J., Miller, B., Cummings, J., Mehringer, C. M., Satz, P., and Meyers, H. 1993. Cerebral Perfusion and Neuropsychological Consequences of Chronic Cocaine Use. *Journal of Neuropsychiatry and Clinical Neuroscience*, *5*, 419–427.

Strub, R. L. and Black, F. W. 1977. *The Mental Status Examination in Neurology*. Philadelphia: F.A. Davis.

Sweeney, J. A., Meisel, L., and Walsh, V. L. 1989. Assessment of Cognitive Functioning in Polysubstance Abusers. *Journal of Clinical Psychology, 45*, 346–350.

Taussig, I. M. and Ponton, M. 1996. Issues in Neuropsychological Assessment for Hispanic Older Adults: Cultural and Linguistic Factors. In Yeo, G. and Gallagher-Thompson, D. (Eds.) *Ethnicity and the Dementias*. Washington, D.C.: Taylor and Francis, pp. 47–58.

Thompson, P. J. and Trimble, M. T. 1982. Non-MAOI Antidepressant Drugs and Cognitive Functions: A Review. *Psychological Medicine, 12*, 530–548.

Trzepacz, P. T. and Baker, R. W. 1993. *The Psychiatric Mental Status Examination*. New York: Oxford Press.

Trzepacz, P. T., McCue, M., and Klein, I. 1988. Psychological Response to Propranolol in Graves Disease. *Biological Psychiatry, 23*, 243–249.

Veiel, H. O. F. 1997. A Preliminary Profile of Neuropsychological Deficits Associated with Major Depression. *Journal of Clinical and Experimental Neuropsychology, 19*, 587–603.

Walker, E., Lucas, M., and Lewing, R. 1992. Schizophrenic Disorders. In Puente, A. E. and McCaffrey, R. J. (Eds.) *Handbook of Neuropsychological Assessment: A Biopsychological Perspective*. New York: Plenum Press, pp. 309–334.

Wroblewski, B., Glenn, M. B., Whyte, J., and Singer, W. D. 1989. Carbamazepine Replacement of Phenytoin, Phenobarbital, and Primidone in a Rehabilitation Setting: Effects on Seizure Control. *Brain Injury, 3*, 149–156.

11 Detection of Deception and Malingering

The validity of the clinical observations and test data obtained from any examination, including the neuropsychological evaluation, depend to a considerable extent on the motivation, effort, and credibility of the patient. The clinical history, medical records, interviews with collateral sources, behavioral observations, and the specialized tests and measures utilized by a neuropsychologist who is performing a comprehensive neuropsychological examination can provide a substantial database to evaluate a patient's motivation, effort, and credibility. This chapter will discuss the concepts and defining characteristics of individuals who attempt to manipulate the neuropsychogical examination process to obtain secondary gains. It will specifically focus upon the detection of deception and malingering.

The detection of deception and malingering in neuropsychology has often been equated with the administration of specialized tests that have purportedly been designed to detect an individual's effort and motivation. While these tests may be helpful in identifying individuals who may be not putting forth adequate effort or are not motivated to perform to the best of their ability, individuals who do not perform well on these tests should not simply be labeled as malingers unless the findings of these tests can be integrated into the context of a much broader and comprehensive neuropsychological examination. For this reason and for reasons related to test security (National Academy of Neuropsychology, 2000), this chapter will focus on the issues inherent in deception and malingering within a much broader clinical context rather than these specialized tests.

CRITICAL CONCEPTS IN OUR UNDERSTANDING OF DECEPTION AND MALINGERING

Any discussion of deception and malingering requires the understanding of several related but distinct concepts such as *symptom validity*, *response bias*, *effort*, *dissimulation*, and *malingering* (Bush et al., 2005). These concepts are presented below.

SYMPTOM VALIDITY

Symptom validity refers to the degree to which the examinee's presentation is a valid and truthful reflection of his or her underlying neuropsychological condition. It also refers to the accuracy or truthfulness of the examinee's behavioral presentation (signs), self-reported symptoms (including their cause and course), and neuropsychological test performance.

RESPONSE BIAS

Response bias is an individual's attempt to mislead the examiner through inaccurate or incomplete responses or suboptimal effort when he or she is administered neuropsychological tests. The presence of response bias adversely impacts the symptom validity.

EFFORT AND MOTIVATION

It is generally assumed that most examinees are trying to perform to the best of their ability when they are administered a neuropsychological test. *Effort refers to the energy invested by the examinee to achieve a particular result as they are being tested during a neuropsychological examination.* While an invalid test performance can result from poor/inconsistent effort, invalid test performance can occur in situations where the effort put forth by the examinee is actually high. Distinguishing an invalid test performance due to poor/variable effort vs. high effort is not only difficult, but requires that the neuropsychologist understand the critical distinction between effort and motivation.

Effort and motivation are not synonymous. For example, some patients may be highly motivated to perform maximally when they are given a neuropsychological test. Despite their high motivation to perform well on the test, their test performance may become seriously compromised if they are in considerable pain, fatigued, or anxious at the time they are tested. Conversely, an individual's motivation to perform to the best of their ability may be low when a monetary incentive or some type of secondary gain is present. A great deal of effort may be expended by this individual to create the spurious appearance that he or she is cognitively impaired or brain-damaged on the basis of their (poor) test performance, which does not accurately reflect their true cognitive abilities.

DISSIMULATION

Dissimulation refers to the intentional misrepresentation or falsification of an individual's cognitive or psychological symptoms. It is typically characterized by an overrepresentation or an underrepresentation of an individual's symptoms. This term bears some similarity to response bias, but infers a greater degree of volitional control to create a certain type of impression, either positive or negative. Response bias, on the other hand, refers to the individual maintaining a particular response set, which may or may not be intentional. For example, an individual who is depressed and lacking in self-esteem may respond in an overly self critical manner to test questions, resulting in a negative and inaccurate assessment of his or her abilities. However, if such a response bias is the result of an intentional attempt to present one's self in a more negative light than warranted by reality, this would be considered dissimilation.

MALINGERING

Malingering refers to the intentional production of false or grossly exaggerated physical or psychological symptoms as a result of the individual being motivated by external incentives such as avoiding military duty, avoiding work, obtaining financial compensation, evading criminal prosecution or obtaining drugs (American Psychiatric Association, 2000). As a consequence, malingering can be viewed to be a form of dissimulation characterized by a negative response bias. This negative response bias results in low symptom validity. As previously noted, a distinction can be made between effort and motivation. For example, in the case of malingering, there is typically a great deal of effort spent to present with psychological problems or cognitive deficits accompanied with low motivation to perform optimally when they are examined or tested.

Manifestations of Malingering

As can be seen from the definition of malingering, the symptoms portrayed by an individual can either be false or grossly exaggerated. Falsification of symptoms can be manifested in two different ways: (1) The symptoms being reported have never previously existed. For example, an individual who claims to have suffered a traumatic brain injury in the absence of head trauma, an alteration of consciousness, and symptoms such as concentration difficulties, dizziness, memory problems, or headaches begins reporting these symptoms for the first time 2 years postaccident. (2) The malingerer experienced an injury at an earlier point in time whose symptoms have resolved.

For example, a patient who has fully recovered from a relatively mild concussion, whose symptoms resolved (e.g., memory or headaches) several years ago, continues to claim ongoing symptoms and disability related to this concussion. Such cases present a greater challenge since the prior injury and its symptoms had been previously documented.

A similar diagnostic dilemma involves the exaggeration of legitimate symptoms. In such cases, although the individual's complaints of memory problems and headaches may be legitimate, malingerers grossly exaggerate them. For example, an individual who sustained a relatively mild concussion describes his or her symptoms as severe and disabling as if he or she had sustained a much more severe brain injury. An intermittent mild headache may be falsely described as a constant severe headache that prevents them from working.

A mild degree of exaggeration can be seen in most personal injury cases. For example, on a ten-point pain rating scale where zero represents no pain and a ten represents the worst pain imaginable, an individual may legitimately suffer from a headache at a severity level of three (relatively mild). However, when they are asked to rate the headache, the severity of the headache may be rated as a four or five instead of a three. While this is not high enough to be called exaggeration, it is high enough to dramatize the negative effects associated with their injury and most likely reflects the incentive caused by the likelihood of obtaining secondary gains.

Gross symptom exaggeration would typically be manifested when an individual claims that his or her headache is constant and always very severe (e.g., rated as a 10 or higher) even though the individual seems well rested and presents as well groomed and nicely dressed. It is certainly easier to identify the presence of exaggeration when it takes this more extreme form. For example, if the litigant's headache is at a severity level of three, there may be little or no physical evidence of pain as such, except for the individual occasionally rubbing his or her temples. An individual's claim that their headache is very severe would be grossly inconsistent with his or her behavior and physical appearance (e.g., they appear well groomed, healthy, and rested). Some malingers, while claiming that the severity of their headache "has always been at a 10 for the past year," will paradoxically state that they refuse to take any pain medications because they are afraid they might get addicted to them, fail to seek out the services of a pain or headache specialist and rarely see their own physician ("I don't like seeing doctors"), or deny that they had ever been treated at an emergency room during the past year.

CONVENIENT FOCUS

Convenient focus (Drukteinis, 2006) is another form of falsification consistent with malingering, but is not technically considered malingering according to the DSM-IV-TR definition. *Convenient focus refers to falsely attributing symptoms and impairments to a situation in which the incentive of secondary gain is involved.* It is not unusual, for example, to see litigants who are troubled by emotional problems such as depression, marital discord, financial difficulties, and feelings of inadequacy and insecurity stemming from unresolved traumatic events that occurred in their childhood (e.g., physical or sexual abuse, abandonment, etc.). Subsequent to these existing emotional problems, they then suffer an injury to which they attribute the cause of their past and present emotional problems. Thus, while their emotional complaints may be legitimate, their attribution as to the specific cause of their complaints is not. In such cases, many of these individuals will deny ever having a history of any problems during their childhood, life, marriages, or with any of the jobs they held in the past. This is illustrated in the case of Mrs. Bonds.

Case of Mrs. Bonds

A 59-year-old female struck her head on a clothes rack while she was reaching down to get her purse while shopping in a large department store. Although she fell to the ground, she quickly got up and reported the incident to the manager before she left the store and drove home. The next day she noticed a small bruise on her forehead. She contacted an attorney who filed a personal injury suit against the store. When she was later seen by a neuropsychologist, she claimed that she was having severe headaches and memory difficulties; felt depressed, tense, and anxious; had sleep difficulties; and was experiencing severe neck and back pain, which she attributes to her accident. During a detailed clinical and background history she indicated that her husband had been diagnosed with terminal cancer, her sister had just died of cancer, her brother had recently died of a heart attack, and her son had recently been discovered to have AIDS. When she asked if she had been troubled by these tragic events, she denied that they had bothered her and attributed all of her symptoms to the injury she sustained in the department store 2 years ago.

Convenient focus often does not involve either feigning or gross exaggeration of the symptoms. Although in these situations symptoms such as feigning or gross exaggeration can be seen, they may not meet the DSM-IV-TR criteria for malingering. On the other hand, the lack of or relatively minimal relationship between the personal injury and the emotional difficulties would tend to indicate that the symptoms are feigned or grossly exaggerated when they are illegitimately attributed to the personal injury to which secondary gain motivation is obvious. The following case illustrates this point.

Case of Mr. Boxer

Mr. Boxer presented for a personal injury evaluation several months after being involved in a motor vehicle accident. There was no question that Mr. Boxer suffered a mild to moderate head injury and definite soft tissue injuries. He had not been able to return to work or resume his normal routine since the injury, offering a number of ongoing complaints including pain, attention and memory problems, irritability, and depression. In the several months interval between the motor vehicle accident and the neuropsychological evaluation, many of Mr. Boxer's complaints had diminished, consistent with the expected course of recovery. He had demonstrated good compliance with treatment and expressed what appeared to be a legitimate motivation to recover and return to his normal routine. His clinical presentation seemed entirely credible. He did not appear to be exaggerating his symptoms. His performance on neuropsychological tests, personality tests, and measures of effort and motivation did not provide a challenge to his credibility.

In responding to questions regarding his personal history, Mr. Boxer acknowledged that he had suffered a prior head injury about a year before the motor vehicle accident in which a heavy box fell several feet, striking him on the crown of the head. This force resulted in a mild concussion and soft tissue injuries. When discussing this prior injury, Mr. Boxer revealed that he suffered several symptoms that were very similar in nature to the symptoms he currently experienced following the motor vehicle accident for which he presented for the personal injury evaluation. However, he was adamant in indicating that only minor annoying residuals of this prior injury remained by the time he was involved in the motor vehicle accident and stated that he had made a full recovery in the weeks and months prior to his accident. He indicated that he had been discharged from the care of his neurologist and his orthopedist and had resumed his normal routine without incident.

His credible presentation in the examination certainly conferred an aura of candor to his self-reported medical history. However, the medical records confirmed that the self-report of the facts of his preexisting injury were accurate in all but one critical way: Mr. Boxer had not fully recovered. In fact, he was still under the care of both his neurologist and orthopedist at the time of the motor vehicle accident. The range, severity, and quality of complaints that were present in the doctors' progress notes were virtually identical to those that he offered several months later in the evaluation related to the motor vehicle accident. While it seemed likely that the motor vehicle accident exacerbated these preexisting symptoms, the records clearly revealed that he continued to suffer almost the entire range and severity of the complaints that he attributed entirely to his motor vehicle accident. Contrary to his representations, he had not returned to work at the time of his motor vehicle accident and remained significantly depressed and disabled in numerous realms of his life, inconsistent with his representation during the evaluation for his motor vehicle accident.

DISTINGUISHING FEATURES OF MALINGERING

The diagnosis of malingering should only be made after a careful review of the potential conditions that could account for an individual's apparent exaggerated or feigned behavior during a neuropsychological examination. For example, individuals with a number of psychiatric and medical disorders often present with significant subjective complaints without objective medical evidence to substantiate an underlying organic or psychiatric etiology. Subjective complaints such as feelings of persecution, memory difficulties, hearing voices, and an inability to sleep by psychiatric patients in the absence of objective medical evidence (e.g., computed tomography [CT] and magnetic resonance imaging [MRI] studies) does not mean that these patients are feigning or grossly exaggerating their symptoms.

Psychiatric factors can complicate the presentation of symptoms and claims of disability even in cases where objective medical evidence exists, resulting in a suspicion of gross exaggeration. For example, a brain injury caused by a stroke can result in a wide range of cognitive, emotional, and physical sequalae. Objective medical evidence of this brain injury can often be readily demonstrated through appropriate diagnostic testing. The evidence substantiating a legitimate medical condition would typically render a diagnosis of malingering moot unless the injury or medical condition was not of sufficient severity to account for the level of symptoms and disability claimed by the patient. In such cases, the disability in excess of what would be expected from the medical condition alone would raise suspicion of malingering as an additional factor influencing the complaints of impairment and disability. However, the excessive complaints can result from other factors besides malingering, such as emotional distress that is superimposed upon the medical disorder.

Malingering would be an inappropriate diagnosis if the magnification of disability was the result of factors such as emotional distress, the exaggeration being the result of a psychiatric component rather than a conscious and purposeful attempt to procure secondary gain. In some rare, very complicated cases, malingering may still be a component of the overall presentation. In such cases, the alleged disability is still significantly greater than that can be attributed to the combination of organic and psychiatric factors. The interaction of organic, psychiatric, and volitional factors is well exemplified in such unusual cases.

The symptoms and disability may arise from multiple sources representing medical/organic, emotional/psychiatric, and volitional components. In cases of multiple etiologies, the identification of malingering and deception can be a challenging process since malingering, volitional gross exaggeration, or feigning of symptoms can coexist with other conditions. Thus, they represent a continuum with multiple contributors, not an all or none or unitary phenomenon.

THE NATURE OF SECONDARY GAIN IN PSYCHIATRIC DISORDERS

Secondary gain is typically equated with the intentional production of symptoms or disability motivated by a tangible external incentive (e.g., feigning the symptoms of a postconcussion syndrome in a personal injury case to obtain monetary gains). The fact that secondary gain can also derive from unconscious and nonvolitional motivations is often not recognized or fully appreciated by nonmental-health professionals. In such cases, the presence of a tangible external incentive may not be obvious either. Such secondary gain derived from an unconscious and nonvolitional motivation without a tangible external incentive is characteristic of several psychiatric disorders. In such cases, the secondary gain relates to psychological or emotional benefits derived from a behavior (Goodwin, 1989).

SOMATOFORM DISORDERS

Somatoform Disorders are a spectrum of psychiatric conditions in which unconscious secondary gain motivation is prominent. *Somatoform Disorders refer to conditions in which the major complaints suggest a physical or medical disorder although the accompanying objective medical findings are either absent or insufficient to explain the complaints* (American Psychiatric Association, 2000). Although patients with a Somatoform Disorder suffer from legitimate disability, they are, understandably, viewed with skepticism by attorneys and many health care professionals. Malingering may often be suspected when a Somatoform Disorder coincidentally also presents within a situation in which external incentives for the complaints are available, such as in medicolegal cases.

There are various subtypes of Somatoform Disorders (American Psychiatric Association, 2000). Undifferentiated Somatoform Disorders and Somatization Disorders are subtypes in which there may be no obviously identifiable organic component whatsoever. The subtype of Hypochondriasis often derives from a medical or physical foundation but this may or may not be pathological. Regardless, the physical or medical signs of the disorder can become a source of disabling worry and concern. For example, mild chronic grumbling of the stomach may be interpreted as a sign of peptic ulcer disease or cancer. Another subtype involves the symptoms of pain. In a pain disorder, the presence of pain proves to be disabling. The lack of an organic generator causing the pain typically suggests the presence of unconscious motivation for the production of the reported disabling pain. The presence of a genuine organic source for the pain does not preclude unconscious motivators serving to perpetuate and exacerbate the pain beyond a reasonable expectation given the nature of the injury or medical problem. Such cases are diagnosed as suffering from a Pain Disorder Associated with Psychological Factors and General Medical Condition.

None of the Somatoform Disorder subtypes involves an intentional or volitional production of physical symptoms. Often the physical complaints represent an unconscious strategy for resolving a psychological conflict in a manner that preserves the individual's self-esteem. For example, a worker may find it unacceptable to acknowledge that he or she feels inadequate to perform his or her job duties or feels overwhelmed by the demands of his or her job. Depression, anxiety, frustration, or anger over the job situation would not be an option for this worker, since these symptoms would be perceived as tacit acknowledgment of his or her feelings of inadequacy and poor self-worth.

Since medical illness is not perceived as a sign of psychological inadequacy, physical symptoms can develop as an unconscious strategy to avoid the demands of the job in a manner that prevents this worker from acknowledging any negative feelings about him or herself. The worker's physical symptoms are reinforced by the secondary gain of absolving the worker from confronting his or her feelings of inadequacy or incompetency. Thus, secondary gain is present, but is measured in terms of psychic or behavioral benefits rather than as a more tangible monetary incentive such as obtaining compensation in personal injury litigation or avoiding prosecution within criminal litigation.

CHARACTERISTICS ASSOCIATED WITH UNCONSCIOUS AND CONSCIOUS SECONDARY GAIN

Although not universal, individuals seeking secondary gain on an unconscious vs. conscious basis can be contrasted by at least three distinguishing behaviors and personality characteristics (Purisch and Sbordone, 1997). First, they differ in their response to performing responsibilities and leisure activities. Second, the degree of approval seeking behavior and socialization often distinguish these two prototypes. Third, the reinforcing role of successfully procured secondary gain impacts their behavior in different ways as well. These characteristics are discussed below.

Performance of Responsibilities and Leisure Activities

Difficulties performing responsibilities, such as work or domestic chores, are common in both groups. The legitimate disability associated with a Somatoform Disorder results in diminished ability to meet responsibilities. In cases in which the symptoms are produced intentionally, however, there is no diminished capacity to engage in responsible behavior, but only a simulated claim of being unable to do so. A diminished ability to engage in preferred leisure activities is also characteristic of the authentic disability associated with a Somatoform Disorder. Such a difficulty in performing discretionary, desirable activities confers a greater sense of legitimacy upon the complaints as no obvious secondary gain can be gleaned. Why avoid reinforcing activities unless the belief in the symptoms is genuine? A sophisticated malingerer will recognize the need to maintain the appearance of being disabled and endeavor to portray a disability for partaking in rewarding activities as well as the more onerous work and domestic responsibilities. However, it requires considerable diligence to maintain this façade over a long period of time such that malingerers are more readily detected engaging in preferred activities, such as playing sports (which can often be seen in subrosa recordings), which should otherwise be precluded if the symptoms and disability were genuine.

Need for Approval and Degree of Socialization

A sense of subjective discomfort and shame over acknowledging psychological problems is a personality vulnerability related to the development of Somatoform Disorders. Individuals with such personalities are often motivated by social approval and external validation, and, inversely are motivated to avoid the perception by others as being seen in a negative light such as being vulnerable, incompetent, or somehow psychologically flawed. Risk of social exposure is to be avoided and when endured elicits embarrassment and shame. Consistently, such individuals behave in a very socially responsible manner and have strong needs for social approval. As noted in the earlier example, one worker developed physical symptoms to avoid his stressful work demands, a coping mechanism that allowed him to avoid confronting his disquieting feelings of incompetence. Any perception by others of his incompetence risked criticism and rejection, a reaction that his vulnerable self-esteem could not easily tolerate. Such individuals are characteristically overly socialized and comport themselves in a highly conforming manner when they are seen for a neuropsychological examination (e.g., they arrive on time or a few minutes early for their appointment, are neatly dressed and well groomed, and very pleasant).

Dependency and deference to authority are traits also related to need for approval and, accordingly, are qualities displayed in many individuals with Somatoform Disorders. As such, the patient with a Somatoform Disorder usually enjoys visiting doctors, a situation conducive to satisfying their dependency needs. Deference to authority is reinforced when the doctor validates her experience of illness, but can also be a two-edged sword when the doctor ultimately questions the legitimacy of her complaints. Challenging the doctor's authority directly would prove to be distressing, such that she may up the ante by developing new symptoms or showing a deterioration of her condition in an unconscious attempt to gain validation (approval) from her doctor. Failing to convince the doctor can lead to "doctor shopping," a perpetual search to find a physician who truly "understands" what is causing their problems.

Such individuals, convinced of the seriousness of their condition, eagerly submit to treatment. Unfortunately, various medical treatments, medications, and surgery do not really get to the core psychological issues that are generating and perpetuating the symptoms and usually are doomed to failure (despite a typical initial placebo effect). Repeated failure to respond to treatment can result in increasing frustration and desperation. This distress can then result in further complications and symptoms. Treating doctors often become exasperated and begin to develop critical attitudes toward the patient, thereby producing a negative, downward spiral in which the patient begins to develop more complaints. Some patients are ultimately treated with suspicion and may be labeled as malingerers.

The malingerer, on the other hand, will visit doctors or submit to treatment only to the extent that it is consistent with the belief that this is necessary to build a case and to present a convincing aura of their disability. Otherwise, there is typically an aversion to visiting doctors for fear of being discovered. In addition, malingerers will avoid treatment because they are well aware that they do not need it and attending treatment, particularly for lengthy periods of time, becomes very inconvenient, similar to the diligence required to avoid engaging in rewarding activities.

While patients with a Somatoform Disorder patient are typically dependent, pleasant, cooperative, and attempt to establish good rapport with the treating or evaluating doctor, malingerers, on the other hand, are frequently guarded, suspicious, have poor rapport, and are often hostile with the doctor (although the latter characteristics vary depending upon the maligner's level of intelligence and sophistication). Many sophisticated malingerers may appear cooperative, but this is frequently superficial and manipulative in its intent, such as in the case illustration of Mr. Boxer discussed above.

The Role of Reinforcement

The role of reinforcement, the reward or payoff, for symptoms such as obtaining secondary gains differs between patients with Somatoform Disorders and malingerers. When individuals who have a Somatoform Disorder receive a disability payment, it often serves to reinforce their belief that they have a legitimate physical disability and strengthens their feelings of dependency. This is known as compensation neurosis. The malingerer, on the other hand, knows quite well that their manipulative behavior to prove that they are disabled will most likely be reinforced by monetary compensation or disability payments, thus encouraging further manipulative behavior.

FACTITIOUS DISORDER

A Factitious Disorder includes features of both malingering and Somatoform Disorder. Common to malingering, there is intentional production or feigning of physical or psychological signs or symptoms. In Factitious Disorder, however, *the motivation for this behavior is the secondary gain related to assuming the sick role, not the obvious external incentive associated with malingering* (American Psychiatric Association, 2000). As such, a Factitious Disorder falls under the heading of those disorders in which the motivating drive derives from the unconscious, bearing some resemblance to a Somatoform Disorder. However, with Somatoform Disorders, the behavior is not produced intentionally. For example, infliction of an acute medical crisis, such as severe hypoglycemia, might be factitiously produced when a patient intentionally self-administers a shot of insulin to dramatically lower his blood sugar, necessitating a visit to the local hospital emergency room.

A major difference between malingering and Factitious Disorder is the degree of self-control that governs the intentional production of symptoms. The malingerer has a great deal of choice in producing the symptoms; they can be turned on or off when deemed advantageous. The Factitious Disorder patient has no such control, producing symptoms in a compulsive manner. This behavior cannot be readily stopped, accounting for the unconscious source of the motivation. Whereas a malingerer may avoid riskier, painful procedures, or self-harm, the Factitious Disorder patient eagerly undergoes such procedures and may inflict personal injury. Whereas malingering is not, by itself, a psychiatric disorder, Factitious Disorder is typically associated with severe psychopathology.

Sometimes the distinction between malingering and Factitious Disorder is difficult to make. This is particularly true in cases in which the incentive can be either external (as in the case of malingering) or internal (as in satisfying the need to play the sick role). For example, both malingerers and patients with Factitious Disorders can feign or exaggerate pain in pursuit of narcotic analgesics, but the underlying motivations would be different.

Rogers (1992) discusses the types of issues that need to be addressed during the clinical evaluation to discriminate the malingering from Factitious Disorder. For example, the external incentives of the malingerer might be revealed in responses to questions such as "What would be the best outcome from this evaluation?" or "What is at stake (e.g., job, psychiatric treatment, money, benefits)?" The motivation to play the sick role may be revealed in responses to questions such as "Do you admire doctors and what they can do for you?" or "Are you sometimes forced to 'play up' your symptoms to get the attention that you deserve?"

Case of Ms. Limb

A rather extreme example of a patient with Factitious Disorder was Ms. Limb, a woman in her early 30s when she was first evaluated as part of a personal injury matter following a motor vehicle accident. She was in a wheelchair because of complications from a prior injury in which she had fractured her femur. Despite appropriate surgery and follow-up care, the fractured femur never completely healed. The surgical wound site became infected and continued to remain infected despite multiple courses of antibiotics. Ultimately, she developed osteomyelitis with complications necessitating the amputation of this lower extremity.

It was suspected that her leg had never healed because she continued to contaminate the wound, resulting in extensive medical treatment. She had subsequently injured her other leg and this leg, too, failed to heal, amazingly resulting in complications such that when she was evaluated she presented as a bilateral lower extremity amputee. Of course, she never acknowledged contaminating the wounds, but this appeared to be the only logical explanation for her failure to respond to numerous medical treatments. As a postscript, it was learned that 3 years later she had died from complications of another self-inflicted injury.

It is puzzling to understand the motivations that would drive someone to such extreme and bizarre behavior as Ms. Limb. Her actions were intentional, but quite obviously out of control. Some perspective can be gained by looking at analogous compulsive behaviors that fall on a lower end of the continuum. An alcoholic, for example, may be fully aware of the negative consequences of his or her drinking but consciously and volitionally engages in drinking. The compulsive nature of the addiction makes it difficult to terminate such self-injurious behavior on a volitional basis.

DSM-IV-TR SUSPICION INDICES FOR MALINGERING

The DSM-IV-TR (American Psychiatric Association, 2000) lists what may be considered red flags to aid in the recognition and diagnosis of malingering. They include medical–legal context of presentation, marked discrepancy between the person's claimed stress or disability and the objective findings, lack of cooperation during the diagnostic evaluation and in complying with the prescribed treatment regimen, and the presence of Antisocial Personality Disorder. The rationale and shortcomings of each of these red flags will be discussed below.

Medical–Legal Presentation

The rationale of including a medical–legal context of evaluation is considered a red flag because of the presence of a readily identifiable external incentive inherent in such situations, a necessary condition for establishing a diagnosis of malingering. However, this criterion makes an implicit assumption that involvement in litigation is strongly associated with malingering. This assumption has no empirical support. For example, one representative survey of forensic psychologists provided their estimate of the base rate of malingering in forensic contexts as only being 15.7% (Rogers et al., 1994). The mere presence of an external incentive does not uniformly motivate most people to malinger and, most individuals in medical–legal context do not malinger. Furthermore, there are numerous other contexts in addition to the medical–legal context in which external incentives for malingering are present. Such a criterion may also be somewhat discriminatory. For example, there are a disproportionate percentage of individuals of low socioeconomic backgrounds in the medical–legal context such as those related to welfare, housing, injuries related to physical labor, and criminal justice. Strict adherence to this flawed criterion for malingering might present a bias against individuals of low socioeconomic status (Sbordone et al., 2000).

Identifying potential malingerers by the context in which they present seems to miss the point. The medicolegal context in general does not strongly predict malingering. However, there are certain specific variables associated with the medical–legal situation that, if present, may be more strongly related to the potential for malingering (Rogers, 1997). One of these is the motivation to engage in malingering, which can be greatly influenced by the magnitude of the incentive, not the mere presence of an incentive itself. The outcome of litigation varies from the low stakes of a small claims suit to the high stakes of a death penalty criminal trial and, accordingly, the potential for malingering would reasonably differ under these two scenarios.

Another variable is the presence of alternative behaviors; the fewer the alternatives to malingering, the greater likelihood that it will occur. For example, feigning insanity may be the only way a defendant can avoid being found criminally guilty of committing murder. A cost-benefits analysis often accompanies such reasoning. For example, what does such a criminal defendant have to lose if he is discovered to have been feigning insanity? He may reason that he would be no worse off than if he had not taken such a risk. Another factor that can enhance the motivation for malingering is when the litigant believes that she may be successful or, at the least, can malinger without the likelihood of being detected. Under such circumstances, there appears to be little downside risk compared to the chance for success.

The adversarial nature of litigation may also be a factor in the decision to malinger but is not likely relevant unless the situation is perceived as being highly adversarial. For example, personal injury litigants often bear ill will toward the opposing attorney or insurance company and, when extreme, this anger can motivate exaggeration and feigning.

Antisocial Personality Disorder

The presence of Antisocial Personality Disorder as a red flag is based upon the fact that malingering itself would be considered a behavior in which there is a violation of societal rules. Individuals with Antisocial Personality Disorders, by definition, do not conform to the accepted rules of broader society and, therefore, would be more likely to engage in behaviors such as malingering. Surprisingly, there is no solid evidence that individuals with Antisocial Personality Disorders have a higher base rate of malingering. The base rate of malingering obviously differs among settings and the result of contextual motivations, but may not be disproportionately high among individuals with Antisocial Personality Disorders, estimated to be only 3 to 8% in this population (Rogers, 1997).

Not all individuals who are diagnosed with Antisocial Personality Disorder are cut from the same cloth, a prominent factor confounding the ability to predict the potential for malingering in this group. This heterogeneity among those diagnosed with Antisocial Personality Disorders largely stems from the failure of the DSM-IV-TR criteria for Antisocial Personality Disorder to adequately distinguish between antisocial behavior and antisocial personality. The diagnostic criteria are based upon behavior and history, not core personality traits characterizing individuals with such histories and behaviors. Thus, many individuals are identified as having an Antisocial Personality Disorder without possessing the core personality traits that are assumed to exist in such individuals. For example, individuals who are economically disadvantaged may engage in antisocial behavior as an adaptation to their life circumstances, for example, selling drugs as a way to make income in an environment with otherwise limited economic opportunities. However, many such individuals may have the flexibility to behave in conforming and socially acceptable ways when given other alternatives. An individual with core personality traits associated with Antisocial Personality Disorder, on the other hand, would have difficulty conforming to the accepted rules and expectations under most circumstances.

The findings from the Hare Psychopathy Checklist — Revised (Hare, 1991) underscores the difference between antisocial personality traits and antisocial behaviors. Group data collected from this psychometric instrument commonly used to identify psychopathy (an analogous, but not identical, concept as Antisocial Personality Disorder) has revealed two major factors underlying psychopathy. The first of these pertains to the core personality traits of the psychopath and relates to a "selfish, callous, and remorseless use of others." Items loading on this factor include glibness/superficial charm, grandiose sense of self worth, pathological lying, conning/manipulative, lack of remorse or guilt, shallow affect, callous/lack of empathy, and failure to accept responsibility for own actions.

A second factor depicts the characteristic history of psychopaths that is emphasized by the DSM-IV-TR criteria for Antisocial Personality Disorder, describing such individuals as being "chronically unstable, antisocial, and (engaging in a) socially deviant lifestyle." Items loading on this factor include need for stimulation/proneness to boredom, parasitic lifestyle, poor behavioral control, early behavioral problems, lack of realistic goals, impulsivity, irresponsibility, juvenile delinquency, and revocation of conditional release. Individuals displaying evidence of core psychopathic personality traits, demonstrated by a high score on factor one, clearly have a proclivity to engage in the chronically antisocial and socially deviant lifestyle illustrated by the second factor. Such individuals are true psychopaths who are not burdened with the products of socialization such as conscience. It may be that it is these individuals who are most likely to engage in malingering. On other hand, individuals with behavioral and historical features exemplified by the second factor may be quite capable of being socialized and developing a sense of conscience but have learned to engage in antisocial behavior due to environmental and contextual factors (Sbordone et al., 2000). Such individuals may not be disproportionately prone to engage in malingered behavior, all other things being equal.

Noncompliance and Lack of Cooperation

Noncompliance to treatment as a red flag is based upon the belief that malingers will show poor motivation to submit to treatments or maintain protracted treatment regimens for their bogus complaints. Lack of cooperation as a red flag is based upon the assumption that malingerers are guarded, not fully participating in examinations for fear of being exposed. Again, this criterion is too general, not applying specifically to malingering.

Noncompliance and lack of cooperation can result from many sources other than malingering. For instance, factors such as pain, fatigue, and depression can interfere with motivation and effort during lengthy or strenuous evaluations and treatment sessions. Lack of compliance and cooperation may also be more common in those from low socioeconomic circumstances who may be less inclined to utilize health services as well as having typically less access to such services. Issues of trust, sophistication and affordability are relevant considerations under such circumstances (Sbordone et al., 2000). Furthermore, it may be difficult to identify noncompliance or lack of cooperation when issues associated to convenient focus are relevant, as exemplified by the case of Mr. Boxer. Under similar circumstances, malingerers may appear cooperative, at least superficially.

Excessive Subjective Complaints vs. Objective Findings

The large gap between complaints and substantiating objective findings is one of the hallmarks of malingering. As such, the inclusion of this red flag is actually redundant with definition of malingering itself. Nonetheless, this criterion, like the others, is overly broad and includes a large number of legitimate conditions that are not associated with significant objective medical findings, for example, Somatoform Disorders and mild traumatic brain injuries. Such disorders demonstrate that an absence of (objective) evidence is not the same thing as evidence of absence for the disorder.

Furthermore, the types of complaints common in neuropsychological disorders are relatively frequent even in nonpatient populations and under conditions that do not present obvious incentives for the complaints. For example, Lees-Haley and Brown (1993) found that 54% of control subjects endorsed anxiety or nervousness, 52% endorsed sleeping problems, 62% endorsed headaches, and so forth. Thus, so-called normal individuals may frequently endorse a number of emotional and physical complaints without an obvious history to support a medical or objective basis for such complaints.

Demographic factors also need to be considered in influencing the frequency of complaints. Certain individuals may be suspected of malingering when other factors may account for apparently unexplained symptoms. On the basis of our experience, for example, females and the elderly are more likely to demonstrate chronic symptoms, but are actually less likely to malinger compared to young and middle-aged males. Economically disadvantaged individuals display a higher base rate of psychiatric disorders and, thus, can more frequently present with complaints that are unsubstantiated by objective medical findings (Sbordone et al., 2000).

Sensitivity and Specificity of the DSM-IV-TR Criteria

The flaws in each of these four DSM-IV-TR red flags dictate a very conservative approach to their application as a diagnostic checklist to identify malingering. Indeed, Rogers (1997) indicates that these four criteria in combination have only moderate sensitivity. About two thirds of malingerers were found to satisfy two or more of these indices. Inversely, about one third of malingerers may satisfy no more than one of these four criteria. Thus, there is a relatively high risk of failing to identify a malingerer on the basis of these four criteria. Of greater concern is their very poor specificity to malingering. Rogers reports that 80% of individuals with two or more of these indices being positive will be falsely accused of malingering. This problem with specificity undoubtedly relates to the over-inclusive nature of each of the four red flags.

SUBTYPES OF MALINGERING

Rogers et al. (1998) indicate that there are a number of factors associated with malingering. Not all malingerers are the same, nor are the factors motivating malingerers the same in all cases. They proposed that malingering may be explained by three different types of motivation, the criminological, the pathogenic, and the adaptational. The criminological model refers to "badness," whereas the pathogenic model refers to "madness." The criminological model is most consistent with the stereotypical view of the malingerer as being a bad person, a psychopath, someone who breaks the rules in a manipulative and cunning manner. In the pathogenic model, however, psychopathy is not the central issue. Rather, malingering is motivated by psychiatric factors, often seen as an attempt to ward off or preempt more serious problems. For example, a socially phobic individual may fake being hard of hearing to excuse withdrawing from a conversation. The adaptational model views malingering as the outcome of a cost-benefit analysis in which the individual weighs her options and the result of an adversarial context in which malingering is utilized to cope with a difficult situation. For example, a homeless person may fake being ill in order to obtain shelter. In the criminological and pathogenic models, there is a certain type of individual who may be more prone to malingering. The adaptational model, on the other hand, would suggest that virtually anyone could be a potential malingerer under certain circumstances related to the cost and benefits and being placed in an adversarial situation.

Rogers et al. (1998) also indicate that the setting in which an individual finds himself, whether forensic or nonforensic is relevant in malingering. Furthermore, they substantiate that malingering can take different forms depending upon the types of symptoms exaggerated or feigned (i.e., cognitive, mental, and medical symptoms). They present evidence of an interaction between the individual, the setting, and the symptoms. For example, medical symptoms were found to be more commonly malingered in females than males in nonforensic settings. Cognitive symptoms were found to be more commonly malingered in males and females in nonforensic settings.

Different methods of malingering were discovered by Heinze and Purisch (2001). They examined 57 male inmates suspected of malingering incompetency to stand trial. Each were administered a number of different tests measuring motivation and effort. These investigators found that not all individuals malingered in the same way. Five different patterns were identified. Global malingerers were identified by an indiscriminate endorsement of problems on symptom questionnaires and inventories and impaired performance on neurocognitive measures. They portrayed problems across the wide spectrum of psychiatric and cognitive procedures. A second subgroup tended toward endorsing displaying symptoms of mental illness but not neurocognitive problems. A third subgroup endorsed and displayed neurocognitive problems but not mental illness. A fourth subgroup did endorse problems related to mental illness and neurocognitive disorder but unlike the global group, they endorsed and displayed less severe forms of mental illness, such as depression, anxiety or posttraumatic stress, but not psychosis. The fifth subgroup displayed evidence of malingering dependent on the measure. These inmates were able to be further subdivided. Some showed evidence of malingering on short tests such as the Rey-15 Item test, but not on longer tests such as the MMPI-2. Other inmates showed evidence of malingering on symptom questionnaires, but not on performance measures.

IDENTIFICATION OF COGNITIVE MALINGERING ON NEUROPSYCHOLOGICAL TESTS

Suspicion of malingering is frequently raised during a neuropsychological evaluation when cognitive test performances are well below expectations given the history and clinical observations. However, assuming that the poor test performance is the result of malingering would be premature and often incorrect. The determination that the poor test results are attributable to malingering can only be made after careful consideration of the multiple reasons other than malingering for cognitive test performance to be below expectations. None of these reasons are mutually exclusive. Malingering should only be identified as the product of a process of elimination in which other potential alternatives are given due consideration.

FACTORS ASSOCIATED WITH POOR NEUROPSYCHOLOGICAL TEST PERFORMANCE

As discussed in other chapters of this book, Sbordone and Purisch (1996) detailed a number of factors that can produce poor performance on neuropsychological tests. The list is extensive, with suboptimal motivation and malingering being only one of these factors. A brief review reveals the first factor to be the presence of a prior brain insult or injury, or congenital or preexisting neurologic conditions that impact neuropsychological tests independent of any injury that may be the subject of litigation. For example, an individual may be evaluated in a personal injury case because of a head injury. Neuropsychological testing may reveal moderate to severe cognitive problems, whereas the facts of the head injury would suggest only that mild deficits should be expected, at worst. A careful history, however, may reveal a prior brain injury or a preexisting neurologic condition that negatively impacted the individual's neuropsychological test performance.

Factors that negative impact attention, such as absence attacks (seizures), acute pain, performance anxiety, depression or other psychiatric problems, sleep deprivation and excessive fatigue, among others, could clearly limit the individual's ability to apply consistent effort, even when the individual is motivated to perform well on the test. The distinction between motivation and effort will be discussed in greater detail later in this chapter.

Cognitive tests are intended to assess the brain. However, many of these tests require intact sensory processing, such as seeing or hearing what information is being presented. Many require some sort of motor response, such as manipulating blocks, drawing, or placing pegs into holes. An examinee who has forgotten her eyeglasses or hearing aid may not be able to sufficiently process the instructions that are given to him or her prior to taking the test. An individual with an orthopedic injury may not be able to manipulate materials well. In both cases, poorer performances would be expected. If this information was ignored, the impaired performance would most likely be attributed entirely to the effects of a brain injury.

Test results may be skewed for normative reasons. The vast majority of neuropsychological, academic, and personality tests administered in the United States were normed upon data collected from individuals raised in the predominant culture, enrolled in the American educational system and speak English as their mother tongue. Application of such norms becomes increasingly questionable as a function of the degree to which an individual being examined significantly departs from proto-typical cultural, educational, or linguistic standards. Scores falling outside of the norm may contain a significant artifact associated with such individual differences and need to be interpreted as reflect-ing a brain injury or psychiatric disorder with due caution and qualification. For example, bilingual speakers with English as a second language frequently perform below the norm on language-based tests, such as word finding or verbal fluency, even when their conversation English proficiency appears normal.

There are multiple other factors that need to be considered as potential adverse influences upon test performance. The bottom line is that there is no test that truly evaluates malingering and there is no test performance that can be exclusively associated with malingering. The factors that can impact test performance are multiple and need to be considered in a comprehensive manner before concluding that the poorer than expected test results were purposeful and motivated by external incentives.

LIMITATIONS IN RESEARCH STUDIES OF MALINGERING

UNCERTAIN EFFICACY OF NEUROPSYCHOLOGICAL TESTS

The past decade has seen an enormous emphasis in the field of neuropsychology in developing methods and tests to identify malingering. This near obsession in the forensic neuropsychological literature has been in part motivated by the sobering findings that traditional neuropsychological tests and test batteries have not definitely demonstrated their effectiveness in discriminating the performances of malingerers from patients with bona fide brain injuries (Faust, 1991; Guilmette and Guilano, 1991). However, the studies demonstrating the poor ability of neuropsychological measures in making such discriminations have been criticized as methodologically flawed (Barth et al., 1991; McCaffrey and Lynch, 1992), such that this issue remains unclear at this time. Even if the research designs were not an issue, there is little doubt that distinguishing real from false neuropsychological test results would still present a formidable problem. Comparisons of test results of brain-injured individuals to subjects considered to be faking or instructed to simulate brain injury reveal signifi-cant overlap in test performances. Although there is great overlap in the group performances, as a group, malingerers typically demonstrate greater variability in performance than patients with brain damage. This makes sense as no two malingerers are likely to be as closely matched as two patients with the same type of brain-damage. Each malingerer may have idiosyncratic beliefs about what it means to be brain-damaged and employ different strategies on how to simulate brain impairment. Unfortunately, this knowledge that malingerers as a group are more variable in performance than individuals with true brain-damage does not particularly help in their identification on a case-by-case basis.

In truth, neuropsychological tests and neuropsychological test batteries were constructed with the intent to uncover impairments associated with brain dysfunction. They were not designed to detect malingering. The research indicating a poor track record in doing so, therefore, can hardly be considered a fatal flaw. Analogously, CTs and MRIs are intended to identify structural lesions of the brain and cannot be faulted for failing to identify neurological disorders that are not structural in nature, such as epilepsy, which is an electrophysiological disorder of the brain.

Despite the fact that neuropsychological tests were not designed to detect malingering, there does appear to be some evidence that particular patterns of performance are more likely to be found in malingerers than true patients. Reitan and Wolfson (1998) demonstrate that the failure of so-called expert clinicians to distinguish the neuropsychological performance of malingerers and true brain-damaged patients in one classic study using the Halstead–Reitan Neuropsychological Battery (Heaton et al., 1978) was an indictment of the methods employed by the diagnosticians rather than a lack of critical differences in test performance derived from each group. They reviewed the same data used in the original study and reported that there were, indeed, significant differences in the patterns of performance demonstrated by the two groups. They criticized the clinicians for focusing on the level of performance (i.e., normal vs. mild, moderate, or severe impairment), which was not particularly revealing, as opposed to the pattern of performance (i.e., certain measures performed better or worse than others). The presence of specific patterns of performance was also utilized to distinguish malingerers from true brain-damaged patients on the Luria–Nebraska Neuropsychological Battery (Mensch and Woods, 1986).

The knowledge that certain patterns of test performance are associated with malingering has fueled the burgeoning research in the development of specialized techniques that has capitalized on identifying such aberrant patterns of performance. As noted in the introductory paragraph to this chapter, a specific discussion of these tests and elucidation of the strategies underlying their development is beyond the scope of this chapter. However, there are inherent problems associated with the research and development of methods for detection of malingering. An appreciation of these issues is necessary to recognize the limitations of the conclusions that can be drawn from such test results.

PROBLEMS DETECTING MALINGERERS FOR USE IN RESEARCH STUDIES

In a general sense, the reliability and validity of any test of malingering is dependent upon research demonstrating that the test results are capable of distinguishing malingerers from subjects whose test performance is impaired by factors such as brain-damage or psychiatric disorder. An inherent problem in this research is the difficulty in identifying a group of subjects who are truly malingering. Malingerers frequently do not admit that they are malingering. Furthermore, most clinicians are not particularly sensitive to the presence of malingering in their patients, malingering running counter to the bond of trust so vital to the doctor–patient relationship. Sensitivity to malingering is likely enhanced in only a small group of physicians and neuropsychologists, those involved in the criminal justice system and the personal injury system. This group could likely be further subdivided into that those who routinely conduct defense oriented evaluation of personal injury plaintiffs and evaluation of criminal defendants with a prosecutorial bent as being most sensitized to the potential for malingering. In an attempt to overcome these inherent problems in identifying malingering, research-set criteria for defining the presence of malingering in research studies is typically based on either certain suspicion indices or simulation of malingering by recruited subjects.

SUSPECTED MALINGERING

The difficulty inherent in identifying true malingering is a significant obstacle in test development and general research into the presentation of malingering. Because a malingerer does not generally identify himself, there is frequently no way to know for sure whether or not he is malingering. As a result, criteria to identify suspected malingering are routinely employed in most research. Many tests of malingering have been developed within the medical–legal context in which the thorny problem of assessment of brain-damage in individuals with mild head injury is common. Typical criteria for suspected malingering in such cases include a history in which mild head trauma is not documented but later alleged. The fact that the individual is involved in litigation is often an inclusion criterion. Such an individual is also suspected of malingering when he or she demonstrates excessive impairment on testing, an improbable symptom history or clinical presentation, and shows evidence of excessive and prolonged disability. Each of these criteria is reasonable and the probability of identifying a true malingerer likely increases when these various criteria are used in combination. Nonetheless, the risk of false positives-identifying someone who is malingering who is not—still exists, thereby contaminating the research in this field.

SIMULATED OR ANALOG MALINGERING

Another strategy employed in malingering research utilizes simulated or what is often referred to as analog malingerers. Analog malingerers are neither patients nor do they suffer from brain injury, but are individuals who are instructed to simulate brain injury when undergoing neuropsychological testing. Such subjects can differ from true malingerers in many ways. They may possess a completely different level of sophistication about brain injury than a true malingerer who may have a greater stake in presenting in a plausible manner. This directly relates to differences in incentives in the two situations. In research studies, an incentive may be some type of course credit or being paid a paltry fee for participation. Certainly, simulated malingerers would have less fear of being detected. It is likely that there are general demographic differences between analog malingerers and real malingerers. The type of individual who presents for research study may likely come from a different background than an individual who finds himself in some type of litigation situation.

Many malingerers in personal injury situations have actually been involved in some type of potential injury type of situation for which they are falsely attempting to portray a brain injury. A simulated malingerer, however, may differ in that she has never been involved in a trauma type of situation, with generalized effects associated with that situation exerting a potential influence upon her approach to testing and clinical presentation. Furthermore, while it is assumed that the analog malingerer has followed instructions, it is frequently impossible to be certain if she actually did attempt to fake bad. Finally, the analog malingerer is assumed to be absent in any type of neuropsychological or physical problems. However, they may have real cognitive impairment. Thus, their impaired test performance may be contaminated by a legitimate organic etiology.

RELATIONSHIP OF LITIGATION TO PSYCHOLOGICAL AND NEUROPSYCHOLOGICAL TEST PERFORMANCE

Reitan and Wolfson (1998) analyzed a large database of neuropsychological test performances on the Halstead–Reitan Neuropsychological Battery and the Wechsler Adult Intelligence Scale. The subjects in this database pool had been administered these measures on more than one occasion. They analyzed the reliability or consistency of test performance of the subjects over repeated testing, analyzing whether there was any difference between subjects involved in litigation vs. those who were not involved in litigation. They found marked variability on test–retest performances on these cognitive tests for litigants compared to nonlitigants. This diminished reliability in test performance over time suggests that litigants may, at the least, demonstrate different strategies and exert different levels of effort when being administered neuropsychological tests at different points in time. For example, a litigant may do well on a memory test during the first session. However, when retested several months later, the litigant now exerts only partial effort on the same measure that results in a lower score.

Because this variability does not appear to be a common finding in nonlitigants, the presence of greater test variability within the litigation context most likely reflects motivation and effort. If test scores vary over time, an attempt to manipulate an impression may influence the litigants more than the nonlitigants. However, the methods in which the test results are manipulated may differ on different occasions as a result of factors such as the inability to remember the tests or strategies for manipulation that were previously utilized when they were tested earlier.

In addition to the variability in test performance over repeated testings, the overall test performance is lower and the number of complaints is greater in litigants. In general, litigants perform worse on cognitive measures than litigants matched for presence or severity of brain injury. Furthermore, litigants endorse more psychopathology on personality measures than matched nonlitigants. Thus, involvement in litigation tends to be associated with poor performance on tests of cognitive functioning and personality when factors such as the presence and severity of injury are controlled.

When the presence and severity of brain injury is not controlled, litigants with undocumented mild head trauma actually perform more poorly than litigants who have a documented brain injury (Pankratz and Binder, 1997). This is also seen in measures of personality in which mild head injury litigants endorse more psychopathology compared to moderate–severe head injury litigants (Youngjohn et al., 1997). While the greater impairment and psychopathology in individuals with undocumented or mild head injury compared to those with documented or moderate to severe head injuries appears counterintuitive, there may be multiple explanations for this finding, one being that individuals with no or only mild head injury may be more litigation minded and have better capability to profit from or remember coaching. Another often present factor is the fact that individuals with mild injuries are typically far more aware of their symptoms and impairments when compared to individuals with moderate to severe injury. For example, the presence of a moderate to severe injury reduces an individual's insight into their cognitive deficits, which results in fewer subjective complaints.

Individuals with mild injuries may be more distressed as a result of their greater awareness of their cognitive deficits. As a consequence, their complaints or test performances are likely to be impacted by their awareness of their cognitive deficits, particularly the problems that they have created in their life. Individuals with moderate to severe cognitive difficulties may offer few complaints, at least on personality tests or symptom inventories, as a direct consequence of their poor awareness of their cognitive problems that reflects the severity of their brain injury.

RELATIONSHIP OF LITIGATION TO MOTIVATION AND EFFORT

The Reitan and Wolfson (1998) findings are significant in that there was no attempt to label the litigants as malingerers. It is quite likely, in fact, that many of the litigants were not malingering, but were less reliable in their response to the test on different occasions. Although malingering likely occurred at a higher base rate in the litigant sample than in the nonlitigant sample, there were likely factors other than malingering that contributed to the greater variability of the litigants over time. Indeed, the presence of malingering in litigation may be over-diagnosed as evidenced by the fact that the percentage of litigants who dramatically improve after settlement is typically low, running contrary to expectations if such individuals were actually malingering.

There is no doubt that litigation has a complex interaction with variables of motivation and effort. While litigants frequently endorse more complaints than nonlitigants with similar injuries or history, this does not equate with malingering. The very involvement in litigation provides a context for cataloguing and remembering symptoms; it is to the litigant's benefit to do so. Litigants often are referred to a number of doctors and evaluators who reinforce this focus on cataloging and remembering symptoms through frequent interviews and provision of questionnaires.

The potential of external incentives likely influences the report not only of the number or frequency of symptoms but also their severity. If headache pain can be characterized on a 0 to 10 scale as either a 3 or a 4, it is more likely that an individual involved in litigation will report it as occurring at a severity level 4. This is far different, however, than that same individual indicating that the headache is 9 or 10, the latter reflecting the gross exaggeration that is associated with malingering. Thus, a higher frequency and severity of complaints for litigants compared to matched nonlitigants is reasonable, given the contextual demands and reinforcers, their greater reports of complaints not necessarily reflecting an attempt to feign or grossly exaggerate their problems, as would be seen in malingering. However, there can be little doubt that litigation can have a significant impact upon overall motivation and effort in how the litigant presents. The evaluation of these two factors becomes a critical component in the determination of the veracity of the patient's complaints and credibility of their test performance and clinical presentation.

The Process of Evaluating Motivation and Effort During the Neuropsychological Evaluation

Motivation and effort need to be considered in judging factors impacting neuropsychological test performance. Motivation can be viewed along a continuum reflecting the degree of desire to perform well on neuropsychological testing. Effort can be viewed along a continuum reflecting the amount of energy or persistence exerted in presenting in a particular manner. Frederick (1997) views these two variables as being interactive such that the evaluation of the factors impacting impaired neuropsychological test performance need to include both motivation and effort. The four outcomes of high and low motivation and effort are depicted in Figure 11.1. At the end of each continuum, the quadrants represent motivation to excel and high effort resulting in a compliant response style and a valid test performance.

The other three combinations of motivation and effort result in invalid test results but, importantly, in only one instance is the presence of malingering likely. Malingerers are often motivated to perform poorly or to demonstrate impairment in their test performance. However, their effort is often quite high, the result of an active attempt to manipulate the test results.

The two remaining quadrants are less definitive as to the presence of malingering. The irrelevant response style is perhaps the least common of these combinations. Such individuals are motivated to

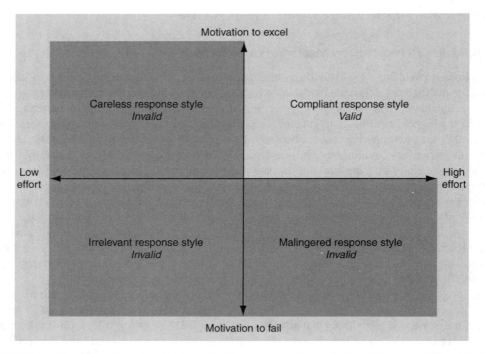

FIGURE 11.1   The interaction of motivation and effort on test performance. From VIP manual copyright 1997, 2003 NCS Pearson Inc. Reproduced by permission of the copyright holder. "VIP" is a registered trademark of NCS Pearson Inc.

fail but do not put the high degree of effort into manipulating a convincing impression of impairment, simply taking the test in a somewhat hasty or haphazard manner, intending to do poorly but not putting much effort into attempting to manipulate a plausible result. These individuals would be considered unsophisticated malingerers. However, many individuals in this group are not specifically malingering. They are not definitively motivated to fail. Rather, they may simply not care about the outcome of the testing one way or the other.

Such an individual may not be engaged in the testing process, simply being motivated to getting the testing over with for whatever reason. An example would be a delinquent male adolescent who reluctantly attends a court-ordered psychological evaluation, who then puts little effort into his test taking behavior. He may complete personality testing, such as the MMPI-A, in only 10 min, where it typically takes considerably longer (1 hour or more) to complete this measure in a valid manner. An examination of the test results reveals that he did not respond to the test items and instead simply filled in the blanks to get the test over as quickly as possible. Other scenarios such as an individual with severe depression or severe pain, or other factors that may make the evaluation process extremely stressful or irritating can result in similar behavior, an attempt to complete the process as quickly and as painlessly as possible without regard or concern for the outcome.

The remaining combination, the careless style, resulting from good motivation and poor effort, is likely the most common reason for invalid test results. In such cases, there is often ample evidence that the subject was generally motivated to perform well, as suggested by a number of test results in various areas falling in the normal or even better than normal range. However, the pattern of test performance is unreliable, showing deficiencies or problems in areas that would not be predicted from the ability to perform well on analogous tests. For example, an individual may be able to recite six digits in the backward direction from which they were read to her, indicating good working memory. However, she performs poorly another test of working memory, Trail Making — Part B, continuing to lose her train of thought when asked to alternate between numbers and letters, that is, 1 to A to 2 to B to 3 to C and so on. Such an individual may demonstrate uneven effort due to a large number of factors such as pain, physical illness, emotional distress, fatigue, and so forth which interferes with her ability to focus and concentrate in a reliable manner, thus resulting in various performances that underestimate her true potential.

Any test that requires some type of voluntary response from the patient will be sensitive to motivation and effort (e.g., a memory test requires a voluntary response whereas a constriction of the pupil to light does not). Malingering represents only a particular constellation of factors impacting motivation and effort that conspire to adversely impact test results. However, there are many reasons other than malingering in which test results below expectations or unreliable test results can be produced. Once again, the diagnosis of malingering involves a process that is multifactorial and involves the integration of the entire database. Reliance on individual measures outside the broader context is frequently misleading. A comprehensive approach to determining the presence of malingering is required.

THE POWER OF A COMPREHENSIVE NEUROPSYCHOLOGICAL EVALUATION TO IDENTIFYING MALINGERING

The comprehensive approach to identifying malingering utilizes specialized tests of motivation and effort as only one piece in a much more complex puzzle. The multiple sources of information gathered as part of the neuropsychological evaluation provide a considerable database that can significantly enhance the process of determining a litigant's credibility, well beyond the results of these specialized test results (Purisch, 2001). Information obtained from self-report, medical records, collateral informants, academic transcripts, employment records, clinical observations, questionnaires, and test results can all be compared and contrasted looking for consistencies and inconsistencies that reflect upon the litigant's credibility and potential for malingering. Inconsistencies are common in patients suffering from psychiatric disorders or brain injury and cannot be regarded as convincing evidence of malingering. However, the inconsistencies associated with malingering are often notable for being self-serving, for example, significantly exaggerating the facts of the injury or denying documented preexisting disability.

Credibility can also be evaluated by inspecting the correspondence among the medical findings, subjective complaints, clinical observations, and test results. Subjective complaints not supported by either test results or clinical observations may be credible but are not likely to be significantly disabling. Claims of significant disability arising from such symptoms should be regarded with suspicion. Major inconsistencies between clinical observations and test results may reflect the different contexts in which they are obtained (qualitative observation vs. standardized testing) or be a definite indication of an attempt to manipulate an impression of impairment. For example, a plaintiff may cry when discussing stressful events giving rise to or part of her litigation, but otherwise not present with depression in interview or on personality testing. The distress may be legitimate, but limited to specific eliciting situations. Any claims of a more pervasive or disabling depression should be regarded with suspicion. Similarly, a plaintiff who complains of severe memory impairment should demonstrate evidence of obvious memory problems during both interview and testing. A plaintiff able to provide a comprehensive history with excellent recall of information should be regarded with suspicion if his performance is poor on tests obviously assessing memory.

While such obvious inconsistencies between the qualitative behavior of the subject and other sources of information raise red flags as to dissimulation, a trained forensic neuropsychologist is often able to detect subtle cues, which suggest that the subject is trying to manipulate an impression. Such cues are illustrated by the work of Ekman (1992) who was able to discern that specific nonverbal and gestural signs universally accompany genuine emotions. In general, he has discovered that reliable telltales of false emotions may be an asymmetrical expression, the onset is too abrupt, the offset is too abrupt or jagged, and the location of the emotion in speech is incorrect. A more specific sign may be, for example, a lack of a reliable forehead expression associated with either fear or sadness. In addition to observing mismatched emotions and expressions of these emotions, the forensic neuropsychologist can look for inconsistencies in the manner in which the subject relates his history that are suggestive of dissimulation. For example, Porter and Yuille (1996) found that liars' accounts tended to be vague in content, with a paucity of details, lacking in coherency and consistency, and they were less likely to admit to forgetting aspects of the target event upon direct questioning.

Credibility can also be evaluated by determining the correspondence between the degree of impairment and expectations. Neuropsychological tests are able to provide tangible information about the degree of impairment necessary for such analyses. Quantification and normative standards of performance are major strengths favoring the use of neuropsychological tests over clinical mental status examinations utilized by neurologists and psychiatrists. The relevance of a litigant's scores on measures of attention, language, memory, and other areas can be judged in comparison to others of similar background on the basis of factors such as age, education, or gender. The degree of subjective interpretation required is significantly reduced compared to relying on clinical observations and qualitative data alone.

Quantification also permits statistical comparisons of performances on tests administered on multiple occasions. Changes in test scores are expected to parallel a change in neuropsychological status. Symptoms associated with brain dysfunction should be detected by abnormal performance on neuropsychological tests. Improvement in symptoms related to recovering brain functioning, as is expected following acute events such as head trauma or stroke, should be reflected in better performance on the same neuropsychological tests administered on multiple occasions. Similarly, no change in test performance over time should be expected when the underlying condition has not changed (other than that improvement that is associated with a practice effect). For example, a patient with a traumatic brain injury should not demonstrate much change in neuropsychological test performance after about 2 years postinjury. Therefore, serial testing at 2 and 3 years postinjury should yield relatively similar test performances. Unexpected change in scores in such cases often raises suspicion that an attempt was made to manipulate the test results on one or more of the test sessions. A plaintiff intent on malingering will find it very difficult to remember and recreate the same performance on multiple occasions unless the strategy is simply to feign severe impairment across the board. Such a pattern would likely be detected as obviously fraudulent when judged within the context of history, observations, and records.

ETHICAL AND CLINICAL ISSUES IN THE IDENTIFICATION OF DECEPTION AND MALINGERING

The need to provide informed consent regarding any treatment and evaluation has become a standard of care and an ethical obligation in medicine and psychology (National Academy of Neuropsychology, 2003). Informed consent provides a potential patient or examinee the relevant information needed to make an informed decision as to whether to proceed with a planned treatment or evaluation, and the advantages and risks of doing so. The type of information provided in our own evaluations include the reason for the evaluation (e.g., to determine if there is anything wrong with your brain following your head injury), the referral source (e.g., the attorney on the other side of the case), our role (e.g., as a forensic evaluator, not as a treating doctor), the differences between a treating and evaluating doctor, limits of confidentiality, and so forth. Our informed consent also includes an admonition that the ability to make sense of the results of the evaluation will be compromised if the litigant does not answer truthfully and does not apply appropriate effort on the tests and procedures that are to be administered to him. Actual disclosure regarding the use of methods to detect dishonesty, however, may not be appropriate if the integrity of the process is to be preserved. The danger of providing complete informed consent in this matter was explained by Youngjohn et al. (1999), who stated, "Warning persons about the presence of (malingering detection) techniques reduces the validity and scientific quality of forensic evaluations. Rather than warn persons that they will be caught if they try to malinger, we recommend that persons be told to do their best (and to) encourage maximum effort . . . ."

Whether or not the clinician or forensic expert should even diagnose the presence of malingering is also a thorny ethical and clinical issue. There are a number of factors that raise concern about the wisdom of identifying a patient as malingering dictating that such a diagnosis should be offered cautiously. The consequences of applying such a pejorative label include the fact that it often results in negative attitudes by others, skepticism about the need for treatment, suspicion about employability, and so forth. This is particularly critical when the patient labeled as a malingerer suffers from legitimate medical or psychiatric problems in addition to the gross exaggeration. In other words, malingering is typically not an all or none phenomenon but may be focused upon particular complaints, behaviors, and test performances. It is not mutually exclusive of other legitimate pathology. If, in fact, such a patient does have a real disturbance, such problems are less likely to be taken seriously. Of course, such a derogatory diagnosis can be particularly harmful when it is incorrect.

On the other hand, there are certainly reasons in favor of providing a diagnosis of malingering. For one, such a label would prevent the individual from abusing the system by inappropriately procuring of secondary gain. In many settings, there are only limited treatment, financial, and other resources that need to be allocated and they should be reserved for those who are truly in need. In a treatment setting, in particular, identifying a patient as a malingerer can provide a mechanism to set limits upon him and redirect his energy into more appropriate methods for meeting his needs.

It is recommended that such a diagnosis be offered very cautiously and only after considering the costs and benefits of doing so. The decision to identify an individual as a malingerer should also consider motivational factors related to the criminological, pathogenic, and adaptational models, discussed earlier in this chapter. Branding someone as a malingerer should require compelling evidence derived from convergent evidence. It should not be diagnosed from a single test or indicator.

Certainly, it is necessary not to overlook any contributory coexisting problems and diagnostic considerations. Recommendations should be made in consideration of these contributory problems and diagnostic conditions.

The diagnosis of malingering is frequently overused in cases with limited evidence, often confined to specific circumstances. The case of Mr. Crash provides an excellent example of this.

Case of Mr. Crash

Mr. Crash was an older adolescent when he suffered a severe frontal lobe injury 2 years earlier after being ejected from the bed of a pick-up truck. He performed very poorly on a defense neuropsychological IME examination in a manner highly consistent with purposeful intent to portray himself as impaired. Certainly, there was no need to do so. His injury and resulting severe disability were well documented. His intentionally poor performance during this one examination stood in contrast to all prior examinations in which his motivation and effort were sound. In all likelihood, his attempt to manipulate the test results on this one occasion was a reflection of the poor judgment associated with his frontal lobe injury.

In such a case, it would be inappropriate to diagnose this patient as a malingerer on the basis of this one episode of poor judgment. It is recommended that a diagnosis of malingering should be reserved for behavior that is pervasive and can be demonstrated across multiple settings. It is recommended that the clinician avoid labeling specific symptoms, behavior, and test performances in malingerers. Consider terms such as overreporting, exaggerating, poorly motivated, and fluctuating effort.

REFERENCES

American Psychiatric Association. 2000. *Diagnostic and Statistical Manual of Mental Disorders: Fourth Edition, Text Revision*. Washington, D.C.: American Psychiatric Association.

Barth, J. T., Ryan, T. V. and Hawk, G. L. 1991. Forensic Neuropsychology: A Reply to the Method Skeptics. *Neuropsychological Review*, 2, 251–266.

Bush, S. S., Ruff, R. M., Tröster, A. I., Barth, J. T., Koffler, S. P., Pliskin, N. H., Reynolds, C. R., and Silver, C. H. 2005. Symptom Validity Assessment: Practice Issues and Medical Necessity. *Archives of Clinical Neuropsychology*, 20, 419–426.

Drukteinis, A. M. 2006. The Growth of Employment Stress Claims: Workers' Compensation, Discrimination, Harassment and Accommodation Problems (Part 2 of 5). *New England Psychodiagnostics*, http://www.psychlaw.com/LibraryFiles/EmploymentStress2.html

Ekman, P. 1992. *Telling Lies: Clues to Deceit in the Marketplace, Politics and Marriage*. New York: W.W. Norton.

Faust, D. 1991. Forensic Neuropsychology: The Art of Practicing a Science That Does Not Yet Exist. *Neuropsychology Review*, 2, 205–231.

Frederick, R. I. 1997. *Validity Indicator Profile Manual*. Minneapolis: National Computer Systems, Inc.

Goodwin, D. M. 1989. *A Dictionary of Neuropsychology*. New York: Springer-Verlag.

Guilmette, T. J. and Guiliano, A. J. 1991. Taking the Stand: Issues and Strategies in Forensic Neuropsychology. *The Clinical Neuropsychologist*, 5, 197–219.

Hare, R. D. 1991. *Manual for the Revised Psychopathy Checklist*. North Tonawanda, NY: Multihealth Systems.

Heaton, R. K., Smith, H. H., Lehman, R. A., and Vogt, A. T. 1978. Prospects for Faking Believable Deficits in Neuropsychological Testing. *Journal of Consulting and Clinical Psychology*, 46, 892–900.

Heinze, M. C. and Purisch, A. D. 2001. Beneath the Mask: Use of Psychological Tests to Detect and Subtype Malingering in Criminal Defendants. *Journal of Forensic Psychology Practice*, 1, 23–52.

Lees-Haley, P. R. and Brown, R. S. 1993. Neuropsychological Complaint Base Rates of 170 Personal Injury Claimants. *Archives of Clinical Neuropsychology*, 8, 203–209.

McCaffrey, R. J. and Lynch, J. K. 1992. A Methodological Review of "Method Skeptic" Reports. *Neuropsychology Review, 3*, 235–248.

Mensch, A. J. and Woods, D. J. 1986. Patterns of Feigning Brain-Damage on the LNNB. *The International Journal of Clinical Neuropsychology, 8*, 59–63.

National Academy of Neuropsychology. 2000. Test Security: Official Position of the National Academy of Neuropsychology. *Archives of Clinical Neuropsychology, 15*, 383–386.

National Academy of Neuropsychology. 2003. *Informed Consent in Clinical Neuropsychology Practice.* NAN Website.

Pankratz, L. and Binder, L. M. 1997. Malingering on Intellectual and Neuropsychological Measures. In Rogers, R. (Ed.) *Clinical Assessment of Malingering and Deception*, 2d ed. New York: Guilford.

Porter, S. and Yuille, J. C. 1996. The Language of Deceit: An Investigation of the Verbal Clues to Deception in the Interrogation Context. *Law and Human Behavior, 20*, 443–458.

Purisch, A. D. 2001. Neuropsychological Evaluation of Neurological Disorders and Malingering Related to Mold Toxicity. *Mealey's Litigation Report: Mold, 1*, 43–51.

Purisch, A. D. and Sbordone, R. J. 1997. Forensic Neuropsychology: Clinical Issues and Practice. In Horton, A. M., Wedding, D., and Webster, J. (Eds.) *The Neuropsychology Handbook Volume 2: Treatment Issues and Special Populations*, 2nd ed. New York: Springer-Verlag.

Reitan, R. M. and Wolfson, D. J. 1998. Detection of Malingering and Invalid Test Results Using the Halstead-Reitan Battery. In Reynolds, C. R. (Ed.) *Detection of Malingering During Head Injury Litigation*. New York: Plenum Press.

Rogers, R. 1992. *Structured Interview of Reported Symptoms.* Odessa, FL: Psychological Assessment Resources.

Rogers, R. (Ed.) 1997. *Clinical Assessment of Malingering and Deception*, 2nd ed. New York: Guilford.

Rogers, R., Salekin, R. T., Sewell, K. W., Goldstein, A., and Leonard, K. 1998. A Comparison of Forensic and Nonforensic Malingerers: A Prototypical Analysis of Explanatory Models. *Law and Human Behavior, 22*, 353–367.

Rogers, R., Sewell, K. W., and Goldstein, A. 1994. Explanatory Models of Malingering: A Prototypical Analysis. *Law and Human Behavior, 18*, 543–553.

Sbordone, R. J. and Purisch, A. D. 1996. Hazards of Blind Analysis of Neuropsychological Test Data in Assessing Cognitive Disability: The Role of Confounding Factors. *Neurorehabilitation, 7*, 15–26.

Sbordone, R. J., Strickland, T. L., and Purisch, A. D. 2000. Neuropsychological Assessment of the Criminal Defendant: The Significance of Cultural Factors. In Fletcher-Janzen, E., Strickland, T. L., and Reynolds, C. R. (Eds.) *Handbook of Cross Cultural Neuropsychology*. New York: Plenum Press.

Youngjohn, J. R., Davis, D., and Wolf, I. 1997. Head Injury and the MMPI-2: Paradoxical Severity Effects and Influence of Litigation. *Psychological Assessment, 9*, 177–184.

Youngjohn, J. R., Lees-Haley, P. R., and Binder, L. M. 1999. Comment: Warning Malingerers Produces More Sophisticated Malingering. *Archives of Clinical Neuropsychology*, 511–515.

12 Neuropsychological Testing

Neuropsychological testing consists of the administration of tests that have been specifically designed to evaluate an individual's functioning in cognitive domains such as abstract thinking, academic skills, attention, cognitive flexibility, concentration, executive functions, language, judgment, intellectual functioning, learning, memory, motor functions, organization, planning, problem solving, speed of cognitive processing, and visual–spatial and visual–constructional skills. The neuropsychologists also administer tests to evaluate a patient's emotional and psychological functioning in response to a brain insult and preexisting personality traits. In medicolegal cases, specialized tests are commonly administered to plaintiffs to assess their effort and motivation to perform to the best of their ability on the concurrently administered neuropsychological tests. The results of these tests can assist the neuropsychologist determine whether an individual's test performances truly reflect cognitive deficits caused by a specific brain insult or are the results of nonneurological factors. These test results can also assist the neuropsychologist determine whether the individual being tested is exaggerating their cognitive and psychological symptoms as a result of their underlying troubled psychological state, need for attention, or malingering (see Chapter 11).

Neuropsychologists typically utilize what have been described as standardized neuropsychological test batteries (see below) or flexible test batteries when assessing individuals who are known or are suspected as having a brain insult. Although many neuropsychologists have stressed that flexible neuropsychological test batteries are as effective as standardized batteries such as the Halstead–Reitan in identifying brain-impaired individuals (e.g., Lezak et al., 2004), Russell et al. (2005) have criticized the use of flexible batteries for not having been validated psychometrically to identify individuals with brain damage. They have also stressed that the tests and norms utilized in flexible batteries are not dependable. Unfortunately, these authors fail to point out that standardized batteries such as the Halstead–Reitan cannot be given to everyone. For example, it was never designed to adequately assess individuals with language, memory, or executive function disorders or accurately predict how an individual can work, live independently, or function in society. It appears inappropriate for individuals who are auditorally, motorically, or visually impaired, have psychiatric disorders, have a low IQ, or are unable to tolerate 8 to 12 hours of testing. Like many standardized test batteries, it does not contain norms for individuals who were raised in a different cultural or linguistic environment, or do not speak English. These authors also fail to point out that many neuropsychologists do not give the complete Halstead–Reitan battery and include supplemental tests to assess cognitive functions that are not adequately assessed by the battery. Once a neuropsychologist fails to administer the entire battery and supplements the battery with other tests then he or she is now utilizing a flexible rather than a standardized neuropsychological battery.

Flexible neuropsychological batteries (Sweet and Moberg, 1990) consist of a composite of neuropsychological tests that have been selected because of one or more of the following factors: the cultural and linguistic background of the individual being tested, the type of brain insult sustained by the individual, the particular expressed complaints of the individual and the individual's significant others, the length of time since injury, specific referral questions or issues, specific tests that have been administered to the individual in the past, the duration of time since previous testing, specific medicolegal issues (e.g., the plaintiff may not be putting forth his or her best effort or is malingering), specific perceptual and motor limitations (e.g., the individual may be visually impaired, deaf, or unable to use his or her right or left arm), current emotional or psychiatric problems (e.g., the individual may be severely depressed or psychotic), the sensitivity and specificity of certain tests designed to assess the individual's cognitive problems, the time allotted for assessment, the individual's endurance and tendency to fatigue, and the patient–examiner interaction (e.g., the examiner may notice a particular cognitive problem during testing, which may result in the administration of another test to further investigate this problem).

USE OF PSYCHOLOGICAL ASSISTANTS OR TECHNICIANS

Many neuropsychologists employ psychological assistants or technicians to administer their psychological and neuropsychological tests. Many psychologists base their evaluations on the neuropsychological questionnaire that is completed by the individual while sitting in the waiting room, the individual's raw test data, and the observations of their assistant or technician. Unfortunately, the use of assistants or technicians not only minimizes the time the neuropsychologist actually spends with the individual who is being examined, but places heavy reliance on the written information provided by the individual (which may be inaccurate for a variety of reasons), the individual's quantitative test scores (which may reflect a variety of nonneurological factors), and the observations of a person whose training in neuropsychology and ability to recognize the neurobehavioral manifestations of brain damage is usually quite limited.

This chapter will critically review many of the widely used neuropsychological tests that are used to evaluate individuals with known or suspected brain insults.

NEUROPSYCHOLOGICAL BATTERIES AND TESTS

STANDARDIZED NEUROPSYCHOLOGICAL TEST BATTERIES

Neuropsychologists may use a standardized neuropsychological battery to evaluate individuals suspected of having brain dysfunction or damage. There are several advantages (and disadvantages) in utilizing such batteries:

1. The battery usually contains norms that compare the individual's test scores to those of brain-damaged patients and normal controls, a manual that describes how to administer and score the various tests contained within the battery, and the specific tests that should be administered.
2. The administration of a standardized neuropsychological test battery may not require that the examiner be well versed in neuroanatomy, behavioral neurology, or neuropsychology because some of these batteries can serve as "stand alone" instruments to detect brain damage.
3. Most standardized neuropsychological batteries are relatively easy to administer and score.
4. They can usually be administered by technicians or psychological assistants (e.g., an individual can be trained to administer and score a neuropsychological battery in a week or two).

TRAINING IN THE USE OF A STANDARDIZED NEUROPSYCHOLOGICAL TEST BATTERY

The vast majority of psychologists and neuropsychologists who use standardized test batteries have usually taken one or more workshops, that teach them how to administer, score, and interpret the results of the tests contained within the battery. These workshops usually last between 2 and 5 days and typically include a cursory overview of the neuroanatomy of the brain, neuropathology, and brain–behavior relationships. These workshops usually focus on the tests-scores obtained from individuals who have previously been administered these tests by one of the instructors. The major emphasis of such courses is typically on how to properly interpret them.

Unfortunately, these workshops usually do not provide students with the opportunity to administer the battery to brain-damaged subjects, and score the test data. Since many psychologists who complete these workshops do not receive supervision from a qualified and experienced neuropsychologist after completing the workshops, errors in test administration, scoring, or the interpretation of the test data that are likely to occur and be repeated without being recognized.

NEUROPSYCHOLOGICAL TEST BATTERIES

HALSTEAD–REITAN NEUROPSYCHOLOGICAL TEST BATTERY AND ITS ALLIED PROCEDURES

The Halstead–Reitan Neuropsychological Test Battery and allied procedures is perhaps the best known and most widely used neuropsychological test battery. This battery was developed by Ward Halstead and his doctoral student, Ralph M. Reitan (Horton and Wedding, 1984). The tests in this battery were initially used by Halstead to investigate the cognitive abilities that were compromised by brain injury. He assessed a group of neurosurgical patients with documented brain injuries and analyzed the test results. Reitan later revised and augmented the core battery of tests developed by Halstead. One of the advantages of the Halstead–Reitan Neuropsychological Test Battery is that it has been researched in more detail than any other set of neuropsychological tests or batteries and has used multivariate statistical techniques to accurately classify patients as brain-damaged or lateralize the location of brain damage (Horton, 1997).

The Halstead–Reitan Battery consists of adult, intermediate child (9 to 14 years), and young child (5 to 8 years) versions. Each battery is designed to include a minimum of 14 neuropsychological tests capable of assessing as many as 26 different brain–behavior relationships. The Halstead–Reitan Battery also includes the Wechsler Adult Intelligence Scale, the Minnesota Multiphasic Personality Inventory (MMPI), and an academic achievement measure such as the Wide Range Achievement Test (Whitworth, 1984). The complete Halstead–Reitan Battery consists of the Halstead Category Test, the Tactual Performance Test, the Seashore Rhythm Test, the Speech–Sounds Perception Test, the Finger Oscillation (Tapping) Test, the Trail Making Test, the Grip Strength Test, the Sensory Perceptual Examination, the Tactual Perceptual Examination (Tactile Finger Localization, Fingertip Number Writing Perception Tests, and Tactile Form Recognition Test), the Modified Halstead–Wepman Aphasia Screening Test, the Wechsler Adult Intelligence Scale, and the MMPI. Each of these tests is described below. The reliability, validity, strengths, and weaknesses of these tests will be discussed later in this chapter.

APHASIA SCREENING TEST

The Aphasia Screening Test consists of a number of different tasks that serve as a brief screening device to evaluate whether the patient has any impairment in language or nonlanguage skills. For example, the patient is asked to name specific objects (e.g., cross, triangle, square); read letters, numbers, and words; perform arithmetic tasks (e.g., 85–27 or 17–3); read and write sentences; pronounce words (e.g., Massachusetts); identify specific body parts; and determine left from right. Scoring is determined by the number of errors made by the patient and by assigning specific weights to the test items that the patient failed (Russell et al., 1970).

Poor performance on this test can be due to a number of factors such as the individual's high level of anxiety during testing, dyslexia, limited educational background, poor command of English, cultural deprivation, borderline or retarded intellectual functioning, poor arithmetic skills, psychiatric problems, histrionic behavior (e.g., the patient may dramatically state, "I can't draw any more. Ever since I had that accident, I can't use my right hand any more. I just can't use it. It just doesn't work any more."), psychotic thinking (e.g., when shown a cross and asked to identify it, the patient may state, "It's a message from God telling me that I am Jesus Christ."), or malingering (e.g., "What is this test supposed to show anyway. Can't you see that I'm brain-damaged? Why are you giving me these tests? They're just a waste of time. Can't you see from my records that I have brain damage and can't do these things?").

HALSTEAD CATEGORY TEST

The Halstead Category Test is a nonverbal test that measures a person's ability to formulate abstract principles based on receiving feedback after each specific test item. The test consists of 208 stimuli that are shown on slides. Each test item suggests a number ranging from one to four. The patient is instructed to determine or guess a particular number based on their conceptualization of the abstract principle represented by the slide. After the patient decides on a particular response, he or she must depress one of four levers on the instrument, which are numbered from one to four. When the subject has depressed the correct number, a door chime will ring. If, on the other hand, the patient depresses one of the incorrect numbers, a buzzer will sound. Based on this feedback, correct or incorrect, the patient must determine the underlying principle in each of seven different subtests. Traditionally, the items for the Category Test have been presented on a relatively small viewing screen located on a box. Some psychologists use the booklet version of this test, which is easier to use because it is portable. However, if the examiner uses the booklet version, he or she must verbally indicate whether the patient's responses are correct or incorrect (Lezak, 1983).

The Halstead Category Test usually requires 45 minutes to 2 hours to complete, depending on the characteristics of the person being administered the test. For example, neurologically intact individuals of average or above average intelligence usually take an hour to complete this test. Individuals who are elderly, or who have sustained severe diffuse brain damage, may require 2 hours or longer. It is important that the individual be told at the beginning of each of the seven subtests that there is an underlying principle that must be deduced that may be the same or different from the principles found in the other subtests. The only exception to this is that when the individuals are given the seventh subtest, they are told to answer the items the same way as they had previously done during the six prior subtests (Whitworth, 1984).

The scoring for this test consists of the total number of errors made by the patient. Reitan (1955) recommended a cut-off score of 51 or more errors based on empirical research to statistically discriminate between brain-damaged and neurologically intact groups of relatively young adult patients. Fromm-Auch and Yeudall (1983) reviewed the literature on the normative data for normal subjects taking the test. They found that the average scores for normal healthy adults across these studies ranged from 22.8 to 59.4 errors. Their review suggests that using the cut-off score of 51 errors may miscategorize normal healthy adults as brain-damaged. In addition, the use of this cut-off score when testing visually impaired or normal elderly individuals may also result in a high percentage of false positive errors, that is, normal individuals erroneously categorized as brain-damaged.

Heaton et al. (1991) found that demographic variables such as sex, age, and education significantly affected an individual's performances on this test. As a consequence, they have recommended that psychologist use norms (that they developed) based on a person's sex, age, and educational background to determine the severity of the individual's cognitive impairment.

FINGER OSCILLATION (TAPPING) TEST

The Finger Tapping Test measures an individual's ability to depress with his or her index finger a lever that is attached to a counter. The individual initially uses his or her preferred hand and then the nonpreferred hand. The individual is given five consecutive trials of 10 seconds each for each hand. Scoring consists of the average number of taps for each hand. Reitan (1955) has recommended that a cut-off score of 10% or more be used for the preferred hand to discriminate between brain-damaged patients and normal controls. Bornstein (1986), on the other hand, found that 30% of normal healthy adults had differences of greater than 10%. His findings indicate that the norms recommended by Reitan erroneously categorize a significant number of normal individuals as brain-damaged. In addition, Thompson and Parsons (1985) have stressed that norms based on the individual's gender, age, and educational background should be utilized to avoid misdiagnosing normal adults as brain-damaged.

A patient's performance on this test can be used to determine the laterality (side of the brain) of brain damage. For example, if an individual's performance with his or her nonpreferred hand is 25% or more slower than the preferred hand (in the absence of any peripheral, neurological, psychological, or orthopedic problems), it is likely that the patient may have sustained a right-hemisphere brain injury. While poor performance on this test can be due to subcortical or diffuse brain damage (when a patient's performance in both hands is very slow) or to unilateral brain damage (confined to one side of the brain), patients who have been placed on high dosages of anticonvulsant medications (e.g., Dilantin or Phenobarbital) are likely to perform slowly. Patients who have a history of injuries to either hand or arm, or who have developed radiculopathies involving the fifth and sixth cervical vertebrae (C5 and C6) will often have difficulty on this task. In addition, patients who are extremely nervous or markedly depressed will often perform relatively poorly. This test is also prone to conscious manipulation since a patient can control the rate of their motor speed by their visual observations of the response counter.

GRIP STRENGTH (HAND DYNAMOMETER) TEST

The Grip Strength (Hand Dynamometer) Test consists of measuring the grip strength of each hand with a dynamometer. The patient is typically given two or three trials with each hand. The average of all trials administered serves as the patient's score for each hand. It has been generally accepted that the strength of the patient's preferred (dominant) hand should generally be 5 to 10% stronger than the nonpreferred hand. If a patient's grip strength in the dominant hand is 50 kg, but only 35 kg in the nondominant hand, it is likely that this patient may have right-hemisphere brain damage, particularly if this is supported by the medical records, neuroimaging studies, and other neuropsychological test data.

Although differences of greater than 10% have been interpreted as evidence of brain damage or dysfunction in the contralateral hemisphere of the significantly weaker hand (Whitworth, 1984), Bornstein (1986) has found that 25 to 30% of healthy adults have differences of greater than 10%. To avoid misclassifying normal healthy adults as brain-damaged, many neuropsychologists use the norms that have been developed by Heaton et al. (1991), which correct for the patient's gender, age, and educational background, rather than the earlier norms developed by Reitan (1955).

Poor performance on this test can also be caused by one or more of the following confounding factors: a physical injury to one of the patient's arms, hands, or fingers; a radiculopathy involving either C5, C6, or C7; peripheral neuropathy (e.g., damage to the ulnar or radial nerve); arthritic pain or discomfort in one of the patient's shoulders, arms, hands, or fingers; histrionic behavior (e.g., the patient loudly states, "I have no strength in this hand. Can't you see how weak it is?"); depression (e.g., the patient fails to put forth the necessary effort because of a depressed mood); or malingering. Because this particular test easily lends itself to conscious manipulation, the neuropsychologist and examiner should carefully observe the individual who is being tested to ensure that he or she is putting forth maximum effort while taking this test. To further ensure that an individual's performance on this test was not due to motivational factors, the patient's performance should be compared to his or her performance on other neuropsychological tests and medical records.

MINNESOTA MULTIPHASIC PERSONALITY INVENTORY

This test will be described in greater detail later in this chapter under Tests of Personality and Emotional Adjustment. While this test is administered as part of the Halstead–Reitan

Neuropsychological Battery, the profile obtained from this test typically plays only a minor role in the interpretation of the patient's scores on other tests contained within this battery. This, of course, may vary considerably and depend on the clinical expertise and experience of the psychologist or neuropsychologist interpreting the profile.

SEASHORE RHYTHM TEST

The Seashore Rhythm Test requires the patient to determine if two pairs of musical rhythms are the same or different. The patient is presented with a tape recording and after a brief practice session is provided with three sets of ten test items. After each pair of rhythms is presented, the patient must decide if they were the same or different and write S (same) or D (different) on a sheet of paper. After the patient is given all three sets, totaling 30 test items, the patient's score can be determined by comparing the patient's actual scores to those in the test manual (Lezak, 1983). While a score of six or more errors has been used in the past as a cut-off point to discriminate between brain-injured and nonbrain-injured patients (Reitan, 1955), to avoid misclassifying normal healthy adults as brain-damaged, many neuropsychologists use the norms developed by Heaton et al. (1991). While poor performance on this test has been reported for patients who have sustained damage to the right temporal lobe (Reitan, 1955), it can also reflect damage to other parts of the brain, particularly subcortical or diffuse brain damage or injuries to the frontal lobes. Individuals who are neurologically intact may also perform poorly on this test if they are nervous, psychotic, or markedly depressed or have hearing problems.

SENSORY–PERCEPTUAL EXAMINATION

The Sensory–Perceptual Examination contains a number of different tests to determine a patient's ability to perceive stimuli to each side of the body. In the tactile perception test, the patient's hands are placed on a table with the palms down. After the patient's eyes are closed, the examiner touches the back of each hand lightly in a random sequence. This same procedure is also done to both sides of the patient's face. The examiner must maintain a similar amount of pressure on the patient's face or the back of the hand. The examiner then touches both hands and both sides of the face simultaneously and asks the patient to indicate which side was touched. When a patient consistently reports that only one side of the body has been touched when both sides have been touched, the patient has given evidence of a suppression error, which suggests a contralateral (the side of the brain opposite to the patient's hand or face that was touched) brain injury. The examiner can often localize the particular hemisphere that has been damaged, particularly when the injury involves one of the parietal lobes (Lezak, 1983).

A similar type of test has been developed to assess the patient's ability to perceive auditory stimuli. For example, the examiner stands directly behind the patient who has his or her eyes closed. The examiner makes a small noise by rubbing his fingers together approximately six inches away from the patient's left or right ear. Initially, this is done to determine whether the patient can perceive the auditory stimuli in each ear. Following this, the examiner simultaneously rubs the fingers of both hands together near both of the patient's ears. The patient is instructed to indicate from which side the sound is coming. If the patient consistently fails to identify the sound arriving at one of the ears, then it is likely that a suppression of the sound arriving in that ear has occurred as a result of an injury to the contralateral hemisphere. It should be noted, however, that this particular test requires considerable experience on the part of the examiner because it is necessary for the examiner to place his hands equidistant from the patient's ears and keep the level of sound made by rubbing the fingers together approximately equal (Whitworth, 1984).

The patient's visual fields are also examined. The examiner sits approximately three feet in front of a sitting patient. The examiner then outstretches his or her arms while the patient's eyes are focused directly on the examiner's nose. The examiner then instructs the patient to indicate whether he or she notices anything moving at the periphery of the visual field while focusing on the examiner's nose. The examiner tests the patient's upper, middle, and lower visual fields by making slight movements with his or her fingers and moving them closer to the patient until they are detected. This is done separately for each side. This is followed by simultaneous movements of the examiner's fingers on both hands in the patient's upper, middle, and lower visual fields.

Scoring is based on the number of sensory suppressions or imperceptions made by the patient during simultaneous stimulation. For example, some patients will show a reduction in their peripheral vision or be totally unable to recognize any movements in their left or right visual fields. This condition is known as homonymous hemianopsia. In other patients, there may be a partial loss in either the upper or lower visual field (upper or lower quadrantanopsia) (Golden, 1979).

SPEECH–SOUNDS PERCEPTION TEST

The Speech–Sounds Perception Test consists of presenting via a tape recorder a total of 60 nonsense words that are variants of the "ee" sound. The subject is instructed to listen to each word and then underline one of four words (one of which is the correct word) on a sheet of paper. After the test instructions are presented and the subject is administered three sample test items, the test begins. Once the test has begun, the examiner cannot stop the tape or interrupt the subject until the entire 60 test items are completed (Whitworth, 1984). The subject receives no feedback from the examiner after beginning the actual test. The subject is given six sets of ten words that are numbered by the speaker on the tape (e.g., the tape states, "The fifth word is freep.").

Scoring consists of matching the subject's responses to the manual to determine the number of errors the subject has made. While Reitan (1955) recommended a cut-off point of eight or more errors to differentiate between brain-damaged patients and normal controls, many neuropsychologists prefer to use the norms developed by Heaton et al. (1991) to avoid misclassifying healthy adults as brain-damaged.

This test tends to be sensitive to both diffuse brain damage and left-hemisphere lesions and to severe frontal lobe pathology because the task requires a fairly high level of concentration and attention. Poor performance on this test can also be due to the following confounding factors: a native language other than English, a preexisting history of dyslexia, a developmental auditory perceptual disorder, impaired visual acuity (i.e., difficulty seeing the written words), psychosis (e.g., the subject attributes a bizarre connotation or meaning to the word that alters his or her response choice), severe depression, or fatigue.

TACTUAL PERCEPTUAL EXAMINATION

During the tests described below, the patient should never be informed that bilateral rather than unilateral stimulation will be given. It is also important that the examiner ensure that the patient cannot "cheat" by not fully closing his or her eyes while the hands or face is touched. This problem can be prevented by placing a visual obstacle, such as a book or piece of cardboard, over the patient's hands so he or she cannot perceive which hand(s) is being touched. Some examiners prefer, however, to use a device in which the patient's hands are inserted into a large open-ended box, which provides a greater visual obstacle.

TACTILE FINGER LOCALIZATION AND FINGERTIP NUMBER WRITING PERCEPTION TESTS

The Tactile Finger Localization Test is a test of finger agnosia, which consists of touching the subject's fingers while his or her eyes are closed or a visual obstacle has been placed in front of the hands. The subject's fingers are touched in a random order four times each. The subject must report the name or number of each finger touched. Scoring consists of the number of errors out of a total of 20 trials.

In the Fingertip Number Writing Perception Test the examiner writes numbers (3, 4, 5, or 6) in random order on the fingertips of the subject's hands, which cannot be seen by the subject, until a total of 20 numbers has been written on each hand. The subject must identify which number he or she perceives the examiner has written. Scoring consists of the number of errors made with each hand. When the subject makes significantly more errors on one hand than the other, unless the subject's performance reflects a chronic medical condition, prior injury to the finger, or psychological or motivational factors, there is a good likelihood that the area of the brain contralateral to that hand has been damaged (Golden, 1979; Lezak, 1983).

TACTILE FORM RECOGNITION TEST

The Tactile Form Recognition Test uses a square, triangle, circle, and cross made of plastic. The examiner places one of these shapes in the patient's hand after the patient has placed his or her hand through a large visual obstacle that prevents visual identification of the object. The patient's task is to identify the particular object by feeling the object and relying on kinesthetic information alone. The patient must then point with the free hand to the matching object located on the visual obstacle directly in front of him or her. This procedure is then repeated for the other hand and then for each hand again. Scoring consists of the number of errors made with each hand and the amount of time required before the patient was able to provide the examiner with a response (Lezak, 1983).

Poor performance on this test can reflect a number of conditions including physical damage or injury, cervical radiculopathy, attention or concentration difficulties, high levels of anxiety or depression, paranoia (e.g., the patient becomes frightened when asked to close his or her eyes when an unfamiliar person is standing directly behind him or her in a small room with the door closed), chronic medical conditions (e.g., diabetes, poor circulation), hysteria (e.g., the patient begins sobbing during the examination and states, "I don't feel anything in my fingers or any part of my body. My body's completely numb."), or malingering (the patient reports feeling no sensation whatsoever on either side of the body in the absence of any type of neurological disease or injury). Because the scoring procedures depend heavily on the experience and expertise of the examiner, it is not uncommon for significant discrepancies to occur when a patient is given this examination by two different examiners (Whitworth, 1984).

TACTUAL PERFORMANCE TEST

This test consists of placing a blindfold on a patient and having the patient place ten blocks of different shapes into a specially designed form board. The patient's task is to place each of the blocks into its respective shaped holes as quickly as possible. The patient begins with his or her preferred hand and uses only that hand until all of the blocks are placed. The patient begins the second trial with the nonpreferred hand until all the blocks are correctly placed. Typically, the patient's score improves between 30 and 40% on the second trial because of learning effects. On the third trial, the patient is instructed to use both hands. After the patient completes all three trials, the blindfold and form board are removed and the patient is instructed to draw a diagram that illustrates the placement of the various blocks as best as he or she can recall. The drawing is then scored for memory (the number of blocks of various shapes recalled) and localization (the exact number of blocks placed in correct relative position).

Scoring also consists of computing the total amount of time the patient required to complete all three trials (Lezak, 1983). While Reitan (1955) recommended a cut-off of 15.7 minutes (942 seconds) to discriminate between brain-injured patients and normal controls, many neuropsychologists prefer to use the norms developed by Heaton et al. (1991).

A patient's score on the localization scale is considered a sensitive indicator of brain injury since it measures a variety of cognitive functions such as speed of cognitive processing, the tactile and kinesthetic abilities, nonverbal learning, and incidental memory (the ability to recall information or events that the patient was not specifically instructed to learn or recall) (Boll, 1982). Studies (Wheeler et al., 1963) have shown that by using the localization cut-off score of five, 85% of the brain-injured group could be differentiated from normal controls, while psychiatric patients could be differentiated from brain-injured patients with 64% accuracy. Other investigators (Golden, 1978) have reported similar findings. Golden (1978, 1979) also found that by using a cut-off score of four or five correct on the memory scale, he was able to achieve similar findings. In addition to quantitative measurements, qualitative evaluation of the patient's performances between preferred and nonpreferred hand, or with both hands, is helpful in determining whether the injury is predominantly in the left or right hemisphere or is present throughout the entire brain (diffuse brain damage).

Poor performance on this test can be due to one or more of the following factors: anxiety (e.g., patients who are insecure or paranoid or have a history of being raped or molested are likely to become very upset and anxious when blindfolded by a virtual stranger in a relatively small room with the door closed); peripheral motor problems (e.g., physical injury to one of the hands, wrists, or arms; motor weakness secondary to cervical radiculopathy; loss of a finger); peripheral neuropathy involving the nerves within the arm or shoulder, sweaty hands (e.g., causing the patient to drop the blocks on the floor); physical pain or discomfort caused by bending or stretching or by remaining seated for 15 to 20 minutes; significant auditory or perceptual difficulties (e.g., the patient is unable to hear or understand the test instructions); a severe headache; or motivational factors.

TRAIL MAKING TEST

The Trail Making Test consists of two parts. On Part A, the patient is instructed to connect in ascending order 25 circles that are distributed on a sheet of white paper and are numbered from 1 through 25. On Part B, the patient's task is to connect circles containing either numbers or letters in alternate sequence, that is, beginning with 1 and going to A, then 2, then B, etc. On both tasks, the patient is instructed to work as quickly as possible and is provided with practice items prior to beginning the test. Scoring is based on the amount of time the patient takes to complete each task. Some neuropsychologists may also use qualitative measures in evaluating a patient's performance on this test. For example, the number of errors the patient makes (after the patient has made an error, the instructor is required to gently provide the patient with a cue, such as "Which letter follows D?" or "You went from number 5 to 6. You should have gone to a letter instead"), the number of times the patient lifts his or her pencil off the paper after having been instructed to keep the pencil on the paper at all times, and the number and type of cues and prompts provided by the examiner during the test. Poor performance on Part A can be due to subcortical or right-hemisphere brain injury. Poor performance on Part B can be due to left-hemisphere brain damage. Poor performance on both Parts A and B can reflect diffuse brain damage (Golden, 1979).

Many neuropsychologists use the norms developed by Heaton et al. (1991) to avoid misclassifying healthy adults as brain-damaged. Poor performance on this test can also be due to the following factors: visual difficulties (e.g., the patient failed to bring his or her glasses to the examiner's office), high levels of anxiety, marked depression, histrionic behavior (e.g., the patient begins crying during the middle of the test, stating, "I can't do this. I can't do this. Oh, God, please help me. Oh, God, please help me"), physical injury or peripheral neurological impairment of the patient's arm or hand (e.g., fractured wrist, C6 radiculopathy, crush injury to patient's arm), inability to recite the alphabet (e.g., limited command of English), a severe headache, other physical pain, or discomfort (that is likely to affect the patient's ability to concentrate), or motivational factors (because this test is under the patient's voluntary motor control, an individual can manipulate his or her performance by deliberately performing slowly to simulate the performance of a brain-damaged patient).

WECHSLER ADULT INTELLIGENCE SCALE

The Wechsler-Bellevue Intelligence Scale/Wechsler Adult Intelligence Scale — Revised was originally used when this battery was first developed. More recently, however, the Wechsler Adult

Intelligence Scale (Revised) or Third Edition has been used, although a few psychologists persist in using the older version of this test. The Wechsler Adult Intelligence Scale — Revised (WAIS-R) and III will be discussed later in this chapter.

SCORING INDICES OF THE HALSTEAD–REITAN BATTERY

HALSTEAD IMPAIRMENT INDEX

The Impairment Index, devised by Halstead (1947), is a summary measure of the proportion of tests that show evidence of brain damage. It ranges from 0.0 to 1.0 (a score of 0.5 means that half of the tests administered to the patient showed evidence of brain impairment). While ten tests were initially used, Reitan (1974) later recognized that some of the test scores were less sensitive to brain damage than others, and eliminated some of the tests that had originally been used by Halstead to calculate this index. This index comprises the Category Test, the Seashore Rhythm Test, the Speech–Sounds Perception Test, the Finger Tapping Test for the dominant hand only, and the Tactual Performance Test scores for total time, memory, and localization. The cut-off score for brain damage used by Reitan for this index is 0.5 (a score of 0.4 is considered borderline impaired). Thus, individuals who score lower than 0.4 are classified as normal, while individuals scoring 0.5 or higher are classified as brain-damaged.

AVERAGE IMPAIRMENT INDEX

One of the difficulties with the use of the Halstead Impairment Index is that an individual, who only barely falls into the impaired range on the tests that make up this index, receives the same score as another individual whose test scores may be far more impaired. To correct for this possibility, an average impairment rating index was developed, which averages the weighted scores on 12 of the Halstead–Reitan tests based on a four-point scale in which a score of 0 indicates that the individual's score was above the mean (average), a score of 1 falls into the normal range, a score of 2 indicates that the score was below 1 standard deviation from the mean, a score of 3 was 2 standard deviations below the mean, and a score of 4 was 3 standard deviations below the mean. The use of the Average Impairment Index provides a better assessment of the level of impaired brain functioning than does the Halstead Impairment Index, because the Halstead Impairment Index focuses completely on the patient's deficits, while the Average Impairment Index provides the patient with credit for performing well on a test. Research on the use of the Average Impairment Index has shown that brain-damaged subjects can be reliably differentiated from control subjects (Goldstein and Shelly, 1972).

GENERAL NEUROPSYCHOLOGICAL DEFICITS SCALE

The General Neuropsychological Deficits Scale is an index of a patient's overall neuropsychological competence. It uses 42 separate test variables derived from the subtests of the Halstead–Reitan Neuropsychological Battery (Reitan and Wolfson, 1988). These variables are based on the patient's level of performance, specific deficits and pathognomonic signs, patterns of performance, and comparisons of the two sides of the patient's body on motor and sensory–perceptual measures (Horton, 1997). Similar to the method used in the Average Impairment Rating Index, each test score is rated on a four-point scale in terms of the indicated degree of brain damage. Research has shown that the General Neuropsychological Deficits Scale is superior to the Halstead Impairment Index in assessing the severity of brain injury (Horton and Sobelman, 1994). Reitan and Wolfson (1992) have also developed a neuropsychological deficit scale for older children, which is based on 45 test variables derived from the Halstead–Reitan Neuropsychological Test Battery for Older Children (Reed et al., 1965).

ALTERNATIVE IMPAIRMENT INDEX

The Alternative Impairment Index is composed of selected scores from a number of the tests contained within the Halstead–Reitan Neuropsychological Battery. Preliminary research with this index found that it produced similar hit rates for the severity of brain damage as did the Halstead Impairment Index and the General Neuropsychological Deficits Scale (Horton, 1995).

INTERPRETATION OF THE HALSTEAD–REITAN NEUROPSYCHOLOGICAL TEST BATTERY

Reitan has proposed that a patient's test scores on the Halstead–Reitan Neuropsychological Battery should begin with an estimation of the premorbid level of functioning based on the patient's performance on the Information, Comprehension, Similarities, and Vocabulary subtests of the Wechsler Adult Intelligence Scale (Reitan and Wolfson, 1986). After this, he recommends a review of the results of the most sensitive measures in the battery, the Halstead Impairment Index (or General Neuropsychological Deficits Scale), the Category Test results, score on Part B of the Trail Making Test, and the Localization score of the Tactual Performance Test. The next step in the interpretation process is a consideration of the indicators of lateralization and localization of functions based on the patient's level of performance, as well as measures of inference (patterns of performance, pathognomonic deficits, and the patient's motor and sensory perceptual performance on the right and left sides of the body). Following this, a prediction is made about the course of the brain lesion (whether it is getting worse, better, or staying the same). Tests that are utilized to predict the course of the lesion are the Speech–Sounds Perception tests, the Seashore Rhythm tests, and Part B of the Trail Making Test. Another method is to perform serial testing over time to demonstrate whether there has been any change in the patient's cognitive functioning. The last step in the interpretation of the test data involves making a prediction as to the underlying neurological etiology (e.g., brain tumor, stroke, head trauma, and Alzheimer's disease). Unfortunately, this last step requires that the individual making this prediction to possess considerable knowledge and understanding of neurology and neuropathology.

Reliability and Validity

Reitan reported that the Halstead–Reitan Battery could discriminate between brain-damaged patients and nonbrain-damaged controls in a statistically reliable manner (Reitan, 1955). Subsequent cross-validation studies (e.g., Vega and Parsons, 1967) found that the Halstead–Reitan Battery was capable of distinguishing between brain-damaged patients and normal controls at a statistically reliable level, but somewhat less than reported earlier by Reitan. While these studies have examined the effectiveness of this battery to distinguish between brain-damaged patients and neurologically intact control subjects, the ability of the battery to discriminate between brain-injured and psychiatric patients is less effective (Lezak, 1995). The effectiveness of the Halstead–Reitan Battery to localize the site of brain damage has been somewhat problematic (see, e.g., Schreiber et al., 1976). However, when multivariate statistical analyses of the test scores have been utilized, the localization of brain damage has improved considerably (Wheeler and Reitan, 1963).

Strengths and Limitations

Among the many strengths of the Halstead–Reitan Neuropsychological Battery are its impressive validity and reliability in discriminating between brain-damaged patients and normal controls. It is the most widely used standardized neuropsychological battery. The time required to learn how to administer and score the battery is usually less than a week. The use of quantitative test scores and measures permits one patient's test scores to be compared with another's and is well suited for clinical settings and for research. While this battery has been effective in determining the extent and severity of brain damage and the lateralization and localization of a brain lesion, its greatest contribution appears to be making psychologists aware of the need to assess many of the patient's cognitive and behavioral functions when addressing neuropsychological issues (Lezak, 1995).

Despite the numerous studies and publications that have attested to the clinical sensitivity, reliability, and validity of the Halstead–Reitan Battery, no "cookbook" has ever been developed to assist the clinician in making accurate interpretations of the test data (Whitworth, 1984). Clearly, clinical interpretation of the complex test data requires many years of training, considerable expertise, and a great deal of clinical acumen.

The validity and reliability of the battery in discriminating between brain-damaged patients and individuals who are attempting to simulate brain damage in personal injury litigation cases is controversial. For example, Heaton, Baade, and Johnson (1978) sent test data from the Halstead–Reitan Neuropsychological Battery to ten experienced neuropsychologists and asked them to determine whether the individual's scores were produced by either a malingerer or a brain-injured patient. Their diagnostic accuracy ranged from chance level to approximately 20% better than chance. However, when qualitative test interpretation methods were utilized, these neuropsychologists had little difficulty discriminating brain-injured patients from malingerers. While McKinzey and Russell (1997) reported that the application of mathematical decision-making formulas developed by Mittenberg et al. (1996) to the Halstead–Reitan test scores could correctly identify 77.5% of brain-damaged patients, these formulas incorrectly categorized 22.5% of these patients as malingerers.

Since many of the tests contained in the Halstead–Reitan Battery appear to be sensitive to the effects of age, education, and gender, many neuropsychologists (e.g., Heaton et al., 1986; 1996) have raised concerns about the need to use demographic normative corrections to interpret the significance of an individual's test scores. As a consequence, Heaton et al. (1991) have developed age, education, and gender correction norms. Reitan and Wolfson (1995), however, have argued that these demographic norms were developed on a normal population and have suggested that the effects of brain damage may actually obviate the need for demographic corrections. Recently, Moses et al. (1999) investigated the adequacy of the Heaton et al. (1991) norms. While they found these norms were clearly superior to Reitan's original norms (1955) in minimizing the confounding effects of age and education, they cautioned against using these norms to determine an individual's level of neuropsychological impairment.

The normal control group that was utilized by Halstead (1947) has been criticized by Lezak et al. (2004) as anything but normal since 10 of the 28 control subjects had been receiving care for minor psychiatric disturbances, some of whom had military combat experience. One control subject was a military prisoner facing imminent life or death imprisonment or execution. Three other control subjects were awaiting lobotomies because of behavioral problems (two of which were described as having homicidal impulses; one had suicidal impulses and was described as having strong homosexual tendencies).

The age of Halstead's normative group ranged from 14 to 50 years of age with a mean age of 28.3. A number of studies (e.g., Cullum et al., 1989) have stressed that Halstead's norms should not be applied to older subjects since these individuals were unlike the control subjects upon which the Halstead–Reitan Battery was originally normed. Since neuropsychological test scores tend to decline as the subjects get older, these norms tend to misclassify normal individuals over the age of 45 as impaired. For example, when healthy volunteers between the ages of 55 and 67 were administered this battery using Halstead's norms, the majority were misclassified as brain-damaged on the Halstead impairment index. When the average impairment index was utilized, 38% of these individuals were misclassified as brain-damaged (Lezak et al., 2004).

Although Heaton et al. (1991) have derived norms based on an individual's age, sex, and educational background from healthy subjects who participated as research controls in a variety of different studies, Reitan and Wolfson (1996, 1997) have argued that age and educational corrections are unnecessary since the tests were designed to be sensitive to brain damage and are less affected by the individual's age and educational background. They justified this by arguing that person's scores on the General Neuropsychological Deficit Score (GNDS) did not correlate significantly with age or education in their sample even though a number of other studies have not found this to be the case (Straus et al., 2006).

Since the Halstead–Reitan Neuropsychological Battery takes between 8 and 12 hours for administration, some neuropsychologists (e.g., Kasznik, 1989) have felt that it is essentially inappropriate for elderly persons whose endurance and stamina are often quite limited. Thus, these individuals may perform poorly because they become too exhausted to perform to the best of their ability.

Another criticism that has been leveled at the Halstead–Reitan Neuropsychological Battery, is that none of the summary scores that are generated can be used to identify the patient's strengths and weaknesses. Unfortunately, for some psychologists, these are the only scores that are utilized in arriving at their opinions about a particular individual's cognitive functioning. This practice, unfortunately, reduces the complexity of the brain to a single score or several summation scores and makes no attempt to provide a detailed analysis of the patient's performance in specific cognitive domains. Thus, while trying to create the impression of scientific objectivity, this approach essentially ignores the complexity of the patient's cognitive functioning, and is not helpful in predicting how the patient will function at work, school, or in the community.

While the Halstead–Reitan Neuropsychological Test Battery appears to have been designed to detect and localize brain lesions or damage, it was never primarily designed to predict everyday and vocational functioning (Sbordone, 1997). While some efforts have been made to predict everyday and vocational functioning from the tests contained with the Halstead–Reitan Neuropsychological Battery, the correlations between neuropsychological measures derived from this battery and everyday functioning have been only modest (Sbordone and Guilmette, 1999).

The Halstead–Reitan Battery has some practical limitations because the equipment necessary to administer the complete battery is fairly expensive and difficult to transport due to its size and bulkiness. Since it may require several hours to administer the entire battery, patients with significant brain injury, particularly in the acute and postacute stages, are likely to become extremely fatigued or frustrated. Many neuropsychologists do not administer the entire battery; therefore, some difficulties may arise if a patient is tested by several different neuropsychologists. For example, if the patient is seen in a hospital or prison setting, the neuropsychologist may use only those tests that can be carried within a briefcase. Thus, the neuropsychologist would then be forced to rely on only those tests that could be conveniently administered (Whitworth, 1984).

Many psychologists who have taken a workshop on the Halstead–Reitan Battery receive little or no supervision after they have completed the workshop. Thus, they may make errors in their interpretation of the neuropsychological test data. Furthermore, many psychologists may administer this battery only once a month or so, which does not permit them the opportunity to develop sufficient expertise or experience in its use. As a result, they may overlook confounding factors such as prior physical injuries (e.g., loss of a finger, surgery, and fractures), pain and discomfort at the time of testing, headaches, poor vision, impaired hearing, cultural and linguistic factors, the deleterious effects of medications and medical diseases (e.g., hypothyroidism, diabetes, and endocrine disorders), psychotic thinking, depression, anxiety, histrionic behavior, or motivation when interpreting the test data (Sbordone and Purisch, 1986).

LURIA–NEBRASKA NEUROPSYCHOLOGICAL BATTERY

The Luria–Nebraska Neuropsychological Battery (LNNB) is a comprehensive neuropsychological test battery that integrates the neuropsychological assessment procedures of the late Professor Alexander Romanovich Luria and the American psychometric tradition through the work of its authors (Golden et al., 1978). This battery contains a total of 269 test items that make up 11 clinical scales motor functions, rhythm and pitch, tactile and kinesthetic functions, visual functions, receptive language, expressive language, reading, writing, arithmetic, memory, and intellectual processes. In addition to these scales, three additional scales have been developed (based on the 269 test items) that are sensitive to brain impairment and recovery following brain injury and are known as the pathognomonic, profile elevation and impairment scales (Golden et al., 1987).

The LNNB contains two lateralization scales — left-hemisphere scale and right-hemisphere scale. In addition, eight scales have been developed to localize brain damage to the following regions of the brain left frontal, left sensory–motor, left parietal–occipital, left temporal, right frontal, right sensory-motor, right parietal-occipital, and right temporal lobes. The LNNB also attempts to integrate the qualitative tradition of Luria by listing 66 different qualitative indices that the test examiner is asked to score. Thus, the Luria–Nebraska combines quantitative and qualitative information about the patient's performance. Learning how to administer this battery generally requires from several days to 2 weeks.

Interpretation of the LNNB is very complex and requires considerable background and training in the neurosciences, behavioral neurology, and neuroanatomy, as well as considerable familiarity with Luria's model of brain–behavior relationships and higher cortical functions. The entire test battery can usually be administered in 2½ to 3 hours.

The test material necessary to administer this battery consists of the test protocol sheet (which contains the test items and their scoring indices), a number of visual stimuli, a set of audiotaped rhythm and pitched stimuli, and such items as a rubber band, a key, a nickel, a protractor, a rubber eraser, and a large paper clip (Franzen, 1985). Unlike the Halstead–Reitan, the Luria–Nebraska is portable and can be administered at the patient's bedside. It contains two forms (I and II) and is designed to be administered to patients 14 years and older.

INTERPRETATION OF THE LNNB TEST SCORES

The test scores of a particular patient for each of the 11 clinical scales can be placed on a profile sheet by which the examiner can visually examine the elevations on each of the clinical scales in terms of normative data (mean and standard deviation). On the basis of the patient's age and educational achievements, the patient's critical level can be statistically determined and scores that exceed this critical level on a scale are considered to be statistically significant. When three or more of the clinical scales exceed the critical level, there is good likelihood that the patient has brain impairment (this is not the same as brain damage, since it indicates that while no structural damage to the brain may be present, the functioning of the brain is impaired).

Unlike the Halstead–Reitan Battery, interpretation of the LNNB must include a careful clinical and background history from the patient to rule out many of the extraneous factors which may cause a particular patient to fail one or more of the test items. When combined with a careful review of the patient's medical, neurological, educational, psychiatric, psychological, and vocational records, this interpretation can, in the hands of a competent and experienced neuropsychologist, provide a wealth of useful information about the patient's cognitive and behavioral impairments.

Test interpretation also involves determining the degree of scatter among the scale scores, the elevation of the localization scales in reference to the critical level, careful examination of the individual test items to determine if the patient's performance is consistent with a pattern of neuropsychological impairment and disorder, and a careful review of the patient's observed qualitative behaviors during testing (Franzen, 1985).

RELIABILITY AND VALIDITY

Studies that have examined the test–retest reliability of the LNNB have reported correlation coefficients ranging as low as 0.77 to as high as 0.96 in each of the clinical and auxiliary scales used in the battery. The interrater reliability of the battery has been reported to be excellent with an overall 95% agreement rate between examiners being reported (Golden et al., 1978).

A number of validity studies (e.g., Hammeke et al., 1978) have shown that the LNNB can discriminate brain-damaged patients from normal controls at a statistically reliable level of confidence. Blackerby (1985) has reported that each of the clinical scales measures a single unidimensional trait across a wide range of item difficulties and appears to have good construct validity. Correlations between the Halstead–Reitan and Luria–Nebraska Neuropsychological Test Batteries have ranged from 0.60 to 0.96 (Shelly and Goldstein, 1982). A discriminant function analysis of the Halstead–Reitan and Luria–Nebraska Neuropsychological Batteries has shown that both batteries have a hit rate of 85% accurate classification in discriminating between brain-injured patients and normal controls (Golden et al., 1978).

STRENGTHS AND LIMITATIONS

The LNNB appears to be a reliable, valid, and sensitive means of assessing higher cortical (cognitive) functions. It rests on Luria's theoretical ideas for brain–behavior relationships based on his investigation of patients with various brain disorders. This test battery can provide valuable data in the analysis of cognitive deficits due to neurological disease, schizophrenia, or other psychiatric disorders and appears to be robust in the face of nonspecific confounding factors such as depression or headaches (Moses, 1997). It utilizes a functional system analysis to investigate a wide variety of higher cortical functions and relates this analysis to Luria's theory of higher cortical functions.

Since the LNNB is portable and can easily be transported to the patient's bedside, it can be used to test patients in less than formal settings (e.g., jails and hospitals). It is relatively easy to administer and takes only 2½ to 3 hours in comparison to 6 hours for the Halstead–Reitan Battery. It relies on both quantitative and qualitative information, as well as a careful clinical and background history of the patient to rule out confounding causes of poor performance. It allows the neuropsychologist to visually examine the patient's performance on each of the clinical and auxiliary scales and consider a particular scale in relation to others. The administration and scoring of the Luria–Nebraska Battery can be learned in less than 2 weeks.

Like the Halstead–Reitan Battery, many neuropsychologists supplement this battery with a variety of other tests such as the Wisconsin Card Sorting Test or the Wechsler Memory Scale to evaluate the integrity of specific functions. The battery can be insensitive in terms of its ability to detect cognitive impairments as the level of the patient's intellectual functioning increases. For example, patients with IQs in excess of 120 may not demonstrate any impairment on this battery since they may be able to utilize their high level of intellectual functioning to compensate or conceal their cognitive deficits in certain areas (Franzen, 1985; Purisch and Sbordone, 1986). A patient's test scores on the LNNB can be affected by a variety of factors such as poor effort, medications, health problems, medical disease, etc (Purisch, 1999).

The LNNB battery has been found to have some shortcomings. For example, studies by Goldstein et al. (1987); Sears et al. (1984) indicated that this battery was not able to satisfactorily identify the laterality of a brain insult. For example, when this battery was administered to patients who had right-hemisphere brain insults, patient's often tested as normal in contrast to patients who had left-sided cerebral insults and showed a pattern consistent with diffuse brain damage. The memory scale has also been criticized (Larrabee et al., 1985) since its short-term memory scale was found to have a major attentional component, which made it difficult to utilize the scale to arrive at a meaningful clinical interpretation of the patient's memory functioning.

Golden et al. (1982) stressed that neuropsychologists using this battery should avoid at arriving at any simplistic interpretations of the test data unless the behavioral observations of the patient are incorporated into the interpretation of this test scores and a pattern analysis of the test data is utilized within the context of the patient's background and history. Lezak et al. (2004) have stressed that the effectiveness of this battery depends on the tester's knowledge of neuropsychology and behavioral neurology as well as an understanding of Luria's theoretical framework. As a consequence, it is not suitable for use by any examiner who does not have an adequate background in these areas. Examiners lacking this background who rely entirely on the test scores are likely to arrive at inaccurate interpretations of the test data.

NEUROPSYCHOLOGICAL ASSESSMENT BATTERY

This test was designed to assess the major functional cognitive domains of attention, language, memory, spatial, and executive functions using an integrated and modular approach (Stern and White, 2003). The test provides norms for each of the modules. The examiner can use a single set of normative tables that allow for within-patient and between-patient's score comparisons across the cognitive domains, which can be compared to the patient's estimated level of intellectual functioning. Some of the advantages of this test include demographically corrected norms to equivalent parallel forms of the test and the inclusion of tasks that assess patient's functioning in real-world type of activities.

This test contains a screening module to assess whether the five major cognitive domains can be administered. Individuals who do poorly on this module may not need to be given any or all of the five tests that assess the five major cognitive domains. The screening module can be used to predict the patient's performance on any of the five major domains.

This test was designed to be administered to adults and elderly patients in approximately 4 hours. The norms for this test were based on 1448 cases that were standardized with respect to patient's education, gender, race/ethnicity, and geographic region.

RELIABILITY AND VALIDITY

The stability of the two test forms was assessed using an average test–retest interval of greater than 6 months utilizing subjects ranging in age from 20 to 97 years old. Healthy individuals were administered both forms 1 and 2 separately. Unfortunately, the test–retest correlations of the primary scores tended to be marginal or low. Composite scores such as screening domain, domain, total screening, and total NAB were found to be more stable than the individual test scores. However, the test–retest reliabilities of cognitive domains such as language, screening, spatial, and executive functions were found to be less than adequate (Strauss et al., 2006). Currently, there is no information available on the test–retest reliability of brain-damaged patients. High interrater reliability was found on all of the subtests (White and Stern, 2003).

STRENGTHS AND LIMITATIONS

This battery can be administered in approximately 4 hours. It produces quantitative summary scores as well as numerous qualitative indices that provide a coordinated norming of the test. It also contains equivalent and parallel forms that are separately normed. Another unique feature of the battery is the inclusion of measures that tap daily living skills. Its ease of administration and portability are helpful. There is also some evidence that the test scores have some ecological validity. This test contains a comprehensive set of demographically corrected normative data, which permits the standardized scores to be compared directly and allows identification of different profiles of strengths and weaknesses.

While the test–retest reliability of the primary test scores tend to be less than optimal, this may reflect the fact that the interval between testing was longer than is usual in most clinical situations (e.g., 6 months). Unfortunately, the test–retest reliability of the spatial, memory, and executive function domain scores are not sufficient for the clinician to utilize in clinical decision making.

While this test was developed based on feedback from the users and neuropsychological experts, this does not represent a fundamental shift in its underlying conceptual framework. For example, the tests themselves incorporate traditional methods of assessment. The test is not theory driven and employs standard testing paradigms. As a consequence, it does not provide new methods of assessing or new conceptualizations of a patient's cognitive functioning (Strauss et al., 2006).

REPEATABLE BATTERY FOR THE ASSESSMENT OF NEUROPSYCHOLOGICAL STATUS

This test was designed to identify dementia ranging from mild to severe in older adults (Randolf, 1998). As it became more widely used, it was modified to include younger adults. It consists of 12 subtests that assess the following cognitive domains: immediate memory (list learning, story memory), visuospatial/constructional (figure copy, line orientation), language (picture naming, semantic fluency — fruits and vegetables), attention (digit span, coding), and delayed memory (list recall, list recognition, story memory, and figure recall). The test can usually be administered in 20 to 30 minutes. The test stimuli are placed in a wire-bound easel-backed booklet, which allows the test to be portable and even administered at the patient's bedside. An alternate form is available should the patient need to be retested at a later occasion. This allows the examiner to monitor the progress of the patient's cognitive impairment or assess the effects of treatment (Randolph et al., 1998).

The norms that are contained in the stimulus booklet are based on a sample of 540 subjects ranging in the age from 20 to 89 years old. Recently, the normative information from this test has been corrected for the patient's age and educational background. The normative data also exist for patients with schizophrenia or schizoaffective disorder (Strauss et al., 2006).

RELIABILITY AND VALIDITY

High reliability coefficients have been found when elderly adults who were retested after 39 weeks. Lower test–retest reliability was found in the language and immediate memory domains. Duff et al. (2005) have provided regression-based equations to assess any changes in the patient's cognitive domains.

The test scores appear highly correlated with WAIS-III full scale IQ and Wechsler Memory Scale — III (WAIS-III) indices (Gold et al., 1999). Since the Wechsler full scale IQ or memory index scores have been found to be substantially higher than the repeatable battery for the assessment of neuropsychological status (RBANS) total scale index score, the RBANS appears to be more sensitive to cognitive impairment than the Wechsler test.

STRENGTHS AND LIMITATIONS

The RBANS has been found to be sensitive to a number of neurological disorders including cerebral concussions (Killam et al., 2005) and dementia (Beatty et al., 2003). It is also helpful in distinguishing between primarily cortical vs. subcortical disorders. It also appears to be a useful screening instrument for psychiatric patients (Gold et al., 1999). While it is a useful screening tool to measure cognitive functioning and appears to be well tolerated by elderly patients, it may not be suitable for a lengthy examination (Hobart et al., 1999).

It appears to be more sensitive to standardized tests such as the Mini-Mental Status Examination, the dementia rating scale, and the Wechsler Memory Scale-IV. It should not, however, take the place of a more comprehensive neuropsychological examination. Since this test was designed to be administered to help the adults as well as individuals who may have moderately severe dementia, it may have limited usefulness in detecting cognitive impairment at the high end and above the intellectual distribution. Since the test–retest reliability of most of the indices appears low, its ability to monitor change in the patient's cognitive functioning may be limited in situations where the patient's progress or decline is relatively subtle (Strauss et al., 2006). Since it tends to place a heavy demand on verbal responses, it may not be appropriate for patients with aphasia (Larson et al., 2005).

SAN DIEGO NEUROPSYCHOLOGICAL TEST BATTERY

The San Diego Neuropsychological Test Battery was developed by Ruff (1985). It was developed as part of a Multicentered National Traumatic Coma Data Bank Program to provide a complete mental status examination to assess neuropsychological functions such as sensory perception, attention, concentration, verbal abilities, spatial integration, intelligence, motor speed and dexterity, memory, learning, and abstract and flexible thinking. The goal was not necessarily to develop new tests, but rather to use tests that had solid psychometric properties. However, within the areas of attention, memory and learning, intelligence, abstract thinking, and flexible thinking, attempts were made to obtain analogous tasks for the visuospatial and auditory–verbal modes of processing. The time for test administration was limited to an average of 3½ hours to avoid excessive fatigue or the need to split testing over two sessions.

The underlying theoretical basis is Luria's three primary functional units (arousal, analyzing and coding, and planning). The battery attempts to employ Luria's well-documented theoretical constructs of human information processing through an investigation of quantitative differences across the three primary functional units. This battery consists of some 21 procedures that together yield a total of 38 scores. The test data is initially interpreted quantitatively in terms of whether a patient's performance falls in the normal, borderline, or impaired range on each of the 38 test scores. These test scores are then qualitatively evaluated based on Luria's model of cortical organization.

RELIABILITY AND VALIDITY

Baser and Ruff (1987) reported that the San Diego Neuropsychological Battery was able to correctly identify 80% of brain-injured patients among normal controls and schizophrenic patients. This study also found, through empirical analyses, that the construct validity of the San Diego Neuropsychological Battery was adequate since it was based on Luria's theory of cortical organization.

STRENGTHS AND LIMITATIONS

The strengths of this battery appear to be its use of function-specific test measures based on their psychometric properties and Luria's model of neuropsychological functioning and information processing. Its major shortcoming appears to be the competence of the neuropsychologist who interprets the clinical significance of the 38 scores. Since this battery was based on Luria's theories of neuropsychological functioning and information processing, the neuropsychologist utilizing this battery should possess considerable expertise with Luria's model of brain–behavior relationships.

MICROCOG ASSESSMENT OF COGNITIVE FUNCTIONING COMPUTERIZED BATTERY

The Microcog is a computer-administered and scored test that was intended to serve as a screening device or diagnostic tool as part of a general neuropsychological examination or examination of cognitive functioning (Powell et al., 1993). The standard form consists of 18 subtests that can be administered in about 1 hour. The short form contains 12 subtests that can be completed in approximately 30 minutes. Nine index scores are derived from the Microcog subtest scores and are conceptually formed to represent functioning in five neurocognitive domains attention/mental control, memory, reasoning/calculation, spatial processing, and reaction time. In addition, indices derived from the subtests can be used to represent overall processing speed and accuracy, as well as information processing speed and accuracy.

The attention/mental control component consists of the following subtests:

1. Numbers forward and numbers reversed — in the Visual Digit Span Test with Serial Presentation of Stimuli, the subject must recall and enter on a computer a string of digits immediately following their serial presentation in the center of the computer screen.
2. Alphabet — the subject must watch for and respond to letters of the alphabet as they appear in sequence within a series of random letters presented at a rate of about 1/s.
3. Word list — the subject is presented with a list of categorized words in the guise of a signal detection task and must later recognize these words.

Memory is assessed by five subtests that measure immediate and delayed verbal memory. Four of these subtests involve immediate and delayed recall of the content of two stories. The fifth subtest involves the delayed recall of a name and address.

Reasoning/calculation is assessed by the following:

1. Analogy subtest — the examinee is presented with three words, two of which have a specific relationship. The examinee must then select from a list of three words which word expresses the same relationship with the word that was originally presented.
2. Object Match subtest — the examinee is presented with four figures on the screen and is required to identify the figure that does not match the other three. The subject is then asked to group the figures according to a different principle.
3. Math Calculation subtest — the examinee is presented with addition, subtraction, multiplication, and division problems that vary in their difficulty and require mental calculations. This subtest records the patient's responses from left to right rather than right to left, as is characteristic of paper and pencil calculations.

Spatial processing is assessed by the following tests:

1. The Tic Tac subtest — the subject is presented with a 1-second display of a 3×3 matrix in which three, four, or five of the nine spaces are colored. The examinee must replicate the spatial configuration by pressing corresponding keys on the computer's numeric keypad. Later, the subject is shown images with different configurations to assess primary spatial memory.
2. The Clock subtest — the subject is shown seven clock faces that have a prominent hour and minute hand set at various times. Although the faces have no numbers, the examinee is required to choose the time setting from a set of numbered responses displayed with each clock.

Reaction time is based on the Timers subtests, which measures the time between the appearance of a signal shown on the computer screen and movement made in response to that signal. Timers 1 and 2 assess simple reaction time in both auditory and visual modalities.

INTERPRETATION OF THE MICROCOG

Interpretation of the patient's test data is generally based on level of performance in comparison to an appropriate normative group. Standard scores are computed for each of the Microcog indices and subtests. An index score of 100 reflects the average performance of a given age group and educational level. Scores of 85 and 115 correspond to 1 standard deviation below and above the mean, respectively. Scores of 70 and 130 deviate 2 standard deviations from the mean. Individuals who have index scores of 70 to 84 fall in the low-average range, while individuals whose index scores are 69 or lower fall in the below-average range. A patient's performance on this battery can also be interpreted in terms of the patterns of the various scores. Thus, the adequacy of an individual's functioning in one cognitive domain can be compared to his or her functioning in another domain. Such comparisons can generate hypotheses about spared and impaired cognitive functions, as well as assist the examiner in identifying the patient's relative strengths and weaknesses.

The Microcog automatically computes a number of pair-wise comparisons between index scores and subtest scores. These comparisons were selected on the basis that significant differences between them would most likely be clinically meaningful. Discrepancies that are both significant and rare most likely represent a meaningful and substantial difference in the abilities being compared. In general, the larger the discrepancy and the less frequently it occurs, the less likely it can be explained as a normal variation. However, it should be recognized that not all comparisons between indices or subtests are interpretable, even when the difference between the indices or scores is statistically significant and rare. Furthermore, since many statistical comparisons are automatically computed, the likelihood of making spurious statistical conclusions is considerable (Spreen and Strauss, 1998).

RELIABILITY AND VALIDITY

The test–retest reliability was assessed in a study involving 262 adults, ranging in age from 18 to 89, who were tested twice. At the subtest level, scale scores were divided into three groups that coincided with the scale score ranges for below-average, low-average, and average-to-above-average categories. Reliability was assessed by examining the consistency of classification from test to retest. This study found that the means from test to retest were very stable and showed little practice effects. Furthermore, the subject's overall performances in each of the indices were found to be relatively stable over time.

While the Microcog subtest and index scores appear to be valid measures of neurocognitive functioning, correlations between the Microcog and a number of widely used neuropsychological tests have ranged from only 0.28 to 0.46. For example, correlations between the Microcog's memory index and the Wechsler Memory Scale — Revised (WAIS-R) verbal and visual memory indices were only 0.37 and 0.34, respectively. Similarly, the correlations between the total score on the Microcog story — immediate and delayed — and the WAIS-R delayed recall index were only 0.38 and 0.40, respectively. These findings suggest that while the correlations are in a positive direction, they are generally lower than expected (Powell et al., 1993).

STRENGTHS AND LIMITATIONS

Clearly the strength of the Microcog is its computerized administration that can take from 30 minutes to an hour. Its normative scores were derived from a nationally representative sample of adults and are available for each subtest. The individual's scores are compared to age- and education-level adjusted norms. The Microcog produces a comprehensive quantitative analysis of the patient's scores, including precise quantification of reaction times. The major limitation in the use of this battery is that it was not designed to provide a comprehensive neuropsychological assessment for patients suspected of having cognitive deficits. Also, the administration of tests via computer may cause some patients to become anxious because of their inexperience or apprehension at being around computers. The presence of another individual in the same room where the patient is being tested, may cause the patient to take his or her eyes off the screen and miss the presentation of the test stimuli, particularly if the stimuli are rapidly presented.

The test battery may not be appropriate for individuals who are visually or motorically impaired or dyslexic. It may also not be appropriate for individuals with different cultural or linguistic backgrounds or whose primary language is not English. Because the Microcog does not have any obvious built-in measures to ensure that the patient was trying to perform to the best of his or her ability, malingering is possible.

NEPSY: A DEVELOPMENTAL NEUROPSYCHOLOGICAL ASSESSMENT TEST TO ASSESS YOUNG AND OLDER CHILDREN

The NEPSY was designed to detect subtle cognitive deficits that can interfere with the ability of a child to learn new information, detect and describe the effects of brain damage or dysfunction in young children, follow-up children with brain damage and dysfunction to determine whether any recovery or improvement has been made, and provide valid test results to assess the neuropsychological development of children (Korkman et al., 1998). This test incorporates Luria's neuropsychological approach with Developmental Neuropsychology.

It was designed to function as a flexible test battery. It contains five core cognitive domains as well as expanded and supplemental subtests, which can be selectively administered based on the fact of the assessment performed and the specific characteristics of the child. It does not yield an overall score, which is consistent with Luria's conceptual model of neuropsychological functioning as composed of independent but related functional systems (Strauss et al., 2006). The five core domains include: attention/executive functions; language; sensory or motor function; visual spatial processing; and memory and learning. Two versions of the test can be utilized depending on the age of the child.

The battery is designed to assess children who range from 3 to 12 years of age. Children ranging in age from 3 to 4 are given a different test battery than children whose ages range from 5 to 12. The addition of supplemental neuropsychological tests allows a more complete interpretation of the significance of a child's scores in these cognitive domains. Unlike other neuropsychological test utilized for children, it utilizes a qualitative assessment of the child's behavior during testing and allows the examiner to perform a complex multidimensional assessment that can be customized to meet the specific needs of the individual child (Kemp et al., 2001).

Although the full administration typically takes 1 hour in children ranging from 3 to 4 years of age and 2 hours in children who are 5 and older, the assessment of the five core domains usually takes approximately 45 minutes in children who are between the ages of 3 and 4, and 65 minutes in children who are 5 and older. One of the major advantages in using this test to assess children is that in addition to standardized administration procedures, it permits the examiner to utilize a process-oriented approach to assess how children arrive at a particular level of performance.

RELIABILITY AND VALIDITY

Test–retest reliability studies have had mixed results. For example, the visual attention, body part naming, comprehension of instructions, and visual motor precision subscales were found to have marginal test–retest reliability in children ranging in age from 3 to 4. The test–retest reliability coefficients were found to be low on the statue, phonological processing, verbal fluency, and block construction subtest in these children. Subtests such as visual attention, phonological processing, block construction, narrative memory, and list learning were found to have marginal test–retest reliability in children ranging from 5 to 12 years of age.

Children between the ages of 5 and 12 were found to have low test–retest reliability on the following subtests: tower, design fluency, speeded naming, comprehension of instructions, imitating hand positions, visual motor precision, arrows, immediate memory prefaces, and delayed memory prefaces subtest (Korkman et al., 1988). Some subtest reliabilities were found to be adequate to high in younger age groups but were reported to be marginal or low in older children (Strauss et al., 2006). Practice effects (an improvement in the patient's performance upon retesting) were found to be greatest in the core memory domain score and the memory and learning subtests scores.

The subtests, which comprise each core domain, were based on Luria's theoretical model of cognitive function and prior research with this test. The correlations between the core subtests tend to be weak with the exception of the two subtests making up the attention/executive core domain, which is only modestly correlated in the 3 to 4 age group. However, the correlations for the 5 to 12 age group are even lower.

Some of the NEPSY subtests in their related core domains such as verbal fluency, statue, phonologic processing, and block construction tend to have poor psychometric properties when administered to children who are 3 and 4 years of age. Similarly, subtests such as visual motor precision, design fluency, tower, speeded naming, comprehension of instructions, imitating hand positions, arrows, and memory prefaces have also been found to have poor psychometric properties in children ranging in age from 5 to 12. As a consequence, this test appears to have some serious psychometric limitations that may to some degree reflect practice effects.

Strengths and Limitations

The NEPSY represents a major advance in the field of Pediatric Neuropsychology. It was specifically designed to assess the neuropsychological functioning of children. It is not simply an extension of an adult neuropsychological battery. It is the only comprehensive neuropsychological battery for children, which is normed on a single, large, randomized, and stratified normative sample. It is modeled to a considerable degree on Luria's theoretical approach to assessment. As a consequence, it has a strong theoretical foundation which allows the examiner to administer this test battery in a flexible manner to children. It also relies heavily on the child's qualitative behavior during testing. It utilizes brightly colored, child-friendly stimuli that appears to maintain the interest of most young children. It can be administered to children as young as 3 years of age (Strauss et al., 2006).

Studies that have examined its test–retest reliability and validity have revealed some serious shortcomings. As a consequence, psychologists utilizing this test should utilize an abundance of caution when interpreting the test data, particularly to determine whether a child's cognitive functioning has changed overtime and whether the core cognitive domains accurately reflect the patient's cognitive functioning.

INDIVIDUAL NEUROPSYCHOLOGICAL TESTS

In this section we will cover individual neuropsychological tests that are frequently used to evaluate an individual's cognitive functioning. This section will examine tests that are frequently used to assess the following cognitive functions: intelligence, attention/concentration, language, academic achievement, learning/memory, visuospatial/perceptual skills, motor functions, abstract thinking, conceptual thinking/problem-solving skills, executive functions, personality/emotional adjustment, and malingering.

TESTS USED TO ASSESS INTELLIGENCE

Kaufman Assessment Battery for Children

The Kaufman Assessment Battery for Children (K-ABC) (Kaufman and Kaufman, 1983) is an intelligence test for children between the ages of 2½ and 12½ years of age. It contains 16 subtests:

1. Magic window — the ability of the child to identify and name an object that has been only partially exposed is measured.
2. Face recognition — a previously shown face must be selected from a group photograph.
3. Hand movements — an exact sequence of taps on a table must be repeated as demonstrated by the examiner.
4. Gestalt closure — a drawing that is only partially complete must be named or described.
5. Number recall — digits must be repeated.

6. Triangles — identical rubber triangles must be assembled to match a picture of an abstract design.
7. Word order — silhouettes and objects must be pointed to in exactly the same order as the objects are named by the examiner.
8. Matrix analogies — a picture design must be selected that best completes a visual analogy.
9. Spatial memory — the location of pictures randomly arranged on a page must be recalled.
10. Photo series — a series of photographs is to be arranged within a specific time sequence.
11. Expressive vocabulary — photographed objects are named.
12. Faces and places — famous persons, fictional characters, or well-known places must be named.
13. Arithmetic — simple counting, recognition of shapes, identifying numbers, and performing simple arithmetic tasks.
14. Riddles — the child must determine the name of a concrete or abstract geometric concept after being given several cues.
15. Reading/decoding — assesses the child's ability to identify letters, read, and pronounce words.
16. Reading/understanding — the child is instructed to perform written commands.

Children who are 6 years of age and younger are given only seven of the above subtests. Children who are 7 years of age and older can be given the 13 subtests. As the child progresses in age, some tests are replaced by others that are more appropriate for the child's level of cognitive development. A child's scores can be converted into age-appropriate norms using tables contained within the manual. The K-ABC manual also contains confidence levels for each subtest. The test has separate norms for African-Americans. Interpretation of the test involves examining the differences between the various subtests to determine the strengths and weaknesses of the child. This test can be administered to children who are over 7 years of age in approximately 75 minutes. Younger children can be administered this test in approximately 30 minutes.

Reliability and Validity

Test–retest reliability coefficients ranging from 0.84 to 0.95 have been reported (Matazow et al., 1991). Numerous studies (e.g., Kamphaus and Reynolds, 1987) have investigated the validity of the K-ABC and are cited in the interpretative manual. These studies have shown that this test possesses adequate discriminant validity.

Strengths and Limitations

This test appears to have been constructed using a neuropsychological model and can be broken down into right- and left-hemisphere functions (Kaufman and Kaufman, 1983). While this test appears to have more relevance to neuropsychologists than do the Wechsler scales, some neuropsychologists (Donders, 1992) have cautioned others not to attribute specific neuropsychological significance to the data obtained by this particular test. For example, Donders administered this test to 43 children who had sustained traumatic brain injuries and found that this test did not discriminate between these children and healthy controls any better than the WISC-R. Furthermore, this test is not equivalent to the Wechsler scales or even the Stanford–Binet (4th ed.) and the test scores have relatively low concurrent validity (Spreen and Strauss, 1998).

KAUFMAN BRIEF TEST OF INTELLIGENCE

The Kaufman Brief Test of Intelligence (K-BIT) is an individually administered intelligence test that is suitable for individuals whose ages range from 4 to 90. It assesses verbal and nonverbal intellectual abilities (Kaufman and Kaufman, 1990). The Vocabulary subtest assesses verbal intellectual skills and can be broken down into expressive vocabulary (which requires the subject to name a pictured object) and definitions (which requires the person to provide the word that best fits two clues). An individual's nonverbal intellectual abilities are assessed by the Matrices Test, which consists of items involving visual stimuli that require the individual to determine the relationship between these stimuli using a multiple-choice format. This test was normed on a nationwide standardization sample of 2022 individuals ranging in age from 4 to 90, which was stratified according to the recent U.S. Census data on four background variables gender, geographic region, socioeconomic status, and race or ethnic group.

The K-BIT can usually be administered in about 15 to 30 minutes, depending on the age of the individual being tested. Children can usually be tested in 15 to 20 minutes, while adults can usually complete the test in 20 to 30 minutes. On the basis of the tables contained within the test manual, the individual scores on each test item can be converted to standard scores with a mean of 100 and standard deviation of 15 for both the Vocabulary and Matrices subtests, as well as the individual's IQ composite. By referring to tables in the manual, the examiner can also compare the individual's performance on the two subtests to determine if the difference between them is significant.

RELIABILITY AND VALIDITY

Test–retest reliability for an interval ranging from 12 to 145 days with a mean of 121 days revealed some practice effects of about 3 standard score points on the IQ composite and 2 to 4 points on the Vocabulary and Matrices subtests during retesting. The scores from this test appear to correlate fairly well with the Wechsler Intelligence Scales, the Stanford–Binet, the Kaufman Assessment Battery for Children, and the Test of Nonverbal Intelligence (Spreen and Strauss, 1998).

STRENGTHS AND LIMITATIONS

This test can provide a helpful screening measure of verbal, nonverbal, and general intellectual ability when time constraints prevent administration of a standardized test battery such as the Wechsler. It is relativity easy to administer and score, and has good normative data. It does not require manual or rapid responses (Kaufman and Kaufman, 2001). While it appears well suited for individuals who are physically handicapped or have significant motor limitations, it may not be appropriate for individuals who have a low level of intellectual functioning (Strauss et al., 2006). One additional limitation is that this test provides less of a differentiation between verbal and nonverbal intellectual functions than the Wechsler (Spreen and Strauss, 1998). It may also produce a spuriously low estimate of verbal intelligence (Burton et al., 1995).

RAVEN PROGRESSIVE MATRICES TESTS (RPMT)

These tests were developed in England and have been widely used in the United States as well as in many other countries throughout the world (Raven, [1938] 1996). They serve as tests of inductive reasoning and require that the patient conceptualize spatial, design, and numerical relationships ranging from very simple and concrete to very complex and abstract. There are three versions of this test Standard, Colored, and Advanced Progressive Matrices Tests.

The Standard version consists of 60 items that are grouped in five sets (A to E) of 12 items. Each test item contains a rectangle with one part removed. The subject's task is to select the correct pattern from either six or eight pictures below. This test is particularly appropriate for individuals who are not fluent in or do not understand English, suffer from physical disabilities, are aphasic, have cerebral palsy, or are deaf (Spreen and Strauss, 1998).

While these tests appear to assess mainly an individual's nonverbal and visuospatial problem-solving skills, some of the more difficult items involve mathematical concepts that involve analytic reasoning utilizing the left hemisphere. Individuals who have right-sided brain lesions are likely to perform less well than individuals with left-hemisphere brain lesions, particularly on visuospatial problems contained in Set A. However, the reverse appears to be true for Set B, which seems to place more emphasis on the individual's verbal conceptual skills. Thus, the seeming visuospatial and nonverbal characteristics of this test appear to be misleading. Therefore, this test is not a good tool for discriminating right- and left-brain-damaged patients or for assessing an individual's visuospatial abilities (Lezak, 1995).

COLORED MATRICES TEST

The Colored Matrices Test (CMT) (Raven, [1947] 1995) consists of only 36 items, which are grouped into three sets of 12 items each. It was developed for use with children above 5½ years of age and for older individuals. Children, however, who are over the age of 11 should be administered the Standard Progressive Matrices Test.

ADVANCED PROGRESSIVE MATRICES TEST

The Advanced Progressive Matrices Test (APMT) (Raven, [1965] 1994) has been designed to be used with people of more than average intellectual functioning or for those who find the Standard Progressive Matrices Test too easy. Both the Standard and Colored Progressive Matrices Tests are untimed. Most individuals require approximately 40 minutes to complete the standardized test or approximately 25 minutes to complete the colored version of the test. Set 2 of the Advanced Progressive Matrices Test, however, has a time limit that is usually set at 40 minutes.

Reliability and Validity

Studies have found that this test possesses adequate test–retest reliability. Concurrent validity studies show a modest correlation between the Raven and conventional tests of intelligence such as the Wechsler and Stanford–Binet scales (Spreen and Strauss, 1998).

Strengths and Limitations

The Raven tests are excellent tests of inductive reasoning (Alderton and Larson, 1990). It is one of the most researched nonverbal tests (McCullum et al., 2000). Because these tests does not require the patient to perform any skilled movements or to verbalize his or her response but to simply point, they can be used to assess individuals whose cultural and linguistic background would place them at a disadvantage if they were administered the Wechsler Intelligence Scales. They can also be administered to individuals with significant motor limitations or who are hearing impaired. The tests are relatively easy to administer and score, are relatively culture-free, and are suitable for patients who were born and raised outside of the United States, speak little or no English, have limited educational backgrounds, or have been culturally deprived. Despite these advantages, it provides relatively little information about an individual's intellectual strengths or weaknesses. Thus, additional tests may need to be administered if the neuropsychologist wishes to gain a true picture of these areas.

An individual's performance on this test can be affected by such factors as visual field defects, unilateral neglect, other visual–perceptual difficulties, and motivational factors (since it does not contain any scales that would alert the examiner that the test-taker was trying to perform poorly). As with many tests the scores for people taking this test have increased since the test was initially published, which indicates that it not only needs new norms, but the use of the older test norms will diminish its ability to detect impairment (Hiscock et al., 2002).

STANFORD–BINET INTELLIGENCE SCALE — REVISED

The Stanford–Binet Intelligence Test — Revised can be used to assess the intellectual functioning of children between 2 and 18 years of age (Thorndike et al., 1986). It consists of 15 subtests:

1. Vocabulary — picture naming and defining words.
2. Comprehension — questions involving reasoning and judgment.
3. Absurdities — describing what is wrong with an absurd picture.
4. Verbal relations — determining how three words are alike and are different from a fourth word.
5. Pattern analysis — placing blocks into form boards and putting together block designs.
6. Copying — copying simple patterns of geometric designs.
7. Matrices — indicating which of three geometric designs or letter patterns fit into a box.
8. Paper folding and cutting — deciding which one of five patterns with folding marks matches one of the shapes when it is unfolded.
9. Quantitative — placing blocks with varying numbers and dots correctly on a tray, counting the number of objects on cards, or performing arithmetic tasks.
10. Number series — finding two subsequent numbers in a printed series.
11. Equation building — arranging numbers with basic arithmetic symbols to arrive at the correct solution.
12. Bead memory — identifying or arranging beads on a stick based on a pictured pattern.
13. Memory for sentences — repetition of sentences.
14. Memory for digits — repeating three to nine digits forwards and backwards.
15. Memory for objects — determining the correct sequence of previously shown objects using a multiple-choice format.

Although the test items are presented in a standardized manner, the examiner may begin administering a different subtest if the subject becomes resistant during a subtest or becomes fatigued. Testing usually requires between 60 and 90 minutes. The manual contains examples of passed, queried, and failed responses, as well as helpful guidelines for scoring. Raw scores for each subtest can be converted into standard age scores based on reference tables contained in the manual. These subtests have been designed to measure a child's skills in four areas verbal reasoning, abstract/visual reasoning, quantitative reasoning, and short-term memory.

The norms on this test were based on a carefully selected sample of over 5000 children, adolescents, and young adults who were representative of the U.S. census in terms of their gender, race, geographic distribution, and parental occupation and education.

RELIABILITY AND VALIDITY

Atkinson (1989) found that the test–retest reliability of the Stanford–Binet Intelligence Scale — Revised, after an average of 16 weeks, ranged from 0.71 to 0.91, and 0.90 for the composite score in preschoolers and elementary school children, respectively. Subtest reliability ranged from 0.28 (quantitative) to 0.86 (comprehension). Its concurrent validity with other tests such as the Wechsler Preschool and Primary Scale of Intelligence — III was 0.80, 0.83 with the WISC-R, 0.79 to 0.91 with the WAIS-R, and 0.89 with the Wechsler Intelligence Scales.

STRENGTHS AND LIMITATIONS

While the Stanford–Binet Revised produces scores that appear to be comparable to the Wechsler Tests when the subject is in the average range of intellectual functioning, it may produce scores that are considerably lower (approximately 10 points) than the WAIS-R or WISC-R when mentally handicapped or gifted subjects are tested. Its use in the neuropsychological assessment of young children in the age group of 2 to 4 appears valuable. Some of these subtests, particularly Absurdities,

Comprehension, Copying Pattern Analysis, Matrices, and Memory for Sentences, may provide the neuropsychologist with useful information about a child's cognitive functioning following a brain insult.

STANFORD–BINET INTELLIGENCE SCALES — FIFTH EDITION

This test is the latest revision of the Stanford–Binet scales, which were initially developed by Binet and Simon in 1905. This test has been revised several times. In the fifth revision, the authors have expanded the range of the test to allow the assessment of very low and very high levels of cognitive ability. The fifth revision also restores the original toys and manipulative stimuli that are used to assess preschoolers. It also has increased clinical utility, contains updated test materials and more nonverbal items, and increases the range of the cognitive domains measured by the test (Roid, 2003).

It produces a full scale IQ score based on ten subtests, which form five factors. Each of the five factors is composed of two subtests (one from the nonverbal domain and one from the verbal domain). Each subtest is composed of five or six separate testlets that measure different levels of ability within a subtest. These testlets contain anywhere from 3 to 6 items that are at the same level of difficulty. During testing, the examinee is administered a series of testlets at each level of functional ability. If the ceiling is not reached on any of these testlets, the examiner moves to a higher level of functioning.

It normally takes between 45 and 75 minutes to administer the full battery. However, the abbreviated battery can be administered in 15 to 20 minutes. The test contains the material used by the examinee, record forms, and examiner's manual. It is divided into three major components that are found in three different item books. For example, Book 1 contains two subtests (object series/matrices and vocabulary) that can be used to determine the examinee's functional ability level. Book 2 contains all of the nonverbal subtests. Book 3 contains all of the verbal subtests.

The test norms were based on 4800 subjects ranging in age from 2 to over 85 years of age. They were stratified according to age, gender, race/ethnicity, geographic region, and socioeconomic level. In addition to this normative sample, it was also administered to 1365 individuals who had been diagnosed with different types of developmental and learning disabilities, mental retardation, motor impairment, autism, attention deficit hyperactivity disorder, auditory receptive difficulties, speech and language impairment, and emotional problems (Strauss et al., 2006).

RELIABILITY AND VALIDITY

The test–retest reliability was found to be quite high. The full scale IQ and reliability IQ coefficient was very high (0.93 to 0.95). The reliability for the nonverbal IQ was slightly lower (0.89 to 0.93). On the other hand, the working memory index (WMI) only achieved adequate test–retest reliability in adults, while the working memory-nonverbal test reliability was only marginal. Practice effects appear to be minimal. It specifically amounted to a full scale IQ improvement of typically 2 to 4 points. Interrater agreement has also been reported as high (0.90).

This test has been found to have excellent content validity based on a number or research studies (Roid, 2003). It also has been found to correlate highly with other intelligence tests such as the Wechsler Intelligence Scale for Children III and the Wechsler Adult Intelligent Scale — III (Strauss et al., 2006).

STRENGTHS AND LIMITATIONS

This test was developed based on a solid theoretical basis, rigorous test development methodology, and the tradition of psychological assessment. It appears to be an impressive test based on its excellent reliability, small practice effects, and minimal floor or ceiling effects. These features make the scale ideal for testing very young children, low functioning individuals, and gifted examinees. It also appears to be relatively free of cultural or other biases and contains a number of novel tasks that have norms for a large range of age groups, which makes it suitable for repeated testing.

Since this test does not measure speed of cognitive processing, it may be less likely to be utilized by neuropsychologists than psychoeducational specialists. For example, determining the patient's processing speed is important in the differential diagnosis of several important neuropsychological disorders. Finally, the test data on the types of patients, which are typically examined by neuropsychologists, is lacking (Strauss et al., 2006).

TEST OF NONVERBAL INTELLIGENCE — III

The Test of Nonverbal Intelligence — III (TONI-III) measures intellectual functioning without the use of language during its administration, irrespective of the test's item content, or the response modality of the patient (Brown et al., 1997). As a consequence, it appears to be well suited for patients who have aphasia, dyslexia, language disabilities, learning disabilities, and speech problems as a result of either developmental disability or neurologic disorder. It is also useful in assessing individuals who have reading difficulties because of their limited exposure to English. Because of the test stimuli utilized in this test, it appears more suitable for individuals who are raised with different linguistic and ethnic backgrounds.

The examiner can avoid using English instructions by pointing, nodding, or gesturing to the examinee. Individuals who have profound motor deficits can utilize eye blinks, head movements, or other methods to select one of the four or six choices available to them. The test is comprised of five training items of increasing difficulty.

This test provides a strong measure of general intelligence and fluid intelligence rather than crystallized intelligence. The problem-solving tasks contained within this test cover several different abstract reasoning and problem-solving skills such as generalization/classification, discrimination, analogous reasoning, seriation, induction, deduction, and detailed recognition (Brown et al., 1997; Strauss et al., 2006).

It has been designed to be administered to subjects ranging from 6 through nearly 90 years of age. There are two equivalent forms of the test containing 45 items each. All of the items require abstract/figural problem solving. It can be administered in 10 or 15 minutes to most individuals. The test score can be converted to a TONI-III nonverbal IQ score. No significant gender effects have been reported. This test is preferable to the Wechsler tests for individuals who speak English as a second language, or were raised in a different cultural or ethnic background.

RELIABILITY AND VALIDITY

Test–retest reliability has been found to be excellent. For example, coefficients ranging from 0.89 to 0.94 after 1 week interval have been reported for three different age groups. The test–retest reliability, however, of individuals who are less than 13 and over 40 years of age is lacking (Strauss et al., 2006). The test items were based on theories of nonverbal intellectual functioning and have been evaluated by item analysis and differential functioning analysis statistical techniques. Correlations with other nonverbal IQ tests appear to be high. Correlations with standard IQ tests are also high.

STRENGTHS AND LIMITATIONS

The TONI-III's lack of reliance on verbal instructions or responses, its largely motor-free format, and its brevity appears suitable for most clinical populations, particularly individuals who have language and motor problems, or were raised in a different linguistic, ethnic, or cultural background.

The TONI-III has a number of limitations. For example, the test–retest reliability for older individuals is scant. Other limitations consist of its reliance on figural reasoning as a measure of intelligence and its limited ability to assess gifted individuals. It was not designed to assess individuals with moderate mental retardation. As a consequence, it should not be used to diagnose intellectual impairments in children or even older adults. Some aspects of the psychometric properties of this test seem weak. For example, although internal reliability and test–retest reliability are excellent, alternate form reliability is less than adequate for some age ranges. Although the test is reportedly intended to identify individuals with intellectual impairments, it is not recommended when intellectual impairment is suspected or when comparisons with other IQ test are needed to serially monitor the patient's intellectual functioning (Strauss et al., 2006).

WECHSLER PRESCHOOL AND PRIMARY SCALE OF INTELLIGENCE — THIRD EDITION

This test was primarily designed to assess the intelligence of preschool and young children. It can be administered to children whose ages range from 2 years 6 months to 7 years 3 months. American norms were based on testing 1700 children according to age, gender, parental education, and geographic region. The third edition (Wechsler, 2002) appears to correct some of the limitations and problems that were found in the first two editions. For example, it seems to fit in well with current factor analytic theories of intelligence and cognitive functioning. The test yields the traditional full scale IQ, verbal IQ, and performance IQ scores in addition to a general language composite (GLC) and a processing speed quotient (PSQ). The test instructions are simpler than the two prior versions of the test. The manual and test materials are easier to use, and the norms have improved.

It usually takes between 30 and 35 minutes to administer the core subtests (Receptive Vocabulary, Information, and Block Design) to the children ranging in age from 2 years 6 months to 3 years 11 months. It normally takes 5 to 7 minutes longer to administer the supplemental subtest (Picture Naming). It usually takes 40 to 50 minutes to administer the core subtests (Information, Vocabulary, Word Reasoning, Block design, Matrix Reasoning, Picture Concepts, and Coding) to children ranging in age from 4 to 7 years and 3 months. An additional 3 to 4 minutes is required if the symbol search subtest is administered. In older children, it usually takes between 70 and 85 minutes to administer all of the subtests that are necessary to produce composite scores and perform a discrepancy analysis (Strauss et al., 2006).

RELIABILITY AND VALIDITY

When a sample of 157 normal children across three age groups were tested twice during an interval averaging 26 days, the test–retest reliability coefficients were found to be high. Practice effects were found to be smallest for verbal test and for the youngest subjects.

The WPPSI-III appears to have excellent validity (Wechsler, 2002). It seems to be highly correlated with the second edition in healthy children with respect to their full scale, verbal IQ, and performance IQ scores. However, the test scores for the object assembly, block design, and similarity subtests were only marginally or adequately correlated to the WPPSI-R (second edition). This test was found to correlate highly with the WISC-III. It was also found to be highly correlated with the Wechsler Individual Achievement Test — II. Research has shown that the validity and clinical utility of the WPPSI-III appear promising.

STRENGTHS AND LIMITATIONS

The WPPSI-III represents a substantial improvement from the WPPSI-R based on the feedback from users, its theoretical underpinnings, clinical utility, and psychometrics. While some clinicians have begun using this test in clinical groups, little research has been done to establish its usefulness in clinical populations. It also appears to be minimally affected by limited English proficiency. Furthermore, the VIQ appears to be minimally affected by motor impairments.

The WPPSI-III possesses little information on test–retest reliability in clinical groups. Furthermore, test–retest correlations do not appear to be adequate for all of the subtests. For example, moderate PIQ subtest intercorrelation suggests that this composite may actually reflect a heterogeneous domain (Strauss et al., 2006). Since the IQs derived from younger children do not appear to be based on the same subtest clusters used for older children, comparing the IQ scores of children across different age ranges might be problematic.

WECHSLER INTELLIGENCE SCALE FOR CHILDREN — FOURTH EDITION (WISC-IV)

The Wechsler Intelligence Scale for Children (WISC-IV) (Wechsler, 2003) is the fourth edition of an intelligence battery for children that originally appeared in 1949 with two subsequent revisions in 1974 and 1991. The WISC-IV is fundamentally different from the previous editions. Although this test has been seen by many as a major improvement over the previous versions of this test, it has also been criticized by traditionalist for not covering all the domains of current factor analytic theories of intelligence. One of the most obvious and dramatic deviations from the traditional Wechsler model is the complete elimination of the VIQ and PIQ indices in favor of four indices verbal comprehension index (VCI), conceptual reasoning index (CRI), WMI, and processing speed index (PSI). Although the full scale IQ score remains, the VCI and the reasoning indexes have replaced the verbal IQ and performance IQ scales (Strauss et al., 2006). The VCI measures verbal knowledge, reasoning and conceptualization. The perceptual reasoning index (PRI) measures the interpretation, reasoning, and organization of visually presented nonverbal information. The WMI measures attention, concentration, and working memory for verbal material. The PSI measures the speed of mental and graphomotor processing.

The WISC-IV contains five core subtests and five supplemental subtests. The full scale IQ is based on the ten core subtests and is used to describe composite scores. In the fourth edition of this test, several subtests were removed from the core index score such as information, arithmetic, picture completion, picture arrangement, and object assembly. Some subtests were redefined as supplemental tests while others were eliminated. This version contains five new subtests: picture concepts, word reasoning, matrix analogies, letter/number sequencing, and cancellation. The VCI includes two supplemental tests Word reasoning (which is a verbally based task involving fluid reasoning skills) and information (which primarily measure crystallized verbal knowledge that originally contributed to arriving at the VIQ score and WISC-III). The PRI evaluates fluid reasoning skills by use of two new subtests (matrix reasoning and picture concepts). It still, however, maintains block design. The picture arrangement, object assembly, and mazes subtests of the WISC-III were either removed or redesigned to eliminate or minimize bonuses given for rapid or speedy performance such as in the arithmetic and block design subtest of the WISC-III.

The norms that were used to develop this test were based on 220 children in 11 age groups ranging from 6 to 16 years and 11 months of age. The norms were stratified by age, gender, race, parental education, and geographic region. This test can usually be administered in about 1½ hours. When testing children with mental retardation, the testing time is usually shorter. However, it is somewhat longer when testing gifted children.

RELIABILITY AND VALIDITY

The test–retest reliability ranges from high to excellent for the index scores. The FSIQ and VCI have the highest reliabilities. Most subtests also have high reliability, although some only fall into the adequate range. Practice effects can be small for the comprehension subtest to considerable for the picture completion subtest. Inter-rater reliability appears be very high particularly for subtests requiring judgment on the part of the examiner for scoring the comprehension, information, word reasoning similarities, and vocabulary subtests. The test has excellent content validity and correlates highly with the WISC-III full scale scores in normal children. It also correlates highly with the WPPSI-III.

STRENGTHS AND LIMITATIONS

The WISC-IV appears to be a suitable replacement of the WISC-III. The latter having been the most commonly used intelligence test used by psychologists. As a consequence, the WISC-IV should become the most widely used IQ test in the world. The technical manual is well written and appears to be quite thorough. Its exact role in neuropsychological assessment remains somewhat unclear at this time. For example, Yeates and Donders (2005) have cautioned that the PRI may not be as sensitive to brain dysfunction as the POI or PIQ as a result of its reduced reliance on motor skills and speed, which are two common deficits in children who have sustained brain trauma or have a neurological disorder. These authors, however, have predicted that the PSI may have the greatest sensitivity to children who suffer from acute brain impairment.

One major limitation is that test–retest reliability in clinical groups is lacking. The WMI does not appear to adequately sample visual working memory since it is composed exclusively of auditory/verbal working memory test. Thus, additional tests will most likely be required to perform a more comprehensive evaluation of working memory. The test still appears generally insensitive to evaluate children with extremely low intellectual functioning particularly in the youngest age ranges (Strauss et al., 2006).

WECHSLER ADULT INTELLIGENCE SCALE — REVISED

WAIS-R was specifically designed to evaluate a patient's intellectual functioning and until recently was the most widely used psychological test (Wechsler, 1981). It consists of six verbal subtests (Information, Comprehension, Arithmetic, Digit Span, Similarity, and Vocabulary) and five performance subtests (Picture Completion, Picture Arrangement, Block Design, Object Assembly, and Digit Symbol). Each of these tests is individually administered by the examiner. The test is appropriate for individuals ranging in age from 16 to 74. The norms utilized on this test were derived from representative groups of the adult population in the United States, based on the 1970 U.S. Census Report. The test authors considered such variables as age, sex, race, occupation, geographic location, education, and urban–rural residence to ensure that the groups selected adequately represented the U.S. adult population (Spruill, 1984).

The WAIS-R Information subtest evaluates the patient's ability to answer questions regarding topics that are academic (e.g., Whose name is generally associated with the theory of relativity?), historical (e.g., Name five presidents of the United States since 1950), and cultural (Who was Martin Luther King, Jr.?). Within the Comprehension subtest are questions regarding the meanings of common sayings, or what types of actions or behaviors to be expected in particular cultural or social situations. The Arithmetic subtest provides the patient with specific mental arithmetic tasks. The Digit Span subtest consists of having the patient repeat strings of numbers forward and backward. The Similarity subtest presents the patient with two common objects and asks how these objects are related (e.g., How are a table and chair related?). The Vocabulary subtest asks the patient to provide a definition of specific orally presented words.

The WAIS-R performance subtests evaluate the patient's visuospatial and constructional skills. In the Picture Completion subtest, the patient is shown drawings of objects that have a part missing and is required to select the missing part. The Picture Arrangement subtest contains a series of pictures, that when properly arranged by the patient will present a pictorial sequence of logical events. The Block Design subtest requires the patient to manipulate small blocks having differently colored sides to reproduce specific printed designs. The Object Assembly subtest involves putting together pieces to form a complete object (e.g., a hand), similar to a jigsaw puzzle. The Digit Symbol subtest is a coding task, in which the patient must substitute one symbol for another, based on a specific code, as quickly as possible. These subtests are administered in a particular order.

For scoring purposes, it is essential that the patient's exact responses be recorded in the test booklet. According to the manual for administration and scoring, the examiner may at times query the patient on specific verbal subtests or when the patient fails to comprehend the test instructions. Within each of the 11 subtests, the easiest items are presented first, to allow the patient to "learn how to take the test." Five of the eleven subtests are timed, which means that the patient receives a higher score if a particular test item is solved quickly.

The WAIS-R manual describes how the test should be administered and the types of responses and prompts permitted by the examiner. The manual also defines how a specific test item will be scored. Occasionally, however, patients will provide responses that are not contained in the manual; hence the examiner must extrapolate a particular score based on the response's proximity to samples contained in the manual. The scoring procedure results in numeric scores for each of the 11 subtests, which are converted into standard scores based on their statistical variability from the norm. The patient's standard score on each of the 11 subtests can also be corrected for age. Thus, the same numeric score for a 20 year old on the Digit Symbol subtest is likely to produce a higher standard score if obtained by a 60 year old.

The patient's scores on the verbal and performance subtests determine the patient's verbal and performance intelligence quotients. The patient's full-scale intelligence quotient represents a composite of the patient's verbal and performance intellectual quotients. Full-scale IQ scores ranging from 90 to 109 represent 50% of the adult population and are considered to fall within the average range. When the patient's IQ exceeds 109 but is less than 120, the patient is regarded as having above-average intelligence. When the patient's IQ exceeds 120, the patient is seen as having superior intellectual functioning. IQs of 130 or higher are considered to represent very superior intellectual functioning. IQs less than 90 but greater than 80 are considered to fall into the range of low-average intellectual functioning. When a patient's score falls between 70 and 79, he or she is considered to have borderline intellectual functioning. Scores of 69 or less fall into the mentally retarded range. Approximately 95% of the population falls between IQ scores of 70 and 130.

The administration of the entire test battery typically requires between 60 and 90 minutes. Some psychologists prefer to use abbreviated forms of the test, in which they will administer fewer than all 11 of the subtests (often only 5 or 6) to save time (Lezak, 1983).

RELIABILITY AND VALIDITY

Research studies have shown that while the overall reliability of the WAIS-R is high, the reliability of the individual subtests ranges considerably (from 0.96 on the Vocabulary subtest to 0.52 for the Object Assembly subtest). The WAIS-R has generally demonstrated very high reliability in assessing normal controls and psychiatric patients (except for their performance on the Arithmetic subtests, because of the use of psychotropic medications). The reliability for psychiatric and brain-injured patients is likely to be somewhat different, depending on the severity of the patient's psychiatric disorder, the type of medications the patient is taking, the type of brain injury involved, the time since injury, and the length of time between test administrations (Spruill, 1984).

Based on research studies, IQ coefficients have been found to correlate well with the patient's grade point average at all levels of education. Thus, the WAIS-R has been frequently used by psychologists and other health professionals to predict academic achievements or success (Spruill, 1984). For example, if a patient expresses an interest in going on to college to study engineering and obtains an IQ of only 92, more than likely he or she may be persuaded by the school psychologist into either going to a junior college or attending a trade school. On the other hand, if a particular student is found to have a very high IQ (e.g., 142); he may be encouraged to enter college, rather than becoming a plumber or a carpenter. However, it should be pointed out that vocational success and a particular person's IQ score have a much lower correlation. This is partly based on the semantic difficulty created by the term vocational success, as well as on the numerous factors that may contribute to one's becoming successful in a particular vocation.

STRENGTHS AND LIMITATIONS

The WAIS-R is a relatively easy test to administer and score. The manual is well-written, easy to read, and generally provides clear directions for scoring. It is effective in determining IQ scores that range from 45 to 150. It is widely used in a variety of settings and has been based on a representative sample of normative population groups within the United States. IQ scores obtained through this test have been shown to correlate highly with the patient's grade point average throughout school (Lezak, 1983).

The chief limitation of the WAIS-R is that it was not designed to evaluate patients who have sustained brain damage. Many of the WAIS-R subtests appear relatively insensitive to brain injury and frequently result in high scores that most likely do not reflect a brain-injured patient's cognitive functioning in "real-world" settings or unstructured situations. Kaplan et al. (1991) tried to rectify this by modifying the WAIS-R scoring system and developed the WAIS-RNI (Revised Neuropsychological Instrument), which permits neuropsychologist to evaluate an individual's qualitative responses and errors to improve their understanding of the test data.

The WAIS-R is inappropriate for individuals who have significant visual or motor impairments (e.g., diplopia, hemiparesis, visual agnosia, or aphasia). An individual's performance on this test can be adversely affected by emotional factors (e.g., depression). Unless this is recognized, it may create the spurious impression that the individual has dementia from a relatively mild traumatic brain injury or that cognitive functioning has deteriorated, even though performance on more sensitive neuropsychological tests has significantly improved. Patients who are raised in different cultures or whose command of English is limited may receive spuriously low IQ scores. The WAIS-R is also not particularly suited for patients who have aphasic difficulties or who are motorically, visually, or auditorally impaired. Finally, patients who are placed on anticonvulsant medications (e.g., Dilantin) or antipsychotic medications are likely to obtain lower IQ scores.

THE WECHSLER ADULT INTELLIGENCE SCALE — THIRD EDITION

The Wechsler Adult Intelligence Scale — Third Edition (WAIS-III) is a revision of the WAIS-R (Wechsler, 1997a). It contains a total of 14 subtests, 11 of which were retained from the WAIS-R. The Symbol Search was adapted from the Wechsler Intelligence Scale for Children — III and two new subtests, Matrix Reasoning and Letter–Number Sequencing, were added. Symbol Search consists of a series of paired groups, each pair consisting of a target group and a search group. The patient must determine, by marking the appropriate box, whether the target symbol appears in the search group. Matrix Reasoning consists of a series of incomplete grid-type patterns that the patient must complete by pointing to or saying the number of the correct response from five possible choices. Letter–Number Sequencing presents the patient with a series of letters and numbers that the patient must simultaneously track and orally repeat with the numbers in ascending order and letters in alphabetical order.

As with the WAIS-R, the WAIS-III also contains verbal and performance scales and produces a full-scale IQ score. The WAIS-III, however, contains index scores for verbal comprehension, perceptual organization, working memory, and processing speed. The VCI is composed of Vocabulary, Similarities, and Information subtests. The Perceptual Organization Index is composed of the Picture Completion, Block Design, and Matrix Reasoning subtests. Working Memory is composed of the Arithmetic, Digit Span, and Letter–Number Sequencing subtests. Finally, Processing Speed is based on the Digit Symbol–Coding and Symbol Search subtests.

While the norms for the WAIS-R do not include individuals above the age of 74, the WAIS-III has norms extending to 89 years of age. Like the WAIS-R, the WAIS-III can be used as a psycho-educational test for secondary and postsecondary school planning and placement. It can also be used as a core test for assessing learning disabilities and for determining exceptionality and giftedness. It was primarily developed to assess an individual's intellectual functioning or to serve as a part of a broad battery of neuropsychological tests that assess multiple domains of neuropsychological functioning. More specifically, it was designed to be used in conjunction with the Third Edition of the Wechsler Memory Scale.

Although the WAIS-R gave patients bonus scores for quick and correct performances, the influence of bonus points has generally been reduced in the WAIS-III. However, three of the subtests (Block Design, Arithmetic, and Object Assembly) have some items for which patients receive bonus points for quick performance. The administration of the WAIS-III takes from 1½ to 2 hours depending on the patient's intellectual abilities, speed of cognitive processing, and age.

The standardization sample for the WAIS-III was based on 2450 adults that were divided into 13 age groups, ranging from 6 to 89. The standardization sample consisted of an equal number of male and female subjects in each age group. For each age group in the standardization samples, the proportion of whites, African-Americans, Hispanics, and other racial/ethnic groups was based on the racial/ethnic proportions of individuals within each age group within the United States population according to 1995 census data. The samples were also stratified according to their educational background (fewer than 8 years of education to over 16 years of education).

Reliability and Validity

The test–retest reliability of the WAIS-III was assessed with intervals ranging from 2 to 12 weeks (average retest interval was 34.6 days). The sample used in this study consisted of 394 participants. This study found reliability coefficients ranging from 0.67 to as high as 0.95 in individuals ranging in age from 16 to 29. When individuals in the 30 to 54 age group were evaluated, their test–retest reliability coefficients were somewhat higher, ranging from 0.78 to 0.96.

The validity of the WAIS-III was assessed by comparing it to the previous editions of this test (WAIS-R and the Wechsler Intelligence Scale for Children — Third Edition). Correlation coefficients of 0.94, 0.86, and 0.93 were obtained for the verbal IQ, performance IQ, and full-scale IQ scores, respectively. A comparison of the average IQs on these tests revealed that the full-scale IQ scores of the WAIS-III were nearly 3 points less than the revised edition, while the verbal and performance IQs were 1.2 points and 4.8 points less than the WAIS-R.

Correlation coefficients between the WAIS-III and the Wechsler Intelligence Scale for Children were found to be very high 0.88, 0.78, and 0.88 for the verbal, performance, and full-scale IQ scores, respectively. Correlation coefficients with the Raven Standard Progressive Matrices Test ranged from 0.49 to 0.79, with the patient's performance IQ correlating 0.79 with the Raven.

Strengths and Limitations

While the normative data in the WAIS-III appears to be superior to the WAIS-R, the time required to administer the WAIS-III appears to have been increased by approximately 30 minutes as a result of increasing the number of subtests from 11 to 14. As a consequence, this test may require up to 2 hours to administer, which may be particularly difficult for patients who have recently sustained a significant traumatic brain injury, since their performance may deteriorate as they are taking this test.

This test may not be suitable for individuals with significant motor impairments, for whom English is not their native language, or who have speaking or hearing impairments. Because of the restrictions placed on the examiner during testing, patients who appear fatigued or become excessively anxious during a test cannot be given a break in the middle of the administration of a subtest without violating the manner in which the original test norms were obtained. Thus, because of its inflexibility, it may not be particularly suitable for patients who have sustained significant brain damage. It may also not be appropriate for individuals who are significantly anxious or depressed at the time of testing.

Many psychologists frequently have arrived at the opinion that an individual has brain damage because of a discrepancy between verbal and performance IQ scores of the WAIS-R or WAIS-III. For example, many have assumed that if the difference between the individual's verbal and performance IQ scores is 15 points or greater, there is a strong likelihood that this individual has brain damage. Unfortunately, 24% of normal individuals who were tested in the development of the WAIS-III had verbal and performance IQ scores that differed by 15 points or more. Thus, differences of 15 points or greater can be found in approximately one out of four of normal individuals and should not be used to determine whether a patient has brain damage (Strauss et al., 2006).

WECHSLER ABBREVIATED SCALE OF INTELLIGENCE (WASI)

The Wechsler Abbreviated Scale of Intelligence (WASI) (Psychological Corporation, 1999) was developed to provide a brief estimate of intelligence. It can also be used as a screening instrument if a more complete assessment of an individual's IQ cannot be performed due to time constraints or for research purposes. The test measures a person's verbal and nonverbal abilities. It consists of four subtests: Vocabulary, Block Design, Similarities, and Matrix Reasoning. These tests were selected because of their high loadings on a general intellectual ability factor (G). These subtests assess both verbal/crystallized and nonverbal/fluid intelligence. The verbal scale consists of the vocabulary and similarity subtests and produces a verbal IQ score. The performance scale consists of the block design and matrix reasoning subtests and yields a performance IQ. The full scale IQ is derived from the verbal and performance IQ scores. Three of the four subtests are not timed. Only the block design test is timed. If time is a limitation, the full scale IQ score can be estimated from the vocabulary and matrix reasoning scores. It takes about 25 to 30 minutes to administer the entire test. The test manual provides the scoring criteria for each subtest. It also provides T-score equivalents for each of the four subtest scores.

Unlike the WAIS-III, the WASI can be administered to individuals who are between the ages of 6 and 89 years of age. The norms have been corrected for in terms of gender, education, and race/ethnicity. Since individuals with insufficient language proficiency, uncorrected hearing or visual impairments, history of drug or alcohol abuse, or patients who are taking antianxiety, antidepressant, or antipsychotic medications were excluded from the normative samples; the test norms may not be applicable for individuals with these problems. In addition, Individuals with medical or psychiatric disorders that were likely to affect their cognitive functioning were not included in the normative sample.

RELIABILITY AND VALIDITY

The test–retest reliability for normal children and adults ranging in age from 6 to 89 who were tested anywhere from 2 to 12 weeks apart was 0.85 for children and 0.88 for adults. Test–retest reliability coefficients with a full scale IQ were 0.93 for children and 0.92 for adults. The interrater reliability was found to be high for both verbal and nonverbal subtests.

The WASI and WISC-III were compared in a sample of 176 children and adolescents ranging from 6 to 16 years of age. Correlations between the corresponding VIQ and PIQ tests were 0.82 and 0.76 respectively. The full scale WISC-III correlated 0.87 with the WASI full scale IQ and 0.81 with the WASI full scale IQ using only two subscales. In the study involving 248 adults ranging in age from 16 to 89 years of age, correlations between the WASI and the WAIS-III subtests ranged from 0.66 to 0.88. For the IQ scores, the coefficients were 0.84 for PIQ and 0.88 for VIQ. The WAIS-III full scale IQ was found to have a correlation of 0.92 with the WAIS full scale IQ-IV and 0.87 with the WASI full scale IQ-II (Strauss et al., 2006).

STRENGTHS AND LIMITATIONS

The WASI is a brief and easily administered test to assess intellectual functioning. It has excellent test–retest reliability, covers a wide age span (6 to 89), and has few practice effects. The WASI is linked to the WISC-III, not to the new WISC-IV. Examiners should be cautious when making clinical inferences between a person's verbal and nonverbal intellectual functioning based on the WASI verbal IQ and performance IQ test scores. The WASI should not take the place of a comprehensive assessment of an individual's intellectual ability. It should be used for screening, research projects, or to provide a global estimate of a person's intelligence when time constraints are an issue.

TESTS TO ASSESS ATTENTION AND CONCENTRATION

A variety of brain insults can affect a patient's attention and concentration skills. For example, many patients who sustain brain injuries are distractible and have difficulty sustaining their attention, responding to more than one task at a time, and shifting their attention to other tasks. A number of neuropsychological tests have been developed to assess a patient's attention and concentration skills.

BRIEF TEST OF ATTENTION

The Brief Test of Attention (BTA) (Schretlen, 1997) has been designed to assess auditory divided attention. It consists of two parallel forms that are presented via an audio cassette. On Form N (numbers), a voice reads ten lists of letters and numbers that increase in length from 4 to 18 elements. The patient's task is to disregard the letters and count how many numbers were read aloud. The same ten lists are presented again as Form L (letters); however, the patient must ignore the numbers and count how many letters were read aloud. The number of correctly monitored lists is summed across Forms N and L, so that the patient's score can range from 0 to 20. This test can be administered in approximately 10 minutes.

Reliability and Validity

Studies that have examined its test–retest reliability have been reported by Schretlen (1997). The first study involved 60 mildly hypertensive but otherwise healthy 60- to 80-year-old adults who were administered the test on two separate occasions. The retest interval ranged from 6 months to 1 year, with an average of 9 months. The test–retest reliability coefficient was found to be moderately high (0.70). In a second study that involved 78 adolescent girls, the test–retest reliability over an interval of 6 months was found to be only 0.45. These studies suggest that repeated testing may lead to improved test performance through the acquisition of general and specific skills or knowledge.

The construct validity was assessed by comparing the Brief Test of Attention with the other widely known tests of attention (Digit Span, Trail Making, and Stroop Color and Word tests). Scores on the Brief Test of Attention were found to be more highly correlated with digits backward (0.53) than forward (0.43) on the Digit Span Test in a sample of 452 patients and 149 normal respondents ranging in age from 6 to 86.

When the results of the normal participants and patients were analyzed separately, the Brief Test of Attention scores consistently correlated more highly with digits backward and digits forward. Scores on the Brief Test of Attention and the Trail Making Test were found to be significantly correlated based on a sample of 311 patients and 73 normal adults, ranging in ages from 15 to 86.

When the normal participants and the patients were analyzed separately, the Brief Test of Attention scores consistently correlated more highly with Part B of the Trail Making Test than with Part A. Correlations between the Brief Test of Attention scores and the Stroop Color and Word Test found that the former correlated significantly with all three parts of the Stroop.

Strengths and Limitations

This test appears to be sensitive to subtle impairments in a patient's auditory divided attentional skills. It can be administered to patients even at their bedside in less than 10 minutes. It possesses norms ranging from 17 to 82 years of age, including those with visual and motor impairments. It has also been standardized for use with hearing-impaired adults between the ages of 17 and 82, who can distinguish between spoken words and letters of the alphabet. It appears to be highly correlated with other tests of attention and sensitive to the attentional impairments of patients who have sustained traumatic brain injuries. It appears to possess some ecological validity in that it may predict the driving outcomes of elderly patients (Strauss et al., 2006).

The BTA correlates highly with other measures of attention and appears to be sensitive to attentional impairments. It has been used to assess patients who have sustained traumatic brain injuries and has been found to be sensitive to the attentional problems of these patients when they were assessed even as long as 8 years later (Schretlen, 1997). This test has also been used to identify elderly individuals who are at risk for driving accidents. When the patient's performance on this test and his or her reported crash history were examined (Keyl et al., 1996), investigators found that an elderly patient's score on this test tended to be linked to his or her crash history. Its chief limitation is that it may not be appropriate for individuals from different cultural backgrounds or whose primary language is not English. It may also not be appropriate for individuals who have significant auditory impairments or who are aphasic. In addition, patients who are significantly anxious or severely depressed may do poorly.

COLOR TRAILS TEST

The Color Trails Test (CTT) (D'Elia et al., 1994) is similar to the Trail Making Test, but appears to be relatively free of the confounding influence of language and cultural bias that can affect a patient's performance on the Trail Making Test. The CTT retains the psychometric properties of the standard Trail Making Test, but substitutes color for the English alphabet letters, making it more suitable for individuals with different cultural backgrounds whose use and knowledge of English is limited. This test contains colored circles and universal sign language symbols (Arabic numerals from 1 to 25). These numbers are superimposed on circles with either vivid pink or yellow backgrounds that are perceptible to color-blind individuals. For Color Trails 1, the subject must use a pencil to rapidly connect circles numbered from 1 through 25 in sequence, ignoring the color of the circle. For the Color Trails 2 trial, the subject must rapidly connect numbered circles in sequence, but alternate between pink and yellow circles. The examiner uses a stopwatch to record the length of time taken to complete each trial and also records on the record form qualitative features of the patient's performance such as near misses, prompts, number-sequence errors, and color-sequence errors. This test possesses excellent norms that have been corrected for the patient's age and educational background. It also has norms for Hispanic- and African-American patients. It is suitable for patients who are 18 years and older and requires approximately 10 minutes to administer. The normative data was based on the performance of 1528 healthy volunteers, including a subsample of 182 African-Americans and sub-sample of 292 Hispanics.

Reliability and Validity

The normative data for the CTT are based on the performance of 1528 healthy volunteers, which included 182 African-Americans and 292 Hispanic-Americans, ranging in age from 18 to 90 living in Los Angeles.

Research has shown that the CTT possesses good test–retest reliability and validity (when compared with the Trail Making Test) (D'Elia et al., 1994). This research has shown that patients require more time on Part 2 of the CTT than on Part B of the Trail Making Test (82 seconds vs. 56 seconds in 20- to 30-year-old subjects). African-American and Hispanic-American subjects were found to test slower than Caucasian Americans; however, this may have been due to the effects of age and education (Spreen and Strauss, 1998). Significant slowing on Parts 1 and 2 has been reported in patients who sustain traumatic brain injuries (D'Elia et al., 1996) or have Human Immuno Deficiency Virus (HIV) (Maj et al., 2003). There was also some evidence that suggests that the Children's Color Trails Test (CCTT) can distinguish normal children from children who have mild neurological disorders, attention-deficits/hyperactivity disorder (ADHD) or are learning disabled (Lorente et al., 2003).

Strengths and Limitations

The CTT tried to eliminate the inherent language bias in the Trail Making test (e.g., subjects taking the Trail Making Test must know the English alphabet). It is unclear as to whether ethnicity affects the test scores or whether the performance on this test varies according to ethnicity (e.g., Caucasian, Hispanic, Cantonese, etc.) or geographic location. The norms utilized for children appear to be taken only from children living in western half of the United States. As a consequence, the use of the test norms for children who were raised in a foreign context is discouraged.

Research studies have not clearly demonstrated that the children's trail making test is the equivalent to the trail making test particularly with respect to Part 2 of the Color Trails Test to Part B of the Trail Making test. It is also unclear as to whether the Color Trails Test is more sensitive to brain damage than the Trail Making Test (Strauss et al., 2006).

CHILDREN'S COLOR TRAILS TEST

The CCTT was designed to be administered to children whose ages range from 8 to 16. The norms were based on a sample of 678 children residing in the Los Angeles area. Some of the children in the sample had mild neurological disorders, learning disability, or comorbid ADHD/learning disorder. Scoring for the children's version is similar to the adult version with the exception of near misses (which are not scored). This test can be administered in 5 to 10 minutes.

Reliability and Validity

Test–retest reliability following intervals of 8 and 16 weeks has been found to be marginal to low; although high correlations were found between the different forms (A and B). Correlations with the Trail Making Test are only moderately high. Correlations with the Test of Variables of Attention (TOVA) have been modest (Llorente et al., 2003).

Strengths and Limitations

This test appears more appropriate for children who were raised in a different cultural or linguistic background since it does not require the test-taker to be familiar with the alphabet. It does, however, require that the test-taker be fairly fluent in Arabic numerals. This test does not contain any data from children who live outside of Los Angeles. It is not clear whether a child's performance on this test varies according to their ethnic background or geographic location. It is also unclear whether this test is better at detecting brain damage than other tests of attention (Strauss et al., 2006).

COMPREHENSIVE TRAIL MAKING TEST

The Comprehensive Trail Making Test (CTMT) was developed to rectify some of the shortcomings of the original Trail Making test. This includes improved norms and reliability as well as increased sensitivity to the separate cognitive components that underlie test performance (Reynolds, 2002). It was also designed to be more sensitive in detecting executive dysfunction than the original Trail Making Test paradigm.

The CTMT consists of five trials. The examinee is asked to connect a series of stimuli in order using a pencil as quickly as possible. This test includes some distractive stimuli in some trials to increase the demands on the individual's inhibitory controls and ability to shifting sets.

This test was designed to be administered to individuals ranging in age from 11 to 74 years and 11 months. Recently, norms have been developed for children between the ages of 8 and 10. Correlations with education are reportedly minimal (Strauss et al., 2006). Scores on this test appear to be correlated with age with faster performances occurring between the ages 11 to 29 followed by a decrease in speed after age 30 and a more marked decreased in speed after age 60 (Reynolds, 2002).

Reliability and Validity

Test–retest reliability following an interval of 1 week produced was found to be high (0.84). Interrater reliability was found to be very high for the composite score (0.99) and for the separate trials (0.96 to 0.98).

Strengths and Limitations

Although this test seems to hold considerable promise and appears to be a worthwhile alternative to the Trail Making Test because of its strong psychometric properties and stratified normative sample, test–retest data are lacking for children. In fact, additional important information about the test's correlation to other test of attention, the Trail Making Test as well as other measures of executive dysfunction is lacking (Strauss et al., 2006).

CONTINUOUS PERFORMANCE TEST

Continuous Performance Test (CPT) was first introduced by Rosvold et al. (1956) to detect lapses in attention. Subjects were asked to press a key when a target letter (X) appeared or when the target letter was preceded by another letter (A to X). Since that time, CPTs have been modeled after this test paradigm, although these tests appear to vary with respect to whether they are administered within the visual–auditory modality, the type of stimuli utilized (e.g., colors, geometric figures, letters, or numbers), the task requirements (e.g., responding to specific stimuli), and the type of data that are evaluated (e.g., omissions and commissions) (Spreen and Strauss, 1998).

Many computerized versions of this test have been developed and are commercially available. In this form, the presentation of the test stimuli is controlled by the computer program that permits the examiner to administer one or more practice tests. Depending on the computerized version utilized, testing will normally require 10 to 20 minutes. The computer program usually provides an overall summary of the test data and may indicate when the subject gave slower responses at the end of the test than at the beginning, which suggests the subject's inability to sustain his or her attention. Scoring is usually broken down into several categories hits (the percentage and number of targets the patient responded to correctly), omissions (the percentage and number of targets the patient failed to respond to), commissions (the percentage and number of times the patient responded to a nontarget stimulus), the mean response time, the consistency of the response times to targets, and the response characteristics expressed in complex signal detection analysis.

This technique has been frequently used with some success to evaluate patients with attention-deficit disorders (see, e.g., Seidel and Joshko, 1991; Ballard, 1997). When it is administered 6 months postinjury, it appears to be sensitive to children who have sustained severe traumatic brain injuries (Kaufmann et al., 1993) as well as adults who have sustained closed head injuries (Burg et al., 1995). This technique also appears to be sensitive to the effects of medication, particularly Ritalin, when it is given to patients who have attention-deficit disorders with hyperactivity (Conners and Multi-Health Systems Staff, 1995).

Reliability and Validity

Studies (e.g., Seidel and Joshko, 1991) have shown that the continuous performance technique appears to have adequate test–retest reliability. There appear to be relatively few, if any, practice effects as a result of repeated testing. Any improvement on repeated testing most likely reflects significant cognitive change rather than familiarity with the test (Conners and Multi-Health Systems Staff, 1995).

Some investigators (e.g., Seidel and Joshko, 1991) have reported low to moderate correlations between the various versions of the CPT and other measures of attention such as the Stroop and Paced Auditory Serial Attention tests, which most likely reflect the multidimensional nature of attention and the fact that these tests may tap different aspects of attention and concentration. Ballard (1997) has found that a patient's scores on the CPT appear to be correlated with academic achievements. Its greatest use appears to be identifying individuals with either attention-deficit disorder or attention-deficit hyperactivity disorder. For example, Spreen and Strauss (1998) reported that this test correctly classified 91% of children and adults with attention-deficit disorders or attention-deficit hyperactivity disorders.

Strengths and Limitations

The major strength of this test appears to be its ability to detect patients with attention-deficit hyperactivity disorders as well as patients who have sustained traumatic brain injuries. Computerized versions of this test are relatively easy to administer and produce rather comprehensive data analysis of a patient's performance using signal detection analyses. One of the shortcomings of this test is that it may fail to distinguish patients who are suspected of having sustained a traumatic brain injury who have a prior history of attention-deficit disorder or attention-deficit hyperactivity disorder. The normative data for these tests appear to have used mainly children and young adults. Therefore, there are relatively few normative studies for adults over the age of 35, and data obtained in individuals who are 35 or older may be difficult to interpret (Strauss et al., 2006).

CONNERS' CONTINUOUS PERFORMANCE TEST — II

The Conners' Continuous Performance Test — II (CPT-II) (Conners and MHS staff, 2000) is a computerized test that measures sustained attention and response inhibition. It can be administered to individuals ranging in age from 6 to over 55. The standardization sample that was used to develop the various norms for this test consists of 1920 individuals. Information on the educational and socioeconomic status of the sample appears to be lacking.

The first CPT (Rosvold et al., 1956) required the examinee to press a key when the letter X was presented and not press the key when any other letters were presented. More difficult version required the examinee to press a key only if the X was preceded by the letter A. This test served as a vigilance task since it required the examinee to maintain his or her attention over long periods of time to detect infrequently occurring test stimuli.

The CPT-II utilizes a different test paradigm. For example, the interval rate between the presentation of the test stimuli and the inter-stimulus event rate varies across trials. In addition, the standard test paradigm utilized in the original test was reversed so that the overwhelming majority of the trials consist of targets instead of nontargets. Thus, the examinee has to press the spacebar whenever they see any letters except for the letter X. Thus, this version of the test requires the examinee to maintain continuous attention to the letters that he or she is presented and inhibit their responses to a specific letter. This apparently increases the target to nontarget ratio and the number of possible correct responses.

The CPT-II has a larger normative sample than the earlier test and includes more adult cases. The clinical sample has been expanded to include a neurologically impaired group. The test has been designed to run on a Windows platform instead of DOS and the signal detection measures have been revised (Strauss et al., 2006).

A signal detection analysis of the data is performed. The scores in percentiles can be obtained relative to nonclinical cases, an ADHD sample, and a neurologically impaired clinical sample, which includes children and adolescents. A computer program produces number of graphs and provides various scoring options.

Reliability and Validity

The test–retest reliability has been based on a sample size of only 121 cases. Only four variables were found to have test–retest reliability that was high enough to justify its use in a clinical context. These include commission, D prime, and confidence indexes for the neurologically impaired and ADHD samples. The remaining CPT-II scores had marginal or extremely low test–retest reliability coefficients. In fact, some of the variables had reliability coefficients that were essentially at the chance level (Strauss et al., 2006).

Although the test manual fails to provide correlations between the CPT-II and other test of attention, a few studies have found support for the convergent validity of the CPT-II (Strauss et al., 2006). Research studies that have investigated the correlations between the CPT-II and rating scales measuring similar constructs (e.g., Riccio et al., 2001) have found moderate correlations in some cases, but only limited correlations in others. In the CPT-II standardization sample, children and adolescents with ADD perform worse on all the CPT-II variables with the exception of commission when their scores were compared to the nonclinical group (Connors and MHS staff, 2000).

Adults with ADHD perform worse than the nonclinical group on all of the CPT-II variables. The evidence that the CPT-II can differentiate between individuals with ADHD and other clinical groups is rather confusing. For example, while Epstein et al. (2001) reported a higher rate of commission errors in adults with ADHD compared to adults with anxiety disorders, other studies (e.g., Walker et al., 2000) have not found any differences between ADHD groups and other clinical groups including patients with mild psychiatric disorders.

Strengths and Limitations

The CPT-II provides a quick computerized assessment of an individual's attention/executive functioning based on adult normative data and data from ADHD and neurologically impaired subjects. The computer program is easy to use and has many interesting features that are invaluable for doing research. There is also evidence that the CPT-II provides a good measure of the patient's executive functions. The test may also have some potential to measure the patient's perseverative tendencies.

While the CPT-II confidence indices (ADHD and neurological) appear to have good reliability, the test results should not be used as primary evidence for the diagnosis of ADHD since the confidence index (ADHD) appears to be prone to misinterpretation. The normative data for this test appear to be subpar and have some major shortcomings. For example, they were not stratified according to the census data and no socioeconomic status or educational data was presented in the manual. There was also no information on the patient's rural/urban status. The environments in which the norms were obtained were often quite different, which makes their usefulness limited. In addition, some of the data was collected at the patients' homes, which are not representative of the general population. There was also an overrepresentation of the number of women included in the normative sample.

The neurologically impaired group was not adequately described. For example, almost one third of the individuals in this group were reported to have a postconcussion disorder; however, no further information was provided such as the severity of this disorder, whether or not the individual is currently in litigation, and time since injury. Given the likelihood of a high base rate of exaggeration in postconcussion patients, the test does not include any procedures that would identify individuals who are malingering. Research studies have shown that the test results do not appear to be affected by the examinees ethnic background (Strauss et al., 2006).

DIGIT SPAN TEST

The Digit Span Test is a subtest of WAIS-R and the WAIS-III (a description of these tests was provided earlier in this chapter). It consists of orally presenting random number sequences, such as "9-4-7-2-6," to the patient at a rate of approximately 1 per second. The patient must repeat the digits in the exact sequence in which they were presented. The examiner typically begins by having the subject repeat only two or three digits and will increase the number of digits in the sequence until the subject is unable to repeat the sequence correctly. Following this, the examiner instructs the patient to repeat the orally presented digits backwards, so that if the examiner states, "5-2-9," the patient should respond, "9-2-5."

The examiner continues to add a digit every time the patient correctly performs the task. Scoring consists of the total number of digits the patient could correctly recall in the exact order they were presented (forward digit span) and the total number of digits the patient could recall in reverse order (backward digit span). Typically, whenever an error is made on a particular sequence, the examiner will provide a different sequence containing the same number of digits. If the patient fails that sequence, the examiner will stop testing the patient or begin the backward digits task. Most patients are able to recall seven digits forward and five digits backward. A difference of three or more digits between the patient's forward and backward score is observed more commonly in brain-damaged patients than in neurologically intact individuals (Lezak, 1983).

Reliability and Validity

The test–retest validity of this test ranges from 0.66 to 0.89, depending on the interval length and the subject's age (Lezak, 1995). Validity studies (e.g., Hom and Reitan, 1984; Black, 1986) have shown that this test tends to be more sensitive to left-hemisphere than right-hemisphere or diffuse brain damage. In the first few months following significant closed head injury, it is not uncommon to see a patient's score on this test fall into the impaired range; however the patient's performance is likely to return to normal over time (Uzzell et al., 1987). It is one of the least sensitive measures of dementia, particularly in the early stages; a patient's performance on this test does not become noticeably impaired until the dementia becomes moderately severe (Botwinick et al., 1986). While patients who have sustained mild traumatic brain injuries are able to do fairly well on this test, patients who have sustained more severe traumatic brain injuries, particularly with significant frontal lobe involvement, are likely to do poorly (Ruff et al., 1986).

Strengths and Limitations

Poor performance on this test in terms of being able to recall only a few digits backward and forward, such as five forward and three backward, can be due to a variety of factors such as anxiety, depression, being preoccupied with unrelated thoughts, or brain dysfunction. The Digit Span Test is more sensitive to left-hemisphere brain damage (Newcombe, 1969). It is fairly resistant to the aging process; that is, an individual's performance will show relatively little deterioration on this test prior to the age of 60 (Kramer and Jarvik, 1979). The Digit Span Test is primarily a test of attention and is not generally regarded as an accurate test of recent memory. For example, patients with Korsakoff's syndrome (a disorder characterized by profound impairments in recent memory) typically perform this test well, but cannot recall what happened 5 minutes earlier.

Even though it is one of the subtests of the Wechsler Adult Intelligence Scale, it has been used for many years by neurologists, psychiatrists, and psychologists during their mental status examinations to evaluate the patient's attention and immediate memory. Poor scores on this test are commonly observed in individuals who are anxious and depressed. Thus, to determine whether a particular patient's score is indicative of emotional problems or a brain injury, the psychologist or neuropsychologist must carefully evaluate the patient's complaints and performance on other neuropsychological tests, the presence of confounding factors and external stressors in the patient's environment, the patient's behavior and motivation during testing, and the patient's profile on tests of personality and emotional adjustment.

The Digit Span Test does not correlate highly with the ten other subtests on the Wechsler Adult Intelligence Scale. It appears to measure a very specific skill or ability. The test appears to be sensitive to brain damage, particularly when the damage is located in the left hemisphere. The Digits Backward score appears to be more sensitive to brain damage and age than the Digits Forward score. However, one should not conclude that a particular patient has brain damage because of poor performance on this test, since poor performance on this test can be due to a variety of nonneurological factors.

PACED AUDITORY SERIAL ADDITION TEST

The Paced Auditory Serial Addition Test (PSAT) was developed by Gronwall (1976, 1977) to assess sustained and divided attentional skills in individuals ranging in age from 16 to 74. It assesses the individual's ability to add 60 pairs of numbers ranging from 1 to 9. Each number is added to the number immediately preceding it. For example, if the individual is read the numbers "3-5-7-2-6-5," the patient must add the first two numbers, then the second and third numbers, then the third and fourth numbers, and so on. Thus, the patient in this example should correctly respond, "8-12-9-8-11." The pace at which the numbers are presented is also varied. They are presented either 1.2, 1.6, 2.0, or 2.4 seconds apart by the use of a tape recorder (or a computer program). The slower rate (2.4 seconds) is presented first with the patient being read 60 digits at this rate. Then the patient is presented with 60 digits at 2.0 seconds apart. On trials three and four, the speed increases to 1.6 and 1.2 seconds, respectively.

The test consists of a total of 240 responses made by the patient. Scoring is the percentage of correct responses for each presentation rate (Lezak, 1983). As one might expect, the rate of correct responses diminishes considerably as the rate of the presentation of the stimuli increases. For example, Gronwall and Wrightson (1974) and Gronwall (1977) reported that the percentage of correct responses decreased from 82% at the slowest rate (2.4 seconds) to 51% at the fastest rate (1.2 seconds) in normal controls. There is also a children's version that allows testing of children ranging in age from 8 to 14.5. The children's version used the same norms as the adult version.

Reliability and Validity

Test–retest correlations involving intervals of 7 to 10 days have been reported to be high (McCaffrey et al., 1995). However, some researchers have reported significant practice effects if patients repeat this test 1 week later. For example, Stuss et al. (1988) have found an increase of six points when subjects were tested 1 week later. While Gronwall (1977) has reported that the practice effects are relatively minimal if the subjects are retested after the second administration, other investigators (e.g., Feinstein et al., 1994) have reported practice effects following repeated administrations of this test. This test has been found to be moderately correlated to the Digit Span, Auditory Consonant Trigrams, Trail Making, and Stroop tests (Spreen and Strauss, 1998).

Strengths and Limitations

This test appears sensitive to relatively subtle attention impairments in patients who have sustained cerebral concussions or mild head trauma (Levin et al., 1982). Gronwall and Wrightson (1981) found, however, that while this test was able to detect subtle deficits in information processing in patients who had recently sustained a cerebral concussion, their scores on this test normalized within 60 days. Using this test has been advocated to determine whether a patient is able to return to his preinjury social and vocational activities following mild head trauma. Normal subjects who are given this test again 1 week later improved their test scores by 18%, which most likely reflect practice effects (Schachinger et al., 2003).

This test is not widely used despite its presumed sensitivity to subtle brain damage. Some individuals who are given this test find it quite frustrating and refuse to complete it.

Poor performance on this test can reflect mechanical difficulties (e.g., difficulties with the tape recorder or quality of sound), anxiety, depression, inattention due to recent stressors (e.g., financial difficulties, divorce, and extramarital affair of spouse), physical pain or discomfort, headache, medications, or hysteria. Poor performance on this test should be corroborated by the patient's performance on other neuropsychological tests that assess sustained and divided attention. Poor performance on this test can also be due to suboptimal motivation since there are no built-in measures to detect the test-taker's effort and motivation as they are taking this test.

RUFF 2 AND 7 SELECTIVE ATTENTION TEST

This test was developed by Baser and Ruff (1987) to assess a patient's selective attentional capacity in the presence of different distractor conditions known to influence selection speed. The test involves a paper and pencil format and can be administered at the patient's bedside in approximately 5 minutes. The patient is asked to cross out as quickly as possible numerical targets (2 and 7) that are embedded in either alphabetical capital letters or in blocks of digits. After satisfactorily completing a practice trial, the subject is told to begin the search from the top left side of the line and then proceed to the second and third lines in a similar fashion. The subject is then told to start a new block whenever the examiner says "next." The test consists of 20 blocks of three lines each, with a time limit of 15 seconds for each block. The blocks are printed on two pages that are taped together back to back. Each line contains ten target and 40 distractor stimuli. The distance between the targets and distractors is equal. The target location is randomized throughout each line.

Scoring of the test consists of the total number of hits and errors (errors of omission and commission) and is computed separately for each distracted condition. The patient's speed is determined by the sum of the hits during each condition (digit–letter and digit–digit) and the accuracy (the total number of hits minus the total number of errors divided by the total number of hits multiplied by 100).

This test was normed on 360 adults, stratified by age, gender, and education. One hundred of these subjects were later retested to establish the test's reliability. Ruff et al. (1992) reported that this test can be easily administered and is also sensitive to patients with brain damage involving portions of the frontal lobe, as well as portions of the temporal, parietal, and occipital lobes. This test has also been shown to be sensitive to patients in the early stages of autoimmune deficiency syndrome (AIDS) (Schmitt et al., 1988) and to be one of the key predictors in whether patients who have sustained traumatic brain injuries are capable of returning to work or school. Ruff (1994) has found that the majority of patients with major depression were not impaired on this test, particularly if they did not exhibit clinical evidence of psychomotor retardation.

Reliability and Validity

This test appears to have adequate to high test–retest reliability. It is highly correlated with the Digit Symbol, and the selective attention tests of the Test of Everyday Attention (TEA). It is poorly correlated with the Digit Span, Stroop, and Seashore Rhythm tests (Ruff and Allen, 1996). It appears quite prone to practice effects (Lemay et al., 2004).

Strengths and Limitations

The major strength of this test appears to be its ease of administration and the fact that it can be given at the patient's bedside. It also appears to be sensitive to selective attention deficits that are commonly seen in patients who have sustained traumatic brain injuries or have other forms of cerebral pathology; to detecting the subtle attentional difficulties which are frequently seen during the early stages of AIDS; and to predicting whether a patient who has sustained a traumatic brain injury is ready to return to work or school.

The normative sample does not represent a national stratified random sample. Thus, clinicians should be careful when interpreting the scores of individual who do match the sample upon which the test norms were based (Strauss et al., 2006). It may not be appropriate for individuals who have poor vision or who are significantly anxious at the time of testing. Patients who exhibit clinical evidence of psychomotor retardation may perform poorly on this test. Since it is prone to practice effects, caution is recommended in interpreting the test results when it readminstered. Since this test does not include any built-in validity scales to detect individuals who are not putting forth their best effort, it may not detect individuals who are simulating cognitive impairment.

STROOP COLOR AND WORD TEST

The Stroop Color and Word Test have been used to differentiate between normals, nonbrain-damaged psychiatric patients, and brain-damaged patients (Stroop, 1935). The test consists of a Word page with Color names printed in black ink, a Color page with Xs printed in colors, and a Word-Color page with words from the first page printed in colors from the second (interference task). There are a number of different versions of and scoring systems for this test. It can be administered in less than 10 minutes and is easily scored. It appears to be fairly effective in distinguishing brain-damaged patients from normal healthy adults and psychiatric patients (Trenerry et al., 1989). Brain-injured patients typically respond more slowly on each of the three sections of this test, although they do not consistently demonstrate difficulties on the Word-Color page (Ponsford and Kinsella, 1992; Batchelor et al., 1995).

Reliability and Validity

The Stroop Test appears to possess satisfactory reliability (Franzen et al., 1987; Spreen and Strauss, 1998). While practice effects have been reported when this test is administered a second time on the Word-Reading Trial, additional practice effects have not been reported on subsequent trials. The trial-to-trial reliabilities and estimated reliabilities of the average of three trials appear to be satisfactory. Test–retest reliability coefficients of 0.90, 0.83, and 0.91 for the three parts of the test have been reported (Spreen and Strauss, 1998).

The Stroop Test appears to be sensitive to the effects of closed head injury. Even when patients appear to have made a good recovery, they may continue to perform abnormally slowly for five or more months post injury. It may also be sensitive to the subtle attentional deficits that are often seen in patients who sustain mild traumatic brain injuries (Bohnen et al., 1992). This test also appears to be sensitive to patients with dementia (Koss et al., 1984).

Strengths and Limitations

Diminished performance has been observed in depressed (Raskin et al., 1982) and anxious patients (Batchelor et al., 1995). Thus, poor performance on this test does not necessarily mean that the person being tested has sustained a brain injury or is neurologically impaired. In addition, advancing age appears to be linked with slowing in color naming (Graf et al., 1995). Its sensitivity to detect cognitive impairment in brain-damaged individuals may decline over time. For example, patients with moderate to severe brain damage tested no differently than controls when they were tested 2 to 5 years postinjury (Spikman et al., 2000).

This test should not be administered to individuals who are color-blind or have significant problems with their visual acuity. It should not be administered to individuals who are unable to read or comprehend the test instructions. Individuals who deliberately perform slowly while taking this test may be inaccurately diagnosed as brain-impaired. As a consequence, the neuropsychologist should carefully observe individuals while they are being tested to see if they are putting forth their best effort. Reviewing an individual's test data without having had the opportunity of observing the individual being testing is not recommended since this test cannot detect suboptimal motivation.

SYMBOL DIGIT MODALITIES TEST

The Symbol Digit Modalities Test (Smith, 1968) is a modification of the Digit Symbol Subtest of the WAIS. The patient must code symbols according to a key that displays nine symbol–numeric relationships. The patient is given a pencil and ten practice items that initially begin with a symbol. The patient is then told that in the box below the symbol he or she must fill in the particular number that is associated with the symbol shown. Having examined the key, the patient is instructed to place that number below the symbol so that it corresponds exactly to the key. After completing all ten practice items, the patient is instructed to begin when the examiner says, "Start," continue working as quickly as possible without skipping any items and immediately stop when the examiner says, "Stop." The test lasts for a total of 90 seconds. Scoring consists of the number of correct responses made within the allowed time. Unlike the Digit Symbol subtest, the patient's oral responses can be substituted and scored in cases where the patient has sustained an injury to a dominant arm or hand. Since an individual's performance on this test decreases with advancing age, norms have been developed for different age groups (18–24, 25–34, 35–44, 45–54, 55–64, and 65–74).

Reliability and Validity

Smith (1968) obtained norms from 420 healthy adults ranging from ages 18 to 74. He also obtained norms from brain-damaged patients and reported that by using a cut-off score of 1.5 standard deviations below the mean for a particular age group, he was able to identify 86% of the brain-damaged group and 92% of the normal controls. For an average retest interval of 29 days, the test–retest reliability for both the written and oral forms of this test was found to be 0.80 and 0.76, respectively (Smith, 1991). A patient's performance on this test has been found to be significantly correlated to the Coding subtest of the Wechsler Intelligence Scale for Children — Revised (Lewandowski, 1984) and the Digit Symbol subtest of WAIS-R (Morgan and Wheelock, 1992). This test is sensitive to various types of neurological disorders in children and adults and appears to be highly correlated with their functioning in real-world activities (Spreen and Strauss, 1998).

Strengths and Limitations

The SDMT is very sensitive to diffuse and subcortical brain damage. It is widely used and appears to be sensitive to a wide range of neurological disorders since this test involves visual scanning, attention, and visual motor activities. It is easy to administer and score. There is written and oral version of the test. The entire test can be administered in less than 5 minutes. More recent norms that include gender, and education stratified norms are clearly superior to the original norms (Jorm et al., 2004). The oral version may be less susceptible to cultural effects. Research studies on the test–retest reliability of children are lacking (Strauss et al., 2006).

Poor performance on this test can be caused by factors other than brain damage. For example individuals who are taking antipsychotic or anticonvulsant medications, are experiencing high levels of anxiety, are severely depressed, or are in considerable pain and discomfort at the time of testing, have a severe headache, chronic untreated medical problems (e.g., hypothyroidism), are extremely fatigued, psychotic typically do not perform to the best of their ability. Since a person's performance on this test is under their voluntary control, poor performance may also reflect suboptimal motivation.

TEST OF EVERYDAY ATTENTION

The TEA was designed to assess attentional processes in individuals ranging from 18 to 80 years of age (Robertson et al., 1994). There is also a children's version of the test. It is primarily based on the attentional model developed by Posner and Peterson (1990), which proposes three attentional systems: attention, vigilance, and selection. TEA consists of the battery of eight subtests that assess selective attention, sustained attention, attentional switching, and divided attention. The normative sample consists of 154 adults ranging in age from 18 to 80, which are broken down into the following age groups 18–34, 35–49, 50–64, and 65–80. It contains two educational levels. It includes three alternate forms if testing needs to be repeated. The TEA usually takes between 45 to 60 minutes to complete, is portable, and does not require a computer for administration (Strauss et al., 2006). There is also a children's version that can be used for children ranging in age from 6 to 16.

The TEA was developed to help predict the recovery of function following brain damage and the patient's ability to attend to a variety of real-world tasks. The manual describes how each subtest should be scored and interpreted in addition to how any performance deficits on each task might affect an individual's ability to function effectively in everyday activities. The TEA also measures an individual's vigilance and selection employing familiar materials designed to simulate everyday activities.

Reliability and Validity

Test–retest reliability information for repeated administrations of version A are not contained in the manual. Test–retest reliability is based on versions A and B administered sequentially. Thus, these test–retest reliability coefficients reflect both alternative form reliability and test–retest reliability. Overall, the test–retest coefficients range from acceptable to high; however, some subtests were found to have marginal to poor reliability (e.g., telephone searching while counting). Despite the low reliability of the telephone search while counting task, this was felt by the authors to be clinically valuable because of its sensitivity and because of the fact that some groups of patients had extreme difficulty with it. There is no data, however, in the manual to support its clinical sensitivity (Strauss et al., 2006).

There is no evidence in the manual for practice effects. However, the manual states that the practice effects were automatically considered when the scale scores were derived for version B. However, the manual contains no information on the clinical significance of version A–version B scale score differences. The manual does show the expected practice effects when version C is administered after version B. Unlike many tests that report to assess attention, the TEA is one of the few tests, which appears to be based on a well-established theory of attention (Bate et al., 2001). At the present time, there have been no studies on the factors or structure of this test (Strauss et al., 2006).

Strengths and Limitations

The TEA tries to rectify some of the major problems inherent in well-recognized tests of attention, namely their multifactorial nature, poor ecological validity, and their lack of underlying theoretical structure (Bate et al., 2001). It is one of the few tests, which is based on established theory of attention that deals with the issue of ecological validity. The test is usually perceived by the examinees having some relevance unlike many other neuropsychological tests. The test manual is fairly well written. There is also a children's version of the test.

The TEA has been used to assess patients with dementia, stroke, traumatic brain injury, and psychiatric disorders. While it appears to be effective in discriminating patients with cognitive deficits from matched controls, it currently does not discriminate between individuals with mild cognitive impairment and individuals who have dementia of the Alzheimer's type. It appears sensitive to the effects of stroke. For example, older patients who sustain unilateral strokes generally perform poorly on all of the TEA subtests than age matched controls. It also appears to be sensitive to attentional problems in individuals who have sustained small white matter infarcts (Van Zandvoort et al., 2003). It has also been reported to be sensitive to attentional impairments in individuals who have sustained a closed head injury. For example, closed head injury patients were found to have poor scores on the TEA subtest, which measured selective and sustained attention (map search, telephone search, telephone search while counting, and lottery) (Chan et al., 2003).

The TEA appears to have some promise with respect to the issue of ecological validity of the test data since moderate correlations were found between two of the TEA subtests (map search and elevator counting) and an attention questionnaire that were completed by close relatives. Unfortunately, the normative sample in the manual is not well described. For example, information on the test relationship to factors such as education, gender, ethnicity, and IQ is either lacking or quite limited. The manual also does not provide sufficient information about the test's reliability.

The influence of practice effects on the TEA subtests for version A cannot be determined based on the information contained in the manual. Although this information is available for version B, it is unclear as to whether versions A and B should be considered equivalent forms. The procedures necessary for determining the significance of any changes upon retesting are poorly described in the manual. There are no clear guidelines for determining the clinical significance of the version A vs. version B scale score differences when the examinees were later retested. Since the norms for version C are made up of only a small number of individuals, version C should not be used in a clinical setting (Strauss et al., 2006).

TEST OF VARIABLES OF ATTENTION

The Test of variables of attention (TOVA) is a computerized test that has been designed to assess an individual's sustained attention and impulsivity. The test uses brief stimulus presentations in short interstimulus intervals. It lasts longer than most other CPTs. It tends to create some testing conditions that some believe may differentiate children with ADHD and normal children. The TOVA can be used as a measure of attention within the context of the neuropsychological evaluation. It can also be used to screen and diagnose attentional disorders as well as measure the effectiveness of medications designed to treat children and adolescents with ADHD (Leark et al., 1999; Strauss et al., 2006).

The test consists of four intervals. The target appears 22.5% of the trials during the first two intervals (stimulus — infrequent condition). It appears on 77.5% of the trials (stimulus — frequent condition) during the second two intervals. Since the interstimulus interval is short the examinee must respond more quickly in addition to responding more frequently.

The first half of the test has been designed to maximize the demands on sustained attention in order to elicit errors of omission. The second half of the test measures the patient's ability to inhibit their behavior and elicits errors of omission. The test generally takes about 22 minutes.

The examiner begins by reading the test of instructions. There is a 3-minutes practice session following this. The examiner usually remains present during the entire administration, although prompting by the examiner is not permitted as the test is being given. The TOVA is usually the first test administered and should be administered in the morning. The TOVA produces number of different scores omissions, commissions, response time, response time variability, D', ADHD score, post commissions response time, anticipatory responses, and multiple responses. The ADHD score is determined by a combination of scores that have been shown to have superior predictive ability in detecting ADHD.

Reliability and Validity

Test–retest reliability on 24 children from the standardization group (Greenberg et al., 2000) following a 90-minutes interval found that correlation for reaction time was high (0.93) and the correlations were moderate to high of the remaining TOVA variables (0.7 to 0.8). The test authors have stated that practice affects were negligible. However, when test–retest correlations were performed on a group of children with ADHD who have been given stimulant medication after 2 months, adequate reliability was only found for one subset of the TOVA variables. After 4 months, the reliability coefficients were even less. Only response time showed adequate reliability (Llorente et al., 2001).

Correlations between the TOVA and the Wechsler index scores and subtests were found to be negligible, which suggest that they are probably measuring different aspects of attention. There is no published correlational data on the relationship between the TOVA and other tests that assess continuous performance (Strauss et al., 2006).

Strengths and Limitations

The TOVA utilizes a nonverbal format, and geometric stimuli instead of letters or numbers, which may minimize cultural effects. It seems appropriate for young children and adults with letter and number identification problems. Its short interstimulus presentation rate seems effective in detecting attentional impairments. It has been studied and used in variety of clinical populations, including individuals who were taking medications.

While the TOVA might be a good at detecting an attention, it does not appear to be as effective as the Conner's scales at detecting attentional impairments that are commonly seen in real-world settings. As a consequence, confirmation of impairment in real-world settings should be assessed with questionnaires or interviews with significant others. The test norms appear to be inadequate for adults. Since some of the standard scores for males in the older age groups appear to be artificially inflated (because of the small size of the samples obtained and lack of subject errors) this test should only be administered to children and adolescents.

The TOVA should be treated as one component of comprehensive diagnostic workup for ADHD, which should include a history of the patient's symptoms, a psychological/neurological screening examination, evaluation of the patient's academic/work environment, structured interviews with the family and teachers, and behavioral ratings from significant others (Greenberg et al., 2000). Finally, great care should be taken in reviewing the TOVA interpretation report that may state that the individual had high ADHD scores "suggestive of ADHD." This should not be taken to mean that the individual has ADHD (Strauss et al., 2006).

TRAIL MAKING TEST

The Trail Making Test consists of two parts (A and B) and is one of the tests given in the Halstead–Reitan Battery (Reitan, 1955). This test was described earlier in this chapter and is widely used as a measure of attention, visual scanning, and visuomotor tracking. Part B is more difficult than Part A, since it requires the patient to shift sets (e.g., go from a number to a letter), rather than connecting only numbers. Whenever a patient makes an error, the examiner points out the error and may provide the patient with a cue or prompt. Scoring of this test is based on the number of seconds required to complete both parts. It is important to note that if the patient makes an error and is corrected or is given a cue or prompt, the timing of the patient must not stop. This test has been shown to be sensitive to brain damage and cognitive deterioration associated with advancing age.

Reliability and Validity

The test–retest reliability of this test has been found to be high for normal adults (Lezak, 1983) and patients with various neurological disorders (Goldstein and Watson, 1989) at retest intervals of 6 months and 1 year, respectively. The test–retest reliability for Part B tends to be lower than for Part A as a result of significant practice effects (McCaffrey et al., 1993). Educational factors appear to play a significant role in a patient's performance on this test (e.g., Bornstein, 1985).

Studies by Hom and Reitan (1990) have reported that Parts A and B of this test appear to be quite sensitive to the progressive cognitive decline seen in patients with dementia. It is also sensitive to diffuse traumatic brain injury (Leininger et al., 1990), alcoholism (Grant et al., 1987), and polysubstance abuse (McCaffrey et al., 1988). When this test was administered to patients who had sustained moderate to severe traumatic brain injuries, it predicted fairly well their ability to live independently in the community (Acker and Davis, 1989).

Strengths and Limitations

One of the chief strengths of this test is that it is widely used and can be easily administered in 5 to 10 minutes. It appears to be sensitive to brain damage. It is backed by a solid body of research. Qualitative observations of a patient's behavior as he or she is taking this test can be helpful in identifying specific types of cerebral pathology providing the examiner has had sufficient training to do this.

It may not be appropriate for individuals whose native language is not English or who have limited familiarity with the English alphabet. Since individuals with psychiatric disorders often perform poorly, it should not be used as a screening test to differentiate brain-injured patients from psychiatric patients. Since there are no built-in measures to detect suboptimal motivation, some individuals may deliberately perform slowly to appear brain-damaged.

TESTS TO ASSESS LANGUAGE

THE APHASIA SCREENING TEST

The Aphasia Screening Test is part of the Halstead–Reitan Battery and contains 51 items that permit the examiner to screen patients for aphasic disturbances in approximately 15 to 20 minutes. A more comprehensive description of the administration of this test can be found earlier in this chapter.

Reliability and Validity

Studies assessing the test–retest reliability of this test are not available. While this test has been utilized in the Halstead–Reitan Battery to screen for aphasia, Snow (1987) found that patients with left-hemisphere brain damage did worse on the verbal items than patients whose brain damage was confined to the right hemisphere.

Strengths and Limitations

The major strength of this test appears to be its ease of administration since it can be easily administered to patients in 5 to 10 minutes. It offers no guidelines for clinical application to the inexperienced examiner. It has been severely criticized by Lezak (1995), who pointed out that it is prone to produce potentially harmful and incorrect interpretations and strongly recommended that it should not be used.

BOSTON DIAGNOSTIC APHASIA EXAMINATION — THIRD EDITION

The Boston Diagnostic Aphasia Examination — Third Edition (BDAE-3) provides a comprehensive assessment of an aphasic patient's language and communication difficulties (Goodglass et al., 2001). Although Boston Diagnostic Aphasia examination test was originally developed by Goodglass and Kaplan (1983), it has been substantially revised since that time to integrate the latest developments in neurolinguistic research. It contains more than 50 subtests that evaluate the patient's communication and communication-related skills. There are three different formats Standard, Short, and Extended. The Short format allows the clinician to make a fairly rapid assessment of a patient's language and communication functioning. The Extended format provides an in-depth assessment of a patient's language and communication functioning. The BDAE-3 allows the user to utilize quantitative and qualitative methods to assess individuals with aphasic disturbances.

The BDAE-3 contains a 44-page booklet that guides the examiner through this test. Scoring instructions are provided in the manual and answer booklet. A score summary sheet provides the examiner with a visual profile of the patient's performance on each of the subtests. Administration of the Standard format usually takes about 90 minutes. The Short format takes between 40 and 60 minutes. The Extended format can take as long as 2½ hours. It can be administered to individuals whose ages range from 16 to old age. There is a Spanish version of this test.

Reliability and Validity

The manual contains no information about test–retest reliability. This omission appears to reflect the fact that aphasic patients can improve in their functioning over time and the authors believe that the reliability of this test is likely to be spuriously low until the patient's functioning has returned to its premorbid baseline level (Strauss et al., 2006). Correlations with other tests of aphasia are missing in some cases. Research studies, however, have shown that the test findings appear to be correlated with specific areas of the brain that have been damaged (e.g., Radanovic and Scaff, 2003).

Strengths and Limitations

The BDAE-3 provides a comprehensive assessment of a patient's language and communication functioning. It contains a Short form that requires 40 to 60 minutes to administer instead of 90 minutes when using the Standard form. The methodology utilized in this test is based on a great deal of research on neuroliguistics and aphasia at the Boston VA Medical Center. The BDAE-3 has no test–retest reliability scores and its validity to other tests of aphasia is limited. There is also a Spanish version of this test.

Boston Naming Test

The Boston Naming Test consists of 60 drawings of objects that become increasingly less familiar and difficult to name (Kaplan et al., 1983). For example, the patient may be presented with a drawing of a harmonica and asked to name it. If the patient is unable to name this object, he or she is given a cue, such as, "It's a musical instrument." If the patient is still unable to name it, he or she is provided with the first syllable of the word "harmonica" and told, "It begins with har." It is essential that the examiner note the amount of time required before the patient was able to provide a correct response and whether the patient was correct or incorrect after being provided with a stimulus cue or phonemic cue. A patient's score is based on the number of objects that were successfully named without having been provided with a phonemic cue.

Reliability and Validity

Sawrie et al. (1996) found that the test–retest reliability of this test, after a duration of 8 months, was high. This test has also been found to have high concurrent validity with other tests of language (Spreen and Strauss, 1998). This test appears to be sensitive to subtle word-finding difficulties, as well as to subcortical brain disease or damage (Lezak et al., 1990).

Strengths and Limitations

The test manual and booklet provide normative data based on the patient's educational achievements (12 years of education or less, or more than 12 years of education) and age (20–29, 30–39, 40–49, and 50–59 years old). The normative data contain means and standard deviations that permit the examiner to determine the degree of the patient's severity. Careful analysis of the patient's responses on each of the test items, as well as the responses to stimulus and phonemic cues, can be of considerable assistance in precisely identifying the nature of the patient's impairment and its clinical significance.

Poor scores on this test can be due to a variety of confounding factors the individual's premorbid cultural or linguistic background and intellectual functioning, limited educational background, anxiety, depression, psychotic thinking, or suboptimal motivation. A poor performance on this test, in the absence of word-finding difficulties during the clinical interview, should be suspect, particularly when it is not supported by the patient's medical records, clinical history, or other neuropsychological test data.

CONTROLLED ORAL WORD ASSOCIATION TEST

The Controlled Oral Word Association Test (COWAT) consists of instructing the patient to name as many words as possible beginning with specific letters of the alphabet (Spreen and Benton, 1977). Typically, the patient is given an example of the task requirements. For example, he is told, "I want you to say as many words as you can that begin with the letter M without giving me people's names." In other words, he might say, "Marble, music, marriage, magic." After this example, the patient is given the letter F and is instructed to state as many words as possible beginning with this letter. The patient is given 1 minutes, during which time he must state as many words as he can that begin with that letter. The examiner must rapidly write down the patient's responses on a sheet of paper as the patient is engaged in this task. Immediately following this, the patient is given the letter A and instructed to provide as many words as possible beginning with that letter. As soon as this is completed, the patient is given the letter S and is given the same instructions. This test can be administered in approximately 5 to 10 minutes.

A patient's score is the total number of words provided during the three trials (F, A, and S). Norms have been developed for both males and females according to educational achievements (fewer than 9, 9–11, 12–15, and 16 or more years of formal education) and age group (25–54, 55–59, and 60–64). Points may be added to the patient's score to adjust for educational and age differences in patients. For example, a 56-year-old woman who has completed less than 9 years of formal education would have ten points added to her score. Conversely, a 25-year-old college graduate would not have any points added to his score. The patient's percentile can be determined on the basis of his or her adjusted score. An adjusted score of 53 or higher would place a patient above the 95th percentile and would indicate superior performance on this task. On the other hand, a patient whose adjusted score is 23 or 24 is considered to have borderline impairment. Patients whose scores are 16 or less are considered to have severely defective performance (Lezak, 1983).

Reliability and Validity

The test–retest reliability has been found to be high when patients are retested approximately 1 month later and moderately high 8 months later. Its concurrent validity, in comparison to the WAIS-R vocabulary subtest, appears to be low (0.15). It appears to be sensitive to frontal lobe damage (Miceli et al., 1981). Patients who have sustained more severe traumatic brain injuries tend to score more poorly than patients with less severe brain injuries (Peck et al., 1992).

Strengths and Limitations

This test has been found to be a sensitive indicator of brain damage, particularly involving the left frontal–temporal area. Patients who have sustained bilateral frontal–temporal lobe injuries typically make the lowest scores on this test. Poor performance on this test may also reflect such factors as test anxiety, depression, fatigue, cultural deprivation, linguistic background, significant physical pain and discomfort, headache, hysteria, malingering, or inadequate motivation. Poor performance on this test should be corroborated by other neuropsychological test data, the patient's medical records, information from significant others, and the patient's clinical history.

MULTILINGUAL APHASIA EXAMINATION

The Multilingual Aphasia Examination (MAE) was designed to provide a relatively brief, but quite detailed, examination of the presence, severity, and qualitative aspects of aphasic language disorders for children ranging in age from 6 to 12 and adults ranging in age from 16 to 97. It was revised by Benton et al. (1994) and contains nine subtests and two rating scales in the following five domains oral expression, spelling, oral–verbal understanding, reading, and rating scales (articulation and praxic features of writing). The revised edition includes norms for children (kindergarten through grade 6). The test corrects for the patient's age and educational background. This test requires approximately 40 minutes or less to administer, and also contains a Spanish version (which takes an additional 20 minutes to administer to normal healthy adults). Scoring is relatively simple and straightforward and is described in the test manual.

Reliability and Validity

There are no data on the reliability of this test. The validity of this test appears to rest on the test's ability to discriminate between normal and aphasic subjects. Using the suggested cut-off scores, between 2.6 and 7% of normal individuals and between 14.4 and 64.6% of aphasics were misclassified on the basis of the individual subtests. However, using the failure of two or more subtests as a cut-off point, the misclassification rates dropped to 3 and 4%, respectively (Spreen and Strauss, 1998). This test has been found to be a sensitive indicator of acute confusional states (Lee and Hamsher, 1988). When used to evaluate patients with traumatic brain injuries who complained of word-finding or naming difficulties, this test was found to be highly correlated with the severity of the brain injury (Levin et al., 1981). This test was standardized on a sample of 360 healthy Iowa subjects, ranging in age from 16 to 69, stratified for age, education, and gender. The norms for this test have cut-off points for high average, average, borderline, defective, and very defective test performances.

Strengths and Limitations

One of the major strengths is that it is relatively easy to administer and score and appears to be useful in evaluating language impairments in patients who have sustained significant traumatic brain injuries. It can be administered to Spanish-speaking individuals. Scoring the individual's subtest performance permits the examiner to use each test separately, particularly if the examiner wishes to study verbal fluency or verbal memory in a patient who is not aphasic.

It does not have any test–retest reliability data that limits its usefulness in making a clinical diagnosis. Since the normative sample is poorly described in the test manual, great care should be taken when applying the norms in the manual to individuals who do not share the demographic characteristics of the normative sample (Strauss et al., 2006).

This test is inappropriate for individuals whose command of English or Spanish is limited. Because it does not contain any formal means to assess whether the individual being tested is performing to the best of his or her ability, the burden of this determination is placed entirely upon the subjective observations of the examiner. If this test is given by a psychological assistant or technician, the neuropsychologist may be hard pressed to indicate that the patient was exhibiting suboptimal motivation during testing.

PEABODY PICTURE VOCABULARY TEST — THIRD EDITION

The Peabody Picture Vocabulary Test — Third Edition (PPVT-III) was designed to assess an individual's receptive vocabulary skills. It can be administered to children as young as 2½ years old to individuals who are over 90 years old. The test is the third edition of a widely used standardized test that was originally published in 1959. It is an individual administered test. It is not timed and utilizes a multiple choice format. The examinee must point to one of four pictures when they given a particular word by the examiner. The test consists of 204 test items that increase in difficulty throughout the test. There is also a Spanish version available. It usually takes between 8 and 16 minutes to administer (Dunn and Dunn, 1997).

Reliability and Validity

Test–retest reliability after a 1 month interval was very high (range 0.91 to 0.94). However, when the youngest subjects were tested after an interval of 8 months, the reliability was found to be only marginal (Reese and Read, 2000). An extensive amount of research was spent in the development of this test. Although the correlations between the second edition and third edition of this test are quite high, the third edition has been found to produce higher test scores than the second edition (Pankratz et al., 2004). Moderately high correlations have been found on other tests of expressive and receptive language (Strauss et al., 2006).

Strengths and Limitations

The PPVT-III is one of the most widely used tests to assess the receptive language skills of individuals ranging in age from 2½ years of age to over 90. It can be administered in 8 to 16 minutes. Scoring is straightforward and simple. Some differences exist in the test scores obtained in the second and third editions of the test with the scores tending to be higher in the third edition. Although this test has often been used to assess an individual's IQ this is not recommended (Hodatt and Gerken, 1999). Even though visual stimuli are used throughout the test, it is not free of cultural bias (Stockman, 2000).

TOKEN TEST

The Token test assesses the patient's ability to perform orally presented commands. The examiner presents a set of tokens that vary in substance — cardboard or plastic, shape — circles or squares, size — large or small, and color. Some or all of the tokens may be placed directly in front of the patient, depending on specific test procedures. The examiner's commands to the patient range from being very straightforward and simple, such as, "Touch the white square," to "Before touching the yellow circle, pick up the red square." The test is composed of five parts that comprise a total of 62 test items. This test can usually be administered in about 10 minutes.

Reliability and Validity

Although the test–retest reliability for normal children over the age of 11 and adults is low, its reliability for individuals with cognitive impairments or receptive language difficulties is higher (Taylor, 1998). This test has been found to be sensitive to patients with subtle receptive language deficits secondary to brain injury (Boller and Vignolo, 1966), is sensitive to even minor impairments in receptive language, and correlates well with other measures of language. It can also be used to evaluate children and adolescents who have sustained closed head injuries (Spreen and Strauss, 1998).

Strengths and Limitations

While norms have been developed to compare the scores of nonaphasic and aphasic brain-damaged patients to normal controls, the normative samples are poorly described and the data was collected over two decades ago. Because this test is fairly simple, neurologically intact patients should obtain near-perfect scores. Patients with aphasic difficulties typically make a significant number of errors. This test tends to be sensitive to left temporal–parietal lobe damage. Patients who perform poorly on this test are likely to exhibit receptive language difficulties during the clinical interview and during the administration of other neuropsychological tests. At times the patient's responses may appear inappropriate, or the patient may seem confused after being asked a lengthy or complex question. The patient's family and significant others and the patient's medical records should corroborate this problem. Poor performance on this test can be due to a number of different reasons — auditory comprehension or hearing difficulties, distractibility, depression, severe anxiety, psychotic thinking, pain and discomfort at the time of testing, language or cultural difficulties, medications, or suboptimal motivation.

TESTS TO ASSESS ACADEMIC ACHIEVEMENT

PEABODY INDIVIDUAL ACHIEVEMENT TEST — REVISED

This test was designed to measure academic achievement from kindergarten through grade 12 in the areas of mathematics, reading, recognition, reading comprehension, spelling, and general information (Dunn and Markwardt, 1970; Markwardt, 1989). It is frequently used as a screening test to determine if a more detailed diagnostic test should be administered to the patient. The test materials contain four volumes of test plates, as well as training exercises, the test items, and the instructions for administering the six subtests. It consists of two response formats (free response and multiple choice). During the General Information subtest the examiner reads 100 questions that can be answered orally by the patient. These items test the patient's general encyclopedic knowledge in the fine arts, humanities, recreation, science, and social studies.

During the Reading Recognition subtest, the patient is provided with a list of 100 words which must be read aloud. In the Reading Comprehension subtest, the patient must read a sentence silently and then select one picture out of four that best illustrates the sentence. In the Mathematics subtest, the examiner reads each item aloud, while the patient must select the correct response from within a multiple-choice format. In the Spelling subtest, the patient must initially recognize letters from their names or sounds. Then, the examiner presents a word out loud and uses it in a sentence, and the patient must select a correct spelling response for the word from a multiple-choice format. The Written Expression subtest examines the patient's written language skills (copying and writing letters, writing words and sentences from dictation, and writing a story in response to a picture prompt).

The Peabody Individual Achievement Test — Revised can usually be administered to the majority of nonbrain-injured individuals in approximately 1 hour. The manual contains the scoring criteria and examples of correct and incorrect responses. A person's score for each subtest is the total number of actual and assumed correct responses up to the ceiling level. A basal level is then determined, below which all items are assumed correct. Items above the ceiling item are assumed incorrect. Composite scores can be produced that summarize the patient's achievement skills in general information, reading recognition, reading comprehension, mathematics, and spelling. A patient's composite scores determine his or her total test score (Spreen and Strauss, 1998).

Reliability and Validity

The standardization sample used to develop this test consisted of approximately 1500 children who were roughly proportional to the U.S. population in terms of sex, geographic region, socioeconomic status, and race or ethnic group. Research studies have demonstrated high test–retest reliability (above 0.90) after intervals of 2 to 4 weeks. This test has been found to correlate highly with other achievement tests such as the Kaufman Assessment Battery for Children, the Wide Range Achievement Test — Revised, and the Stanford Diagnostic Mathematics Test (see, e.g., Prewett and Giannulli, 1991).

Strengths and Limitations

This test possesses excellent test–retest reliability and validity. Because it is fundamentally a screening test, it should not be used as a diagnostic instrument, nor should it be used in the development of individual educational programs (Costenbader and Adams, 1991; Allinder and Fuchs, 1992). The norms contained within this test are based solely on children living in the United States, and neuropsychologists should exercise caution when interpreting the scores of individuals who have been raised or are living outside of the United States. It also tends to inflate the scores for young children and deflate the scores of children at the highest age and grade levels (Costenbader and Adams, 1991).

WECHSLER INDIVIDUAL ACHIEVEMENT TEST

This test was designed to measure a patient's arithmetic, listening comprehension, oral expression, reading, spelling, and writing skills (Wechsler, 1992). It has been designed to evaluate individuals ranging in age from 5 to 19 years and 11 months. It is often used in conjunction with the Wechsler Intelligence Scale for Children — III. The test takes between 30 and 50 minutes to administer to children who have not yet entered the third grade. If the child has entered the third grade, testing will probably take just over an hour. While the scoring procedures to assess basic reading, mathematics reasoning, spelling, and numerical operations are straightforward, scoring for the items in the Reading Comprehension, Listening Comprehension, Oral Expression, and Written Expression subtests is more subjective (Spreen and Strauss, 1998).

Reliability and Validity

Test–retest correlations have been reported to be high for most of the subtests. However, the correlations for the Oral Expression and Language Composite subtests, while adequate, tend to be lower. The scores on this test correlate moderately well with the Wechsler Intelligence Scale for Children test scores, with most of the correlations ranging from 0.30 to 0.70 for the full-scale IQ scores. Correlations with other tests (Kaufman Test of Educational Achievement, Wide Range Achievement Test — Revised, and the Woodcock–Johnson Psycho-Educational Battery — Revised) generally fall in the moderate range. This test was standardized on 4252 Americans according to age (5 to 19 years), regional residence, gender, race/ethnicity, and education of parents. The manual provides normative tables containing standard scores for both age and grade for the different academic terms. It also contains tables to determine confidence intervals, percentile ranks, stanines, and age and grade equivalence (Spreen and Strauss, 1998).

Strengths and Limitations

The scores on this test can be compared to the Wechsler Intelligence Test, as a subset of the standardization sample (1284 subjects) was also administered the Wechsler Adult Intelligence Scales so that ability and achievement discrepancy statistics could be computed. One of the limitations in administering this test to patients with traumatic brain injuries or brain insults is that there are no norms for such patients. Patients who sustain severe traumatic brain injuries may test lower on some of the scales, particularly Arithmetic and Listening Comprehension, because of their attentional and memory difficulties, respectively, and this performance may be used as evidence of a preexisting history of learning difficulties even when not supported by academic records.

WECHSLER INDIVIDUAL ACHIEVEMENT TEST — SECOND EDITION

The Wechsler Individual Achievement Test — Second edition (WIAT-II) (The Psychological Corporation, 2002) is a comprehensive test battery that allows clinicians and school psychologists identify academic problems in young children and adolescents. It is a revision of the original WIAT (The Psychological corporation, 1992). It covers areas such as word reading, reading, comprehension, mathematics calculation, mathematics reasoning, listening comprehension, oral expression, and written expression that traditionally have been used to diagnose learning disabilities. The test produces five composite scores (reading, mathematics, written expression, oral language, and total composite) as well as supplemental scores for some of the subtests.

The U.S. norms for the test were based on 4379 individuals who were stratified based on age, grade, gender, race/ethnicity, geographic region, and parental education. It normally takes 45 minutes to administer to young children, but could take as long as 2 hours to administer to older children, adolescents, and young adults.

Reliability and Validity

The test–retest reliability of the WIAT-II is very high for all ages. Practice effects on the average tend to be relatively minimal. The content of the WIAT-II appears to have been based on comprehensive surveys of achievement test users, recommendations from experts, and a review of the literature. It appears to be highly correlated with the full scale IQ scores from the Wechsler IQ tests. It also appears to be a good predictor of an individual's grades or academic performance (Strauss et al., 2006).

Strengths and Limitations

The WIAT-II psychometric properties appear sound. They are based on a number of research studies, links to the Wechsler scales, and a strong theoretical background. Its strengths include extensive norms, and an easy to administer format with interactive and verbal materials. It has good reliability and validity. Although experienced examiners seem to have little difficulty administering WIAT-II, the scoring and normative data for this test appear quite complex. For example, the manuals contain massive amounts of information, which can overwhelm the reader. Software for scoring is available and is highly recommended.

WIDE RANGE ACHIEVEMENT TEST

The Wide Range Achievement Test — Third Edition (Wilkinson, 1993) has been developed to assess the patient's spelling, reading, and arithmetic competence. Children from ages 5 to 11 years can be evaluated at Level I, while patients from 12 to over 45 years can be assessed at Level II. Some differences exist in the manner in which the patient's spelling and reading skills are evaluated at the two different levels. The spelling test evaluates the patient's ability to spell a list of words of increasing difficulty. The arithmetic subtest includes addition, subtraction, multiplication, and division, as well as arithmetic problems involving fractions, percentages, and conversions. This subtest also contains computation of squares and square roots and a variety of algebraic problems. The patient is given 15 minutes to complete the arithmetic section. The reading section involves having the patient read individual words of increasing length and difficulty (Lezak, 1995).

Reliability and Validity

The test–retest reliability of this test has been reported to be high (0.91 to 0.98). Scores on this test appear to correlate moderately well with the full-scale IQ scores of the Wechsler Intelligence Scale for Children — III. Moderate to high correlations have been reported between this test and the California Test of Basic Skills (4th ed.) and the Stanford Achievement Test (Spreen and Strauss, 1998).

Strengths and Limitations

Scoring on this test is relatively straightforward with the patient's score consisting of the total number of correct items achieved for the Spelling, Arithmetic, and Reading subtests. These scores are then compared to age norms and can be converted into standard scores or percentiles, as well as the patient's grade equivalent. While this test was not specifically designed to evaluate patients with brain damage, it frequently identifies patients who have had a previous history of spelling or reading difficulties. Patients with brain damage frequently do poorly on the arithmetic subtest because of its cognitive demands and the 15-minutes time limit. A careful analysis, however, of the patient's responses and errors on this test can often determine if the errors reflect preinjury arithmetic difficulties or brain injury. Poor performance on this test can also reflect a variety of extraneous factors such as anticonvulsant or psychotropic medications, anxiety, poor vision, depression, psychotic thinking, histrionic behavior, or poor motivation. To determine if the patient's poor performance has been caused by brain damage or was the result of a prior history of academic difficulties, dyslexia, or spelling difficulties, the neuropsychologist must carefully review the patient's academic and medical records, interview significant others, and observe the patient's behavior during testing.

TESTS TO ASSESS VISUOSPATIAL AND PERCEPTUAL SKILLS

BENDER–GESTALT TEST

The Bender–Gestalt Test evaluates the patient's visual perceptual and visual constructional skills (Bender, 1938; Hutt, 1985). It is one of the most frequently used psychological tests in the United States (Lezak, 1995). It consists of nine geometric designs that are presented individually on a 4 × 6″ card to the patient, who then must draw each as accurately as possible on a blank sheet of paper. When the patient completes the first drawing, the second card is placed on top of the first, and so on until all nine cards have been reproduced. The test is used to evaluate the patient's perceptual tendencies to organize visually presented stimuli into configural "gestalts." Exact reproductions of the designs are necessary for reliable evaluation of the patient's visual perceptual and visual constructional skills.

The test can be administered in a relatively short time to individuals who are at least 3 years of age. A number of different scoring systems exist based on the accuracy and organization of the patient's drawing, which considers factors such as the relative size of the drawings in comparison to the test stimuli, relative placement on the sheet of paper, and the particular distortions of the reproductions (which may include inversions or rotations of the figures, indicating perceptual and fine motor problems). Despite its considerable popularity among clinical psychologists who frequently use it as a screening test to determine organicity or brain damage, its use in this capacity appears to be overrated since its effectiveness depends on the skill and training experience of the examiner (Whitworth, 1984).

Reliability and Validity

Investigators such as Koppitz (1964, 1975) have conducted numerous validity and reliability studies using this test with young children. The test–retest reliability of this test, when taken 2 weeks apart by kindergarten children, found coefficients of 0.90. When the same group of kindergarten children were given this test 8 months apart, the test–retest reliability coefficient dropped to approximately 0.50 (Whitworth, 1984). However, it should be pointed out that as children become older, their scores tend to become higher. Koppitz reported correlation coefficients ranging from approximately 0.50 to as high as 0.80 between this test and Wechsler Intelligence Test scores.

Lezak (1976) has found that this test can be effective in discriminating between psychiatric and brain-injured patients, as well as normal controls. For example, Koppitz obtained correct diagnoses ranging from 74 to 91% when using this test to discriminate among psychiatric and brain-injured patients and normal controls. Studies by Heaton et al. (1978) reported that this test could correctly discriminate between psychiatric and organic patient groups with 84% accuracy.

Strengths and Limitations

One of the major strengths of this test is its ease and speed of administration. It has been used for over 60 years. As a consequence, there have been over 1000 studies done on its clinical effectiveness, validity, and reliability. Even though it is a good screening test for organicity or brain damage, it is often been misused when the psychologist relies solely on the results of this test, does not administer other neuropsychological tests or fails to take a careful clinical and background history of the patient. Because of the numerous scoring systems that exist, there is no one accepted scoring system for the diagnosis of organicity. Because it is so easy to administer, this test is too frequently misused or abused by untrained, inexperienced, and even unethical examiners.

Unfortunately, the validity of a patient's scores on this test in clinical settings can be misleading. For example, Russell (1976) found that scores of an aphasic patient with pronounced right hemiplegia, who had sustained a severe depressed skull fracture some 17 years earlier, were actually normal. Bigler and Ehrfurth (1980) reported that three patients with evidence of brain damage that was documented on computed tomography (CT) scans had received scores that were within normal limits. Health status appears to be a factor in the patient's score on this test. For example, Klonoff and Kennedy (1965) found that hospitalized elderly males made higher error scores than healthier males.

BENTON FACIAL RECOGNITION TEST

This test was designed to assess the individual's ability to compare photographs of faces (Benton et al., 1994b). The patient is shown a photograph of a person's face. Directly below this photograph are six photographs, each of which contains a photograph of someone's face. In the first section of the test, the patient is asked to identify the photograph from the six photographs located directly below. During the second section of the task, the patient is shown a photograph that contains only three-quarters of a person's face. The patient is instructed to examine the six photographs below it and pick out three photographs of this individual. In the third section of the test, the patient must match this person's identity to photographs that have been taken under low lighting conditions.

This test appears sensitive to subtle perceptual/visual discrimination impairments. Since the patient need only point to the photographs, this test is only minimally dependent on the patient's linguistic skills and can be given to patients whose knowledge of English is limited. This test also places little emphasis on the patient's visual memory, since the original photograph is always available for matching purposes.

Reliability and Validity

The test–retest reliability over a duration of 1 year has been found to be moderately high (0.60) in the elderly (Levin et al., 1991). Trahan (1997) found that more than half of the patients who had sustained right-hemisphere strokes were impaired on this test in comparison to only one out of four patients who had sustained left-hemisphere strokes. It does not appear to be particularly sensitive to patients who have sustained relatively mild traumatic brain injuries because these individuals typically test within the normal range. However, it does appear to be sensitive to patients who have sustained severe traumatic brain injuries, particularly patients who exhibit posttraumatic dementia (Spreen and Strauss, 1998).

Strengths and Limitations

The test usually takes approximately 15 minutes to administer, depending on whether the patient is cognitively intact or severely brain-injured. The examiner can choose to give the patient the short form, which contains only 13 items, or the long form, which contains 22 items. Correlation studies between scores obtained on the short and long forms have ranged between 0.88 and 0.94, which suggests that the use of the short form may be desirable to save valuable time. Normative data is provided with the test packet to permit the examiner to compare the patient's scores to those of normal controls and brain-damaged patients (Lezak, 1983). This test tends to be particularly sensitive to patients who have sustained posterior right-hemisphere damage, but is generally insensitive to left-hemisphere and frontal lobe damage.

Poor performance on this test can also be produced by poor vision, high levels of anxiety, marked depression, low intellectual functioning, physical pain and discomfort, headache, concentration difficulties, psychotic thinking, histrionic behavior, suboptimal motivation, and malingering. To rule out the likelihood of these factors, it is essential that the patient's score on this test be compared with other neuropsychological tests and that the examiner take a careful background and clinical history, interview significant others, and review the patient's medical records. In addition, the patient's behavior during testing should be carefully observed to determine if it is consistent with individuals with documented brain injury.

BENTON JUDGMENT OF LINE ORIENTATION TEST

This test requires the patient to match a pair of angled lines that are shown on a card to one of 11 numbered lines below. The patient is required to either point to or name the numbers associated with the 11 lines. The test consists of four practice items and 30 test items. It has two forms (F and V) that are approximately equal in difficulty and contain exactly the same test items arranged in a different order (Benton et al., 1994b).

Reliability and Validity

This test has high inter-rater reliability for the number of correct and total error scores. The test–retest reliability has been found to be moderately high. Studies that examine the validity of this test to detect brain damage have shown that while this test is sensitive to brain damage, its predictive validity is not high (Spreen and Strauss, 1998). It appears to be more sensitive to brain damage that is located in the right hemisphere and may not detect brain damage if it is located in the left hemisphere (Lezak, 1995).

Strengths and Limitations

This test tends to be sensitive to posterior right-hemisphere damage, particularly in the right parietal lobe (Lezak, 1983). Scoring is performed by adding the number of correct test items. The test manual contains normative data to allow the examiner to compare the patient's score to determine its clinical significance. Poor performance on this test may reflect visual acuity difficulties, test anxiety, severe depression, physical pain or discomfort, attentional difficulties, headache, medication side effects, fatigue, hysteria, psychotic thinking, malingering, or suboptimal motivation.

BLOCK DESIGN TEST

The Block Design subtest of WAIS-III contains 14 designs. The first four designs have a 30-second time limit; 5 through 9 have a 60-second time limit; and 10 through 14 have a 2-minutes time limit. Subjects are given bonus points for rapid performance on designs 7 through 14. Some neuropsychologists prefer to use a qualitative rather than a quantitative approach with this test to localize the site of a patient's brain injury (Lezak, 1983, 1995).

Reliability and Validity

The test–retest reliability for the Block Design Test appears to be high (Wechsler, 1997a). The test can be used to predict a patient's full-scale WAIS-III IQ score. Practice effects appear to be relatively negligible for patients who have sustained severe traumatic brain injuries at a 1-year follow up

(Rawlings and Crewe, 1992). This test is generally recognized as one of the best measures for visuospatial organization. The patient's score on this test tends to be lower in the presence of any type of brain injury (Lezak, 1995).

Strengths and Limitations

This test has been shown to be sensitive to brain damage, particularly when the injury is located in the frontal or parietal lobes, and also to patients with Alzheimer's disease, strokes, and hypoxic encephalopathy. Patients with subcortical brain damage typically work very slowly and exceed the time limits, whereas patients with left posterior hemisphere brain damage usually maintain the overall 2×2 or 3×3 configuration of their blocks but make considerable errors with regard to the internal details of their designs. Patients with right posterior hemisphere damage typically exhibit a loss of the overall 2×2 or 3×3 block configuration and produce designs that are grossly distorted (Lezak, 1995). Thus, a careful qualitative analysis of the types of errors made by the patient can provide a greater understanding of the site of brain injury and its clinical significance.

Poor performance on this test may also reflect such factors as poor visual acuity, orthopedic injury to one or both arms or hands, test anxiety, severe depression, significant physical pain or discomfort, headache, hysteria, malingering, or inadequate motivation. It is not indicative of the diagnosis of brain damage unless it is supported by other test data, including the patient's medical history, the neurological examination, neurodiagnostic tests, information from significant others, and behavioral observations of the examiner.

HOOPER VISUAL ORGANIZATION TEST

This test consists of showing subjects 30 pictures of objects that have been cut up and placed in different positions (Hooper, 1983). The subject's task is to visually examine each picture and decide what it would be if it were assembled. The subject must write down the name of the particular object, such as fish, ball, or key. The test items are generally arranged in increasing difficulty. Most individuals can usually complete this test in approximately 15 minutes.

Reliability and Validity

This test appears to have good test–retest reliability at 6 and 12 months (Lezak, 1983). The validity of this test as a general screening measure for brain damage is controversial (Spreen and Strauss, 1998).

Strengths and Limitations

This test tends to be sensitive to posterior brain damage; however, patients with frontal lobe damage will often test as impaired on specific items. Patients with severe hypoxic or anoxic encephalopathy tend to do poorest on this test. Patients with frontal lobe pathology, particularly when it is more prominent in the right frontal lobe, will frequently exhibit problems in visual organization because of their tendency to examine only one object, rather than visually organize the different objects into a single gestalt. For example, such patients are likely to have difficulty on Item 28, which forms a key, typically looking at only one of the three pieces, which resembles an Exacto knife, and identifying the entire object as a knife. Research studies have shown that repeated administrations of this test did not result in any appreciable change in the patient's scores (Lezak, 1983, 1995), which indicates that its test–retest reliability is high.

Poor performance on this test can reflect a variety of factors such as poor visual acuity, low intellectual functioning, high levels of anxiety, severe depression, psychotic thinking, brain damage, histrionic behavior, or malingering. A qualitative analysis of a patient's errors can be helpful in determining whether his or her responses are consistent with patients who have sustained brain damage or reflect psychotic thinking, malingering, or histrionic behavior. The patient's score on this test should be compared with medical history, subjective complaints, background history, neurodiagnostic tests, and other neuropsychological tests to determine validity.

OBJECT ASSEMBLY TEST

This test is a subtest of the WAIS (Revised and Third Edition). It requires the subject to assemble cardboard figures of familiar objects. The WAIS-R version contains four figures a mannequin, a profile of a face, a hand, and an elephant. The WAIS-III contains five figures a man, a profile of a face, an elephant, a house, and a butterfly. The subject is not told what the object is and must deduce the identity of the object as he or she begins assembling it. A 2-minute time limit is given for each object in the WAIS-R version, with bonus points given for rapid completion of the task. The WAIS-III version provides a 3-minutes time limit for the elephant, house, and butterfly figures, with bonus points for rapid performance.

Reliability and Validity

The test–retest correlation of the Object Assembly subtest of the WAIS-R and WAIS-III has been found to be moderately high (Wechsler, 1987, 1997a). The Object Assembly and Block Design subtests correlate more highly with each other than with any of the other Wechsler subtests, which most likely reflect the fact that they both require the patient to construct an object or design from discrete parts. Unlike the Hooper Visual Organization Test, this does not appear to be a conceptual task. It appears to be sensitive to damage in the left- and right-parietal and occipital lobes, although it may also be sensitive to frontal lobe damage (Lezak, 1983, 1995).

Strengths and Limitations

This test is one of the performance subtests of the WAIS-R and WAIS-III. It permits the examiner or neuropsychologist to evaluate an individual's visuospatial–perceptual and visuoconstructional skills. When the subject is unable to complete one of the objects within the allotted time, the subject's score is based on how many pieces of the object were put together correctly before the testing time elapsed. Like the Block Design Test, the Object Assembly Test is sensitive to posterior brain injury, particularly in the right-hemisphere, as well as dorsolateral frontal lobe damage. Because this test, like the Block Design Test, requires skilled motor movements to assemble the various pieces, an individual's performance on this test is likely to be poor if he or she had sustained a significant physical injury to either hand, has diplopia (double vision), is extremely anxious, is visually impaired, or has motor ataxia (jerky movements of the arms or hands).

Patients with posterior right-hemisphere damage typically perform poorly on this test. Patients with frontal lobe injuries show poor organization and planning skills. Like the Block Design Test, patients with significant brain injuries may not comprehend the test instructions, which may cause the examiner to provide examples and instructions that considerably exceed the test instructions to the subject as described by the manual. When this occurs, the psychologist or neuropsychologist should provide a record of this including the rationale utilized to violate the instructions as set forth in the test manual. Comparison to test norms under these circumstances may not be appropriate, particularly if the examiner has grossly violated the test instructions or procedures that are set forth in the manual. Should this occur, the neuropsychologist should provide a descriptive, qualitative account of the patient's performance throughout the test. If an individual performs poorly on the Block Design Test, he or she most likely will also perform poorly on the Object Assembly test, since these tests measure very similar abilities and appear to be mediated by similar brain mechanisms.

Seashore Rhythm Test

The Seashore Rhythm Test, which is part of the Halstead–Reitan Neuropsychological Battery, can be used to evaluate a patient's nonverbal auditory perceptual skills (Seashore et al., 1960; Reitan and Wolfson, 1993). The administration of this test was described earlier in this chapter.

Reliability and Validity

The test–retest reliability ranges from 0.50 to 0.77 (Bornstein et al., 1987). It has been reported to be one of the most sensitive tests to attention and concentration deficits. It appears to correlate highly with the severity of traumatic brain injury (Hom and Reitan, 1990). It does not differentiate between right- and left-hemisphere brain damage (Long and Brown, 1979).

Strengths and Limitations

Although this test appears to be sensitive to deficits of attention and concentration, it may not be appropriate for patients who are hearing impaired, significantly anxious, or depressed. Because the stimuli presented to the patient does not appear to have any discrete trials, any hesitation in responding may interfere with the presentation of the next trial. Although normal subjects make between three and five errors on this test (Bornstein, 1985; Reitan and Wolfson, 1989), the original cut-off error score was set between five and six errors (Halstead, 1947). Thus, use of the original norms may result in the misclassification of a significant number of normal healthy individuals as brain impaired.

Smell Identification Test

The Smell Identification Test (Doty, 1998) is sensitive to olfactory deficits caused by a wide range of medical, neurological, and psychiatric disorders. It can be utilized to detect anosmia (inability of the patient to smell, which is frequently seen in patients who have sustained orbitofrontal lobe damage). It consists of four self-administered test booklets, each containing ten stimuli for smell. A patient must select from one of four multiple choices. This test incorporates microencapsulation technology and sound psychometric principles to provide a relatively easy means of quantifying the patient's olfactory functioning. For example, it focuses on the comparative ability of the patient to identify a number of odorants at the suprathreshold level. The test stimuli include a number of odorous components mimicking the types of stimuli experienced by individuals in the general population.

Reliability and Validity

The test–retest reliability of this test has been reported to be in excess of 0.90 (Doty, 1998). It also appears to possess excellent validity in terms of comparison studies with other olfactory tests, including tests for detection of olfactory thresholds.

Strengths and Limitations

One of the strengths of this test is its normative data base of 4000 subjects and the relative ease with which it can be used to assess an individual's olfactory functioning. Although one of the strengths of this test is its ability to detect malingering, this test may not be suitable for individuals who have bad colds or who have a history of cocaine abuse. Its findings should be interpreted in conjunction with the individual's clinical and background history and medical records.

SPEECH–SOUNDS PERCEPTION TEST

The Speech–Sounds Perception Test (Boll, 1981; Reitan and Wolfson, 1993), which is part of the Halstead–Reitan Neuropsychological Battery, can be used to evaluate the patient's auditory perceptual skills. The administration of this test was described earlier in this chapter.

Reliability and Validity

Test–retest correlations have been reported to be moderately high (Bornstein et al., 1987) when testing was repeated three times a week and at 3-month intervals. This test appears to be sensitive to left-hemisphere damage, particularly the temporal lobe (Hom and Reitan, 1990). It also appears to be sensitive to attentional deficits.

Strengths and Limitations

This test is relatively easy to administer and score. Psychologists should avoid concluding that an individual has left-hemisphere damage as a result of making a high number of errors on this test (Lezak, 1995). It is not appropriate for individuals for whom English is not their native language or who are hearing impaired. Individuals who have attention-deficit disorders or who are hyperactive may perform poorly on this test because it tends to be boring. As a consequence, these individuals may have trouble paying attention to the test stimuli. The test may also not be appropriate for elderly patients since a significant number of these individuals suffer from high frequency hearing loss.

TACTUAL PERFORMANCE TEST

The Tactual Performance Test (Halstead, 1947; Reitan and Wolfson, 1993) is one of the tests used in the Halstead–Reitan Neuropsychological Battery. It can be used to evaluate a patient's kinesthetic perceptual skills. The administration of this test was described earlier in this chapter.

Reliability and Validity

Thompson and Parsons (1985) reported that the test–retest reliability was moderate to high with intertest delays ranging from 3 months to 1 year. However, they found that most individuals tended to show significant improvement in their performance when they are later retested. This test appears to be sensitive to patients with both frontal and parietal lobe lesions (Lezak, 1995).

Strengths and Limitations

While this test is widely used as part of the Halstead–Reitan Neuropsychological Battery, its major problem is that some individuals develop significant psychological distress when they are blindfolded, which is likely to interfere with their performance on this test. Another major disadvantage of this test is that it takes a considerable amount of time to administer. Because the equipment needed to test the patient is rather bulky, it cannot be easily transported to a hospital or jail.

VISUAL FORM DISCRIMINATION TEST

The Visual Form Discrimination Test (Benton et al., 1994b) has been designed to assess an individual's complex visual discrimination skills. The test consists of showing a geometric figure to an individual who must match it to one of four sets of designs. One of the designs is an exact replica, while the others may either vary subtly (e.g., one of the peripheral figures is too high or low) or be grossly distorted (e.g., one of the major figures is rotated 180 degrees). A patient's performance on each of the 16-test items can be easily scored since the choices are numbered from 1 to 4. It can be administered to individuals ranging in age from 19 to 74 years of age in 15 to 20 minutes.

Reliability and Validity

No test–retest reliability coefficients are available for this test. It appears to be sensitive to patients with unilateral, bilateral, and diffuse brain damage (Benton et al., 1994b.)

Strengths and Limitations

This test has been found to be sensitive to posterior brain damage, particularly in the left-parietal lobe and dementia. It can be administered to patients who are unable to speak English, because it only requires that they point to one of four sets of figures on a sheet of cardboard. Scoring is based on a three point scoring system. The test also places little emphasis on the patient's visual memory since the patient need not recall the three geometric figures, but only required to match it with one of the four alternatives.

Most healthy individuals typically complete this test in 15 to 20 minutes, although patients with severe diffuse brain damage may take 30 minutes or longer. The test manual contains normative data to permit comparison of an individual's score to normal controls and brain-damaged patients.

The normative sample was only based on 85 subjects with no history or evidence of brain disease. Normal individuals are expected to make near perfect scores on this test. Individuals with brain damage typically make considerably more errors. No corrections have been made for the patient's age that probably reflects the small size of the normative sample. Poor performance on this test may be due to factors besides brain damage visual acuity difficulties, high levels of anxiety, severe depression, histrionic behavior, psychotic thinking, or suboptimal motivation. In the absence of corroborating evidence from other neuropsychological test data, neuroimaging studies (e.g., computed tomography [CT] scan and magnetic resonance imaging [MRI]), the examiner's behavioral observations, and interviews with significant others, poor performance on this test should not be interpreted as evidence of brain damage.

TESTS TO ASSESS MOTOR FUNCTIONS

FINGER TAPPING TEST

The Finger Tapping Test (Reitan and Wolfson, 1993) is frequently used to evaluate an individual's motor speed. It is one of the tests that make up the Halstead–Reitan Battery. The administration of this test was described earlier in this chapter.

Reliability and Validity

The test–retest reliability of the Finger Tapping Test appears to be quite high (0.86 for females and 0.94 for males) when normal individuals were retested after 10 weeks (Gill et al., 1986). It also appears to be high when patients with psychiatric and neurological disorders were tested an average of 2 years later (Goldstein and Watson, 1989). Patients with lesions located in the left or right hemisphere tend to perform worse when tapping with their contralateral hand (Finlayson and Reitan, 1980). It also appears to be sensitive to patients with epilepsy (Dodrill, 1978), as well as patients with other neurological disorders (Heaton et al., 1985).

Strengths and Limitations

It is one of the most widely used tests in the Halstead–Reitan Battery and can be administered in approximately 10 minutes. The patient's performance on this test can be compared to norms based on sex, age, and educational background (Heaton et al., 1991). While it is sensitive to unilateral lesions, particularly in the posterior frontal lobes, patients with subcortical disorders (e.g., AIDS, Huntington's disease, Parkinson's disease, etc.) are also likely to perform poorly on this test. Because an individual's performance on this test depends to a large degree on motivation, it is prone to conscious manipulation. Individuals who are severely depressed or taking high levels of anticonvulsant medications (e.g., Dilantin) may also tap slowly. A neuropsychologist should not conclude that a patient has a lesion in the contralateral hemisphere based solely on poor performance on this test unless a variety of confounding factors can be ruled out and it is corroborated by medical records and other neuropsychological tests.

GRIP STRENGTH TEST

The Grip Strength (Hand Dynamometer) Test was designed to assess the strength of a patient's grip in each hand (Reitan and Wolfson, 1993). It is one of the tests contained within the Halstead–Reitan Battery. The administration of this test was described earlier in this chapter.

Reliability and Validity

The test–retest reliability has been found to be quite high for both men and women (0.91 and 0.94, respectively) when these individuals were tested each week over a period of 10 weeks (Reddon et al., 1985). Although it is frequently used to detect differences in hand strength with the assumption that lateralized brain damage is likely to affect the strength of the contralateral hand, Koffler and Zehler (1985) found that 27% of normal individuals were misclassified as braindamaged when their dominant hand strength exceeded that of their nondominant hand by 5 kg. Bornstein (1986) has also noted that differences between the preferred and nonpreferred hand of 10% or greater were found in approximately 30% of healthy adults. Since this particular test requires the patient to put forth his or her best effort, a patient's performance on this test can be easily manipulated (Lezak, 1995).

Strengths and Limitations

One of the strengths of this test is that it can be easily administered in approximately 5 minutes and is one of the tests used in the Halstead–Reitan Battery. Since this test depends on the individual's effort, it can be consciously manipulated. Individuals with orthopedic injuries or arthritic problems in their hands may perform poorly on this test. Neuropsychologists should exercise considerable caution in categorizing individuals as brain-damaged based on their score on this particular test without carefully reviewing their medical records and other neuropsychological test data.

GROOVED PEGBOARD TEST

The Grooved Pegboard Test (Klove, 1963; Matthews and Klove, 1964) permits an assessment of a patient's fine motor coordination and manual dexterity skills. It consists of a small board that contains 25 slotted holes in a 5×5 configuration. The pegs to be inserted into grooved slots are located in an adjacent metal dish. The patient is instructed to place the pegs into each of the slotted holes as quickly as possible, using only one hand. The patient typically begins with the preferred hand. After the patient has completed the task of filling each of the holes, the pegs are removed and placed back into the metal dish. The patient is then instructed to use the nonpreferred hand to perform the task and to work as quickly as possible. Patients are usually permitted several practice trials with each hand to familiarize them with the task. Scoring is determined by the amount of time the patient requires to complete the task with each hand (Lezak, 1983, 1995).

Because of the manual dexterity required to fit the pegs into the slotted holes, patients who sustain damage to the brain stem, cerebellum, or corticospinal motor pathways are likely to have considerable difficulty on this test. Norms have been developed according to the patient's gender, age, and educational background for the preferred and nonpreferred hands (Heaton et al., 1991).

Reliability and Validity

The reliability and validity of this test to lateralize the site of brain damage to the left or right hemisphere has been seriously questioned (Lezak, 1995).

Strengths and Limitations

The strengths of this test are its ease of administration and scoring. One of the major problems with this test is that the norms are too restrictive and result in 25 to 30% of normal right-handed individuals being misclassified as brain-damaged (Bornstein, 1986). Therefore, neuropsychologists need to be cautious when interpreting a patient's performance on this test, particularly if the patient's medical records are unavailable.

Poor performance on this test can be caused by one or more of the following problems brain damage, visual difficulties, physical injury, orthopedic problems, peripheral neurological impairment, anxiety, depression, physical pain or discomfort, hysterical behavior, malingering, medications, fatigue, or inadequate motivation. Poor performance on this test should not be interpreted as evidence of brain damage unless these other factors can be ruled out and the patient's test performance is supported by medical records and other neuropsychological test data.

TESTS TO ASSESS LEARNING AND MEMORY

AUDITORY CONSONANT TRIGRAMS TEST

The Auditory Consonant Trigrams Test is an adaptation of the Brown–Peterson technique (Baddeley, 1986). It assesses the patient's short-term memory using a distraction task. Three letters (consonant trigrams) are orally presented to the patient at a rate of one letter per second. Immediately following this, the patient is orally presented with a three-digit number and asked to immediately begin subtracting out loud by the number 3 or, if the patient has arithmetic difficulties, by the number 1. After delays of either 9, 18, or 36 seconds, the examiner instructs the patient (usually by knocking on the table) to stop subtracting and recall the three consonants that were originally presented. While the patient is required to remember the consonants after the delay, he or she is not allowed to repeat the consonants aloud while subtracting or counting backwards. All intervals are timed, beginning after the presentation of the last consonant. The patient's responses are recorded verbatim. The number of correct letters recalled is added for each amount of delay. Normal individuals are able to recall 70 to 80% of the consonants correctly with delays of 9 seconds, 50 to 80% with delays of 18 seconds, and approximately 67% with delays as long as 36 seconds (Lezak, 1995). This test can usually be given in 10 to 15 minutes and can be easily scored.

Reliability and Validity

Stuss et al. (1989) have reported that when this test was given to healthy subjects and brain-injured patients on two occasions over an interval of a week, each group significant practice effects upon retesting. While its test–retest reliability appears to be less than adequate, it appears to have good validity in that it can distinguish normal individuals from patients who have suffered traumatic brain injuries. When this test was compared to the brain-injured patient's performances on the PSAT and the Trail Making Test, it was found to be superior in differentiating patients who had sustained mild traumatic brain injuries from neurologically intact controls. It also appears to be less affected by the patient's age and educational background and may be less stressful than the PSAT (Spreen and Strauss, 1998).

Strengths and Limitations

This test can evaluate a patient's verbal memory under conditions of distraction and also provide a means of assessing divided attentional information processing skills (Stuss et al., 1989). It captures everyday experience, particularly momentary distraction and subsequent loss of very recent information (Crowder, 1982). It permits the neuropsychologist to evaluate a patient's ability to retain recently acquired information without rehearsing the material to be remembered (Morris, 1986).

Impaired performance on this test has been observed in patients with a wide variety of neurological disorders including traumatic brain injury, Alzheimer's disease, herpes encephalitis, and Korsakoff's syndrome, and in patients who have undergone frontal leukotomy (Spreen and Strauss, 1998). This test may not be appropriate for patients who are anxious or hearing impaired. This test can be difficult to administer in a consistently standardized manner. Practice effects have been found on retesting. Poor performance on this test does not necessarily mean that the patient's short-term memory is impaired since nonneurological factors (e.g., anxiety, depression, medications, etc.) and/or suboptimal motivation can affect a person's performance on this test.

BENTON VISUAL RETENTION TEST

The Benton Visual Retention Test (Benton, 1974) is designed to assess the patient's visual memory. This test consists of presenting ten cards containing up to three geometric figures. The subject's task is to draw the geometric figures on a separate sheet of paper after the card containing the geometric figures has been removed. There are four different methods of administering this test. During Administration A, the patient is informed that he or she will be asked to draw the contents of a card from memory on a sheet of paper that is the exact size (5 × 8 in.) of the card. Each card is presented for 10 seconds. In Administration B, the patient is permitted only 5 seconds to memorize each card before trying to draw it. Administration C requires the patient to copy the contents of the card onto a sheet of paper, after which the card and the drawing are removed. In Administration D, the patient is shown each card for 10 seconds, but must wait 15 seconds after the card has been removed before beginning the drawing. This test can be administered in about 10 to 15 minutes.

Scoring consists of either the total number of drawings that are correct or calculation of the number of errors on the basis of a scoring system developed by Benton et al. (1994b). The latter scoring system permits a more qualitative analysis of the patient's errors and can provide richer information about the type of injury and its location in the brain. According to Benton's scoring system, a patient's errors involve omission, distortion, perseveration, rotational, misplacement, or size.

The test manual provides norms for patients ranging in age from 15 to 64. The manual also contains expected correct and error scores according to the patient's estimated premorbid intellectual functioning (e.g., IQ). The interpretation of the patient's performance on this test is fairly straightforward and consists of comparing the patient's expected score (based on age and premorbid IQ) and actual score. A score of 3 points below the expected correct score, according to Benton et al. (1994b), suggests the presence of impairment. When the difference is four or more points below the expected score, there is a strong indication of impairment.

Reliability and Validity

Test–retest studies have reported correlation coefficients ranging from 0.79 to 0.84 on the three forms of this test (Sivan, 1992). While a number of studies have examined the sensitivity of this test to detect brain damage, its ability to predict brain damage does not appear to be high. For example, Levin et al. (1990) found that brain-damaged patients did not perform significantly worse than normal controls. This test, however, appears to be most sensitive to patients who have sustained right posterior lesions, usually as a result of a stroke (Spreen and Strauss, 1998). This test has also been used to identify patients with Alzheimer's disease. Storandt et al. (1986) found that patients in the early stages of Alzheimer's disease made significantly more errors than matched controls.

Strengths and Limitations

This test has been highly reliable over repeated administrations (Lezak, 1983, 1995). It also discriminates between brain-injured patients and normal controls with 60 to 70% accuracy and correctly categorizes normal controls with 80 to 90% accuracy. Its ability to discriminate between brain-damaged and psychiatric patients is less impressive, and qualitative analysis of a patient's errors typically reveals a pattern of errors (e.g., bizarre responses) that are idiosyncratic to psychotic or schizophrenic patients, but are rarely exhibited by brain-damaged patients. Benton et al. (1994b), in a series of studies (e.g., Benton and Spreen, 1961), carefully compared the errors made by normal controls who were instructed to simulate brain damage with the errors of brain-damaged patients. The malingerers made a much greater percentage of distortion errors and very few errors of omission and perseveration. Through a qualitative analysis of the errors made by both groups, Benton was able to distinguish malingerers from brain-damaged patients easily. Research studies have also demonstrated that brain-damaged patients tend to omit a peripheral geometric figure and make a high percentage of rotational and size errors unlike normal controls or malingerers.

Intact performance on this test does not rule out the brain damage, since the research studies cited above indicate that this test failed to identify 30 to 40% of the brain-damaged patients. Poor performances, on the other hand, can be caused by a variety of factors including anxiety, psychotic behavior, severe pain and discomfort, headaches, fatigue, visual difficulties, constructional difficulties (e.g., the patient has never been able to draw well), suboptimal motivation, hysteria, and malingering. As a note of caution, the diagnosis of brain damage should not be made on the basis of poor performance on this test unless it is supported by the patient's clinical and medical history, other neuropsychological test findings, and the observations of significant others and the examiner.

BRIEF VISUOSPATIAL MEMORY TEST — REVISED

The Brief Visuospatial Memory Test — Revised (BVMT-R) (Benedict and Groninger, 1955; Benedict, 1997) has been used to assess a patient's visual memory. It consists of six alternative forms each of which produces measures of immediate recall, rate, acquisition, delayed recall and recognition. The patient is shown an $8 \times 11''$ plate containing six simple geometric designs in a 2×3 matrix. Each matrix is presented for 10 seconds, after which the patient is instructed to reproduce as many of the designs as possible in the same location on a blank sheet of paper. The patient is also asked to complete two additional learning trials, using the same plate, in order to improve the performance. After a delay of approximately 25 minutes, during which time the patient is involved in distracting tasks, the patient is asked to reproduce the designs again. This is then followed by a recognition trial in which the patient is shown 12 designs each of which is printed on a $3 \times 5''$ card. The patient is then asked to indicate which designs were included in the original matrix.

Approximately 15 minutes is required to administer this test. An additional 25 minutes is required for delayed recall. The patient's responses are evaluated in terms of their accuracy and location. Criteria for scoring each design are provided in the manual. The patient's recall scores are combined to produce measures of learning and memory. In addition, measures of target discriminability and response bias can be calculated from the total number of yes–no positives obtained from the recognition trial (Spreen and Strauss, 1998).

Reliability and Validity

Although the interrater reliability of this test has been reported to be high in the test manual (Benedict, 1997), the reliability coefficients ranged from marginal to high according to the measures utilized and the test form (Strauss et al., 2006). There are also some practice effects. In a separate study Benedict et al. (1996) found that in patients with nonlateralized cerebral pathology or psychiatric disease the indices of learning and delayed recall correlated most strongly with their performance on tests such as the Hopkins Verbal Learning Test, the Visual Reproduction subtest of the WAIS-R, and the Rey Figure Recall. The correlations, however, were not high when performance on this test was compared with measures of expressive language (the Verbal Fluency and Boston Naming Tests). This test also appears to be sensitive to cerebral pathology. Benedict et al. (1996) found that patients with dementia performed poorly on this test.

Strengths and Limitations

The BVMT-R appears to be effective in detecting memory impairment. The major advantages of this test are its six equivalent forms and the inclusion of learning, delayed, recall, and recognition components. It can be administered in approximately 15 minutes, plus additional 25 minutes to assess delayed memory recall.

The standardization sample used to develop this test included 588 healthy volunteers with an average age of 38.6 years (range 18 to 88) and an average educational level of 13.4 years. The manual contains data on the proportion of normals and patients with neurological disorders who fall within the various score ranges. Its overall test–retest reliability is good. Since this test tends to be moderately correlated with the patient's age and intellectual functioning, it needs to be broken down this way. As a consequence, interpretations of the performance of individuals with low levels of intellectual functioning should be made with caution. This test is inappropriate for patients who have significant visual acuity, constructional, or perceptual difficulties (visual field cuts).

BUSCHKE SELECTIVE REMINDING TEST

The Buschke Selective Reminding Test (SMT) (Buschke, 1973; Buschke and Fuld, 1974) measures verbal learning and memory. It consists of the presentation of a list of 10 or 12 unrelated words. After the list has been presented, the individual is instructed to recall as many words as possible from the list. Words that are not recalled are repeated by the examiner on the next trial. The trials are continued until the individual is able to repeat the entire list. Normal controls are typically able to recall a list of ten unrelated words by the third trial (Buschke and Fuld, 1974). It can be administered to children who are 5 to 15 years of age. It can be administered to adults ranging from 18 to 91 years of age. A number of different versions of this test exist.

Reliability and Validity

As a result of the manner in which this test is administered, it has been difficult to assess its test–retest reliability (Hannay and Levin, 1985). Modest correlations have been demonstrated between this test and other tests of verbal learning and memory (Shear and Craft, 1989). It has also been used with some success to evaluate the memory functioning of patients who have sustained severe traumatic brain injuries. Levin et al. (1979) found that performance on this test was grossly impaired in patients who were moderately or severely cognitively disabled at the time they were tested.

Strength and Limitations

The SMT allows the clinician to distinguish between retrieval from short- and long-term memory (Strauss et al., 2006). It appears to have few practice effects when it is readministered to patients with neurological disorders. Practice effects can be seen when it is readministered to normal subjects. This test has been used to identify patients with dementia or severe brain injuries since these patient groups are usually unable to improve their performance over the learning trials (Levin et al., 1979). Poor performance can also reflect attentional difficulties, hearing loss, anxiety, depression, physical pain and discomfort, use of anticonvulsive or antipsychotic medications, headaches, chronic medical conditions (e.g., endocrine or metabolic disorders), low premorbid intellectual functioning, chronic alcohol use, hysteria, or suboptimal motivation.

CALIFORNIA VERBAL LEARNING TEST

This test was designed to provide an assessment of the strategies and processes involved in learning and remembering verbal material (Delis et al., 1987). It was modeled after the Rey Auditory Verbal Learning Test (RAVLT). The test consists of two 16-item word lists that contain four words from each of four different semantic categories (e.g., fruits and tools). Words from the same category are never presented to the patient consecutively, which forces the patient to use an active semantic clustering strategy in recalling the words. The test measures both the patient's recall and recognition of the word list over five learning trials. After the list of 16 words is presented to the patient over five consecutive learning trials, a different list of 16 words again containing four words from each of four semantic categories is presented for one trial. Two of the semantic categories on the second list are the same categories as the first list, while the other two categories are different. After being given one trial of the new list, the patient must recall words from the first list under both free and category-cued recall conditions. After a 20-minute delay, during which time the patient is involved in a nonverbal task, the patient is asked to recall the first list again under free- and cued-recall conditions.

Through the use of this procedure, the California Verbal Learning Test (C-VLT) is able to determine the patient's levels of total recall and recognition across each learning trial, semantic and serial learning strategies, serial position effects, learning rate across trials, recall consistency across trials, degree of vulnerability to proactive and retroactive interference, retention of information over short and longer delays, enhancement of recall by the use of category cues and recognition testing, indices of recognition performance (e.g., discriminability and response bias) based on the use of signal detection theory, perseverations and intrusions in recall, and false positives in recognition testing (Spreen and Strauss, 1998).

The test is appropriate for individuals between 17 and 80. A children's version has been developed and can be administered to children 15 and 16 (Delis et al., 1994). Although the format is similar to the adult version, the child is asked to learn and recall 15 words (five words from each of three semantic categories). A short nine-word form has been developed to evaluate older patients who are cognitively impaired (Libon et al., 1996). The first list of words consists of three items from three categories (fruits, vegetables, and clothing), and the second nine-word list is drawn from three different categories (fruits, tools, and baked goods).

The instructions for the administration of this test are contained within the manuals. The test can be administered using either a paper-and-pencil or computer format (in the latter the psychologist enters the patient's response into the computer at the time of administration). The test can usually be administered in approximately 35 minutes. Scoring can be done manually or through computer software. The latter is more efficient in tabulating the results of the numerous analyses and is also cost-effective.

Reliability and Validity

Correlation coefficients of the various scores on this test ranged from poor to moderate (0.12 to 0.79), after the test was administered to 21 normal adults who were tested over 1 year later. The practice effects of this test were very pronounced, with an average increase of 12 to 15 words total over the five trials when the test was administered for the second time (McCaffrey et al., 1995). When test–retest correlations were done on children, practice effects were also seen on retesting, but were only modest depending on the age of the child. Thus, retesting is likely to produce higher test scores.

Schmidt (1997) found that the recall consistency index was substantially confounded by the number of words recalled, which is likely to create problems with respect to interpreting the test scores. For example, while the Category Clustering Index may be interpreted with confidence, Spreen and Strauss (1998) recommend that neuropsychologists be cautious in interpreting the Serial Clustering Index, because it tends to increase with the number of words in a patient's recall. When the California Verbal Learning Test was compared to the RAVLT, moderate correlations were found in their respective test variables (Crossen and Wiens, 1994). When normal patients were compared, they tended to score slightly higher on the California than on the Rey, which may reflect the fact that the California contains 16 vs. 15 words for the Rey. This study also suggests the possibility that the California lists are easier to learn since they contain built-in semantic categories.

When comparisons were made in patients who had sustained moderate to severe traumatic brain injuries, no significant differences were found between these batteries with respect to the patients' raw scores or the correlations between the raw scores and these tests. Even when both tests were given on the same day with an interval of 2 to 4 hours between administrations, Crossen and Wiens (1994) found no significant effects based on the order of presentation. The California Verbal Learning Test appears to correlate well with others tests of learning and memory, including the Wechsler Memory Scale, the WAIS-R, the SMT, and the Recognition Memory Test (Spreen and Strauss, 1998).

Strengths and Limitations

This test can be helpful in distinguishing different memory disorders in adults and children. Because it tends to identify the cognitive strategies used by patients who are asked to learn and recall verbal material, it may also be helpful in planning cognitive rehabilitation strategies for patients with significant memory deficits. The manuals are generally well written and provide interpretive guidelines for the various derived test scores.

One of the major limitations of using this particular test is the relatively low, and at times poor, test–retest reliability and a tendency for patients to score significantly higher when they are retested. Delis et al. (1987) cautioned psychologists that their norms may not be representative for the United States population in terms of demographic variables such as education, race, and region and, therefore, should be interpreted with caution. More recently Randolph et al. (1994) found that when the norms for this test suggest a mild deficit, the individual's performance most likely falls in the normal range, particularly if the individual being tested is educationally limited. In addition, the normative sample used in this test has been criticized as being relatively small. Finally, emotional factors such as depression may lower the patient's score 0.5 to 1.0 standard deviations below age- and sex-corrected norms for nondepressed populations (Otto et al., 1994).

CALIFORNIA VERBAL LEARNING TEST — CHILDREN'S VERSION

This test is similar to the California Verbal Learning Test (CVLT) and can be administered to individuals ranging in age from 5 to 16 years and 11 months. There is also a modified Spanish version of this test. This test takes 15 to 20 minutes to administer. In addition, 20 minutes must be allowed to accommodate the delayed–recall interval during which nonverbal unrelated tasks are given. This test also utilizes scoring software, which requires approximately 10 minutes and provides over 20 normed-based scores. A normative sample consisted for 920 children in 12 age groups ranging from 5 years to 16 years 11 months. The test norms were stratified based on demographic information. Additional norms are now available for 4 year olds (Goodman et al., 1999).

Reliability and Validity

Many of the test variables have very low test–retest reliability. Practice effects based on test–retest samples appear considerable. The relationship between the CVLT-C and children's learning tests is scant. Correlations with nonverbal learning paradigms and between the Children's Category Test and CVLT-C were found to be low to moderate indicating that the two tests seem to measure different dimensions of learning (Donders, 1998). This test appears to be predictive of long term educational outcome after closed head injury and appears to account for more variance in the prediction of special education needs than do demographic or neurological variables such as this severity of injury.

Strengths and Limitations

The CVLT-C appears to be an excellent instrument for measuring verbal memory in children. Studies have demonstrated its sensitivity and utility in both clinical and research settings. Predicting special education placement after brain injury is considerably enhanced because of its strong predictive power. This test may also have some utility predicting the outcome of other patient groups.

While this test provides vast number of scores, their psychometric properties are somewhat weak. As a consequence many of the CVLT-C variables have test-reliability coefficients that are below acceptable standards for clinical use, and may be too low for research. This means that the performance of any given individual may reflect factors that do not appear to be fully understood. In addition, there appears to be some question as to whether the CVLT-C process variables accurately reflect the individual's executive functions (Strauss et al., 2006). The interpretation of the test data is confusing. Clinicians should not infer organic pathology if all of these scores are not in the same range because of variations of the pattern.

California Verbal Learning Test — II

The California Verbal Learning Test — II (CVLT-II) tests an individual's recall and recognition of two-word lists over immediate and delayed memory trials (Delis et al., 2000). The second edition incorporates new developments in field and tries to rectify some of the criticisms that had been made about the first edition. The second edition includes new words list that are easier to understand than in the first edition, a larger normative database, new measures to analyze aspects of learning and memory, an optional force choice recognition task, alternate and short forms, and updated scoring software.

The subject is asked to recall words from list A immediately after the list is presented during the first five trials. List A consist of 16 words, 4 from each of 4 semantic categories (furniture, vegetables, ways of traveling, and animals). A 16 word interference list (list B), which includes vegetables and animal words, also introduces two additional categories (musical instruments and parts of a house) and is presented for one trial followed by short delay-free recall of list B and then recall of list A. After a 20 minute delay, during which nonverbal testing takes place, a long delay-free recall, long delay acute recall, yes/no recognition trials of list A are administered. An optional forced-choice recognition trial is given 10 minutes after the yes/no recognition trial (Strauss et al., 2006).

Approximately 50 minutes are required to administer this test. While hand scoring of the CVLT-II is possible, the use of computer software not only markedly decreases the amount of time necessary for test scoring, but also provides raw and standardized scores for more than 50 learning and memory variables. The examiner can also print one or any combination of three different reports. The core report (provides raw and standardized scores for 27 most commonly used CVLT-II measure), the expanded report (provides raw and standardized scores for 66 normed variables in the long form and 51 in the short form), and the research report (which provides raw scores for more than 269 nonnormed variables).

The normative sample for the CVLT-II was based on 1087 normal volunteers ranging in age from 16 to 89 whose educational background ranged from less than grade 9 to more than 16 years. The sample was also matched according to race/ethnicity, education, and region. The norms are derived by converting the raw scores on the list A trials I to V, total measure to age and gender corrected T scores with the mean of 50 and a standard deviation of 10. The raw scores on the other CVLT-II measures have been converted to age and gender corrected Z scores with the mean of 0 and the standard deviation of the 1. The raw scores on the alternate form are calibrated with the standard form.

The computer software provides the following information Levels of total recall and recognition on all trials; learning strategies (e.g., semantic clustering, serial clustering, subjective clustering); primary — recent effects and recall, rate of new learning per trial, consistency of item recall across all trials, degree of vulnerability to proactive and retroactive interference, retention of information over short and longer delays, enhancement of recall performance by category queuing and recognition testing, breakdown of recognition performance (discriminability and response bias) derived from signal — detection theories; indices reflecting the relative integrity of encoding, storage and retrieval processes; analysis of intrusion — types and recall (e.g., semantically related, semantically unrelated, across list intrusions); repetition errors in recall; analysis of false positive types and recognition testing; and indices of test taking effort (Strauss et al., 2006).

Reliability and Validity

The test–retest reliability was assessed by giving the standard form of the CVLT-II to a sample of 78 subjects ranging in the age from 16 to 80 years anywhere from 9 to 49 days later. A reliability coefficient measuring the patient's achievement on the learning or recalling total recognition discrimination were found to be high; however, the reliability for measures such as percent recall total learning, slope, trial 1, total repetitions were poor. Subjects intended to learn but eat more words in the five learning trials when they were later retested.

The CVLT-II correlates highly with this predecessor when the CVLT and the CVLT-II were given on a counter balanced order. The mean interval between test administrations was 7 days. Although most of the test–retest reliability coefficients were adequate to high, free-recall intrusion was only marginal.

The norms used in the CVLT-II appear to be more representative of the educational level of the US population. Since the differences in the CVLT and CVLT-II raw scores appear negligible, the authors have suggested that the best method for comparing a person's relative performance on the two tests is to carefully examine any changes in the raw scores rather than in their standardized scores (Strauss et al., 2006).

Strengths and Limitations

The CVLT-II is among one of the common memory assessment instruments used by neuropsychologists (Rabin et al., 2005). The CVLT-II shows considerable promise of being a valuable tool to characterize the unique learning and memory profiles of various neurological and psychiatric disorders. It has been used to measure the memory of patients with focal frontal lesions (Baldo et al., 2002). These patients showed poor overall recall and showed an increased tendency to make intrusion, reduced semantic clustering errors and were impaired on yes/no recognition. However, their forced choice recognition scores were normal. When this issue was carefully examined, patients with focal frontal lesions tended to mistakenly endorse two types of distractors semantically related words and words from the interference list consistent with the frontal lobes role in the selection of relevant activations and the inhibition of the irrelevant activations.

The normative data in the first edition of the CVLT was criticized for being two stringent probably because of the high level of education in the normative sample. The norms used in the CVLT-II appear to be more representative of the educational level of the US population. Since the differences in the CVLT and CVLT-II raw scores appear negligible; the authors have suggested that the best method for comparing a person's relative performance on the two tests is to carefully examine any changes in the raw scores rather than in their standardized scores (Strauss et al., 2006).

Moore and Donders (2004) have found that individuals who are involved in personal injury litigation or have a prior psychiatric history are likely to produce invalid test performances on the CVLT-II. Individuals who have longstanding emotional problems may also be likely to make reattribution errors associated with the underestimation of their premorbid problems and the augmentation of their cognitive and semantic symptoms. For many clinicians, interpretation of the CVLT-II test results is confusing. Clinicians should not infer pathology if all of these scores are not in the same range because of the variations and patterns of performance that were found in the normative sample. Thus, chance factors may contribute to many of the CVLT-II variables (Donders, 1999).

CHILDREN MEMORY SCALE

The Children Memory Scale (CMS) was designed to assess learning and memory in children and adolescents (Cohen, 1997). It was designed with five primary goals — consistency with current conceptualizations and research on learning and memory; sensitivity to developmental changes; capability for comparison between memory and intelligence; inclusion of clinically and educationally relevant tasks; and inclusion of motivating, child friendly tasks within the context of a standardized assessment tool. This test was designed to help psychologists identify learning and memory disorders in children and adolescents, isolate deficits in their learning and recall strategy, and play an important role in the design of remedial training programs for memory deficits.

The CMS assesses memory in three different ways. The temporal dimension (immediate vs. delayed recall), modality (verbal vs. visual), and testing format (recall vs. recognition). This test provides a general memory score that serves as a single composite score that reflects average memory performance across verbal and visual domains. It consists of nine main subtests, six of which are core subtests that contribute to the index scores. This test usually takes 30 to 45 minutes to administer, not including the 30 minute delay interval. Thus, it usually takes an hour even longer to administer the test. Three supplemental subtests can be administered during the delay interval, which usually takes another 10 to 15 minutes of testing time.

The CMS appears relatively simple to administer. The instructions are clearly printed on the test booklets. The start point, discontinuation point, and scoring information are contained on the test protocols. Slightly different tests or administration procedures are used depending on the age of the child. Children who are between 5 and 8 years of age are administered different tests than children who are 9 years and older.

Scoring the test by hand, although possible, can be lengthy and complex. Fortunately, the test comes with computer software that significantly improves the ease of scoring. The CMS norms were based on a random sample of the 1000 American children ranging from 5 to 16. They were stratified according to age, race/ethnicity, geographic region, and parental education.

Reliability and Validity

Test–retest reliability coefficients over the general memory, attention–concentration, and verbal immediate indices are high. The test–retest reliability of the index scores was based on a sample of 125 children from standardization sample who were tested twice after a mean interval of approximately 60 days. These data unfortunately show very poor test–retest reliability for the visual immediate and visual delayed indices as well as poor reliability for the delayed recognition index. This may be due to some ceiling effects.

For some index scores the practice effects are substantial. This is particularly true for general memory. For example, the test scores for the adolescence subgroup increased by 20 standard score points at retesting. Most other indices increased by ten points or more. Practice effects, however, were found to be minimal on attention/concentration and the delayed recognition indices. Interrelated reliability of the core subtest scores and indices was very high with all the correlations being in excess of 0.98.

Since the CMS and WAIS-III can be administered to 16-year-old adolescents, their performances on these tests were found to be similar on the basis of their correlations between the indices with the two versions supporting the convergent validity of the CMS. For example, the correlations between the CMS verbal indices and the WMS-III auditory memory index ranged from 0.63 to 0.74. Since the convergent and divergent validity scores for the visual index were not as strong and produced only modest correlations between the visual delayed indices on both measures, the visual memory indices of the CMS and WMS-III are difficult to interpret in a clinical context when the same individual has been administered both tests over time.

Strengths and Limitations

The CMS was published in 1997 and is widely used by psychologists who evaluate children and adolescents. It has several strengths; for example, it allows a broad comprehensive assessment of memory and learning. The test materials are well designed and user friendly. The standardization sample appears to be large and well constructed.

The CMS, however, has some limitations. It has very few manipulative and ecological relevant tasks. While it is easy to administer, it is difficult to score by hand. The time needed for test administration is relatively long, which can be problematic for some children, particularly, those who have limited stamina or behavioral problems. It does not provide adequate coverage of visual attention and visual working memory. Interpretation of the index scores and subtests with respect to localizing brain damage is not recommended. No validation studies are available for the proposed neuroanatomical correlates of the CMS index scores (Strauss et al., 2006).

Continuous Visual Memory Test

The Continuous Visual Memory Test (CVMT) (Trahan and Larrabee, 1988) is a continuous visual recognition memory test which consists of three tasks, the acquisition task (which tests recognition memory by requiring the patient to discriminate new vs. old or repeated stimuli from a set of 112 complex designs presented in rapid sequence); the delayed recognition task (after a 30-minute delay the subject must recognize the old stimuli from sets of perceptually similar stimuli); and the visual discrimination task (which assesses the patient's ability to perceive and discriminate the stimuli adequately in order to distinguish visual discrimination deficits from visual memory problems).

Reliability and Validity

The test–retest reliability of this test was examined in a sample of 12 neurologically normal adults after a 7-day retest interval. The reliability coefficients were found to be 0.85, 0.80, and 0.76 for the three tasks, respectively. The construct validity of these tests was examined by Trahan and Larrabee (1984) using 92 neurologically normal adults ranging in age from 18 to 61. They found that a patient's performance on this test was only moderately correlated with performance on the Delayed Visual Reproduction subtest of the WAIS-R. Thus, an individual's score on this test may not correlate well with performance on other tests of memory. Trahan and Larrabee (1988) did, however, find that when this test was administered to patients who had sustained severe traumatic brain injury, dementia of the Alzheimer's type, or significant amnestic disorders, all three patient groups performed significantly below age-matched controls. They argued that this finding supports the use of this test as a measure of visual memory because it demonstrates sensitivity to patient populations that are well known to have significant memory deficits.

Strengths and Limitations

The CVMT appears to be well suited for patients who have significant motor impairments, because the administration of this test does not require them to perform any tasks requiring drawing or construction. While individuals with mild to moderate depression and other mild psychiatric conditions appear to perform normally on this test, it is not appropriate for individuals who are severely depressed or have significant visual impairments or visual field cuts. If any visual designs or stimuli are shown to the patient inadvertently during the 30-minute waiting time before they are administered the Delayed Recognition task, it could impair their recognition of the previously shown test stimuli. Thus, patients who are given this test should be given only verbal tests during this 30-minute delay.

Individuals who have limited intellectual functioning, are severely cognitively impaired, or have significant psychiatric problems should also not be given this test because they may not comprehend the test instructions or pay sufficient attention to the test stimuli presented. Similarly, individuals with significant attention-deficit disorders or frontal lobe pathology may respond impulsively to the test stimuli or display behavioral rigidity (i.e., perseveration) in their test responses.

While this test was designed to be given to individuals ranging in age from 18 to 91, considerable caution should be used when interpreting the scores of persons over the age of 80, since the normative sample contains relatively few individuals in this age range. The educational level in the normative sample ranged from 4 years of education to postgraduate training. The vast majority of the subjects used in the normative sample had at least a high school education. Therefore, some caution should be used when interpreting the scores of individuals who have less than a high school education.

Since this test relies heavily on the patient's visual and auditory skills, subjects with corrected vision that is worse than 20/60 may not have sufficient visual acuity to perform this test. This is also true for patients who have severe visual neglect. This test can usually be administered in approximately 45 to 50 minutes, including a 30-minutes waiting time for the delayed recognition task. During this delay, the patient should not be given any tests that involve the presentation of geometric designs because these stimuli may impair performance on the recognition task or confound an interpretation of the performance on this test.

RECOGNITION MEMORY TEST

The Recognition Memory Test (RMT) (Warrington, 1984) was designed to assess recognition memory for printed words and photographs of faces. Each part consists of a target list of 50 stimulus pictures (50 words or 50 unfamiliar male faces) that are shown to the patient one at a time. The patient is asked to judge whether the word or face is pleasant. Immediately after the 50 items are shown, the patient is given a forced-choice recognition task in which he or she must indicate which items were previously shown. The patient's score is the number of items correctly recognized on each task. The test can usually be administered in approximately 15 minutes. The examiner can also determine the patient's word/face discrepancy score to determine whether the individual's memory is impaired for verbal and visual material.

Reliability and Validity

While test–retest reliability studies are not available, this test appears to be sensitive to the presence of cognitive impairment in neurologically compromised and brain-damaged patients, particularly patients who have Alzheimer's disease or mild brain atrophy (as shown on a CT or MRI scan). Patients with right-hemisphere brain damage did not demonstrate impairment when they were asked to recognize words, but were found to be impaired when they were asked to recognize faces. Patients with left-hemisphere damage were impaired in their ability to recognize both words and faces (Spreen and Strauss, 1998).

Strengths and Limitations

The RMT can be easily administered and scored. It permits the neuropsychologist to evaluate an individual's verbal and nonverbal (visual) recognition memory. Since it does not require specific motor responses, it may be particularly appropriate for individuals who are physically handi-capped or hemiplegic. Unfortunately, the test has no test–retest reliability data or parallel forms. The verbal section of this test may not be appropriate for individuals who are severely dyslexic or who were raised in a different cultural or linguistic environment. Individuals who have severe visual acuity difficulties cannot be administered the visual section of this test. This test appears to provide additional information to neuropsychologists who rely on traditional tests of memory functioning.

While this test was not designed as a test to evaluate the patient's motivation, it appears to have been used with good success in detecting individuals who are exaggerating or feigning memory impairment (Iverson and Franzen, 1994; Millis and Putnam, 1994). Since the test requires the individual to respond either "yes" or "no" during the recognition task, scores that are below chance (fewer than 20 correct) suggest that the individual's performance was most likely due to submotivational factors.

REY AUDITORY VERBAL LEARNING TEST

The Rey Auditory Verbal Learning Test (RAVLT) is a popular and widely used test to assess verbal learning using a fixed order word list (Schmidt, 1996). After the patient has been instructed to remember as many words as possible, the examiner orally presents a list of 15 words (list A) at a rate of 1 per second. After the entire list of words has been presented, the patient must recall them, in any order. The examiner must write down the words in the order the patient recalls them and note whether the patient's responses are incorrect or repeated. When the patient cannot recall any more words, the entire list of words is presented again, and the patient is asked to recall as many words as possible. The list is presented a total of five times (trials I through V). After the patient has completed the fifth trial, the examiner presents the patient with a list of 15 new words (list B). Once again the patient is instructed to remember as many words as possible (trial VI). This second list is presented only once. After the patient is able to recall as many of the new words as possible, the examiner instructs the patient to recall as many words as possible from the original list (trial VII).

Some neuropsychologists will also ask the patient to recall as many words as possible after a delay of 30 minutes. In addition, the patient may later be presented with either a short story or a list of 45 words that contain the 15 words from the first list. The patient is instructed to identify these words as the story is being read slowly or as a list of 45 words is visually presented to them. This serves as a test of recognition memory to determine if the patient's memory impairment is due to faulty encoding (e.g., processing difficulties at the time the information was initially presented or retrieved from memory) or storage loss (e.g., information was lost due to faulty storage).

Scoring consists of the total number of words the patient is able to recall during each of the five learning trials, the number of words recalled from the second list, and the number of words from the first list after the interference trial. The patient's scores can be compared to norms for manual laborers, professionals, students, elderly laborers, and elderly professionals as well as to brain-damaged patients (Lezak, 1995). Norms are available for individuals ranging in age from 7 to 89.

Reliability and Validity

The test–retest reliability with intervals ranging from 6 to 14 days was found to be moderately high for trials IV, V, and VII, delayed recall, and recognition of list A words, but relatively low for trials I, II, and III, and list B words (Geffen et al., 1994). The test–retest reliability for intervals of 1 month was also found to be moderately high for trials I to V (0.61 to 0.86) and delayed recall and recognition trials (0.51 to 0.72) (Delaney et al., 1992), and for intervals of 1 year for trials I through V (Uchiyama et al., 1995). The concurrent validity of this test, in comparison with other measures of memory, has also been reported to be moderately high (Moses, 1986). This test has been reported to be effective in discriminating between normal adults and neurologic patients. Powell et al. (1991) found that a score of 12 or less on trial V could correctly classify 78% of the normals and 70% of the neurological patients.

Strengths and Limitations

Careful analysis of variables such as the patient's learning curve over the learning trials, the type and number of errors made, the relative loss of words recalled after the interference trial, and a comparison of the patient's performance on the fifth trial of the first list with the number of words the patient is able to recognize during the recognition trial can help the neuropsychologist determine if the patient is cognitively impaired or is trying to simulate memory impairment. For example, brain-damaged patients are likely to show a flat learning curve over the first five consecutive learning trials and have difficulty recalling the first list of words after being presented with the second list (interference trial) with relatively intact verbal recognition performance. Most normal controls are usually able to learn between 10 and 14 of the 15 words by the end of five consecutive learning trials based on age and gender norms. Brain-damaged patients typically recall fewer words and often show a flatter learning curve. Normal controls (depending on their age and gender) are usually able to recall between 9 and 12 words after the interference trial and typically are able to recall 90% or more of the originally learned words (list A).

The administration of tests that have been specifically designed to assess motivation and effort of tests of verbal learning such as the Word Memory Test (Green, 2003) should be administered in conjunction with the this test to rule out the likelihood that poor performance on the RAVLT reflects the individual's suboptimal motivation. Poor performance on this test can also be due to nonneurological factors such as severe anxiety, marked depression, psychotic thinking, severe pain or headache, inattention due to excessive ruminative mental activity, medications, alcoholic dependency, or hysteria. Poor performance on this test should be corroborated with the clinical history, the patient's medical records, interviews with significant others, other neuropsychological test data, and observations of the patient's behavior.

REY–OSTERRIETH COMPLEX FIGURE TEST

The Rey–Osterrieth Complex Figure Test (ROCUT) consists of instructing the patient to copy a complex geometric figure onto a sheet of white paper. Although it has been recommended that the patient be given five or six colored pencils when copying this figure, there has been a growing trend to simply give the patient one pencil to copy the figure. The amount of time taken to initially copy the figure is recorded. The standard procedure is to have the patient draw the figure again from memory after a delay of 3 minutes and again after 30 minutes or 1 hour. Some neuropsychologists who have extensive experience with this test may eliminate the 3-minute-delay drawing and have the patient draw the figure from memory following a 30-minute to 1-hour delay.

A scoring system was developed by Taylor (1969), which was adapted from the original work of Osterrieth (1944). This system allows the examiner to score the patient's copy and drawing from memory of the figure using 18 separate criterion units contained within the figure, which can be scored separately. In addition, the examiner can provide partial credit (1/2 to 2 points) for each of the 18 units, depending on whether the unit was copied or drawn correctly, distorted, or absent. A score of 36 would constitute a perfect score during copying, while a score of 32 would place the subject at the 50th percentile with respect to normal controls. A score of 22 on the memory trial would place the subject at the 50th percentile.

Over the past 20 years, several neuropsychologists have attempted to develop a qualitative method of evaluating the patient's performance on this test. For example, Binder (1982) found that patients with left-hemisphere damage tend to break up the design into smaller units, while patients with right-hemisphere damage are likely to omit many of the elements contained within the design. Lezak (1983, 1995) reported that, overall, more patients with left-sided brain damage tended to simplify their copies than did patients with right-hemisphere brain damage. In addition, following a stroke, patients with right-hemisphere damage tended to produce much less accurate copies than did patients with left-hemisphere damage.

Reliability and Validity

The ROCVT was found to have moderate test–retest reliability after a 1-month interval (Spreen and Strauss, 1998). Its concurrent validity was moderately high in comparison with other tests of visual memory. It has been used with good success in identifying patients with various types of neurological disorders. It appears to be sensitive to traumatic brain injury and drug abuse. While patients with posterior brain damage are likely to have difficulty spatially organizing the figure, patients with frontal lobe pathology are likely to have difficulty in planning and organizing their drawing of the figure. There appears to be a tendency for patients with predominantly right-hemisphere brain damage to perform more poorly on the recall section of this test than patients with predominantly left-hemisphere brain damage. Patients with diffuse brain damage tend to perform worse than patients with chronic psychiatric conditions (Meyers and Meyers, 1995).

Strengths and Limitations

One of the major strengths of ROCVT is its ease of administration and scoring Psychologists should be cautious in concluding that an individual has brain damage based on poor test performance until suboptimal motivation can be ruled out by specialized tests and measures. Since poor performance on this test can be due to nonneurological factors such as poor drawing skills, depression, anxiety, or psychosis; motor difficulties secondary to orthopedic problems, physical pain, or hysteria, the neuropsychologist should not conclude that an individual has brain damage based on poor performance on this test unless it is supported by other test data and is consistent with the patient's medical records; information obtained from significant others, and the behavioral observations of the examiner.

RIVERMEAD BEHAVIORAL MEMORY TEST

The Rivermead Behavioral Memory Test (RBMT) was designed to detect impairment of everyday memory functioning, as well to monitor changes in the patient's memory following treatment (Wilson et al., 1985). It consists of 12 subtests that are based on a study of memory problems frequently experienced in traumatically brain-injured patients (Sunderland et al., 1983). Some of the tasks included within this test involve remembering a person's first and last name, where an item is hidden, an appointment, the gist of a short passage, a person's face, and a new route. Two test items such as remembering a short passage and a route around a room can be assessed both immediately and after a delay. The examiner presents the test stimuli, asks questions, traces the route, and records the patient's responses. There are four parallel versions of this test are available so that practice effects due to repeated testing can be minimized. The test can be administered in about 25 minutes.

Means for the patient's scores and standard deviations are provided for persons from ages 16 through 69 (Wilson et al., 1989a; 1989b). Each test may be scored on a three-point scale ranging from 0 to 2. Scores of 2 indicate normal functioning, scores of 1 indicate borderline performances, and scores of 0 indicate poor performance (lower 5%). The total memory score is the sum of the patient's test scores.

Reliability and Validity

Test–retest correlations, based on 118 patients who were tested twice, ranged between 0.78 for the screening score and 0.85 for the profile score. Performances on retesting tended to be slightly higher than initial testing. Test–retest correlations appear to be somewhat lower for the children's versions of this test and fall into the moderate range (Aldrich and Wilson, 1991). A patient's performance on this test has been found to be moderately correlated with other measures of memory (e.g., Corsi Block Span, Digit Span Test, RAVLT, and the Recognition Memory Test) (Spreen and Strauss, 1998). Patients who have sustained traumatic brain injuries appear to test lower than normal controls (Wilson et al., 1989b).

Strengths and Limitations

The RBMT appears to be a useful complement to many of the traditional memory assessment techniques. Its use of everyday tasks makes it a particularly useful measure in brain-injured and elderly patients. It appears to be ecologically valid and accurately predicts everyday memory functioning (Wilson et al., 1989b). It may also be helpful in predicting which patients who have sustained severe traumatic brain injuries can live independently in the community (Wilson, 1991). It does not appear to be significantly affected by the effects of anxiety or depression (Wilson et al., 1989b).

It does not appear to be influenced by high levels of anxiety or depression and appears to correlate fairly well with the duration of coma, duration of posttraumatic amnesia, and the patient's employment status (Geffen et al., 1991). It also seems to be helpful in predicting which severe traumatically brain-injured patients are able to live independently in the community.

One of the shortcomings of this test is that it may not be suitable for individuals who have sustained mild traumatic brain injuries (Wilson et al., 1989b) and may not be particularly sensitive to specific types of memory deficits (Goldstein and Polkey, 1992). As a consequence, it should only be used in conjunction with standardized memory tests, particularly if one is trying to determine an individual's memory or cognitive impairments and strategies for recalling recently acquired information.

RIVERMEAD BEHAVIORAL MEMORY TEST — SECOND EDITION (RBMT-II)

The Rivermead Behavioral Memory Test — Second Edition (RBMT-II) (Wilson et al., 2003) has made only minor changes to the original test an updated set of photographs that are more representative of the multiracial nature of society, a slight change in the scoring procedure for the route task, and use of a plastic rather than a hardboard box. Like the first edition it is not suitable to detect mild cognitive or memory impairment, and is most suitable for individual who have sustained moderate-to-severe cognitive or memory impairment (Strauss et al., 2006).

A children's version of this test has also been developed. It is identical to the adult version except that the two subtests (remembering a story and the orientation) have been modified. In addition, subtest 1 and 2 (name learning) and subtest 4 (remembering an appointment) are not scored for children less than 8 years of age. While the RBMT-II was designed as a screening test it does not appear to be sufficiently sensitive to detect mild cognitive deficits.

RUFF-LIGHT TRAIL LEARNING TEST

This test was designed to assess visuospatial learning and memory in adults and to be integrated into a more comprehensive neuropsychological battery (Baser and Ruff, 1987; Ruff and Allen, 1999). It was developed to avoid the necessity of intact drawing skills, good eyesight and motor control, visual-motor integration, and recognition memory to perform well. It was also designed to minimize verbal mediation, and verbal learning skills, correlate with measures of visual-motor skills and visual memory, and to be sensitive to right-hemispheric dysfunction.

It can be administered to individuals whose ages range from 16 to 70 years of age. Normative data are available for two age groups (16–54 and 55–70). There are no norms available for children or individuals whose ages all outside of this range. It consists of a Professional Manual, Stimulus Cards 1 and 2, and the Test Booklet. The test consists of instructing the subject to trace with his or her index finger a line connecting 17 circles from the Start and End designations. As the subject is in the process of connecting the circles, they are given two to as many as five different choices when going to the next circle. The subject is informed by the examiner whether the choices made are correct or incorrect. If an incorrect choice is made, the subject is instructed to make another choice until the correct choice is made. This procedure allows each subject to make multiple errors throughout the entire test. The test ends when the subject has completed the entire 15-step trail. Successive trials are administered until the subject has gone through the 15-step trail ten times, or until the trail is recalled without an error on two consecutive trials. Long-term recall is assessed by asking the subject to retrace the trail after a 60-minute delay.

Reliability and Validity

Test–retest reliability between the alternative test forms was found to be relatively low, but statistically significant for total correct and total step errors. Since Stimulus Card 2 was initially found to be more difficult than Stimulus Card 1, a new Stimulus Card 2 was developed and experimentally tested. This significantly improved the test–retest reliability. Correlations between this test and a variety of other neuropsychological tests found significant correlations with other tests of visual–spatial memory, and attention (Ruff and Allen, 1999).

Strengths and Limitations

This test has been found to be effective in distinguishing individuals who have sustained damage to their right rather than left hemisphere (Mahalick et al., 1991). The two versions of this test have high test–retest reliability and appear valid. Clinical uses of this test are limited by the background and expertise of the examiner. Interpretations of the test scores for clinical and diagnostic purposes should not be attempted without a clear understanding of brain and behavior relationships and the medical and psychological factors which affect them.

WECHSLER MEMORY SCALE — REVISED

The WAIS-R (Wechsler, 1987) is an updated version of the original Wechsler Memory Scale. Unlike the original Wechsler Memory Scale, this contains delayed recall measures, provides a better assessment of the patient's visual/nonverbal memory, and has better norms. It was intended to be administered to individuals ranging in age from 16 to 74. It contains the following subtests.

1. Information and orientation — simple questions cover biographical data, orientation, and informational questions.
2. Mental control — the patient must recite a series of numbers or letters.
3. Figural memory — the patient must visually examine abstract designs and then later identify them from an array.
4. Logical memory I — the patient must recall information from two orally presented stories.
5. Visual paired associates I — the patient is shown six abstract line drawings that are paired with different colors and then is later asked to indicate the appropriate color associated with the figure during learning trials.
6. Verbal paired associates I — the patient is read a group of eight word pairs, then must recall the second word after hearing the first word during learning trials.
7. Visual reproduction I — the patient is briefly shown geometric designs that must be drawn.
8. Digit span — the patient is required to recall digits forward and backward.
9. Visual memory span — the patient must tap forward and backward in a particular sequence demonstrated by the examiner.

After these nine subtests are administered, two verbal and two nonverbal subtests (Logical Memory II, Visual Paired Associates II, Verbal Paired Associates II, and Visual Reproduction II) are given to assess the patient's recall of information after a delay of approximately 30 minutes. The WAIS-R takes about 45 minutes to administer. After the patient's scores on each subtest are added, the psychologist must weight the patient's raw scores, sum the weighted scores of the subtests, and transfer these sums into the following index scores general memory, attention/concentration, verbal memory, visual memory, and delayed recall.

Reliability and Validity

The test–retest reliability of the WAIS-R has been found to range from only 0.41 (Verbal Paired Associated II) to 0.88 (Digit Span) with the median reliability coefficient of 0.74 (Wechsler, 1987). Chelune et al. (1989) and Mittenberg et al. (1991) found that individuals ranging in age from 20 to 34 improved approximately 12 raw-score points on the delayed memory index if they were retested within a 6-week interval, whereas older adults ranging in age from 70 to 74 improved an average of approximately 6 raw-score points when they were later retested. Thus, repeated testing during a 6-week interval is likely to produce a rather sizeable improvement in delayed recall, particularly in younger subjects.

The validity of the WAIS-R has been evaluated in conjunction with other tests of memory. Delis et al. (1988) found that the WAIS-R correlated highly with the California Verbal Learning Test. They found that the delayed memory index of the WAIS-R correlated 0.93 with the long-delay, free-recall score on the California Verbal Learning Test. In a similar study, Randolph et al. (1994) found that the WAIS-R indices and the California Verbal Learning Test scores for trials 1 through 5 were highly correlated. Butters et al. (1988) found that the WAIS-R indices were impaired when this test was administered to patients with significant neurological disorders.

Strengths and Limitations

An individual's performance on this test can be affected by practice effects if it is later readminstered. For example, Chelune, Bornstein, and Prifiters (1989) found that individuals ranging in age from 20 to 24 improved by 12 raw-score points on the delayed memory index when they were retested within a 6-week interval. Mittenberg (1991) found that individuals ranging in age from 70 to 74 made an average gain of 6 raw-score points when they were retested. Younger individuals are expected to attain the highest delayed recall scores if they are tested within a 6-week interval as a result of practice effects.

The verbal and visual memory indices cannot be used with any confidence to lateralize brain dysfunction (Loring et al., 1989). Emotional factors such as anxiety and depression can affect a patient's performance on this test, particularly on the Logical Memories and Visual Reproduction subtests. Since there are not built-in measures to assess the individual's motivation to perform to the best of their ability, concurrently administered tests and measures should be used to rule out suboptimal motivation.

WECHSLER MEMORY SCALE — III (WAIS-III)

The WAIS-III (Wechsler, 1997b) comprises 11 subtests with six primary subtests and five optional subtests. It was designed to be used with older adolescents ranging in age from 16 to 89. It was based on a representative sample of 1250 healthy adults, retained seven subtests from the WAIS-R, and added four new subtests.

1. Faces — the patient is shown a series of 24 photographs of faces and is told to remember each face. Later, the patient is presented with a second series of 48 faces and asked to indicate the faces he or she was initially asked to remember.
2. Family Pictures — a family photograph and series of scenes are presented. The patient must recall which individuals were in each scene, where they were located, and what they were doing.
3. Word Lists — a list of 12 unrelated words is orally presented to the patient. The patient is asked to recall as many words as possible over four learning trials. Later, a new list of 12 words is presented. The patient is then asked to recall as many words from the first list as he or she can. Finally, the patient is read 24 words and asked to indicate which words were on the first list.
4. Letter–Number Sequencing — the patient is shown a string of alternating letters and numbers and asked to repeat the string by putting the numbers together in ascending order and the letters together in alphabetical order. The length of the string gradually increases over trials.

Similar to the WAIS-R, the scores from the WAJS-III subtests are organized into summary index scores. The primary index scores are

1. Auditory immediate — the patient's ability to remember information immediately after it is orally presented.
2. Visual immediate — the patient's ability to remember information immediately after it is visually presented.
3. Immediate memory — the patient's ability to remember both visual and auditory information immediately after it is presented.
4. Auditory delayed — the patient's ability to recall orally presented information after a delay of approximately 30 minutes.
5. Visual delayed — the patient's ability to recall visually presented information after a delay of approximately 30 minutes.
6. Auditory recognition delayed — the patient's ability to recognize auditory information after a delay of approximately 30 minutes.
7. General memory — the patient's delayed memory capacity based on scores from Logical Memory II, Verbal Paired Associates II, Faces II, and Family Pictures II.
8. Working memory — the patient's capacity to remember and manipulate visually and orally presented information in short-term memory storage based on performance on the Spatial Span and Letter–Number Sequencing subtests.

Unlike the WAIS-R, the WAIS-III contains the following supplementary auditory process composites:

1. Single trial learning — the patient's capacity to immediately recall auditory memory after a single exposure to material.
2. Learning slope — the patient's ability to acquire new auditory information after repeated exposures.
3. Retention — the patient's delayed recall capacity as a function of immediate recall performance after a delay of approximately 35 minutes.
4. Retrieval — the patient's retrieval for recall vs. recognition memory.

Although the test manual indicates that the primary six subtests can be administered in 30 to 35 minutes, the entire battery usually requires approximately 1 hour to administer. However, individuals who are cognitively impaired or significantly depressed may require an hour and a half (Strauss et al., 2006).

Reliability and Validity

The test–retest reliability of the WAIS-III has been found to range from 0.62 to 0.82, with a median of 0.71 for the primary subtest scores, and from 0.70 to 0.88 (median = 0.82) for the primary indices. A patient's performance on retesting increased from approximately 0.33 to 1 standard deviation from the first to second testings. However, smaller improvements on retesting were seen in older patients ranging in age from 55 to 89 in comparison with individuals between the ages of 16 and 54. The correlation coefficients between the WAIS-III auditory immediate index and the WAIS-R verbal memory index, the WAIS-III visual immediate index and the WAIS-R visual memory index, and the WAIS-III immediate memory index and the WAIS-R general memory index were found to be 0.72, 0.36, and 0.62, respectively. Thus, comparisons made between the visual immediate index of the WAIS-III and the visual memory index of the WAIS-R may result in spurious conclusions as a result of the relatively low correlations between these measures.

Correlations between the WAIS-R and the WAIS-III range from 0.35 (visual immediate index) to 0.55 (WMI). However, a high correlation was found between the WMI of the WAIS-III and the WMI of the WAIS-R, because they shared a similar construct in addition to sharing one subtest. The correlations between the WAIS-R index and other measures on the WAIS-III ranged from 0.51 to 0.68.

Correlations between the WAIS-III indices and other measures of memory and cognitive ability have also been studied. For example, correlations between this test and the Microcog were found to be in the moderate range, but were somewhat lower than expected. While moderate correlations were found between this test and other measures of memory such as the California Verbal Learning Test and the Rey–Osterrieth Visual Figure Test, they were also lower than expected.

Strengths and Limitations

The WAIS-III is perhaps two of the most widely used scale to assess an adult's memory. It is relatively easy to administer and score. The WAIS-III has norms up to the age of 89. The test was standardized on a sample considered representative of the United States population. Although the WAIS-R takes approximately 45 minutes to administer, WMS-III can take twice as long, particularly if it is administered to brain-injured patients. Therefore, many neuropsychologists are reluctant to administer the full WMS-III battery.

Individuals who are severely cognitively or physically impaired may be inappropriate for the WMS-III or be at a major disadvantage if it is administered to them in a standardized manner. While some flexibility may be necessary on the part of the examiner in administering this test, particularly if the patient is hearing impaired or has a speech disability, any modifications in the mode of administration or instructions provided to a patient may invalidate the test norms and may impact the test scores.

When this test is administered to patients who are not fluent in English or to individuals for whom English is the second language, any attempt to translate the test items on an individual basis may render the normative data invalid (Strauss et al., 2006).

WIDE RANGE ASSESSMENT OF MEMORY AND LEARNING — SECOND EDITION

The Wide Range Assessment of Memory and Learning — Second Edition (WRAML-II) was designed to assess memory skills in children and adults (Sheslow and Adams, 2003). The WRAML-II contains verbal index subtest (story memory and verbal learning); visual index subtest (design memory and picture memory); and attention/concentration index subtest (windows and number–letter). It contains two optional subtests (sentence memory and sound — symbol) and two working memory subtest that are only given to children who are 9 years or older (Verbal working memory and symbolic working memory).

The Core battery consists of six subtests (two verbal, visual, and attentional/concentration subtests each). It also contains a screening battery that consists of the four of the Core battery subtests that are designed to assess visual and verbal memory. According to the test manual, the screening battery takes approximately 20 minutes while the core battery usually takes just under an hour to administer.

The age range for second edition was extended to adulthood. The visual learning subtest was eliminated. Optional subtests and new subtests that made up the Attention/Concentration Index were added. Subtests that assessed Delay Recall and Recognition were also added. The test was recalibrated on the basis of the basis of item difficulty. The test materials were updated, which included changes to some of the cards that are used during the test. The test manual was made considerably more detailed (Strauss et al., 2006).

The norms for WRAML-II were based on a national stratified sampling technique that included 1200 individuals who were matched according to gender, race–ethnicity, education, and geographic region. From each of the 15 age groups, 80 individuals were selected.

Reliability and Validity

While the test–retest reliability is high for the verbal memory index, WMI, and general memory index, the reliability for other indices (e.g., visual memory index) is unacceptably low and should not be used for clinical decision making. This might reflect the fact that the time between test administrations ranged from 2 weeks to longer than a year. The interrelater reliability for the subtest requiring subjective judgment was found to be quite high.

The WRAML-II was developed following an exhaustive test revision process that included reviews by expert users, preparation of a "try out" battery, the administration of this battery to several hundred children and adults, additional test analysis and refinement, and a full standardization process.

Strengths and Limitations

The original WRAML had some serious technical and methodological problems that included a lack of separate scale scores for delay and recognition memory as well as some theoretical problems (e.g., the test was not derived from any clear cut model of memory). All of these criticisms have been rectified in the second edition.

The WRAML-II manual is well-written and provides an exhausted review of the test psychometric properties. It also includes data in terms of reliability by age, stability coefficients from all scores including optional scores and subtests; and factor analysis for gender and ethnicity. The test allows for continuity between children and adults, which is a necessity in longitudinal studies or for clinical purposes when retesting is necessary.

While the test appears sensitive to memory impairment, there is no evidence that it can distinguish different types of memory disorders in children or adults. It was also questionable whether it is capable of monitoring changes in an individual's memory functioning over time. Finally, there appears to have been little work done on the ecological validity of this test. There are practice affects on the WRAML-II scores with an average gain of 6 to 7 points on most index scores. The largest increase appears to be from the memory screening index, while the attention-concentration index had smallest increase (Strauss et al., 2006).

TESTS TO ASSESS ABSTRACT THINKING

PROVERBS TEST

The Proverbs Test (Gorham, 1956) presents the patient with 12 proverbs of equivalent difficulty. The patient is given a sheet of paper and required to write out what each proverb means. A three-point scoring system is used and the patient receives 0, 1, or 2 points, depending on the level of abstract thinking contained in the answer. There is also a multiple-choice version of this test, which requires the patient to select one of four possible answers. Patients who sustain prominent diffuse brain damage or extensive damage to the frontal lobes typically have difficulty interpreting proverbs. For example, if they are asked to indicate what the proverb "Strike while the iron is hot" means, they will frequently say, "When the iron is hot, you strike it," thus failing to grasp the abstract principle contained within the proverb and instead providing a concrete interpretation based on the perceived physical properties contained within the proverb.

Reliability and Validity

This test appears to have adequate test–retest reliability. It appears to be sensitive to patients with bilateral frontal lobe pathology (Benton, 1968). It may not, however, differentiate between schizophrenic and brain-damaged patients.

Strengths and Limitations

A patient's interpretation of proverbs is highly correlated with level of intellectual functioning. On the other hand, intelligent and well-educated patients who were raised in a different culture or whose native language is not English will often have difficulty interpreting the proverbs. Patients who are psychotic may provide bizarre interpretations. For example, if a psychotic patient is asked to interpret the proverb, "Strike while the iron is hot," the patient may say, "When you get this strike, it just goes strike and it goes up to infinity. That shows you that it's in the seventh dimension and it doesn't have any wheels." Some patients with low premorbid intellectual functioning, limited educational, or culturally deprived backgrounds may not fully understand what a proverb is and may require some examples of proverbs to take this test in a meaningful manner.

SIMILARITIES TEST

The Similarities Test is one of the verbal subtests of WAIS-R and WAIS-III. The patient is asked how two words that represent common objects (e.g., table and chair) or concepts (e.g., democracy and monarchy) are alike. Scoring is based on a three-point scale (0, 1, and 2) according to the criterion examples found in the test manual.

Reliability and Validity

Both versions of this test appear to have high test–retest reliability. Poor scores on this test tend to be associated with left temporal and frontal lobe pathology (Newcombe, 1969). However, patients with left frontal lobe damage seem to do more poorly than patients with right frontal lobe damage (Bogen et al., 1972). A patient's score on this test tends to be sensitive to the effects of dementia (see, e.g., La Rue and Jarvik, 1987).

Strengths and Limitations

The Similarities Test is one of the subtests of the Wechsler Adult Intelligence Scale. It can usually be administered in 10 to 15 minutes. A person's score on this test can be compared with scores on the remaining verbal subtests to evaluate its clinical significance. This test is inappropriate for individuals who have been raised in a different culture or whose native language is not English. It is also inappropriate for individuals who are psychotic or severely depressed. The diagnosis of brain damage should not be made solely on the basis of an individual's performance on this test.

TESTS TO ASSESS CONCEPTUAL THINKING/PROBLEM-SOLVING SKILLS

CATEGORY TEST

The Category Test (Halstead, 1947; Reitan and Wolfson, 1993), which is one of the tests used in the Halstead–Reitan Battery, can be used to assess a patient's conceptual skills in determining the underlying principle in each of six sets of test items. The patient must depress a lever after being shown one of the test items. The patient hears a pleasant door chime for a correct answer or buzzer for an incorrect one. A detailed description of this test was presented earlier in this chapter.

Reliability and Validity

High test–retest reliability coefficients have been reported for both normal and brain-damaged adults (Spreen and Strauss, 1998) for intervals as long as 2 years. However, these coefficients tend to be lower in children and persons with psychiatric disorders. It seems to be sensitive to a variety of brain impairments and appears to be as sensitive as the full Halstead–Reitan battery in determining the presence of brain damage (Adams and Trenton, 1981).

Strengths and Limitations

While this test seems to be quite sensitive at detecting brain damage, it takes nearly 2 hours to administer. There appears to be considerable variability in the performance of healthy normal controls on this test, which suggests that misclassifying a normal individual as brain-damaged on the basis of his or her test performance can occur. Since factors such as age and education can affect a person's scores on this test, it is strongly recommended that a person's performance on this test should be compared to norms corrected for age and education. Unless this done elderly individuals who have a limited educational background are at high risk of being misclassified as brain-damaged. (The reader is strongly encouraged to review the section in this chapter that discusses the Strengths and Limitations of the Halstead Reitan Battery to obtain more information about this issue.)

RAVEN PROGRESSIVE MATRICES TEST

The Raven Progressive Matrices Test (Raven, [1938] 1996) is also a test of conceptual thinking and problem solving. A detailed description of this test can be found earlier in this chapter.

RUFF FIGURAL FLUENCY TEST

The Ruff Figural Fluency Test provides a measure of nonverbal fluency, similar to the Verbal Fluency Test, which requires the patient to generate as many words as possible beginning with specific letters of the alphabet (Ruff, 1988). This test examines a patient's nonverbal capacity for fluid and divergent thinking and ability to shift cognitive sets. The test consists of five parts, each representing a different stimulus pattern of dots, and the patient's task is to draw as many unique designs as possible within a specific period of time. Parts 2 and 3 contain the dot patterns of Part 1 with different distractors, while Parts 4 and 5 contain a variation of the original dot pattern. After the initial instructions have been given, the patient is given 60 seconds to produce as many designs as possible on Part 1. This process is repeated for Parts 2, 3, 4, and 5.

Reductions in the rate of the number of designs produced by a patient appear to be primarily related to inflexibility in producing novel designs. Patients frequently become locked into one or two strategies or never develop a particular strategy, which inhibits their ability to produce new designs. Scoring consists of counting the total number of unique designs and the number of perseverative errors (i.e., repetitions of the same pattern within the single stimulus sheet).

Reliability and Validity

Ruff, Light, and Evans (1987) used a normative sample of 358 volunteers ranging in age from 16 to 70, with educational levels ranging from 7 to 22 years. Test–retest reliability over a 6-month interval was found to be 0.76 for the number of unique designs produced. The test–retest reliability coefficients for perseverative raw scores are only 0.36. Ruff and his associates found that retesting produced higher scores (108.6 vs. 100.6) when the subjects were tested after a 6-month interval; however, they found that the number of perseverative errors the subjects made diminished.

Validity studies on this test have examined normal individuals and head-injured patients (Baser and Ruff, 1987). These studies demonstrated that this test could identify the head-injured patients. Ruff et al. (1994) found that this particular test tends to be sensitive to patients who have sustained damage to the right prefrontal lobe. Factor–analytical studies have shown that this test tends to be highly correlated with a patient's planning and flexibility skills (Baser and Ruff, 1987).

Children have also been assessed using this test. Evans et al. (1985) reported that a child's test performance on this test was correlated with their age. The clinical efficiency of this test was studied by Ruff et al. (1986) by comparing 35 brain-injured patients with 35 normal controls. The brain-injured patients were divided into moderate and severe brain-injured groups. They found that the performance of the severely brain-injured patients on this test was lower than patients with moderate brain injuries.

Strengths and Limitations

The major strengths of this test are its ease in administration and the relative time it takes to administer the entire test (approximately 10 minutes). Validity studies have demonstrated sensitivity to patients who have sustained severe traumatic brain injuries.

It can also be administered to children with fairly good results. This test does not appear to be appropriate for patients with significant motor deficits, particularly involving their dominant hand, or for those who have significant visual impairment. Patients who have high levels of anxiety or are significantly depressed may perform poorly on this test. Since this test has no built-in measure to determine if the individual taking the test is performing poorly due to suboptimal motivation, the use of concurrently administered tests to identify suboptimal motivation is recommended.

WISCONSIN CARD SORTING TEST

The Wisconsin Card Sorting Test (Berg, 1948; Grant and Berg, 1948; Heaton, 1981) evaluates a patient's problem-solving skills, cognitive flexibility, ability to maintain a particular conceptual set, and concept formation (Heaton et al., 1993). The current version of this test consists of 128 cards, each of which contains one to four symbols (triangle, star, cross, or circle) that are in one of four colors (red, green, yellow, or blue). The examiner places four cards in a horizontal array in front of the patient. The patient's task is to match the top card in a pack of 64 cards by placing it directly below one of the four cards above. The patient is given only minimal instructions on this test; however, the purpose of the test is to have the patient deduce the underlying sorting principle based on the feedback provided by the examiner after each card is sorted. After a patient has made ten consecutive correct responses, the underlying category automatically changes. For example, if the patient had been sorting correctly according to color, the underlying concept might change to form or number (Lezak, 1983, 1995).

Patients with frontal lobe damage will frequently continue sorting according to color even though they continue receiving negative feedback from the examiner. The patient, however, is never informed that the underlying category has changed and must deduce this based on the feedback received after making a response.

The patient is given a maximum of 128 cards to complete 6 categories. A patient's score on this test can be based on several different factors — number of categories completed before the supply of cards runs out, total number of errors made by the patient, percentage of correct responses, number of perseverations, number of perseverative errors, trials required to complete the first category, percentage of conceptual level responses, number of failure to maintain set errors, and ability to reduce errors over trials. These classifications permit the examiner to qualitatively analyze the patient's performance to determine the nature of the patient's impairments, as well as their clinical significance. A computerized version of this test is commercially available.

Reliability and Validity

The test–retest reliability for healthy children and adolescents who were tested approximately 1 month apart ranged from 0.37 to 0.72. Retesting may yield different performances on this test and is likely to produce significant practice effects (Lezak, 1995). This test has been found to be sensitive to patients with frontal lobe pathology by some investigators (e.g., Heaton et al., 1993), while other investigators (e.g., Stuss et al., 1983) found that patients with frontal lobe pathology did not differ from normal controls on this test. Patients with diffuse brain damage tend to perform on this test about the same as patients with frontal lobe pathology (Heaton et al., 1993; Strauss et al., 1993). Because of this, a patient's performance on the test is not necessarily indicative of frontal lobe pathology (Spreen and Strauss, 1998). Individuals with a variety of disorders (e.g., alcoholism, autism, multiple sclerosis, Parkinson's disease, and drug abuse) have been reported to test as impaired when administered this test (Adams et al., 1995).

Strengths and Limitations

Validity studies using this test have demonstrated an overall hit rate of 72% in its ability to discriminate between brain-damaged patients and normal controls. The manual that accompanies the test contains norms for normal controls, patients with frontal lobe pathology, patients with brain injuries that do not include the frontal lobes, and patients with diffuse brain damage.

This test has been shown to be sensitive to dorsolateral lesions of the frontal lobes (Stuss and Benson, 1986). On the other hand, it is relatively insensitive to orbital frontal lesions (Stuss and Benson, 1986). For example, individuals who sustain damage primarily to their orbital frontal lobes typically perform well on this test, particularly if they have an average or above average intellectual functioning.

Poor performance on this test can also reflect — visual impairment, color blindness, visual–perceptual difficulties, impaired hearing, psychotic thinking, severe depression or anxiety, histrionic behavior, suboptimal motivation, or malingering. To rule out these possibilities, it is essential that the examiner obtain a careful history from the patient, which includes a review of medical records, interviews with significant others, behavioral observations of the patient during testing and the clinical interview, review the patient's performance on this test with other neuropsychological tests, and administer concurrent test that measure motivation and effort.

TESTS THAT ASSESS THE EXECUTIVE FUNCTIONS OF THE BRAIN

EXECUTIVE FUNCTIONS OF THE BRAIN

The executive functions of the brain are poorly understood by the vast majority of psychologists and neuropsychologists. One of the many reasons for this is that the training of the neuropsychologist strongly emphasizes the administration, scoring, and interpretation of standardized neuropsychological tests and batteries using statistical comparisons to age and educationally corrected norms, rather than understanding the complex alterations of the patient's cognitive, behavioral, and emotional functioning following a brain insult. As a consequence, the assessment of a patient's executive functions is usually based on the particular neuropsychological test or tests that are administered to a patient, rather than an understanding of the neurobehavioral consequences caused by an insult to complex neural circuits and feedback loops that connect the frontal lobes with subcortical and other cortical structures (Sbordone et al., 1996; 1997; 2000).

Psychologists have traditionally relied on the use of one or more of the following neuropsychological tests to assess the frontal lobes or executive functions of the brain — Wisconsin Card Sorting Test, Halstead Category Test, D-KEFS, The Behavioral Assessment of the Dysexecutive Syndrome, COWAT, Ruff Figural Fluency Test, Tinker Toy Test, Stroop Test, Trail Making Test, Color Trails, Rey Complex Figure Test, and various motor tests such as the Finger Tapping, Purdue Pegboard, and Grooved Pegboard tests (Cripe, 1996; Sbordone, 2000).

A description of the more widely administered neuropsychological tests used by psychologists to assess executive dysfunction can be found below.

BEHAVIORAL ASSESSMENT OF THE DYSEXECUTIVE SYNDROME

The Behavioral Assessment of the Dysexecutive Syndrome (Wilson et al., 1996) was developed to predict problems in everyday functioning arising from impaired executive functions. This test consists of a collection of six novel tests and a questionnaire, which are similar to real-life activities likely to be problematic for patients with impaired executive functions

1. Rule shift cards test — examines the patient's ability to respond correctly to rule and shift from one rule to another.
2. Action program test — requires the patient to get a cork out of a tube without using any of the objects in front of him or her; but without lifting up the stand, the tube, or the glass beaker containing water; and without touching the lid with his or her fingers.
3. Key search test — requires the patient to develop a strategy to locate lost keys in an imaginary large square field.
4. Temporal judgment test — contains four open-ended questions.
5. Zoo map test — requires the patient to show how he or she would visit a series of designated locations on a map at a zoo following certain rules.
6. Modified six elements test — tests the subject's ability to perform three tasks, each of which is divided into two parts, attempting something from each subtest within a 10-minutes time period without violating any rules.
7. Dysexecutive questionnaire — a 20-item questionnaire that samples a patient's emotional and personality changes, motivational changes, behavioral changes, and cognitive changes. The entire test can be administered in approximately 30 minutes. The instructions for administration are given within the test manual. Some items have time components. Scoring for the entire battery is obtained by adding together the individual profile scores for each test. The patient's score on this test can range from 0 to 24 (Spreen and Strauss, 1998).

Reliability and Validity

The test–retest reliability for this test ranges from 0.08 (Rule Shift Cards) to 0.71 (Key Search). In general there is a tendency for brain-injured patients to improve on follow-up testing. The authors of the test have suggested that the test–retest correlations are not expected to be high since the first administration contains an element of novelty, which is a critical aspect of the dysexecutive syndrome. Wilson et al. (1996) have found that an individual's performance on this test is able to determine brain injury or normalcy. A patient's performance on this test appears to be associated with objective ratings of everyday executive function problems among brain-injured patients.

Strengths and Limitations

This test appears to be a useful tool for the evaluation of impaired executive functions in traumatically brain-injured patients, particularly those who appear to be cognitively well preserved and function well in highly structured settings. This test has been found to be a better predictor of a patient's executive functions in real-world situations than the Wisconsin Card Sorting Test (Wilson, 1993). Wilson et al. (1996) have also reported that scores on this test were able to differentiate patients with neurological disorders composed largely of closed head injuries from normal, healthy controls. They concluded that a patient's performance on this test was significantly correlated with the ratings of executive functions made by their significant others. Unlike many, if not all, standardized neuropsychological tests, this particular test forces the subject to organize and plan behavior over longer time periods, as well as set priorities in the face of two or more competing tasks. As a consequence, its test–retest reliability tends to be low. It may not be sensitive to patients who have sustained only mild traumatic brain injuries. Patients who are depressed, have significant hearing or visual impairments, or are significantly anxious may perform poorly on this test.

Delis-Kaplan Executive Function System (D-KEFS)

The Delis-Kaplan Executive Function System (D-KEFS) (Delis et al., 2001) has been designed to detect relatively subtle and even mild forms of executive dysfunction. The test utilizes a process-oriented approach, that allows each task to produce multiple scores to identify the source of any difficulties. The authors have also introduced a number of features that can increase the sensitivity of their tests to detect even mild brain damage.

The D-KEFS test was designed to be utilized in a flexible manner. For example, tests contained within this battery — trail making, verbal fluency, design fluency, color-word interference, sorting, 20 questions, word context, tower, and proverb — can be used alone or in combination with other D-KEFS tests. The examiner also has the option of omitting a particular test condition. The D-KEFS includes an alternate form for three of the tests that have been found to be most susceptible to practice effects sorting, 20 questions, and verbal fluency.

The entire battery usually takes about 90 minutes to administer. The scoring guidelines for each test can be found in the examiner's manual and the record form. For most measures, the test scores can be converted into scores that are scaled to the patient's age with a mean of 10 and a standard deviation of 3. The raw scores can also be converted to cumulative percentile ranks, which are corrected for each of these 16-age groups.

The D-KEFS utilizes both primary and operational measures. Primary measures provide a global overall characterization of the patient's test performance on a particular task or provide process scores for key components of the task. An analysis of both primary and operational measures provides for a more comprehensive assessment of executive functions.

This test was designed to be given to individuals ranging in age from 8 to 89 years of age. It was normed on 1750 individuals that were selected to match the U.S. population in terms of age, gender, race/ethnicity, education, and geographic region.

Reliability and Validity

The test–retest studies of the standard form of the D-KEFS based on a sample of 101 cases with the interval between test administration ranging from 9 to 74 days (average of about 25 days) ranged from low (with respect to the trail making and design fluency tests) to adequate/high for the lettering, and category fluency tests. Practice effects were evident for most of the tasks.

The correlations between the various tests tend to be low. This suggests that the tests are not interchangeable raises the possibility that the construct of executive functioning utilized in this battery may have weak convergent validity (Salthouse et al., 2003). Only one study has tried to correlate findings from the D-KEFS with another measure of executive functioning such as the Wisconsin Card Sorting Test. This study found moderate-to-high correlations ranging from 0.31 to 0.59 between the number of categories completed on the Wisconsin Card Sorting Test and the various D-KEFS measures from the nine tests. This finding suggests that the D-KEFS and Wisconsin Card Sorting Test may be assessing similar, but not identical underlying cognitive processes (Strauss et al., 2006).

Strengths and Limitations

The D-KEFS test has been designed to assess important dimensions of the executive functions of the brain while utilizing a wide array of various tasks and measures. Alternative forms are available for three of the tasks.

Whether the D-KEFS test is sensitive to mild forms of executive dysfunction is not known at this time. It is also not clear whether this test can distinguish different executive dysfunction profiles. Although there appears to be some preliminary evidence suggesting that the D-KEFS can distinguish cortical from subcortical disorders, the sample sizes that were utilized in the study were quite small and the study lacked appropriate controls. There is also some concern about the internal consistency in the test–retest properties of many of the measures.

Test–retest reliabilities are not provided for various operational measures. In addition, there is no information regarding inter-rater reliability. Due to the low test–retest reliabilities, the design fluency, sorting, tower, and 20 questions test should not be used for longitudinal assessment. Finally, the D-KEFS does not represent a theoretically driven or comprehensive set of test measures that assess the executive functions. For example, Delis et al. (2004) have admitted that the D-KEFS was never intended to assess all aspects of the executive functions or frontal lobe functions. Finally, there is no rationale why the nine tests were chosen and why other tests or techniques were not chosen instead (Strauss et al., 2006).

BEHAVIORAL RATING SCALES TO ASSESS THE EXECUTIVE FUNCTIONS OF THE BRAIN

Since neuropsychological tests are usually administered in a quiet highly structured one on one environment, an individual's behavior in this setting typically does not allow us to observe their executive functions. As a consequence, specialized questionnaires have been developed that can be completed by family members to assess how an individual behaves in a variety of complex, novel, and unstructured settings. Some of these behavioral rating scales are presented below.

BEHAVIOR RATING INVENTORY OF EXECUTIVE FUNCTION

The Behavior Rating Inventory of Executive Function (BRIEF) (Gioia et al, 2000) was designed to assess the executive functioning in children. It is completed by parents and teachers who have observed the child function in different settings. It produces eight theoretically and empirically derived subscales (inhibit, shift, emotional control, initiate, working memory, plan/organize, organization and materials, and monitor) that reflect some aspects of the executive functions. These subscales can be used to create the behavioral regulation index (BRI) and the metacognition index (MI) as well as the global executive composite (which is an overall score). The BRIEF includes two scales that are designed to assess inconsistency and negativity. The forms that are used by both parents and teachers contain 86 items, 18 of which differ across forms used by parents and teachers.

The BRIEF can be given to subjects ranging in age from 5 to 18. It also has a preschool version (BRIEF-P) that can be given to children ranging from 2 to just under 6 years of age. Each form of the BRIEF takes between 10 to 15 minutes to complete. The respondents are asked to rate a child's behavior on a 3-point scale (never, sometimes, and often).

Reliability and Validity

The Parent form that rated 54 children from the normative sample and 40 children from the clinical sample was readministered after a 2 to 3 week interval. The Teacher form evaluated 41 children and was readministered after a 3.5 week interval. On the average, the teacher interrated reliability was slightly higher than form that was completed by the parent. The teacher form interrated reliability was particularly good for all of the composites as well as the Inhibit and Emotional control scales. Correlations between different raters (parents and teachers) who rated 296 children were generally modest. The correlations, however, were low for the Initiate and Organization of Material scales. Parents consistently tended to rate children as having more difficulties on all scales than did teachers.

The scale structure was initially derived through literature review, consultation with colleagues, and an expert panel. It was later verified by factor analysis. Correlations with neuropsychological tests that measure the executive the functioning of patients ranged from modest or minimal. Correlations with other ratings scales measuring similar dimension of behavior, such as ADHD, were highly correlated. This appears to be consistent with recent theories of ADHD that have proposed that ADHD patients have a problem with their executive functions rather than an attention problem per se (Barkley, 1997). However, the BRIEF parent ratings were not higher in traumatic brain-injured children who had confirmed frontal lobe pathology in comparison to children who did not (Briezen and Pigott, 2002).

Strengths and Limitations

The BRIEF appears to be a psychometrically sound instrument that has been well designed. A number of research studies have been done utilizing this rating scale on children of variety of neurological disorders. These studies all appear to support the validity and clinical utility of the BRIEF.

The manual is well-written and thorough and includes a detailed examination of the psychometric properties of the clinical groups. The test–retest reliability of the composite scores, particularly those from the teacher form, appears to be high enough for reliable diagnostic decision making. The BRIEF also appears to be useful tool to screen children with ADHD. It also appears to be helpful when assessing children who have a variety of neurological and medical disorders.

The BRIEF appears to have a few limitations. For example, the clinical studies only examined the parent form. As a consequence most of the information from the clinical samples that is provided in the manual involves the parent form. The normative sample includes uneven numbers across the age groups. For example, there was only one 18-year-old in the normative sample in the teacher form. The lack of a strong overlap between the BRIEF and standard tests of executive functioning suggest that these measures may be tapping different aspects of behavior (Strauss et al., 2006).

FRONTAL SYSTEMS BEHAVIORAL SCALE

This rating scale has been designed to measure behaviors associated with damage to the frontal lobes and frontal systems of the brain (Grace and Malloy, 2001). This scale tries to identify neurobehavioral symptoms in natural settings which may not be seen on neuropsychological testing. It assesses the individual's behavior related to frontal systems after damage occurs. It allows multiple observers rate changes in an individual's behavior over time.

It consists of two 46-item hand-scorable rating forms (The Family Rating Form and the Self-Rating Form) that measure the following neurobehavioral syndromes Apathy, Disinhibition, and Executive Dysfunction by the use of a five-point Likert scale. This test requires the rater to identify the individual's functioning prior to and after an injury to the brain. It is similar to the BRIEF (described above).

The norms were based on a community based sample of 436 adults ranging in age 18 to 95 years of age. This scale does not require the rater to interview the individual who is being rated since the ratings are based on observations of the individual's behavior in various settings.

Reliability and Validity

This scale's intrascale reliability for the two rating forms have been reported to be high for both normal and clinical samples. The reliability ratings were marginally better in clinical samples. Studies reported by the authors have shown that the ratings are sensitive to frontal lobe pathology. The ratings, however, are not only sensitive to frontal lobe pathology but also appear to reflect damage to other parts of the brain.

Strengths and Limitations

The Frontal Systems Behavioral Scale (FrSBe) was designed to assess neurobehavioral symptoms in real-world settings that are often not detected by neuropsychological tests. It is a rating scale, not a neuropsychological test. It is completed by the family members and the patient. The ratings completed by the former are based on observations of the patient's behavior. The patient's self-rating makes little sense since patients with frontal lobe pathology are typically poor at identifying their behavioral and cognitive symptoms, and comparing their current functioning to their preinjury level of functioning.

While this rating scale can be helpful in identifying changes in an individual's neurobehavioral functioning following a neurological insult, the ratings of family members can reflect their denial or their own emotional problems in dealing with the patient. The ratings can also reflect the patient's psychiatric symptoms rather than problems caused by frontal lobe damage or dysfunction. This scale also has no built-in measures of validity which means that it can be manipulated by the patient and their family. The results of this rating scale should be consistent with the patient's medical history and generally consistent with the results of neuropsychological testing.

RUFF NEUROBEHAVIORAL INVENTORY

The Ruff Neurobehavioral Inventory (RNBI) is a self-report questionnaire which has been designed to measure the current status of individuals whose lives have been altered by a catastrophic event such as a spinal cord or traumatic brain injury (Ruff and Hibbard, 2003). It can assist the clinician identify specific areas of the patient's functioning that have been affected as well as those areas which been preserved. Unfortunately, these issues are not identified on standardized personality tests since these tests are not normed for patients with neurological or physical injuries. The first component of this inventory evaluates the individual's own perception of his or her health. Unlike most questionnaires which focus on physical or mental health, the RNBI places equal emphasis on the patient's emotional, cognitive, and physical health involving the patient's internal resources (Interpersonal Functions). The second component examines the patient's interpersonal functions which include spirituality, financial and vocational stability, and social and recreation functioning. The RNBI also evaluates the patient's perceived social support system and reliance on external resources. The clinical sample utilized consisted of 195 patients who were assessed in a variety of different settings. They included individuals of both sexes with pain disorders, cerebral vascular accidents, traumatic brain damage, and spinal cord injuries and whose ages ranged from 18 to 75 years.

The administration and scoring of this test is rather straight forward and can be completed by qualified mental health professionals who have sufficient background with theories of psycho-pathology and neuropathology, as well as brain–behavior relationships to understand common diagnostic taxonomies.

Reliability and Validity

Ninety-four college students were recruited to test the RNBI test–retest reliability. Both premorbid and postmorbid cognitive scales had good test–retest reliability. The test–retest reliability coefficients for the premorbid and postmorbid scales were also good. The test–retest correlations for the Neurological Status and Pain scales were relatively low. The test–retest correlations for all of the Composite Premorbid Physical scales were lower than the Premorbid Cognitive, Emotional, and Quality of Life scales. The test–retest reliability correlations were moderately high for the postmorbid cognitive, and physical composite scales, but were somewhat lower for the Emotional scale, and relatively low for the Quality of Life scale.

The MCMI-III Desirability scale correlated significantly with the premorbid and postmorbid RNBI validity scales. The MCMI-III Desirability scale was positively correlated with RNBI Positive Impression scales, and negatively correlated with the Negative Impression scales and the Infrequency scale. Correlations between the RNBI Emotional and Quality of Life scales and the MCMI-II scales were usually statistically significant, but tended to be low.

Strengths and Limitations

The RNBI was designed to assess the current psychological status of individuals whose lives have been significantly altered by a catastrophic event such as a brain or spinal cord injury. It greatest strength is that it probes deeper into the patient's concerns, functioning, and strengths than any of the well-known and widely used psychological tests. Unlike traditional psychological tests that were not designed to assess patients with neurological trauma, this test appears unique in that it explores a wide range of issues that should be relevant to clinicians. While its correlations with these tests are in some cases rather weak, this may reflect the fact that they are not measuring the same issues and the fact that the scores on the more traditional psychological tests did not contain any norms for subjects who have sustained catastrophic neurological trauma.

TESTS TO ASSESS PERSONALITY/EMOTIONAL ADJUSTMENT

BECK ANXIETY INVENTORY

The Beck Anxiety Inventory (BAI) (Beck and Steer, 1993a) was designed to measure the subjective symptoms of anxiety in adolescents and adults. It consists of 21 descriptive statements of anxiety symptoms which are rated on a four-point scale — 0 — not at all; 1 — mildly, it did not bother me much; 2 — moderately, it was very unpleasant but I could stand it; and 3 — severely, I could barely stand it. The 21 test items are numbness or tingling, feeling hot, wobbliness in legs, inability to relax, fear of the worst happening, dizziness or lightheadedness, heart pounding or racing, unsteadiness, feeling terrified, feeling nervous, feelings of choking, hands trembling, shaking, fear of losing control, difficulty breathing, fear of dying, feeling scared, indigestion or discomfort in the abdomen, faintness, facial flushing, and sweating (not due to heat).

Scoring of BAI consists of adding the scores for each of the 21 symptoms. The maximum score is 63 points. Scores ranging from 0 to 7 points are considered to reflect a minimal level of anxiety. Scores of 8 to 15 indicate mild anxiety, 16 through 25 moderate anxiety, and 26 or higher severe anxiety. A patient's test score provides only an estimate of the overall severity of anxiety, and the psychologist must consider other aspects of psychological functioning exhibited by the person, particularly any comorbid symptoms of depression. As a consequence, other scales such as the Beck Depression Inventory (BDI) (Beck and Steer, 1993b) and the Beck Hopelessness Scale (Beck and Steer, 1987) should be given in conjunction with this test.

Reliability and Validity

The test–retest reliability, based on an interval of 1 week, has been found to be 0.75 (Beck et al., 1979). The concurrent validity of BAI, in comparison with other clinical rating scales to assess anxiety, has been found to be low to moderately high.

Strengths and Limitations

The BAI can be administered in 5 to 10 minutes. It should be administered with the BDI and the Beck Hopelessness Scale to provide a more comprehensive assessment of the patient's subjective emotional difficulties. A patient's score on this test can be intentionally inflated because of its obvious face validity. Therefore, an individual's score on this particular test needs to be consistent with other personality tests such as the MMPI-2, the Millon Clinical Multiaxial Inventory (MCMI), or the Personality Assessment Inventory. It may not be appropriate for patients who have sustained severe traumatic brain injuries. Because of their cognitive impairments, these individuals may be unaware of their emotional problems.

BECK DEPRESSION INVENTORY

The BDI (Beck and Steer, 1993b) was designed to assess the patient's subjective symptoms of depression. It contains 21 forced-choice statements that assess depressive symptoms — sadness, pessimism/discouragement, sense of failure, dissatisfaction, guilt, expectation of punishment, self-dislike, self-accusation, suicidal ideation, crying, irritability, social withdrawal, indecisiveness, feeling unattractive, work inhibition, insomnia, fatigability, loss of appetite, weight loss, somatic preoccupation, and loss of libido. The patient must circle the number (0, 1, 2, or 3) next to the statement in each group of four that best describes the way he or she has been feeling within the past week or two (BDI-II) including the day of the test.

Approximately 5 to 10 minutes is required for the patient to complete this test. The total score is the sum of the numbers circled for each of the 21 test items. The maximum score is 63. While the test can be scored manually, computer software is available for test administration, scoring and interpretation.

Reliability and Validity

Test–retest reliability of this test has been found to be in excess of 0.90 (Beck, 1970). When patients' scores on this test were compared with their scores on other measures of depression, their scores were found to be highly correlated with the other tests (Spreen and Strauss, 1998).

Strengths and Limitations

This test can be easily administered to patients to assess their subjective symptoms of depression. It can be administered in 5 to 10 minutes and is easily scored. One of the major limitations of this test is that individuals involved in litigation or being evaluated by the courts may purposely test as severely, if not profoundly, depressed, because of the test's obvious face validity. Patients with severe closed head injuries may not test as depressed because they may be unaware of their cognitive difficulties (Sbordone et al., 1998). This test was not specifically designed to evaluate depression in elderly patients.

DETAILED ASSESSMENT OF POSTTRAUMATIC STRESS

The Detailed Assessment of Posttraumatic Stress (DAPS) (Briere, 2001) was designed to evaluate individuals who have undergone a significant psychological stressor or trauma. Unlikely existing psychological tests such as the PAI and MMPI-2, it has been specifically designed to assess for the presence of acute stress and posttraumatic stress disorders. Unlike traditional psychological tests, the DAPS contains norms for 400 individuals who have been exposed to at least one trauma event. It consists of 104 test items. It contains two validity scales (positive and negative bias) and nine clinical scales (relative trauma exposure, onset of exposure, peritraumatic dissociation, reexperiencing, avoidance, hyperarousal, posttraumatic stress — total, and posttraumatic impairment). It also contains three additional scales to assess trauma-specific dissociation, substance abuse, and suicidality.

The entire test can be completed in 15 to 20 minutes. Computer software is available to test administration, scoring, and generating a comprehensive narrative report which contains charts, and graphs. The use of this software program increases the accuracy of test scoring and saves considerable time.

Reliability and Validity

The alpha coefficients of the clinical scales ranged from low (0.57) to high (0.96) in the normative sample. The average coefficient was found to be 0.83. The reliability (alpha) coefficients were actually somewhat in the clinical samples. These results indicate that with the exception of the Negative Bias and Relative Trauma Exposure Scales, the scales are internally consistent. No data is available in the test manual about test–retest reliability.

Validity was determined in terms of whether the DAPS clinical scale would correlate with trauma exposure variables in ways that would be predicted by the trauma literature. Specifically, the relationship between the total number of traumas and posttraumatic outcome was examined by examined the correlation between the Trauma Exposure Scale (which assess the total lifetime trauma exposure) and the various symptom scales of the DAPS. As expected, greater the number of previous trauma exposure, more are the subjective PTSD symptoms.

Strengths and Limitations

The DAPS appears to measure symptoms typically associated with acute and posttraumatic stress disorders. Since it does not measure psychological symptoms such as generalized anxiety, depression, psychosis, and personality disorders, traditional psychological tests also need to be administered to identify and evaluate these symptoms. The diagnosis of either an acute or posttraumatic stress disorder should not be made simply on the basis of a patient's clinical profile on this test, particularly in forensic cases. The examiner should perform a careful clinical history and examination, review the patient's medical and psychiatric records, and interview significant others before a diagnosis of PTSD can be made.

MILLON CLINICAL MULTIAXIAL INVENTORY (MCMI-I, MCMI-II, AND MCMI-III)

The MCMI (I, II, and III) is a personality inventory that requires the patient to respond in a true/false format (Millon, 1977, 1987, 1994). It contains 175 questions. Unlike the MMPI (which will be discussed later in this chapter), the questions and the patient's responses are contained within the same booklet. This test has been designed for patients who are 17 or older. Unlike the MMPI, it attempts to directly assess preexisting personality traits or disorders. As a consequence, it may be valuable in medico-legal cases.

The MCMI-III, the most recent version, also contains a total of 175 test items with potentially objectionable statements screened out. The reading and vocabulary skill levels required for this test are approximately at eighth-grade level. Each of its 24 clinical scales was constructed as an operational measure of a syndrome derived from the theory of personality and psychopathology developed by Millon (1990). This test also incorporated changes in the diagnostic criteria contained in the Diagnostic and Statistical Manual of Mental Disorders — IV and can produce a computer-generated interpretive narrative report.

Reliability and Validity

The test–retest reliability of the MCMI-III ranges from 0.82 (debasement) to 0.96 (somatoform). The median test–retest reliability coefficient was found to be 0.91. Its validity was assessed by calculating correlations between the base rate scores for each scale and clinical ratings and collateral test scores. Scores on this test have been found to be moderately correlated to the Diagnostic and Statistical Manual and other personality tests (Millon, 1994).

Strengths and Limitations

The MCMI has been shown to be a valid test, partly through the cross-validation sample techniques developed by its authors. It is a relatively new test in comparison to the MMPI, and research studies on its use and effectiveness are, therefore, limited. Like the MMPI, this test was not designed to identify or diagnose brain injury. Its primary value for the neuropsychologist lies in its ability to describe the various emotional and adjustment problems the patients are likely to have following a posttraumatic stress disorder or brain injury.

Because the test relies on the patient's responses (true/false) to specific test items to determine current emotional problems, the neuropsychologist should exercise great caution in assuming that the Axis II profile produced by this test, which describes premorbid or longstanding personality traits, accurately reflects these traits after a significant duration of time has elapsed between the time of the injury or accident and when the patient is actually tested. For example, item #43, "My own 'bad temper' has been a big cause of my troubles," was designed to identify longstanding antisocial and borderline personality traits. If after sustaining a traumatic brain injury that results in poor frustration tolerance, irritability, and aggressive outbursts toward others the patient recognizes this problem and responds, "Yes," then the patient is likely to be diagnosed as having longstanding antisocial or borderline personality traits even though such traits were not present prior to the individual's brain injury. Therefore, considerable caution is recommended in determining whether an individual's current personality traits were or were not present prior to their traumatic brain injury.

Such a determination should not be based solely on the results of the patient's MCMI, or MMPI-2 test profile, but instead should be based on a thorough clinical investigation that includes — a review of the patient's prior academic, legal, medical, military, and occupational records; a detailed interview of the patient; and interviews with significant others. If the test profile corroborates this information, then it should be regarded as valid. If it contradicts this information, then the psychologist should interpret the test profile as a reflection of the neurobehavioral symptoms the individual has developed as a result of their brain injury.

MINNESOTA MULTIPHASIC PERSONALITY INVENTORY (MMPI, MMPI-2, MMPI-A)

The MMPI is the most widely used personality inventory to assess a patient's level of adjustment, personality dynamics, attitude towards self and the world, and current emotional problems. The MMPI was not designed, nor should it ever be used, to diagnose brain damage. The MMPI consists of 566 items, of which 16 items are repeated for scoring purposes (Hathaway and McKinley, 1943). The test provides questions or statements which must be answered within a true/false format.

The latest version of the test (MMPI-2) contains a total of 567 items (Hathaway et al., 1989) and has reworded and modified some of the questions. Both the old and new versions contain three validity scales, the L (Lie), the F (Faking), and the K (Defensiveness) scales. A patient's profile on these scales can provide valuable insights as to whether the patient is exaggerating or denying psychological problems, and whether the patient is defensive or seeking out help for the emotional problems.

The MMPI and the MMPI-2 contain ten clinical scales — hypochondriasis, depression, hysteria, psychopathic deviate, masculinity/femininity, paranoia, psychasthenia, schizophrenia, mania, and social introversion. Scoring can be done by placing special templates over the patient's answer sheet or by entering the patient's raw score for each item into a computer for scoring. The patient's scores for the three validity and ten clinical scales are entered onto a profile sheet after the patient's raw scores are adjusted in terms of the elevation of the K scale. The psychologist can then examine the relative elevations of each of these scales in relationship to each other and determine the clinical significance of the patient's profile.

The MMPI-A (Butcher et al., 1992; 1995) was developed for adolescents between the ages of 14 and 18. It consists of 478 test items that were primarily derived from the MMPI, but rewritten for adolescents. It contains the validity and clinical scales of the MMPI as well as its subscales and additional scales (Spreen and Strauss, 1998).

Significance of the Clinical Scales

Patients who experience a great deal of concern over their bodily functions and who are likely to complain of a wide variety of physical problems, including pain and discomfort, are likely to have elevated scores on the Hypochondriasis scale. Significant elevations on this scale can be due to real or imagined physical problems. Patients who experience suicidal thoughts, depression, poor self-esteem, sleep difficulties, loss of appetite, feelings of helplessness, dejection, lack of positive feelings, and apathy tend to score high on the Depression scale. Patients who are unable to tolerate hostility and stress but tend to be very friendly, sociable, egocentric, immature, have unhappy marriages, and little insight into their emotional problems or needs tend to score high on the Hysteria scale. Patients who have a history of criminal behavior, drug abuse, a general disregard for the rules of society, and problems with law enforcement authorities; exhibit impulsive behavior or poor judgment; and are markedly egocentric tend to score high on the Psychopathic Deviate Scale.

Males who score high on the Masculinity/Femininity scale are either homosexual or confused about their sexual identity. They also feel insecure when placed in masculine roles. It should be noted, however, that well-educated males who are artistic, creative, or highly intellectual may also score high on this scale. Males who score low on this test typically have deep-seated feelings of insecurity about their masculinity and may attempt to compensate for these feelings of insecurity by acting "macho." Females who score high on this scale tend to be highly competitive, unemotional, and aggressive. They often resent males and are actively engaged in competition with them. Women who score low on this scale tend to be submissive, passive, sensitive, emotionally constricted, and self-pitying. Such women frequently have doubts regarding their femininity and prefer to date "macho" males.

Individuals who are hostile, resentful, and tend to blame others for their own failures; appear guarded; or display excessive moral rigidity are likely to score high on the Paranoia scale. It should also be noted that extremely low scores on this scale may represent a covert form of paranoia, as patients may attempt to conceal or deny their paranoia.

Patients who are excessively anxious, nervous, perfectionistic or have phobias, trouble concentrating, or difficulty coping with their environment often score high on the Psychasthenia scale. Individuals who experience hallucinations and bizarre thoughts, appear odd, have difficulty expressing or dealing with their feelings, and frequently act inappropriately are likely to score high on the Schizophrenia scale. Many brain-injured patients tend to score high on this scale, particularly if they are confused, have difficulty regulating their behavior and emotions, and have difficulty organizing their thinking.

Individuals, who tend to be grandiose, jump from one topic to another, appear happy virtually all of the time, yet display poor judgment and an endless supply of energy are likely to score high on the Mania scale. Patients with brain injuries are also likely to show elevations on this scale, particularly if they are coping with their diminished cognitive functioning by excessive overactivity. Individuals who enjoy being alone, are hard to get to know, and are seen by others as very sensitive tend to score high on the Social Introversion scale. Low scores on this scale are frequently seen in individuals who are opportunistic, manipulative, highly intelligent, and confident of their abilities.

Reliability and Validity

The test–retest reliability for the MMPI-2 scales after 7 days has been reported to range from 0.51 (Paranoia) to 0.92 (Social Introversion). Studies of high-point-code stability after 1 to 2 days have reported only a 50 to 63% agreement (Graham, 1993). Recent studies have shown good discriminant validity between the MMPI-2 and the Diagnostic and Statistical Manual — III (Graham, 1993).

The MMPI-2 has been administered to individuals with moderate-to-severe traumatic brain injury. These individuals tended to show elevated scores on the Schizophrenia and Mania scales. However, patients who have sustained only mild traumatic brain injuries tend to show elevations on the Hypochondriasis, Depression, and Hysteria scales. Elevations on the Hypochondriasis scale and low scores on the Masculinity/Femininity scale tend to predict poor outcome of resumption of employment following a traumatic brain injury (Goldstein and Primeau, 1995).

A frequent criticism on the use of the MMPI and MMPI-2 in medicolegal cases is that the scale elevations may reflect neurological damage or dysfunction, rather than the patient's emotional state. As a consequence, a number of investigators have recommended caution when interpreting the MMPI-2 profiles of patients who have neurological disorders. Some investigators (Alfano et al., 1991; Alfano et al., 1993) have recommended that certain items of the MMPI-2 need to be deleted in patients who have sustained closed head injury. However, the deletion of these test items has been criticized by other investigators (Spreen and Strauss, 1998).

Strengths and Limitations

Numerous research studies have demonstrated the validity and reliability of the MMPI to diagnose patients with personality or emotional disorders. Psychologists who use this test should have extensive clinical training and expertise in making such interpretations. These interpretations should generally be consistent with the patient's clinical and background history, the observations of significant others, the patient's profile on other personality measures (e.g., MCMI-III or PAI), and the behavioral observations of the examiner.

While the MMPI and the MMPI-2 were not designed to diagnose brain damage, some psychiatrists and psychologists may unfortunately rely on a patient's MMPI profile to diagnose brain damage or organicity. A patient's profile on this test can often be used to determine the presence of significant emotional problems which may account, at least in part, for his or her relatively poor performance on the neuropsychological tests which are affected by emotional factors.

The psychologist administering MMPI-2 should be sure that the individual being tested can read well enough to comprehend the item content (a sixth-grade reading level is required to understand the MMPI-2 items, whereas a seventh-grade reading level is required for the MMPI). If the examiner suspects that the patient's reading skills are below this level, reading or achievement tests should be administered to assess the patient's level of reading proficiency. If the examiner finds that the patient's reading skills are below the sixth grade level, an audiocassette version of the MMPI-2 can be used in order for the patient to understand the test items. Many psychologists prefer to score this test on a computer, which tends to be more accurate, reliable, and less time consuming than hand scoring.

If the patient was raised speaking another language or in a different culture, particularly individuals who are unable to read or understand English, appropriate foreign language versions of this test have been developed. The standard MMPI-2 norms, however, may not be appropriate for these individuals since their responses on this test may reflect their cultural and linguistic background. It is important evaluate the test protocols of an individual who has taken this test for any invalid response patterns before attempting to interpret the clinical profile with confidence.

Some individuals may be motivated to present their psychological problems in an exaggerated manner. Evaluation of the patient's validity scales in comparison with other ecological measures, and the clinical observations of the patient, may help identify individuals who are exaggerating their psychological difficulties.

Psychologists should not rely solely on this test to determine whether an individual has psychological or psychiatric difficulties. Such an assessment should be based on a detailed clinical and background history, behavioral observations, interviews with significant others, and a review of the patient's medical and psychiatric records.

PERSONALITY ASSESSMENT INVENTORY

The Personality Assessment Inventory (Morey, 1991) is a self-administered objective test of personality and psychopathology that has been designed to provide information on critical patient variables. It was developed to provide measures of constructs that are essential in treatment, planning, implementation, and evaluation.

The clinical syndromes assessed by this test were selected on the basis of their history of importance within the nosology of mental disorder and their significance in contemporary diagnostic practice (Morey, 1996). These criteria were determined through a review of the historical and contemporary literature, as well as through a survey of practicing diagnosticians. Scores on this test are presented in the form of linear T scores that have a mean T score of 50 and a standard deviation of 10. The test contains 344 test items that make up 22 nonoverlapping full scales 4 validity, 11 clinical, 5 treatment, and 2 interpersonal (see Table 12.1).

TABLE 12.1
Personality Assessment Inventory Scales and Subscales

Scales and subscales	Focus
Validity	
Inconsistency	Determines if the patient is answering questions consistently throughout the task
Frequency	Determines if the patient is responding carelessly or randomly
Negative impression	Determines whether the patient is exaggerating or malingering
Positive impression	Suggests whether the patient is trying to make a very favorable impression or is reluctant to admit to minor flaws
Clinical	
Somatic complaints	The patient's preoccupation with health matters and somatic complaints
Conversion	Symptoms associated with conversion disorder, particularly sensory or motor dysfunctions
Somatization	The occurrence of various common physical symptoms and vague complaints of ill-health and fatigue
Health concerns	The patient's preoccupation with health issues and physical problems
Anxiety	Observable signs of anxiety
Cognitive	The patient's ruminative worries and concerns about current issues that impair concentration and attention
Effective	The patient's levels of tension, problems in relaxing, and the presence of fatigue as a result of high levels of perceived stress
Physiological	Overt physical signs of tension and stress such as sweaty palms, trembling hands, complaints of irregular heartbeats, and shortness of breath
Anxiety-related disorders	Symptoms and behaviors related to phobias, traumatic stress, and obsessive–compulsive symptoms
Obsessive–compulsive	Intrusive thoughts or behaviors, rigidity, indecision, perfectionism, and effective constriction
Phobias	Assesses common phobic fears
Traumatic stress	Traumatic events which have produced continuing distress and left the patient changed or damaged
Depression	Symptoms of depressive disorders
Cognitive	Feelings of worthlessness, hopelessness, and personal failure, as well as indecisiveness and concentration difficulties
Effective	Feelings of sadness, loss of control in normal activities, and anhedonia
Physiological	The patient's level of physical functioning, activity, and energy including disturbances in sleep, changes in appetite, and weight loss
Mania	Symptoms of mania and hypomania
Activity level	Over-involvement in a wide range of activities in a somewhat disorganized manner
Grandiosity	Inflated self-esteem, expansiveness, and the belief in the possession of special unique skills or talents
Irritability	The presence of strained relationships due to frustration with the inability or unwillingness of others to keep up their plans, demands, and possibly unrealistic ideas
Paranoia	Symptoms of paranoia and more enduring characteristics of a paranoid personality

TABLE 12.1
Continued

Scales and subscales	Focus
Clinical (continued)	
Hypervigilance	Suspiciousness and a tendency to monitor the environment for real or imagined slights by others
Persecution	Belief of being treated inequitably and that there has been a concerted effort among others to undermine personal interest
Resentment	Bitterness and cynicism in interpersonal relationships, as well as a tendency to hold grudges and externalize blame for any misfortunes
Schizophrenia	Symptoms consistent with schizophrenic disorders
Psychotic experiences	The experience of unusual perceptions or sensations, magical thinking, and other unusual ideas that may involve delusional beliefs
Social detachment	Social isolation, discomfort, and awkwardness in social situations
Thought disorder	Confusion, concentration difficulties, and disorganization of thought processes
Borderline features	Attributes consistent with borderline personality disorder
Effective instability	Emotional responsiveness, rapid mood changes, and poor emotional control
Identity problems	Uncertainty about major life issues and feelings of emptiness, unfulfillment, and absence of purpose
Negative relationships	Examines for history of ambivalent, intense relationships with the feeling of exploitation and betrayal
Self-harm	Impulsivity in areas that have a high potential for negative consequences
Antisocial features	History of illegal acts and authority problems
Antisocial behaviors	Examines whether the patient has had a history of antisocial acts or involvement in illegal activities
Egocentricity	A lack of empathy or remorse along with a generally exploitive approach to interpersonal relationships
Stimulus seeking	The patient's craving for excitement and sensation, a low tolerance for boredom, and a tendency to reckless and risk-taking behavior
Egocentricity	Lack of empathy and loyalty, instability and excitement seeking
Alcohol problems	Problems with alcohol use and dependence
Drug problems	The consequences of prescription and illicit drug use and features of drug dependence
Treatment	
Aggression	Characteristics and attitudes related to anger, assertiveness, hostility, and aggression
Aggressive attitude	Hostility, poor control over the expression of anger and the belief in the instrumental utility of aggression
Verbal aggression	Verbal expressions of anger ranging from assertiveness to abusiveness and the patient's readiness to express anger toward others
Physical aggression	A tendency toward physical displays of anger, including damage to property, physical fights, and threats of violence
Suicidal ideation	Suicidal ideation ranging from hopelessness to actual thoughts and plans for committing suicide
Stress	The impact of recent stressors in major life areas
Nonsupport	The patient's perceived level of social support, particularly the level and quality
Treatment rejection	The patient's interest and motivation for making personal changes of a psychological or emotional nature
Interpersonal	
Dominance	The extent to which the patient is controlling and independent in interpersonal relationships
Warmth	The degree to which the patient is interested, supportive, and empathetic in personal relationships

Source: Adapted from Morey, L. C. 1996. *An Interpretative Guide to the Personality Assessment Inventory (PAI)*. Odessa, FL: Psychological Assessment Resources, Inc.

This test was developed to assess patients from age 18 through adulthood. Because the standardization sample did not include individuals under the age of 18, there is no data to support the interpretation of the test scores for adolescents. Unlike the MMPI or the MMPI-2, the reading level necessary for patients to take this test is only at the fourth grade level. This test can usually be administered in 45 to 60 minutes.

Reliability and Validity

Test–retest studies of reliability over a 4-week interval for the 11 full clinical scales found the reliability to be 0.86 (Morey, 1991). However, Boyle and Lennon (1994) reported a median test–retest reliability of only 0.73 in their normal sample over the same time period. A number of correlational studies have shown that the scales on this test have good convergent and discriminant validity in comparison with other tests of personality (Morey, 1996).

Strengths and Limitations

This test appears to be psychometrically superior to the MMPI-2 and assesses a wide range of clinical domains. Patients who are proficient at reading at only the fourth grade level should be able to take this test. This test appears to possess good test–retest reliability and to have good concurrent validity with other widely used personality inventories and measures. It contains only 344 items in comparison to the 567 items for the MMPI-2. Since the test questions are more straightforward than those on the MMPI-2, the entire test can usually be completed in approximately 45 minutes compared with nearly 1½ to 2 hours for the MMPI. A computerized interpretative profile and narrative report is commercially available and can assist the psychologist in scoring and interpreting this test.

As with the MMPI-2, this test was not designed to determine whether a patient has brain damage and should not be used for this purpose. Caution should be exercised in testing patients whose first or native language is not English. Valid administration of this test assumes that the patient is physically and emotionally capable of meeting the normal demands of testing with self-report instruments. The test may also not be appropriate for patients who are easily distracted, under extreme emotional distress at the time of testing, are unable to read or comprehend the test questions or who have significant visual handicap. Interpretation of the clinical profiles of individuals with impaired cognitive abilities as a result of brain insults caused by drug use, alcohol, or exposure to toxic chemicals, or who are disoriented due to a neurological disorder at the time of testing should be done with great caution since this test was not normed on such individuals.

Psychologists should not rely solely on this test to determine whether an individual has psychological or psychiatric difficulties. Such an assessment should be based on a detailed clinical and background history, behavioral observations of the patient, interviews with significant others, and a review of the patient's medical and psychiatric records. The results of this test should be used in conjunction with other personality measures (MMPI-2, BAI, BDI, etc.).

TRAUMA SYMPTOM INVENTORY

Trauma Symptom Inventory (TSI) has been designed to evaluate acute and chronic symptoms of psychological trauma. It can be given to individuals who are 18 years and older. It contains 100 items that measure an individual's subjective distress, dysphoric mood, posttraumatic stress symptoms, sexual difficulties, and self dysfunction. Each symptom must be rated according to its frequency of recurrence over the preceding 6 months using a four-point scale ranging from 0 (never) to 3 (often). It also contains three validity scales. Twelve critical items have been developed to identify issues such as self mutilation, potential for suicide, and the potential for violence against others.

Three of the TSI scales appear to be most relevant to posttraumatic stress disorder intrusive experiences, defensive avoidance, and anxious arousal (Briere and Elliott, 1998). Interpretations of the various scales may be helpful to distinguish between individuals who have symptoms following a recent trauma from individuals who have longstanding identity and affect regulation difficulties such is often the case in individuals with borderline personality disorders. These latter individuals tend to present as a complex trauma victim who is chronically distressed, overwhelmed by intrusive symptoms and potentially more likely to act out painful internal states because of lower self resources. There are three validity scales — response level, atypical response, and inconsistency response. There are nine clinical scales — anxious arousal, depression, anger/irritability, intrusive experiences, defensive avoidance, disassociation, sexual concerns, dysfunctional sexual behavior, impaired self reference, and tensional reduction behavior. This test can usually be administered in 20 minutes.

Reliability and Validity

No information about the test–retest reliability coefficients is reported in the manual. The validity of the test was examined by correlating the TSI scales with indices from other measures thought to measure similar constructs. For example, the validity scales correlated ideally with the validity scales on the personality assessment inventory in the MMPI-II.

The validity of TSI was also demonstrated by examining the differences between traumatized and nontraumatized groups (Briere, 1995; Merrill, 2001; Elliott et al., 2004). Psychiatric patients who have a history of child abuse or adult assault tended to have higher raw scores, female university students with a history of childhood abuse had higher scores than women who were not abused. Individuals who had experienced multiple traumatic events were found to be more distressed than those who have experienced fewer distressing traumatic events (Green et al., 2000).

It is often difficult for the validity scales on the TSI to distinguish between individuals who are honestly reporting traumatic experiences and those who are exaggerating or fabricating trauma-related symptoms.

Strengths and Limitations

The TSI provides the clinician with information about the various aspects of the patient's psychological state that includes posttraumatic stress, to support mood and self functioning. It is based entirely on the patient's self report that can in some cases be fabricated. Over the inclusion of the validity scales to examine underreporting or overreporting of clinical symptoms distinguishes the TSI and all other standardized measures of trauma-related symptomology (Strauss et al., 2006).

Since it is often difficult for the validity scales on the TSI to distinguish between individuals who are honestly reporting traumatic experiences and those who are exaggerating or fabricating trauma related symptoms, this instrument should not be used as the sole basis in diagnostic evaluations of patients who have experienced psychological trauma. Other tests such as the MMPI-II or the Personality Assessment Inventory should be given in conjunction with the TSI and a careful clinical interview is needed to provide information useful for a differential diagnosis.

TEST SUMMARY

Appendix B presents a summary of the strengths and limitations of the widely used neuropsychological tests discussed in this chapter.

REFERENCES

Acker, M. B. and Davis, J. R. 1989. Psychology Test Scores Associated With Late Outcome in Head Injury. *Neuropsychology*, 3, 1–10.

Adams, K. M., Gilman, S., Koeppe, R., Klain, K., Junck, L., Lohman, M., Johnson-Greene, D., Berent, S., Dede, D., and Kroll, P. 1995. Correlation of Neuropsychological Function with Cerebral Metabolic Rate in Subdivisions of the Frontal Lobes of Older Alcoholic Patients Measured With [18F] Fluorodeoxyglucose and Positron Emission Tomography. *Neuropsychology*, 9, 275–280.

Adams, R. L. and Trenton, S. L. 1981. Development of a Paper-and-Pen Form of the Halstead Category Test. *Journal of Consulting and Clinical Psychology, 49*, 298–299.

Alderton, D. L. and Larson, G. E. 1990. Dimensionality of Raven's Advanced Progressive Matrices Items. *Educational and Psychological Measurement, 50*, 887–900.

Aldrich, F. K. and Wilson, B. 1991. Rivermead Behavioural Memory Test for Children (RBMT-C): A Preliminary Evaluation. *British Journal of Clinical Psychology, 30*, 161–168.

Alfano, D. P., Finlayson, M. A. J., Sterns, G. M., and MacLennan, R. N. 1991. Dimensions of Neurobehavioral Dysfunction. *Neuropsychology, 5*, 35–41.

Alfano, D. P., Paniak, C. E., and Finlayson, M. A. J. 1993. The Neurocorrected MMPI for Closed Head Injury. *Neuropsychiatry, Neuropsychology, and Behavioral Neurology, 6*, 111–116.

Allinder, R. M. and Fuchs, L. S. 1992. Screening Academic Achievement Review of the Peabody Individual Achievement Test — Revised. *Learning Disabilities Research and Practice, 7*, 45–47.

Atkinson, L. 1989. Three Standard Errors of Measurement and the Stanford–Binet Intelligence Scale, Fourth Edition. *Psychological Assessment, 1*, 242–244.

Baddeley, A. 1986. *Working Memory*. Oxford: Clarendon Press.

Baldo, J. V., Delis, D., Kramer, J., and Shimamura, A. P. 2002. Memory Performance on the California Verbal Learning Test — II Findings from Patients with Focal Frontal Lesions. *Journal of the International Neuropsychological Society, 8*, 539–546.

Ballard, J. C. 1997. Computerized Assessment of Sustained Attention a Review of Factors Affecting Vigilance Performance. *Journal of Clinical and Experimental Neuropsychology, 18*, 843–863.

Barkley, R. A. 1997. *ADHD and the Nature of Self-Control*. New York: Guildford.

Baser, C. A. and Ruff, R. M. 1987. Construct Validity of the San Diego Neuropsychological Test Battery. *Archives of Clinical Neuropsychology, 2*, 13–32.

Batchelor, J., Harvery, A. G., and Bryant, R. A. 1995. Stroop Color–Word Test as a Measure of Attentional Deficit Following Mild Head Injury. *The Clinical Neuropsychologist, 9*, 180–186.

Bate, A. J., Mathias, J. L., and Crawford, J. R. 2001. Performance on the Test of Everyday Attention and Standardized Test Attention Following Severe Traumatic Brain Injury. *The Clinical Neuropsychologist, 15*, 405–422.

Beatty, W. W., Ryber, K. A., Gontkovsky, S. T., Scott, J. G., McSwan, K. L., and Bharucha, K. J. 2003. Analyzing the Subcortical Dementia Syndrome of Parkinson's Disease Using the Rbans. *Archives of Clinical Neuropsychology, 18*, 509–520.

Beck, A. T. 1970. *Depression Causes and Treatment*. Philadelphia: University of Pennsylvania Press.

Beck, A. T. and Steer, R. A. 1987. *Beck Hopelessness Scale Manual*. San Antonio, TX: Psychological Corporation.

Beck, A. T. and Steer, R. A. 1993a. *Beck Anxiety Inventory Manual*. San Antonio, TX: Psychological Corporation.

Beck, A. T. and Steer, R. A. 1993b. *Beck Depression Inventory*. San Antonio, TX: Psychological Corporation.

Beck, A. T., Rush, A. J., Shaw, B. F., and Emery, G. 1979. *Cognitive Therapy of Depression*. New York: Guilford.

Bender, L. 1938. A Visual Motor Gestalt Test and Its Clinical Use. *American Orthopsychiatric Association Research Monographs, 3*.

Benedict, R. H. B. 1997. *Brief Visuospatial Memory Test — Revised*. Odessa, FL: Psychological Assessment Resources.

Benedict, R. H. B. and Groninger, L. C. 1995. Preliminary Standardization of a New Visuospatial Memory Test with Six Alternative Forms. *The Clinical Neuropsychologist, 9*, 11–16.

Benedict, R. H. B., Schretlen, D., Groninger, L., Dobraski, M., and Shpritz, B. 1996. Revision of the Brief Visuospatial Memory Test Studies of Normal Performance, Reliability, and Validity. *Psychological Assessment, 8*, 145–153.

Benton, A. L. 1968. Differential Behavioral Effects in Frontal Lobe Disease. *Neuropsychologia, 6*, 53–60.

Benton, A. L. 1974. *Revised Visual Retention Test Clinical and Experimental Applications*. New York: Grune and Stratton.

Benton, A. L. and Spreen, O. 1961. Visual Memory Test the Simulation of Mental Incompetence. *Archives of General Psychiatry, 4*, 79–83.

Benton, A. L., Hamsher, K. de S., Rey, G. J., and Sivan, A. B. 1994a. *Multilingual Aphasia Examination*, 3d ed. Iowa City, IA: AJA Associates.

Benton, A. L., Sivan, A. B., Hamsher, K. de S., Varney, N. R., and Spreen, O. 1994b. *Contributions to Neuropsychological Assessment a Clinical Manual*, 2nd ed. New York: Oxford University Press.

Berg, E. A. 1948. A Simple Objective Technique for Measuring Flexibility in Thinking. *Journal of General Psychology*, *39*, 15–22.

Berry, D. T. R., Wetter, M. W., Baer, R. A., Youngjohn, J. R., Gass, C. S., Lamb, D. G., Franzen, M. D., MacInnes, W. D., and Bucholz, D. 1995. Over Reporting of Closed Head Injury Symptoms on the MMPI-2. *Psychological Assessment*, *7*, 517–523.

Bigler, E. D. and Ehrfurth, J. W. 1980. Critical Limitations of the Bender–Gestalt Test in Clinical Neuropsychology. *Clinical Neuropsychology*, *2*, 88–90.

Binder, L. M. 1982. Constructional Strategies on Complex Figure Drawing after Unilateral Brain Damage. *Journal of Clinical Neuropsychology*, *4*, 51–58.

Black, F. W. 1986. Digit Repetition in Brain-Damaged Adults Clinical and Theoretical Implications. *Journal of Clinical Psychology*, *42*, 770–782.

Blackerby, W. F. III. 1985. A Latent-Trait Investigation of the Luria–Nebraska Neuropsychological Battery. *Dissertation Abstracts*, *46*, 342B. (University Microfilms No. 85-05, 223).

Bogen, J. E., DeZure, R., Tenhouten, W. D., and Marsh, J. F. 1972. The Other Side of the Brain IV the A/P Ratio. *Bulletin of the Los Angeles Neurological Societies*, *37*, 49–61.

Bohnen, N., Jolles, J., and Twijnstra, A. 1992. Modification of the Stroop Color–Word Test Improves Differentation between Patients with Mild Head Injury and Matched Controls. *The Clinical Neuropsychologist*, *6*, 178–188.

Boll, T. J. 1981. The Halstead–Reitan Battery. In Filskov, S. B. and Boll, T. J. (Eds.) *Handbook of Clinical Neuropsychology*. New York: Wiley–Interscience, pp. 577–607.

Boll, T. J. 1982. Behavioral Sequelae of Head Injury. In Cooper, P. R. (Ed.) *Head Injury*, 2d ed. Baltimore: Williams & Wilkins, pp. 363–375.

Boller, F. and Vignolo, L. 1966. Latent Sensory Aphasia in Hemisphere-Damaged Patients an Experimental Study with the Token Test. *Brain*, *89*, 815–831.

Bornstein, R. A. 1985. Normative Data on Selected Neuropsychological Measures from a Nonclinical Sample. *Journal of Clinical Psychology*, *41*, 651–659.

Bornstein, R. A. 1986. Normative Data on Intermanual Differences on Three Tests of Motor Performance. *Journal of Clinical and Experimental Neuropsychology*, *8*, 12–20.

Bornstein, R. A., Baker, G. B., and Douglas, A. B. 1987. Short-Term Retest Reliability of the Halstead–Reitan Battery in a Normal Sample. *Journal of Nervous and Mental Disease*, *175*, 229–232.

Botwinick, J., Storandt, M., and Berg, L. 1986. A Longitudinal Behavioral Study of Senile Dementia of the Alzheimer's Type. *Archives of Neurology*, *43*, 1124–1127.

Boyle, G. J. and Lennon, T. J. 1994. Examination of the Reliability and Validity of the Personality Assessment Inventory. *Journal of Psychopathology and Behavior Assessment*, *16*, 173–188.

Briere, J. 1995. *Trauma Symptom Inventory*. Odessa, FL: Psychological Assessment Resources.

Briere, J. 2001. *Detailed Assessment of Posttraumatic Stress Professional Manual*. Lutz, FL: Psychological Assessment Resources.

Brown, L., Sherbenoq, R. J., and Johnson, S. K. 1997. *Test of Nonverbal Intelligence a Language — Free Measure of Cognitive Ability*, 3d ed. Austin, TX: Pro-Ed.

Burg, J. S., Burright, R. G., and Donovick, P. J. 1995. Performance Data for Traumatic Brain-Injured Subjects on the Gordon Diagnostic System (GDS) Tests of Attention. *Brain Injury*, *9*, 395–403.

Burton, D. B., Naughe, R. I., and Schuster, J. M. 1995. A Structural Equation Analysis of the Kaufman Brief Intelligence Test and the Wechsler Intelligence Scale — Revised. *Psychological Assessment*, *7*, 538–540.

Buschke, H. 1973. Selective Reminding for Analysis of Memory and Learning. *Journal of Verbal Learning and Verbal Behavior*, *12*, 543–550.

Buschke, H. and Fuld, P. A. 1974. Evaluating Storage Retention and Retrieval of Disordered Memory and Learning. *Neurology*, *24*, 1019–1025.

Butcher, J. M., Williams, C. L., Graham, J. R. 1992. *MMPI-A (Minnesota Multiphasic Personality Inventory — Adolescent)*. Minneapolis: University of Minnesota Press.

Butcher, J. N. and Williams C. L. 1992. *Essentials of the MMPI-2 and MMPI-A Interpretation*. Minneapolis: University of Minnesota Press.

Butcher, J. N., Graham, J. R., and Ben-Poratz, Y. S. 1995. Methodological Problems and Issues in MMPI, MMPI-2, and MMPI-A Research. *Psychological Assessment, 7,* 320–329.

Butters, N., Salmon, D. P., Cullum, C. M., Cairne, P., Troster, A. I., Jacobs, D., Moss, M., and Cermak, L. S. 1988. Differentiation of Amnesic and Demented Patients with the Wechsler Memory Scale — Revised. *The Clinical Neuropsychologist, 2,* 133–148.

Chan, R. C. K., Hoosain, R., Lee, T. M. C., Fan, Y. M., and Fond, D. 2003. Are There Subtypes of Attentional Deficits in Patients with Persisting Post-Concussive Symptoms? A Cluster Analytic Study. *Brain injury, 17,* 131–148.

Chelune, G. J., Bornstein, R. A., and Priftera, A. 1989. The Wechsler Memory Scale — Revised Current Status and Application. In Rosen, J., McReynolds, P., and Chelune, G. J. (Eds.) *Advances in Psychological Assessment.* New York: Plenum Press.

Cohen, M. J. 1997. *Children's Memory Scale.* San Antonio, TX: The Psychological Corporation.

Conners, C. K. and Multi-Health Systems Staff. 1995. *Conners' Continuous Performance Test.* Toronto: Multi-Health Systems.

Conners, C. K. and Multi-Health Systems Staff. 2000. *Conners' Continuous Performance Test (CPT-II) Computer Programs for Windows. Technical Guide and Software Manual.* North Tonewanda, NY: Multi-Health Systems Inc.

Costenbader, V. K. and Adams, J. W. 1991. A Review of the Psychosomatic and Administrative Features of the PIAT-R Implications for the Practitioner. *Journal of School Psychology, 23,* 219–228.

Cripe, L. I. 1996. The Ecological Validity of Executive Function Testing. In Sbordone, R. J. and Long, C. J. (Eds.) *Ecological Validity of Neuropsychological Testing.* Boca Raton, FL: CRC Press, pp. 171–202.

Crossen, J. R. and Wiens, A. N. 1994. Comparison of the Auditory–Verbal Learning Test (AVLT) and the California Verbal Learning Test (CVLT) in a Sample of Normal Subjects. *Journal of Clinical and Experimental Neuropsychology, 16,* 190–194.

Crowder, R. G. 1982. The Demise of Short-Term Memory. *ACTA Psychologica, 50,* 291–323.

Cullum, C. M., Thompson, L. L., and Heaton, R. K. 1989. The Use of the Halstead–Reitan Test Battery with Older Adults. In Pirozzola, N. F. J. (Ed.) *Clinics and Geriatric Medicine (Vol. 5, No. 3).* Philadelphia: Saunders.

D'Elia, L., Satz, P., Uchiyama, C., and White, T. 1994. *Color Trails Test. Professional Manual.* Odessa, FL: Psychological Assessment Resources.

Delaney, R. C., Prevey, M. L., Cramer, J. 1992. Test–Retest Comparability and Control Subject Data for the Rey Auditory Verbal Learning Test and the Rey–Osterrieth/Taylor Complex Figures. *Archives of Clinical Neuropsychology, 7,* 523–528.

Delis, D. C., Cullum, C. M., Butters, N., Cairns, P., and Prifitera, A. 1988. Wechsler Memory Scale — Revised and California Verbal Learning Test Convergence and Divergence. *The Clinical Neuropsychologist, 2,* 188–196.

Delis, D. C., Kaplan, E., and Kramer, J. H. 2001. *Delis-Kaplan Executive Function System.* San Antonio, TX: The Psychological Corporation.

Delis, D. C., Kramer, J. H., Kaplan, E., and Holdnack, J. 2004. Reliability and Validity of the Delis-Kaplan Executive Function System An Update. *Journal of the International Neuropsychological Society, 10,* 301–303.

Delis, D. C., Kramer, J. H., Kaplan, E., and Ober, B. A. 1987. *California Verbal Learning Test Adult Version Manual.* San Antonio, TX: Psychological Corporation.

Delis, D. C., Kramer, J. H., Kaplan, E., and Ober, B. A. 1994. *CVLT-C California Verbal Learning Test — Children's Version.* San Antonio, TX: Psychological Corporation.

Delis, D. C., Kramer, J. H., Kaplan, E., and Ober, B. A. 2000. *California Verbal Learning Test, 2nd ed. Adult Version.* San Antonio, TX: The Psychological Corporation.

Dodrill, C. B. 1978. A Neuropsychological Battery for Epilepsy. *Epilepsia, 19,* 611–623.

Donders, J. 1992. Validity of the Kaufman Assessment Battery for Children When Employed with Children with Traumatic Brain Injury. *Journal of Clinical Psychology, 48,* 225–230.

Donders, J. 1998. Performance Discrepancies between the Children's Category Test (CCT) and the California Verbal Learning Test — Children's (CVLT-C) Version in the Standardized Sample. *Journal of the International Neuropsychological Society, 4,* 242–246.

Donders, J. 1999. Performance Discrepancies on the California Verbal Learning Test — Children's Version and the Standardization Sample. *Journal of the International Neuropsychological Society, 5,* 26–31.

Doty, R. L. 1998. *The Smell Identification Test*. Odessa, FL: Psychological Assessment Resources.

Duff, K., Beglinger, L. J., Schoenberg, M. R., Patton, D. E., Mold, J., Scott, J. G., and Adams, R. L. 2005. Test–Retest Ability and Practice Effects of the Rbans in a Community Dwelling Elderly Sample. *Journal of Clinical and Experimental Neuropsychology, 27*, 565–575.

Dunn, L. M. and Markwardt, F. C. 1970. *Peabody Individual Achievement Test Manual*. Circle Pines, MN: American Guidance Service.

Dunn, L. M. and Dunn, L. M. 1997. *Examiner's Manual for the Peabody Picture Vocabulary Test*, 3d ed. Circle Pines, MN: American Guidance Service

Elliott, D. M., Mok, D. S., and Briere, J. 2004. Adult Sexual Assault Prevalence, Symptomology, and Sex Difference in the General Population. *Journal of Traumatic Stress, 17*, 2003–2211.

Epstein, J. N., Johnson, D. E., Varia, I. M., and Conners, C. K. 2001. Neuropsychological Assessment of Response Inhibition in Adults with ADHD. *Journal of Clinical and Experimental Neuropsychology, 23*, 362–371.

Evans, R. W., Gualtieri, C. T., and Ruff, R. M. 1985. Verbal Fluency and Figural Fluency in Bright Children. *Perceptual and Motor Skills, 61*, 699–709.

Feinstein, A., Brown, R., and Ron, M. 1994. Effects of Practice of Serial Tests of Attention in Healthy Adults. *Journal of Clinical and Experimental Neuropsychology, 16*, 436–447.

Finlayson, M. A. J. and Reitan, R. M. 1980. Effect of Lateralized Lesions on Ipsilateral and Contralateral Motor Functioning. *Journal of Clinical Neuropsychiatry, 2*, 237–243.

Franzen, M. D. 1985. Luria–Nebraska Neuropsychological Battery. In Keyser, D. J. and Sweetland, R. C. (Eds.) *Test Critiques*, Volume III. Kansas City, MO: Test Corporation of America, pp. 402–414.

Franzen, M. D. and Iverson, G. L. 1998. Detecting Negative Response Bias and Diagnosing Malingering: The Dissimulation Exam. In Snyder, P. J. and Nussbaum, P. D. (Eds.) *Clinical Neuropsychology: A Pocket Handbook for Assessment*. Washington, DC: American Psychological Association, pp. 88–101.

Franzen, M. D., Tishelman, A. C., Sharp, B. H., and Friedman, A. G. 1987. An Investigation of the Test–Retest Reliability of the Stroop Color–Word Test Across Two Intervals. *Archives of Clinical Neuropsychology, 2*, 265–272.

Fromm-Auch, D. and Yeudall, L. T. 1983. Normative Data for the Halstead–Reitan Neuropsychological Tests. *Journal of Clinical Neurospychology, 5*, 221–238.

Geffen, G. M., Butterworth, P., and Geffen, L. B. 1994. Test–Retest Reliability of a New Form of the Auditory Verbal Learning Test (AVLT). *Archives of Clinical Neuropsychology, 9*, 303–316.

Geffen, G. M., Encel, J. S., and Forrester, G. M. 1991. Stages of Recovery During Post-Traumatic Amnesia and Subsequent Everyday Deficits. *Cognitive Neuroscience and Neuropsychology, 2*, 105–108.

Gill, D. M., Reddon, J. R., Stefanyk, W. O., and Hans, H. S. 1986. Finger Tapping Effects of Trials and Sessions. *Perceptual and Motor Skills, 62*, 674–678.

Gioia, G. A., Isquith, P. K., Guy, S. C., and Kenworthy, L. 2000. *Behavioral Rating Inventory of the Executive Function*. Lutz, FL: Psychological Assessment Resources.

Gold, J. M., Kueern, C., Iannone, Z. M., and Buchanan, R. B. 1999. Repeatable Battery for the Assessment of Neuropsychological Status as a Screening Test in Schizophrenia Sensitivity, Reliability, and Validity. *American Journal of Psychiatry, 158*, 1944–1950.

Golden, C. J. 1978. *Diagnosis and Rehabilitation in Clinical Neuropsychology*. Springfield, IL: Thomas.

Golden, C. J. 1979. *Clinical Interpretation of Objective Psychological Tests*. New York: Grune and Stratton.

Golden, C. J., Ariel, R. M., McKay, S. E., et al. 1982. The Luria–Nebraska Neuropsychological Battery Theoretical Orientation and Comment. *Journal of Consulting and Clinical Psychology, 50*, 291–200.

Golden, C. J., Hammeke, T. A., and Purisch, A. D. 1978. Diagnostic Validity of a Standardized Neuropsychological Battery Derived from Luria's Neuropsychological Tests. *Journal of Consulting and Clinical Psychology, 46*, 1258–1265.

Goldstein, D. and Primeau, M. 1995. Neuropsychological and Personality Predictors of Employment after Traumatic Brain Injury. *Journal of the International Neuropsychological Society, 1*, 370 (Abstract).

Goldstein, G. and Shelly, C. H. 1972. Statistical and Normative Studies of the Halstead–Reitan Neuropsychological Test Battery Relevant to a Neuropsychiatric Hospital Setting. *Perceptual and Motor Skills, 34*, 603–630.

Goldstein, G. and Watson, J. R. 1989. Test–Retest Reliability of the Halstead–Reitan Battery and the WAIS in a Neuropsychiatric Population. *The Clinical Neuropsychologist, 3*, 265–273.

Goldstein, G., Shelly, C, McCue, M., and Kane, R. L. 1987. Classification with the Luria–Nebraska Neuropsychological Battery: An application of Cluster and Ipsative Profile Analysis. *Archives of the Clinical Neuropsychology, 2*, 215–235.

Goldstein, L. H. and Polkey, C. E. 1992. Behavioural Memory after Temporal Lobectomy or Amygdalo-Hippocampectomy. *British Journal of Clinical Psychology, 31*, 75–81.

Goodglass, H. and Kaplan, E. 1983. *Boston Diagnostic Aphasia Examination.* Philadelphia: Lea & Febiger.

Goodglass, H., Kaplan, E., and Barresi, B. 2001. *Boston Diagnostic Aphasia Examination*, 3d ed. Philadelphia: Lippincott Williams and Wilkins.

Goodman, A. M., Delis, D. C., and Mattson, S. M. 1999. Normative Data of Four-Year-Old Children on the California Verbal Learning Test — Children's Version. *The Clinical Neuropsychologist, 13*, 274–282.

Gorham, D. R. 1956. *Clinical Manual for The Proverbs Test.* Missoula, MT: Psychological Test Specialists.

Grace, J. and Melloy, P. F. 2001. *Frontal Systems Behavioral Scale (FrSBe) Professional Manual.* Lutz, FL: Psychological Assessment Resources.

Graf, P., Uttl, B., and Tuokko, H. 1995. Color-and-Picture-Word Stroop Tests Performance Changes in Old Age. *Journal of Clinical and Experimental Neuropsychology, 17*, 390–415.

Graham, J. R. 1993. *MMPI-2 Assessing Personality and Psychopathology*, 2d ed. New York: Oxford University Press.

Grant, D. A. and Berg, E. A. 1948. A Behavioral Analysis of Degree of Impairment and Ease of Shifting to New Responses in a Weigh-Type Card Sorting Problem. *Journal of Experimental Psychology, 39*, 404–411.

Grant, I., Reed, R., and Adams, K. M. 1987. Diagnosis of Intermediate Duration and Subacute Organic Mental Disorders in Abstinent Alcoholics. *Journal of Clinical Psychiatry, 48*, 319–323.

Green, P. 2003 Green's Word Memory Test for Microsoft Windows. Edmonton, Alberta: Green's Publishing Inc.

Green, B. L., Goodman, L. A., Crupnick, J. L., Corcoran, C. B., Petty, R. M., Stockton, P., and Stern, N. M. 2000. Outcomes of Single versus Multiple Trauma Exposure in a Screening Sample. *Journal of Traumatic Stress, 13*, 271–286.

Greenbery, L. M., Kindschi, C. L., and Corman, C. M. 2000. Test of Variables of Attention: Clinical Guide. Los Alamitos, CA: Universal Attention Disorders.

Gronwall, D. 1976. Performance Changes during Recovery from Closed Head Injury. *Proceedings of the Australian Association of Neurologists, 5*, 72–78.

Gronwall, D. and Wrightson, P. 1981. Memory and Information Processing Capacity after Closed Head Injury. *Journal of Neurology, Neurosurgery and Psychiatry, 44*, 889–895.

Gronwall, D. A. and Wrightson, P. 1974. Delayed Recovery of Intellectual Function after Minor Head Injury. *The Lancet, 2*, 605–609.

Gronwall, D. M. A. 1977. Paced Auditory Serial Addition Task: A Measure of Recovery from Concussion. *Perceptual and Motor Skills, 44*, 367–373.

Gruen, A. K., Frankle, B. C., and Schwartz, R. 1990. Word Fluency Generation Skills of Head-Injured Patients in an Acute Trauma Center. *Journal of Communication Disorders, 23*, 163–170.

Halstead, W. C. 1947. *Brain Intelligence: A Quantitative Study of the Frontal Lobes.* Chicago: University of Chicago Press.

Hammeke, T. A., Golden, C. J., and Purisch, A. D. 1978. A Standardized, Short and Comprehensive Neuropsychological Test Battery Based on the Luria Neuropsychological Evaluation. *International Journal of Neuroscience, 18*, 135–141.

Hannay, J. H. and Levin, H. S. 1985. Selective Reminding Test: An Examination of the Equivalence of Four Forms. *Journal of Clinical and Experimental Neuropsychology, 7*, 251–263.

Hathaway, S. R. and McKinley, J. C. 1943. *Booklet for the Minnesota Multiphasic Personality Inventory.* New York: Psychological Corporation.

Hathaway, S. R., McKinley, J. C., Butcher, J. N., Dahlstrom, W. G., Graham, J. R., Tellegren, A., and Kaemmer, B. 1989. *Minnesota Multiphasic Personality Inventory Manual for Administration and Scoring.* Minneapolis: University of Minnesota Press.

Heaton, R. K. 1981. *Wisconsin Card Sorting Test Manual.* Odessa, FL: Psychological Assessment Resources.

Heaton, R. K., Baade, L. E., and Johnson, K. L. 1978. Neuropsychological Test Results Associated with Psychiatric Disorders in Adults. *Psychological Bulletin, 85*, 141–162.

Heaton, R. K., Chelune, G. J., Talley, J. L., Kay, G. G., and Curtis, G. 1993. *Wisconsin Card Sorting Test (WCST) Manual Revised and Expanded.* Odessa, FL: Psychological Assessment Resources.

Heaton, R. K., Grant, I., and Matthews, C. G. 1991. *Comprehensive Norms for an Expanded Halstead–Reitan Battery Demographic Corrections, Research Findings, and Clinical Applications*. Odessa, FL: Psychological Assessment Resources.

Heaton, R. K., Grant, I., and Matthews, C. G. 1986. Differences in Neuropsychological Test Performance Associated with Age, Education and Sex. In Grant, I. and Adams, K. (Eds.) *Neuropsychological Assessment of Neuropsychiatric Disorders*. New York: Oxford University Press, pp. 100–120.

Heaton, R. K., Nelson, L. M., Thompson, D. S. 1985. Neuropsychological Findings in Relapsing-Remitting and Chronic-Progressive Multiple Sclerosis. *Journal of Clinical and Experimental Neuropsychology*, *53*, 103–110.

Heaton, R. K., Ryan, L., Grant, I., and Matthews, C. G. 1996. Demographic Influences on Neuropsychological Test Performance. In Grant, I. and Adams, K. M. (Eds.) *Neuropsychological Assessment of Neuropsychiatric Disorders*, 2d ed. New York: Oxford University Press.

Heaton, R. K., Smith, H. H., Lehman, R. A., and Vogt, A. T. 1978. Prospects for Faking Believable Deficits on Neuropsychological Testing. *Journal of Consulting and Clinical Psychology*, *46*, 892–900.

Hobart, M. P., Goldberg, R., Bartko, J. J., and Gold, J. M. 1999. Repeatable for the Assessment of Neuropsychological Status as a Screening Test in Schizophrenia Convergent–Divergent Validity and Diagnostic Group Comparisons. *American Journal of Psychiatry*, *1956*, 1951–1957.

Hodatt, A. F. and Gerken, K. C. 1999. Correlations between Scores for Peabody Picture Vocabulary Test — III and the Wechsler Scale for Children III. *Psychological Reports*, *84*, 1139–1142.

Hom, J. and Reitan, R. M. 1984. Neuropsychological Correlates of Rapidly vs. Slowly Growing Intrinsic Cerebral Neoplasms. *Journal of Clinical and Experimental Neoplasms*, *6*, 309–324.

Hom, J. and Reitan, R. M. 1990. Generalized Cognitive Function after Stroke. *Journal of Clinical and Experimental Neuropsychology*, *12*, 644–654.

Hooper, H. E. 1983. *Hooper Visual Organization Test (VOT)*. Los Angeles: Western Psychological Services.

Horton, Jr., A. M. 1995. The Alternative Impairment Index: A Measure of Neuropsychological Deficit. *Perceptual and Motor Skills*, *80*, 336–338.

Horton, Jr., A. M. 1997. The Halstead–Reitan Neuropsychological Test Battery Problems and Prospects. In Horton, Jr., A.M., Wedding, D., and Webster, J. (Eds.) *The Neuropsychology Handbook*, Vol. 1. New York: Springer, pp. 221–254.

Horton, Jr., A. M. and Sobelman, S. A. 1994. The General Neuropsychological Deficit Scale and the Halstead Impairment Index Comparison of Severity. *Perceptual and Motor Skills*, *78*, 888–890.

Horton, Jr., A. M. and Wedding, D. 1984. *Clinical and Behavioral Neuropsychology*. New York: Praeger.

Hutt, M. L. 1985. *The Hutt Adaptation of the Bender–Gestalt Test Rapid Screening and Intensive Diagnosis*, 4th ed. Orlando, FL: Grune & Stratton.

Iverson, G. L. and Franzen, M. D. 1994. The Recognition Memory Test, Digit Span and Knox Cube Test as Markers of Malingered Memory Impairment. *Assessment*, *1*, 323–334.

Jorm, A. F., Anstey, K. J., Christensen, H., and Rodgers, B. 2004. Gender Differences and Cognitive Abilities: The Mediating Role of Health State and Health Habits. *Intelligence*, *32*, 7–23.

Kamphaus, R. W. and Reynolds, C. R. 1987. *Clinical and Research Applications of the K-ABC*. Circle Pines, MN: American Guidance Service.

Kaplan, E., Fein, D., Morris, R., and Delis, D. C. 1991. *WAIS-R NI Manual*. San Antonio, TX: Psychological Corporation.

Kaplan, E. F., Goodglass, H., and Weintraub, S. 1983. *The Boston Naming Test*, 2d ed. Philadelphia: Lea & Febiger.

Kaszniak, A. W. 1989. Psychological Assessment of the Aging Individual. In Birren, J. E. and Schaie, K. W. (Eds.) *Handbook of the Psychology of Aging*. New York: Academic Press.

Kaufman, A. S. and Kaufman, N. L. 1983. *K-ABC Kaufman Assessment Battery for Children*. Circle Pines, MN: American Guidance Service.

Kaufman, A. S. and Kaufman, N. L. 1990. *Kaufman Brief Intelligence Test Manual*. Circle Pines, MN: American Guidance Service.

Kaufman, A. S. and Kaufman, N. L. 2001. Time for Changing of the Guard: A Fair Well to Short-Forms of Intelligence. *Journal of Psychoeducational Assessment*, *19*, 245–267.

Kemp, S. L., Kirk, U., and Korkman, M. 2001. *Essentials of the Nepsy Assessment*. New York: John Wiley & Sons, Inc.

Keyl, P. M., Rebok, G. W., and Gallo, J. J. 1996. Screening Elderly Drivers in General Medical Settings toward the Development of a Valid and Feasible Assessment Procedure (Final Report). *Andrus Foundation of the NRTA/AARP*, Los Angeles.

Killam, C., Cautin, R. L., and Santucci, A. C. 2005. Assessing the Enduring Residual Neuropsychological Affects of Head Trauma in College Athletes Who Participate in Contact Sports. *Archives of Clinical Neuropsychology*, 20, 599–611.

Klonoff, H. and Kennedy, M. 1965. Memory and Perceptual Functioning in Octagenarians and Nonagenarians in the Community. *Journal of Gerontology*, 20, 328–333.

Klove, H. 1963. Clinical Neuropsychology. In Forster, F. M. (Ed.) *The Medical Clinics of North America*. New York: Saunders.

Koffler, S. P. and Zehler, D. 1985. Normative Data for the Hand Dynamometer. *Perceptual and Motor Skills*, 61, 589–590.

Koppitz, E. M. 1964. *The Bender–Gestalt Test for Young Children*. New York: Grune & Stratton.

Koppitz, E. M. 1975. *The Bender–Gestalt Test for Young Children, Volume II Research and Applications, 1963–1973*. New York: Grune & Stratton.

Korkman, M., Kirk, U., and Kemp, S. 1998. *Nepsy a Developmental Neuropsychological Assessment Manual*. San Antonio, TX: The Psychological Corporation.

Koss, E., Ober, B. A., Delis, D. C., and Friedland, R. P. 1984. The Stroop Color–Word Test Indicator of Dementia Severity. *International Journal of Neuroscience*, 24, 53–61.

Kramer, N. A. and Jarvik, L. 1979. Assessment of Intellectual Changes in the Elderly. In Raskin, A. and Jarvik, L. (Eds.) *Psychiatric Symptoms and Cognitive Loss in the Elderly*. Washington, DC: Hemisphere, pp. 221–272.

La Rue, A. and Jarvik, L. F. 1987. Cognitive Function and Prediction of Dementia in Old Age. *International Journal of Aging and Human Development*, 25, 79–89.

Larrabe, G. J., Kane, R. L., Schuck, J. R., and Francis, D. J. 1985. Construct Validity of Various Memory Testing Procedures. *Journal of Clinical and Experimental Neuropsychology*, 7, 239–250.

Larson, E. B., Kirschner, K., Bode, R., Hainemann, A., and Goodman, R. 2005. Construct and Predictability of the Repeatable Battery for the Assessment of Neuropsychological Status in Evaluation of Stroke Patients. *Journal of Clinical and Experimental Neuropsychology*, 27, 16–32.

Leark, R. A., Dupuy, T. R., Greenberg, L. M., Corman, C. L., and Kindsehi, C. L. 1999. *Test of Variables of Attention Professional Guide*. Los Alamitos: California Universal Attention Disorders.

Lee, G. P. and Hamsher, K. 1988. Neuropsychological Findings in Toxicometabolic Confusional States. *Journal of Clinical and Experimental Neuropsychology*, 10, 769–778.

Leininger, B. E., Gramling, S. E., Farrell, A. D., Kreutzer, J. S., and Peck, E. A. 1990. Neuropsychological Deficits in Symptomatic Minor Head Injury Patients after Concussion and Mild Concussion. *Journal of Neurology, Neurosurgery and Psychiatry*, 53, 293–296.

Lemay, S., Bedard, M. A., Rouleau, I., and Tremblay, P. L. G. 2004. Practice Effect and Test–Retest Reliability of Attentional and Executive Tests in Middle Aged Elderly Subjects. *The Clinical Neuropsychologist*, 18, 240–302.

Levin, B. E., Llabre, M. M., and Reisman, S. 1991. Visuospatial Impairment in Parkinson's Disease. *Neurology*, 41, 365–369.

Levin, H. S., Benton, A. L., and Grossman, R. G. 1982. *Neurobehavioral Consequences of Closed Head Injury*. New York: Oxford University Press.

Levin, H. S., Gary, H. E., Eisenberg, H. M. 1990. Neurobehavioral Outcome 1 Year after Severe Head Injury Experience of the Traumatic Coma Data Bank. *Journal of Neurosurgery*, 73, 699–709.

Levin, H. S., Grossman, R. C., Rose, J. E., and Teasdale, G. 1979. Long-Term Neuropsychological Outcome of Closed Head Injury. *Journal of Neurosurgery*, 50, 412–422.

Levin, H. S., Grossman, R. G., Sarwar, M., and Meyers, C. A. 1981. Linguistic Recovery after Closed Head Injury. *Brain and Language*, 12, 360–374.

Lewandowski, L. J. 1984. The Symbol Digit Modalities Test: A Screening Instrument for Brain-Damaged Children. *Perceptual and Motor Skills*, 59, 615–618.

Lezak, M. D. 1976. *Neuropsychological Assessment*. New York: Oxford University Press.

Lezak, M. D. 1983. *Neuropsychological Assessment*, 2d ed. New York: Oxford University Press.

Lezak, M. D. 1995. *Neuropsychological Assessment*, 3d ed. New York: Oxford University Press.

Lezak, M. D., Howieson, D. B., and Loring, D. W. 2004. *Neuropsychological Assessment*, 4th ed. New York: Oxford University Press.

Lezak, M. D., Whitham, R., and Bourdette, D. 1990. Emotional Impact of Cognitive Insufficiencies in Multiple Sclerosis (MS). *Journal of Clinical and Experimental Neuropsychology, 12*, 50 (Abstract).

Libon, D. J., Mattson, R. E., Glosser, G., Kaplan, E., Malamut, B. M., Sands, L. P., Swenson, R., and Cloud, B. S. 1996. A Nine-Word Dementia Version of The California Verbal Learning Test. *The Clinical Neuropsychologist, 10*, 237–244.

Llorente, A. M., Williams, J., Satz, P., and D'Elia, L. F. 2003. *Children's Color Trial Test (CCTT)*. Odessa, FL: Psychological Assessment Resources.

Long, C. J. and Brown, D. A. 1979. *Analysis of Temporal Cortex Dysfunction by Neuropsychological Techniques*. Paper presented at the annual convention of the American Psychological Association, New York.

Loring, D. W., Lee, G. P., Martin, R. C., and Meador, K. J. 1989. Verbal and Visual Memory Index Discrepancies from the Wechsler Memory Scale — Revised Cautions in Interpretations. *Psychological Assessment, 1*, 198–202.

Mahalick, D. M., Ruff, R. M., and Sang, H. S. 1991. Neuropsychological Sequelae of Arteriovenous Malformations. *Neurosurgery, 29*, 351–357.

Markwardt, F. C. 1989. Peabody Individual Achievement Test — Revised. Circle Pines, MN: American Guidance Service.

Matazow, G. S., Kamphaus, R. W., Stanton, H. C., and Reynolds, C. R. 1991. Reliability of the Kaufman Assessment Battery for Children for Black and White Students. *Journal of School Psychologists, 29*, 37–41.

Matthews, C. G. and Klove, H. 1964. *Instruction Manual for the Adult Neuropsychology Test Battery*. Madison, WI: University of Wisconsin Medical School.

McCaffrey, R. J., Cousins, J. P., Westervolt, H. J., Martynowics, M., Remick, S. C., Szebenyi, A., Waghe, W. A., Bottomly, P. A., Hardy, C. J., and Hardy, R. F. 1995. Practice Effects with NIMH AIDS Abbreviated Neuropsychological Battery. *Archives of Clinical Neuropsychology, 10*, 241–250.

McCaffrey, R. J., Krahula, M. M., Heimberg, R. G. 1988. A Comparison of the Trail Making Test, Symbol Digit Modalities Test, and the Hooper Visual Organization Test in an Inpatient Substance Abuse Population. *Archives of Clinical Neuropsychology, 3*, 181–187.

McCaffrey, R. J., Ortega, A., and Haase, R. R. 1993. Effects of Repeated Neuropsychological Assessments. *Archives of Clinical Neuropsychology, 8*, 519–524.

McCauulum, S., Bracken, B., and Wasserman, J. 2000. *Essentials of Nonverbal Assessment*. New York: John Wiley & Sons.

McKinzey, R. K. and Russell, E. W. 1997. Detection of Malingering on the Halstead–Reitan Battery: A Cross-Validation. *Archives of Clinical Neuropsychology, 12*, 585–590.

Merrill, L. L. 2001. Trauma Symptomology among Female. US Navy Recruits. *Military Medicine, 166*, 621–624.

Meyers, J. and Meyers, K. 1995. Rey Complex Figure Test under Four Different Administration Procedures. *The Clinical Neuropsychologist, 9*, 63–67.

Miceli, G., Caltagirone, C., Gainotti, G., Masullo, C., and Silveri, M. C. 1981. Neuropsychological Correlates of Localized Cerebral Lesions in Non-Aphasic Brain-Damaged Patients. *Journal of Clinical Neuropsychology, 3*, 53–63.

Millis, S. R. and Putnam, S. H. 1994. The Recognition Memory Test in the Assessment of Memory Impairment after Financially Compensable Mild Head Injury: A Replication. *Perceptual and Motor Skills, 79*, 384–386.

Millon, T. 1977. *Manual for the Millon Clinical Multiaxial Inventory (MCMI)*. Minneapolis, MN: National Computer Systems.

Millon, T. 1987. *Manual for the Millon Multiaxial Inventory — II (MCMI-II)*, 2d ed. Minneapolis, MN: National Computer Systems.

Millon, T. 1990. *Toward a New Personology*. New York: John Wiley & Sons.

Millon, T. 1994. *Manual for the Millon Clinical Multiaxial Inventory — III (MCMI-III)*, 3d ed. Minneapolis, MN: National Computer Systems.

Mittenberg, W., Rothole, A., Russell, E., and Heilbronner, R. 1996. Identification of Malingered Head Trauma on the Halstead–Reitan Battery. *Archives of Clinical Neuropsychology, 11*, 271–281.

Mittenberg, W., Thompson, G. B., and Schwartz, J. A. 1991. Abnormal and Reliable Differences among Wechsler Memory Scale — Revised Subtests. *Psychological Assessment, 3*, 492–495.

Moore, B. A. and Donders, J. 2004. Predictors of Invalid Neuropsychological Test Performance after Traumatic Brain Injury. *Brain Injury, 18*, 1965–1984.

Morey, L. C. 1991. *Personality Assessment Inventory Manual*. Odessa, FL: Psychological Assessment Resources.

Morey, L. C. 1996. *An Interpretative Guide to the Personality Assessment Inventory (PAI)*. Odessa, FL: Psychological Assessment Resources, Inc.

Morgan, S. F. and Wheelock, J. 1992. Digit Symbol and Symbol Digit Modalities Tests Are They Directly Interchangeable? *Neuropsychology, 6*, 327–330.

Morris, R. G. 1986. Short-Term Forgetting in Senile Dementia of the Alzheimer's Type. *Cognitive Neuropsychology, 3*, 77–97.

Moses, Jr., J. A. 1986. Factor Structures of Benton's Test of Visual Retention, Visual Construction and Visual Form Discrimination. *Archives of Clinical Neuropsychology, 1*, 147–156.

Moses, Jr., J. A. 1997. The Luria–Nebraska Neuropsychological Battery Advances in Interpretation. In Horton, Jr., A. M., Wedding, D., and Webster, J. (Eds.) *The Neuropsychology Handbook (Vol. 1)*, 2d ed. New York: Springer-Verlag, pp. 255–290.

Moses, Jr., J. A., Pritchard, D. A., and Adams, R. L. 1999. Normative Corrections for the Halstead–Reitan Neuropsychological Battery. *Archives of Clinical Neuropsychology, 14*, 445–454.

Newcombe, F. 1969. *Missile Wounds of the Brain*. London: Oxford University Press.

Osterrieth, P. A. 1944. Le Test de Copie d'une Figure Complex Contribution a L'Eetude de la Perception et de la Memoire. *Archives de Psychologie, 30*, 286–356.

Otto, M. W., Bruder, G. E., Fava, M., Delis, D. C., Quitkin, F. M., and Rosenbaum, J. F. 1994. Norms for Depressed Patients for The California Verbal Learning Test Associations with Depression Severity and Self-Report of Cognitive Difficulties. *Archives of Clinical Neuropsychology, 9*, 81–88.

Pankrtz, M., Moorison, A., and Plante, E. 2004. Difference in Standard Scores of Adults on the Peabody Picture Vocabulary Test (Revised Third Edition). *Journal of Speech, Language and Hearing Research, 47*, 714–718.

Peck, E. A., Mitchell, S. A., Burke, E. A., and Schwartz, S. M. 1992. Post Head Injury Normative Data for Benton Neuropsychological Tests. *Paper presented at the American Psychological Association*, Washington, DC.

Ponsford, J. and Kinsella, G. 1992. Attentional Deficits Following Closed Head Injury. *Journal of Clinical and Experimental Neuropsychology, 14*, 822–828.

Posner, M. I. and Peterson, S. E. 1990. The Attention of the Human Brain. *Annual Review of Neuroscience, 13*, 25–42.

Powell, D. H., Kaplan, E. F., Whitla, D., Weintraub, S., Catlin, R., and Funkenstein, H. H. 1993. *Microcog Assessment of Cognitive Functioning (Manual)*. San Antonio, TX: Psychological Corporation.

Powell, J. B., Cripe, L. I., and Dodrill, C. B. 1991. Assessment of Brain Impairment with the Rey 8Auditory Learning Test: A Comparison with Other Neuropsychological Measures. *Archives of Clinical Neuropsychology, 6*, 241–249.

Prewett, P. N. and Giannulli, M. M. 1991. The Relationships among the Reading Subtests of WJ-R, PIAT-R, K-TEA, and WRAT-R. *Journal of the Psychoeducational Assessment, 9*, 166–174.

Purisch, A. D. 1999. Forensic Use of the Luria–Nebraska Neuropsychological Battery. In Golden, C. J., Warren, W. L., and Espe-Pfeiffer, P. (Eds.) *The Luria–Nebraska Neuropsychological Battery: A Guide to Clinical Interpretation and Use in Special Settings*, Vol. 1. Los Angeles: Western Psychological Services, pp. 165–186.

Purisch, A. D. and Sbordone, R. J. 1986. The Luria–Nebraska Neuropsychological Battery. In Goldstein, G. and Tarter, R. A. (Eds.) *Advances in Clinical Neuropsychology*, Vol. 3. New York: Plenum Press, pp. 291–316.

Rabin, L. A., Barr, W. B., and Burton, L. A. 2005. Assessment Practices of Clinical Neuropsychologist in the United States and Canada: A Survey of INS, NAN, and APA Division 40 Members. *Archives of Clinical Neuropsychology, 20*, 33–65.

Radanovic, M. and Scaff, M. 2003. Speech and Language Disturbances Due to Subcortical Lesions. *Brain and Language, 84*, 337–352.

Randolph, C. 1998. *RBANS Manual*. San Antonio, TX: Psychological Corporation.

Randolph, C., Gold, J. M., Kozora, E., Cullum, C. M., Hermann, B. P., and Wyler, A. R. 1994. Estimating Memory Function Disparity of Wechsler Memory Scale — Revised and California Verbal Learning Test indices in Clinical and Normal Samples. *The Clinical Neuropsychologist, 8*, 99–108.

Randolph, C., Tierney, M. C., Mohr, E., and Chase T. M. 1998. The Repeatable Battery for the Assessment of Neuropsychological Status (RBANS) Preliminary Clinical Validity. *Journal of Clinical and Experimental Neuropsychology, 20*, 310–319.

Raskin, A., Friedman, A. S., and Di Mascio, A. 1982. Cognitive and Performance Deficits in Depression. *Psychopharmacology Bulletin, 18*, 196–202.

Raven, J. C. [1965] 1994. *Advanced Progressive Matrices Sets I and II*. Oxford, U.K.: Oxford Psychologists Press.

Raven, J. C. [1947] 1995. *Colored Progressive Matrices Sets A, AB, B*. Oxford, U.K.: Oxford Psychologists Press.

Raven, J. C. [1938] 1996. *Progressive Matrices: A Perceptual Test of Intelligence, Individual Form*. Oxford, U.K.: Oxford Psychologists Press.

Reddon, J. R., Stefanyk, W. O., Gill, D. M., and Renney, C. 1985. Hand Dynamometer Effects of Trials and Sessions. *Perceptual and Motor Skills, 61*, 1195–1198.

Reed, H. B., Reitan, R. M., and Klove, H. 1965. The Influence of Cerebral Lesions on Psychological Test Performance of Older Children. *Journal of Consulting Psychology, 29*, 247–251.

Reese, E. and Read, S. 2000. Predictive Validity of the New Zealand MacArthur Communicative Development Inventory Words and Sentences. *Journal of Trial Language, 27*, 255.

Reitan, R. M. 1955. Investigation of the Validity of Halstead's Measure of Biological Intelligence. *AMA Archives of Neurology and Psychiatry, 73*, 28–35.

Reitan, R. M. 1974. Methodological Problems in Clinical Neuropsychology. In Reitan, R. M. and Davidson, L. A. (Eds.) *Clinical Neuropsychology Current Status and Application*. New York: John Wiley & Sons, pp. 19–46.

Reitan, R. M. and Wolfson, D. 1986. The Halstead–Reitan Neuropsychological Test Battery. In Wedding, D., Horton, Jr., A. M., and Webster, J. S. (Eds.) *The Neuropsychology Handbook*. New York: Springer-Verlag, pp. 134–160.

Reitan, R. M. and Wolfson, D. 1988. *Traumatic Brain Injury. Recovery and Rehabilitation*, Vol. 2. Tucson, AZ: Neuropsychology Press.

Reitan, R. M. and Wolfson, D. 1989. The Seashore Rhythm Test and Brain Functions. *The Clinical Neuropsychologist, 3*, 70–78.

Reitan, R. M. and Wolfson, D. 1992. *Neuropsychological Evaluation of Younger Children*. Tucson, AZ: Neuropsychology Press.

Reitan, R. M. and Wolfson, D. 1993. *The Halstead–Reitan Neuropsychological Test Battery Theory and Clinical Interpretation*. Tucson, AZ: Neuropsychology Press.

Reitan, R. M. and Wolfson, D. 1995. Influence of Age and Education on Neuropsychological Test Results. *The Clinical Neuropsychologist, 9*, 151–158.

Reitan, R. M. and Wolfson, D. 1996. Relationship of Age and Education to Wechsler Adult Intelligence Scale IQs and Brain-Damaged and Non-Brain-Damaged Groups. *The Clinical Neuropsychologist, 10*, 293–304.

Reitan, R. M. and Wolfson, D. 1997. The Influence of Age and Education on Neuropsychological Performances of Persons with Mild Head Injuries. *Applied Neuropsychology, 4*, 16–33.

Reynolds, C. R. 2002. *Comprehensive Trail-Making Test*. Austin, TX: Pro-Ed Inc.

Riccio, C. A., Reynolds, C. R., and Lowe, P. A. 2001. *Clinical Applications of Continuous Performance Test Measuring Attention and Impulsive Responding in Children and Adults*. New York: John Wiley & Sons.

Robertson, I. H., Ward, T., Ridgeway, B., and Nimmo-Smith, I. 1994. *The Test of Everyday Attention*. Bury St. Edmunds, England: Thames Valley Test Center.

Roid, J. H. 2003. *Stanford–Binet Intelligence Scales*, 5th ed. Itasca, IL: Riverside Publishing.

Rosvold, H. E., Mirski, A. F., Sarason, I., Bransome, E. D., and Beck, L. H. 1956. A Continuous Performance Test of Brain Damage. *Journal of Consulting Psychology, 20*, 343–350.

Ruff, R. M. 1985. *San Diego Neuropsychological Test Battery (Manual)*. San Diego, TX: University of California.

Ruff, R. M. 1988. *Ruff Figural Fluency Test*. San Diego: Neuropsychological Resources.

Ruff, R. M. 1994. What Role Does Depression Play on the Performance of the Ruff 2 and 7 Selective Attention Test? *Perceptual and Motor Skills, 78*, 63–66.

Ruff, R. M. and Allen, C. C. 1996. *Ruff 2 and 7 Selective Attention Test Professional Manual*. Odessa, FL: Psychological Assessment Resources.

Ruff, R. M. and Allen, C. C. 1999. *The Ruff–Light Trial Learning Test*. Odessa, FL: PAR.

Ruff, R. M. and Hibbard, K. M. 2003. *The Ruff Neurobehavioral Inventory*. Lutz, FL: Psychological Assessment Resources.

Ruff, R. M., Allen, C. C., Farrow, C. E., Niemann, H., and Wylie, T. 1994. Differential Impairment in Patients with Left versus Right Frontal Lobe Lesions. *Archives of Clinical Neuropsychology*, 9, 41–55.

Ruff, R. M., Evans, R., and Marshall, L. F. 1986. Impaired Verbal and Figural Fluency after Head Injury. *Archives of Clinical Neuropsychology*, 1, 87–101.

Ruff, R. M., Light, R., and Evans, R. 1987. The Ruff Figural Fluency Test: A Normative Study with Adults. Developmental *Neuropsychology*, 3, 37–51.

Ruff, R. M., Niemann, H., Allen, C. C., Farrow, C. E., and Wylie, T. 1992. The Ruff 2 and 7 Selective Attention Test: A Neuropsychological Application. *Perceptual and Motor Skills*, 75, 1311–1319.

Russell, E. W. 1976. The Bender–Gestalt and the Halstead–Reitan Battery: A Case Study. *Journal of Clinical Psychology*, 32, 355–361.

Russell, E. W., Neuringer, C., and Goldstein, G. 1970. *Assessment of Brain Damage a Neuropsychological Key Approach*. New York: Wiley-Interscience.

Russell, E. W., Russell, S. L. K., and Hill, B. D. 2005. The Fundamental Psychometric Status of Neuropsychological Batteries. *Archives of Clinical Neuropsychology*, 20, 785–794.

Salthouse, T. A., Atkinson, T. M., and Berish, D. E. 2003. Executive functioning as a Potential Mediator of Age-Related Cognitive Decline in Normal Adults. *Journal of Experimental Psychology: General*, 132, 566–594.

Sawrie, S. M., Chelune, G. J., Naughe, R. I., and Luders, H. O. 1996. Empirical Methods for Assessing Meaningful Change Following Epilepsy Surgery. *Journal of the International Neuropsychological Association*, 2, 556–564.

Sbordone, R. J. 1991. *Neuropsychology for the Attorney*. Boca Raton, FL: CRC Press.

Sbordone, R. J. 1996. Ecological Validity Some Critical Issues for the Neuropsychologist. In Sbordone, R. J. and Long, C. J. (Eds.) *Ecological Validity of Neuropsychological Testing*. Delray Beach, FL: GR/St. Lucie Press, pp. 15–42.

Sbordone, R. J. 1997. The Ecological Validity of Neuropsychological Testing. In Horton, Jr., A. M., Wedding, D., and Webster, J. (Eds.) *The Neuropsychology Handbook (Vol. 1)*, 2d ed. New York: Springer, pp. 365–392.

Sbordone, R. J. 2000. The Executive Functions of the Brain. In Groth-Marnat, G. (Ed.) *Neuropsychological Assessment in Clinical Practice: A Practical Guide to Test Interpretation and Integration*. New York: John Wiley & Sons.

Sbordone, R. J. and Guilmette, T. J. 1999. Ecological Validity: A Prediction of Everyday and Vocational Functioning from Neuropsychological Test Data. In Sweet, J. J. (Ed.) *Forensic Neuropsychology Fundamentals and Practice*. Lisse, Netherlands: Swets & Zeitlinger, pp. 227–254.

Sbordone, R. J. and Purisch, A. D. 1996. Hazards of Blind Analysis of Neuropsychological Test Data in Assessing Cognitive Disability the Role of Confounding Factors. *Neurorehabilitation*, 7, 15–26.

Sbordone, R. J., Seyranian, G., and Ruff, R. M. 1998. Are the Subjective Complaints of Tramatic Brain-Injured Patients Reliable? *Brain Injury*, 12, 505–515.

Schachinger, H., Cox, D., Linder, L., Brody, S., and Keller, U. 2003. Cognitive and Psychomotor and Hypoglycemia Response Error Patterns and Retest Reliability. *Pharmacology Biochemistry and Behavior*, 75, 915–920.

Schmidt, M. 1996. *Rey Auditory–Verbal Learning Test*. Los Angeles: Western Psychological Services.

Schmidt, M. 1997. Some cautions on interpreting qualitative indices for word-list learning tests. *The Clinical Neuropsychologist*, 11, 81–86.

Schmitt, F. A., Bigley, J. W., McKinnis, R., Logue, P. E., Evans, R. W., Drucker, J. L., and the AZT Collaborative Working Group. 1988. Neuropsychological Outcome of Zidovudine (AZT) Treatment of Patients with AIDS and AIDS-Related Complex. *New England Journal of Medicine*, 319, 1573–1578.

Schreiber, D. J., Goldman, H., Kleinman, K. M. 1976. The Relationship between Independent Neuropsychological and Neurological Detection and Localization of Cerebral Impairment. *Journal of Nervous and Mental Disorders*, 162, 360–365.

Schretlen, D. 1997. *Brief Test of Attention (Manual)*. Odessa, FL: Psychological Assessment Resources.

Sears, J. D., Hirt, M. L., and Hale, R. W. 1984. And Cross Validation of the Luria–Nebraska Neuropsychological Battery. *Journal of Consulting and Clinical Psychology*, *52*, 309–310.

Seashore, C. E., Lewis, D., and Saetveit, D. L. 1960. *Seashore Measures of Musical Talents (Revised)*. New York: The Psychological Corporation.

Seidel, W. T. and Joshko, M. 1991. Assessment of Attention in Children. *The Clinical Psychologist*, *5*, 53–66.

Shear, J. M. and Craft, R. B. 1989. Examination of the Concurrent Validity of the California Verbal Learning Test. *The Clinical Neuropsychologist*, *3*, 162–168.

Shelly, C. and Goldstein, G. 1982. Psychometric Relations between the Luria–Nebraska and Halstead–Reitan Neuropsychological Battery in a Neuropsychiatric Setting. *Clinical Neuropsychology*, *4*, 128–133.

Sheslow, D. and Adams, W. 2003. *Wide Range of Assessment of Memory and Learning, Administration and Technical Manual*, 2d ed. Wilmington, DE: Wide Range.

Sivan, A. B. 1992. *Benton Visual Retention Test*, 5th ed. San Antonio: Psychological Corporation.

Smith, A. 1968. The Symbol Digit Modalities Test: A Neuropsychologic Test for Economic Screening of Learning and Other Cerebral Disorders. *Learning Disorders*, 3, 83–91.

Smith, A. 1991. *Symbol Digit Modalities Test*. Los Angeles: Western Psychological Services.

Snow, W. G. 1987. Aphasia Screening Test Performance in Patients with Lateralized Brain Damage. *Journal of Clinical Psychology*, *43*, 266–271.

Spikman, J. M., Deelman, B. G., and Van Zomeren, A. H. 2000. Executive Functioning, Attention and Frontal Lesions in Patients with Chronic CHI. *Journal of Experimental Neuropsychology*, *22*, 325–338.

Spreen, O. and Benton, A. L. 1977. *Neurosensory Center Comprehensive Examination for Aphasia (NCCEA)*. Victoria, British Columbia University of Victoria: Neuropsychology Laboratory.

Spreen, O. and Strauss, E. 1998. *A Compendium of Neuropsychological Tests*. New York: Oxford University Press.

Spruill, J. 1984. Wechsler Adult Intelligence Scale — Revised. In Keyser, D., Storandt, M., Botwinick, J., and Danzinger, W. L. (Eds.) *Test Critiques*. Kansas City, MO: Test Corporation of America.

Stern, R. A. and White, T. 2003. *Neuropsychological Assessment Battery Administration, Scoring, and Interpretation Manual*. Lutz, FL: Psychological Assessment Resources.

Stockman, I. J. 2000. The New P Body Picture Vocabulary Test-III: An Illusion of Unbiased Assessments? *Language, Speech, and Hearing Services in the Schools*, *31*, 340–353.

Storandt, M., Bowinick, J., and Danzinger, W. L. 1986. Longitudinal Changes Patients with Mild SDAT and Matched Healthy Controls. In Poon, L. W. (Ed.) *Handbook for Clinical Memory Assessment of Older Adults*. Washington, DC: American Psychological Association.

Strauss, E., Hunter, M., and Wada, J. 1993. Wisconsin Card Sort Performance Effects of Age of Onset and Laterality of Dysfunction. *Journal of Clinical and Experimental Neuropsychology*, *15*, 896–902.

Strauss, E., Sherman, E. M. S., and Spreen, O. 2006. *A Compendium of Neuropsychological Tests*, 3d ed. New York: Oxford Press.

Stroop, J. R. 1935. Studies of Interference in Serial Verbal Reaction. *Journal of Experimental Psychology*, *18*, 643–662.

Stuss, D. T. and Benson, D. F. 1986. *The Frontal Lobes*. New York: Raven Press.

Stuss, D. T., Benson, D. F., Kaplan, E. F., Weir, W. S., Naeser, M. A., Lieberman, I., and Ferrill, D. 1983. The Involvement of Orbitofrontal Cerebrum in Cognitive Tasks. *Neuropsychologia*, *21*, 235–248.

Stuss, D. T., Stetham, L. L., and Pelchat, G. 1988. Three Tests of Attention and Rapid Information Processing an Extension. *The Clinical Neuropsychologist*, *2*, 246–250.

Stuss, D. T., Stetham, L. L., Hugenholtz, H., and Richard, M. T. 1989. Traumatic Brain Injury: A Comparison of Three Clinical Tests, and Analysis of Recovery. *The Clinical Neuropsychologist*, *3*, 145–156.

Sunderland, A., Harris, B., and Baddeley, A. D. 1983. Do Laboratory Tests Predict Everyday Behavior? A Neuropsychological Study. *Journal of Verbal Learning and Verbal Behavior*, *22*, 341–357.

Sweet, J. J. and Moberg, P. J. 1990. A Survey of Practices and Beliefs among ABPP and Non-ABPP Clinical Neuropsychologists. *The Clinical Neuropsychologist*, *4*, 101–120.

Taylor, L. B. 1969. Localization of Cerebral Lesions by Psychological Testing. *Clinical Neurosurgery*, *16*, 269–287.

Taylor, R. 1998. Indices of Neuropsychological Functioning and Decline Over Time in Dementia. *Archives of Gerontology and Geriatrics*, *27*, 165.

The Psychological Corporation. 1992. *Wechsler Individual Achievement Test*. San Antonio, TX: Author.

The Psychological Corporation. 2002. *Wechsler Individual Achievement Test*, 2d ed. San Antonio, TX: Author.

Thompson, L. L. and Parsons, O. A. 1985. Contribution of the TPT to Adult Neuropsychological Assessment: A Review. *Journal of Clinical and Experimental Neuropsychology*, 7, 430–444.

Thorndike, R. L., Hagen, E. P., and Sattler, J. M. 1986. *Stanford–Binet Intelligence Scale*, 4th ed. Chicago: Riverside Publishing.

Trahan, D. E. 1997. Relationship between Facial Discrimination and Visual Neglect in Patients with Unilateral Vascular Lesions. *Archives of Clinical Neuropsychology*, 12, 57–62.

Trahan, D. E. and Larrabee, G. J. 1984. *Construct Validity and Normative Data for Some Recently Developed Measures of Visual and Verbal Memory*. Paper presented at the 12th Annual Meeting of the International Neuropsychological Society, Houston, TX.

Trahan, D. E. and Larrabee, G. J. 1988. *Continuous Visual Memory Test*. Odessa, FL: Psychological Assessment Resources.

Trenerry, M. R., Crossen, B., DeBoe, J., and Lember, W. R. 1989. *Stroop Neurological Screening Test*. Odessa, FL: Psychological Assessment Resources.

Uchiyama, C. L., D'Elia, L. F., Dellinger, A. M., Becker, J. T., Selnes, O. A., Wesch, J. E., Chen, B. B., Satz, P., Van Gorp, W., and Miller, E. N. 1995. Alternative Forms of the Auditory–Verbal Learning Test Issues of Test Comparability, Longitudinal Reliability, and Moderating Demographic Variables. *Archives of Clinical Neuropsychology*, 10, 147–158.

Uzzell, B. P., Langfitt, T. W., and Dolinskas, C. A. 1987. Influence of Injury Severity on Quality of Survival after Head Injury. *Surgical Neurology*, 27, 419–429.

Van Zandvoort, M., De Haane, E., Van Gijm, J., and Catpelle, L. J. 2003. Cognitive Function Indications with a Small Infarct in the Brain Stem. *Journal of the International Neuropsychological Society*, 9, 490–494.

Vega, Jr., A. and Parsons, O. A. 1967. Cross Validation of the Halstead–Reitan Tests for Brain Damage. *Journal of Consulting Psychology*, 31, 619–623.

Walker, A. J., Shores, E. A., Trollor, J. M., Lee, T., and Sachdev, P. S. 2000. Neuropsychological Functioning Adults with Attention Deficit Hyperactivity Disorder. *Journal of Clinical and Experimental Neuropsychology*, 22, 115–124.

Warrington, E. K. 1984. *Recognition Memory Test Manual*. Windsor, U.K.: NFER–Nelson.

Wechsler, D. 1981. *Wechsler Adult Intelligence Scale — Revised*. New York: Psychological Corporation.

Wechsler, D. 1987. *Wechsler Memory Scale — Revised*. San Antonio: Psychological Corporation.

Wechsler, D. 1992. *Wechsler Individual Achievement Test*. San Antonio, TX: Psychological Corporation.

Wechsler, D. 1997a. *Wechsler Adult Intelligence Scale*, 3d ed. San Antonio, TX: Psychological Corporation.

Wechsler, D. 1997b. *Wechsler Memory Scale*, 3d ed. San Antonio, TX: Psychological Corporation.

Wechsler, D. 2002. *WPPSI-III Technical and Interpretive Manual*. San Antonio, TX: The Psychological Corporation.

Wechsler, D. 2003. *WISC-IV Technical and Interpretive Manual*. San Antonio, TX: The Psychological Corporation.

Wheeler, L., Burke, C. J., and Reitan, R. M. 1963. An Application of Discriminant Functions to the Problem of Predicting Brain Damage Using Behavioral Variables. *Perceptual and Motor Skills*, 15, 789–799.

Wheeler, L. and Reitan, R. M. 1963. Discriminant Functions Applied to the Problem of Predicting Cerebral Damage from Behavioral Testing: A Cross-Validiation Study. *Perceptual and Motor Skills*, 16, 681–701.

White, T. and Stern, R. A. 2003. *Neuropsychological Assessment Battery, Psychometric and Technical Manual*. Lutz, FL: Psychological Assessment Resources.

Whitworth, R. H. 1984. Bender Visual Motor Gestalt Test. In Keyser, D. J. and Sweetland, R. C. (Eds.) *Test Critiques*, Vol. I. Kansas City, MO: Test Corporation of America, pp. 90–98.

Wilkinson, G. S. 1993. *WRAT3 Administration Manual*. Wilmington, DE: Wide Range, Inc.

Wilson, B. A. 1991. Long-Term Prognosis of Patients with Severe Memory Disorders. *Neuropsychological Rehabilitation*, 1, 117–134.

Wilson, B. A. 1993. Ecological Validity of Neuropsychological Assessment: Do Neuropsychological Indices Predict Performance in Everyday Activities? *Applied and Preventive Psychology*, 2, 209–215.

Wilson, B. A., Alderman, N., Burgess, P. W., Emslie, H., and Evans, J. J. 1996. *Behavioral Assessment of the Dysexecutive Syndrome*. Bury St. Edmunds, U.K.: Thames Valley Test Company.

Wilson, B. A., Baddeley, A., Cockburn, J., and Hiorns, R. 1989a. *Rivermead Behavioural Memory Test Supplement Two*. Bury St. Edmunds, U.K.: Thames Valley Test Company.

Wilson, B. A., Baddeley, A., Cockburn, J., and Hiorns, R. 1989b. The Development and Validation of a Test Battery for Detecting and Monitoring Everyday Memory Problems. *Journal of Clinical and Experimental Neuropsychology, 11*, 855–870.

Wilson, B. A., Cockburn, J., and Baddeley, A. 1985. *The Rivermead Behavioural Memory Test.* Bury St. Edmunds, U.K.: Thames Valley Test Company.

Wilson, P. A., Cockburn, J., Baddeley, A., and Hiorns, R. 2003. *Rivermead Behavioral Memory Test — Supplement Two.* Bury St. Edmunds, U.K.: Thames Valley Test Company.

Yeates, K. O. and Donders, J. 2005. The WISC-IV and Neuropsychological Assessment. In Prifitera, A. Saklofsky, D. H., and Weiss, L. G. (Eds.) *WISC-IV Clinical Use and Interpretation Scientist — Practitioner Perspectives.* New York: Elsevier Academic Press.

13 The Interpretation of Neuropsychological Test Data: Assessment Issues

In Chapter 10 the importance of gathering a comprehensive database when conducting a neuropsychological evaluation was discussed; the background, history, qualitative clinical observations, quantitative neuropsychological and personality test results, and information obtained from collateral sources and review of records, all being critical components of a thorough exam. We favor an approach in which each component of the evaluation can be used to generate hypotheses that can be supported or rejected by integrating all possible sources of data.

Neuropsychological tests are viewed as only one component of the total evaluation, not the central focus of the evaluation itself. It has been our unfortunate experience in reviewing many neuropsychological reports that errors in the interpretation of the neuropsychological test results are frequent. Such interpretations can be readily challenged only if the full database inclusive of the interview, observations, collateral data, and record review are considered. This chapter will focus on critical issues in evaluating the quality of the neuropsychological data, the interpretations derived from this data, and the process of integrating this information within the broader context.

DIFFERENT LEVELS OF EVALUATING NEUROPSYCHOLOGICAL TEST DATA

There are different levels in which neuropsychological test data can be evaluated. The rationale, strengths and weaknesses of each level of evaluation need to be appreciated to make optimal use of the data to arrive at opinions regarding a patient's neurocognitive functioning. These levels can be labeled as follows: screening to identify cognitive impairment; identifying the strengths and weaknesses of a patient's test performance; identifying underlying factors on the basis of pattern analysis; and performing a comprehensive integration of the historical, qualitative, quantitative, and collateral data. Only the latter constitutes a comprehensive neuropsychological evaluation. However, each level, in its own way, has utility, given the context and skills of the examining psychologist.

SCREENING: SENSITIVITY AND SPECIFICITY

Screening typically refers to the use of cognitive tests to identify the presence of brain impairment. Screening for "organicity" was the first and most important clinical application of cognitive tests. The reported sensitivity of these tests to detect brain dysfunction established clinical psychology, and later neuropsychology, as a recognized diagnostic specialty within neurological and psychiatric contexts. The concept of "organicity" derived from the assumption that the common impairments of most patients suffering from brain disease or damage could be detected on the basis of their performance of cognitive tests. Tests that were later developed under this assumption were constructed to be sensitive to the cognitive manifestation of brain-damage or dysfunction. For example, the Bender–Gestalt, one of the earliest and most popular of these screening tests, examines the patient's ability to copy a series of designs of varying complexity and detail. The sensitivity of the Bender–Gestalt to brain impairment is based on the observation that visual–motor integration, a composite of neuropsychological skills underlining the copying of designs, is often disrupted in many patients with brain-damage or disease. Like many other screening tests, elaborate scoring systems were developed to examine a patient's drawings for the presence of "organic signs" such as rotation, dog-ears, tremors, and so forth (Lacks, 1999).

The degree to which a test is able to detect the phenomenon for which it is designed is called its *sensitivity*; in the previous example, the sensitivity of the Bender–Gestalt would relate to the degree to which it proved its ability to identify patients with known brain-damage or dysfunction. The sensitivity of a test is typically expressed in percentages. For example, if the Bender–Gestalt was administered to 50 patients with known brain-damage and, according to the scoring system, 40 of these patients scored in the range deemed to be consistent with organicity, the sensitivity would be deemed to be 80% (40/50). As with many similar tests, attempts were made to increase the sensitivity of the Bender–Gestalt, for example, adding a background interference procedure, that is, having a patient copy the designs on a paper with light squiggly lines to serve as a distraction (Boake and Adams, 1982). Similarly, other procedures have been developed to enhance the sensitivity of the Bender–Gestalt, such as adding a memory condition in which patient is asked to draw the designs from memory immediately after they had copied them or at a delay.

The use of screening tests does not require particular expertise in neuropsychology. Indeed, training in clinical psychology typically includes training in the use of such screening measures, the purpose being to enable the psychologist to identify patients who may be suffering from some form of brain-damage or dysfunction. The clinical psychologist's function in this case is analogous to a general medical practitioner who must be capable of recognizing the hallmarks of a large number of medical conditions with sufficient expertise so that a referral to an appropriate specialist can be made. Unfortunately, psychologists often do not refer patients whom they have identified as "organic" to neuropsychologists for a more comprehensive evaluation of the patient's cognitive functioning.

The sensitivity of any screening test will never be 100%. There is no test that can identify all forms of neuropsychological impairment. For example, a patient with a right temporal lobe lesion may have difficulty in perception of nonverbal auditory stimuli, such as music or intonations of voice. It is unlikely that these impairments would be identified by the Bender–Gestalt, which focuses upon visual–motor integration skills. Consequently, sensitivity to a wide range of brain disorders cannot be obtained from a single measure or procedure. Optimally, a variety of measures, each with proven sensitivity to some forms of brain disorder, should be included in a screening battery.

The Halstead–Reitan (Reitan, 1993) and the Luria–Nebraska (Golden et al., 1985) Neuropsychological Batteries have been developed as relatively comprehensive procedures that could form the core of a neuropsychological evaluation. Each battery evaluates a wide range of neuropsychological functions, including skills related to motor, perceptual, language, memory, intellectual, and executive functions. By casting a wide net, these batteries are generally very sensitive to many forms of brain disorder. In one study, Filskov and Goldstein (1974) found that the Halstead–Reitan was capable of correctly identifying neuropsychological impairment in every single case of a large sample of hospitalized brain-damaged patients.

Although sensitivity is a critical component in determining the utility of a neuropsychological instrument, it needs to be balanced with the *specificity* at which particular disorders are identified. Specificity is the opposite of sensitivity. It refers to the ability of a test procedure or battery to identify subjects as *not* suffering from "organicity." For example, if the population assessed contained 50 subjects without brain-damage and the test demonstrated scores within the normal or nonbrain damage range for 40 of this group, its specificity would be 80% (40/50). The Filskov and Goldstein (1974) study did not address the issue of the specificity of the Halstead–Reitan. There was no control group of patients without brain disorder; all were patients with confirmed brain-damage. Thus, even though the sensitivity in this study was 100%, the Halstead–Reitan would have proven virtually useless if the significant majority of nonpatients also scored in the organic range. While sensitivity would be perfect, the specificity to brain-damage would be very low.

Care must be taken to examine the *hit rates* of any given neuropsychological procedure or battery in identifying organicity. The hit rate is the percentage of patients who are correctly placed into their clinical group. Thus, a test that correctly identifies 45 out of 50 patients as brain-damaged would have a sensitivity of 90%. If this same test identifies 35 out of 50 nonpatients as falling within the normal range, its specificity would be 70%. The hit rate represents the overall effectiveness, combining the sensitivity and specificity of the test. In this particular example, the hit rate would be 80% in that 80 out of 100 of the overall sample were correctly placed into their group.

Use of comprehensive neuropsychological test batteries such as the Halstead–Reitan and Luria–Nebraska have documented hit rates hovering around 90% in studies contrasting performance of patients with identified brain-damage to control patients (Golden et al., 1985; Reitan, 1993). Not surprisingly, tests that assess a single or limited number of functions, such as the Bender–Gestalt, typically have hit rates significantly lower than those derived from broad batteries in which a wide range of functions are assessed (Spreen and Benton, 1965). Empirical cookbook rules have been developed to address even more specific issues such as the *laterality* (right or left side of the brain) or specific *locus* (lobe or even more specific location) of brain injury (as opposed to merely identifying the *presence* of brain-damage). However, as the diagnostic questions become more specific, hit rates generally tend to diminish (Russell et al., 1970). Thus, the hit rates of identifying whether a person has brain dysfunction are greater than those for determining whether the dysfunction is in the left or right hemisphere, which in turn is typically greater in determining which lobe is maximally impaired.

A number of factors influence the sensitivity and specificity of neuropsychological tests. The level of the cutoff score between normal and impaired performance is one such factor. The establishment of a stringent or conservative cutoff score reduces the sensitivity of a test, that is, the performance has to demonstrate a greater level of impairment in order to be deemed as abnormal. Conversely, a more liberal cutoff score will enhance the sensitivity of the test, that is, the performance needs to demonstrate a lower level of impairment in order to be deemed as abnormal. The level of the cutoff score has the opposite effect on a test's specificity; conservative cutoffs result in improved specificity while liberal cutoffs result in diminished specificity.

The failure to identify a patient with brain-damage as being organic by a given cutoff score is referred to as a *false negative* error. Conversely, the false identification of organicity in a nonbrain damaged subject is referred to as a *false positive* error. Setting of the cutoff scores usually considers maintaining the highest hit rate possible while striking a reasonable balance between false positive errors and false negative errors. However, certain circumstances may require a more conservative or liberal cutoff to be established. A more conservative cutoff runs the risk of false negative errors (failing to identify real cases of brain-damage), but may be appropriate under certain circumstances. For example, in a health clinic operating with limited funding, patients who will receive services need to be selected carefully. Only patients with a high potential of having brain-damage would be referred for further workup. On the other hand, situations in which there may be consequences for failure to diagnose or identify patients with brain-damage, the cutoff point should be more liberal, running the risk of more false positives (falsely identifying nonbrain damaged cases as brain-damaged). Despite the risks, such a liberal approach would minimize the potential for overlooking patients with bona fide brain-damage who require further workup.

Cutoff scores can also affect decisions in medicolegal situations. Thus, a plaintiff claiming brain injury after a motor vehicle accident may be deemed as falling in the normal or impaired range depending upon the cutoff scores utilized by the evaluating psychologist. Differences in opinion between the psychologists retained by the defense and the plaintiff may be more apparent than real. The defense-retained psychologist may set a very stringent cutoff point, thereby lowering the sensitivity of the battery to identify brain-damage. The plaintiff-retained psychologist may, on the other hand, set a very liberal cutoff point, increasing the sensitivity of the test to brain-damage. For example, a criminal defendant in a capital murder case underwent two neuropsychological evaluations for the purpose of determining his competency to stand trial, one for the defense (arguing incompetency) and one for the prosecution (arguing competency). His performance on a critical measure of problem solving and reasoning fell 1.7 standard deviations below the population average, or at the fourth percentile. The prosecution-retained neuropsychologist considered this performance to fall within the borderline range of impairment using classifications derived from the Wechsler Intelligence Scales, whereas the defense-retained neuropsychologist considered this performance as being clearly impaired using a categorization system in which levels of impairment are gauged upon standard deviations from the average performance. (These categorization systems will be discussed in greater detail below.) As such, the prosecution-retained neuropsychologist's interpretation did not support a definitive diagnosis of brain dysfunction as a factor in determining the defendant's competency. The defense-retained neuropsychologist reached an opposite conclusion on the basis of the same set of test results.

There are other factors that impact sensitivity and specificity in addition to the cutoff point. The decision to use a particular cutoff point is often influenced by hit rates for the test reported in published studies. However, hit rates can be easily inflated or deflated by the design of the study. If the groups compared in a study are very different, then the hit rate may be spuriously inflated. For example, a study utilizing cognitive tests to discriminate patients with middle-stage Alzheimer's disease from young healthy college-educated controls could be expected to obtain a hit rate of 100%.

If the groups compared in a study are very similar, then the hit rates may be deflated. For example, if two organically impaired groups of patients were contrasted, such as those with acquired brain injury and chronic schizophrenics, then the hit rate may be considerably lower, hovering around 65% (Heaton et al., 1978). A significant percentage of schizophrenics are brain impaired, a condition that a sensitive neuropsychological test should detect. This same sensitive test should also be capable of identifying the patients with acquired brain-damage as being impaired. Thus, a significant proportion of schizophrenics and patients with acquired brain-damage perform in the abnormal range; the hit rate for discrimination of these groups is negatively affected.

A test should not be automatically discarded if its ability to discriminate between groups of patients is relatively low. The decision to use or discard the particular instrument will depend upon its ability to discriminate the groups beyond the *base rate* of each condition. The base rate is the frequency at which something occurs. Thus, if there are 50 chronic schizophrenics and 50 patients with mild acquired brain injury, the base rate of schizophrenia is 50% and the base rate of mild acquired brain injury is 50% in that population. Simply flipping a coin would result in a classification rate of 50%, no better than the base rate. However, if a neuropsychological test is able to obtain a hit rate of 65% then this exceeds the base rate and the test may, in fact, be of some utility.

DESCRIPTION OF STRENGTHS AND WEAKNESSES

The second level of neuropsychological assessment is one in which test results are used to provide a relatively cursory and superficial description of strengths and weaknesses. In this model, each test or subtest performance is typically interpreted individually rather than as a constituent part of a broader battery of test performances. Interpretation frequently consists of a description of what each individual test is intended to measure along with the level of performance obtained on that test. For example, the Picture Arrangement subtest of the Wechsler Intelligence Scales is frequently considered a measure of "social intelligence" (Wechsler, 1997a). Thus, a performance on this measure 2 standard deviations above the mean (98th percentile) might be described as reflecting superior social intelligence, whereas a performance on the other end of the spectrum 2 standard deviations below the mean (second percentile) might be interpreted as reflecting impaired social intelligence.

Such descriptions are superficial and can be quite misleading. *No neuropsychological test measures only a single construct, such as social intelligence* (Luria, 1980). An analysis of the demands of the Picture Arrangement subtest of the Wechsler Adult Intelligence Scale, in this example, illustrates this point. On this particular test, the subject is presented with about four or five pictures, similar to individual frames in a cartoon. These pictures are out of sequence and the subject's task is to put them in a sequence that will result in a meaningful story line. It is not difficult to appreciate why this particular test is believed to tap into aspects of what might be considered social intelligence. In order to perform well on the test, the subject needs to be able to analyze the characters, their expressions, their actions, and the environmental context to determine the flow of the story, all elements that likely contribute to a comprehension of the social environment in daily life. However, there are numerous abilities that are required for sequencing the cards in the appropriate manner: visual perception, sequencing skills, working memory, attention to detail, language skills (where there are contextual elements such as signs in the pictures), fine motor skills (to actually manipulate and place the cards), and executive skills related to hypothesis formation and testing, among others. Furthermore, *no single test can capture all the elements of a global ability, such as social intelligence.*

If the subject proves deficient in any one of the component skills required to perform the Picture Arrangement subtest, sequencing the cards will be impaired. Yet, the subject may still possess intact social intelligence, particularly under circumstances in which the deficient component skill can be circumvented. For instance, an individual with poor working memory skills may not be able to sequence the cards correctly, being unable to keep all the elements in mind at the same time, but yet prove quite capable of navigating social situations in which mental manipulation and sequencing skills are not requisites.

Associating any particular task with a single construct can be highly misleading. Most neuropsychological tasks are simply too complex or multifactorial to be considered direct measures of a single construct (such as exemplified by the Wechsler Picture Arrangement subtest, discussed above). Furthermore, the depiction of a particular test as being a measure of a certain construct is usually based upon inference, not empirical research. Thus, it seems reasonable that a task such as Picture Arrangement test could tap into social intelligence; however, such claims are usually not validated empirically. As noted, social intelligence is a very complicated construct. There is no doubt that there are elements of the Picture Arrangement test that contribute to social intelligence. However, this test does not comprehensively assess all elements under all circumstances. For example, there are many social situations in which the appropriate social response relies upon interpreting the tone of voice, a factor not assessed by the Picture Arrangement subtest. Furthermore, the deficiency in any particular component of Picture Arrangement test *will not ensure that social intelligence is impaired in the real world, in which the demands and prompts often differ significantly from those in the highly structured and artificial test environment.*

Despite these inherent problems, this superficial description of a patient's cognitive strengths and weaknesses is very often contained in neuropsychological reports. Such a level of interpretation typically reflects a relatively low level of neuropsychological sophistication. Unfortunately, many psychologists, whose background and training in neuropsychology is inadequate, often provide such neuropsychological reports. Their reports should only be considered useful as a preliminary description of potential neuropsychological strengths and weaknesses, but should not be seen as reflecting a true neuropsychological analysis. A true neuropsychological analysis endeavors to identify underlying factors of performance on the basis of pattern analysis.

For example, poor performance on the WAIS-III Block Design might be superficially described as demonstrating problems in replicating geometric designs using colored cubes. At a somewhat higher level the deficit might be described as reflecting a problem in visual–motor integration. A superficial description of a poor performance on Object Assembly might indicate the existence of a problem in assembling puzzles. At a somewhat higher level, a commonality with Block Design could be offered as a breakdown in visual–motor integration. The most superficial interpretations offer nothing more than a description of each task, hardly useful in conveying the essence of the impairment underlying each task. The less superficial description, a breakdown in visual–motor integration, is only marginally more informative. While it does provide insight into the general type of task that can prove challenging to the test taker, it suffers from the lack of specificity. Are the impaired performances due to problems in visual perception, spatial organization, motor coordination, or the ability to translate visual–spatial perception and organization into a meaningful motor output? Specifications of such underlying factors are far more informative to the consumer of the report.

IDENTIFICATION OF UNDERLYING FACTORS BASED UPON PATTERN ANALYSIS

The discussion above makes it clear that any single neuropsychological test or measure assesses multiple factors such as provided in the example of the Picture Arrangement subtest of the Wechsler Intelligence Scale. Every neuropsychological test or measure can be dissected in the same manner. For example, on the Controlled Oral Word Association Test (Benton and Hamsher, 1989), the subject is asked to generate as many words beginning with a certain letter of the alphabet in a 1-min time span. While poor performance on this task is frequently assumed to represent impairment in verbal fluency, this would be no more than a superficial and misleading description. The executive functions of the brain (see Chapter 5) are required to actively generate the words on the basis of retrieval process from a person's lexical store or words according to specific rules. There is a need to keep the particular letter in mind. The instructions exclude proper names and numbers or using the same word twice with a different suffix. Thus, these particular rules need to be kept in mind during the performance. Sensorimotor aspects of speech are also important such that any impairment affecting the generation or reception of nerve impulses or muscular control to the speech apparatus would result in poor performance on this task. Spelling abilities are required, which includes among other things phonetic analysis and synthesis. An ability to categorize words according to sounds, proper names, numbers, and suffixes is required. Additional components contribute to this task as well. The breakdown of any of these individual components would result in impaired performance on the Controlled Oral Word Association Test. The interpretation of the poor performance as reflecting a breakdown in verbal fluency is, thus, superficial, and can clearly be misleading.

A true neuropsychological approach endeavors to identify the underlying component contributing to the impaired test performance. At times, this may be clearly evident when an individual suffers from an obvious motor problem with speech, known as dysarthria. In such cases, speech is often slow, hesitant, and slurred, not requiring particular neuropsychological expertise to recognize that dysarthria (motor impairment of speech) underlies the impairment on this verbal fluency task.

In most instances, the identification of the component underlying impaired test performance is not so easily surmised. Identification of the underlying components requires a pattern analysis of the full set of test results. Patterns emerge when there is impairment in a skill common to multiple tests on the battery. For example, the California Verbal Learning Test (CVLT) (Delis et al., 2000) and the Faces subtest of the Wechsler Memory Scale-III (Wechsler, 1997b) differ in that they are measures of verbal and visual learning, respectively. However, they possess the common need to organize information presented in a sequential manner. (The CVLT requires learning of a list of 16 words read in sequence. The Faces subtest requires the recognition of 48 faces presented in sequence.) Poor performance on the CVLT may reflect some type of verbal problem, a hypothesis supported when other verbal tests also demonstrate poor performance. Poor performance on the Faces subtest may reflect some type of visual problem, a hypothesis supported when other visual tests also demonstrate poor performance. When both of these tests are performed poorly, it suggests a breakdown in a skill other than verbal or visual, in this case the ability to organize information in a sequential manner.

The relationship between global functions such as social intelligence and the brain is quite complex and involves multiple processes and the working of many brain regions in concert with one another. Identification of underlying *neuropsychological factors* indicates a linkage between cognitive functions and the anatomy of the brain. For example, a pattern of impaired spelling, reading, word finding, and language comprehension may result from a breakdown in a common underlying factor of phonetic analysis and synthesis that, in turn, can be localized to a region in the left temporal lobe.

The identification of the underlying factors that are causing impaired neuropsychological test performance requires a pattern analysis, which necessitates a high level of neuropsychological sophistication. A competent neuropsychologist needs to understand the components underlying successful performance on any given measure. There needs to be a clear understanding of the common components relating any two tests as well as an ability to distinguish their differences, which may seem obvious, but frequently tend to be more subtle. For example, the Block Design and Object Assembly subtests of the Wechsler Intelligence Scales both require visuospatial perception and ability to manipulate materials to make particular constructions; in the case of Object Assembly, puzzles, and in the case of Block Design, two-dimensional geometric designs. Breakdowns of either manipulation capacity or visuospatial perception are reasonable hypotheses when both of these tests are performed poorly. However, performances on these two tests do not always correlate; Block Design may be performed well and Object Assembly poorly, or vice versa. In such cases, the different demands underlying performance of both tests need to be clearly understood. One such difference relates to the degree of structure, Block Design being more structured because the subject is working off a model, absent in the Object Assembly test constructions. Better performance on Block Design may indicate that the subject profits from structure. On the other hand, the Block Design task is often considered more abstract than Object Assembly. Poor performance on Block Design in the presence of intact Object Assembly may be the result of impaired capacity for abstraction.

The breakdown of global cognitive functions such as social intelligence, verbal fluency, memory, comprehension, perception and so on into their component elements is known as the *functional systems* approach (Luria, 1980). In essence, the brain functions on two levels. At the global level, it enables adaptive functions such as intelligence, perception, and memory. At the component level, it mediates the multiple factors contributing to the performance of the global functions. This network of multiple brain regions/component functions working in a concerted manner to produce global adaptive behaviors is known as a *functional system*.

The neuropsychologist utilizes knowledge of functional systems underlying any global ability to make inferences about brain functioning using the processes of *syndrome analysis* and *double dissociation* (Luria, 1980). Syndrome analysis refers to the process of identifying patterns within a set of neuropsychological test results that reflect a breakdown in a particular component factor. In other words, a breakdown in a particular component factor will result in a certain pattern of test results or a syndrome of impairments. For example, injury to the left parieto–occipital region of the brain results in impairment in what is known as simultaneous synthesis, or the ability to understand the meaning of information within a broader context (Luria, 1980). If the context changes, the meaning of individual bits of information also changes. For instance, we know that the 2 in 21 is larger than the 2 in 12 because of its relative position being in the ten's place rather than the unit's place. Without going into the reasoning, suffice it to say that a breakdown in simultaneous synthesis will result in problems with mathematics, reading, spelling, word finding, understanding logical–grammatical relationships, telling time, left–right orientation, constructional praxis, and finger gnosis (identifying fingers by touch). When the test results and clinical observations reveal impaired performances on these measures, it is reasonable to hypothesize that this represents a syndrome associated with damage to the left parieto–occipital region of the brain.

Neuropsychological hypotheses are evaluated by a process of double dissociation (Teuber, 1955). Double dissociation requires the elimination of competing hypotheses by eliminating other factors that could potentially account for the pattern or syndrome that is observed. A practical example can be found in preliminary research conducted by one of the authors comparing neuropsychological performance of paranoid and nonparanoid schizophrenics (Purisch and Langell, 1978). It was hypothesized that nonparanoid schizophrenics would perform more poorly than paranoid schizophrenics on measures of executive functioning (due to previous research findings implicating deficient frontotemporal lobe functioning in this group, associated with a breakdown in executive skills). A comparison of selected test performances assessing executive function did reveal the expected pattern, supporting the hypothesis. Despite the confirming results, the conclusion that the poor performance by the nonparanoid schizophrenics on these measures resulted from a breakdown in executive function was not supported within the range of scientific probability. It was entirely possible that the nonparanoid schizophrenics would have performed poorly on most or all tasks, even ones that did not require executive functioning. The process of double dissociation requires elimination of competing theories. Thus, both groups were administered tasks in which their executive functions were not critically demanded. The performance of the two groups on these measures demonstrated few differences. Thus, it was unlikely that the poor performance by the nonparanoid schizophrenics on the tests of executive functioning represented a more general deficiency; rather the deficiency likely stemmed from a breakdown of their executive functions, as demonstrated by the ability to eliminate the competing hypothesis through double dissociation.

The application of functional systems, syndrome analysis, and double dissociation are the hallmarks of a competent neuropsychological analysis. However, a full neuropsychological evaluation requires the integration of the hypotheses generated from clinical observations and test results within the broader context of the historical, qualitative, quantitative, and collateral data.

COMPREHENSIVE INTEGRATION OF HISTORICAL, QUALITATIVE, QUANTITATIVE, AND COLLATERAL DATA

As discussed in Chapter 10, a comprehensive neuropsychological evaluation consists of the integration of multiple sources of information. It does not rely solely upon test results. For this reason, it is more appropriate to refer to the neuropsychologists' activities as being a process of performing a neuropsychological *evaluation* rather than merely neuropsychological *testing*. The testing is only one component that fits within a broader context. While the results of the testing may enhance the understanding of the individual, accurate interpretation of the test results needs to consider the test data within the context of the patient's clinical and background history, qualitative behavior during the interview and testing, and the information obtained from collateral sources. This can be well illustrated by the difficulties that frequently occur when using only the test results to infer the etiology of the disorder in question (e.g., brain-damage caused by a motor vehicle accident).

Neuropsychological tests are frequently nonspecific to the etiology of an impaired test performance, frequently sacrificing specificity for sensitivity. Neuropsychological testing by itself cannot discriminate multiple concurrent factors impacting the patient's test performance (Sbordone and Purisch, 1996). For example, an individual with a traumatic brain injury may demonstrate a neuropsychological pattern reflective of frontotemporal and subcortical impairment, consistent with the etiology. However, this particular individual may also have a history of alcohol abuse and learning disorder, the effects of which will also be reflected on the patient's performance on neuropsychological tests. Simply looking at the neuropsychological test results alone without knowledge of the patient's history can result in confusion and inaccurate opinions about the etiology of the patient's poor test results. In this case, processes such as syndrome analysis and double dissociation may be inadequate because there are too many contaminating and confounding factors to permit the identification of the underlying component impairment.

Similarly, factors such as concurrent medical disorders, medications, peripheral problems such as difficulty in seeing or hearing, illness, fatigue, motivation, and emotional factors, among others, can clearly contaminate the reliability and validity of neuropsychological test results, particularly when the task is to determine what types of problems, if any, are directly related to a brain injury. Without utilizing this broader context, it would be difficult or virtually impossible to identify and account for the contribution and role of these other factors.

RECOGNIZING BIASED NEUROPSYCHOLOGICAL TEST RESULTS

LIES, DAMN LIES, AND STATISTICS

The above quotation by Mark Twain is well appreciated in any endeavor where statistics are used to demonstrate or prove a point. The truth of the matter may be obscured or even dismissed by quantitative sophistry. Neuropsychological data is quantifiable and interpretation typically relies on transforming or converting the raw data through statistical means. It is not surprising, then, that neuropsychological test data can be subject to abuse, resulting in conclusions that otherwise may not be warranted by the data. The various methods by which neuropsychological data can be analyzed and the conclusions that can be derived from each method need to be considered when determining whether the interpretations are contaminated by bias. Such factors that impact upon the interpretation of test data include the establishment of cutoff scores, using absolute vs. relative levels of performance, adjusting for demographics, assumptions of consistencies and inabilities in the patient's test performance, and the assumption of a normal distribution.

SETTING CUTOFF SCORES: SENSITIVITY VS. SPECIFICITY

The issue of sensitivity vs. specificity was discussed in some detail earlier in this chapter. Briefly, setting cutoff scores at a low threshold to detect impairment increases the sensitivity of the test. Setting the cutoff point at a high threshold to detect impairment increases the specificity of the test. Accordingly, in clinical practice, the level at which the psychologist deems the score to be falling in the impaired range will obviously affect his or her interpretation of the patient's neuropsychological performance.

Nowhere is the issue of the cutoff score more pertinent than in medicolegal evaluations in which there are numerous influences consorting to distort objectivity. In civil personal injury litigation, the plaintiff-retained neuropsychologist is reinforced for detecting cognitive impairment while the defense-retained neuropsychologist is reinforced for the opposite. The level at which the cutoff points are established can obviously impact the decision of whether or not impairment is present, such that the same set of test data can be interpreted differently by the neuropsychologist retained on each side. For example, one neuropsychologist may consider performance at the 16th percentile (i.e., 1 standard deviation below the mean) as representative of impaired performance. Another neuropsychologist may not consider impairment to be present unless the performance is at the second percentile (2 standard deviations from the mean). Thus, any score from the 3rd to the 16th percentile would be deemed to fall within the normal (or unimpaired) range by the neuropsychologist utilizing the more conservative criterion for judging the presence of impaired test performance.

It is critical that the consumer of the neuropsychological report appreciate the specific cutoff points that are being utilized by the interpreting neuropsychologist in determining the presence and level of impairment. For example, the neuropsychologist may consider anything below 1 standard deviation to be impaired in the mild range, scores 2 standard deviations to be in the moderate range, and 3 standard deviations below the mean to be in the severely impaired range. Scores may be expressed in percentiles, scale scores, T-scores, or standard scores. Scale scores for any test indicate that the average performance is a scale score of 10 and the standard deviation is 3. T-scores indicate that the average is a T of 50 and the standard deviation is 10. Standard scores are typically indicative of average scores set at 100 with a standard deviation of 15. Thus, a score at the 16th percentile is considered 1 standard deviation below the mean on the basis of the normal curve. When expressed in scale scores, this would represent a score of 7; when expressed in T-scores, this would represent a score of 40; and when expressed in standard scores, this would represent a score of 85.

Another commonly used scale follows the continuum utilized on the Wechsler Intelligence Scales (e.g., WAIS-III). On these measures, standard scores from 90 to 109 are considered to be in the average range. This would fall about two thirds of a standard deviation on either side of the average of 100 or between the 25th and 75th percentile. A low average score would fall between 80 and 89 or 0.67 and 1.3 standard deviations below the mean or between the 9th and 25th percentiles. A borderline score would fall in the range of 70 to 79 or 1.3 standard deviations to 2 standard deviations below the mean or between the second and ninth percentiles. Anything below the standard score of 70, or greater than 2 standard deviations below the mean, would be considered to be in the impaired or deficient range. A similar scale is represented for scores above the mean such that scores from 110 to 119 or

0.67 to 1.3 standard deviations above the mean or between the 75th and 91st percentiles would be considered to be above average; scores from 120 to 129 or 1.3 to 2 standard deviations above the mean or between the 91st and 98th percentiles would be considered to be in the superior range; and scores of 130 and above or more than 2 standard deviations above the mean would be considered to be in the very superior range.

These are not the only continuums that are used, and the consumer of the report, again, is cautioned to determine the specific criteria that are being utilized by the interpreting neuropsychologist in rating the presence of impairment and the various labels associated with the performance (e.g., average, mildly impaired, superior, etc.). It is noted, however, that in the authors' experience, research on most neuropsychological tests generally discriminate between the control groups and brain-injured patients when the score falls somewhere between 1 and 1.5 standard deviations below the mean (e.g., Heaton, et al., 2004; Golden, et al., 1985). As such, establishing an impaired score at the 16th percentile or at 1 standard deviation below the mean may be too liberal and result in too many false positives, exchanging specificity for sensitivity. On the other hand, using a conservative cutoff at the second percentile or 2 standard deviations below the mean would seem too conservative, potentially resulting in too many false negatives, exchanging sensitivity for specificity.

It is common practice for neuropsychologists to utilize the same cutoff score across all tests in a neuropsychological test battery. This may not be warranted given the research on each individual test in the battery, which may establish that the best cutoff point for one test is not necessarily the same for another test or any other test in the battery. This is typically done for convenience sake, as it would be too cumbersome to evaluate each test individually.

ADJUSTMENTS FOR DEMOGRAPHICS

Impaired test performance can either be judged in comparison to a population norm or in comparison to expectations derived from the subject's own test performances. The former is referred to as *absolute level of performance*. The latter is referred to as *relative level of performance*. The absolute level of performance contrasts the subject with a particular demographic group of interest; the validity of the inferences derived by this comparison method is contingent upon the relevance of the normative group. For example, the Wechsler Adult Intelligence Scale (WAIS) transforms raw score performances on each subtest to scale scores (average $= 10$ and standard deviation at 3) on the basis of a comparison of the subject's performance to the mean and standard deviation for a reference group of adults aged 20 to 34. This group was selected to represent young adults considered to be at the peak of neuropsychological functioning. Such a comparison provides information about how the subject compares to an optimally functioning group. However, age is a powerful factor impacting the brain and, therefore, a patient's performance on neuropsychological tests and their functioning in real-world settings. Working memory and speed of processing diminish with increasing age and, as such, an older adult would be at a competitive disadvantage when their test scores are compared to norms derived from the reference group of young adults.

For example, performance on the WAIS-III Digit Symbol Subtest decreases with age. This is a measure that demands speed of processing, requiring the subject to quickly associate symbols with numbers within a 2-min time span. The number of symbols that are associated with the numbers within this time span decreases over the decades to the point that an average performance (50th percentile) of someone in the reference group would be 76 to 80 items completed in 2 min, whereas an average performance for someone who is in their 70s would be 49 to 53 items in 2 min. A normal individual in his 70s who obtained an average score on Digit Symbol for his age would fall at about the sixth or seventh percentile compared to the reference group. As such, an average performance for this normal elderly adult would be considered impaired compared to the normal young adult, reflecting a competitive disadvantage on related tasks placing a premium on speed of performance. Using the criterion of absolute level of performance, this impairment could be relevant when making predictions about the functioning of the older adult in the real world. This competitive disadvantage reflects the reality of diminished functioning as a product of the normal aging process. However, this deterioration in certain skills is normal when people age and should not be considered the result of a pathological brain condition.

Education has also been demonstrated to be a powerful factor associated with neuropsychological test performance (Lezak et al., 2004). Many tests designed for use in pediatric populations provide norms for either age or education. Tests for adults will almost always provide age norms, but not always education norms. Education norms for adults are rarely provided without age norms. The norms in such cases typically include consideration of both age and education. For example, a set of norms may look at individuals in their 40s, with further subdivisions for education less than high school, high school, and greater than high school. Education is strongly associated with accumulation of knowledge related to reading, writing, arithmetic, vocabulary, store of general information, and other skills that can be developed with experience as well as schooling. It may also reflect the fact that the persons of relatively low intelligence often are less likely to graduate from high school or attend college.

Accumulation of knowledge and aptitudes through experience and learning is referred to as crystallized intelligence (Cattell, 1963). Measures of crystallized intelligence generally resist the deleterious effects of aging such that one's vocabulary level, for example, would not be expected to be any worse in the eighth decade of life than it is in the fourth decade of life (Wechsler, 1997a). On the other hand, skills that are more inherent to brain functioning, and more difficult to acquire through learning and experience, such as speed of organization and working memory, evidence a steady decline with age. Such skills tap into what is known as fluid intelligence (Cattell, 1963).

Two factors associate crystallized intelligence with level of education. The first factor is the common sense notion that more years of schooling result in accumulation of more knowledge and higher proficiency on crystallized types of tasks. The second factor is not as straightforward, but also appears to be an important variable. On the average, people with better brains (demonstrating higher levels of fluid intelligence) are more successful in different realms of life, including academic and vocational attainment. Those with higher levels of fluid intelligence profit from experience more than those with lower levels of fluid intelligence. High fluid intelligence is associated with accumulating more information and skills in life. Comparing subjects with low education to norms derived from subjects with higher levels of education can lead to the spurious conclusion of brain-damage when, in fact, their test performances may very well fall within the expected range for their level of education. On the other hand, brain-damage may be masked when a highly educated person is compared to norms derived from a lower education group.

This picture becomes more complex when the normative factors, such as age and education, are not the same for each test within a battery of tests. Differences in performance can be more apparent than real, an artifact of different standards of comparison. For example, a 45-year-old man with 12 years of education may be deemed to perform differently on two measures of vocabulary, a finding that on its face does not appear to make sense. Closer examination may reveal that the normative group may average 3 years of college for one test, but 10 years of schooling for the other test. When compared against other individuals in their 40s, this person with 12 years of education would likely perform better in absolute sense on the test in which the norms were developed using subjects with 10 years of education and worse in absolute sense compared to the norms for the test utilizing subjects with 3 years of college.

Age and education are the most common demographic variables used in normative studies (O'Bryant et al., 2004). Some test performances are associated with other variables. For example, any measure of strength should provide norms for gender (e.g., Heaton et al., 2004). Differences in test performances associated with variables such as cultural background and primary language (particularly if a test is administered in a different language, e.g., a test of English language comprehension administered to a Spanish–English bilingual) are recognized but, unfortunately, these are factors that are rarely controlled in collection of norms. While some norms account for race or ethnicity, such a correction is often not warranted.

There is evidence that group differences associated with race or ethnicity are typically secondary to factors such as differences in socioeconomic and education status associated with such group membership (Mercer, 1977). In such cases, the purpose of specific normative comparisons can become meaningless if the individual differs significantly from the general group characteristics that are assumed to exist.

The use of absolute level of performance is appropriate when the issue relates to determining how well an individual compares to a certain population of interest. As in the illustration above, it might be useful to determine how an elderly person compares to a younger optimally functioning group in order to derive inferences regarding their ability to compete with such a group. Such an issue may be important, for example, when assessing airline pilots at the age of 65. Although a given pilot may perform perfectly normally compared to his or her age group, demands of his or her job, with critical public safety concerns, mandates a higher level of performance in such cases. In situations such as this, comparison to the young adult reference group is justified.

Confidence in the interpretation of neuropsychological test performance increases as a function of the degree of match of the subject with the demographics of the normative group of comparison. With a close match, lower than expected performances compared to the norms are more likely to represent impairment in neuropsychological functioning. For a person who is 35-years-old and with a doctoral degree, comparison to general population norms, with an average age of 45 and an average education of 12 years, would not be a close match. Such a young adult with high education could suffer a brain injury and still perform normally compared to the general population norms. The opposite situation exists with an 85-year-old individual with 3 years of education. Such an elderly individual with a low level of education would predictably perform poorly on many neuropsychological measures compared to the general population. However, this impairment may represent their baseline functioning; any interpretation of deterioration in their performance due to brain-damage would, therefore, be incorrect. Such a conclusion would be defensible only if their neuropsychological test performance was lower than expected given norms obtained from elderly individuals with low levels of education.

In neuropsychological utopia, norms would exist across the age and education spectrums as well as for other relevant variables such as gender and socioeconomic status. While appreciation of the need for such demographic adjustments has stimulated efforts to develop appropriate norms for a variety of tests, most norms still adjust only for age and, perhaps, education (Heaton et al., 2004). The paucity of appropriate norms to determine an individual's absolute level of performance requires, then, a different standard, a relative level of performance comparison. A relative level of performance employs an ipsative strategy whereby the individual's test performances are compared to each other rather than to an external population norm. In essence, this approach emphasizes a comparison of the person's best and worst performances. Theoretically, an individual's best performances represent his or her potential, providing a baseline expectation of performance across the battery of neuropsychological tests. The individual serves as his or her own control for comparison in determining whether there has been any change in functioning from baseline, even in the absence of appropriate population norms.

For example, the 35-year-old person with the doctoral degree may perform in the superior range on some neuropsychological tests compared to general population norms. This superior level of performance would be considered the potential baseline of neuropsychological functioning used as the comparison standard applied to performance on other neuropsychological tests. Thus, any performances falling within the average range of the general population would still be significantly lower than this superior baseline prediction and, therefore, represent a potential impairment, at least in a relative sense. Similarly, a poorly educated or low functioning individual may perform poorly across a wide range of tests, but there might be little variability between the best and worst performances. In such a case, the individual is likely performing within expectations compared to their own ipsative baseline and would not be considered impaired relative to expectations.

While an ipsative comparison of test scores can serve as a useful strategy in interpreting levels of performance in the absence of appropriate external population norms, the validity of such interpretations relies upon two assumptions. The first of these assumes that it is normal to display consistency in performance across measures in a neuropsychological test battery. The second is the assumption of the normal distribution.

ASSUMPTIONS OF CONSISTENCY IN ABILITIES ON TEST PERFORMANCES

A fundamental assumption underlying neuropsychological test interpretation is that an individual with a normal brain should be able to manifest relatively consistent aptitudes across the range of neuropsychological abilities. The fallacy of this assumption is obvious upon simple common sense reflection. There are many domains of neuropsychological aptitude including verbal, mathematical, musical, artistic, athletic, social, emotional, and executive skill domains (Gardner, 2004). Very few, if any, individuals could be considered equally proficient in all realms. People naturally display greater proficiency in some areas than others. Accepting the assumption that the normal brain is characterized by a relative equivalency of aptitude across all realms, it must also be assumed that individuals who do not manifest this relative equivalency must not have normal brains. (Indeed, it may be argued that relative areas of deficiency, such as an individual's poor artistic skills, may represent a form of brain dysfunction. If so, then brain dysfunction seems to be an important element associated with the range of individual differences.) On the other hand, the assumption that the normal brain is characterized by relative evenness of function across the different realms is probably incorrect.

Although highly flawed, the assumption of relative equivalency of neuropsychological aptitudes appears to be applied by many clinicians in an uncritical manner, providing a dubious foundation for determination of neuropsychological strengths and weaknesses. This strategy of interpretation assumes that there should be relatively little variability in performance across a battery of neuropsychological tests. Thus, an individual who performs in the superior range on certain measures would be expected to perform close to that range on all other measures. An individual in the average range should be within the average range on all other measures, and a person who performs below the norm should consistently perform within that range on all measures. Larger than expected variability in test performances, therefore, is commonly considered a significant indicator of neuropsychological impairment. The range of scores on neuropsychological tests is often referred to as *scatter*. Identification of learning disabilities, such as reading (dyslexia) or math (dyscalculia) problems often relies upon the analysis of the scatter of test results. For example, a student with a Wechsler FSIQ of 115, at the 84th percentile, would also be expected to perform in this range on academic achievement tests such as reading, spelling, or arithmetic. Achievement of test scores falling significantly below this prediction, typically demonstrating scatter of 1.5 to 2 standard deviations lower than the FSIQ, are presumed to be indicative of a learning disability (American Psychiatric Association, 2000).

The validity of inferences based upon the scatter of test results relies upon separating real differences in performance vs. those produced by statistical artifacts. Judging the influence of statistical artifact involves the consideration of the *standard error of measurement* — the range of the lowest and highest score within 1 standard deviation that a patient can be expected to obtain if taking the same test on multiple occasions (Franzen, 2000). The "true" score is considered to be somewhere within this range. For example, an individual may obtain a scale score of 10 on the Digit Span subtest of the Wechsler Adult Intelligence Scale, which has a standard error of measurement of approximately 1.25 scale score points. This indicates that the "true" score likely lies somewhere between 8.75 and 11.25 with a confidence of 64% (the area of the normal curve falling between -1 and $+1$ standard deviations from the mean) and between 7.50 and 12.50 with a confidence of 95% (the area of the normal curve falling between -2 and $+2$ standard deviations from the mean). The same individual being tested on Digit Span at a later point in time should be expected to obtain a score between 7.50 and 12.50 ninety-five percent of the time if there has been no change in his cognitive status. Scores outside of this range can be expected to occur by chance only 5% of the time and, as such, likely represent a true difference in performance, rather than a difference based upon the statistical artifact.

Controlling for statistical artifact is also critical in drawing inferences when contrasting scores on different tests administered within the same session. For example, if the score on the Object Assembly test is 6 and the standard error measurement is 1.6, then the true score would be considered to be within the range of 2.8 and 9.2 within the 95% confidence interval (i.e., 2 standard error of measurement units on either side of the obtained score). In the example above, the "true" score on Digit Span was between 7.5 and 12.5 at the 95% confidence interval. Thus, there is an overlap between the upper range of the true score of Object Assembly and the lower range of Digit Span between 7.5 (the low end of Digit Span) and 9.2 (the higher range of Object Assembly). Scores below this range on Object Assembly and above this range on Digit Span are unlikely to have occurred by chance and, therefore, the difference in test performances would be more likely real rather than due to a statistical artifact. Unfortunately, the determination of real differences from those occurring by chance involves calculations that require knowledge of standard error of measurement, proving cumbersome for the clinician analyzing an extensive set of test results. Fortunately, many computer scoring software programs now calculate such statistics for the clinician.

Armed with knowledge of significant statistical differences between pairs of scores, however, does not always prove useful in a clinical situation. A statistically significant difference is not necessarily the same thing as a practically significant difference. For example, on the WASI (Psychological Corporation, 1999), an average difference of 8.51 points between Verbal IQ and Performance IQ is expected to occur less than 5% of the time by chance, reaching the level of statistical significance. However, a difference of such magnitude can be expected in greater than 30% of normal adults. The decision to identify a VIQ–PIQ scatter of 9 points as indicative of abnormal scatter because such a difference is unlikely to occur by chance on a statistical basis needs to be tempered by the knowledge that such a difference is also relatively common in the normal population.

Expressing the difference in magnitude between scores in terms of frequencies obtained by the normal population utilizes the concept of the base rate (the frequency at which something occurs), discussed above. In the illustration above, the base rate of a 9 point difference between the WASI VIQ and PIQ is 30%. Without knowledge of the base rate of a particular observation, it is difficult to conclude whether the result on a neuropsychological test or a clinical observation is significant. For example, complaints such as anxiety or nervousness, sleeping problems, depression, headaches, and several other symptoms are generally recognized as being associated with neuropsychological impairment in brain-injured patients. However, a survey by Lees-Haley and Brown (1993) found that 170 personal injury claimants with *orthopedic* injuries also had a very high base rate of complaints typically associated with a brain injury. In particular, 93% of the claimants reported anxiety or nervousness; 92%, sleeping problems; 89%, depression; 88%, headaches; 79%, fatigue; 78%, concentration problems; 77%, irritability; 65%, impatience; 61%, feeling disorganized; 59%, confusion; 56%, loss of efficiency with everyday tasks; 53%, memory problems; 44%, dizziness; 39%, numbness; and 34%, word-finding problems. Reliance upon such subjective complaints is not particularly useful in the differential diagnosis of brain injury, at least in the litigation context. Unfortunately, the base rate of differences between scores on various tests is frequently unknown and those that have been demonstrated are typically greater than would be expected. In another example, Matarazzo and Prifitera (1989) discovered that the average scatter between best and worst subscale performances on the Wechsler Adult Intelligence Scale was in the range of 6 to 7 points, well in excess of the standard deviation of 3 points. Thus, a base rate of about 2 standard deviations separating best and worst performances can be expected in normals. A similar finding was demonstrated on the Luria–Nebraska Neuropsychological Battery, in that normals typically demonstrate 25 T-score points, or 2.5 standard deviations, between their best and worst performances (Golden et al., 1985). Such scatter is considerably larger than expected, such that most neuropsychologists would interpret of the presence of impaired performance without knowledge of the base rate.

The presence of significant scatter is not sufficient to conclude the presence of neuropsychological impairment. Similarly, the absence of significant scatter does not rule out the presence of neuropsychological impairment. The pattern of scores is more important than the presence of significant scatter in inferring the presence of underlying brain dysfunction. The pattern that is obtained needs to make neuropsychological sense. Thus, a high degree of scatter between two highly correlated measures such as Block Design and Object Assembly does not make sense and would likely find an explanation in factors other than brain dysfunction. However, minimal scatter may be significant if the pattern does make sense. For example, scores on Wechsler Information, Vocabulary and Similarities verbal scales may be in the average range while scores on Wechsler Object Assembly, Block Design, and Picture Completion performance scales may be in the below average range. The average difference between these two factors may be no more than 3 or 4 points, clearly less than the 6 to 7 points base rate scatter found in normals, yet, the pattern makes sense based upon a functional systems and a syndrome analysis approach.

Another consideration in determining the validity of the assumption of consistency among test scores and performances relates to test construction issues. Tests are constructed for different purposes and, as discussed, frequently employ different types of normative groups. The Wechsler Intelligence Scales, for example, were developed to assess selected proficiencies in the normal general population and were designed to assess a nearly the full range of aptitude from very low to very high (Matarazzo, 1972). Each of the subtests presents items or tasks that run the gamut from extremely easy to highly challenging. In psychometric jargon, the Wechsler subtests are designed to have low floors and high ceilings. Thus, scores may range from 3 to 4 standard deviations below the mean to 3 to 4 standard deviations above the mean. As a result, an individual with a very superior Full Scale IQ score (FSIQ) of 150 falls more than 3 standard deviations above the mean (based upon an average score of 100 and a standard deviation of 15), whereas an individual with a Mentally Deficient FSIQ of 50 would fall more than 3 standard deviations below the mean. There are more than a 6 standard deviation between these high and low performers.

Most neuropsychological tests are not constructed with the same purpose as intelligence tests. A primary goal of most neuropsychological tests is the identification of the presence and degree of impairment, and not to distinguish varying levels of normalcy, from average to very superior. These tests can usually have a low floor, enabling the ability to discern various levels of impairment. However, the ceiling level of task or item demand is typically much lower than would be found on an intelligence test. As such, it may require no more than an above normal aptitude to do well on the most demanding task on a neuropsychological test; neuropsychological tests displaying relatively low ceilings make it difficult to discern the wide range of normal performance from above average to very superior. Individuals with superior or very superior intelligence may not be distinguished from individuals with above average intelligence. In each of these cases, they would be deemed to be functioning within the normal range, not reflective of brain impairment, thus satisfying a primary purpose and goal of the neuropsychological test.

FSIQ is often assumed to be the baseline for judging whether or not performances on neuropsychological tests depart from expectations. Thus, an individual with above average FSIQ would be predicted to perform in the above average range on neuropsychological tests, average FSIQ within the average range, below average FSIQ in the below average range, and so forth. This strategy can be particularly misleading in individuals with superior and very superior FSIQs due to the limited ceiling of most neuropsychological tests (Dodrill, 1997). For example, an individual with an FSIQ of 130, or 2 standard deviations greater than the mean, could incorrectly be predicted to perform in this range on a host of neuropsychological measures. Obtaining a score 2 standard deviations above the mean on a given neuropsychological test would be impossible if the ceiling of this test is only 1 standard deviation above the mean. In this case, this individual could perform without error on the neuropsychological test but only obtain a score 1 standard deviation above the mean, less than predicted by his or her FSIQ of 130. Unless the psychometric difference between the Wechsler Intelligence Scale and the particular neuropsychological test is recognized, using the FSIQ as the baseline expectation would result in the misinterpretation that this neuropsychological test performance falls 1 standard deviation below expectations and, therefore, may represent the presence of a relative level of impairment.

This inherent danger of using IQ scores, particularly those that fall well above the norm, as a baseline expectation for performance on neuropsychological measures is being increasingly recognized. The Psychological Corporation, a prominent publisher of psychological and neuropsychological tests, for example, has endeavored to co-norm a number of measures, including intelligence, memory, and academic achievement. In doing so, statistical analyses are able to provide predicted scores for memory and achievement based upon the Wechsler IQ. For instance, an individual with a Wechsler FSIQ of 130 may be predicted to obtain a Wechsler Memory Scale Auditory Memory Index score of 115, or 1 standard deviation below their obtained FSIQ. In such a case, obtaining a Verbal Memory Index of 115 would be interpreted as meeting expectations, not evidence of impairment.

ASSUMPTION OF NORMAL DISTRIBUTION

Many variables conform to a normal distribution, such as height, weight, and intelligence. A variable that is normally distributed is one in which the greatest number of subjects fall at the average with a decreasing frequency of subjects found as the variable increasingly departs from the average either in the positive or negative direction. The frequency of subjects falling at each point along the continuum of the variable defines the variable as being normally distributed. Thus, 1 standard deviation from the mean contains 34% of subjects on either side of the mean. In other words, 1 standard deviation below the mean falls at the 16th percentile and 1 standard deviation above the mean falls at the 84th percentile. One standard deviation below the mean falling at the 16th percentile means that 84 out of 100 subjects should place higher on the given variable. One standard deviation above the mean falling at the 84th percentile means that 84 out of 100 subjects should place lower on the given variable. Similar symmetry is found as the variable increases or decreases along this continuum.

Many neuropsychological skills, however, are not normally distributed. For example, stereognosis, or the ability to recognize objects by touch, is not normally distributed. Virtually any individual with normal tactual perception should be able to identify a wide range of objects placed in their hands by touch alone, whether they are of low average intelligence or superior intelligence. Failure to recognize even a few of these objects, in many cases, is clearly abnormal and, again, may not depend upon IQ level. The distribution of scores on this measure would be considered to be *skewed*, rather than normally distributed. The inability to perform near optimal levels on these types of tasks is often considered to be a sign of impairment, of which there may be a continuum from no ability up to that which would be considered to be mildly impaired.

There is a clear problem with assuming normal distribution on tasks where the scores can reflect a skewed distribution in that the percentiles cannot be interpreted in the same manner as those derived from a normally distributed task. For example, the ability to copy a complicated design, such as the Rey Complex Figure Test (RCFT) (Meyers and Meyers, 1995), is not normally distributed. For a normative group of say 100 subjects, an individual may perform at the 16th percentile, simply meaning that 84 of the 100 subjects performed better than him. This 16th percentile, however, cannot be considered to be 1 point along a normally distributed continuum. Rather, it would be seen that the vast majority of normal individuals score at the average or above, making such a curve "top heavy." Performance at or below the 16th percentile in such a case could be considered to be evidence of impairment, but not one in which subjects placed along a continuum can be inferred.

The problem with assuming a normal distribution for tasks in which the distribution is actually skewed develops when the percentile scores on all tests are treated as if they are normally distributed.

For example, if the subject who is at the 16th percentile on the RCFT also obtained a FSIQ of 115, the untrained neuropsychologist would appropriately consider the IQ of 115 to be 1 standard deviation above the mean, but would inappropriately consider a score at the 16th percentile on the RCFT to be 1 standard deviation below the mean. The 16th percentile does define 1 standard deviation below the mean for a variable that is normally distributed but may represent a completely different point on the continuum of a variable with a skewed distribution. Thus, the comparison of the performance on the IQ test, which is normally distributed, with the performance on the RCFT, which demonstrates a skewed performance, cannot assume that the meaning of the standard deviation is identical. As such, the conclusion that the difference in these performances was 2 standard deviations from the mean would not be justified. Using the same standards and definitions that apply to a normal distribution to a skewed distribution is unjustified, and is similar to comparing apples to oranges.

Many variables are not normally distributed; particularly psychological constructs such as the magnitude of depression or the presence of borderline personality features. On a personality test such as the MMPI-2 (Butcher et al., 2001), there are a number of items that are associated with depression. The mean and standard deviation in a normal group of these items is then obtained and scores 2 standard deviations greater than the mean are considered to be clinically significant, as if depression was normally distributed. A similar procedure would be conducted in terms of deriving a scale for schizophrenia in which scores 2 standard deviations above the normal mean would be considered to be clinically significant. However, closer analysis would reveal that there may be far more normals lying 2 standard deviations above the mean for depression than there would be normals falling 2 standard deviations above the mean for schizophrenia. These variables are not normally distributed and the attempt to compare the scores on the basis of normal distribution is, therefore, unwarranted. The authors of the MMPI-2 have recognized this fallacy and have changed the distributions of several scales from a normal distribution to a uniform distribution (Butcher et al., 2001), which is based upon frequencies rather than the normal distribution. As such, scores 2 standard deviations above the mean for depression or schizophrenia are reserved for only the highest 2% of the population. This way, then, the scores become meaningful in terms of frequency distributions and, therefore, become comparable.

Another method of interpreting the significance of scores that are not normally distributed employs knowledge of base rates. For example, the base rate of patients with a schizoid personality disorder is far less than patients with borderline personality disorder. Assuming a normal distribution or even a uniform distribution does not, therefore, reflect the frequency in which groups identified as having each of the disorders fall within a continuum. In fact, many times the diagnostic decision making process considers qualitative features of a given disorder, not how high the patient falls on some quantitative continuum. Such decisions rely upon categorical considerations rather than dimensional or continuous distributions. Using a continuous distribution assumes that someone with a score of 50 on a borderline personality disorder scale would be half as borderline as someone with a score of 100. This would not be appropriate for a diagnosis, which would be established more on a qualitative than a quantitative basis. Various personality measures developed by Theodore Millon and his colleagues (e.g., MCMI-III) have controlled this problem by means of base rate or prevalence rate scores in which scores above a certain level are set to be relatively specific to a certain diagnosis (Millon et al., 1994). At lower levels the likelihood of such a diagnosis becomes increasingly unlikely. These categorical variables in the measurement of personality are analogous to the skewed variables referred to above in assessing neuropsychological functions. Such scaling is intended to identify whether or not a trait or impairment exists; it is not simply a matter of placing it on a continuum. The existence of such a trait or impairment would be considered to be a *pathognomonic sign*. The pathognomonic sign approach is typical of medicine, which frequently evaluates patients on a more qualitative basis looking for presence of impairment, rather than gauging the performance on a continuum and without an assumption that the various signs observed are normally distributed.

REFERENCES

American Psychiatric Association. 2000. *Diagnostic and Statistical Manual of Mental Disorders*, 4th ed., Text Revised. Washington, D.C.: American Psychiatric Association.

Benton, A. L. and Hamsher, K. 1989. *Multilingual Aphasia Examination*. Iowa City, IA: AJA Associates.

Boake, C. and Adams, R. L. 1982. Utility of the Background Interference Procedure for the Bender–Gestalt. *Journal of Clinical Psychology*, *36*, 627–631.

Butcher, J. N., Graham, J. R., Pen-Porath, Y. S., and Dahlstrom, W. G. 2001. *MMPI-2 Manual for Administration, Scoring, and Interpretation*, Revised Edition. Minneapolis: University of Minnesota Press.

Cattell, R. B. 1963. Theory of Fluid and Crystallized Intelligence: A Critical Experiment. *Journal of Educational Psychology*, *54*, 1–22.

Delis, D. C., Kramer, J. H., Kaplan, E., and Ober, B. A. 2000. *California Verbal Learning Test (2nd Edition): Adult Version*. San Antonio: Psychological Corporation.

Dodrill, C. B. 1997. Myths of Neuropsychology. *Clinical Neuropsychologist*, *11*, 1–17.

Filskov, S. B. and Goldstein, S. G. 1974. Diagnostic Validity of the Halstead–Reitan Neuropsychological Battery. *Journal of Consulting and Clinical Psychology*, *42*, 382–388.

Franzen, M. D. 2000. *Reliability and Validity in Neuropsychological Assessment*, 2d ed. New York: Plenum Press.

Gardner, H. 2004. *Frames of Mind: The Theory of Multiple Intelligences*. New York: Basic Books.

Golden, C. J., Purisch, A. D., and Hammeke, T. A. 1985. *Luria–Nebraska Neuropsychological Battery: Forms I and II Manual*. Los Angeles: Western Psychological Services.

Heaton, R. K., Baade, L. E., and Johnson, K. L. 1978. Neuropsychological Test Results Associated with Psychiatric Disorders in Adults. *Psychological Bulletin*, *85*, 141–162.

Heaton, R. K., Miller, S. W., Taylor, M. J., and Grant, I. 2004. *Revised Comprehensive Norms for an Expanded Halstead–Reitan Battery: Demographically Adjusted Neuropsychological Norms for African American and Caucasian Adults*. Lutz, FL: Psychological Assessment Resources.

Lacks, P. 1999. *Bender–Gestalt Screening for Brain Dysfunction*, 2d ed. New York: John Wiley & Sons.

Lees-Haley, P. R. and Brown, R. S. 1993. Neuropsychological Complaint Base Rates of 170 Personal Injury Claimants. *Archives of Clinical Neuropsychology*, *8*, 203–209.

Lezak, M. D., Howieson, D. B., and Loring, D. W. 2004. *Neuropsychological Assessment*, 4th ed. New York: Oxford University Press.

Luria, A. R. 1980. *Higher Cortical Functions in Man*, 2d ed. New York: Basic Books.

Matarazzo, J. D. 1972. *Wechsler's Measurement and Appraisal of Adult Intelligence*. Baltimore: Williams & Wilkins.

Matarazzo, J. D. and Prifitera, A. 1989. Subtest Scatter and Premorbid Intelligence: Lessons Learned from the WAIS-R Standardization Sample. *Psychological Assessment: A Journal of Clinical and Consulting Psychology*, *1*, 186–191.

Mercer, J. R. 1977. Identifying the Gifted Chicano Children. In Martinez, J. L. (Ed.) *The Chicano Psychology*. New York: Academic Press.

Meyers, J. E. and Meyers, K. R. 1995. *Rey Complex Figure Test and Recognition Trial: Professional Manual*. Odessa, FL: Psychological Assessment Resources.

Millon, T., Millon, C., and Davis, R. 1994. *Millon Clinical Multiaxial Inventory — III Manual*. Minneapolis: National Computer Systems, Inc.

O'Bryant, S. E., O'Jile, J. R., and McCaffrey, R. J. 2004. Reporting of Demographic Variables in Neuropsychological Research: Trends in the Current Literature. *Clinical Neuropsychologist*, *18*, 229–233.

Psychological Corporation. 1999. *Wechsler Abbreviated Scale of Intelligence Manual*. San Antonio: Psychological Corporation.

Purisch, A. D. and Langell, M. E. 1978. Differences in Frontal Lobe Functions in Nonparanoid and Paranoid Schizophrenics, Unpublished Manuscript.

Reitan, R. M. 1993. *The Halstead–Reitan Neuropsychological Test Battery: Theory and Clinical Interpretation*. Tucson: Neuropsychology Press.

Russell, E. W., Neuringer, C., and Goldstein, G. 1970. *Assessment of Brain-Damage: A Neuropsychological Key Approach*. New York: John Wiley & Sons.

Sbordone, R. J. and Purisch, A. D. 1996. Hazards of Blind Analysis of Neuropsychological Test Data in Assessing Cognitive Disability: The Role of Psychological, Pain and Other Confounding Factors. *Neurorehabilitation*, 7, 15–26.

Spreen, O. and Benton, A. L. 1965. Comparative Studies of Some Psychological Tests for Cerebral Damage. *Journal of Nervous and Mental Diseases*, *140*, 323–333.

Teuber, H. L. 1955. Physiological Psychology. *Annual Review of Psychology*, *6*, 267–296.

Wechsler, D. 1997a. *Wechsler Adult Intelligence Scale — Third Edition: Administration and Scoring Manual.* San Antonio: Psychological Corporation.

Wechsler, D. 1997b. *Wechsler Memory Scale — Third Edition: Administration and Scoring Manual.* San Antonio: Psychological Corporation.

14 The Limitations of Neuropsychological Tests

LIMITATIONS OF IQ TESTS TO ASSESS BRAIN-DAMAGE

Many psychologists commonly administer the Wechsler Adult Intelligence Scale to patients who have sustained brain-damage to determine whether there has been any change in the patient's intellectual functioning even though IQ tests were never designed to assess brain-damaged patients and are typically insensitive to their neurobehavioral problems and cognitive deficits. As a consequence, the results from such tests often provide inaccurate and misleading information about the patient's ability to function in real-world settings. The following case example illustrates this.

Case Example

An 18-year-old male had sustained a severe closed head injury as a result of a serious motor vehicle accident on the night of his high school graduation. He was referred by his treating neurologist for neuropsychological testing approximately 6 months postinjury to determine if he was able to attend college that spring. Prior to his accident he had been given an academic scholarship to attend a prestigious East Coast University based on his excellent high school grades and SAT scores. He had planned on becoming either a physician or attorney. He was administered the Wechsler Adult Intelligence Scale and was found to have a full scale IQ of 140, which placed him in the very superior range (99th percentile). As soon as he had completed this test, the examiner went to the restroom. Upon his return a few minutes later, the patient did not recognize the examiner and denied that he had ever previously seen him or had undergone any testing that day. Interviews with his family corroborated this patient's severe cognitive deficits.

On the basis of his IQ score, one would be tempted to say that he was capable of going to college and becoming either an attorney or physician. Had the neuropsychologist recommended that this patient attend college on the basis of his high IQ score, this patient would have most likely flunked out of school.

LIMITATIONS OF UTILIZING PSYCHOLOGICAL ASSISTANTS OR TECHNICIANS

Many neuropsychologists employ psychological assistants or technicians to administer their psychological and neuropsychological tests. As a consequence, neuropsychologists may spend only a limited amount of time with patients who have been referred for testing. They typically base their evaluations on a neuropsychological questionnaire that is completed by the patient while he or she is sitting in the waiting room, the patient's raw test data, and the observations of their assistant or technician as the patient is tested. Unfortunately, the use of assistants or technicians not only minimizes the time the neuropsychologist actually spends with the patient, but forces the neuropsychologist to rely almost entirely on the written information provided by the patient (which may be inaccurate for a variety of reasons), the patient's quantitative test scores, and the observations of an assistant or technician, whose understanding of the neurobehavioral symptoms of a closed head injury is frequently quite limited. This practice limits the psychologist's ability to recognize many of the patient's cognitive deficits and neurobehavioral symptoms, not to mention predict how this patient will function in real-world settings.

LIMITATIONS OF WIDELY USED NEUROPSYCHOLOGICAL TESTS AND THEIR NORMS

Neuropsychologists often administer standardized neuropsychological tests to individuals; irrespective of cultural, ethnic, or linguistic background even when their command of English is marginal or fair. They will utilize the norms of these tests to score the individual's test performance. When this occurs, psychologists, not uncommonly, arrive at inaccurate and misleading interpretations of the test data and make recommendations that can be detrimental to the individual's welfare.

Case Example

A 53-year-old male accountant had sustained a mild closed head injury. He was referred for neuropsychological testing by his physician. He was born and raised in the Philippines. He completed his education in the Phippines and relocated to Hawaii 5 years ago. Although he spoke with a heavy accent, his command of English seemed adequate. He was administered a variety of standardized neuropsychogical tests in English rather his native language to assess his cognitive and intellectual functioning. He tested with a full-scale IQ of 88 on the Wechsler, and performed poorly on tests of confrontational naming, language, verbal memory, and on a test that was used to assess his "executive functioning" (e.g., Controlled Oral Association test). These results convinced the psychologist who examined him that he sustained an injury to his left hemisphere. The psychologist concluded that this patient was severely impaired and was unable to return to work as an accountant. After being informed that he could not return to work as an accountant, the patient became quite depressed and entertained thoughts of committing suicide since he could not support his family.

When he was retested by another psychologist 2 months later, he was found to have an IQ of 133 on the Test of Non-Verbal Intelligence. When the stories on the Logical Memories subtest of the Wechsler were administered to him in his native language, he tested in the 98th percentile. When he was asked to name the pictures on the Boston Naming Test in his native language, he made a score of 59 out of 60 rather than 42 when he had been earlier tested in English. When he was asked to generate words in his native language on the Controlled Oral Word Association Test, he tested in the 95th percentile rather than the 12th percentile, when he earlier had been asked to respond in English. On the basis of these findings the psychologist recommended that this patient could return to work as an accountant. A 6-month follow-up revealed that he had successfully returned to work duties and responsibilities and no longer felt depressed.

Psychologists often fallaciously assume that the norms of standardized neuropsychological tests should apply to all individuals irrespective of their age, educational, cultural, ethnic, or linguistic background even though research has shown that variables such as the patient's age, prior level of intellectual functioning, educational background, geographic location, and the patient's cultural, ethnic, and linguistic background account for most of the variability in the test scores of the vast majority of widely used neuropsychological tests and measures (Mitrushina et al., 1999).

How appropriate is it to utilize norms obtained from college graduates born in the United States ranging in age from 25 through 39 to a foreign-born 64-year-old individual whose command of English is only fair and has only completed 6 years of formal education? Such invidious comparisons are likely to result in the latter individual's test scores falling in the impaired range and the psychologist concluding that this individual would have significant difficulty functioning in their community even though this individual's functioning in his or her environment is seen as normal by the vast majority of people who reside in his or her environment.

LIMITATIONS OF NEUROPSYCHOLOGICAL TESTS TO ASSESS BRAIN-DAMAGE

Most psychologists who are practicing today use neuropsychological tests to identify a patient's cognitive strengths and deficits, rather than determining whether the patient has brain-damage since this is typically determined by the patient's medical history and neuroimaging studies. Neuropsychological testing is primarily used today to determine whether a patient has sustained brain-damage when the neurological examination is normal, and the neuroimaging studies are negative as often occurs when an individual has sustained a concussion or mild traumatic brain injury. However, with the advent of increasing sophistication in neuroimaging, it is unlikely that neuropsychological testing will be utilized in the future to determine whether a patient who is believed to have sustained a concussion is brain-damaged if the brain-damage can be accurately identified, localized, and quantified by functional neuroimaging. On the positive side, this is likely to place more emphasis on the development of innovative methods of assessing how the brain injury or dysfunction effects the patient's functioning in real-world situations.

Although many psychologists have assumed that poor scores on neuropsychological tests following a motor vehicle accident are indicative of brain-damage and cognitive dysfunction, poor test performance can be caused by a variety of other causes other than a brain injury caused by the accident. For example, Sbordone and Purisch (1996) identified a number of confounding factors that can cause an individual to perform poorly during testing, regardless of whether or not they sustain a brain injury in their accident. These factors include: prior brain injury or insult, congenital or preexisting neurological conditions, absences (seizures), acute pain, symptoms and impairments secondary to physical injuries, peripheral sensory impairment, peripheral motor impairment, current and chronic medical illness, sleep deprivation, excessive fatigue, history of alcohol/drug abuse, medications, psychiatric illness, recent psychosocial stressors, suboptimal motivation or malingering, negative patient/examiner interactions, cultural/linguistic discrepancies, the patient's vocational and avocational background, test sophistication, and practice effects.

Psychologists who arrive at the opinion that a particular patient has sustained brain-damage solely based on their relatively poor test performance without carefully considering these factors are likely to inaccurately categorize such individuals as brain-damaged. They are also likely to make inaccurate and misleading predictions of the patient's ability to function in real-world settings, particularly when the factors which accounted for the patient's poor performance are no longer present.

Case Example

A 49-year-old male was referred for neuropsychological testing after he began to complain of headaches, dizziness, concentration and memory difficulties, irritability, fatigue, and sleep difficulties after being involved in a motor vehicle accident 7 months ago. His medical records revealed that he had a questionable loss of consciousness, but did not appear confused or disoriented at the scene of the accident or when he was later seen in the ER. He was placed on medical leave by his physician as a result of his complaints. Neuropsychological testing indicated that his attention and recent memory were mild to moderately impaired. The psychologist, who relied on the patient's complaints and test results, decided that this patient had sustained a closed head injury and should not return to work at this time. Unfortunately, the psychologist did not obtain a history of the patient's injury or background, review the patient's medical records, or interview any significant others.

This patient was evaluated by another psychologist who took a careful clinical history, reviewed the patient's medical records, and interviewed the patient's 24-year-old daughter. On the basis of this information, this psychologist learned that at time of the last examination the patient had been going through a nasty divorce, had been taking a variety of anxiety, anti-depressant, and pain medications; and had been in a great deal of pain and discomfort as a result of injuring his lower back after he had fallen down a flight of stairs while he was heavily intoxicated.

Since his last examination, he had met an attractive woman who he was now dating. He had been sleeping much better and was considerably less anxious and depressed than he had been at the time of his prior examination. He was no longer drinking, taking medications, and was no longer experiencing back pain and discomfort. His neuropsychological test scores fell into the normal range. This psychologist recommended that this patient should return to work.

This case demonstrates that this patient's test results when he was initially tested were most likely due to several factors which had a deleterious effect on his cognitive functioning at the time he was examined. These factors were not present at the time of the second examination.

LIMITATIONS OF NEUROPSYCHOLOGICAL TESTING TO ASSESS NEUROBEHAVIORAL SYMPTOMS

Although standardized neuropsychological tests are commonly used to assess patients with frontal lobe injuries, Damasio (1985) reported that patients who had most of their prefrontal lobes surgically removed, often tested in the normal range on IQ and other standardized neuropsychological tests. He found, however, that in real-world settings these patients often exhibited the following neurobehavioral symptoms: a loss of initiative, curiosity, exploratory behavior, motivation, creativity, and libido; an inability to regulate their behavior and emotions, organize their thoughts, plan, remain on task, monitor their actions, solve problems, recognize their mistakes, or rectify them when they were later pointed out to them. They also exhibited impaired social behavior, inflexible thinking, poor judgment, impulsivity, egocentricity, an inability to show affection or feel compassion toward others, and frequently used crude or coarse language in the presence of their children or parents. They had no plans or concern for future events, were unable to profit from experience, and tend to confabulate when they were asked to recall remote information. Thus, the neuropsychological tests that were administered did not recognize these neurobehavioral symptoms.

Neuropsychologists frequently assume that whatever cognitive deficits the patient has such deficits can be detected by neuropsychological tests. In other words, the patient's test performance should provide us with reliable information about their cognitive functioning. Unfortunately, in many cases, neuropsychological testing often fails to detect the patient's neurobehavioral and cognitive deficits. The following story illustrates this point:

A man, upon arriving home at approximately 2 A.M., sees a man in the middle of the street on his hands and knees apparently searching for something on the street. Out of curiosity, he walks over and asks the other man if he needs assistance. The man replies that he has lost his car keys. The passerby asks where he had lost them. The man kneeling on the asphalt responds "about two blocks away." Puzzled by this response, he asks "why are you looking here if your keys are two blocks away? The man states, "the light here is better."

This amusing story illustrates how we are often bound by the insensitivity of the many of the tests we use to detect a patient's cognitive deficits and neurobehavioral symptoms. As a consequence, many of the patient's neurobehavioral and cognitive deficits go undetected, particularly when neuropsychologists rely heavily on the patient's scores on standardized neuropsychological tests that may not show any cognitive deficits and give us little information about the patient's neurobehavioral symptoms.

LIMITATIONS OF NEUROPSYCHOLOGICAL TESTS TO ASSESS THE FRONTAL LOBES OF THE BRAIN

Stuss and Benson (1986) have stressed that neuropsychological tests were not specifically designed to evaluate the frontal lobes of the brain. They emphasized that identification of the behavioral and cognitive symptoms of frontal lobe pathology depended to a large degree on the competence and experience of the neuropsychologist. They stressed that the patient's neuropsychological test data needed to be supplemented by interviews with significant others, observations of the patient's behavior in real-world settings, and the patient's medical records to determine how the patient was functioning while they were hospitalized or receiving treatment in a brain injury rehabilitation program.

A number of prominent neuropsychologists and behavioral neurologists have also pointed out how inadequate neuropsychological testing is to assess damage to the frontal lobes and the regions connected to the frontal lobes. For example, Bigler (1988) stressed that traditional neuropsychological tests and measures are generally insensitive to alterations in the patient's behavior caused by frontal lobe damage. He stressed that the patients themselves lacked awareness that such alterations had occurred. As a consequence, he strongly emphasized the importance of careful observations of the patient's behavior and detailed interviews of family members and significant others who have observed the patient to assess any alterations in the patient's executive functions.

Mesulam (1986) felt that the behavioral changes associated with frontal lobe damage were almost impossible to quantify through traditional neuropsychological tests and batteries. He felt that our traditional methods of testing the frontal lobes were often overly simplistic (e.g., Trail Making Test). Thus, if the patient's test scores fall in the average or expected range, they will often conclude that the patient's frontal lobes are intact. Other psychologists may administer the Wisconsin Card Sorting Test to assess the functional integrity of the patient's frontal lobes, even though individuals who sustain significant damage to their orbital frontal lobes typically perform well on this test (Stuss and Benson, 1986).

Luria (1966) observed that while many patients with frontal lobe lesions did fairly well on neuropsychological tests, they approached problem-solving tasks quite differently in that they were generally unable to formulate a plan that was needed to solve the problem when the task required a preliminary analysis of the problem itself. Zangwill (1966) had earlier pointed out those patients who had sustained frontal lobe injuries would often perform in the normal range on standardized neuropsychological tests. He strongly felt that these tests were inadequate to assess the cognitive deficits caused by these injuries.

Many neuropsychologists do not understand the effects of damage to the medial or lateral orbital frontal lobes even though injuries to these regions of the brain are common when patients have struck their heads on the ground as a result of falling from a ladder or are struck by a motor vehicle while walking across the street. Although individuals who sustain damage to the medial orbital frontal lobes typically perform in the normal range on standardized neuropsychological tests, they frequently exhibit a loss of motivation, loss of energy and drive, loss of pleasure from the environment, depression (pseudodepression), psychomotor retardation, a change in their eating habits, loss of sex drive, loss of curiosity, and obsessive–compulsive behavior.

Although these patients with lateral orbital frontal lobe will usually deny any behavioral or cognitive symptoms and test in the normal range on standardized neuropsychological tests, they commonly exhibit a dramatic change in their personality, which is observed by their family and significant others, but not by the patient. They are unable to control their behavior and regulate their emotions, exhibit a loss of social tact, are unable to empathize with others, exhibit marked egocentricity, frequently use crude and coarse language at home, exhibit poor frustration tolerance, exhibit frequent mood swings, and are unaware of how their symptoms affect others.

Why are not patients with these injuries identified by psychologists? This typically occurs when they fail to interview the patient's significant others; base their opinions on the patient's performance on standardized tests that are often administered by a technician or someone in training often without the psychologist being present, have a poor understanding of the behavioral symptoms of orbital frontal lobe pathology, take inadequate histories, fail to review the patient's medical and rehabilitation records, and assume that poor performance on neuropsychological tests indicates brain-damage and relatively normal performance indicates no brain-damage. It also occurs when they do not observe the patient's function outside the test environment, particularly in unstructured, noisy, complex, and novel settings.

Although some neuropsychologists (e.g., Reitan and Wolfson, 1993) have stressed the importance of not biasing the interpretation of the patient's test data by reviewing the patient's clinical history and medical records, this practice often can result in the neuropsychologist forming opinions based solely on tests that are insensitive to the neurobehavioral consequences of orbital frontal lobe damage. This increases the likelihood that the neuropsychologist's predictions about the patient's ability to function in real-world settings will be inaccurate and misleading. This practice also has the potential of arriving at opinions that are potentially harmful to the patient and the patient's significant others.

Case Example

A 27-year-old male sustained a blunt head trauma as a result of falling from a ladder and striking his head on the ground. He sustained a brief loss of consciousness, and was observed to be combative at the scene of the accident. He was taken to the ER and released later that day after his CT head scan was normal. Within a few weeks his wife observed a dramatic change in her husband's personality in that he now had a great deal of difficulty controlling his emotions and temper and would often hit her or throw things with little or no provocation. She denied that he had ever acted this way prior to his accident. He was referred by his family physician for neuropsychological testing. He denied any cognitive symptoms or problems controlling his emotions. All of his test scores fell into the normal range. The psychologist contacted the referring physician and indicated that this patient showed no evidence of brain-damage or cognitive deficits. Three weeks later this patient struck his wife with a heavy metal crowbar during an argument and killed her. The psychologist had not interviewed the patient's wife, or had ever observed this patient's behavior outside of his office, or in a stressful situation.

LIMITATIONS OF NEUROPSYCHOLOGICAL TESTS TO ASSESS THE EXECUTIVE FUNCTIONS OF THE BRAIN

The executive functions are a complex process of integrated cognitive activities. For example, Sbordone (2000) has proposed that the executive functions of the brain be defined as the complex process by which an individual goes about performing a novel problem-solving task from its inception to its completion. This process includes the awareness that a particular problem or need exists, an evaluation of the particular problem or need, an analysis of the conditions of the problem, the formulation of specific goals necessary to solve this problem, the development of a set of plans that determine which actions are needed to solve this problem, evaluation of the potential effectiveness of these plans, the selection and initiation of a particular plan to solve the problem, evaluation of any progress made toward solving the problem or need, modification of the plan if it not effective, disregarding ineffective plans and replacing them with more effective plans, comparing the results achieved by the new plan with the conditions of the problem, terminating the plan when the conditions of the problem have been satisfied, storing the plan, and retrieving it later if the same or similar problem appears.

Neuropsychological tests were primarily designed to assess whether a patient had brain-damage. They were not designed to assess the executive functions of the brain. Much like the man on the street trying to find his keys that are located two blocks away, psychologists frequently rely on neuropsychological tests that are believed to be sensitive to frontal lobe damage to assess the executive functions of the brain since they apparently assume that the executive functions are located in the frontal lobes. This assumption is faulty since injuries to subcortical and other nonfrontal brain structures that have connections to the frontal lobes can produce executive dysfunction even though the patient's frontal lobes are intact (Cummings, 1995). For example, subcortical disorders such as Parkinson's disease, progressive supranuclear palsy, Huntington's disease, Korsakoff's syndrome, and dementia caused by carbon monoxide exposure, and inhalation of organic solvents produce executive dysfunction (Sbordone, 2000).

Many neuropsychologists seem to believe that the best way to assess the executive functions of the brain is to administer one or more of the following tests: The Wisconsin Card Sorting Test, the Halstead Category Test, System, the Verbal Concept Attainment Test, Controlled Oral Word Association Test, the Verbal Fluency Test, Designed Fluency, Ruff Figural Fluency Test, Porteus Maze Test, Tinker Toy Test, Stroop Test, Trail Making Test, Purdue Pegboard Test, Finger Tapping Test, Rey Complex Figure Test, and more recently the Delis–Kaplan Executive Function System.

The patient's performance on these tests may not provide accurate information about their executive functions since they may only assess some, but not all of the complex steps that are involved in the executive functions of the brain (Cripe, 1996; Sbordone, 2000). By analogy, using these tests to assess a patient's executive functions is comparable to being asked to write a review of the movie *Titanic* after watching only 10 min of the 3 hour film. This would not provide sufficient time to comprehend the complexity, richness, and drama of this movie. The only way to fully appreciate the movie and write a meaningful review would be to watch the entire movie from start to finish. Unfortunately, the manner in which neuropsychologists currently practice today (e.g., administering tests rather than observing a patient function in real-world settings) is the primary reason why we do not understand the executive functions of the brain, or how to adequately assess them.

REFERENCES

Bigler, E. D. 1988. Frontal Lobe Damage and Neuropsychological Assessment. *Archives of Clinical Neuropsychology*, 3, 279–297.

Cripe, L. I. 1996. The Ecological Validity of Executive Function Testing. In Sbordone, R. J. and Long, C. (Eds.) *Ecological Validity of Neuropsychogical Testing*. Delray Beach, FL: GR/St. Lucie Press, pp. 129–146.

Cummings, J. L. 1995. Anatomic and Behavioral Aspects of Frontal–Subcortical Circuits. In Grafman, J., Holyoak, K. J., and Boller, F. (Eds.) *Structure and Function of the Human Pre-Frontal Lobes. Clinical Neuropsychology*, 2d ed. New York: Oxford Press, pp. 409–460.

Damasio, A. R. 1985. The Frontal Lobes. In Heilman, K. M. and Valenstein, E. (Eds.) *Clinical Neuropsychology*, 2d ed. New York: Oxford University Press, pp. 409–460.

Luria, A. R. 1966. *Human Brain and Psychological Processes*. New York: Harper & Row.

Mesulam, M. M. 1986. Frontal Cortex and Behavior: Editorial. *Annals of Neurology, 19*, 320–325.

Mitrushina, M. N., Boone, K. B., and D'Elia, L. F. 1999. *Handbook of Normative Data for Neuropsychological Assessment*. New York: Oxford University Press.

Reitan, R. M. and Wolfson, D. 1993. Validity of the Trail Making Test as an Indicator of Organic Brain-Damage. *Perceptual and Motor Skills, 8*, 271–276.

Sbordone, R. J. 2000. The Executive Functions of the Brain. In Groth-Marnat, G. (Ed.) *Neuropsychological Assessment in Clinical Practice: A Guide to Test Interpretation and Integration*. New York: John Wiley & Sons, pp. 437–456.

Sbordone, R. J. and Purisch, A. D. 1996. Hazards of Blind Analysis of Neuropsychological Data in Assessing Cognitive Disability. *Neurorehabilitation, 7*, 15–26.

Stuss, D. T. and Benson, D. F. 1986. *The Frontal Lobes*. News York: Raven Press.

Zangwill, O. L. 1966. Psychological Deficits Associated with Frontal Lobe Lesions. *International Journal of Neurology, 5*, 395–402.

15 Samples of Medicolegal Neuropsychological Reports

This chapter contains six neuropsychological reports that were written by neuropsychologists involved in medicolegal cases. Three of these reports were written at the request of the plaintiff's attorney. The remaining three were written at the request of the defendant's attorney. The names, dates, and various hospitals and treatment centers listed in these reports have been changed to conceal their identities. Any resemblance to actual persons or places is purely coincidental. Each of these reports has been critically reviewed to help the reader recognize its strengths and limitations.

SAMPLE #1

May 21, 1997

Harry C. Carter, M.D.
1400 Fairview Street
Milwaukee, Wisconsin 92351

RE: Joan Allan

Dear Dr. Carter:
I have performed a comprehensive neuropsychological evaluation of Ms. Allan at your request. She was seen at my office for testing. She understood that she was being examined with regard to her claim of having suffered neuropsychological problems from her accident of 12-15-96. She further understood that a report would be prepared for this examination and would be forwarded to you and to the attorneys for the insurance carrier in this case. She also understood that this examiner might be required to testify either in a Deposition or at the time of trial. She was fully agreeable with all of these procedures and it was with her consent that this examination took place.

CHIEF COMPLAINTS

Ms. Allan denied the presence of any significant emotional problems. In general, she stated that she felt well and that she was ready to get on with her life. In particular, she felt that she was ready to return to her previous employment and that she could do so without any problems.

HISTORY OF PRESENT ILLNESS

Ms. Allan had been working as a security guard when she suffered an accident on the job in which she sustained a facial fracture. There was a possibility that she may have sustained a neuropsychological injury since testing performed shortly after her accident suggested this possibility. Yet, when she had been examined more recently, she felt that she was functioning at a much higher level. As a consequence, neuropsychological testing was requested to assess her condition at this time. When she was asked if she had any emotional problems about the accident, she admitted that she had been initially short tempered, but was much better now. She voiced some complaints about occasional problems with her memory, which appear to be more than only normal types of memory problems. For example, at times she forgets simple activities in her home.

PERSONAL HISTORY

She had a very unhappy childhood. There was a history of physical abuse and possible molestation. Her father was an alcoholic and quite abusive. Her mother had a history of emotional problems. Although she had a number of problems while growing up, she was able to complete high school with a 2.8 GPA. After graduating from high school, she held a series of different jobs. She denied any history of counseling prior to the accident and does not feel the need for any counseling at this time.

REVIEW OF MEDICAL RECORDS

The records of Fowler Medical Center indicate that she was admitted after having sustained a closed head injury and a right frontal skull fracture. Her Glasgow Coma Scale score was 7 at the time of her admission. During her hospitalization, she was noted to have severe cognitive impairments, poor judgment, emotional lability, and poor awareness of her cognitive and behavioral impairments. She underwent testing at that time, which revealed a full-scale Intelligence Quotient (IQ) of 78, a performance IQ of 71, and a verbal IQ of 88. Her IQ appears to be generally consistent with the fact that she received Cs and Ds in high school. She was administered the Category Test and made a total of 107 errors. Numerous perseverative errors were noted on the Wisconsin Card Sorting Test. She was impaired on both Parts A and B of the Trail Making Test. She was also administered the full Halstead–Reitan Battery. She scored an impairment index of 1.0, which placed her in the severely impaired range. Since her discharge from the hospital she has not returned to work and has been supported by her husband.

TESTS ADMINISTERED

She was administered the Wechsler Adult Intelligence Scale — Revised (WAIS-R), the Wechsler Memory Scale — Revised, and the Trail Making Test. She was also administered the Millon Clinical Multiaxial Inventory — III (MCMI-III).

TEST RESULTS

On the WAIS-R, she obtained a verbal IQ of 93 and a performance IQ of 80 to produce a full-scale IQ of 86. These findings represent a substantial improvement from previous testing. Qualitative analysis suggested that she was not manifesting any signs of verbal impairment. These results also indicate that she is able to attend and concentrate, her vocabulary is intact, and her abstract verbal skills are good. Her performance on this test also indicates that while she may have some problems with visuospatial analysis, she is able to perform very simple and concrete visual and spatial tasks without any problem. Although her visual motor speed was somewhat slow, her general abilities were within normal limits. Her performance on the Wechsler Memory Scale — Revised indicates that her ability to attend, concentrate, and remember is within normal limits. While qualitative analysis suggests that her visual memory is impaired, because she has difficulty paying attention to details, errors relating to detail are quite common. Her findings suggest that her visuospatial integration deficits are most likely due to the residual problems with her right eye. She was administered the Trail Making Test. She scored at the 75th percentile on Part A and at the 50th percentile on Part B. These findings indicate a marked improvement over the previous test measures.

Personality

Her profile on the MCMI-II suggests chronic problems with adaptation and adjustments in life. Her profile suggests evidence of a personality disorder with prominent sadistic, narcissistic, and obsessive–compulsive traits. Her profile also suggests that she is prejudiced and self-centered and has deep feelings of insecurity about her own self-worth. Furthermore, her deep feelings of resentment are typically projected outward, which is likely to create conflicts with others. The guiding principle for her is that of outwitting others before they can dominate her. Her profile also suggests that alcoholism or drug abuse may be a problem.

Impression

When she was asked about her performance on the testing that was done while she was in the hospital, she reported, "I was not trying at all" and recalled that she also had had an argument with her father on the day of testing and had actually asked the psychologist to leave the room. As a result she did not feel like putting forth her full effort. In comparison with previous testing, there is a steady and consistent pattern of improvement. The results of current testing suggest that she is experiencing significant problems that are related only to her visual skills, which appear to be secondary to her right eye injury. Her right hemisphere appears to be functioning normally and her basic neuropsychological functioning is now within normal limits. Given her background of having done very poorly during high school, her current test results would suggest that there has not been a significant decline in her overall intellectual functioning. Aside from her visual problems, she warrants the diagnosis of an underlying personality disorder because sadistic, narcissistic, and obsessive–compulsive features were indicated by her MCMI profile. However, she does not appear to be having any significant acute emotional problems and appears to be coping quite well. Therefore, it appears that she has returned to her baseline level of functioning.

RICHARD CRUMB, PH.D.

Critique

Dr. Crumb makes no mention in his report of the fact that the patient's computed tomography (CT) scan at the time of her admission to the hospital revealed bilateral frontal lobe contusions or that she had been rendered comatose for 7 days. He fails to mention that, shortly after she was admitted to the hospital, she developed an acute subdural hematoma, which was surgically evacuated. He also fails to mention that her Glasgow Coma Scale score was as low as 3 following surgery. He failed to take a detailed history and did not interview any collateral informants or significant others. He also ignored this patient's symptoms of impulsivity, poor judgment, and disinhibited behavior that she exhibited during his examination. He failed to mention that the medical staff at the inpatient rehabilitation center, where she had spent 3 months, had observed the following symptoms: poor judgment, severe cognitive deficits, impulsivity, disinhibited behavior, an inability to regulate her emotions or behavior, poor organization and planning skills, severe problems with her recent memory (including confabulation), and poor problem-solving skills. These records also note that on several occasions she verbally insulted several of the staff and once threw a chair at another patient.

Dr. Crumb appears to rely heavily on this patient's subjective assessment of her cognitive and behavioral functioning, even though her medical records consistently describe her awareness of her cognitive and behavioral impairments as poor. While he relies on this patient's description of her high school transcript and the fact that he believes that she had been a C and D student in high school, he never actually reviewed her high school transcript, which reveals that she actually graduated from high school with a C+ average. Furthermore, her junior college transcripts revealed that she made As and Bs in many of her classes.

While prior neuropsychological testing identified her as having severe deficits with respect to her problem-solving and executive-function skills, he did not administer any tests during his examination to assess these functions. Instead, he apparently chose to administer tests that are relatively insensitive to traumatic brain injury. Even though she performed poorly on some of these tests, he attributed her poor performance to visual difficulties rather than her brain injury. Dr. Crumb selectively used computer-generated narrative statements taken from her MCMI-II report to describe her in a negative manner (e.g., sadistic, narcissistic, self-centered) to suggest that she had these problems prior to the accident. He also suggests in his report that as a result of having such personality traits, she might have been responsible for causing her brain injury. He failed to point out that this patient had an excellent work history, had an excellent work attendance record, and had received outstanding job performance evaluations prior to her accident. He also failed to consider the possibility that her MCMI-II profile most likely reflected the behavioral manifestations of her brain injury, rather than her preexisting personality traits. For example, her parents, supervisors, and friends described her as a mature and level-headed person prior to her accident, one who made friends easily and was very fair and kind to others.

Finally, he tried to minimize her previous neuropsychological test findings by claiming that she was not trying at the time they were administered to her, when, in fact, they were consistent with the behavioral observations of the medical and rehabilitation staff who had treated her. Thus, he appears to be deliberately minimizing her cognitive and behavioral symptoms. Although he concludes that her "basic neuropsychological functioning is now within normal limits," his choice of tests along with his failure to review her medical records and academic records, to interview collateral sources, to include observations of her behavior, and to administer neuropsychological tests to adequately assess her cognitive and behavioral impairments clearly reflects his strong biases and overadvocacy.

SAMPLE #2

September 5, 1996

John W. O'Brien
Attorney at Law
Law Offices of Cheatam and Howe
One Shady Plaza
Dallas, Texas

RE: Angelo Giovanni

Dear Mr. O'Brien:

Mr. Giovanni was referred for neuropsychological assessment as a result of difficulties he encountered following a motor vehicle accident that occurred on July 7, 1994. The examination also included an interview with Mr. Giovanni's wife, Dodie.

A review of Mr. Giovanni's records indicates that he was rendered unconscious for 2 or 3 min and was noted to be combative at the scene of the accident. He was taken by ambulance to Royal Oak Hospital, where he was noted to be extremely confused and combative and had a Glasgow Coma Scale score of 12. A CT scan revealed a right frontal lobe contusion. He remained hospitalized for 3 days and was discharged with the diagnosis of closed head injury.

After he went home, he began cursing, throwing furniture, and attacking others with little or no provocation. His wife became frightened, because her husband had always been a very gentleman who virtually never lost his temper. She also reported that he no longer seemed interested in having sex and had lost interest in many of the activities he had previously enjoyed such as bowling, going to the movies, and dancing. She complained that her husband had become very egocentric and no longer seemed concerned about her welfare or happiness. While he appeared apathetic most of the time, his apathy would be punctuated by brief, aggressive outbursts that would occur with little, if any, provocation. During these outbursts, he would break windows, punch walls, throw furniture, and curse loudly. Prior to his accident, he had required only 6 or 7 hours of sleep and now he was sleeping 14 to 15 hours a day. Even though he had enjoyed weight lifting and had competed in a number of competitions in the past, he was no longer interested in this activity. While he had had numerous friends prior to the accident, he now made no effort to contact them and refused to return their phone calls.

Prior to his accident, he had worked for several years as a journeyman electrician. He had a good work history and was well thought of by his supervisors and individuals in the trade industry. Now he spends most of his time watching the same videos over and over again and no longer seems interested in helping his wife around the house, which he had done on a regular basis prior to the accident.

When he was interviewed, he denied any cognitive or behavioral impairments. When he was questioned about some of the problems and difficulties his wife had described, he became volatile and tried to assault the examiner, and the police were summoned. After the police arrived, he seemed confused as to why they were necessary and did not appear to recall his violent temper outburst. According to his medical records, he had gained over 40 pounds since his accident. Even though he had been a "health food nut," prior to the accident, he no longer ate healthy foods and would typically eat whatever was placed in front of him.

Although he denied that he had had any problems in driving since his accident, his wife stated that he had been involved in three motor vehicle accidents, all of which were his fault, which she felt reflected his poor judgment. For example, during one of these accidents he went through a red light and struck another vehicle that was in the process of making a turn. In another accident, he failed to yield to an oncoming vehicle before making a left-hand turn. Fortunately, he was not seriously injured in any of these accidents.

He was administered the WAIS-R, which gave him a full-scale IQ of 105, a verbal IQ of 104, and a performance IQ of 105. This score appeared to be consistent with testing done within 6 months following his motor vehicle accident and seemed to be consistent with his job duties as an electrician. His performance on the Wechsler Memory Scale — Revised revealed no significant abnormalities. His Minnesota Multiphasic Personality Inventory (MMPI) profile identified him as a rather tense, anxious, and somewhat depressed individual who lacked insight into his psychiatric and emotional problems. He was also administered the Halstead–Reitan Neuropsychological Battery. His score on the Neuropsychological Deficits Scale was 23, which placed him within the normal range (0 to 25). Within 6 months of his accident, he was tested on the Halstead Category Test and scored in the moderately impaired range. Current testing reveals that his score falls in the mildly impaired range. He tested in the normal range on the Seashore Rhythm, Trail Making, Finger Tapping, and Grip Strength tests and on the Sensory Perceptual Examination.

Based on his neuropsychological test data, he appears to exhibit some mild residual cognitive deficits, particularly on tasks involving problem solving. However, his overall neuropsychological performance placed him within the normal range. He is seen as requiring individual psychotherapy to help him with his emotional difficulties. His wife is also seen as requiring counseling to help her cope with his emotional difficulties.

HARVEY PRINCE, PH.D.

Critique

Although Dr. Prince took a fairly good history from Mr. Giovanni and interviewed his wife, he failed to recognize this patient's orbitofrontal lobe syndrome. As a result of his lack of specialized training in clinical neuropsychology and his poor understanding of behavioral neurology, he failed to appreciate the clinical significance of the history that was provided to him by Mrs. Giovanni, particularly the dramatic change she observed in her husband's personality and behavior since his accident. He also failed to note the clinical significance of this patient's medical records (e.g., that this patient had sustained a prominent frontal lobe contusion and had been combative at the scene of the accident and at the time he had been admitted to the emergency room). To conceal his ignorance about these issues, Dr. Prince appears to selectively ignore this patient's behavioral problems and instead focuses on his neuropsychological test data.

Unfortunately, patients who sustain prominent orbitofrontal lobe damage typically do not perform poorly on standardized neuropsychological tests and show little, if any, change in their intelligence on tests of intellectual functioning. They do, however, manifest an inability to regulate their emotions and behavior, which was clearly obvious to Mrs. Giovanni and to Dr. Prince, who had to summon the police after Mr. Giovanni tried to assault him. However, Dr. Prince dealt with these problems by attributing them to this patient's feelings of anxiety and depression rather than to his brain injury. While Dr. Prince found some evidence that this patient was mildly impaired on the Halstead Category Test, he stressed that this patient's performance on the entire Halstead–Reitan Battery placed him within the average range (which would have been expected because this test is generally insensitive to orbitofrontal lobe damage).

Dr. Prince's opinions appear to reflect his lack of experience and competence in assessing patients who have sustained traumatic brain injuries. Given his lack of experience and understanding, rather than accepting this case, he should have referred this case to another psychologist who possessed the background, training, and experience to evaluate this type of patient.

SAMPLE #3

April 24, 1996

Arturo Guerrero, Esq.
Law Offices of Guerrero and Solis
598 King Street, #310
Dallas, Texas 48934

RE: Reynaldo Cabrera

Dear Mr. Guerrero:
Mr. Cabrera is a 26-year-old, left-handed Hispanic male who has completed only one year of formal education. He was rendered unconscious for an unspecified period of time after he was struck in the head by an elevator on 10-6-93. At the time of his examination on 4-15-96, he seemed alert and oriented and was accompanied by his sister-in-law.

CHIEF COMPLAINTS AS OBTAINED FROM MR. CABRERA VIA A TRANSLATOR

1. His left leg and knee feel cold approximately once per week.
2. Dizziness occurs on the average of once a day and lasts for approximately 1 h. He denies any associated vomiting or vertigo.
3. He is very forgetful.
4. He has had pain and soreness in his left ankle since his accident.

ADDITIONAL COMPLAINTS OF HIS SISTER-IN-LAW

Mr. Cabrera complains of headaches on the average of once or twice per month, which are usually resolved with Tylenol.

CURRENT MEDICATIONS

He denies consuming any alcoholic beverages or taking any medications during the past week.

HISTORY OF INJURY AS OBTAINED FROM MR. CABRERA VIA AN INTERPRETER WITH THE ASSISTANCE OF HIS SISTER-IN-LAW

Mr. Cabrera has no recollection of the accident. He indicated that while he was working on October 6, 1993, he was struck by an elevator and rendered unconscious for an unspecified period of time. He was taken to Greater Dallas Medical Center, where he remained hospitalized for 2 weeks until being transferred to Rio Grande Medical Center, where he was hospitalized for an additional week. While hospitalized he underwent a craniotomy and surgery to his right hip and left ankle. Since his discharge from Rio Grande Medical Center, he has been followed by Dr. Blackwood, a neurologist, and Dr. Moto, an orthopedist. He has also been seen by Dr. Stevens, a neuropsychologist. He has not returned to work.

Prior to his accident, he had never held a driver's license or driven an automobile. He was unable to read, spell, or write anything other than his name. He has never gone out on a date and has completed only the first grade. He has been living with his brother and sister-in-law and has never lived on his own.

Since his accident, he watches a Spanish variety television show and performs household duties, such as cleaning up the house, washing dishes, watering plants, washing his own clothes, and cooking simple meals. He is able to bathe and dress himself. He also enjoys playing cards and games. He is able to cut the grass and clean up the yard. He is able to take a bus on his own and ride a mountain bike. However, his sister-in-law states that he often becomes upset with people. He had five male friends prior to his accident with whom he has continued to maintain contact via telephone.

BACKGROUND AS OBTAINED FROM MR. CABRERA VIA A TRANSLATOR WITH THE ASSISTANCE OF HIS SISTER-IN-LAW

Developmental

Mr. Cabrera was born in Mexico. He grew up in a small province as the youngest of four children. He came to Texas in 1989, but has not learned any English despite enrolling in English as a second language course. He had the usual childhood illnesses. He denies any surgeries or hospitalizations during his childhood. He denies a childhood history of physical, sexual, or psychological abuse. Although his family was described as being very poor, he described his childhood as happy. He is unable to read or spell in his native language. He is able to perform only very simple arithmetic tasks (e.g., $1 + 1, 2 + 2$). He is strongly left handed, speaks only Spanish, and has completed only the first grade.

Occupational History

At the time of his accident, he had been employed as a landscape helper for his father and was earning $6 an hour.

Hobbies/Interests

He enjoys basketball.

Living

Prior to his accident, he was living with his brother and sister-in-law. Since his accident he has continued to reside with them.

Military Service

He denies ever having served in the military.

Legal

He denies ever having been arrested or having had any difficulties with law enforcement authorities.

Family History

He did not know the ages of either of his parents or their educational background. According to his sister-in-law, his mother is 59 years old and his father is 62. His father is a self-employed landscaper. The patient has three brothers. His 31-year-old brother is a high school graduate and is an apprentice electrician. His 33-year-old brother is a high school graduate and works part-time as a carpenter. His 36-year-old brother is a high school graduate and attended trade school to become a carpenter. Each of his brothers is married.

Marital History

Mr. Cabrera is single and has never been married. He denies that he has ever gone out on a date.

Psychiatric

He denies ever receiving any prior psychiatric treatment or counseling. After his accident, he received counseling at Rio Grande Rehabilitation Hospital. He was placed on antidepressant medication for 2 months. He denies a history of suicidal ideation or behavior.

Substance Use

Prior to the accident, he consumed two beers on social occasions. He did not smoke. He denies ever using street drugs or nonprescribed medications. He was hospitalized in 1991 for anemia and was given blood transfusions. He denies ever having been involved in any motor vehicle accidents. He nearly drowned as a child. He denies a prior history of head trauma, respiratory problems, vascular problems, endocrine problems, diabetes, coronary problems, hypoglycemia, toxic exposure, or hypertension.

REVIEW OF MEDICAL RECORDS

The consultation report of Martin Ostheimer, M.D., dated March 12, 1991, indicates that Mr. Cabrera has a history of syncope. He was at work as a landscaper and apparently had two episodes of syncope. He was brought to the emergency room of Santa Maria Hospital where he was noted to have a low hemoglobin count. On admission, his rectal examination revealed guaiac positive stools. They noted that it was difficult to communicate with him because of a language barrier. However, he did admit to black, soft stools several times a day for the past 3 or 4 days prior to admission. He did not complain of nausea, vomiting, abdominal pain, fever, chills, or diarrhea.

The Discharge Summary of Santa Maria Hospital indicated that Mr. Cabrera was admitted on March 11, 1991 under the care of Dr. Ostheimer for severe symptomatic anemia, gastrointestinal bleeding, and acute gastritis. During his hospitalization, he underwent esophagogastroduodenoscopy and colonoscopy and had a blood transfusion. At the time of his admission, he was noted to have melena of 3 to 4 days' duration. He also had syncope on two occasions with exertion. Testing showed mild gastritis and lymphoid hyperplasia, without evidence of ischemic or irritable bowel disease. There was no evidence of acute bleeding during his admission. Biopsy of his colon showed chronic inflammation with lymphoid hyperplasia. There was no evidence of malignancy. He was discharged on March 21, 1991.

The emergency department report of Greater Dallas Medical Center, dated October 6, 1993, signed by Calvin Messer, M.D., indicated that Mr. Cabrera had been transported to the emergency room by the paramedics on that date. Approximately 3 min prior to their arrival, the paramedics had been notified that Mr. Cabrera was a trauma victim who had been struck by a descending or falling elevator from approximately one story above him. At the time of his admission, he was found to be unresponsive. His respiratory rate was approximately 8 and shallow. He was given 100% oxygen, which caused his respirations to increase to 20. His pupils were round, equal, and reactive to light, sluggishly reacting from approximately 4 mm down to 3 mm with direct light. His gaze was dysconjugate and roving. He was noted to have an abrasion on the right cheek. Examination of his ears did not reveal any blood in the canals or behind the tympanic membranes, which were intact. He was diagnosed as having multiple trauma secondary to crush injury from a falling elevator, possible closed head injury, right femur fracture, open left tibial fracture, and probable intrathoracic and intraabdominal injuries with bleeding.

The history and physical report, completed by Kenneth Livingston, M.D., on October 6, 1993, indicated that Mr. Cabrera had been working when an elevator fell approximately 16 ft, crushing him. His friends ran over and lifted the elevator off him, which was estimated to weigh approximately 500 pounds. He was moaning at the scene of the accident but not responsive. When the paramedics arrived, he had a stable blood pressure and was breathing spontaneously. He did not respond to commands. They attempted to intubate him, however this was not successful. At the time of his accident, he was not working at his usual job but at a side job. He was noted to be comatose with dysconjugate gaze. His pupils were 4 mm bilaterally and reactive. He had a positive gag reflex. He was able to move his upper extremities and his left leg with pain. He was diagnosed as having a closed head injury, altered mental status, right subdural hematoma, scalp hematoma, multiple abrasions, femur fracture, open tibia and fibular fracture, bilateral clavicle fractures, blunt chest and abdominal trauma, anemia, hypokalemia, mild metabolic acidosis, and microscopic hematuria. It was felt that he required neurosurgical evaluation for a subdural hematoma and would most likely need a craniotomy decompression.

The neurological consultation report of Gary Willis, M.D., dated October 7, 1993, indicated that Mr. Cabrera had opened his eyes and occasionally followed simple commands with his hands. His pupils were equal, round, and responsive to light. He had questionable right upper quadrant weakness. Since both lower extremities were splinted, his sensory, gait, and cerebellar examinations could not be performed. He underwent a CT scan without contrast, which demonstrated an approximately 1 cm left frontotemporal parietal acute subdural hematoma, with left shift of the midline structures of 1 cm. There was no evidence of skull fracture. His basal cisterns were visible. Dr. Willis felt that Mr. Cabrera had a left frontotemporal parietal acute subdural hematoma, with significant mass effect. He felt that Mr. Cabrera was at risk for further neurological deterioration due to an increasing mass effect and swelling. However, he felt that the prognosis was favorable if the subdural hematoma was evacuated.

The transfer summary of Greater Dallas Medical Center, signed by Aaron Finestein, M.D., indicated that Mr. Cabrera was admitted on October 6, 1993 and was transferred to Rio Grande Medical Center on October 20, 1993. During his hospitalization he underwent a craniotomy with evacuation of a subdural hematoma on October 6, 1993; irrigation and debridement of his left leg on October 7, 1993; closed reduction of the left tibia on October 7, 1993; right tibia pin insertion on October 7, 1993; irrigation and debridement of the left tibia on October 10, 1993; delayed closure of the left tibia on October 10, 93; and rodding of the left and right tibial fractures on October 10, 1993. After Mr. Cabrera had undergone evacuation and decompression of the subdural hematoma, his clinical course improved; that is, he was noted to be neurologically intact with no motor deficits. However, he described slight paresthesia of the distal right foot. His family described him as appropriate, stating that he had returned to baseline functioning.

The consultation report of Mervyn Blackwood, M.D., dated October 21, 1993, indicated that Mr. Cabrera was noted to be in no apparent distress. He was alert and oriented to person and place. However, he was unable to provide the day, month, or year. He was able to name objects and their function. He was not able to read written commands, but could follow simple and complex commands without difficulty. He was able to perform only simple math calculations such as $2 + 2$ and $3 + 3$. He was unable to perform subtraction or multiplication. Examination revealed his cranial nerves to be intact. His motor strength was 5/5 in his upper extremities bilaterally and his right lower extremity. Dr. Blackwood felt that Mr. Cabrera appeared to be doing remarkably well considering the injuries he had sustained on October 6, 1993.

Mr. Cabrera underwent a speech and language evaluation on October 23, 1993, which revealed mild cognitive and communication deficits. He was discharged from Rio Grande Medical Center on October 27, 1993, and was scheduled to be followed on an outpatient basis.

Mr. Cabrera saw Dr. Blackwood on November 8, 1993. At that time, Dr. Blackwood noted that, according to his sister-in-law, Mr. Cabrera's mental status was improving. He was walking with a walker and was weight bearing as tolerated on both lower extremities. He did complain of a little discomfort at the site of his previous left clavicular fracture. However, no distal weakness or numbness had been noted by the patient in his upper or lower extremities.

The outpatient progress note signed by Dr. Blackwood on November 14, 1993 indicated that Mr. Cabrera was noted to be alert and oriented to place and person, but not to time. The remainder of his neurological examination was unremarkable.

Dr. Moto's note, dated January 16, 1994, indicated that Mr. Cabrera came to the clinic for a recheck of his right femur and left tibial fractures. Dr. Moto noted that Mr. Cabrera had done "really very well" since his last visit. He was only complaining of trochanteric discomfort on the right side from his hardware. Otherwise, he was walking without much of a problem and denied any pain in his legs. Dr. Moto noted, however, that Mr. Cabrera had a slightly antalgic gait on the right side with an abductor lurch, which was felt to be in part due to the irritation of his hardware proximally about the right hip. However, he was able to squat and do a deep knee bend with both legs without any particular problems.

Dr. Moto's follow-up report, dated May 16, 1994, indicated that Mr. Cabrera had done remarkably well since his last visit. He also noted that Mr. Cabrera's mental status had improved. His fractures had healed and he was "really quite functional." His main complaint was that of some trochanteric irritation from the proximal end of the right femoral nail. However, this was more of an annoyance than a dysfunctional problem. On physical examination, he had a non-antalgic gait. There were negative Trendelenburg signs bilaterally in his legs. He had good hip, knee, and ankle range of motion bilaterally. His neurovascular examination appeared to be intact distally.

Dr. Moto's follow-up report, dated August 12, 1994, indicated that Mr. Cabrera still had some tenderness to palpation in the trochanteric region of his right hip. He had good range of motion of the hip, with minimal discomfort. X-rays taken of his right femur and tibia on that date showed satisfactory healing of both fractures. It was recommended that he be scheduled for removal of his right femoral nail.

Mr. Cabrera was admitted to Greater Dallas Medical Center on October 10, 1994 to remove the screws from his right femur. He underwent surgery on this date and was discharged on October 20, 1994.

Dr. Moto's progress note, dated October 27, 1994, indicated that Mr. Cabrera came into the clinic 7 days status after discharge from the hospital. Dr. Moto stated that he was unable to remove Mr. Cabrera's intramedullary left femoral nail because of equipment malfunction. In any case, Mr. Cabrera had not had any recurrence of his proximal hip or trochanteric discomfort that he had had preoperatively. However, he was still restricted in his activities and was still ambulating with crutches at home. His pain was less than what it was immediately after surgery. He was getting better range of motion and was experiencing less pain.

The handwritten notes of Dr. Blackwood, dated November 20, 1994, indicated that Mr. Cabrera had not returned to work as a landscaper. He had a lawsuit still pending regarding the accident in the elevator shaft. According to his sister-in-law, Mr. Cabrera was still forgetful. She described an episode in which he mowed the lawn and trimmed the hedges of the house and forgot to clean up afterwards.

His sister-in-law reported that he was exhibiting occasional outbursts of anger. Dr. Blackwood's mental status examination noted that Mr. Cabrera was awake, alert, and oriented to person, place, and time. He exhibited fluent speech and had good naming. He was able to recall three items after 5 min. He was able to name the governor and the president. His neurological examination was normal.

Dr. Blackwood's report, dated December 20, 1994, indicated that Mr. Cabrera's current complaint was that of headache. He no longer had any complaints of any shoulder pain, but still had occasional neck pain. He also complained of bilateral leg pain, worse in the morning when first awakening. He stated that he was not able to do as many activities as he had been able to do prior to his injury. His headaches were accompanied by nausea, but no visual symptoms, and were located in the frontal area bilaterally. He was unable to state how often his headaches occurred. He stated that he had ringing in his ears on an intermittent basis and dizzy spells. However, he denied any syncopal episodes. He could not remember all of the things that he was no longer capable of doing, but stated that there were many things that fit into this category. His neck pain was described as bilateral, without any radiation into his arms or hands, and was not associated with any paresthesia or hyperesthesia. His left leg was painful at the shin and his entire right leg was painful. He has paresthesia and hyperesthesia in both legs with cold weather. The pain is worse in the morning and sometimes worsens with walking. He has a sensation of heat in his legs with sitting. He can walk only short distances before his legs begin hurting. The pain is alleviated by resting. He was still off work and was not taking any medications.

On the basis of his examination, Dr. Blackwood was unable to identify any specific localizing neurologic findings. Nonetheless, he felt that there was sufficient evidence of a head injury to warrant neuropsychological testing of this patient and a neurology consultation. However, he felt that Mr. Cabrera had made an excellent recovery of range of motion and function. He also noted that all of Mr. Cabrera's fractures appeared to have healed. He felt that Mr. Cabrera had some localized pain at the fracture sites or areas of insertion of the intramedullary rods. He cautioned that if the latter proved to be significantly symptomatic, elective removal of the internal fixation devices would be warranted after a minimum of 18 months postfracture. He did not anticipate that Mr. Cabrera's orthopedic fractures would create any significant functional disabilities and felt that Mr. Cabrera should eventually be able to return to gainful employment.

Dr. Blackwood's handwritten notes, dated January 16, 1995, indicated that Mr. Cabrera was accompanied by his brother, who noted that Mr. Cabrera was still forgetful and exhibited occasional outbursts of anger. Mr. Cabrera spent most of his day watching television or playing video games. His brother indicated that Mr. Cabrera has a poor recall of recent events.

Dr. Moto's follow-up report, dated May 5, 1995, indicated that Mr. Cabrera came in for a reexamination of his right femur and left tibial fractures. He had had no particular problem since his last visit. On physical examination, he had a nonantalgic gait and was able to perform a full symmetrical deep knee bend and had normal hip flexion, knee flexion, and ankle dorsiflexion.

BEHAVIORAL OBSERVATIONS

Mr. Cabrera presented as a 26-year-old, left-handed Hispanic male in no acute distress. He was accompanied by his sister-in-law and was interviewed with the assistance of a translator. He was oriented to person, place, time, and purpose. He showed signs of apparent mental retardation that most likely had preexisted his accident. For example, he indicated that prior to the accident he was unable to read or spell and could write only his name. He was able to perform only very simple arithmetic operations such as $2+2$ and $3+3$. He had never operated a motor vehicle or had a driver's license. He had never dated. Although he knew the names of the president and the governor, he did not know how many days in a week or how many hours in a day. He was also unable to name the colors of the American or Spanish flags. He was unable to identify the numerical value of a quarter (he thought it was worth 50 cents). When he was given several coins, he could not put them together in combinations to produce 43 or 59 cents. He could not state how many cents a penny, a nickel, and a dime totaled. His low level of intellectual functioning was also corroborated by the interpreter, who noted that Mr. Cabrera's command of Spanish was poor and he frequently had difficulty comprehending relatively simple words. He did not appear significantly anxious or depressed. He did not appear to be experiencing any significant pain or discomfort. He exhibited a craniotomy scar on the left side of his head. He appeared to be trying to the best of his ability on each of the neuropsychological tests that were administered to him.

NEUROPSYCHOLOGICAL TESTING

Tests Administered

The Raven Progressive Matrices Test

The Reading and Arithmetic Sections of the Wide Range Achievement Test (Revision 3)

Tests of Simple Arithmetic

Judgment of Line Orientation Test

The Rey Auditory Verbal Learning Test

The Rey Complex Figure Test

The Hand Dynamometer Test

Luria's Motor Examination

The Beck Depression Inventory — II

The Personality Assessment Inventory

TEST RESULTS

Mr. Cabrera was administered the Raven Progressive Matrices Test to assess his level of intellectual functioning since this particular test is nonverbal, generally culture-free, and only minimally affected by brain damage. His score on this test placed him in the moderate mentally retarded range. He was also administered the Wide Range Achievement Test (Revision 3) to determine his premorbid reading and arithmetic skill levels, since it is generally well known that a patient's performance on these tests is only minimally compromised by a traumatic brain injury. Testing revealed that Mr. Cabrera was able to perform only simple one-digit arithmetic tasks. He was unable to subtract, multiply, or divide. He could not read simple words such as in, cat, book, or tree even in his own native language. He was unable to make simple change or determine the total numerical value of a penny, nickel, and dime.

He was administered the Judgment of Line Orientation Test. His score on this test was found to be severely impaired. His verbal learning and memory scales were assessed by the Rey Auditory Verbal Learning Test (which was translated into Spanish). He was able to learn only a maximum of 8 out of 15 words over the course of five learning trials, whereas individuals of his sex and age are expected to learn an average of 12 words. He was able to recall six out of the eight words after a brief interference task. His visual memory could not be assessed because of his poor drawing and constructional skills.

His motor skills were assessed by the Hand Dynamometer Test and were found to be appropriate for persons of his sex and age. He was also asked to perform a variety of complex motor tasks. He required extensive practice to learn a task and exhibited a tendency to lose his motor set as the tempo of the task increased.

He was orally administered the Beck Depression Inventory — II (which was translated into Spanish). He obtained a score of 21 on this test, which places him in the moderate to severely depressed range.

He was also orally administered the Personality Assessment Inventory, which was translated into Spanish. His profile on this test was invalid since his score on the Inconsistency Scale exceeded the cut-off for profile validity, which suggested that he responded inconsistently to a number of items with highly similar content.

IMPRESSION

Mr. Cabrera sustained multiple trauma on October 6, 1993 while he was working under an elevator, which apparently fell and crushed him. His coworkers were able to lift the elevator and drag him out from underneath it. When the paramedics arrived at the scene of the accident, he was noted to be moaning and had purposeful responses to painful stimuli. His pupils were equal, round, and responsive to light. He was brought to Greater Dallas Medical Center and was intubated upon arrival. He was noted to have sustained multiple trauma, which included a left frontotemporal acute subdural hematoma, open left tibial/fibula fracture, right femur fracture, and bilateral clavicle fractures.

Shortly after his arrival at the hospital, he underwent decompression of the left frontoparietal subdural hematoma that had been causing a midline shift. After surgery, he was noted to be neurologically intact, with no motor deficits. When he was observed approximately 2 or 3 days following surgery, his family felt that his functioning had returned to his premorbid baseline. He was transferred to Rio Grande Medical Center on October 20, 1993.

He underwent a speech and language evaluation on October 23, 1993, which revealed that he had mild cognitive and communication deficits. He was discharged from Rio Grande Medical Center on October 27, 1993 and was followed on an outpatient basis. A review of the records of his treating physiatrist and orthopedist reveals that Mr. Cabrera appears to have made an excellent recovery from his orthopedic injuries. These records, however, also reveal that his family had observed some residual cognitive difficulties and occasional outbursts following his injury, even though his neurological examination was unremarkable.

When Mr. Cabrera was seen by this examiner on April 15, 1996, he complained of a sensation of intermittent coldness in his left knee and leg, pain and soreness in his left ankle, dizziness that occurs on the average of once a day, without vomiting or vertigo, and forgetfulness. His sister-in-law also added that Mr. Cabrera complains of headaches on the average of once or twice a month, which typically resolve with the use of Tylenol. Mr. Cabrera denied that he was taking any medications at the time he was seen or that he had consumed any alcoholic beverages during the past week. A translator was used throughout the examination since Mr. Cabrera spoke virtually no English.

It is highly unlikely that the head injury Mr. Cabrera sustained in his accident caused him to become mentally retarded since it is generally well known that the IQs of patients who sustain even severe traumatic brain injuries typically return to their premorbid baseline within 1 to 3 years postinjury. It appears instead that Mr. Cabrera was mentally retarded prior to his accident. Neuropsychological testing corroborated his preexisting mental retardation. His performance on the Raven Progressive Matrices Test, which is generally insensitive to cultural, educational, and linguistic factors, as well as the effects of brain injury, was extremely low and estimated his premorbid IQ to be in the 50 to 60 range.

Since it is generally well known that a person's level of intellectual functioning plays a major role in performance on neuropsychological tests, his retarded intellectual functioning would have been expected to cause him to perform poorly on neuropsychological tests of learning, memory, perception, problem solving, and executive functions. For example, persons with IQs of 70 (borderline retarded range) will typically test as impaired on most, if not all, neuropsychological measures. In Mr. Cabrera's case, his estimated premorbid IQ of between 50 and 60 would predict that he would be expected to perform very poorly on virtually any neuropsychological test he was administered. Thus, his neuropsychological test performances would have been expected to be very poor even if he had not sustained a closed head injury. However, despite his low premorbid level of intellectual functioning, Mr. Cabrera was able to work as a landscape helper prior to his accident. Thus, he may still be capable of working at this job from a neuropsychological perspective.

It is my understanding that Mr. Cabrera had undergone neuropsychological testing by Dr. Stevens prior to my evaluation. Since I have not had the opportunity of reviewing Dr. Steven's report and opinions, I would like to review his records prior to arriving at my final opinions in this case. I would also like to have the opportunity of reviewing Mr. Cabrera's Deposition transcript and the Deposition transcripts of his family members prior to arriving at any final opinions in this case.

DIAGNOSES

Axis I   1. Probable moderate mental retardation, preexisting.
            2. Closed head injury, by history.
Axis II   Deferred.
Axis III   Multiple trauma, per review of his medical records.
Axis IV   Severity of psychosocial stressors: minimal.
Axis V   Highest level of adaptive functioning prior to accident: GAF = 40; Current GAF = 38.

Abbreviation: GAF = Global Assessment Functioning.

RAYMOND ROBLOWSKI, PH.D.

Critique

Although Dr. Roblowski obtained a fairly complete history from Mr. Cabrera and interviewed Mr. Cabrera's sister-in-law, the use of a translator combined with the fact that Mr. Cabrera had sustained a significant brain injury during his accident raises the possibility that the background information that Mr. Cabrera provided to Dr. Roblowski may have been inaccurate, particularly about his premorbid level of functioning. Since Dr. Roblowski appears to base his opinion that Mr. Cabrera was retarded prior to his accident on this information, any inaccuracies would most likely affect Dr. Roblowski's opinions. In all fairness to Dr. Roblowski, he apparently recognized that he needed additional information from Mr. Cabrera's family before he could arrive at his final opinions.

Dr. Roblowski utilizes the issue of Mr. Cabrera's mental retardation to justify Mr. Cabrera's poor neuropsychological test performance. While this might be accurate, the interaction between Mr. Cabrera's premorbid retardation (even if accurate) and his significant traumatic brain injury is essentially ignored. For example, one would expect that a severe traumatic brain injury should have further lowered Mr. Cabrera's low premorbid level of intellectual and cognitive functioning. Therefore, he might never be able to be employed in any gainful capacity as a result of his injury since the accident would most likely have placed his cognitive functioning below the level that is necessary for him to ever work as a landscaper's helper.

Dr. Roblowski fails to mention any changes in Mr. Cabrera's cognitive and behavioral functioning that would have been expected following his brain injury. Although Mr. Cabrera did not complain of such problems, it is generally well known that patients who sustain significant brain trauma are likely to deny or minimize such difficulties and would not be expected to exhibit such difficulties during a highly structured neuropsychological examination. Although Mr. Cabrera's sister-in-law did not mention observing such problems, Dr. Roblowski did not specifically ask her whether Mr. Cabrera had ever exhibited such problems since his accident or whether such problems had ever been observed by any family members since his accident. The presence of such behavioral difficulties would most likely place an additional burden on his family, which could make it necessary to place Mr. Cabrera in a long-term care facility at some point in the future.

SAMPLE #4

July 18, 1995

Georgia Madison, Esq.
5000 Layton Boulevard
Suite 230
Cincinnati, Ohio

RE: Donald Meredith

Dear Ms. Madison:
Mr. Meredith is a 53-year-old, right-handed Caucasian male who has completed 12 years of formal education. He was evaluated on 7-1-95 at your request. He arrived on time for his scheduled appointment.

CHIEF COMPLAINTS AS OBTAINED FROM MR. MEREDITH

1. Headaches, secondary to stress that originate in the back of his head and travel over the top of his head and into the periorbital area of his right eye. They are experienced as a dull ache. He usually develops these headaches when he drives long distances in heavy traffic. He stated that he drove to his appointment this morning from Victorville, after leaving at 6:00 A.M., and arrived here at 9:30 A.M. He said that the trip caused him to experience a headache.
2. Sexual difficulties since accident. He reported an inability to maintain an erection during intercourse. He denied, however, a loss of libido since his accident.
3. Memory difficulties for recent events. He denied any difficulties with remote memory.
4. Balance difficulties since accident, particularly when bending over or leaning backwards. He stated that he felt like vomiting at times.

CURRENT MEDICATIONS

Procardia 50 mg A.M.

HISTORY OF INJURY AS OBTAINED FROM MR. MEREDITH

Mr. Meredith stated that he was going to a job site at approximately 7:00 A.M. on the morning of December 6, 1992. As he was walking to pick up his concrete tools at a construction site, he tripped over an elevated edge of the sidewalk and fell forward, striking his right forehead. He claimed, however, that he had no recollection of striking his head. He was told by his son, who had been walking with him, that he was knocked unconscious for approximately 5 min. His son helped him into his pick-up truck and drove him home shortly after that. Mr. Meredith recalled that on the way home, they stopped at a grocery store approximately 3 miles from the site of his accident. His son went into the store, brought him back some water, and then drove him home.

After he arrived home, Mr. Meredith immediately went to bed. His wife woke him at approximately 5:00 P.M. Mr. Meredith got up and passed out while sitting at the dinner table. His wife did not call an ambulance, but took him to a small walk-in clinic, where he underwent an x-ray study of his skull. He was diagnosed as having a concussion. Immediately following this, he went home and went back to bed again. He stayed home for the next 2 or 3 days, during which time he experienced severe nausea, dizziness, blurred vision, and severe headaches.

Mr. Meredith returned to the walk-in clinic for a follow-up visit, did not return to work for approximately 5 weeks after his fall, but told the home builder that he was unable to complete his home. He did not do any work following this for 1½ years because he continued to experience symptoms such as severe nausea, dizziness, blurred vision, and severe headaches.

As a result of financial difficulties, he eventually lost his home and car. Following this, he and his wife moved to the Lake Mead area, where they rented a small home, but he claims that he and his wife were evicted because they got behind on the rent. He and his wife then moved to Covington, where they are currently renting a house. After they had lived there for 6 months, he was offered a job as a project manager in Iran, working in a refinery on a drill island. He was paid $97,000 a year tax free, as well as living expenses. He went to Iran to work on this job, but claimed that he was terminated after only 4 months because he could not handle the requirements of the job. He claimed that he lost his temper twice with the owners and attributed this to his diminished organizational skills and patience, which created difficulties for him at work and in handling stress.

Mr. Meredith started doing odd jobs as a handyman after he got back from Iran, until he began working for Sunnyfield Construction in March 1994, as a foreman and construction worker. He claims that he earns $900 a week (gross salary), with take-home pay of $750. He claims that prior to his accident, he was earning approximately $87,000 a year.

Mr. Meredith began seeing Brian Bremer, M.D. When Mr. Meredith was asked how he ended up getting referred to Dr. Bremer, he stated that he believed that he began seeing him approximately 1 month after his injury. Mr. Meredith also stated that during the time he was being treated by Dr. Bremer, he repaired Dr. Bremer's boat. Mr. Meredith believes that he has been seen by a number of doctors since he began seeing Dr. Bremer.

He reports that he has five dogs at home and enjoys a good relationship with his wife.

BACKGROUND AS OBTAINED FROM MR. MEREDITH

Developmental

Mr. Meredith was born in Springfield, Ohio, the oldest of three children. He weighed 10 pounds at birth and reported normal developmental milestones. In addition to having the usual childhood diseases, he underwent a tonsillectomy when he was 8 or 9 years of age. He describes himself as a very healthy child. Although he goes on to state that he fell 80 ft at work in 1967 and landed in a large pile of sand, he denies that he sustained any injuries during this fall and claims that he just got up and walked away.

Mr. Meredith described his childhood as "normal." He grew up in a Catholic family and attended Catholic elementary and junior high schools. He attended a trade high school where he studied carpentry and architectural drawing. After completing trade school, he graduated from high school in 1960 as a journeyman carpenter and enlisted in the Air Force in 1962. He states, however, that he was given a general discharge from the Air Force after he punched out a first lieutenant who struck him.

Mr. Meredith denied a history of hearing, speaking, stuttering, reading, writing, spelling, arithmetic, motor, behavioral, or attentional difficulties during his childhood or adolescence. He is strongly right-handed. He grew up in an English-speaking family and was raised by his biological parents.

Education

He graduated from high school in 1960 with a 3.7 grade point average and did his best in mathematics and shop and poorest in English classes. He denied that he was ever placed in any special education or remedial classes or was ever held back. While in high school, he played football and basketball. He claimed that he received a football scholarship to Ohio State University, but decided against taking it. He denied that he was ever expelled from school for any conduct or behavioral problems.

Occupational History

According to Mr. Meredith, while he was in the Air Force, he worked at a variety of what he described as odd jobs for a couple of years around the country. He had done construction work since 1961 and had a general contractor's license. He earned between $80,000 and $90,000 a year on the average over the years prior to his accident. He currently works as a foreman and construction worker for Sunnyfield Construction and earning $900 a week (gross salary).

Living

He and his wife live in a three-bedroom rented home.

Legal Problems

He reported that he got in some legal difficulties with the Internal Revenue Service in 1984 as a result of failing to pay taxes that he felt were unfair. He then went into a long discourse about the U.S. government and how the government can do anything it wants to people.

Family History

Both parents are deceased. His father died in 1967 of emphysema secondary to heavy smoking. His mother died in 1993 at 85 years of age as a result of a cerebral vascular accident. His father was employed as a truck driver. His mother was a homemaker. Both parents were high school graduates. Neither parent had ever been previously married or was described as having a history of substance abuse, criminal, psychiatric, or significant health problems. His mother never remarried after his father's death in 1967. His parents were described as having a good marriage and relationship.

Siblings

Mr. Meredith has a 50-year-old brother, who works for General Motors. He has a 53-year-old sister, who resides in Oregon. Neither of his siblings was described as having a history of substance abuse or criminal behavior.

Marital History

He was married for the first time in January 1967 and divorced in 1975. He was married in 1987 for the second time. His wife is a 49-year-old homemaker who has two children from a previous marriage. Mr. Meredith has a 25-year-old son, who has a history of alcoholism. His son is single and is employed as a construction worker.

Sexual

Mr. Meredith is a heterosexual male. He denied a prior history of sexual dysfunction. While he denied a change in sexual libido since his accident, he reported that he has been unable to maintain an erection since his accident.

Psychiatric

He denied a prior history of psychiatric or emotional problems. Since his accident, he has been treated by Brian Bremer, M.D. He denied that he has ever been hospitalized for psychiatric or emotional problems or that he was currently taking any psychiatric medications. He denied that he had ever seriously contemplated suicide.

Substance Use

He denied that he has ever used alcohol, smoked tobacco, or experimented with recreational drugs.

Medical

He denied a history of medical problems prior to his accident, stating that he was in good health. He denied that he had ever been hospitalized for any problems or difficulties. He also denied that he had ever had a motor vehicle accident or ever received a speeding ticket. He denied a prior or subsequent history of stroke, head trauma, respiratory problems, gastrointestinal problems, vascular problems, endocrine problems, diabetes, coronary problems, hypoglycemia, anoxia/hypoxia, or toxic exposure. He reported, however, that he has developed hypertension since his accident.

Behavioral Observations

Mr. Meredith presented as a very large and powerfully built 53-year-old, right-handed Caucasian male, in no acute distress. He was alert and oriented to person, place, time, and purpose. He was casually dressed in appropriate attire, with good personal grooming and hygiene. He indicated that he had driven from Covington to this examiner's office earlier that morning (between 6:00 and 9:00 A.M.) through heavy traffic. He indicated that the driving had caused him to develop a headache. He spoke clearly and in an articulate manner and exhibited no evidence whatsoever of any cognitive difficulties during his interview, which lasted approximately 3 hours. His recent and remote memory appeared intact as he appeared to have no difficulty recalling recent and remote events. He did not appear anxious or depressed during his interview. Several times during the interview, he spoke in a very knowledgable manner about the U.S. Constitution, government, tax system, and other topics, indicating that he is a highly intelligent individual. When he was asked how he knew these things, he indicated that he had done a lot of reading on these topics.

He exhibited no evidence of auditory or visual hallucinations, psychotic behavior, frank paranoia, ataxia, balance difficulties, perseverative behavior, or any pain or discomfort. He refused to take a lunch break, stating that he eats only one meal a day. Mr. Meredith spent over 8 hours in this examiner's office (10:00 A.M. to 6:10 P.M.). During this time, he was continuously active, either during the interview or during testing, except for an occasional break to the restroom. He appeared to be a very personable and engaging individual. During neuropsychological testing, he became very tense and anxious when he was given any test to assess his memory. His performance on these tests was in marked contrast to the excellent memory he demonstrated during his interview. In fact, he stated, in a rather histrionic manner, "My mind goes blank — like somebody closed the door." He emphasized how he "couldn't remember." On other occasions, his performance raised questions in this examiner's mind as to whether or not he was engaging in dissimilation (deliberately attempting to perform poorly). His performance on tasks involving manual dexterity were confounded by his very large and thick fingers.

NEUROPSYCHOLOGICAL TESTING

Tests Administered

The Symbol Digit Modalities Test

The Trail Making Test (Parts A and B)

The Stroop Color and Word Test

The Boston Naming Test

The Controlled Oral Word Association Test

The Hooper Visual Organization Test

The Rey Auditory Verbal Learning Test

The Logical Memories Test

The Taylor–Rey Visual Figure Test

The Finger Tapping Test

The Grooved Pegboard Test

Luria's Motor Examination

Tests of Abstract Thinking

Tests of Proverb Interpretation

Tests of Judgment

Tests of Problem Solving

The Draw-a-Bicycle Test

The Wisconsin Card Sorting Test

The Raven Progressive Matrices Test

The Beck Depression Inventory

The Minnesota Multiphasic Personality Inventory — II

TEST RESULTS

Attention–Concentration

His sustained attention and concentration skills were assessed by asking him to perform a variety of serial arithmetic and nonarithmetic tasks. His performance on these tasks was intact. For example, he had no difficulty performing alternate serial 3 and 5 addition, serial 7 subtraction, serial 13 subtraction, or alternate 3 and 5 subtraction from 100 or indicating which letters in the alphabet contain only straight lines or rhyme with the word tree. His visual motor tracking and sustained attention skills were assessed by Parts A and B of the Trail Making Test. He required only 21.14 seconds to complete Part A, which placed him 1.5 standard deviations above expectation (above average range). He required 70.35 seconds to complete Part B, which placed him 0.4 standard deviations above expectation (average range). Although he made one error on this test, he was able to self-correct and get back on track.

Speed of Cognitive Processing

He was administered the Symbol Digit Modalities Test to assess his ability to rapidly code symbols. He made a score of 51, which placed him 1.1 standard deviations above expectation (above average range). He was also given the Stroop Color–Word Test which required him to rapidly name words and identify colors. While his performance placed him at the low end of the average range, he was observed to become tense and anxious during the test, which appeared to significantly interfere with his performance. His tension and anxiety increased when he was given Part III of this test, which required him to inhibit competing response tendencies. As a consequence, his performance placed him in the mildly impaired range.

Language

He was administered the Boston Naming Test to assess his confrontational naming skills. His score on this test placed him within the normal range with respect to persons of his age and educational background. He was also given the Controlled Oral Word Association Test, which required him to generate as many words as possible beginning with specific letters of the alphabet. He became very tense as the test began and after he had provided this examiner with ten words after only approximately 25 seconds, he stopped and stated, "My mind goes blank" in a histrionic manner. It was noted that Mr. Meredith's performance on this test appeared to be in marked contrast to the verbal adroitness he demonstrated during his interview when he appeared much more relaxed. Nonetheless, his performance on this test placed him within the normal range using norms for persons of his age and educational background.

Visual Organization

He was given the Hooper Visual Organization Test to assess his ability to recognize pictures of objects that had been cut up and placed in different positions. He made a score of 26.5 out of a possible 30, which placed him within the normal range.

Learning and Memory

He was administered the Rey Auditory Verbal Learning Test which required him to learn 15 common words over five consecutive learning trials that were orally presented to him. His performance on this test was confounded by his high level of anxiety during testing and his claim that his mind was going blank during testing "like somebody closed the door." His performance on this test was in marked contrast to the excellent memory he demonstrated for recent events during his interview. In addition, there also seemed to be an element of dissimilation when he was asked to recall words he had learned during the first five trials. For example, he claimed that he could only recall three of the eight words he had learned, stating, "I can't remember."

When he was asked to learn a second list of 15 words, he exhibited no evidence of proactive interference, which is typically seen in patients who have sustained closed head injuries in that the ability to learn a second list of words is typically reduced. However, in Mr. Meredith's case, he tested in the opposite direction, which suggests that his performance during the first list was significantly affected by emotional factors. When asked to recognize the first list of words, when he was orally presented a story that contained words from this list, he became very tense and anxious and was only able to recognize 11 out of the 15 words and made two errors.

When asked to recall two short stories immediately after they were presented to him and after a delay of approximately 30 minutes, he became very tense and anxious during testing. This was manifested by the fact that his recall of the second of the two stories (which is a more difficult story to recall) was significantly better than his first story (12 vs. 8.5 bits of information). Nonetheless, his overall performance placed him well above expectation for persons of his age.

When he was asked to recall the first of these two stories, after a delay of approximately 30 minutes, he initially claimed that he had no recollection of this story. Even after he had been given a cue, "It's about a woman," he still claimed he had no recollection of the story. He was then given another cue, "It's about a woman who was robbed." Immediately following this, he stated, "This guy hired this woman who was robbed of $15. She had two children and didn't have enough money to feed her children. Officer felt sorry for her and gave her some money." He had recalled 76.5% of the originally presented story.

He was asked to copy a complex geometric figure (Taylor–Rey figure). His drawing of this figure revealed no evidence of constructional dyspraxia, although it was done in a hasty manner. His ability to copy this figure from memory, after a delay of approximately 30 minutes, was actually quite good and indicated that his visual memory appears to be intact.

Motor

He was administered the Finger Tapping Test to assess his motor speed. Testing revealed that the motor speed of his dominant right hand was 2.3 standard deviations above expectation. When he was tested with his nondominant left hand, he exhibited a dramatic decline in his performance for reasons that seemed deliberate and indicative of dissimilation. For example, on Trial 1, he made 63 taps, on Trial 2 he made 60 taps, and on Trials 3, 4, 5, 6, and 7, he made 41, 45, 47, 42, and 43 taps, respectively.

On the Grooved Pegboard Test, his performance was confounded by his very large and thick fingers. For example, he complained during the task about how small the pegs were and the difficulty he had handling them. Nonetheless, the performance of his dominant right hand placed him within the normal range, while the performance of his nondominant left hand placed him in the mildly impaired range.

Higher Order Motor/Executive Functions

He was administered a variety of tests, developed by Luria and his associates to assess ability to perform complex motor tasks, which are dependent on the integrity of the anterior frontal lobes and involve one or both hands. Mr. Meredith's performances on these tasks were suspicious for malingering in that he made rather blatant errors that raised some serious questions in this examiner's mind about whether they were being deliberately made in an attempt to perform poorly on these tasks. Even when he was given extensive cues and practice, he continued making blatant errors and showed no sign of improvement in his performance, which would not have been expected even if he had sustained a very severe brain injury. Furthermore, the blatant quality of Mr. Meredith's errors would not have been even remotely expected, given a review of his medical records and his performance on many of the other neuropsychological tests he was administered.

Abstract Thinking/Conceptualization

His responses to verbal similarities were grossly intact. His interpretation of proverbs revealed a mild tendency toward concrete thinking. (Comment: This appeared to be in distinct contrast to the excellent conceptualization and thinking skills Mr. Meredith had exhibited during a lengthy 3 hour interview with this examiner.)

Judgment

His judgment was assessed by asking him what he would do in a variety of hypothetical situations. His responses indicated that he has poor judgment.

Problem Solving

His problem-solving skills were assessed by tasks involving logical–grammatical analysis, mental arithmetic that required him to restructure the problem statement, the Wisconsin Card Sorting Test, and the Raven Progressive Matrices Test. His overall performance on these tasks was generally intact. While he completed only three of the six categories on the Wisconsin Card Sorting Test, a review of Dr. King's raw test data reveals that Mr. Meredith was able to complete all six categories and made fewer errors when he had been previously tested by Dr. King within the first year following his accident. In addition, Mr. Meredith had also been given this test by Dr. Martin and had actually done worse on follow-up testing than when he was originally tested by Dr. King. This is highly unusual since patients typically do much better on follow-up testing. Mr. Meredith received a score of 38 on the Raven Progressive Matrices Test, which was also used to assess his problem-solving skills dealing with abstract figures and designs. His performance on this test placed him at the 78th percentile (above average range).

PERSONALITY/EMOTIONAL

He was administered the Beck Depression Inventory to assess his subjective level of depression. His score (7) indicates that he does not test or see himself as depressed at this time.

He was also administered the MMPI-2. His scores on this test were evaluated by a computer program developed by the author. His profile indicates that he is not admitting to many psychological symptoms or problems; however, he reported some personality characteristics such as great consciousness, a tendency toward self-doubt and indecisiveness that may make him vulnerable to developing symptoms of anxiety or tension under stress. He also endorsed some statements that show some inability to control his anger, thus he is capable of physically or verbally attacking others when he is angry. In addition, his interpersonal behavior may be problematic at times, and he may lose his temper in frustrating situations. He feels intensely angry, hostile, and resentful of others and would like to get back at them. He also tends to be competitive, uncooperative, and very critical of others. It should be noted that while his overall clinical profile was within normal limits, he appears to be somewhat preoccupied and worries excessively about minor matters.

Impression

Mr. Meredith is a 53-year-old, right-handed male, who is currently employed as a construction supervisor and foreman for Sunnyfield Construction. He stated that on the morning of December 6, 1992, he was involved in an accident when he tripped over an elevated edge of the sidewalk and fell, striking his right forehead. Later that day, he was seen at the Emergicare Medical Group where he complained that he had hit his head on the sidewalk and complained of hearing a ringing inside of his head. He also stated that he felt very nervous and complained of drowsiness and pain behind his eyes.

With the issue of Mr. Meredith's credibility in doubt, his performances on the neuropsychological tests administered should not be taken at face value since poor performances can be due to a variety of nonorganic factors, including deliberate attempts to portray himself as injured for purposes of secondary gains. With this in mind, it should be recalled that when Mr. Meredith was tested by this examiner, such difficulties were observed on a number of occasions. In addition, Mr. Meredith was observed to become quite tense and anxious during testing, which appeared to confound his test performance. Mr. Meredith's test performances were in marked contrast to the excellent cognitive functioning he demonstrated during his interview, in which he appeared to be a very intelligent man who possessed considerable knowledge in a wide variety of topics. Furthermore, his ability to discuss recent events, such as the O. J. Simpson trial and other events occurring throughout the world, demonstrated that his recent memory appeared quite intact.

Since I have not had the opportunity of reviewing Mr. Meredith's educational, medical, and vocational records, I am unable to diagnose his condition or offer any opinions at this time about the relationship between his accident and his complaints. After I have had the opportunity of reviewing such records, I will prepare a supplemental report that will contain my diagnostic impression and opinions.

JAMES HEATON, PH.D.

Critique

Dr. Heaton's report contains Mr. Meredith's chief complaints and his description of his accident. Although Dr. Heaton points out a number of confounding factors and inconsistencies between Mr. Meredith's behavior during the examination and neuropsychological test performance, he wisely refrains from offering any diagnoses or opinions about Mr. Meredith's injury until he has had the opportunity of reviewing Mr. Meredith's academic, medical, and vocational records. Unfortunately, many neuropsychologists are often willing to diagnose the individual's condition and offer opinions regarding its causation without reviewing such records.

In this particular case, when these records were later reviewed, they failed to corroborate the history and background Mr. Meredith had provided. They also revealed that he had not been employed for 5 years prior to his "accident." A later review of his legal and criminal records revealed that Mr. Meredith had served time in prison for forgery, embezzlement, and fraud.

SAMPLE #5

March 1, 1997

John Jenkins, Esq.
Law Offices of Jenkins and Sweeney
The Southland Building
Third Floor
Atlanta, Georgia 36420

RE: Eugene Thomas

Dear Mr. Jenkins:
Thank you for referring your client for neuropsychological testing. He was evaluated on 2-26-97. He presented as a confused 43-year-old, right-handed male, with a history of carbon monoxide exposure at work on 1-14-93. He was accompanied by his wife who appeared to be a reliable informant.

CHIEF COMPLAINTS AS OBTAINED FROM MR. THOMAS

1. "I can't remember." (Mr. Thomas had difficulty describing what he meant by this.)
2. "Awkward — I just don't do what I used to." When he was asked to describe what kinds of things, he indicated "everything."

ADDITIONAL COMPLAINTS FROM PATIENT'S SPOUSE

1. Her husband is capable of doing only one thing or task at a time. For example, she indicated that if she tells him to go downstairs and see if his jeans are dry, he will go downstairs and forget what he is supposed to do.
2. He is extremely apathetic and shows a lack of initiative and motivation.
3. He is unable to demonstrate any affection toward her.
4. He has loss of libido and sexual difficulties. She must take the initiative during sex and get him sexually aroused. He is unable to engage in any foreplay since it causes him to lose his erection. He is also clumsy and awkward during sex. She stated that sex is no longer satisfying for her, because her husband has to focus his thoughts entirely on reaching an orgasm, rather than satisfying her needs. She stated that if the phone rings, he loses his orgasm.
5. He has become extremely self-centered.
6. He has become immature and childish. For example, he will not share his food or candy with his children.
7. He is no longer concerned with the welfare of others or his family.
8. She has observed a dramatic change in his personality.
9. He is frequently forgetful.
10. He has poor social judgment, particularly around his family.
11. He has poor problem-solving skills.
12. He is frequently awkward and clumsy.
13. He has poor planning and social skills.
14. He has poor safety judgment.
15. He requires 24 hour supervision.

16. He has poor fine motor and manual dexterity skills.
17. He becomes frustrated and easily upset.
18. He exhibits emotional lability.
19. He exhibits frequent mood swings.
20. His cognitive and behavioral functioning diminish dramatically whenever he becomes ill.
21. He has poor awareness of his cognitive and behavioral problems.
22. His abstract and conceptual thinking skills are poor and his thinking tends to be concrete.
23. He is unable to follow through on things if left alone.
24. He requires frequent cues and prompts in order for him to complete any task.
25. At times, he is unable to comprehend what others are saying to him and is unable to communicate his thoughts to others.

HISTORY OF INJURY AS OBTAINED FROM THE PATIENT AND HIS SPOUSE

Mr. Thomas was laying block in the basement of a building on January 14, 1993 when he felt like he was coming down with the flu. He also felt pain in his chest and thought he was having a heart attack. In addition, he experienced breathing difficulties. He believes that he fell several times, managed to get up, but felt very unsteady on his feet. He kept working until his foreman came in at the end of the day because he wanted to make a good impression since it was his first day working for the Greystone Construction Company. His wife recalls receiving a telephone call from his foreman, who told her that her husband was sick and to come and get him. She obtained a ride to the job site from a neighbor. She estimates that she arrived at the job site about 1 to 1½ hours after she received the telephone call. When she arrived at the job site, she noticed that her husband seemed "rubberish," very confused, disoriented, and in a daze.

She put her arm around him and assisted him as they walked out to their neighbor's car. She noticed that her husband was unable to lift his legs to get into the neighbor's car and "just fell into the vehicle" after she had helped him into it. Although her husband wanted to go home, her neighbor drove them to the emergency room of St. Mary's Hospital, where Mrs. Thomas helped her husband into the emergency room. Mr. Thomas, however, has no recollection of being in the emergency room or seeing any doctors. According to his wife, he was taken to the hyperbaric oxygen chamber after he was found to be suffering from carbon monoxide poisoning. After additional blood tests had been run, he was sent home. The patient and his wife were driven home.

His wife recalls that her husband spent the entire night vomiting and complained of an excruciating headache. The next morning, his wife noticed that her husband began to urinate brown colored urine and that the veins in his arms seemed enlarged. Her husband was taken back to the emergency room of St. Mary's Hospital. While there, she was told by her husband's treating physician that her husband would have died if they had not taken him to the hospital in the first place. Over the next several days, his wife noticed that he began to complain of a severe headache and seemed apathetic and listless. She also observed that his personality had changed and that "things didn't seem to register," and that he was unable to carry out volitional movements, such as putting away the dishes.

Mr. Thomas went to work on Monday, but came home early. Over the next several weeks, he complained that he was unable to recall how to perform familiar tasks such as bricklaying and claimed that he had to think things through before he was actually able to perform them. His wife also observed that he seemed oblivious to what was going on around him and that his ability to process information had been significantly reduced to the point where he could process only a limited amount of information at one time, which caused him to lose information. For example, he described to her seeing a one-line caption on television and indicated that he could process only one part of the caption. Over the next several weeks, his wife and family noticed that his condition continued to deteriorate, even though he continued to work for approximately 2 months during which time he was seen by Dr. Blumenthal, his treating neurologist. According to his wife, his condition continued to deteriorate until some time in the fall of 1993, when it appeared to plateau. During the past year, she has observed that he has had more difficulty understanding what was going on around him, as well as the significance of these events.

BACKGROUND AS OBTAINED FROM MR. THOMAS, WITH THE ASSISTANCE OF HIS WIFE

Developmental

The patient was born in Deerfield, Michigan, as the third oldest of four children. He believes that he was the product of a full-term, uncomplicated delivery. He reports normal developmental milestones and having the usual childhood diseases. He underwent a tonsillectomy during his childhood. He denies a history of head trauma or fractures during his childhood or adolescence. He also denies a childhood history of psychological, physical, or sexual abuse. He denies a childhood history of hearing, speaking, stuttering, reading, writing, spelling, arithmetic, motor, behavioral, or attentional difficulties; hyperactivity; or seizures. He described his childhood as happy. He was close to both of his parents and his siblings. His family moved to Atlanta, Georgia, during his childhood. They also moved several other times because of his father's job. He denies that moving frequently during his childhood bothered him. He had three or four close friends while growing up. While in high school, he was on the wrestling team and played basketball during the summer. He graduated from high school with average grades.

Employment

He started working as an apprentice bricklayer under his father. He became a journeyman bricklayer when he was approximately 21 or 22 years of age, and had worked as a bricklayer since that time. At the time of his injury, he had just started working for the Greystone Construction Company and was earning $20 an hour.

Hobbies/Interests

His hobbies and interests in the past have included hunting and fishing.

Military

He has never served in the military.

Legal

He was arrested at the age of 17 for stealing a guitar and was placed on probation. He denies any other arrests since that time.

Family History

He indicated that his father was currently 63 years of age (his wife later indicated that his father had died 2 years ago of prostatic cancer). His father was a bricklayer. He indicated that his mother was 64 years of age (his wife indicated that his mother was actually 65 years of age). She is a retired office worker. This is the first marriage for both of his parents. Neither parent was described as having a history of substance abuse, criminal behavior, or psychiatric or emotional problems. The patient indicated that his parents were still married.

Siblings

The patient has a 46-year-old brother who is employed as a bricklayer. He has two sisters, who are 40 and 38 years of age. All of his siblings are high school graduates. He denies that any of his siblings has a history of substance abuse, criminal behavior, or psychiatric or health problems.

Marital History

The patient has been married for the past 15 years. His wife is 40 years of age and has completed 11 years of formal education. Since his carbon monoxide poisoning incident, she has been placed on Zoloft for depression and has taken medications for ulcers, insomnia, and hypertension (she indicated that her blood pressure was 170/120). They have two children, a 19-year-old daughter and a 16-year-old son. His daughter has a history of endometriosis and recently underwent surgery for this problem. His 16-year-old son has a history of allergies.

Sexual

While the patient denied a history of sexual difficulties since his accident, his wife provided a lengthy description of her husband's sexual difficulties, which include a loss of libido, inability to maintain an erection, particularly if his attention is distracted, loss of initiative, and an inability to satisfy her. She indicated that prior to the carbon monoxide poisoning incident, their sex life was enjoyable.

Psychiatric

The patient denied a prior or subsequent history of psychiatric or emotional problems. He denied that he has ever contemplated suicide. He denied a family history of psychiatric illness.

Substance Abuse

The patient does not drink, smoke, or use recreational drugs.

Medical History

He denied a history of chronic medical problems prior to the carbon monoxide poisoning incident. He denied sustaining any injuries during any motor vehicle accidents. He also denied a history of stroke, head trauma, respiratory problems, gastrointestinal problems, vascular problems, endocrine problems, diabetes, coronary problems, hypoglycemia, anoxia/hypoxia, toxic exposure, hypertension, or surgery.

REVIEW OF ACADEMIC RECORDS

The records of Atlanta School District indicated that the patient graduated from high school 218th in a class of 269, with a 1.97 (C) grade point average out of a possible 4.0. These records indicate that he obtained a Lorge–Thorndike total IQ score of 95, with a verbal IQ of 87 and a nonverbal IQ of 103, which placed him within the average range of intellectual functioning.

REVIEW OF MEDICAL RECORDS

The emergency room records of St. Mary's Hospital, dated January 14, 1993, indicated that the patient was seen in the emergency room with complaints of chest pain, shortness of breath, weakness, dizziness, headache, nausea, and vomiting, since being exposed to carbon monoxide fumes earlier that day at a construction site. He had been using a gasoline-powered tool to cut concrete in an enclosed space. He had thought he was being overcome by fumes somewhat, but continued to work despite his symptoms. At the time of the examination, he felt very weak, had a headache, and had a rushing sensation in his ears, as well as some discomfort across his chest and nausea. He denied ever having similar symptoms in the past. Although he smoked, when he had a cigarette it did not seem to have any effect on his discomfort. He was observed to be alert, pleasant, and cooperative. His neurological examination was grossly intact. His carboxyhemoglobin level was 31.7, and he was diagnosed as having acute carbon monoxide poisoning. He underwent immediate hyperbaric oxygenation. When he returned from this treatment, he was still somewhat nauseated, but his carboxyhemoglobin level had come down to 1.2.

These records indicated that Mr. Thomas was admitted at 5:46 P.M. His arterial blood gas was drawn at 6:05 P.M. At 6:12 P.M., his carboxyhemoglobin level was reported back. After he was treated in the hyperbaric oxygen chamber, he was discharged at 9:35 P.M. that same evening.

The patient returned to the emergency room of St. Mary's Hospital on January 15, 1993. He complained that his urine was very dark that day and that the veins in his arms were dilated. He denied any headache, but reported some nausea and vomiting the previous day after hyperbaric oxygenation. His neurological examination was unremarkable. An arterial blood gas study revealed a carboxyhemoglobin level of 4.1. Mr. Thomas had smoked that day. He was diagnosed as having postcarbon monoxide exposure.

The patient was seen by Marc C. Blumenthal, D.O. on April 6, 1993 for neurological consultation because of behavioral changes subsequent to carbon monoxide exposure. The patient complained of problems with coordination, slowness of motor movements, and personality changes. His wife indicated that her husband was not thinking clearly, and had exhibited slowness of movement and emotional lability, and that his hands had been shaking. The patient went back to work on Monday, but has been much slower on the job because of decreasing coordination. His wife stated that at home it took her husband 20 min to fold three towels. The patient reported occasional lightheadedness. His memory and concentration have continued to be poor. He has been more irritable. His speech continues to be somewhat slurred. He reports occasional tingling.

Dr. Blumenthal observed that the patient appeared to be slow in his mental processing. His affect was slightly suppressed. He observed that the patient appeared to have normal language fluency, comprehension naming, and repetition. He also observed that the patient's insight and judgment appeared normal, with good verbal recall. His neurological examination was significant for mild slowing of motor movements, with slight postural tremor. The patient was unable to perform tandem walking or balance on either leg. Dr. Blumenthal felt that the patient's clinical examination demonstrated the residuals of his carbon monoxide exposure, consisting of either cerebellar and more probably basal ganglion dysfunction. He felt that it was possible that the patient has evolved a Parkinson-like dysfunction as a result of his carbon monoxide exposure. Dr. Blumenthal planned to order an electroencephalogram (EEG) and cognitive evaluation, as well as an occupational therapy evaluation to assess the patient's motor speed and manual dexterity.

The patient underwent cognitive evaluation on May 1, 1993 at Hillsborough Medical Center. This evaluation revealed diminished activities of daily living (ADL), gross and fine motor coordination, motor strength, and functional endurance. The patient reported difficulty fixing a meal since his carbon monoxide poisoning. Neuromuscular testing revealed that the patient scored more than 2 standard deviations below the norm, which suggested moderate/severe impairment in his gross and fine motor coordination skills.

The patient underwent an EEG on May 10, 1993, which was interpreted as normal in the awake and asleep states.

On May 12, 1993, the patient underwent a cognitive evaluation by Patricia Landers, M.A., who observed mild to moderate cognitive deficits, primarily decreased short-term memory, concentration, and attention to detail. She also observed that the patient exhibited an overall slowness in his verbal responses and had problems with sensory overload. She interviewed the patient's wife, who reported that the patient has had considerable difficulties with his job since the carbon monoxide exposure and was unable to concentrate. She reported that she has observed frequent decreases in her husband's memory for everyday facts and routines. Ms. Landers indicated in her report of May 14, 1993 that she felt that the patient and his wife were very motivated to work on improving these deficits, as well as learning compensatory techniques to help him with his deficits.

The patient was seen again by Dr. Blumenthal on May 14, 1993. The patient and his wife continued to complain of the patient's slowness of movements and his emotional lability. In addition, the patient had experienced a significant amount of noise intolerance and had become short-tempered and irritable. He had difficulty focusing and paying attention. In addition, the patient continues to experience a lot of tremulousness and slight instability. Furthermore, it appeared to take more effort for him to accomplish the same tasks he has done in the past. Dr. Blumenthal's mental status examination revealed that the patient exhibited slowed mental processing and mild problems with short-term recall. His motor examination continued to show some mild bradykinesia, although his motor tone was fairly normal. His reflex and sensory examinations were unchanged. Dr. Blumenthal felt that the patient had probable basal ganglion dysfunction as a result of carbon monoxide poisoning. He placed the patient on Sinemet.

The functional capacity evaluation report of Jill Baker, O.T.R. and Wendy Cummings, O.T.R., dated May 20, 1993, indicated that the patient performed extremely poorly on tasks involving strength and endurance. While the patient did not report any physical symptoms of pain or fatigue, he was observed to have shaking hands during the "heavy" and "very heavy" subtests. The patient also reported that following a day of work, he felt that his brain was being overloaded as a result of trying to think of too many things at once. He did not complain of being physically tired.

The report indicated that he had been administered the Rivermead Perceptual Assessment Battery to assess his visual perceptual skills. His scores on this test were compared to average intelligence norms and his premorbid level as a bricklayer and high school graduate. His performance on this test revealed deficits on 3 of the 16 subtests, which fell under the classification of inattention. As a result, he was felt to have difficulty gathering all of the necessary information, including attention to detail, in a timely manner. A visual screening test was performed to rule out the likelihood of visual acuity difficulties. Although the patient's visual acuity was found to be normal, he demonstrated slight difficulty with saccades searching in the left visual field, difficulty with pursuits, and appeared to minimally lose his fixation. As a consequence, it was recommended that he be formally evaluated by a neurophthalmologist. They felt that the patient appeared to have a possible central field deficit, common with patients with diffuse brain injury, and recommended that he be placed in a structured cognitive retraining program under the care of a neuropsychologist.

Dr. Blumenthal's chart notes, dated May 24, 1993, indicated that the Hillsborough Medical Center Occupational Therapy Evaluation reported that the patient's ADL status, gross and fine motor coordination, and functional endurance skills had decreased. He also indicated that a cognitive assessment, which was performed on May 20, 1993, utilizing the Rivermead Perceptual Assessment Battery, demonstrated visual inattention and perceptual dysfunction. He indicated that this evaluation noted decreased saccadic searching and left visual field and pursuit dysfunction.

Dr. Blumenthal's notes, dated May 25, 1993, indicated that an EEG report from the Hillsborough Medical Center, dated May 10, 1993, was normal.

Dr. Blumenthal's chart notes, dated June 3, 1993, indicated that the patient said that Sinemet had helped his hand tremor and that he was able to work more steadily with the medication. However, when he takes two tablets, he experiences some diarrhea, mild nausea, and stomach aches. There had been no notable improvement in concentration or attention and his memory was about the same. He had daily headaches in the frontal region, which occurred at various times each day, which were usually relieved with Tylenol. He was also having some shadowy vision. The patient, according to his wife, had lost approximately 10 pounds. She had also observed that he had had a noticeable decrease in appetite. The patient was complaining of blotchy hands earlier that week on one occasion. The patient, though mentally alert, was somewhat inattentive. He appeared shy and withdrawn. His short-term memory was reduced. His cranial nerve, motor, reflex, and sensory findings remained normal, except for some mild bradykinesia. Dr. Blumenthal felt that the patient was showing some mild improvement, but still had a long way to go to recover from his encephalopathy.

The patient underwent a cognitive evaluation on June 15, 1993 by Patricia Landers, M.A. The patient continued to report memory and concentration difficulties and stated that his job continued to be "much harder to do than before." His wife continued to report a slowness of her husband's motor responses and speech, as well as decreased memory. The patient was administered the Rivermead Behavioral Memory Test, which was designed to detect impairment of everyday memory functioning. Testing revealed difficulty in all sections of the examination, including remembering facts from paragraph information read to him, remembering faces that he had been shown, remembering names from presented information, remembering a presented route, and following directions after an approximately 10-min lapse. As a consequence, she diagnosed him as having moderate to severe cognitive difficulties secondary to decreased immediate and short-term memory. She also indicated that the patient had decreased ability to concentrate on presented information. She recommended memory and compensatory cognitive rehabilitation treatment on a 3-days-a-week basis for 2 weeks.

The patient was seen again by Patricia Landers on June 30, 1993, after having received 2 weeks of cognitive rehabilitation. Although the patient was noted to have made improvements as a result of treatment, he continued to display deficits in short-term memory in the areas of remembering factual information from presented paragraph information under conditions of immediate and delayed recall, remembering faces or presented names, repeating digits, following presented location directions, and remembering to use his memory notebook.

The reevaluation report of July 5, 1993, signed by Patricia Landers indicated that the patient was administered the Rivermead Behavioral Memory Test and that his scores indicated moderate impaired memory function. She noted that while the patient had made improvements as a result of 2 weeks of cognitive rehabilitation, he continued to exhibit moderate cognitive impairments with respect to his short-term memory, concentration, and attention to details. She noted that the patient had demonstrated excellent motivation for treatment and in completing homework assignments.

Dr. Blumenthal saw the patient on July 10, 1993. His mental status examination revealed the patient to have "a lot of emotional lability." He observed that the patient frequently stumbled over words and had some difficulty in simple conversation. Also, the patient's flatness of facial features continued. While the patient's motor performance was fairly normal, though slowed, he exhibited mild apraxia. He felt that the patient continued to show decrements in his fine motor coordination and speed of performance in mental processing, which he felt was most likely due to his anoxic insult.

Patricia Landers' reevaluation and discharge report, dated July 22, 1993, indicated that although the patient had made improvement in some areas since his initial evaluation, this improvement had not been consistent since final reevaluation scores revealed lower scores in a number of areas. She indicated that testing revealed severe cognitive deficits. She recommended that formal cognitive treatment be discontinued due to the lack of significant continued progress and recommended that the patient receive a vocational rehabilitation consultation, since his memory and concentration deficits were creating great problems for him in his current occupation.

The results of a magnetic resonance imaging (MRI) scan of the head, dated July 25, 1993, revealed a single small focus of increased signal intensity on T2, involving the white matter adjacent to the frontal horn of the left lateral ventricle.

Dr. Blumenthal's chart notes, dated July 27, 1993, indicated that he had reviewed the patient's MRI findings.

The report of Trevor Tindall, M.D., dated August 1, 1993, indicated that he had examined the patient on July 28, 1993. Since the accident, the patient had complained of occasional binocular transient visual obscurations, which consist of both eyes becoming blurry, lasting from 2 to 3 h. This occurs at irregular intervals and currently occurs every few days. Dr. Tindall concluded that he could see no ocular sequelae to the patient's carbon monoxide poisoning.

Dr. Blumenthal's chart notes, dated August 4, 1993, indicated that he had reviewed Dr. Tindall's report of August 1, 1993. He indicated that he would attempt to refer the patient for neuropsychological assessment.

Dr. Blumenthal's chart notes, dated August 7, 1993, indicated that he had received a call from Jill Baker, O.T.R., who indicated that the patient has made sporadic gains, but had been inconsistent; however, she stated that his inconsistencies could not have been duplicated on purpose. She felt that his speech had plateaued. Jill Baker's notes, dated August 9, 1993, indicated that the patient's manual dexterity, as measured by the Pegboard Test, indicated severe impairment. She recommended the patient be evaluated by a neuropsychologist.

Patricia Landers' reevaluation and discharge report, dated August 15, 1993, noted that a comparison of the patient's recent test scores on July 22, 1993 to his initial scores on May 12, 1993 indicated that the patient's scores had decreased in some areas. For example, the final evaluation revealed a decrease in the patient's ability to remember to complete a task after a delay, a decrease in the recalled amount of factual information presented from paragraphs, increased difficulty remembering a location correctly after a delay, and a slight increase in ability to remember to ask a question for which he had been instructed after a delay. She indicated that the patient had remained faithful to treatment, had attended all scheduled sessions, and had completed homework assignments.

Dr. Blumenthal's chart notes, dated August 23, 1993, indicated that the patient and his wife noted no change in the patient's clinical status, as he continued to have problems with his memory and slowed mentation. Dr. Blumenthal noted that the patient continued to be mentally slow for short-term verbal recall. He reviewed the reevaluation reports of July 22, 1993 and August 15, 1993 from Patricia Landers and noted that the final reevaluation revealed that the patient had severely impaired memory functioning and made lower scores in a number of areas, even though the patient had been very involved in cognitive rehabilitation since his initial evaluation.

The patient underwent a Brain Electrical Activity Mapping (BEAM) Study on August 25, 1993, which was interpreted by Dr. Blumenthal on August 26, 1993. The results of this study revealed borderline to mildly abnormal beam study, with central and right temporal dysfunction noted on spectral analysis and the evoked response portion of the record, although the standard EEG had been interpreted as normal.

The patient underwent a cognitive reevaluation by Patricia Landers. She indicated that the patient was readministered the Rivermead Behavioral Memory Test on August 16, 1993 and August 26, 1993. She noted that the patient's performance on this task decreased from August 16, 1993 to August 26, 1993. For example, his standardized profile score on August 16, 1993 was consistent with moderate impaired memory, while his score on August 26, 1993 was consistent with severely impaired memory.

Dr. Blumenthal's chart notes, dated August 30, 1993, indicated that he had communicated with Jill Baker, O.T.R, at the Hillsborough Medical Center, who indicated that the patient was not improving. His chart notes reflected that Ms. Baker asked whether Dr. Blumenthal felt that the patient might be malingering. Dr. Blumenthal indicated that he did not think this was the case.

Dr. Blumenthal's letter to Jack Mills, Workers' Compensation Specialist, dated September 3, 1993, indicated that at the present time the patient's deficits include visual and cognitive dysfunction, resulting in a slowing of motor skills and abilities.

Dr. Blumenthal's chart notes, dated September 6, 1993, indicated that the patient continued to have cognitive difficulties, manifested by difficulty naming objects, people, etc. He noted that when the patient was taken off the Sinemet, there was a mild increase in his shaking, but not to a disabling degree. He also noted that the patient had been having insomnia, sleeping only 2 to 3 h a night, finding himself getting confused with multiple inputs, and having headaches. He indicated that he had reviewed the cognitive assessment findings of the Speech Pathology Department at the Hillsborough Medical Center, which revealed that the patient's cognitive performance had actually decreased with respect to his short-term memory and ability to remember faces, route location, and information.

He diagnosed the patient as having significant postanoxic cognitive dysfunction. Dr. Blumenthal expressed a desire to have this patient be assessed by a clinical neuropsychologist to confirm the patient's cognitive deficits.

Dr. Blumenthal's chart notes, dated October 1, 1993, indicated that the patient and his wife were seen during a follow-up visit. He indicated that the patient's wife did most of the talking during the interview and stated that her husband was getting worse, particularly with respect to his memory. She also said that he became very frustrated and anxious when attempting to do complex mental processing tasks. She indicated that his headaches were about the same and were being helped with Catoprofen. Dr. Blumenthal observed that while the patient appeared mentally alert, he seemed dull and quiet. Although he spoke in full sentences, he was often halting and had a lot of word-finding difficulties. He also observed that the patient's short-term verbal recall was poor and that the patient had some difficulty in sequencing complex mental tasks. He appeared somewhat slow in his motor performance, although his cranial nerve, motor, reflex and sensory findings remained normal.

Dr. Blumenthal's chart notes, dated November 1, 1993, indicated that the patient and his wife were seen again. The patient's wife has not noted any change in her husband's clinical condition. The patient expressed few complaints, other than some low back pain, consisting of stiffness when he sits in one position for long periods of time. Dr. Blumenthal's mental status examination revealed the patient to be a very quiet and withdrawn individual, who seemed somewhat dull in response, with very short answers. He observed that all of the patient's motor movements and mental processing were "very slow." He felt that the patient had had significant cognitive dysfunction from his anoxic injury. He placed the patient on Hydergine, 3 mg t.i.d., in an attempt to improve his condition, although he stated that he did not hold much hope for this particular medication. He indicated that if there was no improvement in the patient's cognitive functioning by the end of April, that the probability of return of functioning of any sort was quite minimal.

The neuropsychological assessment report of Kenneth Solomon, Ph.D., dated January 7, 1994, noted that while the patient appeared to be fully cooperating during neuropsychological testing, he seemed extremely slow and mentally limited. His wife indicated that her husband had become very confused and forgetful and that even relatively simple tasks overwhelmed him. As a consequence, she had to supervise virtually any task he did around the house. The patient reported that he gets a headache very easily whenever he has to work or think hard at all. He was somewhat aware of the cognitive changes that have taken place in him, but often needed some prompting from his wife. He had become rather dependent on her to structure his time and supervise what he did. His wife indicated that her husband exhibited balance problems, some subtle visual difficulties (he sees shadows), incoordination, and a markedly decreased activity level; he tired easily, had problems dropping things, was impatient, and had trouble controlling his temper. He had very impaired memory, a markedly changed personality, and trouble with common sense; he spoke and thought slower and felt very stressed. His wife went on to state that doing virtually anything took him three to four times as long as it did before. Even then, the quality of his work was much inferior to what it used to be. The patient denied ever having had any learning problems at any time during his childhood. He had begun working as a bricklayer after finishing high school and had performed that work ever since. He stated that he enjoyed this work and wanted to return to it.

Dr. Solomon observed that the patient's thinking and response times were exceptionally long. He observed that the patient required inordinate repetitions and some elaboration of test instructions. Furthermore, once an instruction was set in his mind, he could not modify it easily. He felt that the need for supervision to maintain the patient's task orientation was moderate. He felt that the patient's self-awareness of his cognitive processes was questionable. For example, he felt that while the patient did know something was different, he did not always seem to recognize subtle things, such as the extended length of time it took him to think or respond.

Motor testing revealed marked slowness for finger tapping. In addition, the Grooved Pegboard Test was also performed extremely slowly and awkwardly. However, grip strength was normal bilaterally. Time sense estimation revealed extreme deficiency in that the patient estimated the passage of 1 minute as only 10 seconds. This suggested extreme impairment of attention and concentration. The patient required 210 seconds to complete Part A of the Trail Making Test, however he did not make any sequencing errors. On Part B, testing was discontinued, after the patient had only completed a third of the test after 6 minutes. Dr. Solomon observed that the patient could not grasp this task. Based on his average of mental processing, latency of responses, alertness, concentration, depth of thinking, ability to sustain motivation and level of consciousness, he felt that the patient's global mentation and mental control were moderately to severely impaired. Because of this, he felt that the potential for stimulus overload was very high, and, conversely, the patient's potential for initiation of activity and conversation was minimal. The patient could not even repeat a string of four numbers. Repeating digits backwards was extremely difficult and the patient could do only one set of three digits accurately. Dr. Solomon felt that this represented severely impaired mental control.

Dr. Solomon found that the patient's inability to learn lexical symbol associations quickly, as measured by the Digit Symbol subtest, was consistent with severe impairment. He reported that the patient's ability to recall two short stories that had orally been presented to him without any time delay between presentation and recall, was severely impoverished. Mr. Thomas was found to be moderately impaired with respect to his ability to draw relatively simple geometric designs following a brief visual exposure. Furthermore, the quality of his design rendering was impaired for details. His performance on the California Verbal Learning Test revealed severe impairment for memory capacity and ability to benefit from multiple repetitions of information. This suggests marked deficits in the brain's ability to acquire new learning. The patient's receptive language skills for word recognition and reading tested at the sixth grade level. However, his auditory comprehension and understanding was adequate with some repetition or elaboration. Furthermore, his ability to follow verbal directions was felt to be adequate. The patient's writing and spelling skills tested at the fourth grade level. He exhibited marked word-finding difficulties, and his conversation, expression, and verbal fluency was limited to only a few phrases.

The patient's ability to solve orally presented practical arithmetic problems was extremely poor and he frequently stated that he knew what he needed to do, but simply could not mentally carry out the operational processes. Dr. Solomon felt that the patient's ability for arithmetic reasoning was severely impaired. The patient's ability to recognize and differentiate figure–ground patterns and identify essential from nonessential elements visually was markedly impaired, even though time limits were disregarded. The patient's task planning and sequence anticipation in arranging block designs were markedly impaired due to extreme slowness and difficulty executing the task. The patient seemed to know what he was supposed to do, but could not execute his intentions. The patient's visual form perception and global visual integration skills tested as moderately impaired.

Dr. Solomon reported that the patient's IQ tested between 65 and 70 on both the Ammons Picture Vocabulary Test and WAIS. He noted that recall of old learned information was extremely difficult and that the patient's verbal production was halting and complicated by word-finding difficulties. He observed that thinking was obviously very much of an effort for this patient.

Dr. Solomon concluded that his qualitative and quantitative findings suggested marked impairment in virtually all higher mental processes. He indicated that given this patient's educational and work history, testing reflected a significant decline in cognitive and intellectual functioning. He also indicated that the patient's working memory was severely impaired and that his thinking speed was so slow as to be ineffectual in any competitive work situation. He felt that the patient would most likely be unemployable and that despite the fact that he might be trained for some unskilled labor, he would never return to any type of skilled employment. Finally, he indicated that the patient fell into a range characterized by "a degree of impairment of complex integrated cerebral functions that limits daily activities to directed care under confinement at home or in another domicile." He recommended that the patient participate in an extensive brain injury rehabilitation program to maximize his potential for independence and quality of life. He hoped that this program would assist the patient and his wife preserve their marriage by teaching him skills that would minimize his almost total dependence on her.

Dr. Blumenthal's letter to Jack Mills, Workers' Compensation Specialist, dated February 10, 1994, indicated that the patient had recently been assessed by Dr. Solomon, who found marked impairment of virtually all higher cognitive and mental functions, reflecting significant decline from premorbid levels. The patient had difficulty performing even the most basic motor skills and visual and spatial analysis necessary to carry out bricklaying. His working memory was also severely impaired. He indicated that his findings, when combined with Dr. Solomon's test results, indicated that the patient was totally disabled, with a rating of 100%. He indicated that his additional findings were those of problems with motor control, speed, and coordination. It was his medical opinion that the patient's deficits were permanent, that the patient had reached his maximum level of medical improvement, and that his deficits were irreversible.

Dr. Solomon's letter, dated March 14, 1994, to Mrs. Thomas, indicated that according to his neuropsychological assessment her husband demonstrated severe neurofunctional deficits that placed him 100% disabled for returning to competitive employment. He stated that his functional assessment indicated that the patient would not be able to work in any competitive fashion consistent with his prior employment.

Dr. Blumenthal's letter to Jack Mills, dated May 2, 1994, indicated that the patient's cognitive abilities were so impaired that it made it very difficult for him to function in any work capacity. Therefore, any attempt by this patient at working must be accompanied by an adequate assessment of his performance capabilities.

Dr. Blumenthal's chart notes, dated July 1, 1994, indicated that he had received a telephone call from the patient's wife, who stated, "I do not know how much longer Gene can take it." She stated that her husband was crying frequently and was not sleeping at night.

Dr. Blumenthal's chart notes, dated July 15, 1994, indicated that he had seen the patient and his wife during a follow-up examination. He indicated that the patient was not sleeping and was depressed, crying, withdrawing from family contacts, and restless during the day. However, there had been no more weight loss and his appetite was fair. He continued to be confused, especially as to place. Dr. Blumenthal stated that the patient was extremely depressed and was crying in his office. He felt that the patient's disorientation, concentration, and memory difficulties persisted. He indicated that he would administer amitriptyline 25 mg at bedtime to assist the patient's sleep and hopefully improve his depression.

Dr. Blumenthal's notes, dated September 15, 1994, indicated that the patient returned for another follow-up visit. He indicated that he was sleeping better and that his attitude had improved. He complained of some mild headaches; otherwise there had been no change in his cognitive or functional ability as noted by him or his wife. Dr. Blumenthal's physical examination noted that the patient, while mentally alert and moderately oriented, continued to experience a number of problems in cognitive processing. He spoke very minimally and reacted quite slowly to verbal requests and input. Motor examination revealed good strength, tone, coordination, and gait.

The report of Anthony Derringer, M.D., Department of Neurology, Georgia State University Neurological Foundation, dated January 21, 1995, indicated that the patient has been followed by Dr. Blumenthal and has undergone formal neuropsychological testing. The patient had had difficulty with memory, concentration, and general understanding of events in his environment ever since the carbon monoxide poisoning. According to his wife, he often could not remember from 1 min to the next and even when asked to perform a simple task such as vacuuming a carpet in a room or going into a store to pick up a single item, he was unable to do it. He was virtually never able to carry out anything more complex, such as a two-step operation. His judgment is impaired, according to his wife. For example, he would roughhouse with his children in an inappropriate fashion in public places. On one occasion, when she asked him to remove something from the oven, he simply reached in with his bare hands. He was emotionally very labile and his emotions varied from being withdrawn and passive, particularly in unfamiliar surroundings, to very active and demonstrative.

While the patient did do some reading, according to his wife, she would find him reading the same article again and again.

On neurological examination, Dr. Derringer observed that the patient often appeared bewildered and was very passive. He was very hesitant in answering questions and often did so with only one or two words. He could not recall any details of his injury and seemed to lose track of the course of questions and conversation during the interview. On higher function testing, he was oriented as to the month and year, but could not indicate where they were located or anything about the route taken to get to Dr. Derringer's office. He could not perform serial 7 subtractions or tell Dr. Derringer anything about current events, and he had difficulty reading even a simple paragraph. Part of his difficulty seemed to be keeping track of where he was, as he would skip from one line to another. After reading a simple paragraph in an advertisement for an automobile, he could not describe anything about what he had read. He was able to distinguish left from right, but when asked to do so, he was able to put his left thumb on his right ear only after a considerable delay.

It was Dr. Derringer's opinion that the patient was 100% disabled for gainful employment. Furthermore, Dr. Derringer did not believe that the patient would be able to carry out any light duty or work activities. He indicated that the patient had difficulty carrying out even the simplest household chores and activities and indicated that this patient, if left alone, would not be able to live and function on his own.

The patient underwent an MRI scan of the brain without contrast on November 9, 1996. This study revealed subtle areas of low signal on the T1 weighted images, which demonstrated a bright signal on fluid-attenuated inversion recovery (FLAIR) sequences at the posterior limb of the internal capsules bilaterally. This was felt to occur in the setting of carbon monoxide exposure. There was a third focus of increased signal on T2 and FLAIR sequences immediately adjacent to the left frontal horn, measuring 5 mm in diameter, without mass effect. This was felt to represent a focal infarcted area of the brain.

The neuropsychological evaluation report of Jeremy Rankin, Ph.D., dated December 10, 1996, indicated that the patient was alert and interacted appropriately with the examiner. He indicated that the patient displayed a tendency to give up on some tasks, produced excessive response latencies, showed frequent hesitations, and often looked at the examiner and stated, "I don't know," "I forget," or "Can't remember." Dr. Rankin indicated that the patient sometimes asked him to repeat test instructions or appeared confused by task directions and claimed to completely forget what was asked or presented. The patient spoke in a quivering, monotonous voice that suggested a lack of spontaneity and self-assurance. The patient denied the presence of depressive symptoms, but simultaneously demonstrated a paucity of thought since he repeatedly failed to elaborate his responses, even when encouraged to do so.

During the 4-h examination, the patient never initiated conversation nor did he show evidence of fatigue. Likewise, he never showed frustration, even in the face of repeated failure. Dr. Rankin indicated that he had a brief interview with Mrs. Thomas, which revealed that the patient had gained weight in the recent past, slept throughout the night when he took amitriptyline, and showed no evidence of suicidal ideation or behavior. His wife also noted that he frequently got "mad and upset" with himself because "he couldn't do the things he once did." However, she also pointed out that "things don't bother him anymore; he's not the same man." "He no longer is a concerned parent; he acts childlike with the kids and can't be left home alone."

Dr. Rankin indicated that on an extremely simple vigilance task in which the patient was instructed to indicate each time he heard the letter A, he made three errors of omission and at one point claimed to have forgotten the target letter. The patient was able to recall only three digits forward and two backward. However, during the forward span trials, the patient tried to repeat the digits in backward order three times and on one occasion failed to recall even a single digit. During backward span attempts, the patient claimed to forget one or more digits on three occasions, and on another he repeated the digits without reversing the order. On the Line Cancellation Test, the patient was instructed to cross out all the lines as quickly as possible. He made 21 omissions, with an essentially equal distribution of errors in both hemispatial fields. When he was asked to count backwards from 20 to 1, he required 95 s, and on two occasions stopped performing, looked at the examiner and commented, "What did I just say?" Finally, Dr. Rankin observed that while performing automatic tasks (such as counting from 1 to 20 or reciting the alphabet), the patient required excessive time and was unable to complete the tasks without assistance.

Dr. Rankin reported that the patient demonstrated temporal disorientation and failed to state the day of the month or day of the week. He estimated the time of day as "noon," when it was actually 8:56 A.M. He also incorrectly reported his age as 39 and could not name the current or previous U.S. presidents and reported that a year consisted of 30 weeks. On measures of immediate paragraph and figural memory, his scores placed him at the first percentile. After 30 min of interpolated activity, he retrieved absolutely none of the previously registered paragraph and figural material. On the Rey Auditory Verbal Learning Test, his performances suggested grossly impaired registration and encoding. For example, he remembered a total of only 12 words over five trials and produced a marked recency recall pattern.

Following an interference task, his scores on free recall and recognition trials were both zero. He also tested as defective on the Digit Symbol Recall task, which measures incidental learning for rehearsed material. After repeatedly copying nine number–symbol pairs for approximately 6 min, he remembered none of the individual symbols and none of the number–symbol pairs. Specialized measures for the detection of functional memory loss yielded significant results. He noted that on a forced-choice memory test, the patient's total score was 28 out of a possible 72, which revealed a progressive decline across the second and third blocks. The results of the Word Recognition Test indicated an immediate recall score of 3 and a recognition accuracy of 2.

Dr. Rankin noted that the patient demonstrated fluent conversational speech, with grossly intact language comprehension. However, on language repetition tasks, the patient displayed long response latencies and repeated only the last few words of each sentence. For instance, when he was asked to repeat "He shouted the warning," he replied, "The warning." When directed to repeat the entire sequence, the patient completed the task correctly. A few minutes later, when he was asked to say, "Let's go downtown for an ice cream," he reproduced "town for ice cream." He slowly but satisfactorily completed tests of oral sentence reading, right–left discrimination, ideokinetic praxis, writing a sentence to dictation, and basic subtraction. Dr. Rankin noted difficulties on tasks of oral spelling, simple multiplication, and visual confrontation naming. After the patient had successfully read a brief sentence aloud, he was directed to do what it said, and then hesitated for an extended period and calmly replied, "Wasn't paying attention to what it read." On measures of constructional praxis, his reproductions of a Greek cross and skeleton key were mildly distorted. When asked to draw a clock face and set the hands at 10 after 11, his overall production showed subtle distortions, but the specified time and number placements were correct.

Dr. Rankin reported that the patient tested within the severely impaired range on both Parts A and B of the Trail Making Test, which he felt reflected a slow response style and suggested problems with efficient set shifting and the simultaneous processing of two pieces of competing information. On the abbreviated form of the WAIS-R, Dr. Rankin reported that the patient tested with a full-scale IQ of 66, which he felt was well below expectations based on the patient's age, race, school records, and previous occupation. He noted that during testing, the patient exhibited excessively long response times and a tendency to give up at the first hint of difficulty.

When Dr. Rankin compared the patient's test results from the previous evaluation (by Dr. Solomon), he noted that there was no evidence that any meaningful change had occurred during the intervening 35 months. He also noted that the patient's IQ scores, memory, and performance on tests of executive functioning showed similar levels of performance from prior testing. However, he noted that the patient's score on a measure of immediate figural memory dropped from the 11th to the 1st percentile.

Dr. Rankin concluded that if the patient's scores were accepted uncritically, these scores could be interpreted as evidence of severe temporal disorientation and significant deficits in attention, concentration, psychometric intelligence, general memory, and new learning. However, based on his clinical impression, the patterns of test scores, and performance on forced-choice memory tests, he indicated that he had serious doubts concerning the veracity of the test results. As a consequence of the patient's behavior during testing, he stated that he could not formulate a definitive conclusion regarding the presence, type, and extent of neuropsychological deficits secondary to carbon monoxide poisoning.

DEPOSITION OF DONALD STURGESS, M.D.

The deposition transcript of Donald Sturgess, M.D., taken on November 25, 1996, was reviewed. Dr. Sturgess indicated that he is an internist who specializes in pulmonary and occupational medicine. He indicated that he received training in the treatment of patients with carbon monoxide poisoning at Atlanta City Hospital, where he was the Chief Resident. He also stated that he had written a chapter on carbon monoxide poisoning, which addressed the problems with smoke inhalation and associated problems with carbon monoxide poisoning, particularly how to recognize and treat it, what the acute symptomatology was related to, and the necessary treatment.

Dr. Sturgess indicated that individuals develop chronic toxicity from acute poisoning resulting from chronic carbon monoxide poisoning. He stated that such individuals develop short- and long-term memory loss. He indicated that there was no effective treatment for such patients.

Dr. Sturgess indicated that carbon monoxide binds to hemoglobin and in the binding to hemoglobin it limits the amount of oxygen the hemoglobin can carry around the body. It also makes the amount of oxygen bound to hemoglobin less available to the tissue such that tissues most dependent on oxygen are unable to receive oxygen during the time of high levels of carbon monoxide. He stated that these tissues are present in the brain, eyes, nerve endings, and potentially the heart. He said that a person begins feeling the toxic effects of carbon monoxide at carboxyhemoglobin levels of 10 to 15%. He indicated that one of the factors that is important is how hard the person was working at the time of exposure. In other words, if someone is working very hard and breathing more air in and out of the lungs, more carbon monoxide is being breathed in. One of the dangerous factors of carbon monoxide poisoning, he said, is that there is no limit to the amount of carbon monoxide that can diffuse across the lungs, since it is not rate limited. Therefore, the more that is breathed, the more that person is exposed to, and the amount exposed to will not reach a saturation point until death. He stated that the half life of carboxyhemoglobin is about 4 to 8 h. So, the higher the concentration of oxygen, the lower the half life is. The general rule of thumb is that it takes about seven half lives to eliminate carbon monoxide or almost any other toxin, and this would generally be about 42 h.

Dr. Sturgess indicated that Mr. Thomas was suffering from memory deficits and carbon monoxide encephalopathy, which he described as brain dysfunction, brain damage, generalized brain damage, and focal brain damage related to carbon monoxide exposure that he was subjected to on January 14, 1993. He stated that the carbon monoxide emanated from the concrete saw that was being used in an enclosed area in which he was working.

Dr. Sturgess indicated that this is a permanent condition and, based on the history of his injury, will not improve. Based on his neuropsychological test results, the patient is unable to function and has the emotional problems that are very characteristic of people with brain damage, such as emotional lability and easy frustration.

Dr. Sturgess stated that often after carbon monoxide poisoning there is a return to normal and then there is a demyelinating process that occurs in the brain itself. During this process, which takes several months, the nerve cells demyelinate and conduct poorly. He also indicated that MRI scans are occasionally abnormal in individuals with carbon monoxide poisoning. He had reviewed the MRI study of July 25, 1993 and noted that there were some nonspecific findings in the frontal horn of the left lateral ventricle. Even though there was nothing from the first MRI study that would verify or deny carbon monoxide poisoning, the second MRI, performed on November 9, 1996, indicated that the posterior portion of the internal capsule showed bright areas bilaterally, which is consistent with carbon monoxide poisoning. He felt that this was indicative of an ischemic injury to the brain.

DEPOSITION OF MARC C. BLUMENTHAL, D.O.

The deposition transcript of Marc C. Blumenthal, D.O., taken on November 26, 1996, was reviewed. Dr. Blumenthal stated that his specialty is medical neurology. He indicated that the patient has a static encephalopathy and that it worsened to a point and then has been fairly stable. Dr. Blumenthal said the patient had been referred to him by Jack Mills, of London Life Insurance Company. Although he had not received any specialized type of training in carbon monoxide poisoning and the resulting injuries, he had done specific literature searches on carbon monoxide poisoning several years earlier. He indicated that the patient's initial exposure was between 300 and 700 parts of carbon monoxide per million.

It was Dr. Blumenthal's understanding, based on his original consultation, that the patient was in a basement laying concrete block and was running a gasoline-powered concrete saw. The patient had stated that he was in the basement for several hours, without adequate ventilation, and gradually became lightheaded and woozy; had difficulty standing up, chest pain, shortness of breath, near loss of consciousness; and then was taken to St. Mary's Hospital. During his initial examination, he noted that the patient had mildly significant slowing of his fine motor coordination, had an unsteady gait, and was unable to balance on either leg, as well as having some problems doing deep knee bends.

Dr. Blumenthal emphasized that the patient exhibited almost early Parkinsonian features, such as you would find if a person had an injury to some deep brain structure such as the basal ganglion. Dr. Blumenthal indicated that the basal ganglion is a portion of the brain that is responsible for motor function that integrates motor set and movement. He indicated that the cerebellum is another portion of the brain that is responsible for movement and targeting and the like. He felt that the patient had either cerebellar or possible basal ganglion dysfunction, based on his slowness of movement, his flattened affect, and his emotional lability. He felt that all of these symptoms seemed to point toward basal ganglion dysfunction. When Dr. Blumenthal was asked if the EEG would be beneficial in attempting to determine whether the patient had any dysfunction, he indicated that it would be helpful in determining whether or not he had an encephalopathy. However, he pointed out, the EEG would show cortical dysfunction, and the basal ganglion is subcortical. Dr. Blumenthal emphasized that following carbon monoxide exposure, there is delayed demyelination or axonal dropout that can occur weeks and even a few months following exposure.

Dr. Blumenthal indicated that on follow-up examination, he observed evidence of bradykinesia (slowing of motor function). He stated that bradykinesia is not normal for someone of this patient's age. He indicated that he determined this by watching the patient move, noting his lack of arm swing and the blank look on his face. He also observed the speed with which the patient was able to put nine pegs into nine holes. He felt that the patient was having basal ganglia dysfunction similar to Parkinson's disease and had placed the patient on Sinemet, which he typically uses to treat Parkinson's patients. Dr. Blumenthal noted that the patient's cognitive and behavioral functioning appeared to be getting worse over time. While he pointed out that the EEG had come back normal, he emphasized the problems that were occurring in this patient's brain were subcortical.

Dr. Blumenthal indicated that he had reviewed the results of the patient's MRI brain scan performed on July 25, 1993, which showed a single small focus of increased T2 signal adjacent to the frontal horn and lateral ventricle. Dr. Blumenthal felt that this was a small area of demyelination. He requested the BEAM study, because he felt that brain mapping was a more sensitive way of evaluating brain dysfunction than was the EEG. The brain mapping study was borderline to mildly abnormal and showed evidence of central and right temporal dysfunctions on spectral analysis in the evoked responses.

Dr. Blumenthal stated at no time did he ever suspect that the patient might be malingering. He based this on his clinical experience.

Dr. Blumenthal had referred the patient to Dr. Solomon, stating that he felt Dr. Solomon was the best neuropsychologist to examine the patient because he had published several articles and a book on neuropsychological assessment. Plus, he had used Dr. Solomon extensively over the years for various types of patients and felt that Dr. Solomon did a very credible job.

Dr. Blumenthal indicated that he had reviewed the second MRI, which was abnormal as a result of subtle areas of low signal on T1 weighted images, demonstrating a bright signal on FLAIR sequences at the posterior limb of the internal capsule bilaterally. The report stated that this can occur in the setting of carbon monoxide exposure. He indicated that the differences between the first and second scans reflected the FLAIR sequencing technique, which allows one to see the areas very close to the ventricles. He indicated that the initial MRI, performed in July 1993, did not use this technique.

Dr. Blumenthal indicated that it was his opinion that the patient's condition would not change. He stated that as the patient grows older, his condition may worsen with normal aging of the brain on top of his deficits. He felt that the patient has bilateral frontal lobe dysfunction, with severe cognitive impairments.

Dr. Blumenthal pointed out that Parkinson's disease produces cognitive changes that are not the same as Alzheimer's dementia. He indicated that some people would characterize it as a true dementia, while others would characterize it as a problem in processing. He stated that the patient does not have Parkinson's disease.

Dr. Blumenthal admitted he had not had any conversations with any of the patient's employers or coworkers after the patient had returned to work following his carbon monoxide exposure. He also indicated that at no time did he ever learn or attempt to learn whether there had been any complaints about the patient's work after his return to work following the incident. He stated that the patient was unable to work as a bricklayer or perform light duty work after the carbon monoxide incident because he was unable to acquire new memories, was unable to learn, and had no way of processing new knowledge, attaching it to his present knowledge and carrying it forward with a plan of action.

He felt that the patient's memory and learning capabilities for incidents and information after the time of his injury were markedly impaired. He emphasized that laying bricks requires one to look at a plan that tells where the bricks are to go and then follow through with this plan. While he felt that the patient was physically able to pick up the bricks, he could not follow a particular plan. He indicated that while the patient may be able to lay a line of bricks, once he got to the end of the line someone would have to come back and say, "Now, lay the next line of bricks, the next line of bricks," and even with this he might stop halfway through this. Dr. Blumenthal cited Dr. Solomon's test findings as supporting his opinions.

He indicated that after carbon monoxide poisoning, there is a period of time, which can even be several months long, where demyelination can continue to occur. He felt that the patient was cognitively more impaired than he was immediately after the accident. He indicated that immediately after the accident, for a period of 3 or 4 weeks, the patient seemed to function reasonably well. Then he stopped being able to function. Dr. Blumenthal pointed out that the patient was referred to Dr. Derringer, who arrived at identical conclusions.

DEPOSITION OF ANTHONY DERRINGER, M.D.

The deposition transcript of Anthony Derringer, M.D., taken on November 29, 1996, was reviewed. Dr. Derringer indicated that he had reviewed the patient's medical records and thought it was significant that Dr. Blumenthal had not reported any difficulty with the patient's emotional or intellectual functions during his first visit. However, within days after this the medical record begins to reflect such problems that have become more severe and persistent. Dr. Derringer felt that this was most likely an indication of the delayed effect of carbon monoxide exposure and hypoxia. It was his opinion that the patient had been exposed to carbon monoxide. While Dr. Derringer indicated that he had no basis for an opinion as to how long the patient had been exposed to carbon monoxide or the level of carbon monoxide the patient might have been exposed to, he stated that the patient had had a very high carboxyhemoglobin level when he had been seen at St. Mary's Hospital. Dr. Derringer indicated that he did not feel that the patient was depressed, but that the patient seemed bewildered and severely incapacitated. He also did not recommend psychotherapy since he felt that psychotherapy requires intact personality, intelligence, and brain function.

Dr. Derringer indicated that during his interview with the patient, he had observed that the patient could not recall any details of his injury and seemed to lose his train of thought during the course of the interview. He stated that the patient had a better recall of the events prior to the injury and that his recall of events after the injury was very sketchy. He indicated that the patient could not perform serial 7 subtraction, in fact he could not even subtract 7 from 100. He also observed that the patient could not respond appropriately and had difficulty reading simple paragraphs. Even though he was able to read a simple paragraph aloud, he could not indicate what he had read.

Dr. Derringer indicated that the patient's neurological examination, with the exception of higher functions, was normal. He said that Dr. Blumenthal felt that the patient had shown indications of basal ganglion or cerebellar findings. Dr. Derringer indicated that the first MRI scan demonstrated an abnormal signal intensity in the white matter, which he felt represented an area of demyelination, which is typically seen in cases involving carbon monoxide exposure or hypoxia. The second MRI indicated that there had been some initial deterioration since the first MRI, showing evidence of bilateral deep basal ganglia and deep structure abnormalities, as well as abnormalities in the white matter. He stated that this second scan demonstrates further evolution of the demyelination process. He indicated that there are very few things that can produce this type of pattern that is typical for carbon monoxide exposure. He pointed out that trauma would not look like this. As a result, he felt that the patient was and still remained 100% disabled for gainful employment.

Dr. Derringer described the patient's brain injury as a diffuse brain injury involving demyelination of the white matter of the brain. The importance of noting the basal ganglia lesions is that this is one of the hallmarks of carbon monoxide exposure and hypoxia. However, he pointed out that this does not mean that the damage is restricted to those areas seen on the MRI. Dr. Derringer reiterated that this patient followed the clinical course of carbon monoxide exposure with a delay in the onset of deterioration of higher cortical functions. He estimated that following carbon monoxide exposure and hypoxia, approximately 50% of patients had delayed symptoms.

Dr. Derringer indicated that he never suspected Mr. Thomas of malingering. He indicated that there was nothing about this patient that made him suspect the patient was not doing anything other than the very best he could during his examination. He indicated that he based this on 25 years of experience doing these types of assessments. Dr. Derringer indicated that the patient would not improve and should not deteriorate more unless depression becomes a problem. He indicated that the patient's wife had informed him that the patient had difficulties with memory and concentration and generally understanding events in his environment since his carbon monoxide poisoning. According to his wife, the patient could not remember from 1 min to the next, even when asked to do a single task. He is virtually unable to carry out anything more complex, such as a two-step operation. His judgment is impaired. He demonstrates emotional lability and is withdrawn and passive. Dr. Derringer pointed out that Dr. Solomon's testing indicated evidence of severe cognitive impairment. The patient had dementia, and one of the consequences of dementia was the loss of ability to plan and decide what sequence to follow. Dr. Derringer also felt that the issue of whether this patient was motivated to go back to work was essentially a trivial issue, since he was unable to function in this capacity. He also felt that depression was not a major issue in this case.

DEPOSITION OF RANDY NIELSEN

The deposition transcript of Randy Nielsen, taken on December 1, 1996, was reviewed. Mr. Nielsen indicated that he has been a bricklayer for the past 10 years and was currently employed by Heartland Masonry. He indicated that he had known Mr. Thomas for approximately 18 years. Mr. Nielsen indicated that Mr. Thomas and he had gone hunting every weekend over the previous couple of months. When Mr. Nielsen was asked if Mr. Thomas hunts now, he indicated that he just goes and sits with the boys and does not carry a weapon.

Mr. Nielsen indicated that Mr. Thomas had been a good worker, was a very dependable and hard worker, and got along well with all his coworkers. He described Mr. Thomas as "just a good guy, very easy to work with." He indicated that prior to January 14, 1993, Mr. Thomas did good work and described him as "pretty sharp" in that he caught on quickly and did not take long to figure out things pertaining to whatever they were building. He said that Mr. Thomas had served as a foreman over him. He stated that Mr. Thomas' father had worked for the same company and was one of their lead foremen, so Mr. Thomas had had a pretty good teacher.

He indicated that Mr. Thomas had kept a notebook in which he would take notes of the day's events, so he could discuss them later with others.

BEHAVIORAL OBSERVATIONS

Mr. Thomas presented as an alert, 43-year-old, right-handed, white male, in no acute distress. He was accompanied by his wife, who appeared to be a reliable historian. He was casually dressed in appropriate attire, with fair personal hygiene and grooming. His ability to comprehend this examiner's questions and respond in a timely manner was markedly compromised. Questions frequently had to be repeated and rephrased, particularly if they were somewhat complex or lengthy. The patient typically demonstrated extremely long response latencies before he would reply to this examiner's question. His motor responses were exceedingly slow. He became confused easily and frequently had to be redirected back to the task. He required numerous cues and prompts to maintain his attention and concentration.

While he did not appear depressed, he exhibited a blunt affect and seemed extremely apathetic to the events that were going on around him. For example, when I asked his wife in his presence to describe his current cognitive and behavioral difficulties, he seemed oblivious to her discussion of his problems and the examples that she provided. In fact, when he was asked to indicate what his wife and I had been discussing, he seemed confused and stated, "Something about me?" in a manner that betrayed his poor understanding of his cognitive and behavioral problems, his awareness of his surroundings, and his sense of being overwhelmed by what was going on around him. This was corroborated by the fact that when he was asked to describe all of the problems he saw himself as having, he only complained of memory difficulties and stated that he felt "awkward" since he could not do what he used to do. These complaints were in stark contrast to his wife's observations and complaints and the obvious severe cognitive impairments he exhibited during the interview.

At no time did he appear anxious or depressed. There was no evidence of auditory or visual hallucinations, paranoia, physical pain or discomfort, bizarre thinking, or psychotic behavior. He never initiated any conversation or showed any sign of frustration, even when he had performed poorly. When he was asked to evaluate his performance during neuropsychological testing, he indicated that he thought he was doing well, even though he was performing poorly. While he appeared cooperative, his entire demeanor appeared consistent with patients who have developed a severe dementia following carbon monoxide poisoning; that is, he appeared apathetic, hypokinetic, amnestic, disoriented, and emotionally flat. At no time did he complain of having to take unpleasant tests, or exhibit any evidence whatsoever of suboptimal motivation.

ADDITIONAL INFORMATION OBTAINED FROM THE PATIENT'S SPOUSE

Mrs. Thomas was asked to complete the Significant Other's Questionnaire while I was administering neuropsychological tests to her husband in an adjacent room. While this questionnaire was designed to pick up a variety of cognitive, behavioral, and emotional problems in patients who sustain traumatic brain injuries, it seemed appropriate for Mrs. Thomas to complete it because of her husband's severe cognitive and behavioral impairments and the obvious effect such impairments have had on her health and emotional functioning.

She indicated that her husband has the following "severe" problems: doing things slowly, headaches, word-finding difficulties, circumstantial and tangential thinking, speaking clearly, being easily distracted, concentration difficulties, memory difficulties, planning and organization, setting realistic goals, following through or finishing tasks, apathy, lack of initiative, irritability, impatience, restlessness, temper outbursts, mood swings, difficulty bringing his emotions under control, getting into arguments with others, being dependent on others, requiring supervision, diminished libido, and personality changes. She indicated that virtually all of these problems had placed a "severe strain on her." She also reported that her husband had "moderate" problems in the following areas: balance, becoming tired easily, complaining about things, anxiety, and depression.

With respect to "Activities of Daily Living," she indicated that her husband was "unable to perform the following tasks, even with assistance": shopping for food, preparing meals, washing his own clothes, keeping track of money, paying his bills, balancing a check book, making necessary purchases for himself, performing yard work and repairs, and living independently. He was able to do the following tasks "only with maximal assistance from others": cleaning his room and helping with household chores. He was able to clean up after meals with "minimal assistance." She indicated that her husband was able to perform the following tasks on his own, "but requires prompting": choosing his own clothes, dressing himself, showering/bathing, and brushing his teeth. He was able to perform the following tasks independently, "without prompting": feeding himself, washing his hair, and going to the bathroom.

Mrs. Thomas was asked to complete a questionnaire that required her to judge her husband's ability to perform a variety of very practical skills at the present time. She indicated that her husband was "unable to perform" the following skills: washing dishes, doing laundry, taking care of finances, keeping appointments on time, starting a conversation in a group, staying involved in work activities, remembering what he ate for dinner, driving, handling arguments, accepting criticism, recognizing that something he has said has upset someone else, scheduling daily activities, and keeping his emotions from affecting his ability to go about his day's activities.

She indicated that her husband had a "very difficult time" preparing meals, taking care of personal hygiene, remembering his daily schedule, remembering important things that he needed to do, obtaining help when he became confused, adjusting to unexpected changes, controlling his crying, showing affection toward others, understanding new instructions, meeting his daily responsibilities, controlling his temper, and keeping from becoming depressed. She indicated that her husband is able to perform the following skills "with some difficulty": dressing himself, participating in group activities, and controlling his laughter.

NEUROPSYCHOLOGICAL TESTING

Tests Administered

The Raven Progressive Matrices Test

The Trail Making Test

The Symbol Digit Modalities Test

The Boston Naming Test

The Verbal Fluency Test

The Hooper Visual Organization Test

The Judgment of Line Orientation Test

The Digit Span Test

The Logical Memories Test

The Rey Auditory Verbal Learning Test

The Continuous Visual Memory Test

The Grooved Pegboard Test

The Grip Strength Test

The Finger Tapping Test

Luria's Motor Examination

Tests of Motor Sequencing

Tests of Abstract Thinking

Tests of Proverb Interpretation

Tests of Judgment

Tests of Problem Solving

The Beck Depression Inventory

The Millon Clinical Multiaxial Inventory — III

TEST RESULTS

Attention–Concentration

Mr. Thomas was administered a variety of arithmetic and nonarithmetic tasks that placed heavy emphasis on his sustained attention and concentration skills. His performance on these tasks was characterized by extremely slow response latencies, the need for considerable warm-up time and practice, frequent need for cues and prompts, and frequent repetition and rephrasing of the test instructions. He required 91.27 seconds to count backwards from 20 to 1. When he was asked to perform serial 3 additions, he required considerable practice and warm-up time. Even so, his responses were extremely slow. He required frequent cues and prompts from the examiner because he appeared to easily lose his train of thought or become distracted.

Similarly, when he was asked to perform serial three and five addition, he showed a tendency to add only by three until the instructions were repeated again. He was unable to perform serial 7 subtraction from 100. Instead, he was asked to perform serial 7 subtraction from 20. He had considerable difficulty performing this task, had to be continually reminded of the task instructions, and had to be given frequent cues and prompts throughout this task. He demonstrated a very long latency between responses and was exceedingly slow. He was unable to perform serial 13 subtraction from 100. He was extremely slow when he was asked to recite the alphabet, requiring 78.09 s to complete this task.

He was administered Parts A and B of the Trail Making Test to assess his sustained attention, concentration, and visuomotor tracking skills. He required 147.64 seconds to complete Part A, which placed him in the severely impaired range for persons of his age, sex, and educational background. He required 289.39 seconds to complete Part B, which placed him in the severely impaired range, even though this examiner provided him with frequent cues and prompts throughout the entire test. In the absence of such cues and prompts, it is highly unlikely that this patient would have been able to complete this test. Despite these cues and prompts, the patient was observed to make at least four sequencing errors.

He was administered the Digit Span Test to assess his passive range of attention. He was able to recall only three digits forward, which placed him in the first percentile (severely impaired range). He could not recall even two digits backward. In order to test the veracity of his test performance, he was asked to recall "1–2–3–4–5," which he did. Had he been engaging in malingering on this task, no difference would have been observed between his performance on normal digits forward and his ability to recall the five digit sequence (1–2–3–4–5). The speed of his attentional processing was assessed by the Symbol Digit Modalities Test. He made a score of only 10 on this test, which placed him 5.07 standard deviations below norms for persons of his age (severe to profound impairment).

Language

His confrontational naming skills were assessed by the Boston Naming Test and were found to be markedly impaired. He made a score of only 37 out of a possible 60, which placed him 4.17 standard deviations below norms for persons of his educational background and 5.01 standard deviations below norms for persons of his age (severely impaired range). He was administered the Verbal Fluency (FAS) Test to assess his ability to generate words beginning with specific letters of the alphabet. He was able to generate a total of only 13 words over three trials, which placed him below the first percentile (severely impaired range).

Visual Perception/Organization

He was administered the Judgment of Line Orientation Test to assess his ability to judge the spatial orientation of two pairs of lines. Testing revealed that he made a score of only 9 out of a possible 30, which placed him in the severe to profoundly impaired range. Observations of his behavior noted that he tried to use his fingers to judge the spatial orientation of two pairs of lines. He exhibited extremely slow response latencies during testing. He was also administered the Hooper Visual Organization Test to assess his ability to recognize pictures of objects that had been cut up and placed in different positions. Testing was discontinued after 30 min, when he had completed only 10 of the 30 items.

Learning/Memory

He was administered the Rey Auditory Verbal Learning Test to assess his ability to learn a list of 15 words over five consecutive learning trials. Testing revealed an essentially flat learning curve across the five trials; that is, the patient could recall a maximum of only 4 out of the 15 words, which placed him in the severely impaired range in comparison to norms for persons of his age and sex. Furthermore, observations of his test performance revealed a strong recency effect in that he recalled only the last four items of the 15-item word list. After he was given a brief verbal interference task, he was unable to recall any of the four words he had recalled only a few minutes earlier.

His ability to recall more meaningful information, such as two short stories, was assessed by the Logical Memories subtest of the Wechsler Memory Scale — Revised. His immediate recall of these stories tested as severely impaired; he could recall an average of only three bits of information from each story. Furthermore, his responses revealed a strong recency effect in that five of the six total bits of information recalled came from the end of the story. His ability to recall these stories, after a delay of approximately 30 min, was profoundly impaired; that is, he had no recollection of either story, despite being given several cues to try to jog his memory.

His visual memory was assessed by the Continuous Visual Memory Test, which required him to recognize pictures of objects that he had been visually presented throughout the test. His performance on this test was profoundly impaired.

Motor

He was administered the Grip Strength Test to assess the strength of his dominant and non-dominant hands. Testing revealed average strength bilaterally, without any significant lateralizing differences. His motor speed was assessed by the Finger Tapping Test. Testing revealed that his motor speed was moderate to severely impaired bilaterally, without any significant lateralizing differences. He was also administered the Grooved Pegboard Test to assess his manual dexterity and fine motor skills. His performance placed him in the moderate to severely impaired range bilaterally, and his movements were often very clumsy and awkward.

Executive Functions

He was administered a variety of tests, developed by Luria and his students, to assess ability to perform complex movements involving one or both hands that are mediated primarily by his frontal lobes. His performance on these tests was severely impaired; he demonstrated a marked inability to maintain his motor set and was simply unable to perform these tasks, despite being given considerable practice and warm-up time. Furthermore, he could perform these tasks only in an exceedingly slow manner. When he was asked to perform a three-stage motor movement with his right or left hand, his motor set quickly deteriorated into a two-stage movement without any apparent awareness on his part. To test this, the examiner asked him to evaluate his performance. His response indicated that he was completely unaware of his poor performance and inability to maintain the original motor set, even when the examiner demonstrated the correct motor set and asked him if he had been performing the same set. His ability to perform a simple motor sequencing task that required him to repetitively write M and N in a cursive manner, was severely impaired and careful analysis of his performance revealed numerous errors of perseveration.

Abstract Thinking/Conceptualization

His abstract thinking and conceptualization skills were assessed through tasks involving logical–grammatical analysis and proverb interpretation. His responses on tasks involving verbal similarities tended to be concrete. He was unable to interpret a single proverb.

Judgment

His judgment was assessed by asking him what he would do in a variety of hypothetical situations. Even though the situations that were presented to him were repeated several times and often were rephrased, his judgment was impaired. For example, when he was asked what he would do if someone he recently met offered to sell him a new car for $2000, he responded (after a lengthy delay), "Check on buying it — after another lengthy delay — get a loan on it."

Problem Solving

His problem-solving skills were assessed through tasks involving logical–grammatical analysis, mental arithmetic that required him to restructure the problem statement, and the Raven Progressive Matrices Test. Despite the fact that each of the questions was repeated several times, he indicated that he did not know the answer to any of them. Careful observation of his behavior revealed that the questions seemed too complex for him and appeared to simply overwhelm him. His performance on the Raven Progressive Matrices Test (which is an untimed test that relies heavily on the patient's visual perceptual, problem-solving skills) placed him at the 12th percentile (low average range) with respect to persons of his age.

PERSONALITY/EMOTIONAL

He was administered the Beck Depression Inventory, which required him to read 21 groups of statements and indicate which of the four statements best described the way he had been feeling during the past week, including today. He made a total score of 5 on this test, which indicates that he does not perceive himself as being depressed. He was also administered the MCMI-III to assess his long-standing personality traits and current psychiatric problems. His profile on this test revealed that he answered the test items in a manner that suggested either an unwillingness to divulge matters of a personal nature, poor introspection, or significant cognitive difficulties. Nonetheless, his profile on this test suggested that he tends to lean on others for guidance and security and is likely to assume a passive role in most relationships. While he may attempt to appear calm, these underlying tensions and emotional dysphoria are likely to create feelings of anxiety, sadness, and guilt. His complaints of weakness, fatigability, and a tendency to succumb easily to physical exhaustion suggest the possibility of an underlying depression. However, his profile did not reveal the presence of any significant psychiatric disorders or problems at this time.

Impression

The patient is a 43-year-old, right-handed white male, who had been employed as a bricklayer for the Greystone Construction Company on January 14, 1993. According to his medical records, he was working in the unventilated basement of a building, laying masonry blocks, and using a gasoline-powered concrete saw. He recalls that he felt like he was coming down with the flu and began experiencing pain in his chest, which seemed like he was having a heart attack. He also experienced breathing difficulties and fell to the ground several times, but managed to get up and continue working since it was his first day on the job and he wanted to create a favorable impression. He continued working until his foreman came in at the end of the day. His foreman telephoned the patient's wife and informed her that her husband was sick and asked her to come down and get him. She eventually obtained a ride from a neighbor to the job site and arrived approximately 1½ h later. Upon her arrival, she noticed that her husband seemed "rubberish," as well as disoriented and dazed. She helped him walk out to the car and then observed that he was unable to lift his legs to get into the car but just fell into the vehicle after she had helped him into it. Even though her husband indicated that he wanted to get home, he was taken to the emergency room of St. Mary's Hospital, where his arterial blood gas was drawn at approximately 6:05 P.M. At 6:12 P.M., his carboxyhemoglobin level was reported as 31.7. Immediately following this, he was placed in a hyperbaric oxygen chamber and was discharged at 9:35 P.M. that evening.

After he was driven home by his in-laws, he spent the entire night vomiting and complained of an excruciating headache. The next morning, he began urinating brown urine and the veins in his arms appeared dilated. He returned to the emergency room of St. Mary's Hospital where his carboxyhemoglobin level was measured again and revealed a level of only 4.1, although he admitted that he had smoked earlier that day. He was diagnosed as having post-carbon monoxide exposure.

The patient complained of having problems with coordination, slowness of motor movements, and personality changes. His wife also complained that her husband was not thinking clearly and was suffering from emotional lability. Although the patient tried to return to work on January 16, 1993, he complained of being slower on the job and had difficulty with coordination. On April 6, 1993 he was seen at his employer's request by Dr. Blumenthal, a neurologist. Over the next several weeks, he underwent a number of cognitive evaluations by a speech pathologist, which revealed that his cognitive functioning was actually deteriorating rather than improving.

Mr. Thomas continued to be followed by Dr. Blumenthal, who noted that the patient's cognitive functioning had deteriorated since the time of his carbon monoxide exposure. As a consequence, Dr. Blumenthal referred the patient to Dr. Dennis Solomon for neuropsychological testing. Dr. Solomon's report of January 7, 1994 indicated that the patient was markedly to severely impaired in virtually all of his higher mental processes, particularly on tasks involving speed of mental processing, short-term and recent memory, intelligence, problem solving, and executive functions. As a consequence, Dr. Solomon felt that this patient would be unable to work in any competitive job situation and was completely disabled.

The patient also underwent neurological examination by Dr. Derringer, Professor of Neurology at Georgia State University Medical Center on January 21, 1995, who corroborated Dr. Blumenthal's impression of dementia following carbon monoxide exposure. Dr. Derringer felt that the patient was 100% disabled for gainful employment and indicated that he did not feel that the patient would be able to work at even light duty work activities and he would not be able to live and function independently. In addition, he indicated that the patient would have difficulty carrying out even the simplest household chores and activities.

The patient underwent neuropsychological assessment by Dr. Jeremy Rankin on December 5, 1996. Dr. Rankin's report of December 10, 1996 indicated that although this patient's test results were very poor from a performance perspective and could be interpreted as evidence of severe temporal disorientation and significant deficits in attention–concentration, psychometric intelligence, general memory, and new learning, based on his clinical impression, he had doubts about the validity of these test scores, the pattern of test scores, and the patient's performance on forced-choice memory tests.

Neuropsychological testing by this examiner on February 26, 1997 revealed a similar pattern of test results that had been previously reported by both Drs. Solomon and Rankin. For example, the patient tested as severely impaired on cognitive tasks that assessed his attention–concentration, speed of cognitive and motor processing, confrontational naming, initiation, verbal fluency, verbal and visual learning, recent memory, perceptual organization, spatial organization, manual dexterity, motor speed, motor sequencing, abstract thinking, conceptualization, and executive-function skills.

It is the impression of this examiner that the neuropsychological test results obtained by this examiner, as well as by Drs. Solomon and Rankin, are the manifestations of the severe dementia resulting from the patient's carbon monoxide exposure and subsequent deterioration. A review of the carbon monoxide literature reveals that approximately 11% of the acute carbon monoxide poisoning patients admitted to hospitals develop delayed encephalopathy after a period of "pseudo recovery," lasting from 2 to 60 days. This literature indicates that the most frequent symptoms in such patients are apathy, dull facial expressions, dementia such as amnesia and disorientation, and hypokinesia. This literature also reveals that in approximately half of the cases, the EEGs of these patients are normal, because the major insult appears to be primarily subcortical, involving the globus pallidus and demyelination of white matter. MRI and case studies have shown that patients who demonstrate delayed encephalopathy will frequently develop lesions in the hippocampus, as well as the cortical grey matter, which are manifested by signs of frontal lobe dysfunction, memory disturbance, dysphasia, and visual perceptual difficulties. Unfortunately, it has been this examiner's experience that the neuropsychological or neuropsychiatric sequelae of carbon monoxide poisoning, particularly its delayed effects, are not well understood by the vast majority of neuropsychologists practicing in the community. Having seen hundreds of such patients over the past 20 years, I am familiar with the manifestations of this disorder, particularly with how it differs dramatically from the problems of patients who have sustained closed head injuries. Therefore, it comes as no surprise to this examiner that individuals who have had little or no experience will often base their opinions on their expectations and experiences with patients who have sustained either strokes or closed head injuries. They will frequently misdiagnose these patients, and even perceive them as malingering because these patients do not demonstrate the typical improvements seen in stroke or closed head injury patients within the first 6 months postinjury. Although I regard Dr. Rankin as a competent neuropsychologist, based on his training and background, I suspect that his opinions in this case reflect his limited experience with carbon monoxide patients.

Patients who sustain subcortical brain damage as a result of carbon monoxide exposure will typically develop the following cognitive and behavioral symptoms: poor performance on automatic or well-learned tasks; exceedingly long response latencies; markedly diminished auditory capacity, particularly with respect to the amount and rate of information processed; poor ability to retrieve recently acquired information; markedly decreased speed of cognitive processing; severe temporal disorientation; poor visual scanning; marked motor slowness; and incoordination in the face of relatively intact verbal communication and language comprehension skills. However, when such patients develop delayed encephalopathies, they typically demonstrate more evidence of frontal lobe dysfunction, dementia, dysphasia, and visual perceptual difficulties. It is my opinion that this patient has shown clear evidence of these neurobehavioral sequelae and is severely demented as a result of his carbon monoxide exposure and subsequent delayed encephalopathy. As a result of his severe cognitive and behavioral impairments, he should be considered completely disabled from any competitive employment. Because of the etiology of his condition, his age, and the duration of time since his original neurological insult, I would not expect any improvement in his condition. In fact, I would expect his condition to worsen over the next 10 to 15 years, as his remaining healthy brain cells begin to die with advancing age.

I am very concerned about this patient's wife, who unfortunately has been forced to bear the entire burden of her husband's disability. This has caused her to become anxious, depressed, and hypertensive, as well as to develop ulcers and sleep difficulties. I fear that unless his wife receives some counseling and psychiatric treatment, as well as assistance in caring for her husband, she will be unable to care for her husband and become a casualty herself.

LEYLAND CASSIDY, PH.D.

Critique

Dr. Cassidy's comprehensive and well-written report contains information from Mr. Thomas and his wife, a description of the injury, a careful review of Mr. Thomas' academic and medical records, observation of Mr. Thomas' behavior during the interview and testing, and a quantitative and qualitative analysis of Mr. Thomas' test performances. Dr. Cassidy attempts to integrate the diverse opinions of the two other neuropsychologists who had previously examined Mr. Thomas and obtained similar test findings. The strength of Dr. Cassidy's report appears to be his understanding of the acute and delayed effects of carbon monoxide exposure on the brain based on his experience with such patients. While Dr. Rankin is a competent neuropsychologist, his unfamiliarity with the neurobehavioral sequelae of carbon monoxide exposure placed him in a position where he interpreted Mr. Thomas' neuropsychological test data as malingering since the information did not fit his expectations of recovery following a traumatic brain injury (i.e., the traumatically brain-injured patient is expected to improve over time rather than get worse).

Dr. Cassidy's careful review of the medical records clearly documents Mr. Thomas' deteriorating cognitive and behavioral functioning within the time course that is expected for this particular neurobehavioral syndrome. His understanding of the subcortical manifestations of carbon monoxide exposure was particularly helpful in assisting the trier of fact understand Mr. Thomas' unique cognitive and behavioral impairments. While this report is quite long, it integrates all of the sources of information and data in a clear and cogent manner.

SAMPLE #6

February 18, 1991

Matthew Riley, Esq.
Law Offices of Riley and Bannister
1400 Kensington Boulevard
Second Floor
Providence, Rhode Island

RE: Shirley Simmons

Dear Mr. Riley:
Your client, Shirley Simmons, was seen in this office on 2-6-91 per your request. She presented as a rather confused 23-year-old, right-handed female in no acute distress. She was accompanied by her mother.

CHIEF COMPLAINTS AS OBTAINED FROM PATIENT

1. Unable to find a job.
2. Unable to be viewed as a "person."
3. "My left arm and leg don't work like they should."
4. "Head pain — feels like my head is in a vice at times."
5. "Can't shave left armpit or hold my pet rabbit with my left hand."

Additional Complaints from the Patient's Mother

1. Shirley exhibits frequent mood swings.
2. Shirley frequently exhibits angry feelings that are frequently directed toward her or her siblings.
3. Shirley has no concept of time or money.
4. Shirley has exhibited a loss of initiative and motivation since the accident.
5. Shirley's judgment is poor.
6. Shirley changes her clothes constantly.
7. Shirley's preexisting personality problems and habits have intensified since her accident.
8. She has difficulty with interpersonal relationships.
9. Shirley's goals and expectations are inappropriate.
10. Shirley's language is often vulgar or inappropriate.
11. Shirley fails to follow through on things.
12. Shirley exhibits attention and concentration difficulties.
13. Shirley has a history of suicide attempts since the accident.
14. Shirley is unable to drive since the accident.
15. Shirley is unable to use her left arm since the accident.
16. Shirley has become aggressive/violent at times since the accident.
17. Shirley's recent memory has become impaired since the accident.
18. Shirley requires considerable time for personal grooming, dressing, etc., as a result of her dysfunctional left arm and leg.

HISTORY OF INJURY AS OBTAINED FROM THE PATIENT

Ms. Simmons believes that she was driving her car to school on February, 11, 1987. She has no recollection of the accident. She believes that she woke up at Langdon Community Hospital. She believes that this occurred approximately 2½ months following her motor vehicle accident. She believes that she went home in August 1987, where she was cared for by her mother. She believes that she was transferred to the New Brunswick Traumatic Brain Injury Program in Pennsylvania in September 1988. She believes that she was later transferred to the Renew Brain Injury Rehabilitation Program in Arkansas, where she believes she spent approximately 1½ undergoing extensive rehabilitation. After her discharge home, she continued to receive outpatient psychotherapy that she describes as "bitch sessions."

INTERVIEW WITH PATIENT'S MOTHER

The patient's mother was interviewed on February 6, 1991. She indicated that prior to her daughter's accident, her daughter loved music, her brothers, and animals. While she tended to have a chip on her shoulder, she was generally thoughtful and affectionate toward others. She thought, however, that she was fat, unattractive, and not intelligent. She had only one close friend other than her older brother, but had lots of acquaintances. She was never really sure where she fit in, as she put it, and at times appeared despondent.

Her mother indicated that since her daughter's accident, her short-term memory had become poor. While her attention span and concentration skills were not particularly good prior to her accident, her mother claimed that these problems had markedly intensified. Her reading comprehension skills were poor. Her writing was particularly difficult to read because she could not hold the paper with her left hand. Her math was poor, but her mother claimed that she was never good in arithmetic. She had observed coordination and balance difficulties. At the emotional level, her mother felt that while her daughter did not become tearful, she had emotions but was unable to express them. Her mother felt that the patient did not see herself as having any problems. The patient frequently displayed considerable anger toward her siblings.

The patient's mother appeared very depressed during her interview and broke down and cried several times. She indicated that she had been accused by her sons as having become a martyr. She also admitted that she had not had any type of personal life and had not dated since her daughter's accident. She had also gained over 30 pounds. Her self-esteem had deteriorated. She found herself feeling extremely protective toward her daughter. She also found it difficult to cope with her daughter's numerous deficits.

Because of Mrs. Simmons' apparent emotional problems that appeared to stem from her daughter's accident and subsequent cognitive, emotional, and behavioral difficulties, she was asked to complete the MCMI-II to assess her current emotional functioning and personality traits. A computerized printout of her scores indicated a profile characterized by marked dependency needs, an anxious seeking of attention and reassurance from others, and intense fear of separation from those who provide support. Her dependency strivings were seen as causing her to be overly compliant, to be self-sacrificing, to downplay her personal strengths and attributes, and often to place herself in inferior or demeaning roles. More recently, significant relationships had become increasingly insecure and unreliable, which had caused her to experience increased moodiness, prolonged periods of futility and dejection, and episodes of intense anxiety, as well as to seek out concrete situations to which she could attach her general feelings of unworthiness. She was seen as a self-denying, self-debasing, and pessimistic individual, who was likely to vacillate between being socially agreeable, sullen, aggrieved, passive–aggressive, and contrite. She was seen as exhibiting self-defeating habits, likely to have the attitude that she deserved to suffer, and likely to alienate those upon whom she depended. When threatened by separation or disapproval, she was seen as likely to express guilt and self-condemnation in the hope of regaining support, reassurance, and sympathy.

Mrs. Simmons was seen as feeling helpless, experiencing anxious periods and prolonged depressive moods, and experiencing feelings of emptiness and loneliness and recurrent thoughts of death and suicide, which were expressions of her low self-esteem, preoccupations with her failures, physical unattractiveness, guilt, and feelings of unworthiness. Although she complained about being mistreated, she was likely to assert that she deserved mental anguish and abuse. Such self-debasement was consistent with her self-image, as was tolerance and perpetuation of relationships that fostered and aggravated her misery. This insecure and troubled woman reported a variety of symptoms that included an anxiety disorder in addition to a major depression. In addition, she was likely to experience periodic panic attacks and agoraphobia. Expecting the worst to happen, she not only looked for confirmation, but might have precipitated events that generate self-defeating stressors that further intensified her anxieties. On the basis of this test, it can be assumed that this patient was experiencing severe psychological problems that varied depending on the presence of external stressors (e.g., her daughter's behavior).

BACKGROUND

Developmental

Shirley Simmons was born in Applegate, Wisconsin, as the product of a full-term, uncomplicated delivery. She weighed 8 pounds, 9 ounces at birth. Her mother denies using alcohol or smoking during her pregnancy. The family moved to Rhode Island when Shirley was 4 years old. Her mother reports that while Shirley was somewhat late in her walking, her language, toilet training, and overall development were generally normal. As a child, Shirley began exhibiting attention and concentration difficulties when she was in the first grade. She had a history of reading difficulties, however her mother does not believe that Shirley was ever diagnosed as having dyslexia. Her mother denied that Shirley had a childhood history of clumsiness, frequent ear infections, head injury, hearing problems, hyperactivity, muscle tightness or weakness, speech problems, or visual difficulties. Shirley had a history of chicken pox.

Her mother indicated that Shirley sustained several head injuries as a result of falls that produced lacerations in her head that necessitated taking her to the emergency room, where she received several stitches. Her mother, however, denied that Shirley had ever been rendered unconscious as a result of any of these injuries or exhibited symptoms such as headaches, vomiting, mental confusion, irritability, lethargy, or forgetfulness following these injuries. While Shirley was never psychologically or physically abused as a child, her mother indicated that Shirley was sexually fondled when she was 12 by her biological father, who apparently touched her breasts while she was lying in bed. Shirley described her childhood as "OK" and believed that she was generally happy. She described herself as a "daddy's girl." She described her father as a quiet, soft spoken, and passive individual.

Family History

Her parents divorced when she was 16. Her mother is a 47-year-old floral designer who is a high school graduate and has completed floral design school. Her mother indicated that she, herself, was physically and psychologically abused during her childhood by her alcoholic mother. The patient's father is a 48-year-old high school graduate who is employed as a senior sales assistant. The patient's father was described as an introverted man who has a history of bisexuality. While he apparently was warm and close to his children during their early years, his wife indicated that he became emotionally withdrawn from them as he became older, arguing that his own father died when he was ten. The patient's mother had never remarried. The patient has two brothers who are 19 and 24 years of age.

The patient's father and paternal grandmother have a history of sinistrality. The patient's maternal great-grandmother has a history of Parkinson's disease. The patient's maternal grandmother has a history of alcoholism. The patient was raised by her biological parents who are both fluent in English.

Education

The patient is a high school graduate, although she reported that school was "a challenge" and described herself as being a below average student. When asked why she did not get better grades, she stated that she was a "frequent daydreamer" in class and was not popular among her peers. She also indicated that she was often easily hurt by criticism. While in school, she was placed in reading improvement classes. She reported, however, that her weakest subject in school was mathematics. She denied, however, that she had ever been held back or placed in any special education or remedial classes.

Occupational History

The patient is currently unemployed due to her disability. Prior to her accident, she worked as a telephone operator for Target for approximately 2 months. She worked as a receptionist for a health spa for over a year and was employed as a waitress for approximately 6 months. She denied any work-related injuries or that she had ever been exposed to any toxic, hazardous, noxious, or unusual substances during the course of her employment.

Military

The patient denied that she has ever served in the military.

Recreation

Prior to her accident, she enjoyed jogging, swimming, and social activities with friends.

Marital History

The patient is single and has never been married. She denied a history of dating or sexual intercourse prior to her injury. She admitted that she did not see herself as being attractive or intelligent prior to her accident. She also indicated that she feared being rejected by males and was easily hurt by criticism.

Substance Abuse History

The patient claims that she used alcohol only once in her life while she was in her freshman year in college. She denies ever experimenting with recreational drugs or nonprescribed medications.

REVIEW OF ACADEMIC RECORDS

The patient's academic records were reviewed. These records indicate that she had a Thorndike–Lorge IQ of 90, which placed her in the low end of the normal range of intellectual functioning. A review of her academic transcript revealed that she had consistently been a below average student and had received Cs and Ds, which appears to reflect her level of intellectual functioning and passive–aggressive and dysthymic personality traits.

REVIEW OF MEDICAL RECORDS

The discharge summary of Rhode Island State University Hospital indicated that the patient was admitted on February 11, 1987 and was discharged on March 24, 1987 with the diagnosis of multiple trauma. At the time of her admission, she was noted to be a 19-year-old white female with decerebrate posturing of all extremities, the left being greater than the right. Physical examination revealed a right frontal abrasion, left parietal laceration with boggy scalp and a 6 cm laceration. Neurological examination revealed decerebrate movements of the left arm. She had purposeful responses of the right leg and arm to pain. She was noted to be comatose. Her pupils were equal and reacted to light with roving eye movements. The patient's breathing was assisted with a ventilator.

The patient underwent a CT scan that showed a small amount of blood in the right basal ganglion area. She was taken to the Intensive Care Unit, where she was placed on Mannitol and Decadron and was hyperventilated. She continued to have more decerebrate activities of both sides that evening and had a repeat CT scan that demonstrated an increase in the size of the right intracerebral hematoma with significant midline shift. At that time, she was taken for an emergency craniotomy with evacuation of the clots. During surgery, a ventriculostomy was performed for intracerebral pressure monitoring. Postoperatively, she remained unchanged. She continued to have decerebrate movements of her left side to noxious stimuli while her right side had spontaneous movements that were semipurposeful. She had a dysconjugate gaze and roving eye movements. Her intracranial pressure remained at 7 to 10 with good drainage. She was continued on hyperventilation as well as Mannitol and Decadron.

She was slowly being weaned from the ventilator and underwent a tracheostomy on February 18, 1987. She suffered a pneumothorax from left central venous line placement and underwent chest tube placement with good lung reexpansion. She continued to be weaned off the ventilator and slowly weaned off Mannitol. Her repeat CT scans showed resolution of the right intracerebral hematoma. Sputum cultures were positive for staph aureus, and she was started on Keflin and Gentamicin for 2 weeks. She continued to undergo physical therapy and some rehabilitation. At the time of her discharge, her neurological status improved to the point that she opened her eyes spontaneously and could follow some commands and move her right side purposefully. Her left side continued to be spastic.

The records of Langdon Community Hospital indicated that the patient was admitted from Rhode Island State University Hospital on March 24, 1987 and remained hospitalized until August 11, 1987. These records note that at the time of her admission, she exhibited some right-sided purposeful movement. She was admitted with a tracheostomy, a G-tube, and Foley catheter in place. She had a neurogenic bowel and bladder. A follow-up CT scan on March 25, 1987 showed marked overall improvement with diminished mass affect of the right lateral ventricles and minimal midline shift. Because of the neurological deficits and neurogenic bowel and bladder, the patient was left functionally impaired with diminished mobility and ability to perform her ADL skills. For this reason, she was admitted to Providence Regional Rehabilitation Center for a comprehensive inpatient physical rehabilitation program to improve her level of independence and functional status. Upon admission to this program, she was totally dependent in her care and unable to be mobile or walk. Upon discharge, she was ambulating with moderate assistance, predominantly on her noninvolved right lower extremity. She had a spastic left upper and lower extremity that interfered with her progress. She was noted to have cognitive deficits with problems in attention and memory, which also interfered with her progress. As a consequence, she required verbal cuing when preparing for transfers, particularly when going too fast from a sitting to a standing position.

The Social Work Assessment Report, dated March 25, 1987, indicated that at the time the patient was injured she was a freshman at Rhode Island State University and was coming from a babysitting job to class. The patient's mother described her as an "average" student, but stated that, "If Shirley likes something, she really does well. Shirley has problems in mathematics. It's her least favorite subject." She enjoyed athletics and was a runner.

Prior to starting college, she was working at a health spa. In college, her major was child development. According to her mother, she had hoped to open a child care center one day. Her parents had been separated for about 3 years and divorced for 2 years. Mr. Simmons is a senior sales representative, while Mrs. Simmons is self-employed. The patient has two brothers. The patient's family appears to have had major crises over the past few years, including divorce of the patient's parents and Shirley's accident. In spite of this, Mrs. Simmons appears to have an understanding of the patient's circumstances and rehabilitation process. The patient received counseling at age 12, after her mother overreacted to Shirley's comments about hurting herself.

The initial evaluation report of Barbara Hunt, M.A., C.C.C., dated November 24, 1987, indicated that the patient had been admitted to the Sunland Health Care Center on November 4, 1987. Prior to her admission, she had been residing with her mother and two brothers and had been receiving outpatient physical therapy, occupational therapy, and speech treatment on a twice-a-week basis. Testing revealed moderate deficits in problem identification, goal formation, selection of appropriate alternatives to a given problem, prioritization of solutions to a given problem, simultaneous processing of information as related to "comparison of presented items/similarities/differences," and determination of the main idea of a complex visual picture arrangement and lengthy paragraph presentation. Conversational discourse throughout the evaluation was often characterized by inappropriate verbalizations, numerous off-topic remarks, and frequent attempts to shift the topic of conversation. She was easily verbally redirected to the task with repetition of task expectation while simultaneously ignoring inappropriate utterances.

The notes of Steven Lorimar, M.D., Family Practice, dated November 18, 1987, indicated that the patient had suicidal thoughts even before her injury when she attempted to commit suicide at home 3 years before her accident. Prior to this, the patient had been noted to be depressed. Dr. Lorimar's notes of December 9, 1987 indicated that the patient has multiple minor complaints but is basically depressed and knows her functional limitations. She has a sad looking expression and has significant instability in her left ankle, which prevents her from walking.

The psychosocial evaluation report of Peter Cunningham, A.C.S.W., dated December 3, 1987 stated that at the time of her admission to Sunland, she was noted to have a Rancho Los Amigos level of VI to VII. After the patient returned home following her hospitalization, she was noted to be very impulsive, immature, and lacking in common sense/judgment. She also began to experience increasing conflict with her mother, with her premorbid dynamics coming significantly into play.

According to her parents, they divorced in 1983 after 26 years of marriage. Their marriage had been in trouble for a number of years. There still remains a considerable amount of mutually shared bitterness and antagonism. Infidelity, incompatibility, and interpersonal/emotional problems were the primary reasons cited for the divorce. The patient has two siblings, an older brother, Randy (24), and a younger brother, Brian (19). Her older brother is attending Western State University and resides on campus. He and Shirley were rather close prior to the accident. Shirley and her younger brother have more conflict between them and have been quite sensitive to the amount of parental attention the other has received.

Both parents reported that Shirley's emotional problems first became evident at age six, when she was moved into a separate bedroom, away from her baby brother, Brian. The separation came as a result of a family move to a new home. Following this, Shirley experienced a developmental regression and returned to thumb sucking, obsessive interest in her stuffed animals, and clinging behavior indicative of insecurity. Due to her thumb sucking, she developed an overbite that required several years of braces during the third and fourth grades. These problems led to a significant loss of self-esteem with resulting interpersonal problems. She considered herself an "ugly duckling" who often preferred solitary activities.

She was also described as accident-prone. She was described by her mother as being very sensitive, caring of others, but flighty and tending to be unable to finish anything she started. When she was 12, she was referred for counseling due to increased signs of maladjustment and mounting depression. When she was 17 after her parents' divorce, she cut both of her wrists, although not deeply, after writing her parents a suicide note. In that note, she expressed feelings of worthlessness and of being a burden on them. She also developed early signs of an eating disorder with bulimic-like behavior. Meanwhile, Shirley's father had moved in with his girlfriend; Mrs. Simmons became quite depressed and sought counseling and relief through medication.

Although Shirley was described as a poor student, she graduated from high school and enrolled in Rhode Island State University. She apparently had difficulty adjusting to life away from home and the academic demands of college course work. Compounding an already stress-ridden first year was illness, during which time she contracted mononucleosis causing her to withdraw from school and move back home. She tried to return to school during the fall of 1985.

Shirley had never dated while a teenager but was beginning to show interest in boys while in college. She became particularly fond of a young man who visited the health spa where she was employed. They never dated, but a friendship had developed. After her head injury, she became infatuated with the desire to see this boy, who is presently attending school in another county. Her cognitive deficits, coupled with her strong premorbid desires, led to very obsessive and unrealistic behavior on her part. It was the opinion of Mr. Cunningham that this boy served as a rescue figure which was based more on fantasy than reality. Shirley had interest in sports and exercise and competed on the track team at her high school. However, she was not a star athlete. She enjoyed popular and rock music. Pets were important to her, particularly her many rabbits. She did not smoke or consume alcohol on a regular basis. In addition, she was not involved in many community activities or organizations.

The initial rehabilitation progress report, dated December 4, 1987, of the New Brunswick Neurologic Center at Sunland indicated that shortly after admission, Shirley was described by staff as demonstrating attention-seeking behavior such as ringing the call button repeatedly. Concerns were also noted regarding verbalizations about suicide and were relayed to the consulting psychiatrist who recommended suicide precautions and antidepressant medications. She received five individual counseling sessions. She showed signs of poor self-esteem with an overinfatuation with stuffed animals and males. Difficulties about eating continued to be present. She exhibited an unrealistic body image. Individual counseling would continue to focus on her self-esteem and body image. There was also concern to monitor behaviors with regard to depression and expression of suicide.

While she has made satisfactory adjustment to the program, she was placed on Aventyl, an antidepressant medication, due to signs of depression. Her emotional problems (poor self-image, depression, family conflicts particularly with her mother) are of a long-standing nature. They have only been complicated and intensified by the cognitive sequelae following her February 11, 1987 closed head injury.

The report of Joel Davidson, M.D., dated December 15, 1987, indicated that behaviorally Shirley demonstrated a very insecure image. She had a low opinion of herself and of her capabilities in the future. She was often depressed. She was cooperative but needed minimal redirection on occasion. She exhibited occasional problems with word finding. She demonstrated appropriate communication skills. She was also oriented to day, month, year, and season. Her basic verbal comprehension was appropriate. She was able to follow directions, verbally and written, at the two-step level. She could identify parts of the body, recognize colors, and letters and numbers in different forms.

Ms. Simmons demonstrated preacademic skills in reading and mathematics. On the Key Math Diagnostic Profile, she scored at a grade level of 5.2 and demonstrated deficits in the areas of numeration, fractions, mental computations, and numerical reasoning. She demonstrated deficits in the areas of problem solving which required abstractions using short-term and long-term memory simultaneously. Sequencing of more than three steps presented a problem for her. In the area of problem identification, she exhibited significant deficits in her ability to take key salient features and distinguish them from irrelevant material. She presented no problems in her basic reading skills. Her reading comprehension and general information skills placed her within the normal range. She did, however, show deficits in her ability to work with expressive language components, as well as word-finding difficulties. She also had difficulty summarizing a paragraph. She exhibited difficulty in reading tasks that require high abstraction and a working memory. Her therapist concluded that from a cognitive standpoint, she demonstrates difficulties in her problem-solving skills, abstract thinking, and memory.

The neuropsychological evaluation report of Robert Gordon, Ph.D., and Patrick Jennings, Ph.D., dated April 28, 1988, indicated that the patient's performance on measures of cognitive functioning was found to be consistent with her having a history of closed head injury. Her performance on tests of basic attention and concentration was moderately to severely impaired for her age and grade level. While her ability to respond to timed demands of a simple visual tracking task was mildly impaired, she was severely impaired on a more demanding conceptual tracking task where she was required to shift her attention. She was unable to effectively utilize verbal feedback to bring her back on track while performing this latter task. In addition to conceptual confusion, her performance reflected impairments in motor speed, coordination, and visual scanning. She also demonstrated poor mental efficiency that was supported by severely impaired performance on tasks requiring the conversion of geometric designs into written and oral numbers. The examiners noted that her severe performance on these latter tasks was a negative predictor for success in a high demand work environment and that her lack of persistence and vigilance would predict poor occupational adjustment.

Ms. Simmons tested as severely impaired in her eye–hand coordination and fine motor dexterity. She also tested as severely impaired in terms of her motor speed. However, it was not possible to test her nondominant left hand due to paralysis. When using her intact right hand, she was able to manipulate items but several times lost the sequence of placement of the various test pieces.

Her performance indicated that when she was confronted with fine motor dexterity tasks, she would require more time than normal to complete the task successfully.

Her performance on tasks of visuoperceptual and visuospatial functioning were quite variable. When she was asked to recognize fragmented representations of common objects, she tested as moderately impaired. Her ability to visually scan and attend to detail was noted to be in the severely impaired range when she was asked to find and manually cancel out one of two target letters within an array of letters. Although her response times were slow and reflected a deliberate response style, there was no sign of neglect for space in either the left or right visual fields. The examiners also noted that she was likely to lose detailed information if she were presented with tasks that required conceptual manipulation or mediation. Under these conditions, she was expected to become careless and distracted by her own internal confusion.

Her ability to recall orally presented, meaningful information was found to be relatively intact; however, she tested as moderately impaired in terms of her ability to recall lists of words. Her ability to retain learned information after a brief distraction or over passage of time was found to be poor. Her visual memory was found to be severely impaired.

Ms. Simmons tested as grossly intact in her language comprehension and spontaneous expression. Her conversational speech was generally fluid and adequately organized. In the functional context of communicating with others, she did not exhibit evidence of any difficulty in finding words or expressing her thoughts.

Her ability to solve arithmetic problems without the benefit of paper and pencil was mildly impaired. She was noted to be severely impaired in her ability to "shift sets" during problem-solving tasks and was unable to correctly identify the principle of a simple matching task. Her responses reflected a perseverative style, indicating problems in her ability to form concepts. She also demonstrated inflexibility in her responses.

On the WAIS-R, she obtained a verbal IQ of 72, a performance IQ of 63, and a full-scale IQ of 74, which placed her overall level of intellectual functioning in the borderline range. Her scores on the performance subtests indicated that she may frequently misinterpret subtle social cues or nonverbal behaviors. She tested poorly when she was asked to convert numbers into abstract unfamiliar symbols. Her performance on this test indicated that she was unable to learn new and familiar symbols and had a difficult time sustaining her attention and concentration. Her performance on this test indicated impaired functioning in her right cerebral hemisphere. She was diagnosed as having an organic personality syndrome characterized by adynamia. The examiners felt that she was a good candidate for a residentially based facility that focused on maximizing skills of independent living. They felt that the patient would benefit from a course of intensive rehabilitation in order to focus on developing functional life competencies. Although they did not feel that she would be a candidate for independent living at this time, her current abilities indicated that she may benefit from continuing rehabilitation efforts.

The discharge summary of New Brunswick Rehabilitation and Skilled Nursing Center indicated that the patient was discharged on September 3, 1988 and that she had made excellent progress with regard to her physical, occupational, and cognitive therapies.

The records of Renew, Inc., indicated that the patient was admitted to the program on September 5, 1988. At the time of her admission, she was noted to ambulate fairly slowly and deliberately. She was oriented to person, place, and day, but had difficulty with the date and year. Her left pupil was slightly larger than her right. She was hemiparetic on the left. She had a foot drop on the left and some increased muscle tone, particularly in the left upper extremity and possibly contractures of the left hand. Her left upper extremity was essentially nonfunctional. She had clonus in the left lower extremity. While her strength on the right was very good, it was noted to be very poor on the left. Her left leg was somewhat stronger than her left arm. She was given the diagnosis of status postclosed head injury with right-sided hematoma, depressed skull fracture, status postcraniotomy for evacuation of the hematoma, status posttracheostomy resolved, status post-G-tube resolved, history of depression that preceded her head injury, cognitive deficits including short-term memory difficulties, and left hemiparesis.

The assessment report of Rachel Perkins, O.T.R., dated September 6, 1988, indicated that the patient displayed some short-term memory deficits. Ms. Simmons was oriented with the exception of day of the month and year. She was easily distracted and appeared to use humor as a means of minimizing and coping with her current limitations. She displayed moderate–severe perceptual deficits involving size, location, and space discrimination. She also displayed deficits in visual sequential memory exercises. She requires supervision for safety in shower tasks and verbal cuing to wash herself in correct sequences. She ambulates with the use of a cane. Her left shoulder is subluxed approximately 3/4 to 1 inches. She wore a sling to help approximate her shoulder. Her left hand was nonfunctional. She was identified as having problems with her short-term memory, perceptual deficits, decreased use of the left side of her body, and decreased muscle strength proximally on the right side of her body (shoulder). Her goals are to be able to jog again and to return home.

The initial psychological assessment report of Pamela Herald, M.S., dated September 13, 1988, indicated that the patient's scanning appeared to be within normal limits. Ms. Simmons reported that she is unable to see regular print very well and that her eyes often feel strained. Her eye–hand coordination was within normal limits. She was able to recall five digits forward and five digits backward. She easily remembered three objects after removal from her sight. Her speech was low in volume, but her expressive and receptive language seemed to be generally in keeping with her education and experience. Her judgment tended to be impulsive, but she was able to remain on topic. She seemed eager to discuss a variety of topics. She seemed to have a sharp wit conversationally, when comfortable in a situation. She appeared to block specific information that was contrary to her held opinions. At times she showed maturity of thought, but her emotional immaturity seemed to block her intellectual processes. She was somewhat outspoken in her desire to make her thoughts known. She tended to be offended easily and to feel very unattractive, somehow not measuring up to her mother's or other's expectations. She was very concerned about attention by or interest in the opposite sex. She had become attracted to a young man who resided in a building close to hers and became very nurturing in her attitude toward him. (Note: With the exception of the Digit Span and Informal Memory Tests, no formal psychological or neuropsychological testing was included within this report.)

The report of Terrence Gilmore, M.D. (psychiatric evaluation), dated December 20, 1988, noted that when the patient was first seen following her admission, she complained of feeling depressed and having little energy. On examination, Ms. Simmons exhibited a dense left hemiparesis and left grasp, a left Hoffmann, and left palmomental reflex and right sock. She had diffuse hyperreflexia, especially on the left. Neuropsychological evaluation showed significant deficits in motor coordination and speed, even on the right. Deficits were also shown on the Wisconsin Card Sorting Test and the Benton Visual Retention Test. A review of an EEG study revealed a slow wave focus in the right frontal and temporal lobe. A review of her CT scan revealed hemorrhage in the internal capsule, especially on the right. She has had no seizures. She continues to have difficulties with a very negative attitude, lack of interest and motivation in things, feelings of depression, and suicidal talk.

The case conference report (Renew, Inc.), dated March 14, 1989, noted that the patient's frustration tolerance had increased. Ms. Simmons had difficulty with self-initiation, but she responded well to peer pressure. In a cooking group, she exhibited problems with initiation. Time management was also an issue with her ADL. A timer was being used to assist with this. She needed cues to get to class on time and remember personal items. She exhibited problems with self-esteem. She showed improvement in her weight bearing. She made inappropriate remarks during group discussions but responded well to redirection. She showed improvement in tasks involving sustained attention and retaining information.

The occupational therapy discharge report, dated May 2, 1989, indicated that Ms. Simmons displayed some short-term memory deficits. She was oriented with the exception of the day of the month and year. She was easily distracted and appeared to use humor as a means of minimizing and coping with her current limitations. She displayed moderate to severe perceptual deficits involving size, location, and space discrimination. She also displayed deficits in visual sequential memory exercises. She required supervision for safety in shower tasks and verbal cuing to wash herself in correct sequence. She ambulated with the use of a cane. Her left shoulder was subluxed approximately ≤3/4. She wore a sling to help approximate her shoulder. Her left hand was nonfunctional. Increased tone was present in the wrist and hand.

The Social Services discharge report, dated May 5, 1989, indicated that at the time of her admission, she appeared to have a hypercritical relationship with her mother, which appeared to be a hostile dependent relationship. There appeared to have been significant family problems even prior to her accident. She was described by family members as manipulative. Some of this was evident on her admission. She also appeared to have a poor self-concept and a poor body image. While she maintained contact with both parents, her relationship with her brothers had become very distant. During the course of therapy, she made several suicidal gestures and would become sarcastic and refuse therapies. However, overall she became more cooperative and seemed to gain some insight into her problems. As a consequence, her initial negativism and sarcasm appeared to decrease and her suicidal ideation appeared to have subsided. Nonetheless, she continued to be somewhat manipulative and had difficulty with initiation and motivation. She also tended to overreact and had some difficulty with obsessing. She demonstrated excellent communication skills and was very personable and friendly.

The psychological treatment discharge report, dated May 14, 1989, indicated that the patient had a number of premorbid psychological problems that included depressive tendencies, poor self-image and body image problems, a tendency to be complaining and critical of others, and impaired family and peer relationships. She also exhibited a number of cognitive difficulties, particularly with short-term memory and ability to initiate tasks. During her treatment, she exhibited poor emotional coping skills manifested as aggressive and self-destructive behaviors. She frequently expressed violent feelings/threats toward others, primarily other clients. However, she struck or attempted to strike the direct care staff on only three or four occasions and did not strike any other clients. She occasionally made suicidal statements and exhibited one suicidal gesture: she barely scratched her throat, reportedly with a dull razor blade. This was related to a disappointment with a romantic interest. She showed a pattern of developing a romantic "crush" on one male at a time and of investing a great deal of energy and attention in the relationship, even though her romantic feelings were not reciprocated, apparently a long-standing problem.

She admitted to strong preference for males and formed no significant bonds with female peers, although she appeared superficially friendly with some female peers. Her primary personal goals included forming a romantic relationship, marriage, and the traditional role of housewife and mother. She resisted the attempts of the staff to refocus herself more on self-orientation such as self-appreciation, independent living skills, and career goals. She tended to view self-love and self-appreciation as undesirable qualities and viewed goals for independent functioning negatively as meaning that she would have to live alone.

Her premorbid eating disorder symptoms remained in remission although an overall increase in her appetite and weight was noted during her stay. Although she made progress in recognizing and curbing some of her maladaptive behaviors, she was not able to completely control them. She was unable to initiate behaviors necessary to achieve her goals in spite of expressing good motivation and confidence in her abilities. As a consequence, she displayed significant residual problems initiating tasks.

The occupational therapy evaluation report of Laura Williams, O.T.R., dated June 15, 1989, indicated that the patient reported needing assistance for housekeeping skills, preparing food, managing finances, shopping, and doing laundry. Ms. Simmons was not able to identify obstacles to participation and interest nor was she able to identify specific short-term goals, except to work toward improving her left arm function. She was able to relate some information during the evaluation, but showed difficulty remembering events from her recent past. While she has made much improvement, she continues to require continued intense rehabilitation.

The letter of Leonard Benton, M.D., dated August 29, 1989, indicated that Ms. Simmons demonstrated some decreased attention skills, decreased memory skills, decreased abstract thinking skills, impulsivity, and a tendency toward periodic problems with depression, due to the patient's traumatic brain injury. Additionally, she exhibited a tendency toward concrete thinking. She demonstrated awareness of her actions and of the impact her actions/decisions have on herself and others. She was capable of making realistic and rational decisions when provided with the necessary information and options. Dr. Benton felt that the patient was competent to make decisions regarding her legal responsibilities, particularly if these responsibilities were explained to her in such a manner that she could consider them clearly. (It should be noted that patients who sustain severe traumatic brain injuries, such as has occurred in the case of this patient, are frequently able to verbalize plans and intentions, but are unable to initiate them or carry through with them. It should be noted that these specific problems have been clearly identified by many of her treating therapists. It should also be noted that based on a review of the above records, it is highly unlikely that this patient would be able to make decisions that are appropriate for her welfare in the absence of external cues and structure.)

The report of Adam Brinton, Jr., M.D., dated November 27, 1990, indicated that his neurologic examination revealed the patient to be alert, oriented, and cooperative, but with a flat affect and monotonic speech. He noted that elements of behavior throughout the interview were consistent with frontal lobe release mechanisms and regressive elements. Motor examination showed left hemiparesis. Dr. Brinton felt that the patient exhibited evidence of bilateral brain dysfunction, which influenced her intellectual functioning, judgment, memory, insight, and affect. He also noted that the way her left arm is carried reveals an element of anosognosia or a physiologic inattention to the left side of her body due to the brain injury in the right parietal area. The patient underwent an MRI study, which indicated significant and considerable loss of brain tissue in the right posterior frontal, right mid-temporal, and right basal ganglia and right anterior parietal lobe. In addition, there was brain injury in the left superoparietal occipital area. Dr. Brinton felt that the degree of brain damage or dysfunction was sufficient to produce impairment of intellectualization, insight, judgment, affect, and behavior, as well as superimposed motor deficits. He felt that these problems had become permanent and stationary. He felt that the patient would be employable at a semi-sheltered environment where her behavioral and cognitive deficits could be compensated by sheltered workshops.

The Emergency Care Center report of Dr. Ogilvie, dated December 12, 1990, indicated that the patient came in because of chest pain. While being driven home by a smoker, she had had a hard time tolerating the cigarette smoke. She has no history of chest disease. She denied shortness of breath. She also denied nausea, vomiting, diarrhea and dysuria, urgency, frequency, or hematuria. She was discharged home in a satisfactory condition after she felt better.

BEHAVIORAL OBSERVATIONS

The patient presented as an alert, oriented, 23-year-old, right-handed female in no acute distress. Ms. Simmons arrived at 8:45 A.M. accompanied by her mother. She was oriented to person, place, time, and purpose. She did not appear significantly depressed or anxious. Her affect appeared flat. Her speech had a monotone quality. There was no evidence of word-finding or expressive or receptive language difficulties. She exhibited left-sided hemiparesis that appeared to be more prominent in her left upper extremity than her left lower extremity. She walked with the assistance of a cane and various braces on her left leg. She also exhibited left-sided facial paresis.

Her thinking was noted to be mildly circumstantial and tangential. At times, her responses and questions appeared inappropriate. Her recent memory was impaired with some evidence of confabulation. She expressed poor awareness of her cognitive deficits and exhibited anosognosia for her left-sided motor deficits and signs of abulia. She exhibited evidence of impulsive behavior on several occasions by leaving the testing room without permission after she had been instructed to complete a paper-and-pencil test. She required extensive verbal cuing and structure. She demonstrated poor awareness of her errors and required external cuing to initiate tasks and responses. There was no evidence of auditory or visual hallucinations, seizures, or bizarre thinking, although during the latter part of the day, she asked several times if they could cure people with brain injuries by cutting out their brains.

Ms. Simmons expressed a strong verbal desire to regain her physical functioning, particularly the ability to run again. She made no mention, however, of wanting to improve her cognitive functioning. Her judgment seemed poor in light of her apparent unawareness of her numerous cognitive, behavioral, and emotional problems. As she became somewhat fatigued toward the end of the day, her cognitive functioning markedly deteriorated in terms of her ability to carry on conversations with this examiner. Her thinking became more fragmented, tangential, and illogical. As this occurred, she required more structure from this examiner to the point where she required almost constant external cuing and prompting, particularly as she was performing the Wisconsin Card Sorting Test.

She appeared to be trying to the best of her ability on each of the tests given. She was also given frequent rest periods to minimize the effects of fatigue. On the positive side, she appeared very pleasant and spoke in a soft voice. However, as the day progressed, she began exhibiting decreased frustration tolerance and began showing signs of irritability. At no time did this examiner observe any evidence of malingering or histrionic behavior. A total of 9 hours was spent with the patient in this examiner's office. Approximately 7 hours were spent performing neuropsychological testing with the remaining 2 hours spent interviewing the patient and her mother.

NEUROPSYCHOLOGICAL TESTING

Tests Administered

The Raven Progressive Matrices Test

The Trail Making Test (Parts A and B)

The Stroop Color and Word Test

The Symbol Digit Modalities Test

The Rey–Osterrieth Visual Figure Test

The Letter Cancellation Test

The Judgment of Line Orientation Test

The Visual Form Discrimination Test

The Hooper Visual Organization Test

The Boston Naming Test

The Controlled Word Association Test

The Grip Strength Test

Finger Tapping Test

Grooved Pegboard Test

Luria's Motor Examination

Test of Executive Functions

The Wisconsin Card Sorting Test

The Millon Clinical Multiaxial Inventory — II

TEST RESULTS

Intelligence

Ms. Simmons was administered the Raven Progressive Matrices Test to assess her level of intellectual functioning. She obtained a score of 31 of a possible 60, which placed her at the 14th percentile with respect to persons of her age. Her score on this test indicated an IQ of 84, which placed her in the below average range of intellectual functioning. Qualitative analysis of her errors on this test indicated that she made an overwhelming number of errors to stimuli located in her right visual field, particularly the lower quadrant. This finding suggests the likelihood of left parietal–occipital lobe damage.

Attention–Concentration

Ms. Simmons was given a variety of different tasks to assess her attention–concentration skills. She was administered a test to assess her ability to count backwards from 20 to 1. Her responses on this test indicated strong evidence of loss of set and perseverative errors on the latter part of the task. For example, her responses were: "6, 5, 4, 3, 2, 2, 3, 1." While her performance on serial three addition and alternating serial three and five addition appeared only slightly impaired, it was discovered that she was using her fingers to assist her in performing this task. When she was not permitted to use her fingers, she tended to make a large number of loss of set and perseveratory errors. When she was asked to indicate which capital letters in the alphabet contained only straight lines, she omitted the letters E, F, and Y.

Her visual motor tracking skills were assessed by the Trail Making Test. She required 112 s to complete Part A, which placed her 9.1 standard deviations below expectancy (severe to profound impairment). She required 257 seconds to complete Part B, which placed her 14.1 standard deviations below expectancy (severe to profound impairment). It should also be noted that this patient made two loss of set errors and required extensive cuing from the examiner while performing this task. She was administered the Stroop Test to assess her ability to rapidly name words, identify colors, and inhibit competing stimuli. Her performance on this task showed evidence of marked impairment on each task. Her speed of cognitive processing was assessed by the Symbol Digit Modalities Test. She obtained a score of only 16, which placed her 5.7 standard deviations below expectation (severe impairment).

Perception

Ms. Simmons was asked to copy a complex geometric figure. Even though she spent more than 8 min copying the figure, her drawing was severely impaired, particularly with respect to the right side of the figure that was distorted and missing several important external and internal details. It should be noted that the patient was unaware that her drawing was inaccurate. She was then given the Letter Cancellation Test in which she was asked to cancel out each occurrence of the letter A, on a sheet of paper surrounded by numerous other letters of the alphabet. Visual examination of her performance indicated mild to moderate neglect of her right visual field.

She was administered the Judgment of Line Orientation Test to match the spatial orientation of two pairs of lines. She obtained a corrected score of 17, which placed her within the moderately defective range. She was administered the Visual Form Discrimination Test to assess her ability to discriminate between different geometric forms. She obtained a score of only 22, which placed her in the severely defective range. A qualitative analysis of her performance on the latter test showed that most of her errors were made in the lower right quadrant of her visual field. She was administered the Visual Hooper Organization Test to assess her ability to recognize pictures of objects that had been cut up and placed in different positions. She obtained a score of 25, which placed her in the borderline range.

Language

Ms. Simmons was administered the Boston Naming Test to assess her confrontational naming skills. She obtained a score of 57 of a possible 60, which placed her within the normal range for persons of her age. She was administered the Controlled Word Association Test to assess her ability to generate as many words as possible beginning with specific letters of the alphabet. She obtained a corrected score of 30, which placed her between the 25th and 29th percentile (mild impairment).

Memory

Ms. Simmons was given a computerized memory battery to assess her overall memory functioning. Her performance on this entire battery was found to be highly consistent with traumatic brain damage. More specifically, her ability to learn new information was markedly impaired in that she was able to learn a maximum of only 6 of a possible 15 alphanumeric stimuli (e.g., W7, J5) over five consecutive learning trials. After she was given a second list of words to learn for only one trial (which served as an interference task), she was asked to recall the first list of words again. She could recall only 2 of the 15 words and demonstrated a retroactive interference memory loss of 66.7% (marked impairment).

Qualitative analysis of her errors on this test indicated that she made a high number of extraneous errors and several intrusion errors (from the second list), which suggested that she is likely to make errors of confabulation in her recall of recent events. Her visual and verbal recognition skills were found to be moderately to severely impaired, particularly as the delay between the presentation of the material and its recall increased. While she demonstrated significant impairment in her recall of visual or verbal information, her visual memory tested as more impaired than her verbal memory. This was corroborated by the Rey–Osterrieth Visual Figure Test in which she was asked to draw from memory a complex geometric figure that she had copied approximately 30 min earlier. Her recall of this figure was profoundly impaired.

Motor

Ms. Simmons was administered a variety of motor tests to assess the strength, speed, manual dexterity, and higher motor functions of both hands. Testing revealed that her left hand was completely nonfunctional and her dominant right hand was significantly impaired in terms of its motor speed, manual dexterity, and ability to perform higher level motor functions. It should be noted that the patient exhibited evidence of perseveration and loss of set errors on a variety of higher order motor tasks that involved inhibiting specific movements with her fingers and performing three-stage motor movements. On a task involving motor sequencing with her dominant right hand, she exhibited prominent evidence of loss of set and perseveratory errors.

Executive Functions/Problem Solving

While her responses to verbal similarities were generally intact, her interpretations of proverbs were concrete. It should be noted that the patient showed she had been given virtually the same verbal similarities test in the past and knew what the correct answers were. Her judgment, as determined by her responses to hypothetical situations, was found to be impaired. For example, when she was asked what she would do if she became lost in the forest during the daytime, she stated, "Try to find my way out before dark. Walk back and see if I remembered something."

Her problem-solving skills were assessed through a variety of logical–grammatical tasks, mental arithmetic that required her to restructure problem statements, and the Wisconsin Card Sorting Test. While her responses on tasks involving logical–grammatical analysis were found to be intact, she tested as severely impaired on the mental arithmetic and Wisconsin Card Sorting Tests. For example, on the Wisconsin Card Sorting Test (even though she has been given this test several times in the past), she failed to complete any of the six categories and made a total of 92 errors of which 65 were perseverative.

PERSONALITY/EMOTIONAL

The patient was administered the MCMI to assess her long-standing personality traits and current emotional problems. Her profile on this test indicated that her long-standing personality traits were likely to be characterized by pessimistic moods, an edgy irritability, impatience, and surliness that may overlie feelings of being cheated, misunderstood, and unappreciated. Her need for dependency conflicts, combined with her need for autonomy, have contributed to alternating behaviors of passive–aggressive disrespect and an impulsive and quixotic abusiveness. In the past, she was likely to have expressed momentary thoughts and feelings capriciously and to have been outspoken and rude at times. She was also likely to have been a negative, sullen, fault-finding individual who often behaved in a stubborn manner. She often had a "chip on her shoulder" attitude. Her personal relationships, particularly with her family, were fraught with wrangles and antagonism.

At the time of testing, she was seen as being testy and demanding and exhibited evidence of an agitated form of dysthymic behavior characterized by moodiness and vacillation. She was likely to comment disparagingly about herself, anxiously express feelings of futility about her future, and give vent to outbursts of bitter resentment interwoven with a demanding irritability toward those around her. Her profile indicated that she was likely to periodically voice severe self-recriminations and self-loathing. These behaviors, however, might induce guilt in others and effectively manipulate them, thus providing her with a measure of retribution. She also reported contemplating suicide in the past and having given thought to doing away with herself recently.

Impression

The results of neuropsychological testing revealed strong evidence that this patient had sustained severe focal and diffuse cortical and subcortical brain damage. She showed evidence of significant cognitive impairments generally severe in the following areas: concentration, visual motor tracking, cognitive flexibility, speed of cognitive processing, visual perceptual skills, visual scanning, spatial orientation, visual discrimination, learning new information, retention of newly learned information under conditions of interference or delayed recall, left-sided motor functioning, motor speed, higher order motor functions, abstract thinking, judgment, mental arithmetic, intellectual processes, executive functions, and problem solving.

In addition to these deficits, Ms. Simmons showed prominent abulia, impulsive behavior, flat affect, poor initiation skills, the need for extensive external cuing, and inattention to stimuli located in her right visual field, particularly in the lower right quadrant. Her awareness of her cognitive errors was seen as poor. At no time did she exhibit any recognition of her errors or make any attempt to correct them. The above cognitive and behavioral impairments would be consistent with extensive damage involving the right temporoparietal lobe, frontal lobes, right basal ganglia, and left parietal–occipital lobe, as well as with a focal coup and contrecoup and diffuse axonal injuries, which she most likely sustained in her February 11, 1987 motor vehicle accident.

CONCLUSION

Shirley Simmons is a 23-year-old, right-handed, white female, who was involved in a head-on automobile collision on February 11, 1987. She was rendered unconscious and taken to Columbus Hospital, where she was noted to have sustained a severe closed head injury with right hematoma and depressed skull fracture. She underwent a craniotomy and evacuation of hematoma on February 12, 1987. She remained in a coma for approximately 3 weeks. On February 18, 1987, a tracheostomy was performed. Repeat CT scans of the brain revealed intracerebral hemorrhaging with brain edema and compression with distortion of the adjacent brain structures with some evidence of herniation. The patient underwent a right craniotomy and evacuation of the right intracerebral bleed with a left ventriculostomy placement.

She was transferred to Langdon Community Hospital on March 24, 1987 where she underwent inpatient rehabilitation until her discharge on August 11, 1987. Her significant cognitive deficits and spastic left upper and lower extremities were noted to interfere with her ability to fully participate in rehabilitation. The patient was transferred to the New Brunswick Neurologic Traumatic Brain Injury Rehabilitation Program on November 4, 1987, where she underwent inpatient rehabilitation until September 3, 1988. She was transferred to the Renew Inpatient Rehabilitation Program on September 5, 1988 where she received extensive inpatient rehabilitation until her discharge in May 1990. Since her discharge, she has been living at home with her mother and brothers.

The patient was seen in this examiner's office on February 6, 1991. She was accompanied by her mother. While the patient appeared alert and oriented, her affect was flat and her speech had a monotonic quality. She exhibited left-sided hemiparesis. She demonstrated anosognosia with respect to her left-sided motor problems, particularly her inability to use her left upper extremity. Her awareness of her cognitive deficits was poor, as determined by her chief complaints. Her recent memory was impaired with indications of confabulation. She demonstrated inappropriate and impulsive behavior during the interview. During neuropsychological testing, she demonstrated severe cognitive impairments in a variety of areas including: concentration, visual motor tracking, cognitive flexibility, speed of cognitive processing, complex attentional skills, visual scanning, visual constructional skills, inattention to the right visual field, spatial orientation, visual discrimination, learning new information, retention of newly acquired information particularly under conditions of interference and delayed recall, visual memory, motor impairments involving her left and right side, abstract thinking, conceptualization skills, mental arithmetic, judgment, and problem-solving skills. These impairments were felt to be generally consistent with an MRI study that was reported by Dr. Brinton as showing evidence of significant damage to the right posterior frontal, right mid-temporal, right basal ganglia, right anterior parietal lobe, and left superoparietal and occipital area.

The patient's mother was interviewed on February 6, 1991 by this examiner. Her mother indicated that she has observed a number of significant cognitive, emotional, and behavioral problems in her daughter since her injury, consisting of frequent mood swings, angry and hostile behavior, irresponsibility, poor judgment regarding financial matters, loss of initiative and motivation, aggravation of her premorbid personality problems and traits, severe difficulties with interpersonal relationships, inappropriate goals and unrealistic expectations, use of inappropriate or vulgar language, a failure to follow through on verbally stated plans or intentions, attention–concentration difficulties, history of suicidal gestures and attempts, left-sided motor problems, cognitive difficulties particularly with her recent memory, and marked psychomotor slowing.

The patient's mother was also interviewed regarding the impact that these problems have had upon her since her daughter's injury. She admitted that she had become a martyr and had denied herself any pleasurable activities. She also admitted that she had felt depressed and given serious thought to ending her life. As a result of these problems, her mother was administered the MCMI-II to assess her long-standing personality traits and current emotional problems. Her profile on this test demonstrated evidence of a major depression including self-defeating attitudes. She was seen as experiencing feelings of emptiness and loneliness, as well as recurring thoughts of death and suicide accompanied by feelings of low self-esteem, preoccupation with her failures and physical unattractiveness, and feelings of guilt and unworthiness. She also was seen as suffering from a variety of symptoms consistent with an anxiety disorder. It should also be noted that her mother began crying and sobbing during the interview and revealed that she had had a very unhappy life in the past and did not appear to have any visible means of emotional support at this time. Based on these findings, this examiner strongly recommended that the patient's mother be referred to an appropriate mental health professional for psychotherapy/psychiatric treatment. I have given her the name of a former student and colleague of mine who practices in Rhode Island. I have instructed her to contact him in order to get the name of a therapist in her geographic area.

In reviewing the extensive medical records, it seems apparent that Shirley Simmons has made slow but fairly consistent progress as a result of being placed in inpatient rehabilitation programs for traumatically brain-injured patients. It is the opinion of this examiner that she continues to require inpatient rehabilitation in a highly structured, behaviorally oriented residential rehabilitation program for patients with severe traumatic brain injuries. This examiner highly recommends the Tyler Program, in Santa Anita, California, which has an outstanding reputation in this field. On the basis of her performance on neuropsychological testing, combined with the behavioral observations of this examiner and those of her mother, it is highly unlikely that this patient will be able to live independently on her own or ever work in other than a highly structured or sheltered environment in the foreseeable future. More than likely, this patient will require lifetime placement in a program such as the Tyler Program, which provides the opportunity for brain-injured patients to live in a highly structured, behaviorally oriented environment where they will be treated with respect and dignity.

Although this patient most likely had a personality disorder prior to her motor vehicle accident, the injuries she sustained in her accident appear to have aggravated her personality problems and created a large number of cognitive behavioral, motor, social, and emotional problems that she did not have prior to her accident. She continues to demonstrate behavioral problems that reflect a combination of her preexisting personality traits and her traumatic brain injury. Because of these problems, she is seen as requiring a behaviorally oriented rehabilitation program that will gradually eliminate the use of these behaviors to gain attention and disrupt activities. The severity of these problems further warrants, in this examiner's opinion, the necessity of long-term placement in a highly structured residential setting for patients with traumatic brain damage.

DIAGNOSES

Axis I	1. Severe closed head injury, by history.
	2. Frontal lobe syndrome, severe.
	3. Severe cognitive deficits, secondary to step 1 (as described above).
	4. Organic affective disorder.
	5. Left hemiparesis, by history.
Axis II	Mixed personality disorder with prominent avoidant, dysthymic, and passive–aggressive features.
Axis III	As determined by appropriate medical specialists.
Axis IV	Severity of psychosocial stressors: severe, due to frequent conflicts with her mother and siblings, social isolation, and motor impairments.
Axis V	Highest level of adaptive functioning prior to accident: GAF = 70; Current GAF = 25.

RECOMMENDATIONS

1. It is strongly recommended that this patient be referred to the Tyler Rehabilitation Program in Santa Anita, California, as soon as possible.
2. The patient's mother is severely depressed and shows evidence of suicidal ideation. It is strongly recommended that she be referred to an appropriate mental health specialist as soon as possible for psychotherapy/psychiatric treatment.

CHARLES STERLING, PH.D.

Critique

Dr. Sterling's report documents the discrepancy between Ms. Simmons' subjective complaints and her mother's observations of her behavior. Although Ms. Simmons did not complain of any cognitive or behavioral problems, her mother reported observing numerous such problems. This as well as her sparse history of her injury is consistent with patients who have sustained severe traumatic brain injuries. The information Dr. Sterling obtained from her mother is consistent with her medical records and documents her mother's emotional difficulties as a result of coping with her daughter's cognitive and emotional difficulties since her brain injury. Dr. Sterling actually administered the MCMI-II to assess Mrs. Simmons' emotional functioning, which revealed that she had taken on the role of a martyr while caring for her daughter, which caused her to become quite anxious and depressed.

Although Dr. Sterling pointed out in his report that Ms. Simmons had a preexisting history of attentional and reading difficulties, sexual molestation, and head trauma, these problems are overshadowed by her severe traumatic brain injury that exacerbated her prior cognitive and emotional problems and created a large number of significant cognitive, behavioral, motor, social, and emotional problems that she did not have prior to her accident. Dr. Sterling's report integrates the information he obtained from a variety of different sources and provides the trier of fact with a clear understanding of how this accident has significantly affected Ms. Simmons and her mother and what remedies (treatments) are needed.

Glossary of Neurological and Neuropsychological Terms

A

Abnormal: Maladaptive behavior detrimental to the individual and the group.

Absence seizures: Brief paroxysmal attacks of impaired consciousness, primarily occurring in children. Also known as petit mal.

Acalculia: Impaired calculation abilities, more often associated with left posterior parietal lesions.

Achromatopsia: Impaired perception of colors due to cerebral dysfunction. Can be hemianopic or involve both entire visual fields.

Acute alcoholic hallucinosis: State of alcoholic intoxication characterized by hallucinations.

Acute paranoid disorder: Psychoses characterized by transient and changeable paranoid delusions, usually related to an identifiable stressor and transient in nature.

Acute posttraumatic stress disorder: Disorder in which symptoms develop within 6 months of an extremely traumatic experience instead of entering the recovery state.

Adipsia: A condition in which an individual refuses to drink fluids.

Adjustment disorder with depressed mood: Moderately severe affective disorder behaviorally identical to a dysthymic disorder or depressed phase of a cyclothymic disorder but having an identifiable, though not severe, psychosocial stressor occurring within 3 months prior to the onset of depression.

Afferent fibers/tracts: Neuronal pathways going toward the brain from the peripheral areas of the central nervous system.

Ageusia: Loss of the sense of taste.

Aggression: A forceful or assaultive verbal or physical action toward another person or object; the motor component of anger, hostility, or rage.

Agitation: Marked restlessness and psychomotor excitement.

Agnosia: A disorder characterized by impairment or loss of the ability to interpret sensory stimuli, for example, object recognition, not due to primary sensory system dysfunction, confusion, or dementia.

Agoraphobia: A mental disorder characterized by an irrational fear of leaving the familiar setting of home or venturing into an open area; frequently associated with panic attacks.

Agrammatism: A form of Broca's aphasia, characterized by the reduction of spoken and written language to nouns and verbs with the omission of modifiers, articles, prepositions, and inflectional forms.

Agraphia: A motor programming or linguistic impairment of writing skills in the absence of a primary motor or sensory deficit; usually associated with aphasia and alexia, due to a lesion in the angular gyrus or adjacent posterior parietal cortex.

Akathisia: A general motor restlessness together with elevated inner tension, subjectively reported by the patient; a frequent side effect of antipsychotic medication.

Akinesia: Absence or loss of the power of voluntary movement due to an extrapyramidal disorder, frequently seen in Parkinsonism.

Akinetic mutism: Subacute or chronic state of altered consciousness, in which the patient appears intermittently alert but is not responsive; associated with lesions involving the medialfrontal–subcortical circuit.

Alien hand syndrome: Also termed the "Dr. Strangelove effect," a conflict between the two hands is seen with the patients learning to use their "obedient" hand to control the unpredictable but purposive movements of the alien hand. Contralateral supplementary motor area (SMA) and corpus callosum lesions have been implicated.

Alexia: An acquired inability to read, that is, to comprehend written symbols or word meanings, due to damage in angular gyrus or adjacent posterior cerebral cortex.

Alexia without agraphia: Inability to read with preserved writing capability in the absence of other language deficits.

Allesthesia: Sensation of being touched on the side ipsilateral to a lesion when contralateral stimulation was, in fact, presented.

Alpha rhythm: A regular wave pattern in the EEG in the 8 to 12 Hz range that occurs, especially at the back of the head, during relaxed wakefulness with eyes closed.

Alzheimer's disease (AD): A diffuse degenerative brain disease characterized by the presence of neurofibrillary tangles and senile plaques. It initially presents as a progressive memory loss in late middle life and later develops into a profound dementia with death in 5 to 10 years.

Amblyopia: Reduced visual acuity not caused by optical or retinal impairment.

Amenorrhea: The absence of menses.

Amines: A class of biologically active compounds, including neurotransmitters, that have a component formed from ammonia.

Amnestic syndrome: A disorder characterized by an inability to recall events more than a few minutes after they have occurred, coupled with a variable ability to recall remote events; invariably associated with an impairment of new learning.

Amorphosynthesis: Loss of ability to synthesize more than a few properties of a stimulus; multiple sensory stimuli cannot be processed simultaneously; typically caused by parietal lobe dysfunction.

Amusia: A disorder characterized by the impaired production or recognition of music, including singing, humming, tapping out rhythms, recognition of individual tones and tonal patterns, due to acquired temporal lobe damage.

Amygdala: A structure of the limbic system located at the base of the temporal lobe that adds affective tone (emotion) to sensory input and memories.

Amyotrophic lateral sclerosis (ALS): See motor neuron disease.

Analgesia: Loss of sensitivity to pain.

Anarithmetria: Impaired primary calculation skills due to brain damage; left hemisphere lesions are typically implicated.

Anergia: Decreased or absent motivation or drive.

Anesthesia: Loss of sensation.

Aneurysm: A sac formed by the circumscribed dilation of the walls of an artery, due to a congenital or acquired weakness of the wall. It is filled with blood and is prone to rupture, causing a cerebral hemorrhage.

Angiography: A technique for radiographic imaging of blood vessels that have been filled with an injected contrast medium; designed to produce enhanced pictures of the cerebral vasculature.

Angular gyrus: A cortical convolution, located in the posterior–inferior parietal lobe. The left angular gyrus is critically involved in the integration of spoken and written language.

Angular gyrus syndrome: A disorder following destruction of the angular gyrus of the left hemisphere, characterized by alexia, agraphia, acalculia, right–left disorientation, difficulty naming or recognizing fingers, ideomotor apraxia, anomia, and constructional disorder.

Anomia: Inability to name objects due to brain dysfunction.

Anomic aphasia: A fluent aphasia, characterized by difficulty in naming objects on confrontation; comprehension and articulation may be unimpaired.

Anosmia: Loss of ability to smell.

Anosodiaphoria: Unconcern over, but admission of, an actual neurological impairment. See also Anton's syndrome.

Anosognosia: Impaired ability to recognize or acknowledge an illness or bodily defect, frequently associated with right parietal lesions and the left hemi-neglect syndrome.

Anterior aphasias: A group of nonfluent acquired speech and language disorders with relatively preserved comprehension, including Broca's, transcortical motor, and SMA aphasia, associated with frontal–parietal lesions of the left hemisphere.

Anterior cerebral artery (ACA): One of the two major vascular networks of the frontal and parietal lobes; the ACA and its branches feed the medial aspects of the cerebral hemispheres.

Anterior pituitary: The anterior lobe of the pituitary gland that secretes trophic hormones; also called adenohypophysis.

Anterograde amnesia: Inability to recall life events from the time of traumatic injury; inability to learn and poor short-term memory are associated features.

Anton's syndrome: See also anosognosia. Lack of awareness and frequently adamant denial of blindness; associated with bilateral occipital lobe damage.

Apathetic–akinetic–abulic behavior: This syndrome is characterized by low drive and reduced thought, emotion, speech, and movement; produced by extensive bilateral and predominantly deep midline frontal lobe damage.

Aphagia: An inability to eat, often related to damage to the lateral hypothalamus.

Aphasia: Impaired or absent comprehension or production of speech, writing, or signs, due to an acquired lesion of the cerebral hemisphere, dominant for speech and language, usually the left hemisphere in nearly all right-handed and the majority of left-handed individuals.

Aphemia: A disorder characterized by poorly articulated, slow, hypophonic, breathy speech with no syntactic deficits; usually follows initial mutism and is associated with a lesion involving or undercutting Broca's area in the left posterior inferior frontal lobe.

Apoplexy: A classic but obsolete term for a major cerebral stroke, especially a hemorrhage with loss of consciousness.

Apperceptive visual agnosia: The ability to synthesize or integrate visual input; awareness of discrete parts may be intact.

Apraxia: Refers to impaired ability to perform a learned skilled movement to command or imitation in individuals with unimpaired comprehension and primary motor skills; an inability to make appropriate use of an object.

Apraxia of speech: Known also as verbal apraxia and a frequent component of Broca's aphasia. Speech movement/articulation problems may include (1) articulation errors, (2) phoneme substitution, (3) greater latency of response, (4) greater difficulty with initial than subsequent phonemes, (5) no major vocal musculature problems, (6) sparse output, (7) poor melody, and (8) articulation with much effort.

Apraxic agraphia: Deficit in forming graphemes when writing to dictation or spontaneously; lesions are in the parietal lobe contralateral to the dominant (writing) hand.

Aprosodias: Deficits in the comprehension and expression of affect and emotion; traditionally associated with right hemisphere dysfunction.

Aqueduct: A canal for the conduction of a liquid; the cerebral aqueduct of Sylvius connects the third and fourth ventricles of the brain.

Arachnoid: A delicate fibrous membrane forming the middle of the three coverings (meninges) of the brain.

Arcuate fasciculus: A long, predominantly parietal fiber bundle connecting Broca's and Wernicke's areas.

Arteriovenous malformation (AVM): A congenital vascular lesion, with arterial and venous components. A major cause of intracerebral hemorrhage and epilepsy.

Asphyxia: A state of impaired or absent blood oxygenation.

Assertiveness training: A behavior therapy technique for helping individuals become more self-assertive in interpersonal relationships.

Association areas: Large areas of cortex next to the motor or sensory cortex; involved in advanced stages of sensory information processing, multisensory integration, or sensorimotor integration; damage causes patterned rather than specific deficits.

Associative visual agnosia: Inability to visually recognize objects with ability to copy, draw, or match to sample intact.

Astasia abasia: A psychogenic disorder, characterized by a drunken-type gait but no actual falls to ground.

Astereognosis: Inability to identify objects by touch in spite of intact appreciation of tactile sensation; also called tactile agnosia.

Asthenia: Weakness.

Ataxia: An inability to coordinate muscle activity during voluntary movement, resulting in jerky, imprecise limb movement or impaired balance; most often due to disorders of the cerebellum or the posterior columns of the spinal cord.

Athetosis: Slow, involuntary, successive writhing movements, often seen in the hands; may occur either during movement or at rest; associated with lesions of the basal ganglia.

Atrophy: A wasting or diminution in the size of a part of the body or brain.

Attention deficit disorder: Maladaptive behavior in children characterized by impulsivity, excessive motor activity, and an inability to focus attention for appropriate periods of time; also called hyperactive syndrome or hyperkinetic reaction.

Auditory affective agnosia: Impaired ability to recognize or comprehend affectively intoned speech due to a cerebral disorder.

Auditory agnosia: Impaired recognition of auditory stimuli due to cerebral dysfunction with intact receptive abilities, as measured by audiometry or other means.

Auditory cortex: A region of the temporal lobe that receives auditory input from the medial geniculate nucleus of the thalamus.

Auditory sound agnosia: Impaired ability to recognize nonspeech sounds owing to cerebral dysfunction.

Aura: Subjective sensation, perceptual or cognitive experience, or motor phenomenon occurring at the onset of a partial epileptic seizure or migraine headache.

Automated assessment: Psychological test interpretation by electronic computer or some other mechanical means.

Automatism: (1) Stereotypic units of behavior, linked in a fixed sequence and which may be produced without effort or delay, for example, material learned by rote in childhood or for a given temporal period (e.g., alphabet, number series). (2) A partial complex epileptic attack consisting of stereotyped cognitive, sensory, or motor phenomena; carried out in a state of impaired consciousness and of which the individual usually has no knowledge.

Autonomic nervous system: Part of the peripheral nervous system that supplies neural connections to glands and to smooth muscles of internal organs; composed of two divisions (sympathetic and parasympathetic) that act in opposite fashion.

Autotopagnosia: Inability to recognize or name parts of the body, for example, finger agnosia; typically associated with parietal lobe damage.

Axon: The thin elongated neuronal process that transmits electrical impulses from the cell body to other neurons, muscles, or glands.

B

Balint's syndrome: A syndrome consisting of (1) oculomotor apraxia, or difficulty shifting focus from a near to a distant stimulus; (2) optic ataxia, shown by impaired visually guided movements; and (3) impaired visual attention in the absence of general attentional deficits, with initial random gaze until a stimulus is fixated upon; it results from large bilateral parietal lesions.

Ballism: A type of involuntary movement affecting the proximal limbs, manifested by jerky, flinging movements of the extremity, due to basal ganglia dysfunction.

Basal forebrain: Comprises the septal nuclei, diagonal band of Broca and substantia innominata.

Basal ganglia: A group of nuclei, including the amygdala, caudate nucleus, claustrum, globus pallidus, putamen, subthalamic nucleus of the forebrain, and substantia nigra in the brain stem.

Basilar artery: An artery formed by the fusion of the vertebral arteries; its branches supply blood to the brain stem and to posterior–inferior portions of the cerebral hemispheres.

Behavioral teratology: Impairments in behavior produced by early exposure to toxic substances.

Benzodiazepines: A group of psychoactive compounds that have sedating, calming, or muscle relaxant effects; also known as mild tranquilizers.

Beta rhythm: Irregular EEG activity in the 13 to 30 Hz range, generally associated with an alert state.

Binocular disparity: The slight difference between the views from the two eyes, important in depth perception.

Bitemporal hemianopsia: Optic chiasm damage resulting in visual field loss in both temporal (as opposed to nasal) areas.

Blindsight: Denial of recognition in the face of previous correct recognition and stimulus responses.

Blind spot: A place through which blood vessels enter the retina. Because there are no receptors in this region, light striking it cannot be seen.

Blood–brain barrier: A functional barrier produced by glial cells and cells in the capillary walls of the brain that protects the brain from exposure to potentially toxic substances found in the blood.

Body schema: Body image.

Boxer's encephalopathy: A chronic traumatic brain disorder, characterized by cognitive impairment, Parkinsonism, tremor, dysarthria, and impaired impulse control. May progress to a more severe form, known as dementia pugilistica.

Bradycardia: Abnormal slowness of the heart or pulse.

Bradykinesia: Decreased movement and spontaneity; a cardinal feature of Parkinsonism.

Brain abscess: Localized collection of pus in the brain, formed from disintegrating infected tissue.

Brain stem: The thalamus, hypothalamus, basal ganglia, midbrain, pons, medulla, and associated structures.

Brain stem reticular formation: Nerve cells and fiber pathways in the central core of the brain stem, extending from the spinal cord to the thalamus, involved in arousal of the forebrain.

Broca's aphasia: An expressive nonfluent speech disorder with relatively intact auditory comprehension. Exhibited speech is slow, labored, dysarthric, concrete, and agrammatic. Considered an anterior aphasia that results from a lesion in the inferior posterior left frontal lobe.

Broca's area: An area in the inferior–posterior frontal region of the left hemisphere involved in the production of speech.

Brown–Peterson distractor technique: Counting backwards by two's or three's upon presentation of a verbal or nonverbal stimulus to prevent rehearsal.

Buccolinguofacial apraxia: An oral apraxia affecting voluntary movements of the larynx, pharynx, tongue, lips, and related suborgans in which simple, automatic movements are intact. Commanded tasks may yield deficits (e.g., swallowing, laughing) in the presence of noncommanded, contextual responses (e.g., swallowing food after eating, smiling).

C

Capgras syndrome: A delusional belief involving the reduplication of relatives, friends, possessions, and the like, which may have an organic etiology; the target person, almost always a close relative, is considered an impostor.

Catastrophic reaction: Intensely negative but temporary emotional reaction associated with left hemisphere lesions; often occurring when subjects are informed of their limitations or shortcomings, in response to task demands; a heightened sensitivity to one's limitations.

Caudal: An anatomical term meaning toward the tail end; opposed to rostral.

Caudate nucleus: One of the basal ganglia with a long extension or tail.

Central deafness: Hearing impairment due to a disorder of the auditory system of the brain stem or temporal lobe cortex.

Central nervous system (CNS): The portion of the nervous system that includes the brain and the spinal cord.

Central sulcus: Known also as the Fissure of Rolando, this sulcus divides the anterior from the posterior (frontal and parietal) areas of the brain.

Cephalalgia: Headache.

Cephalic: An anatomical term referring to the head end; also called rostral.

Cerebellar cortex: The outer surface of the cerebellum.

Cerebellar fits: An antiquated term referring to movements representing episodes of decerebrate rigidity. Not true epileptic seizures, they are typically associated with large herniating mass lesions.

Cerebellar cognitive–affective syndrome: Results from cerebellar lesions. Characterized by impairments in executive function, spatial cognition, emotional control and linguistic processing.

Cerebellar syndrome: A syndrome characterized by dysarthria, limb incoordination, nystagmus, unsteady staggering gait, and loss of equilibrium resulting from cerebellar impairment.

Cerebellum: The large posterior brain mass lying dorsal to the pons and medulla and ventral to the posterior portion of the cerebrum. It consists of two lateral hemispheres united by the midline portion, the vermis; involved in the central regulation of movement.

Cerebral contusion: A brain bruise with edema and capillary hemorrhages; refers to superficial damage to crests of the cortical gyri, which often extends to the underlying lobar white matter.

Cerebral cortex: The outer (bark) cortex of the cerebral hemispheres that consists largely of nerve cell bodies and their branches.

Cerebral hemispheres: The right and left halves of the forebrain.

Cerebrospinal fluid: The fluid, secreted by the ventricular choroid plexus, that fills the ventricles inside the brain and circulates around the brain and spinal cord beneath the arachnoid layer in the subarachnoid space.

Cervical: Pertaining to the neck region.

Cheiro-oral: Refers to the simultaneous twitching of the thumb and same-sided corner of the mouth; occurs in partial epilepsy owing to close proximity of motor execution zones for these body parts (i.e., the motor homunculus has its thumb in its mouth).

Chiasma: A crossing; specifically, the crossing of the optic nerve fibers from the medial halves of the retinae.

Chlorpromazine: An antipsychotic drug, one of the class of phenothiazines.

Cholinergic: Refers to nerve cells or fibers that use acetylcholine as their neurotransmitter.

Choreic movements: Uncontrollable, spasmodic, and irregular involuntary movements of the limbs or facial muscles related to basal ganglia dysfunction.

Cingulate cortex and gyrus: Limbic system tissue above or superior to the corpus callosum along the medial walls of the cerebral hemispheres.

Cingulum: A fiber bundle passing longitudinally in the white matter of the cingulate gyrus; a component of the Papez circuit.

Circadian rhythms: Behavioral, biochemical, and physiological fluctuations during a 24-h period.

Circle of Willis: A vascular structure at the base of the brain, formed by the joining of the carotid and basilar arteries through interconnecting channels.

Circulocution: The substitution of an incorrect word for another word; the substitution may itself demand a specific but unobtainable word, thus producing a convoluted output; often seen in fluent aphasia.

Cistern: A closed space adjacent to the brain serving as a reservoir for cerebrospinal fluid.

Cochlea: A snail-shaped structure in the inner ear that contains the primary receptors for hearing.

Coma: A state of profound unconsciousness from which one cannot be aroused.

Coma vigil: A subacute or chronic state of altered consciousness in which the patient appears alert, with eyes often open and moving, but otherwise immobile and unresponsive, associated with medial frontal or upper brain stem damage.

Common carotid arteries: Arteries that ascend the left and right sides of the neck; the branch that enters the brain is called the internal carotid artery.

Complex cortical cells: Cells in the visual cortex that respond best to a bar of a particular width and direction anywhere within a particular area of the visual field.

Complex partial seizures: Epileptic seizures in which consciousness is altered (complex) and which are restricted to or at least arise from a circumscribed area of the brain (partial); often associated with automatisms.

Compulsion: Repetitive behaviors (e.g., hand washing, rechecking if the lights are out) or mental activities (e.g., counting) that the patient feels compelled to do.

Computerized transaxial tomography (CAT): A technique for examining brain structure in intact humans through computer synthesis of x-ray transmission data obtained in many different directions in a given plane. This technique affords a direct three-dimensional view of the brain.

Concussion: A disorder characterized by widespread paralysis of brain function that occurs immediately after a blow to the head. There is typically a transient loss of consciousness with bradycardia, hypotension, and respiratory arrest for a few seconds, followed by posttraumatic and retrograde amnesia.

Conduct disorder: A mental disorder of childhood or adolescence in which the child is disobedient, hostile, and highly aggressive; cruelty to animals, vandalism and robbery, truancy, cheating, and lying may be exhibited.

Conduction aphasia: A fluent aphasic syndrome produced by a parietal lesion in the white matter fibers connecting the posterior/anterior language zones of the left hemisphere. A severe repetition deficit is apparent despite relatively good comprehension of spoken language.

Confabulation: Production of bizarre, false, or unverifiable verbal/written responses, usually in association with amnesia; a close correlation exists between confabulatory tendencies and impairment in self-correction.

Congenital: Existing at or before birth.

Consolidation: A state of memory formation in which information in short-term or intermediate memory is transferred to long-term memory.

Constructional disorders: Deficits in constructional tasks (e.g., drawing, assembling) in which the spatial form of the target object may be lost; primarily associated with pathology in the nondominant or right hemisphere.

Contralateral: Situated on, or pertaining to, the opposite side.

Contrecoup: Refers to the contusion (bruise) in the area opposite the point of impact (coup).

Coronal (plane): The vertical plane dividing the body or brain into front and back parts.

Corpus callosum: Large white matter tract crossing the midline and connecting the right and left cerebral hemispheres.

Cortical deafness: Difficulty recognizing both verbal and nonverbal stimuli due to cerebral dysfunction; most often associated with a stroke; also called cortical auditory disorder.

Cortical dementia: Intellectual deterioration characterized by impairment of language, memory (including retrieval and recognition), new learning, visuospatial function, reasoning, and calculating ability; Alzheimer's disease is a typical example.

Corticobulbar fiber tracts: Connecting pathways between the cortex and the lower brain stem.

Cranial nerves: Originating from the brain, the 12 pairs of nerves that transmit motor and sensory neuronal impulses to and from the cranium or skull.

Creutzfeldt–Jakob disease: A rare, rapidly progressive and invariably fatal dementing disorder; initially manifested by anxiety and memory loss; myoclonic jerking subsequently appears in conjunction with signs of motor, cerebellar, basal ganglia, and pyramidal tract dysfunction. It is caused by a transmissible prion (slow virus).

Crossed aphasia: Aphasic symptoms occurring, usually temporarily, in a right-handed person with a right-hemisphere lesion.

Cyanosis: A dark purplish coloration of the skin and the mucous membrane caused by deficient oxygenation of the blood.

Cyclothymic disorder: Mild affective disorder, characterized by extreme mood swings of nonpsychotic intensity.

Cytoarchitectonics: The study of anatomical divisions of the brain based on the organization, structure, and distribution of cells.

D

Dacrystic epilepsy: Seizures where crying is the predominant ictal event.

Decerebrate rigidity (posturing): A postural change that occurs in some comatose patients, consisting of episodes of rigid extension of the neck and limbs, internal rotation of the upper extremities, and marked plantar flexion of the feet; typically caused by acute intracranial pathology involving the midbrain. Decorticate posturing by contrast is characterized by unilateral or bilateral flexion and adduction of the arms with leg extension and results from structural pathology at a higher thalamic or cerebral hemispheric level.

Declarative memory: The ability to recount what one knows, specifically the details of events, including time, place, and circumstances; frequently lost in amnesia; opposite of procedural memory.

Deja vu: A feeling that an event has been previously experienced; usually a normal phenomenon, but also a typical aura preceding a complex partial seizure in temporal lobe epilepsy.

Delirium: An altered state of consciousness, consisting of confusion, distractibility, disorientation, impaired thinking, memory, and perception (illusions and hallucinations); usually associated with prominent hyperactivity, agitation, and autonomic nervous system overactivity; caused by toxic, metabolic, or structural brain disorders.

Delirium tremens: Acute delirium associated with prolonged alcoholism; characterized by intense anxiety, tremors, and hallucinations.

Delusion: Firm belief opposed to reality but maintained in spite of strong evidence to the contrary.

Delusion of persecution: False belief that one is being mistreated or interfered with by one's enemies; often found in schizophrenia.

Delusional system: An internally coherent, systematized pattern of delusional beliefs.

Demyelination: Loss of myelin with preservation of the axons or fiber tracts in the central and peripheral nervous system. Central demyelination is the underlying pathology of multiple sclerosis.

Dendrites: The multiple short branching processes of a nerve cell.

Dependent personality: A personality disorder marked by lack of self-confidence and feelings of acute panic or discomfort at having to be alone.

Depersonalization disorder: A dissociative disorder, usually occurring in adolescence or young adults, in which individuals lose their sense of self and feel unreal or displaced to a different location.

Depressive disorder: A temporary or chronic disorder characterized by feelings of sadness, loneliness, despair, low self-esteem, and self-reproach; accompanying signs include psychomotor retardation or, less frequently, agitation, withdrawal from social contact, and vegetative states such as loss of appetite and insomnia.

Depressive stupor: Extreme degree of depression characterized by marked psychomotor underactivity.

Desensitization: Therapeutic process by means of which reactions to traumatic experiences are reduced in intensity by repeatedly exposing the individual to them in mild form, either in reality or in fantasy.

Dextral: Refers to right-handedness; opposed to sinistral, or left-handedness.

Dialysis dementia: A progressive often fatal encephalopathy that may be manifested by aphasia, memory difficulties, seizures, and motor signs (e.g., facial grimacing), seen occasionally as the result of long-term renal dialysis.

Dialysis disequilibrium syndrome: An acute encephalopathy characterized by development of intermittent slowed speech, stuttering, and word-finding problems; progression to apraxia, memory loss, impaired attention, and (occasionally) psychosis.

Diaschisis: A condition in which brain areas connected to the damaged area show a transitory arrest of function. Associated with acute, focal brain injuries, for example, stroke, trauma.

Diathesis: A predisposition or vulnerability toward developing a given disorder.

Diathesis–stress model: View of abnormal behavior as the result of stress operating on an individual with a biological, psychosocial, or sociocultural predisposition toward developing a specific disorder.

Dichotic listening: A testing procedure in which different auditory input are simultaneously presented to each ear of the subject through stereophonic headphones.

Diencephalon: The central core of the brain, which together with the telencephalon, forms the cerebrum. Consists of the thalamus, subthalamus, hypothalamus, and epithalamus.

Diffuse axonal injury (DAI): Widespread stretching or shearing of nerve fibers in the cerebral hemispheres and brain stem resulting from traumatic brain injury; frequently associated with capillary hemorrhages and cerebral edema.

Diffusion tensor imaging: A magnetic resonance imaging technique that provides information about the architecture and integrity of white matter fiber tracts.

Dilantin® (see Appendix A): The proprietary name of an anticonvulsant medication often used for the treatment of epileptic seizures; side effects include diplopia or double vision due to eye muscle imbalance, dysarthria, ataxic gait, and metabolic disturbances.

Disconnection syndromes: Disorders involving a severing, by damage or by surgery, of fiber tracts connecting two or more areas of the brain, interfering with neuronal transmission and communication. Corpus callosum disconnections are the most dramatic form.

Disinhibition syndrome: Inability to stop actions or impulses once initiated; often attributed to frontal system deficits in exerting an inhibitory effect on ongoing mental or behavioral processes.

Disorganized schizophrenia: Subtype representing most severe disintegration of personality and poor prognosis for recovery, characterized by marked incoherence or silly or inappropriate responses; also known as hebephrenia.

Dissociation: Separation or "isolation" of mental processes in such a way that they become split off from the main personality or lose their normal thought and affect relationships.

Dissociative disorder: A disorder characterized by a disturbance in functions of identity, memory, and consciousness. Specific forms include psychogenic amnesia, psychogenic fugue, depersonalization, and multiple personality disorders.

Distal: An anatomical term meaning toward the periphery or toward the end of a limb.

Diurnal: Pertaining to daylight hours, opposite of nocturnal.

Divergence: A system of neural connections that allows one cell to send signals to many other cells.

Dopamine (DA): A neurotransmitter produced mainly in the basal forebrain and midbrain substantia nigra that is active in the basal ganglia and the cerebral cortex, primarily the frontal regions; a deficiency results in Parkinson's disease.

Dopaminergic: Refers to cells that use dopamine as their synaptic neurotransmitter.

Dorsal: An anatomical term meaning toward the back of the body or the top of the brain; opposite of ventral.

Dorsal root: The proximal portion of the sensory nerve entering each segment of the dorsal portion of the spinal cord.

Double-dissociation: Differential effects of lesions, allowing for comparison of both independent and dependent variables; for example, lesion X causes X¢ but not Y, whereas lesion Y causes Y¢ but not X.

Double tracking: The simultaneous operation of two mental operations. Digits backward on the Wechsler Adult Intelligence Scale (WAIS), for example, calls for memory and reversing operations at the same time.

Down's syndrome: A form of mental retardation usually associated with an extra chromosome 21. The incidence of leukemia is increased and Alzheimer's disease is almost inevitable by age 40.

DSM-IV: An American Psychiatric Association publication that classifies mental illnesses. Currently in its fourth edition, the manual provides health practitioners with a comprehensive system for diagnosing mental illnesses on the basis of specific ideational and behavioral symptoms. It consists of five axes covering clinical syndromes, developmental and personality disorders, physical disorders, severity of psychosocial stressors, and global assessment of functioning.

Dura: The tough outermost layer of the three layers of meninges that cover the brain.

Dynamic formulation: An integrated evaluation of a patient's traits, attitudes, conflicts, and symptoms that attempts to explain the individual's problem.

Dysarthria: Refers to speech disorders based on central or peripheral motor deficits; the quality of speech is affected, as in hypernasality, breathy phonation, and stridor (flaccid paretic dysarthria), slow, low pitch and harsh (spastic paretic dysarthria), or explosive speech (ataxic or cerebellar dysarthria).

Dysfluency: Difficulty in generating words.

Dysmetria: A movement abnormality typically associated with cerebellar disorders. There is impairment of the distance, power, and speed of a motor act, as seen in performance of the finger–nose–finger test.

Dysnomia: Word-finding disability; shown by failure to correctly name objects or by choosing words that are "off center."

Dysphagia: Difficulty swallowing.

Dysthymic disorder: Mild to moderate affective disorder characterized by extended periods of nonpsychotic depression and brief periods of normal moods.

Dystonia: A movement disorder characterized by prolonged abnormal postures of the neck, trunk, or limbs as a consequence of involuntary muscle contraction and excessive muscle tone; often a side effect of antipsychotic (neuroleptic) medication.

E

Echolalia: The involuntary and compulsive repetition of another's speech.

Echopraxia: The involuntary imitation of another's movements; indicates that extant motor problems are not due to lack of inactivity.

Edema: An abnormal excessive accumulation of clear, watery fluid in cells and tissues of the nervous system.

Electroencephalography (EEG): The recording of the electrical potentials of the brain from electrodes placed on the scalp.

Embolic stroke: A sudden neurological deficit resulting from an embolic blockage of a cerebral artery or one of its branches. Cerebral emboli most often have their origin in the heart atrium or the internal carotid artery.

Embolus: A blood clot or other foreign body, deposited by the blood current, that blocks an artery or vein.

Encephalitis: An inflammation of the brain.

Encephalomalacia: Cerebral tissue softening, resulting from a vascular disorder causing inadequate blood flow.

Encephalopathy: Brain disorder.

Encoding: A process of memory formation in which the information, transmitted through sensory channels, is placed into short-term memory.

Environmental agnosia: An inability to recognize familiar environments despite intact perception; results from a medial temporal occipital lesion.

Epilepsy spectrum disorder: A controversial condition, characterized by paroxysmal behavioral features resembling those seen in temporal lobe epilepsy; not currently considered a form of clinical epilepsy, it may, however, reflect temporal limbic dysfunction.

Epileptiform discharges: Referring to recorded electrical potentials on EEG (primarily spikes, spike-waves, and sharp waves), which are frequently but not invariably associated with clinical epilepsy.

Episodic dyscontrol syndrome: An uncommon disorder, characterized by repeated acts of violent, aggressive behavior directed toward persons or property, in otherwise normal persons that is markedly out of proportion to the event that provokes it. It may be due to temporal–limbic dysfunction; associated features include hypersensitivity to alcohol, multiple traffic accidents, and sexual impulsiveness.

Episodic memory: Recall for events in one's life and experiences; unique and anchored to distinct points in time and space.

Evoked potential (EP): An EEG electrical potential, elicited by and time-locked to a specific stimulus, for example, a click or light flash. Abnormal EPs may indicate the presence of focal pathology impairing the transmission of neural impulses via specific sensory pathways to the brain.

Extinction: The failure to perceive one of a stimulus pair simultaneously presented to different parts of the body, ears, or visual fields.

Extinction to double simultaneous stimulation: Failure to report the stimulus.

Extracerebral: Extrinsic to or lying outside of the cerebral hemispheres.

Extrapyramidal system: A motor system that includes the basal ganglia and some closely related brain stem structures.

F

Face–hand test: Touching the face simultaneously with another body part, particularly same-sided; suppression or displacement of the more peripheral stimulus indicates possible parietal lobe dysfunction.

Falx cerebri: The scythe-shaped fold of dura mater in the longitudinal fissure between the two hemispheres of the brain.

Finger agnosia: Inability to identify the fingers of one's own hand, or those of another person, due to brain impairment.

Flaccid: Relaxed, flabby, soft muscles; opposite of spastic.

Fluent aphasia: A major type of aphasia with impaired comprehension of spoken and written language; associated with effortless, well-articulated, but often incomprehensible, speech, resulting from word/syllable substitutions and grammatical errors. The patient often appears unaware of his deficit; often associated with left posterior temporal–parietal lesions, encroaching on Wernicke's area.

Foramen magnum: The large opening in the occipital bone through which the spinal cord becomes continuous with the medulla.

Foramen Munro: The paired openings between the third and lateral ventricles of the brain.

Forced grasp reflex: The involuntary act of grasping the examiner's hand when moved across the patient's palm and experiencing difficulty letting go; associated with a contralateral medial frontal lesion.

Forebrain: The frontal division of the neural tube that contains the cerebral hemispheres, the thalamus, and the hypothalamus; also called the prosencephalon.

Fornix: One of the paired fiber tracts that runs from the hippocampus in the temporal lobe to one of the mammillary bodies in the inferior hypothalamus and to the septal region.

Free radicals: A group of elements or atoms in a transient uncombined state that react with nearby molecules causing cell damage. Released following traumatic or other forms of brain injury, they contribute to neuronal death, but may be counteracted by antioxidant drugs.

Frontal amnesia: Difficulty in switching from one set of memory traces to another in the face of intact operating memory; "forgetting to recall," as in disregarding instructions is an illustration.

Frontal gait disorder: A disorder resulting from bilateral frontal lobe dysfunction, characterized by difficulty initiating and maintaining the act of walking; the patient's feet appear glued to the floor. See utilization behavior.

Frontal psychosurgery: Includes leukotomies aimed at severing frontal–thalamic connections, undercutting of orbital frontal cortex, cingulotomy, and stereotactic ablation of selected frontal areas.

Frontal "release" signs: These are primitive reflexes, often associated with midline frontal pathology. Normally present in infancy and in advanced age, they include hand/foot grasp, rooting, sucking, and snout reflexes.

Frontotemporal dementia (FTD): A degenerative disorder that produces atrophy of the frontal and temporal lobes; has an insidious onset with behavioral alterations at an earlier age than Alzheimer's with cognitive and motor deficits occurring at a later stage. There are three principal types: Pick's disease, frontal lobe degeneration without Pick cells, and dementia with motor neuron disease (ALS).

Fugue: A neurotic dissociative disorder that entails a loss of memory accompanied by physical flight from one's present life situation to a new environment or less threatening former one.

Functional psychoses: Severe mental disorders attributed primarily to psychological stress.

Future shock: A condition brought about when social change proceeds so rapidly that the individual cannot cope with it adequately.

G

Gamma-amino butyric acid (GABA): The major inhibitory neurotransmitter found throughout the brain; deficits are found in seizure and anxiety disorders.

Ganglion: A collection of nerve cell bodies; also called a nucleus.

Ganglion cells: Cells in the retina whose axons form the optic nerve.

Ganser syndrome: Dissociative disorder, characterized by approximate answers to questions. Amnesia and disorientation often present.

Gastaut–Geschwind syndrome: An interictal behavioral disorder associated with temporal lobe epilepsy. Characterized by deepened emotions, obsessive concerns, circumstantiality, social viscosity (stickiness), hyperreligiosity, hyposexuality, and hypergraphia.

General paresis: A progressive mental deterioration due to syphilitic invasion of the central nervous system, marked by progressive dementia, tremor, speech disturbances, and increasing muscular weakness; in many cases, there is a preliminary stage of irritability, often followed by exaltation and delusions of grandeur.

Generalized seizures: Epileptic seizures that arise, based on clinical features and EEG, from brain sites that project to widespread regions of the brain; these seizures involve loss of consciousness and symmetrical involvement of body musculature.

Gerstmann's syndrome: The symptom cluster of acalculia, agraphia, left–right spatial disorientation, and finger agnosia; results usually from pathology involving the left posterior parietal region, especially the angular and supramarginal gyri.

Glabellar tap sign: The subject is tapped lightly and repeatedly just above and between the eyebrows in order to see whether blinking will normally and quickly habituate; Parkinson's patients will continue to blink with each tap.

Glasgow coma scale (GCS): A clinical scale to assess impaired consciousness; assessment usually includes motor responsiveness, verbal performance, and eye opening; frequently used to gauge the severity of coma and its progression or resolution following severe traumatic brain injury.

Glial cells: Nonneural brain cells that provide structural, nutritional, and other supports to the brain; also called glia or neuroglia.

Glioblastoma multiforma: A neoplasm arising from the glial cells, characterized by high degree of lethality and malignancy.

Gliomas: Brain tumors resulting from the aberrant production of glial cells.

Global alexia: Inability to read letters or words.

Global aphasia: A severe form of nonfluent aphasia with markedly impaired spoken and written language comprehension and articulation deficits associated with a large lesion involving the entire perisylvian area of the left frontal, temporal, and parietal lobes; prognosis for recovery is poor.

Global steropsis: Depth perception in the presence of ambiguous stimulus forms; presumed to be mediated by right hemisphere; is differentiated from stereoacuity.

Globus pallidus: The inner and lighter portion of the lenticular nucleus; part of the basal ganglia.

Glossopharyngeal nerve: A cranial nerve that serves taste perception and sensation in the posterior pharynx and posterior third of the tongue.

Golgi tendon organs: Receptors located in tendons that send impulses to the central nervous system when a muscle contracts.

Grand mal seizures: A type of generalized epileptic seizure that involves nerve cells firing in synchrony; causing loss of consciousness and stereotyped severe diffuse muscle contractions.

Gyri: The ridged or raised portions of a convoluted brain surface; contrast with sulci.

H

Hematoma: An accumulation of extravasated blood; most often caused by head trauma or arterial rupture secondary to hypertension.

Hemiparesis: Weakness on one side of the body.

Hemiplegia: Complete paralysis of one side of the body.

Hemi-spatial neglect: Neglect of external space contralateral to a hemispheric lesion, usually extensive and involving the right parietal lobe; also termed visuospatial agnosia or neglect, unilateral spatial neglect, or hemispatial agnosia.

Herpes encephalitis: The most common acute encephalitis involving the orbital frontal and inferomedial temporal lobes; surviving patients often have a severe amnestic disorder.

Hippocampus: A complex internally convoluted cortical structure lying in the anterior medial region of the temporal lobe; actively concerned with memory consolidation functions, a major component of the Papez circuit.

Histrionic personality: Personality pattern characterized by excitability, emotional instability, and self-dramatization.

Homonymous hemianopsia: Total loss of one half of the corresponding visual field in each eye, right- or left-sided (e.g., right temporal/left nasal; right nasal/left temporal); usually due to a lesion of the medial temporal or occipital cortex.

Huntington's disease: A progressive, hereditary, dementing condition that affects the basal ganglia with atrophy of the frontal lobes and caudate nucleus; involuntary and spasmodic movements are associated features, along with declining cognitive and personality/social skills.

Hydrocephalus: A condition characterized by accumulation of excessive cerebrospinal fluid, resulting in dilation of the cerebral ventricles; increased intracranial pressure, enlargement of the cranium, and compensatory atrophy of the brain may occur.

Hyperacusis: The perception of sounds as abnormally loud.

Hypergraphia: Overwriting, as when too many words are written in response to task demands.

Hypermetamorphosis: Tendency to attend and react to every visual stimulus, leading to mental distraction and confusion.

Hypnosis: Trance-like mental state induced in a cooperative subject by suggestion.

Hypnotherapy: Use of hypnosis in psychotherapy.

Hypnotic regression: Process by which a subject is brought to relive, under hypnosis, early forgotten or repressed experiences.

Hypochondriacal delusions: Delusions concerning various horrendous disease conditions, such as the belief that one's brain is rotting or turning to dust.

Hypochondriasis: Condition dominated by preoccupation with bodily processes and fear of specific diseases.

Hypophonia: Lowered voice volume; contrasted to aphonia, or total lack of voice. The most common cause of both disorders is laryngitis.

Hypothalamus: The ventral and medial region of the diencephalon, lying below the thalamus; it has a major role in nearly all behavior, including feeding, sleeping, sexual activity, temperature regulation, emotional expression, and endocrine regulation.

Hypothermia: Low temperature; especially a state of low body temperature induced for the purpose of decreasing metabolic activities and need for oxygen; employed as treatment for severe traumatic brain injury.

Hypotonia: A diminution or loss of muscle tone. Typically associated with cerebellar lesions.

Hypoxia: Refers to insufficient oxygen in inspired gases, blood, or tissue; contrasted to anoxia, which refers to a total lack of blood oxygen.

Hysterical amnesia: A psychogenic loss of memory without an organic basis.

Hysterical disorder: Disorder characterized by involuntary psychogenic dysfunction of motor, sensory, cognitive, or visceral processes; considered an expression of a psychological conflict or need.

I

Iconic memory: A very brief type of memory that stores the sensory impression of a scene.

Ideational apraxia: Loss of the ability to execute a multistepped act, for example, striking a match and blowing out the flame; associated with diffuse cortical disease and dementia.

Ideographic methodology: A method of study emphasizing the individual case and the uniqueness of each personality.

Ideomotor apraxia: Inability to perform a learned movement (e.g., hitchhiking sign, salute, whistling) to verbal command or imitation in the presence of intact comprehension, motor power, and coordination. Bilateral apraxia is associated with a left inferior parietal lesion; apraxia of the left limbs occurs with left frontal or callosal lesions.

Idiopathic epilepsy: A seizure disorder of unknown origin; opposed to symptomatic epilepsy, whose cause is known.

Illusion: Misinterpretation of sensory data; a false perception.

Implicit memory: Memory in which individuals can demonstrate knowledge in specific circumstances, but cannot actively retrieve the information, for example, a motor skill; opposite of explicit memory.

Inattention: Decreased/absent awareness of events occurring on the side of the body contralateral to a parietal lesion.

Indifference reaction: Denial, unawareness, or minimizing psychological/neuropsychological deficits, traditionally associated with right hemisphere lesions; inappropriately elevated affect may be present.

Infarct: Impoverished or dead brain tissue associated with vascular occlusions.

Inferior colliculus: The auditory center in the midbrain; it receives input from the brain stem auditory nuclei and sends output to the medial geniculate nucleus of the thalamus.

Inflection: Change of pitch or tone of speech.

Infundibulum: A funnel-shaped structure or passage; the stalk of the pituitary gland.

Intention tremor: Also called kinetic, the tremor occurs at the end of a movement, as on the finger–nose maneuver and usually reflects cerebellar dysfunction; contrasted to "resting" tremor, which occurs in the stationary limb and is associated with basal ganglia dysfunction.

Interictal: Refers to behaviors/events in the period between epileptic seizures; adversive personality traits (e.g., irritability, obsessional traits) are associated features.

Intermediate coup lesions: Scattered areas of focal tissue damage in line with the point of trauma impact (coup) and possible terminal point of the damage (contrecoup).

Intermediate-term memory: A form of memory lasting longer than short-term and requiring no rehearsal, but not lasting as long as long-term memory.

Internal capsule: A massive white matter fiber tract separating the caudate nucleus and thalamus (medial) from the more laterally situated lentiform nucleus (globus pallidus and putamen); consists of (1) fibers ascending from the thalamus to the cerebral cortex and (2) fibers descending from the cerebral cortex to the thalamus, subthalamic region, midbrain, hindbrain, and spinal cord. The internal capsule is the major route by which the cerebral cortex is connected with the brain stem and spinal cord.

Internal carotid arteries: See common carotid arteries.

Intracerebral: Within the brain hemispheres.

Intracranial steal: The shunting of blood by an arteriovenous malformation away from normal brain tissue to the AVM site; function in the unaffected area may be impaired, resulting in neuropsychological deficit.

Intravascular: Within a vessel or vessels.

Ipsilateral: Same side; homolateral; opposed to contralateral (opposite side), bilateral (both sides), unilateral (one side).

Ischemia: Cut-off of blood flow to an area of the brain or body organ, usually from mechanical obstruction of a feeding vessel.

Ischemic infarction: A disruption of blood flow (infarction) creating dead or damaged tissue (infarct), resulting more from impaired or absent blood flow rather than from insufficient nutrients in the blood.

J

Jargon aphasia: A severe aphasic disorder, characterized by unintelligible but fluent verbal output, devoid of meaning.

K

Kinesthetic: Pertaining to muscle sense or to the sense by which muscular movement, weight, and position are perceived.

Kluver–Bucy syndrome: A condition manifested by hyperorality, hypersexuality, visual agnosia, and inability to form new memories; associated with bilateral medial temporal lobe lesions.

Korsakoff's syndrome: A severe amnestic disorder resulting from bilateral pathology involving the anterior thalamic nuclei, the mammillary bodies, and their interconnections; triggered by a B-1 thiamine deficiency, usually secondary to severe and chronic alcohol abuse; it is characterized by disorientation, gross memory defects and confabulation; also called Wernicke–Korsakoff syndrome.

L

Labile memory: An early state during which formation of a memory can be easily disrupted by conditions that influence brain activity.

Lacunar state: Multiple but small infarctions in the subcortical regions leaving lacunae; one of the end stages of hypertensive, small vessel, cerebrovascular disease.

Lateral: An anatomical term meaning toward the side; opposite of medial.

Lateral hypothalamus (LH): A hypothalamic region involved in the facilitation of eating behavior; a lesion produces an inability to eat.

Lateral inhibition: A phenomenon produced by interconnected neurons that inhibit their neighbors, producing contrast at the edges of the stimulus.

Lentiform nucleus: The large cone-shaped mass of gray matter forming the central core of the cerebral hemisphere. The base of the cone consists of the putamen, which together with the caudate nucleus composes the striatum; the apical part consists of the two segments of the globus pallidus. The nucleus is ventral and lateral to the thalamus and caudate nucleus, from which it is separated by the internal capsule. Also known as lenticular nucleus.

Leukoencephalopathy: Syndrome characterized by structural involvement of the cerebral white matter from a wide variety of disorders.

Lewy body dementia: A progressive dementia, characterized by intraneuronal inclusions in pigmented brain stem and cortical neurons, with clinical features of both Alzheimer's and Parkinson's diseases. The more common form of the disorder is known as the Lewy body variant of Alzheimer's disease.

Lexical agraphia: A form of acquired agraphia with impaired ability to spell irregular or unknown words and an intact ability to spell regular words; associated with lesions in the parietal–occipital region.

Limb-kinetic apraxia: A form of apraxia, characterized by a clumsiness in the execution of distal limb movements that cannot be attributed to weakness or sensory loss; associated with a lesion in the contralateral hemisphere; also known as motor apraxia. See also apraxia, echopraxia, apraxia of speech.

Limbic system: A heterogeneous array of brain structures at or near the edge (limbus) of the medial wall of the cerebral hemisphere, including the hippocampus, amygdala, and the interconnections of these structures with the septal area, thalamus, hypothalamus, and midbrain. These primarily subcortical structures are involved in memory formation and in motivational and emotional responses through their regulation of the endocrine and autonomic motor system.

Literal paraphasia: Production of off-target sounds with effortless articulation, seen in conduction and Wernicke's aphasia. Associated with left inferior parietal or posterior superior temporal lesions.

Localization of function: The concept that specific brain regions are responsible for various types of experience, behavior, and psychological processes.

Locked-in syndrome: Also known as de-efferentation syndrome, this condition is due to a bilateral basal pontine infarction from a basilar artery occlusion; characterized by aphonia and quadriplegia, the patient's consciousness is preserved. All control of voluntary movement is lost, except for horizontal eye movement, which can be used for limited communication.

Long-term memory: An enduring form of memory lasting for weeks, months, or years.

Lumen: The space in the interior of a tubular structure such as an artery or the intestine.

M

Magnetic resonance imaging (MRI): A diagnostic radiological modality, using nuclear magnetic resonance technology, in which the magnetic nuclei of a patient are aligned in a strong, uniform magnetic field, absorb energy from radio frequency pulses, and emit radio frequency signals as their excitation decays. These signals, which vary in intensity according to the molecular chemical environment, are converted into sets of tomographic images, which permit three-dimensional localization of the point sources of the signals. The technique provides superior three-dimensional images of the brain and other body organs, cerebrospinal fluid, nerves, blood vessels, and tissue pathology, for example, strokes and tumors.

Magnetic resonance spectroscopy (MRS): A technique for detecting and measuring the concentration of important metabolites in different regions of the central nervous system.

Major affective disorders: Category of affective disorders in which a biological defect or other aberration renders a person liable to experience episodes of a more or less severe affective disorder.

Major depression (unipolar disorder): A severe affective disorder in which only depressive episodes occur.

Malaise: A feeling of general discomfort or uneasiness; an "out-of-sorts" feeling, often the first indication of an infection.

Mammillary bodies: Paired hypothalamic nuclei at the base of the brain slightly posterior to the pituitary stalk.

Manic–depressive psychoses: Older term denoting a group of psychotic disorders characterized by prolonged periods of excitement and overactivity (mania) or by periods of depression and underactivity (depression) or by alternation of the two.

Masked facies: An unblinking, bland, expressionless stare; typically seen in Parkinson's disease.

Masochism: Sexual variant in which an individual obtains sexual gratification through infliction of pain.

Medial: An anatomical term meaning toward the middle; opposite of lateral.

Medial geniculate nucleus: A nucleus in the thalamus that receives input from the inferior colliculus and sends output to the auditory cortex.

Medulla: The lowest part of the brain stem; also called myelencephalon.

Meninges: Thin membranous coverings of the brain and spinal cord, including the dura mater, arachnoid, and pia mater.

Meningioma: Neoplastic growth arising from the meninges.

Meningitis: Inflammatory disease of the meninges with associated signs of fever, headache, and stiff neck.

Mesencephalon: The midbrain.

Metencephalon: A subdivision of the hindbrain that includes the cerebellum and the pons.

Midbrain: The middle division of the brain; also called the mesencephalon.

Middle cerebral artery (MCA): One of the two terminal branches of the internal carotid artery; supplies a large part of the cortical convexity of the frontal, temporal, and parietal lobes and major deep structures, including the basal ganglia, internal capsule, and thalamus.

Migraine: A symptom complex occurring periodically and, in its classic form, characterized by predominantly unilateral headache, vertigo, nausea and vomiting, photophobia, and scintillating scotomas (blind spots in the visual field).

Misoplegia: A type of unilateral inattention where the individual, usually hemiplegic, exhibits a strong dislike for the affected limbs or portions of the body; intense hatred resulting in self-mutilation may be expressed.

Mood: The pervasive feeling, tone, and emotional state of an individual, for example, sadness, elation.

Motor aprosody: Inability to sing or to change pitch or voice tempo with intact ability to recognize melodies.

Motor cortex: A region of cerebral cortex controlling movements of the face, neck, trunk, arm, and leg. The origin of the motor neurons of the pyramidal tract.

Motor extinction: Increased contralateral limb akinesia when simultaneously using the ipsilateral extremities, due to cerebral dysfunction.

Motor impersistence: Inability to sustain an initiated voluntary movement; examples include failure to maintain tongue protrusion, eyelid closure, mouth opening, breath holding, hand-grip pressure, and central gaze.

Motor neuron: A brain stem or spinal cord neuron with an axon that exits the central nervous system to establish a functional connection with an effector muscle or gland.

Motor neuron disease: A disease of the motor tracts of the brain stem and spinal cord, causing progressive muscular atrophy and fibrillary twitching of the limbs and tongue, increased reflexes and muscle spasticity; frontal dementia may be seen, usually at an advanced stage.

Motor unit: A single motor neuron and all the muscle fibers innervated by its axon.

Multi-infarct dementia: A stepwise progressive deterioration in intellectual function with focal neurological signs due to multiple cerebral infarcts, typically scattered and relatively small lesions involving deep subcortical structures.

Multiple personality: Type of dissociative disorder characterized by the development of two or more relatively independent personality systems in the same individual. Also known as dissociative identity disorder.

Multiple sclerosis (MS): A common demyelinating disease involving the white matter of the central nervous system and the optic nerves; multiple cognitive and emotional deficits are noted; often initially characterized by exacerbations and remissions, and protean clinical features, for example, blurred and double vision, dysarthria, weakness, and ataxia, which result from plaque-like lesions separated in time and space.

Myasthenia gravis: A neurological disease characterized by easy fatiguability and weakness of muscles.

Myelencephalon: A subdivision of the hindbrain consisting of the medulla.

Myelin: The fatty insulation around an axon that improves the speed of conduction of nerve impulses.

Myelinization: The process of formation of myelin.

Myelin sheath: A thin cover on the axons of many neurons.

Myoclonic seizures: Seizures consisting of single or repetitive myoclonic jerks.

Myoclonus: One or a series of brief shock-like muscle contractions sufficient to move a body part.

N

Narcolepsy: A disorder involving frequent episodes of irresistible sleep, which last from 5 to 30 min, that can occur anytime during the usual waking hours.

Necker cube: An optical illusion using "rate of apparent change" (RAC) to differentiate normal from brain-injured; fewer and slower reversals are reported by individuals with right hemisphere or frontal lobe lesions.

Necrosis: Local death of tissue.

Neocortex: The relatively recently evolved portions of the cerebral cortex.

Nerve impulse: Movement or propagation of an electrical potential away from the cell body of a neuron and down its axon to the axonal terminal at the synapse.

Neural tube: A prenatal structure with subdivisions that correspond to the future forebrain, midbrain, and hindbrain. The cavity of this tube will include the cerebral ventricles and the passages that connect them.

Neurasthenic neurosis: Neurotic disorder characterized by complaints of chronic weakness, easy fatigability, and lack of enthusiasm.

Neurofibrillary tangles: Abnormal whorls of neurofilaments within nerve cells that are characteristically seen in Alzheimer's disease.

Neuroglia: "Nerve glue" or glia; these cells make up about half the volume of the central nervous system and provide structural and metabolic support to neurons. See glial cells.

Neuroleptic drug: A drug with antipsychotic action.

Neurological examination: Examination to determine presence and extent of organic damage to the nervous system.

Neuron: The basic unit of the nervous system, composed of a cell body, receptive extensions (dendrites), and a transmitting extension (axon).

Neuron doctrine: A hypothesis that states that the brain is composed of separate cells that are structurally, metabolically, and functionally distinct.

Neuropathy: A disorder involving the cranial nerves, the peripheral nerves, or the autonomic nervous system.

Neurotic style: A general personality disposition toward inhibiting certain anxiety-causing behaviors; distinguishable from anxiety, somatoform, and dissociative disorders in that neurotic styles do not manifest themselves in specific, disabling neurotic symptoms.

Neurotoxin: Any substance that is poisonous or destructive to nerve tissue.

Neurotransmitter: A chemical released from the synapse in response to an action potential and acts on a postsynaptic receptor, transmitting information chemically from one neuron to another.

Nigrostriatal bundle (NSB): A dopaminergic tract that runs from the substantia nigra of the midbrain to the striatum (caudate and putamen).

Nihilistic delusion: Fixed belief that everything is unreal.

Nociceptors: Receptors that respond to stimuli that produce tissue damage or pose the threat of damage.

Nomadism: Withdrawal reaction in which the individual continually attempts to escape frustration by moving from place to place or job to job.

Norepinephrine (NE): A neurotransmitter produced mainly in brain stem nuclei, also called noradrenalin.

Normal pressure hydrocephalus (NPH): A type of hydrocephalus developing usually in older people, due to impaired absorption of cerebrospinal fluid and characterized clinically by progressive dementia, unsteady gait, urinary incontinence, and, usually, a normal spinal fluid.

Nosology: The classification of diseases, including mental diseases.

Nucleus: An anatomical collection of neurons, for example, caudate nucleus.

Nucleus accumbens: Also known as ventral striatum, forms the ventral medial union of the caudate and putamen. Implicated in incentive and motivational reward and conditioned reinforcement.

Nystagmus: Abnormal to and fro movements of the eye during attempts to fixate; rhythmic oscillation of the eyeballs, either horizontal, rotary, or vertical.

O

Obsessions: Recurrent and intrusive thoughts, impulses, and images, often of a violent or sexual nature, that occur involuntarily.

Occipital cortex: The cortex of the occipital (posterior) lobe of the brain.

Ondine's curse: A type of sleep apnea where automatic breathing during sleep is disrupted; lesions of the brain stem have been implicated in this condition.

Oneirism: Prolonged dream state despite wakefulness.

Optic aphasia: Inability to name visually presented objects with intact recognition; spared recognition is shown by demonstration of use or matching (pointing) to the object when named.

Optic ataxia: Inability to reach objects in space by visual guidance; difficulty in shifting (stimulus boundedness) is an associated feature.

Optic chiasm: The site where the optic nerve from one eye partially crosses to join the optic nerve from the other eye; located at the base of the brain near the pituitary gland.

Optic radiation: Axons of the lateral geniculate nucleus of the thalamus that travel through the temporal and occipital lobes to terminate in the primary visual areas of the occipital cortex.

Optic tract: The axons of the retinal ganglion cells after they have passed the optic chiasm; most terminate in the lateral geniculate nucleus.

Optokinetic system: A closed-loop system controlling eye movement and keeping the gaze on target.

Orbitofrontal cortex: Inferior region of the frontal lobe that mediates associative processing involving emotion, personality, social cognition, and empathy.

Organophosphates: A group of phosphorus-containing highly neurotoxic organic compounds.

Osmoreceptors: Cells in the hypothalamus that were thought to respond to changes in osmotic pressure.

Otorrhea: A discharge from the ear.

P

P 300 wave: An evoked electrical potential recorded on the scalp and derived by computer analysis; reflects a process of cognitive appraisal of a stimulus; a measure of the speed and efficacy of brain information processing.

Paleocortex: Evolutionary old cortex, for example, the hippocampus.

Panic disorder: Recurrent unpredictable panic attacks.

Papez circuit: A major limbic system closed circuit, involved in the formation of long-term memory; it consists of the hippocampus–fornix–mammillary bodies–mammillothalamic tract–anterior thalamic nucleus–cingulate gyrus–cingulum–hippocampus.

Papilledema: Edema of the optic disk, associated with increased intracranial pressure.

Paradoxical sleep: See rapid-eye-movement (REM).

Parahippocampal gyrus: A component of the limbic system, located in the medial temporal lobe adjacent to the hippocampus, which integrates incoming sensory information with internally generated data. See uncus.

Parallel processing: Using several different circuits at the same time to process the same stimulus.

Paralysis: A loss of power of voluntary movement in a muscle through the injury or disease of its nerve supply.

Paranoia: Psychosis characterized by a systematized delusional system.

Paranoid personality: Individual showing behavior characterized by projection (as a defense mechanism), suspiciousness, envy, extreme jealousy, and stubbornness.

Paranoid schizophrenia: Subtype of schizophrenic disorder characterized by absurd, illogical, and changeable ideas or hallucinations of grandeur and persecution.

Paranoid state: Transient psychotic disorder in which the main element is a delusion, usually persecutory or grandiose in nature.

Paraphasias: Errors in word usage associated with aphasia; substitutions for a correct word (e.g., "I ate night") or substitution for syllables (e.g., "I ate rupper") may occur; neologisms, nonexistent words, may occur (e.g., "I ate ronks").

Parasympathetic division: One of the two systems that composes the autonomic nervous system; the parasympathetic division arises from both the cranial and sacral parts of the spinal cord.

Paraventricular nucleus: A nucleus of the hypothalamus.

Paresthesias: Numbness or tingling in the limbs.

Parkinson's disease: A degenerative neurological disorder involving dopaminergic neurons of the substantia nigra, characterized by tremor, rigidity, bradykinesia, and loss of postural reflexes.

Partial seizures: Epileptic seizures characterized by localized onset; the symptoms experienced are dependent on the cortical area of ictal onset or seizure spread; they often include focal repetitive muscle spasms and do not involve a loss of consciousness.

Perceptual defense: A process in which threatening stimuli are filtered out and not perceived by the organism.

Peripheral nerves: Neurons that lie outside the central nervous system.

Peripheral nervous system: The portion of the nervous system that includes all the nerves outside the brain and spinal cord.

Perseveration: Persistent continuation of a line of thought or activity once it is underway; clinically inappropriate repetition.

Perseveration–consolidation hypothesis: A hypothesis stating that information passes through two stages in memory formation. During the first stage the memory is held by perseveration of neural activity and is easily disrupted; during the second stage the memory becomes fixed, or consolidated, and is no longer easily disrupted.

Personality disorder: A group of maladaptive behavioral syndromes originating in the developmental years and not characterized by neurotic or psychotic symptoms.

Petit mal seizures: Type of generalized epileptic seizure characterized by a spike-and-wave electrical pattern; during these seizures the person is unaware of the environment and later cannot recall what happened.

Phantom limb: The experience of sensory messages attributed to an amputated limb.

Phoneme: A basic sound unit that forms a word or part of a word.

Phonological agraphia: Impaired ability to spell nonwords with intact ability for familiar words; associated with lesions of the supramarginal gyrus or associated areas.

Phrenology: The belief that bumps on the skull reflect enlargement of the brain regions responsible for certain behavioral faculties.

Pick's disease: A degenerative and progressive dementing disorder, similar to Alzheimer's disease, with neuronal damage typically confined to the frontal and anterior temporal lobes. Personality changes usually precede memory loss. Affects twice as many women as men.

Pitch: A dimension of auditory experience in which sounds vary from low to high.

Pituitary gland: A small complex endocrine gland located in a socket at the base of the skull. The anterior pituitary and the posterior pituitary are separate in function.

Planum temporale: A region of superior temporal cortex adjacent to the primary auditory area.

Plexus: A network or tangle of interweaving nerves, veins, or lymphatic vessels.

Pneumoencephalogram: A technique for examining brain structure by taking x-rays after a gas is injected into the ventricles.

Pons: A portion of the metencephalon.

Positron emission tomography (PET) scan: A technique for examining brain structure and function by combining tomography with injections of radioactive substances, for example, oxygen, glucose used by the brain. An analysis of metabolism of these substances reflects regional differences in brain activity.

Postcentral gyrus: Involved in sensory mediation, this cortical convolution is located just posterior to the Fissure of Rolando.

Postconcussion syndrome: Constellation of somatic and psychological symptoms, which typically follow recovery from a brief period of disturbed consciousness, usually caused by a blow to the head.

Posterior cortical atrophy: A progressive focal dementia syndrome associated with occipital–parietal cortical atrophy, characterized by complex visual perceptual-motor and related cognitive deficits.

Posterior pituitary: The rear division of the pituitary gland; also called neurohypophysis.

Posttraumatic amnesia (PTA): A form of anterograde amnesia seen as a postconcussional effect of head trauma; correlates well with the coma length and severity. Some retrograde amnesia may accompany PTA.

Posttraumatic stress disorder (PTSD): Category of disorder in which severe and residual symptoms occur following the traumatic experience.

Postural tremor: A tremor that occurs when a person attempts to maintain a posture such as holding an arm or a leg extended, resulting from pathology of the basal ganglia or cerebellum.

Precentral gyrus: Involved in the mediation of motor activity, this cortical convolution is located just anterior to the Fissure of Rolando.

Prion: An infectious proteinaceous particle, also known as a slow virus, responsible for several transmissible degenerative diseases, including Creutzfeldt–Jakob dementia.

Procedural memory: Memory for skilled movements or modifiable cognitive operations; knowing how as opposed to knowing that, considered independent of declarative memory.

Prodrome: Behavioral/mood change preceding onset of a seizure; prodromal signs may be apparent for several days before the seizure.

Progressive supranuclear palsy: An uncommon Parkinsonism-like condition that usually begins in a person's 50s with emotional lability, imbalance, and problems with downward gaze; a subcortical dementia develops with relative sparing of language and reasoning abilities.

Prosody: Rhythm, pitch, and tempo characteristics of speech; important in communication of affective content; typically seen as a right hemisphere function.

Prosopagnosia: Inability to recognize faces of those with whom one was previously familiar; associated with bilateral temporal occipital lesions; loss of ability to recognize unfamiliar faces is a variant of this disorder.

Proximal: An anatomical directional term meaning near the trunk or center; opposite of distal.

Pseudobulbar state: Strong affective expressions including laughing and crying, often simultaneously but also incongruous to the stated feeling of the person; associated with lesions of connecting pathways between the frontal lobes and lower brain structures.

Pseudodementia: A pattern of deficit behavior resembling organically produced dementia; depression is the primary factor causing intellectual impairment.

Pseudodepression: A behavioral pattern characterized by flat affect, diminished motor responses, reduced spontaneity and initiative, resembling a psychiatric depressive disorder; associated with pathology involving the dorsal–lateral frontal convexity, severe bilateral frontal pathology, or disruption of frontal–thalamic pathways. The subject may be aware of the behavior.

Pseudohemianopsia: Lack of attention to visual stimulation from the contralateral side despite intact visual fields.

Pseudopsychopathy: A behavioral syndrome associated with pathology involving the orbital frontal region with motor excess (e.g., puerile acts, restlessness, bursting into motion, impulsive antisocial acts). The subject is aware of the motor behavior, but cannot control it.

Psychogenic amnesia: A dissociative disorder characterized by a disproportionate deficit in retrograde memory and an ability to use information that cannot be recalled.

Psychomotor epilepsy: An epileptic disorder with seizures consisting of a state of disturbed consciousness in which the individual may perform various actions of a repetitive nature, for which he or she is later amnesic.

Ptosis: Drooping eyelid caused by a lesion of the third or oculomotor cranial nerve.

Pure agraphia: Writing deficit caused by brain damage in the absence of other significant language disturbances.

Pure word deafness: Inability to understand spoken words with an intact ability to read, write, and speak; usually does not occur in isolation of other defects and is typically associated with stroke.

Purkinje cell: A type of large nerve cell in the cerebellar cortex.

Putamen: One of the basal ganglia, the outer larger part of the lenticular nucleus. The putamen and caudate compose the striatum.

Pyramidal cell: A type of large nerve cell in the cerebral cortex.

Pyramidal system: A motor system including neurons within the cerebral cortex and their axons that forms the pyramidal tract.

Q

QEEG: Quantitative analysis of brain electrical activity, using computer technology. See topographic mapping.

R

Rapid-eye-movement (REM): A state of deep sleep characterized by low amplitude, fast EEG waves, absence of postural muscle tension, rapid eye movements, and dreaming.

Reaction formation: Ego-defense mechanism in which the individual's conscious attitudes and overt behavior are opposite to repressed unconscious wishes.

Reality principle: Awareness of the demands of the environment and adjustment of behavior to meet these demands.

Receptor: Nerve ending that receives a stimulus.

Reduplicative paramnesia: Associated with right parietal and frontal damage; involves relocating a place (e.g., hospital) to another place (e.g., one's hometown).

Reflex: A simple, highly stereotyped, and unlearned response to a particular stimulus (e.g., an eye blink in response to a puff of air).

Regression: Ego-defense mechanism in which the individual retreats to the use of less mature responses in attempting to cope with stress and maintain ego integrity.

REM behavior disorder: A sleep disorder seen in middle-aged men who, spontaneously aroused in REM sleep, engage in vigorous coordinated and often violent motor acts.

Repression: Ego-defense mechanism by means of which dangerous desires and intolerable memories are kept out of consciousness.

Residual schizophrenia: Category used for persons regarded as recovered from schizophrenia but manifesting some residual symptoms.

Resistance: Tendency to maintain symptoms and resist treatment or uncovering of repressed material.

Reticular activating system: Brain stem area that mediates level of arousal.

Reticular formation: A region of the brain stem, extending from the medulla through the thalamus, which is involved in arousal.

Retrieval: A process in memory during which a stored memory is used.

Retrograde amnesia: Inability to recall events previous to the onset of a trauma or condition; recovery of remote events usually occurs first.

Rhinorrhea: Nasal leakage of cerebrospinal fluid following cranial trauma.

Rostral: An anatomical term meaning toward the head end; opposite of caudal.

S

Schizo–affective psychosis: Disorder characterized by schizophrenic symptoms in association with pronounced depression or elation.

Schizoid personality: Personality pattern characterized by eccentricity, shyness, oversensitivity, and seclusiveness.

Schizophrenia: Psychosis characterized by disturbances in thought and behavior, the breakdown of integrated personality functioning, withdrawal from reality, emotional blunting, and distortion.

Schizophreniform disorder: A subtype of schizophrenic psychosis, usually in an undifferentiated form, of less than 6 months' duration.

Schizophrenogenic: Qualities in parents that appear to promote the development of schizophrenia in their children; often applied to rejecting, cold, domineering, overprotective mothers or passive, uninvolved fathers.

Selective vigilance: A tuning of attentional and perceptual processes toward stimuli relevant or central to goal-directed behavior, with decreased sensitivity to those irrelevant or peripheral to this purpose.

Semantic memory: Memory of general knowledge, considered "timeless and spaceless" (e.g., a number system, a foreign language), a subtype of declarative memory.

Senile dementia: An older term denoting any neurological disorder of the aged (defined as over 65) involving progressive behavioral deterioration including personality change and profound intellectual decline.

Sensorineural deafness: A hearing impairment arising from cochlear or auditory nerve pathology.

Septal region: Midline limbic structure lying anterior to the third ventricle, associated with pleasurable and addictive behavior.

Serotonin: A major neurotransmitter involved in mood and impulse control.

Short-term memory: A form of memory that usually lasts only for seconds or as long as rehearsal continues.

Significant others: In interpersonal theory, individuals such as parents or friends on whom a person is a dependant for meeting physical or psychological needs.

Simultanagnosia: A disorder characterized by an inability to recognize multiple elements in a visual presentation, that is, one object or elements of a scene can be appreciated but not the display as a whole; often associated with inertia of gaze and optic ataxia in Balint's syndrome.

Single photon emission computed tomography (SPECT): A technique for assessing brain function; an administered radioactively labeled tracer interacts with brain tissue, releasing radiation, which is detected by a rotating camera; through tomographic reconstruction an image of brain flow is obtained.

Sleep apnea: A disorder that involves slowing or cessation of respiration during deep sleep, manifested by loud snoring. May result in cerebral hypoxia and daytime hypersomnolence from frequent nocturnal awakenings.

Slow-wave sleep: Stages of sleep including stages 1 through 4, defined by presence of slow EEG activity, midline sharp waves, and frontal–parietal spindles.

Somatesthetic: Pertaining to somatesthesia, or awareness of having a body.

Somatoform disorder: A group of disorders in which physical symptoms suggest physical disorders for which there are no demonstrable organic findings or known physiologic mechanisms. There is frequently evidence that the symptoms are linked to psychologic factors; major subtypes include conversion disorder, hypochondriasis, and pain disorder.

Somatosensory modalities: Body sensations (e.g., touch, pain, pressure), other than auditory and visual.

Spasm: An involuntary, convulsive muscular contraction.

Spatial acalculia: Spatial misalignment of the numbers during arithmetic calculation with intact knowledge of the correct principle; associated with right parietal lesions.

Spatial agraphia: Deficits in spatial–motor aspects of writing due to nondominant parietal lobe pathology; frequently associated with the hemi-neglect syndrome.

Split-brain: Individuals who have had surgical section of the corpus callosum and other cerebral commissures for intractable epilepsy; results in severed communication between the right and left hemisphere.

Stage 1 sleep: The initial stage of slow-wave sleep involving low amplitude EEG waves of irregular frequency, slow heart rate, and a reduction of muscle tension.

Stage 2 sleep: A stage of slow-wave sleep defined by spindle bursts, regular 14 to 18 Hz EEG waves that progressively increase and decrease in amplitude.

Stage 3 sleep: A stage of slow-wave sleep defined by admixed spindles and larger amplitude slow-waves.

Stage 4 sleep: A stage of slow-wave sleep defined by the presence of very high amplitude slow waves of 1 to 4 Hz.

Statistical test of significance: A probability standard, stating that an experimental finding is significant if, by chance alone, it could have occurred fewer than one or five times in 100 occurrences. Five times in 100 is usually the scientific standard of acceptability for statistical significance.

Stenosis: Narrowing or constriction of a bodily canal or opening.

Stereopsis: The perception of depth, using the slight difference in visual information from the two eyes.

Striate cortex: A portion of the visual cortex receiving input via the optic radiation from the lateral geniculate nucleus.

Subarachnoid hemorrhage: An extravasation of blood into the subarachnoid space, often from a ruptured aneurysm or arteriovenous malformation that usually spreads throughout the cerebrospinal fluid pathways.

Subarachnoid space: The space between the arachnoid and pia mater meningeal layers of the brain.

Subcortical dementia: Intellectual deterioration characterized by slowed psychomotor speed, a retrieval memory disorder, variable degree of executive dysfunction, apathy, and depression with language relatively spared; examples include Huntington's disease, AIDS, encephalopathy, and lacunar state; also known as frontal subcortical dementia. See cortical dementia.

Substantia nigra: A large cell mass extending from the rostral pons to the subthalamic region; a major source of dopamine, it is involved in the metabolic disorders associated with Parkinson's disease.

Sulci: The grooves on the brain surface bounding the gyri.

Superior colliculus: Paired rounded structure in the dorsal midbrain that receives visual information from the optic tract.

Superior olivary complex: A structure in the pons that receives input from the cochlear nuclei, providing the first binaural analysis of auditory information.

Supplementary motor area (SMA) location: A motor area on the medial surface of the frontal lobe with bilateral representation involved in tonic and postural motor activity; considered also to be a secondary speech area.

Supraoptic nucleus: A nucleus of the hypothalamus, involved in the secretion of vasopressin that produces a contraction of smooth muscle.

Synapse: The junctional region subserving the transmission of neurochemical messages between neurons. Composed of the presynaptic (axonal) terminal, the postsynaptic (usually dendritic) membrane, and the space (or cleft) between them.

Synaptic transmitter: The chemical in the presynaptic bouton that serves as the basis of interneuronal communication. It travels across the synaptic cleft and reacts with receptors on the postsynaptic membrane when triggered by a nerve impulse; also called neurotransmitter.

Synaptic vesicles: The small, spherically shaped structures near the presynaptic membrane of a synaptic junction that contain molecules of neurotransmitter.

Syncope: A loss of consciousness and postural tone due to reduced cerebral blood flow.

Syndrome: A constellation of signs and symptoms that occur at a statistical level greater than chance and unite to form a recognizable entity with definable characteristics.

T

Tactile: Pertaining to the sense of touch.

Tactile agnosia: An inability to recognize objects by touch, in the presence of intact cutaneous and proprioceptive hand sensation resulting from a lesion in the contralateral parietal lobe.

Tactile hallucination: Hallucinations involving the sense of touch, such as feeling insects crawling over one's body.

Tardive dyskinesia: Abnormal involuntary movements involving the oral structures (e.g., tongue, jaw, lips, cheek) and extremities; a late side effect of prolonged neuroleptic drug treatment, frequently irreversible.

Tegmentum: The dorsal part of the midbrain that extends from the substantia nigra to the cerebral aqueduct.

Telencephalon: Consists of the cerebral cortex, subcortical nuclei, and corpus striatum; the frontal subdivision of the forebrain that includes the cerebral hemispheres when fully developed.

Tentorium cerebelli: A fold of dura mater separating the cerebellum from the cerebrum.

Tetany: Intermittent tonic muscular contractions of the extremities, due to low serum calcium; laryngeal spasm and seizures can occur when severe.

Thalamic syndrome: A sensory disorder, typically due to a thalamic infarct, characterized by a severe loss of superficial and deep sensation with preservation of severe often intractable pain, especially to touch, in the affected contralateral limbs.

Thalamus: The large ovoid mass of diencephalic gray matter surrounding the third ventricle, comprised of nuclei that relay sensory and motor information to different parts of the brain or form critical components of the limbic and reticular activating system.

Thrombotic stroke: A sudden focal neurologic deficit due to diminished blood flow from partial blockage or occlusion of a vessel; occurs most often where blood vessels branch.

Thrombus: A blood clot in the cardiovascular or cerebrovascular system, usually caused by slowing of the circulation, alteration of the blood itself, or changes in the vessel walls.

Thyroxin: A hormone secreted by the thyroid gland.

Tinnitus: A ringing or buzzing sound in the ears.

Tomogram: See computerized transaxial tomography.

Topographic mapping: A procedure for the graphic display of scalp electrical activity by computer analysis of the EEG.

Transcortical aphasia: An aphasic disorder due to the isolation of unaffected motor and sensory language areas from the surrounding hemispheric cortex, often caused by lesions in the watershed zones between major arterial territories. There are two subtypes: motor transcortical aphasia is characterized by impairment of spontaneous speech with intact repetition and comprehension; in sensory transcortical aphasia, speech is fluent, repetition is also intact but language comprehension is severely impaired.

Transient global amnesia: A relatively brief (several hours to several days) amnestic disorder with few neurologic sequelae; associated features include (1) profound anterograde amnesia, (2) some retrograde amnesia, (3) confusion and disorientation, with (4) speech and orientation to person unimpaired. There is usually a sudden onset and an equally rapid termination with no prodromal symptoms; a vascular etiology is suspected.

Transient ischemic attacks (TIA): Neurologic deficits of sudden onset from reduced vascular perfusion within the carotid or basilar vertebral territory; less severe than a major stroke, usually reversible within a period of 24 h, and generally of much shorter duration; often herald a complete thrombotic stroke with permanent brain infarction.

Tremor-at-rest: A tremor that occurs when the affected region, such as a limb, is fully supported.

Tremors: Repetitive and usually involuntary oscillating movements, caused by contraction of opposing muscle groups; often associated with basal ganglia or cerebellar disorder.

Trigeminal neuralgia: Severe paroxysmal bursts of pain in area of a trigeminal nerve lesion; episodic pain may be triggered by light stimulation such as touching the mouth or the face.

U

Unconscious motivation: Motivation for an individual's behavior of which he or she is unaware.

Uncus: The anterior hooked protuberance of the parahippocampal gyrus in the temporal lobe; part of the olfactory cortex.

Undifferentiated schizophrenia: Subtype in which the patient either has mixed symptoms or moves rapidly from one type to another.

Unilateral apraxia: Apraxia affecting one side of the body, usually the left; sympathetic and callosal types have been postulated. Sympathetic apraxia is a transient left-sided apraxia associated with Broca's aphasia and a right hemiparesis, produced by an acute left frontal stroke with destruction of motor association cortex and interruption of callosal pathways.

Unipolar disorder: A severe affective disorder in which only depressive episodes occur, as opposed to bipolar disorders in which both manic and depressive processes are assumed to occur.

Unmyelinated: Refers to fine diameter axons that lack a myelin sheath.

V

Ventral: An anatomical term meaning toward the belly or front of the body or the bottom of the brain; opposite of dorsal.

Ventricles: Cavities in the brain that contain cerebrospinal fluid.

Ventriculo–peritoneal shunt: A surgical procedure that diverts CSF from the brain to the peritoneal cavity for treatment of hydrocephalus.

Ventromedial hypothalamus (VMH): A hypothalamic region involved in eating and chewing among other functions; a lesion may produce obesity.

Vertigo: A type of dizziness, characterized by a spinning or whirling sensation, involving rotation of the patient or the surrounding environment.

Viscosity: A behavioral pattern characterized by stickiness in interactional contexts; associated with frontal system damage and temporal lobe epilepsy.

Visual anosognosia: Denial of blindness caused by a brain lesion. The subject attempts to behave as if the deficit is not present. See Anton's syndrome.

W

Wada technique: A procedure designed to assess which hemisphere is language-dominant. Sodium amytal is injected into one carotid artery in order to deactivate an entire hemisphere. Changes in counting and other verbal output while the injection is in process indicate which hemisphere is dominant for speech and language.

Wernicke–Korsakoff syndrome: Result of damage to the mamillary bodies and the dorsomedial nucleus of the thalamus. Implicated in causing episodic memory impairment.

Wernicke's aphasia: A fluency disorder with severe auditory comprehension and language-processing deficits. Speech and writing is garbled and often incomprehensible because of word and phoneme substitution errors. A naming deficit resulting in empty speech is seen in the mild form. Considered a posterior aphasia.

Wernicke's area: A cortical region in the superior temporal lobe of the left hemisphere involved in language comprehension.

White matter: Consists of densely packed conduction fibers that transmit neural messages between the cortex and lower centers (projection fibers), between the hemispheres (commissural fibers), or within a hemisphere (association fibers).

Wilson's disease: Genetic disease affecting the basal ganglia, due to failure of copper metabolism.

Word deafness: Also called pure word deafness; nonspeech sounds are recognized but not spoken words; usually produced by subcortical lesion disconnecting auditory input from auditory processing regions.

Appendix A:
Psychotropic Agents

Generic name	Principal brand name	Manufacturer
Antidepressants		
Amitriptyline	Elavil	Zeneca, Wilmington, DE
Clomipramine	Anafranil	Novartis, East Hanover, NJ
Desipramine	Norpramin	Hoechst Marion Roussel, Kansas City, MO
Doxepin	Sinequan	Pfizer, New York, NY
Imipramine	Tofranil	Novartis, East Hanover, NJ
Nortriptyline	Pamelor	Novartis, East Hanover, NJ
Citalopram	Celexa	Parke Davis, Morris Plains, NJ
Fluoxetine	Prozac	Eli Lilly, Indianapolis, IN
Fluvoxamine	Luvox	Solvay, Marietta, GA
Paroxetine	Paxil	SmithKline Beecham, Pittsburgh, PA
Sertraline	Zoloft	Pfizer, New York, NY
Phenelzine	Nardil	Parke-Davis, Morris Plains, NJ
Tranylcypromin	Parnate	SmithKline, Beecham, Pittsburgh, PA
Amoxapine	Amoxapine	Watson, Corona, CA
Bupropion	Wellbutrin	Glaxo-Wellcome Research, Triangle Park, NC
Maprotiline	Ludiomil	Novartis, East Hanover, NJ
Mirtazapine	Remeron	Organon, West Orange, NJ
Nefazadone	Serzone	Bristol-Myers Squibb, Princeton, NJ
Trazadone	Desyrel	Bristol-Myers Squibb, Princeton, NJ
Venlafaxine	Effexor	Wyeth-Ayerst, Philadelphia, PA
Duloxetine	Cymbalta	Eli Lilly, Indianapolis, IN
Escitalopram	Lexapro	Forest, St. Louis, MO
Trimipramine	Surmontil	Odyssey, East Hanover, NJ
Protriptylene	Vivactyl	Odyssey, East Hanover, NJ
Mirtazapine	Remeron	Organon, West Orange, NJ
Mood stabilizers — Anticonvulsants		
Lithium	Eskalith	SmithKline, Beecham, Pittsburgh, PA
Carbamazepine	Tegretol	Novartis, East Hanover, NJ
Valproic acid	Depokene/Depakote	Abbott, Abbott Park, IL
Phenytoin	Dilantin	Parke-Davis, Morris Plains, NJ
Primidone	Mysoline	Wyeth-Ayerst, Philadelphia, PA
Gabapentin	Neurontin	Parke-Davis, Morris Plains, NJ
Lamotrigine	Lamictal	Glaxo-Wellcome Research, Triangle Park, NC
Tiagabine	Gabitril	Cephalon, Westchester, PA
Levetiracetam	Keppra	Smyrna, GA
Pregabalin	Lyrica	Pfizer, New York, NY

Continued

Generic name	Principal brand name	Manufacturer
Topirimate	Topamax	Ortho-McNeil, Raritan, NJ
Oxcarbazepine	Trileptal	Novartis, East Hanover, NJ
Ethosuximide	Zarontin	Parke-Davis, Morris Plains, NJ
Zonisamide	Zonegran	Eisai, Teaneck, NJ
Anxiolytics		
Alprazolam	Xanax	Pharmacia, Upjohn, Kalamazoo, MI
Chlordiazepoxide	Librium	ICN, Costa Mesa, CA
Clonazepam	Klonopin	Roche, Nutley, NJ
Diazepam	Valium	Roche, Nutley, NJ
Lorazepam	Ativan	Wyeth-Ayerst, Philadelphia, PA
Oxazepam	Serax	Wyeth-Ayerst, Philadelphia, PA
Buspirone	Buspar	Bristol-Myers Squibb, Princeton, NJ
Hydroxyzine	Vistaril	Pfizer, New York, NY
Clorazepate	Tranxene	Ovation, Deerfield, IL
Hypnotics		
Flurazepam	Dalmane	Roche, Nutley, NJ
Temazepam	Restoril	Novartis, East Hanover, NJ
Triazolam	Halcion	Pharmacia/Upjohn, Kalamazoo, MI
Diphenhydramine	Benadryl	Parke-Davis, Morris Plains, NJ
Zolpidem	Ambien	G.D. Searle, Chicago, IL
Eszopiclone	Lunesta	Sepracor, Marlborough, MA
Estazolam	Prosom	Abbott, Abbott Park, IL
Ramelteon	Rozerem	Takeda, Deerfield, IL
Zaleplon	Sonata	King, Bristol, TN
Antipsychotics		
Chlorpromazine	Thorazine	SmithKline, Beecham, Pittsburgh, PA
Thioridazine	Mellaril	Novartis, East Hanover, NJ
Fluphenazine	Prolixin	Apothecon, Princeton, NJ
Perphenazine	Trilafon	Schering, Kenilworth, NJ
Trifluoperazine	Stelazine	SmithKline, Beecham, Pittsburgh, PA
Haloperidol	Haldol	Ortho-McNeil, Raritan, NJ
Thioxanthene	Navane	Pfizer, New York, NY
Clozapine	Clozaril	Novartis, East Hanover, NJ
Olanzapine	Zyprexa	Eli Lilly, Indianapolis, IN
Quetiapine	Seroquel	Zeneca, Wilmington, DE
Risperidone	Risperdal	Janssen, Titusville, NJ
Aripiprazole	Abilify	Bristol-Myers, Squibb, Princeton, NJ
Ziprasadone	Geodon	Pfizer, New York, NY
Anti-Parkinson agents		
Benztropine mesylate	Cogentin	Merck, West Point, PA
Trihexyphenidyl	Artane	Lederle, Philadelphia, PA
Carbidopa-levodopa	Sinemet	Dupont, Wilmington, DE
Amantidine	Symmetrel	Dupont, Wilmington, DE
Bromocriptine	Parlodel	Sandoz, East Hanover, NJ
Entacapone	Comtan	Novartis, East Hanover, NJ
Selegiline	Eldepryl	Somerset, Tampa, FL
Pramipexole	Mirapex	Boehringher-Ingelheim, Ridgefield, CN
Pergolide	Permax	Valeant, Costa Mesa, CA
Ropinirole	Requip	GlaxoSmithKline, Research Triangle Park, NC
Tolcapone	Tasmar	Valeant, Costa Mesa, CA

Generic name	Principal brand name	Manufacturer
Psychostimulants		
Dextroamphetamine	Dexedrine	SmithKline, Beecham, Pittsburgh, PA
Methylphenidate	Ritalin	Novartis, Basle, Switzerland
Pemoline	Cylert	Abbott, Abbott Park, IL
Pimozide	Orap	Gate Pharmaceuticals, Sellersville, PA
Amphetamine	Salt Combo Adderall	Shire, Newport, KY
Methylphenidate	Concerta	Ortho McNeil, South Raritan, NJ
Dexmethylphenidate	Focalin	Novartis, Basle, Switzerland
Modafinil	Provigil	Cephalon, Westchester, PA
Atomoxetine	Strattera	Eli Lilly, Indianopolis, IN

Appendix B: Strengths and Limitations of Neuropsychological Tests

STANDARDIZED NEUROPSYCHOLOGICAL TEST BATTERIES

HALSTEAD–REITAN NEUROPSYCHOLOGICAL BATTERY (HRNB)

Description

The HRNB is one of the most widely used neuropsychological test batteries. It consists of adult, intermediate child (9 to 14 years), and young child (5 to 8 years) versions. Each battery is designed to include a minimum of 14 neuropsychological tests capable of measuring up to 26 brain–behavior relationships. The entire battery takes between 6 and 8 hours to administer.

Strengths

1. Numerous reliability and validity studies have demonstrated that it can reliably discriminate between brain-damaged patients and normal healthy controls.
2. It is the most widely used neuropsychological battery.
3. Extensive research has been done on the battery.
4. It contains quantitative data and is ideal for research.
5. It can be utilized to determine the extent or severity of brain damage as well as its lateralization and localization.
6. It can be administered by psychological assistants or technicians.
7. The administration and scoring of this battery can be learned in 1 week.
8. It has made psychologists aware of the need to assess many of the patient's cognitive and behavioral functions when addressing neuropsychological issues.

Limitations

1. No "cookbook" has ever been developed to assist the clinician make accurate interpretations of the test data.
2. Clinical interpretation of the complex test data requires many years of training, considerable expertise, and a great deal of clinical acumen.
3. The ability of the battery to detect malingering is controversial.
4. It was never designed to predict everyday and vocational functioning.
5. Testing may require as long as 10 hours to evaluate patients who have sustained severe brain damage.
6. The battery appears to be insensitive to orbitofrontal lobe brain damage.

7. Because the equipment necessary to administer the complete battery is bulky and difficult to transport, it may not be suitable to evaluate patients in their home, at a hospital bedside, or in jail.
8. Many psychologists who have taken a workshop on the HRNB receive little or no supervision after completing the workshop.
9. The battery needs to be supplemented by other neuropsychological tests since it is relatively poor at assessing memory.
10. Because the test strongly emphasizes quantitative measurement of a patient's cognitive deficits, psychologists using this battery may ignore a number of confounding factors when interpreting the test data.

Luria–Nebraska Neuropsychological Battery (LNNB)

Description

The LNNB is a comprehensive neuropsychological test battery based on the assessment procedures of the late Professor Luria and the American psychometric tradition. It contains a total of 269 test items that comprise 11 clinical scales and can be administered in 2.5 to 3 hours.

Strengths

1. The rationale for the tests used in this battery was based on the neuropsychological assessment methods developed by Luria.
2. It possesses adequate validity and reliability.
3. It can be administered in 2.5 to 3 hours.
4. It permits localization of brain impairment.
5. It corrects for the patient's age and educational achievement.
6. The administration and scoring of this battery can be learned in less than 2 weeks.
7. The battery is portable and can easily be transported to the patient's bedside or can be used to test patients in less than formal settings (e.g., jails).

Limitations

1. Test interpretation requires a good understanding of behavioral neurology, neuropathology, and neuroanatomy.
2. Test interpretation is difficult.
3. It needs to be supplemented by other neuropsychological tests.
4. It tends to be insensitive to mild cognitive dysfunction in patients with IQs of 120 or higher.
5. The patient's clinical and background histories are necessary to arrive at accurate test interpretations.

Microcog Assessment of Cognitive Functioning Computerized Battery

Description

The Microcog is a computer-administered and scored test that was intended to serve as a screening device or diagnostic tool for use as part of a general neuropsychological examination of cognitive functioning. The standard form consists of 18 subtests that can be administered in 1 hour. The short form contains 12 subtests that can be administered in approximately 30 minutes.

Strengths

1. Its norms were derived from a nationally representative sample of adults.
2. It produces a comprehensive quantitative analysis of the patient's scores including precise quantification of reaction times.
3. It can be administered in approximately 1 hour.

Limitations

1. The administration of tests by a computer may cause some patients to become anxious because of their inexperience at being around computers or as a result of a "computer phobia."
2. The presence of another individual in the same room where the patient is being tested may cause the patient to miss the presentation of the test stimuli on the computer screen.
3. It may not be appropriate for individuals who are visually or motorically impaired or dyslexic.
4. It may not be appropriate for individuals with different cultural or linguistic backgrounds or whose primary language is not English.
5. It does not have any obvious built-in measures to ensure that the patient was motivated to perform to the best of his or her ability while taking this test.
6. The manual does not contain norms for patients who have sustained traumatic brain injuries.

A DEVELOPMENTAL NEUROPSYCHOLOGICAL ASSESSMENT TEST TO ASSESS YOUNG AND OLDER CHILDREN (NEPSY)

This battery was designed to assess children who range from 3 to 12 years of age who have subtle cognitive deficits that can interfere with the ability of the child to learn new information and detect and describe the effects of brain damage or dysfunction. It can be administered between 45 and 65 minutes depending on the age of the child.

Strengths

1. This battery was designed specifically to assess the neuropsychological functioning of children.
2. It is normed on a single large randomized and stratified normal sample.
3. It has been modeled to a considerable degree on Luria's theoretical approach of cognitive assessment.

Limitations

1. It has serious test–retest reliability shortcomings.
2. Clinicians should be cautious in interpreting the test data to determine whether a child's cognitive functioning has changed over time.

REPEATABLE BATTERY FOR THE ASSESSMENT OF NEUROPSYCHOLOGICAL STATUS (RBANS)

This test battery was designed to identify dementia ranging from mild to severe in adults ranging from 20 to 89 years of age.

Strengths

1. It appears to be sensitive to a number of neurological disorders including cerebra concussions and dementia.
2. It appears helpful in distinguishing primary cortical and subcortical disorders.
3. It seems to be a useful screening tool for psychiatric patients.

Limitations

1. It may be limited in detecting impairment in individuals with high levels of intellectual functioning.
2. Since its test–retest reliability is low, its ability to monitor changes in the patient's cognitive functioning seem limited, particularly in situations in which the patient's progress or decline is relatively subtle.

SAN DIEGO NEUROPSYCHOLOGICAL TEST BATTERY (SDNTB)

Description

The SDNTB was designed to assess neuropsychological functions such as sensory perception, attention, concentration, verbal abilities, spatial integration, intelligence, motor speed and dexterity, memory, learning, and abstract and flexible thinking. It consists of 21 procedures that yield a total of 38 scores. Approximately 3.5 hours are required to administer these tests.

Strengths

1. It appears to be based on Luria's model of neuropsychological functioning and information processing.
2. It provides a comprehensive assessment of a wide range of neuropsychological functions.
3. It possesses adequate construct validity.
4. It requires only 3.5 hours to administer.

Limitations

1. It requires that the neuropsychologist interpreting the test scores have considerable expertise in Luria's model of brain–behavior relationships.
2. It is not widely used.
3. It is not designed to detect malingering.

TESTS OF INTELLIGENCE

KAUFMAN ASSESSMENT BATTERY FOR CHILDREN

Description

This test is an intelligence test for children between the ages 2.5 and 12.5 years. It contains 16 subtests that can be administered to children who are over 7 in approximately 75 minutes. Younger children can be administered this test in approximately 30 minutes.

Strengths

1. Test development was based on a neuropsychological model.
2. It possesses adequate test–retest reliability and discriminant validity.
3. It has separate norms for African-Americans.

Limitations

1. Comparisons to the Wechsler Intelligence Scale for Children and the Stanford–Binet Intelligence Test may be problematic.
2. Some questions have been raised as to whether this test can be used to discriminate between brain-injured and healthy children.

KAUFMAN BRIEF TEST OF INTELLIGENCE

Description

This test assesses an individual's verbal and nonverbal abilities and is suitable for individuals whose ages range from 4 to 90. Children can be tested in 15 to 20 minutes, and adults can usually complete the test in 20 to 30 minutes.

Strengths

1. Scores on this test appear to correlate fairly well with other tests of intelligence.
2. It can be administered to individuals between the ages 4 and 90 in 15 to 30 minutes.
3. It serves as an efficient screening measure to assess an individual's verbal, nonverbal, and general intellectual functioning, particularly when there are time constraints.
4. It is well suited for individuals who are physically handicapped or who have significant motor impairments since it does not require a motor response from the patient.
5. It is easy to administer and possesses good normative data.

Limitations

1. It provides less of a differentiation between verbal and nonverbal intellectual functions than the Wechsler Adult Intelligence Scales.
2. It may produce a spuriously low estimate of verbal intelligence.

RAVEN PROGRESSIVE MATRICES TEST

Description

It serves as a test of inductive reasoning and requires the patient to conceptualize spatial, design, and numerical relationships ranging from very simple and concrete to very complex and abstract. It consists of 60 test items that are grouped into five sets. Each test item contains a rectangle with one part removed. The subject's task is to select the correct piece from either six or eight pictures below the item. While it is an untimed test, most individuals are able to complete it in approximately 25 minutes.

Strengths

1. It appears to be an excellent test of inductive reasoning.
2. It can be administered to individuals with significant motoric limitations or hearing impairment.
3. It is relatively easy to administer.
4. It appears to be appropriate for individuals who are born and raised outside of the United States, speak little or no English, have limited educational backgrounds, or have been culturally deprived.

Limitations

1. It provides relatively little information about the individual's intellectual strengths or weaknesses.
2. An individual's performance on this test can be significantly compromised by visual field defects, unilateral neglect, or other visual–perceptual difficulties.
3. It does not assess a patient's verbal intellectual skills.

STANFORD–BINET INTELLIGENCE SCALE — FIFTH EDITION

Description

This test can be used to assess the intellectual functioning of children between the ages 2 and 85 years. It produces a full-scale IQ score and can be administered in 45 to 75 minutes.

Strengths

1. This edition appears to be based on strong theoretical foundations and considerable research.
2. It appears to be ideal for testing young children.
3. It can provide the neuropsychologist with clinically useful information.

Limitations

1. Young children with limited attention spans may find that this test takes too long to administer.
2. It does not measure speed of information processing that limits its ability to identify subcortical neurological disorders.

TEST OF NONVERBAL INTELLIGENCE — THIRD EDITION

Description

This is a language-free measure designed to assess an individual's abstract/figural problem-solving and intellectual skills. It can be administered to subjects between the ages 5 and 90.

Strengths

1. It can be administered to subjects in about 15 to 20 minutes.
2. There is no listening, speaking, reading, or writing required when giving this test or responding to the test items since the subject is only required to make a minimal motoric response.
3. It is specifically designed to assess the intellectual functioning of individuals who speak little or no English or who were raised in a different cultural background.
4. It is particularly valuable in assessing the intellectual functioning of patients whose test performances may be confounded by language or motor impairments arising from cerebral palsy, or stroke and conditions such as aphasia, hearing impairment, or lack of proficiency with spoken or written English.
5. The test results can be easily scored and normed.

Limitations

1. It is not appropriate for patients who have poor visual acuity.
2. Patients who have visual field cuts or demonstrate unilateral neglect may perform poorly as a result of their perceptual difficulties.
3. It does not provide a measure of the individual's verbal intellectual skills.

WECHSLER ABBREVIATED SCALE OF INTELLIGENCE (WASI)

Description

This test was designed to provide a brief estimate of intelligence. It can be used as a screening instrument when a complete assessment of an individual's IQ cannot be performed due to time constraints. It can be administered to individuals ranging from 6 to 89 years of age in 25 to 30 minutes.

Strengths

1. The norms for this test have been corrected for gender, education, and race/ethnicity.
2. It has excellent test–retest reliability.
3. It covers a wide age span (6 to 89 years).

Limitations

1. Examiners should be cautious when making clinical inferences between an individual's verbal and nonverbal IQ scores.
2. It should not take the place of a comprehensive assessment of an individual's intellectual functioning.

WECHSLER PRESCHOOL AND PRIMARY SCALE OF INTELLIGENCE — REVISED

Description

This test assesses the intellectual functioning of children between the ages 3 and 7 years, 3 months. It produces verbal, performance, and full-scale IQ scores and can be administered in about 75 minutes.

Strengths

1. This test can assess the intellectual functioning of children as young as 3 years.
2. It possesses good test–retest reliability and validity.

Limitations

1. It is not appropriate for children whose primary language is not English or who were raised in a different cultural background.
2. It is not appropriate for children who are aphasic or hearing or motorically impaired.
3. Children who are psychotic, severely anxious, or depressed are likely to perform poorly.
4. Some of the concepts contained in the test may be difficult for children with below average intelligence.

WECHSLER INTELLIGENCE SCALE FOR CHILDREN — FOURTH EDITION

Description

This test can be administered to children between the ages of 6 and 16 years, 11 months. It contains five core subtests and five supplemental subtests. It can be administered to children and adolescents in 1 to 1.5 hours.

Strengths

1. It is the most widely used test to assess intelligence in children and young adolescents.
2. Its norms were based on a standardization sample of 2220 children based on gender, age, parental educational level, geographical region, and race/ethnicity.
3. It generates a full-scale IQ score.

Limitations

1. It is not appropriate for children or adolescents whose primary language is not English or who were raised in a different cultural background.
2. It is not appropriate for children who are motorically impaired, aphasic, psychotic, or severely anxious at the time of testing.
3. A child's IQ as measured by this test may not reflect the presence or severity of brain damage.
4. The test–retest reliability in clinical groups is lacking.

WECHSLER ADULT INTELLIGENCE SCALE — REVISED (WAIS-R)

Description

The WAIS-R is one of the most widely used psychological tests and contains six verbal subtests (Information, Comprehension, Arithmetic, Digit Span, Similarity, and Vocabulary) and five performance subtests (Picture Completion, Picture Arrangement, Block Design, Object Assembly, and Digit Symbol). The test is appropriate for individuals ranging in age from 16 to 74 and can be administered in 1 to 1.5 hours to normal healthy adults.

Strengths

1. The test manual describes how the test should be administered, the types of responses or prompts permitted by the examiner, and how a specific test item will be scored.
2. Testing produces a verbal, performance, and full-scale IQ score.
3. It possesses high test–retest reliability and concurrent validity.
4. The IQs produced by this test have been found to correlate well with an individual's grade point average at all levels of education. It has also been used with good success to predict academic achievements or success.
5. It is a relatively easy test to administer and score.
6. It is widely used in a variety of settings and has been based on a representative sample of normative population groups within the United States.

Limitations

1. Many of the subtests are relatively insensitive to brain injury and may not reflect a brain-injured patient's cognitive functioning in "real-world" settings.
2. It is inappropriate for individuals who have significant visual or motor impairments (e.g., diplopia, hemiparesis, visual agnosia, or aphasia).

3. An individual's performance on this test can be affected by emotional factors (e.g., anxiety, depression, psychosis).
4. Individuals who are raised in different cultures and whose command of English is limited may receive spuriously low IQ scores.
5. Individuals who are placed on anticonvulsant medications (e.g., Dilantin) or antipsychotic medications may obtain lower IQ scores as a result of the deleterious effects these medications have on cognitive functioning.

Wechsler Adult Intelligence Scale — Third Edition

Description

It is the most recent revision of the Wechsler Adult Intelligence Scale. It contains a total of 14 subtests and can be administered to individuals ranging in age from 16 to 89 in 1.5 to 2 hours.

Strengths

1. It can be used to assess individuals between the ages of 16 and 89.
2. Like its predecessor, the WAIS-R, it is the most widely used test to assess intellectual functioning.
3. It possesses good test–retest reliability and concurrent validity.
4. The standardization sample used to construct norms for this test was based on 2450 adults and included the proportion of whites, African-Americans, Hispanics, and other racial/ethnic groups based on the racial/ethnic proportions of these individuals in each group living within the United States population according to the 1995 census data.
5. The normative data in the third edition appear to be superior to the Wechsler Memory Scale — Revised.

Limitations

1. As a result of increasing the number of subtests from 11 to 14, the length of time to administer this test was increased by approximately 30 minutes from 1.5 to 2 hours to administer.
2. It may not be appropriate for individuals who have sustained a significant traumatic brain injury since their performance may deteriorate while they are taking this test.
3. It may not be suitable for individuals with significant motor impairments or individuals for whom English is not their native language.
4. It may not be appropriate for individuals who have speaking or hearing impairments.
5. Because of the restrictions placed on the examiner during testing, patients who appear fatigued or become excessively anxious toward the middle of the test cannot be given a break without violating the manner in which the original test norms were obtained.
6. As a result of its inflexibility, it may not be particularly suitable for individuals who have sustained significant brain damage.
7. It may not be suitable for individuals who are significantly anxious or depressed at the time of testing.

Wechsler Preschool and Primary Scale of Intelligence — Third Edition

Description

This test was primarily designed to assess the intelligence of preschool and young children ranging in age from 2 years and 6 months to 7 years and 3 months. It usually takes between 30 and 35 minutes to administer the core subtests to children under the age of 4. It takes 40 to 50 minutes to administer the core tests to children who are least 4 years old. It can take as long as 85 minutes to administer all of the subtests that are necessary to produce composite scores and perform a discrepancy analysis.

Strengths

1. The third edition of this test appears substantially better than the second edition.
2. It has excellent validity.
3. It possesses high test–retest reliability.
4. It appears to be minimally affected by limited English proficiency.

Limitations

1. Little research has been done to establish its clinical usefulness.
2. Comparing IQ scores across different age ranges may be problematic.
3. Little information is known about its test–retest reliability in clinical groups.

TESTS OF ATTENTION AND CONCENTRATION

BRIEF TEST OF ATTENTION

Description

This test was designed to assess auditory divided attentional skills. It consists of two parallel forms that can be presented via an audiocassette. On Form N (Numbers), a voice reads ten lists of letters and numbers that increase in length from 14 to 18 elements. The patient's task is to disregard the letters and count how many numbers were read aloud. The same ten lists are presented again as Form L (Letters). The patient must ignore the numbers and count how many letters were read. Approximately 10 minutes are required to administer this test.

Strengths

1. This test can be easily administered in approximately 10 minutes.
2. It appears to be sensitive to subtle impairments in auditory divided attention.
3. It possesses norms ranging in age from 17 to 82, including those with visual and motor impairments.
4. It has been standardized for use with adults with relatively intact hearing between the ages of 17 and 82 who can distinguish between spoken words and letters of the alphabet.
5. It is highly correlated with other tests of attention and appears to be sensitive to attentional impairments that are found in patients who have sustained traumatic brain injuries.

Limitations

1. It may not be appropriate for individuals from different cultural backgrounds or whose primary language is not English.
2. It may not be appropriate for individuals who have significant hearing impairments or who are aphasic.
3. Individuals who are significantly anxious or severely depressed may do poorly.
4. Individuals who have attention deficit–hyperactivity disorders may do poorly on this test.
5. Since a person's performance on this test is under the individual's control, it is prone to conscious manipulation.

COLOR TRAILS TEST

Description

This test presents colored circles (pink or yellow) that contain numbers from 1 through 25. For Color Trails 1, the subject must use a pencil and rapidly connect circles numbered from 1 through 25 in sequence, while ignoring the color of the circle. For Color Trails 2, the subject must rapidly connect numbered circles in sequence, but alternate between pink and yellow colors. This test can be administered in approximately 10 minutes.

Strengths

1. It is suitable for individuals from different cultural backgrounds who have a limited command of English.
2. It possesses excellent norms that have been corrected for individual age and educational background.
3. It possesses norms for African-American and Hispanic-American subjects.
4. It possesses good test–retest reliability and validity.

Limitations

1. Individuals who are anxious may find Color Trails 2 somewhat overwhelming since it contains twice as many circles as Color Trails 1.
2. Individuals who are depressed at the time of testing may perform poorly on this test, particularly if they exhibit psychomotor retardation.
3. It is not suited for individuals who have significant motoric impairments.
4. It is not suitable for individuals who have visual field cuts or unilateral neglect.

COMPREHENSIVE TRAIL MAKING TEST

Description

This test was developed to rectify some of the shortcomings of the original Trail Making test. It was designed to be administered to individuals between the ages 11 and 74 years and 11 months. Recently norms have been developed for children between the ages 8 and 10.

Strengths

1. Scores on this test appear to be correlated with age.
2. It has high test–retest reliability.
3. It has strong psychometric properties.

Limitations

1. Test–retest reliability are lacking for children.
2. Correlations with other tests and measures of attention and executive functions are lacking.

CONNER'S CONTINUOUS PERFORMANCE TEST — II

Description

This computerized test has been designed to measure sustained attention and response inhibition. It can be administered to individuals ranging in age from 6 to over 55.

Strengths

1. It provides a quick computerized assessment of an individual's attention/executive functioning.
2. It is relatively easy to use and can be used for research purposes.
3. The test results do not appear to be affected by the examinees ethnic background.

Limitations

1. This test does not include any procedures that would identify individuals who are malingering.
2. The norms for this test have some major shortcomings.

CONTINUOUS PERFORMANCE TEST

Description

This test has been designed to detect lapses in attention and is typically administered by a computer in about 20 minutes.

Strengths

1. It appears sensitive to attentional deficits that are frequently seen in patients who have attention deficit or attention deficit–hyperactivity disorders.
2. The computerized version of this test is relatively easy to administer and produces a rather comprehensive data analysis using a signal detection analysis.
3. It can be administered in approximately 20 minutes.
4. It appears to be sensitive to attentional deficits in individuals who have sustained traumatic brain injuries.

Limitations

1. It may fail to distinguish patients who are suspected of having sustained a traumatic brain injury if they have a prior history of attention deficit disorder or attention deficit–hyperactivity disorder.
2. The normative data for this test appears to be based on children and young adults, and there are relatively few normative studies for adults over 35.
3. Emotional factors may affect an individual's performance on this test.
4. Research studies have found that it possesses only low to moderate concurrent validity with other tests of attention.

DIGIT SPAN TEST

Description

The Digit Span Test is a subtest of the Wechsler Adult Intelligence Scale. The test consists of orally presenting random number sequences to the patient at the rate of one per second. The patient must repeat the digits in the exact sequence they were presented. The examiner continues to add a digit every time the patient correctly performs the task. Scoring consists of the total number of digits the patient can correctly recall in the exact order they were presented (Forward Digit Span) and the total number of digits recalled in reverse order (Backward Digit Span).

Strengths

1. This test tends to be more vulnerable to left hemisphere than right hemisphere or diffuse brain damage.
2. It possesses fairly good test–retest reliability depending on the interval duration and the subject's age.
3. This test is widely used by a wide range of medical specialists as part of their mental status examination.
4. It is fairly resistant to the aging process in that an individual's performance on this test will show very little deterioration prior to the age of 60.

Limitations

1. It is not an accurate test of recent memory since patients with Korsakoff's syndrome typically perform well on this test, even though they cannot recall what happened a few minutes earlier.
2. Poor scores on this test are commonly observed in individuals who are anxious or depressed.
3. It may be difficult to determine whether a particular individual's score is indicative of emotional problems or brain damage based solely on his or her performance on this test.
4. It is not suitable for individuals who are hearing impaired or aphasic.
5. It is one of the least sensitive measures of dementia, particularly in the early stages.
6. Individuals who have sustained a mild traumatic brain injury are usually able to do well on this test.

PACED AUDITORY SERIAL ADDITION TEST

Description

This test was designed to assess an individual's sustained and divided attentional skills. It assesses the individual's ability to add 60 pairs of numbers ranging from 1 to 9. Each number is added to the number immediately preceding it. The numbers are presented at intervals of 1.2, 1.6, 2.0, or 2.4 seconds by the use of a tape recorder or computer program. The test consists of a total of 240 responses made by the patient. This test can be administered in approximately 20 minutes.

Strengths

1. This test is sensitive to relatively subtle divided attentional impairments in patients who have sustained cerebral concussions or mild head trauma.
2. It has been used to determine whether a brain-injured patient is able to return to his preinjury social and vocational activities following a mild head trauma.
3. It has been found to have moderate to moderately high concurrent validity with other measures of attention.

Limitations

1. It is not widely used despite its sensitivity to mild brain damage.
2. The scores of individuals who have sustained mild traumatic brain injuries tend to normalize within 50 to 60 days.
3. Significant practice effects have been reported if this test is given 1 week apart.
4. Poor performance on this test can reflect mechanical difficulties or other distracting physical or mental problems.

5. Some individuals who are administered this test find it quite stressful because of the rapid presentation of the test stimuli and the task requirements.
6. Individuals who have attention deficit–hyperactivity disorder may do poorly on this test.

Ruff 2 and 7 Selective Attention Test

Description

This test has been designed to assess an individual's selective attentional capacity during different distractor conditions known to influence selection speed. It uses a pencil and paper format. The subject is asked to cross out as quickly as possible numerical targets (2 and 7) embedded either in alphabetical capital letters or in blocks of digits. This test can be administered in approximately 5 minutes.

Strengths

1. It can be easily administered, even at a patient's bedside.
2. It appears to be sensitive to selective attention deficits that are commonly seen in patients who have sustained traumatic brain injuries and other forms of cerebral pathology.
3. It appears to be sensitive to subtle attentional difficulties that are frequently seen during the early stages of AIDS.
4. It possesses some ecological validity in that it has been used to predict whether a patient who has sustained a traumatic brain injury is ready to return to work or school.

Limitations

1. It may not be appropriate for individuals who have poor vision or who are severely anxious at the time of testing.
2. Patients who exhibit clinical evidence of psychomotor retardation may perform poorly on this test.
3. It is not known whether this test can detect patients who are simulating cognitive impairment or malingering.
4. The reliability and validity of this test has not been fully established.

Stroop Color and Word Test

Description

This test assesses the patient's ability to rapidly process simple information and the ability to shift from one perceptual set to another in the face of interference. It consists of a word page with the names of colors printed in black ink, a color page with Xs printed in color, and a word–color page with words from the first page printed in colors from the second page. This test can be administered in 10 minutes or less.

Strengths

1. This test appears to possess satisfactory reliability and validity.
2. It appears to be sensitive to the subtle attentional deficits seen in patients who have sustained traumatic brain injuries, as well as patients with dementia.
3. It can be administered in 5 to 10 minutes.
4. It is fairly effective in distinguishing brain-damaged patients from healthy adults and psychiatric patients.

Limitations

1. Poor performance on this test can be observed in depressed or anxious patients.
2. Brain-injured patients do not consistently demonstrate difficulties on the word–color page (interference task).
3. Individuals who are severely dyslexic may have difficulty on the first section of this test.
4. Individuals who are significantly anxious or depressed at the time of testing may perform poorly.
5. It is not suitable for individuals who have significant visual impairments or who are aphasic.
6. It is not suitable for individuals who have visual field cuts or have unilateral neglect.

SYMBOL DIGIT MODALITIES TEST

Description

The patient must code symbols according to a key that displays nine symbol–numeric relationships. After completing ten practice items, the patient is instructed to work as quickly as possible without skipping any items. The test lasts a total of 90 seconds. Scoring consists of the number of correct responses made within the allotted time.

Strengths

1. Norms have been developed for different age groups.
2. It has been used with good success in differentiating brain-damaged patients from normal healthy controls.
3. It is sensitive to a variety of neurological disorders in both children and adults.
4. A person's performance on this test appears to be highly correlated with their ability to function in the real world.

Limitations

1. Individuals who are well educated and have high premorbid intellectual functioning may score within the normal range, even though they have sustained a brain injury.
2. It is not suitable for individuals who have significant visual difficulties.
3. Poor performance on this test can be caused by antipsychotic or anticonvulsant medications, pain and discomfort, headache, and chronic medical problems.
4. Individuals who are severely anxious or depressed at the time of testing may perform poorly.
5. Since performance on this test depends on the level of motivation, individuals with suboptimal motivation may perform poorly.

TEST OF EVERYDAY ATTENTION

Description

This test was designed to rectify the lack of ecological validity in many widely used tests of attention. It can be administered to adults ranging in age from 18 to 80. There is also a children's version that can be used for children ranging in age from 6 to 16. It usually takes 45 to 60 minutes to administer.

Strengths

1. It is one of the very few memory tests that deals with the issue of ecological validity.
2. It is perceived by examinee as having some relevance.

3. It can be used to assess patients with dementia, stroke, traumatic brain injury, and psychiatric disorders.

Limitations

1. The normative data upon which the test is based is poorly described in the test manual.
2. The manual does not provide sufficient information about the test's reliability.

TEST OF VARIABLES OF ATTENTION (TOVA)

Description

This computerized test has been designed to assess an individual's sustained attention and impulsivity. It is often utilized to assess individuals with attention deficit hyperactivity disorder. It can be administered in about 22 minutes.

Strengths

1. It seems appropriate for young children and adults with letter and number identification problems.
2. It appears to be good at detecting attentional impairments.
3. It utilizes a nonverbal format and geometric stimuli that may minimize verbal and cultural issues.

Limitations

1. The test norms appear inadequate for adults.
2. It may not to be as effective in detecting attentional deficits that occur in real-world settings.
3. The TOVA interpretative report should be reviewed with caution and should not be taken at face value.

TRAIL MAKING TEST

Description

This test is part of the HRNB and is widely used as a measure of attention, visual scanning, and visual motor tracking. It contains two parts. Part A requires the individual to connect circles containing numbers ranging from 1 through 25 in serial order. Part B requires the patient to shift sets (e.g., go from a number to a letter rather than connecting numbers). Scoring of this test is the number of seconds required to complete both parts.

Strengths

1. The test–retest reliability of this test has been found to be high for normal adults and patients with various neurological disorders.
2. This test appears to be quite sensitive to progressive cognitive decline in patients with dementia.
3. It can be easily administered to patients in 5 to 10 minutes.
4. It appears to be sensitive to diffuse brain damage.

Limitations

1. It may not be appropriate for individuals whose native language is not English or who have limited familiarity with the English alphabet.

2. It may not be appropriate for individuals who are severely anxious, depressed, or even psychotic at the time of testing.
3. It should not be used as a screening test to differentiate brain-injured patients from psychiatric patients because of its unreliability in discriminating between these patient populations.
4. An individual's performance on this test can be consciously manipulated.
5. It is not suitable for individuals with significant visual or motoric impairments.

TESTS TO ASSESS LANGUAGE

Aphasia Screening Test

Description

This test is part of the HRNB and contains 51 items that permit the examiner to screen patients who have aphasic disturbances in approximately 15 to 20 minutes.

Strengths

1. It can be easily administered to patients in 5 to 10 minutes.
2. It is part of the HRNB.
3. Patients with left-hemisphere brain damage appear to do worse on this test than patients with right-hemisphere brain damage.

Limitations

1. This test is prone to misclassify normal healthy adults as having aphasic difficulties.
2. There are no guidelines for its clinical use or interpretation.
3. Data on its test–retest reliability are not available.
4. It is not a particularly good screening instrument to assess aphasic difficulties.

Boston Diagnostic Aphasia Examination

Description

This test provides a comprehensive assessment of an individual's aphasic difficulties. It contains a total of 34 subtests and evaluates the individual's communication and communication-related skills. It takes approximately 1.5 to 2 hours to administer to relatively normal adults.

Strengths

1. This test was designed primarily to evaluate disturbances in communication and language functioning in individuals who have had strokes or sustained extensive damage to their left hemisphere.
2. It is based on the clinical and research experience of a number of well-known aphasiologists.

Limitations

1. This test can take several hours to administer to aphasic patients or individuals who have sustained severe traumatic brain injuries.
2. There is no test–retest reliability data available.

3. Neuropsychologists using this instrument should have a strong background in aphasiology and familiarity with the "Boston School" approach to aphasia classification.
4. Because it takes so long to administer, it may create motivational difficulties or physically exhaust the test taker. As a consequence, the obtained data may not be reliable.

BOSTON NAMING TEST

Description

This test consists of 60 drawings of objects that become increasingly less familiar and difficult to name. The patient's score is based on the number of objects that are successfully named without having to provide the subject with a phonemic cue. This test can be administered to healthy adults in 10 to 15 minutes.

Strengths

1. The test manual provides normative data based on the individual's educational achievements and age.
2. This test appears to be sensitive to subtle word-finding difficulties.

Limitations

1. Poor scores can reflect a variety of non-neurological factors.
2. A patient's performance on this test should be corroborated by observations of the patient's behavior during interview.
3. This test is inappropriate for patients who were raised in a different culture or speak English as a second language.
4. Individuals with low premorbid intellectual functioning or limited educational background may perform poorly.

CONTROLLED ORAL WORD ASSOCIATION TEST

Description

This test requires the patient to orally generate as many words as possible beginning with specific letters over three 1-minute trials.

Strengths

1. Normative data for both males and females are based on age and educational achievements.
2. It is sensitive to subtle verbal fluency deficits following left-hemisphere brain damage.

Limitations

1. Poor performance can reflect such factors as test anxiety, depression, fatigue, prior linguistic background, physical pain and discomfort, and suboptimal motivation.
2. Poor performance should be corroborated by other test data, medical records, and observations of the behavior.

Multilingual Aphasia Examination

Description

This test has been designed to provide a relatively brief but quite detailed examination of the presence, severity, and qualitative aspects of aphasic language disorders for patients between the ages 6 and 69. This test requires approximately 40 minutes or less to administer and corrects for the patient's age and educational background.

Strengths

1. It can be administered to Spanish-speaking individuals.
2. It is relatively easy to administer and score.
3. It appears to be useful in evaluating language impairments in patients who have sustained significant traumatic brain injuries.

Limitations

1. This test is not appropriate for individuals whose command of English or Spanish is limited.
2. It does not contain any formal means to ensure that the individual being tested is performing optimally.
3. Using the suggested cut-off scores results in a high misclassification rate.

Token Test

Description

This test assesses a subject's ability to perform specific instructions by manipulating tokens of differing shapes, sizes, and colors. The entire test consists of five sections, containing a 62 test items, and can be administered in approximately 20 minutes to healthy adults.

Strengths

1. This test is relatively easy to administer and score.
2. It tends to be very sensitive to left temporal–parietal lobe damage.
3. It correlates well with other measures of language and can be used to evaluate children and adolescents who have sustained closed head injuries.

Limitations

1. Poor performance on this test can be due to hearing difficulties.
2. This test should not be administered to individuals for whom English is a second language or who were raised in a different cultural background.
3. Poor performance on this test can be due to non-neurological factors.

TESTS TO ASSESS ACADEMIC SKILLS

Peabody Individual Achievement Test — Revised

Description

This test was designed to measure academic achievement from kindergarten to grade 12 in the areas of mathematics, reading recognition, reading comprehension, spelling, and general information.

Children in the primary grades will usually require 30 to 40 minutes to complete this test. Older children will usually take 40 to 50 minutes.

Strengths

1. This test possesses excellent test–retest reliability and validity.
2. An individual's score on this test has been found to correlate highly with other achievement tests.
3. Composite scores produced by this test can summarize the patient's achievement skills in general information, reading recognition, reading comprehension, mathematics, and spelling.

Limitations

1. This test should not be used as a diagnostic instrument or to develop individual educational programs.
2. Neuropsychologists should exercise caution when interpreting the scores of individuals who were raised outside of the United States.
3. It tends to inflate the scores for young children and deflate the scores of children at the highest age and grade levels.

WECHSLER INDIVIDUAL ACHIEVEMENT TEST

Description

This test was designed to measure the arithmetic, listening comprehension, oral expression, reading, spelling, and writing skills of individuals ranging in age from 5 to 19 years, 11 months of age. It takes between 30 and 50 minutes to administer to children who have not yet entered the third grade. Testing will probably take over an hour if the child has entered the third grade.

Strengths

1. The scores on this test correlate moderately well with intelligence measures.
2. It possesses high test–retest reliability for most of its subtests.

Limitations

1. There are no norms for individuals who have sustained traumatic brain injuries or brain insults.
2. Since patients who sustain severe traumatic brain injuries may test lower on the arithmetic and listening comprehension subtests because of their attention and memory difficulties, their lower than expected performance on this test may erroneously be used as evidence that they had a preexisting history of learning difficulties.

WIDE RANGE ACHIEVEMENT TEST

Description

This test assesses the individual's spelling, reading, and arithmetic levels of competence. Level 1 evaluates children aged 5 to 11; Level 2 is for children 12 and older.

Strengths

1. An individual's scores can be compared with age norms and converted into percentiles to determine grade equivalency.

2. This test can be used to evaluate individuals with a previous history of learning difficulties.

Limitations

1. It was not specifically designed to evaluate brain-damaged individuals.
2. Brain-damaged individuals can perform poorly on the arithmetic section of this test because of their cognitive difficulties and time limitations.
3. Poor performance can be due to a variety of non-neurological factors.

WECHSLER INDIVIDUAL ACHIEVEMENT TEST — SECOND EDITION

Description

This test was designed to measure arithmetic, listening comprehension, oral expression, reading, spelling, and writing skills in individuals ranging in age from 5 to 19 years, 11 months. It takes between 30 and 50 minutes to administer to children who have not yet entered the third grade. If the child has entered the third grade, testing will usually take just over an hour.

Strengths

1. Scores on this test can be compared with the Wechsler Intelligence Test.
2. Test–retest correlations are high for most of the subtests.

Limitations

1. Patients who sustain severe traumatic brain damage may test lower on some of the subscales even though they had no prior history of learning difficulties.
2. There are no norms for brain-damaged individuals.

TESTS TO ASSESS VISUAL PERCEPTUAL/VISUAL CONSTRUCTIONAL SKILLS

BENDER–GESTALT TEST

Description

The Bender–Gestalt Test evaluates an individual's visual perception and visual constructional skills. It consists of nine geometric designs that are presented individually to the patient, who must draw them as accurately as possible on a blank sheet of paper.

Strengths

1. This test has been found to be effective in discriminating between psychiatric and brain-injured patients, as well as normal controls.
2. This test is relatively easy to administer and score.

Limitations

1. A diagnosis of brain damage should not be made solely on the basis of this test.
2. Because of the numerous scoring systems that exist, there is no one accepted scoring system for the diagnosis of organicity.
3. It is frequently misused or abused by untrained, inexperienced, and unethical examiners.

BENTON FACIAL RECOGNITION TEST

Description

This test assesses the individual's ability to compare pictures of faces.

Strengths

1. It is sensitive to subtle visual perceptual impairments.
2. It can be administered to individuals whose knowledge of English is limited.
3. It places little emphasis on an individual's memory.
4. Normative data allows the examiner to compare an individual's score with those of normal controls.

Limitations

1. It tends to be insensitive to left-hemisphere frontal lobe damage.
2. Poor performance can be caused by visual acuity difficulties, high levels of anxiety, poor motivation, pain, or psychotic thinking.
3. Test scores should be corroborated by the individual's medical records and other neuropsychological test data.

BENTON JUDGMENT OF LINE ORIENTATION TEST

Description

This test requires the individual to match a pair of angled lines shown on a card, containing 11 numbered lines that form a semicircle. The subject is required to either point to or name the numbers associated with the 11 lines.

Strengths

1. This test tends to be sensitive to posterior right-hemisphere brain damage, particularly the right parietal lobe.
2. This test can be easily administered and scored.
3. The test manual contains normative data with which to compare the patient's score to determine its severity and clinical significance.

Limitations

1. Poor performance on this test may reflect visual acuity deficits, test anxiety, depression, physical pain or discomfort, attentional difficulties, headache, medications, fatigue, hysteria, psychotic thinking, or suboptimal motivation.

BLOCK DESIGN TEST

Description

This test consists of assembling blocks with different colored sides to reproduce a specific printed design that may require four or nine blocks.

Strengths

1. This test has been shown to be sensitive to brain damage, particularly when the damage is located in the frontal or parietal lobes.
2. This test is also sensitive to Alzheimer's disease, strokes, and hypoxic encephalopathy.

Limitations

1. Poor performance on this test may be due to such factors as poor visual acuity, orthopedic injury to one or both arms or hands, test anxiety, depression, significant physical pain or discomfort, headache, hysteria, malingering, or suboptimal motivation.
2. Poor performance on this test is not indicative of brain damage unless it is supported by the patient's medical history and other neuropsychological test data.

HOOPER VISUAL ORGANIZATION TEST

Description

This test consists of showing subjects 30 pictures of objects that have been cut up and placed in different positions. The subject's task is to visually examine each picture and decide what it would be if it were assembled. The test items are generally arranged in order of increasing difficulty. Most individuals can complete this test in 10 to 15 minutes.

Strengths

1. This test tends to be particularly sensitive to severe hypoxic or anoxic encephalopathy, posterior brain damage, and patients with prominent right frontal lobe damage.
2. It is relatively easy to administer and score.
3. Repeated administrations of this test do not appear to produce significant practice effects.

Limitations

1. Poor performance on this test can reflect a variety of non-neurological factors such as poor visual acuity, low intellectual functioning, high levels of anxiety, severe depression, psychotic thinking, histrionic behavior, and suboptimal motivation.
2. An individual's performance on this test needs to be compared to his or her medical history and other neurological test data to determine its validity.

OBJECT ASSEMBLY TEST

Description

This test requires the individual to assemble cardboard figures of familiar objects.

Strengths

1. This test is sensitive to posterior brain injury, particularly in the right hemisphere, as well as the dorsolateral frontal lobes.
2. It also appears to be sensitive to parietal lobe damage in the right or left hemisphere.
3. This test can be easily administered and scored.

Limitations

1. Poor performance on this test may be due to a variety of non-neurological factors such as a physical injury to hand, diplopia, anxiety, visual impairment, or motor difficulties.
2. Individuals who are severely brain injured may not comprehend the test instructions.

Seashore Rhythm Test

Description

This test requires the individual to determine if two pairs of musical rhythms are the same or different.

Strengths

1. It appears to be sensitive to attention and concentration deficits.
2. It appears to correlate highly with the severity of traumatic brain injury.

Limitations

1. It may not be appropriate for individuals who are hearing impaired, significantly anxious, or depressed.
2. It does not appear to differentiate between right-hemisphere vs. left-hemisphere brain damage.

Smell Identification Test

Description

This test consists of four self-administered test booklets, each containing ten stimuli for smell. The patient must select one of four multiple choices. The test stimuli include a number of odorous components mimicking the types of stimuli experienced by individuals in the "real world."

Strengths

1. Its norms were based on 4000 subjects.
2. It can be easily administered and scored.

Limitations

1. It may not be suitable for individuals who have a cold or a history of cocaine abuse.
2. Its findings should be interpreted in conjunction with the individual's clinical and background history and medical records.

Speech-Sounds Perception Test

Description

This test consists of presenting a total of 60 nonsense words that are variants of the ee sound via a tape recorder. The subject is instructed to listen to each word and then on a sheet of paper asked to underline one of four words that the he or she believes to be the correct word.

Strengths

1. This test tends to be sensitive to left-hemisphere and diffuse brain damage.
2. It is relatively easy to administer and score.

Limitations

1. It is not appropriate for individuals whose native language is not English or who are hearing impaired.
2. Individuals who have attention deficit–hyperactivity disorder may perform poorly on this test since they are likely to find the test boring.

3. This test may not be appropriate for elderly patients since a significant number of these individuals suffer from high frequency hearing loss.
4. Individuals whose visual acuity is impaired or who are severely depressed, extremely fatigued, or psychotic may do poorly on this test.

VISUAL FORM DISCRIMINATION TEST

Description

This test was designed to assess visual discrimination skills. It evaluates the patient's ability to match three geometric figures to one of four sets of designs.

Strengths

1. It is sensitive to posterior brain damage, particularly in the left parietal lobe.
2. It places little emphasis on the patient's visual memory.
3. It requires only 15 to 20 minutes to administer.
4. Normative data allows comparison with normal controls and brain-damaged patients.

Limitations

1. Poor performance may be due to a wide range of factors including visual difficulties, anxiety, psychotic thinking, or malingering.
2. An individual's poor performance on this test should be corroborated by medical records, neurodiagnostic imaging studies, and other neuropsychological test data.

TESTS TO ASSESS MOTOR FUNCTIONING

FINGER TAPPING TEST

Description

This test measures the individual's ability to depress with his or her index finger a lever that is attached to a counter. The subject is given five consecutive trials of 10 seconds each for both hands. Scoring consists of the average number of taps for each hand. This test can be administered in 5 to 10 minutes.

Strengths

1. An individual's performance on this test can be compared to norms based on sex, age, and educational background.
2. Individuals who have sustained subcortical, brain stem, or posterior frontal lobe damage are likely to perform poorly on this test.

Limitations

1. Individuals who have subcortical brain disease of nontraumatic etiology are also likely to perform poorly on this test.
2. Individuals who are severely depressed or who are taking high levels of anticonvulsant medications may perform poorly.
3. Since an individual's performance on this test depends to a large degree on motivation, it is prone to conscious manipulation.

4. An individual's performance on this test should be corroborated by medical records and other neuropsychological test data.

Grip Strength (Hand Dynamometer) Test

Description

This test measures the grip strength of each hand with a dynamometer. The subject is typically given two or three trials with each hand. The average of all the trials administered for each hand serves as the individual's score.

Strengths

1. It can easily be administered in 5 minutes and is one of the tests utilized in the HRNB.
2. An individual's performance on this test can be compared to norms based on gender, age, and educational background.

Limitations

1. Individuals with orthopedic injuries, a history of arthritis in the hands, or peripheral neuropathy are likely to perform poorly on this test.
2. An individual's performance on this test should be corroborated by a review of their medical records and other neuropsychological test data.

Grooved Pegboard Test

Description

This test assesses the individual's fine motor coordination and manual dexterity. It consists of a small board that contains a total of 25 slotted holes in a 5 × 5 configuration. The pegs located in an adjacent metal dish are inserted into grooved slots. The subject is instructed to place the pegs in each of the slotted holes as quickly as possible using only one hand at a time. Scoring is determined by the amount of time the individual requires to complete the task with each hand. This test can be administered in 5 to 10 minutes.

Strengths

1. This test can be easily administered and scored.
2. An individual's performance on this test can be compared to norms for gender, age, and educational background.

Limitations

1. Poor performance on this test can be due to visual difficulties, physical or orthopedic difficulties, peripheral neuropathy, anxiety, depression, hysteria, medications, fatigue, or suboptimal motivation.
2. The reliability of this test to lateralize the site of brain damage to the left or right hemisphere has been seriously questioned.
3. Neuropsychologists need to be cautious when interpreting an individual's performance on this test, particularly if medical records are unavailable.

TESTS TO ASSESS LEARNING AND MEMORY

AUDITORY CONSONANT TRIGRAMS TEST

Description

This test assesses the individual's short-term memory by using a distraction task. Three letters (consonant trigrams) are orally presented at a rate of one letter per second. Immediately following this, the subject is orally presented with a three-digit number and asked to immediately begin subtracting out loud by the number three, or subtract by the number one. After delays of 9, 18, or 36 seconds, the examiner instructs the individual to immediately stop subtracting or counting backwards and to recall the three consonants that were originally presented.

Strengths

1. This test can evaluate an individual's verbal memory under conditions of distraction, as well as provide a means of assessing divided attentional processing skills.
2. Impaired performance on this test has been observed in a wide variety of neurological disorders.
3. This test can be administered in approximately 15 minutes.

Limitations

1. This test can be difficult to administer in a consistently standardized manner or in the same manner to each subject.
2. Poor performance on this test does not necessarily mean that an individual's short-term memory or divided attentional skills are impaired since motivational factors may play a role in test performance.
3. This test may not be appropriate for individuals who are hearing impaired or have a history of significant arithmetic difficulties.
4. Individuals who are significantly anxious or depressed at the time of testing are likely to perform poorly.

BENTON VISUAL RETENTION TEST

Description

This test consists of presenting ten cards containing up to three geometric figures. The subject's task is to draw the geometric figures on a separate sheet of paper after the card has been removed.

Strengths

1. This test has been found to discriminate between brain-damaged patients and normal controls with 60 to 70% accuracy and correctly categorize normal controls with 80 to 90% accuracy.
2. It is a relatively easy test to administer and score.

Limitations

1. Its ability to discriminate between brain-damaged and psychiatric patients is questionable.
2. Poor performance on this test can be caused by a variety of factors including anxiety, psychotic behavior, severe pain and discomfort, headache, fatigue, visual difficulties, constructional difficulties, suboptimal motivation, hysteria, and malingering.

3. The diagnosis of brain damage should not be made on the basis of poor performance on this test unless it is supported by the individual's clinical and medical history and other neuropsychological test data.

BRIEF VISUOSPATIAL MEMORY TEST — REVISED

Description

This test assesses the individual's immediate recall rate, acquisition, delayed recall, and recognition of visual information.

Strengths

1. This test contains six equivalent forms for serial testing.
2. It can be administered in approximately 15 minutes.
3. It contains data on the proportion of normal subjects and patients with neurological disorders who fall within the various score ranges.
4. It appears to be sensitive to cerebral pathology.

Limitations

1. Individuals who are visually, auditorially, or motorically impaired should not be administered this test.
2. Individuals who are significantly anxious, depressed, or psychotic at the time of testing may do poorly.
3. This test does not have any built-in measures to assess the individual's motivation while taking this test.

BUSCHKE SELECTIVE REMINDING TEST

Description

This test consists of presenting the individual with a list of words. After the list is presented, the individual must recall as many words as possible from the list. Words that are not recalled are repeated by the examiner on the next trial. Trials are continued until the individual is able to repeat the entire list.

Strengths

1. It has been used to assess brain-damaged patients.
2. Brain-damaged patients frequently show impaired learning over trials.

Limitations

1. Poor performance can reflect attentional difficulties, hearing loss, anxiety, depression, physical pain and discomfort, anticonvulsants or antipsychotic medications, headaches, chronic medical conditions, low premorbid intellectual functioning, chronic alcohol use, hysteria, or malingering.
2. This test is not widely used.

CALIFORNIA VERBAL LEARNING TEST — II

Description

This test consists of two 16-item word lists that contain four words from each of four different semantic categories. The test measures both the patient's recall and recognition of the word list over five learning trials. It was designed to be given to individuals ranging in age from 16 to 89. It takes about 50 minutes to administer.

Strengths

1. This test tends to identify the cognitive strategy used by subjects who are asked to learn and recall verbal material. As a consequence, it may be helpful in planning cognitive rehabilitation strategies for individuals with significant memory deficits.
2. The test manuals are well written and provide interpretative guidelines for various derived scores.
3. A computer program has been developed to assist the neuropsychologist in evaluating an individual's performance on this test.

Limitations

1. The norms for the second edition are better than the first edition.
2. It was not designed to identify individuals who are malingering.

CALIFORNIA VERBAL LEARNING TEST — CHILDREN'S VERSION

Description

This version of the test was designed to be administered to individuals ranging in age from 5 to 16 years and 11 months. It takes 15 to 20 minutes to administer the test. Administration of the delayed recall is performed 20 minutes later.

Strengths

1. This test appears to be excellent at assessing verbal memory in children.
2. It can be helpful in predicting special education placement after brain injury.

Limitations

1. Its weak test–retest reliability does not support its use to determine whether a child's verbal memory has improved.
2. Interpretation of the test data is confusing.
3. Clinicians should not infer organic pathology if all the test scores do not fall into the normal range.

CHILDREN'S MEMORY SCALE

Description

This test was designed to assess learning and memory in children and adolescents. It can be administered to children between the ages 5 and 16 in 30 to 45 minutes.

Strengths

1. It provides a broad assessment of learning and memory in children and adolescents.
2. The test materials are well designed and user friendly.
3. The standardization sample appears to be large and well constructed.

Limitations

1. Manual scoring is difficult.
2. It contains few manipulative and ecologically relevant tasks.
3. The time necessary to administer may be problematic for younger children or for children or adolescents with limited stamina or behavioral problems.

CONTINUOUS VISUAL MEMORY TEST

Description

This test requires an individual to discriminate between new vs. old (repeatedly shown test stimuli) from a set of 112 complex designs that are presented in rapid sequence and require the subject to recognize old stimuli after a delay of 30 minutes.

Strengths

1. It appears to be well suited for individuals who have significant motoric impairments because this test does not require them to perform any tasks requiring drawing or construction.
2. Individuals with mild to moderate depression or other mild psychiatric conditions appear to perform normally.

Limitations

1. Caution should be used when interpreting the scores of individuals who have less than a high school education.
2. This test is inappropriate for individuals who have significant visual acuity difficulties or who have severe visual neglect.
3. The subject should not be administered any visual material during the 30-minutes waiting time prior to the delayed recognition task. The presentation of visual material during this period of time is likely to confound an interpretation of the individual's performance on this test.
4. Individuals with limited intellectual functioning, who are severely cognitively impaired, or who have significant psychiatric problems should not be given this test since they may not comprehend the test instructions or pay significant attention to the test stimuli that are shown to them.
5. Individuals with significant attentional deficit disorders or frontal lobe pathology may respond impulsively to the test stimuli and perform poorly.

RECOGNITION MEMORY TEST

Description

This test consists of a target list of 50 stimulus pictures that are shown to the subject one at a time. The subject is asked to judge whether the word or picture is pleasant. Immediately after the items are shown, the subject is given a forced-choice recognition test in which the items previously shown must be recognized. The subject's score on this test is the number of items correctly recognized on each task.

Strengths

1. This test can be easily administered in approximately 10 to 15 minutes.
2. This test does not require specific motor responses and therefore may be appropriate for individuals who are physically handicapped or hemiplegic.

Limitations

1. This test has no test–retest reliability data or parallel forms.
2. The verbal section of this test may not be appropriate for individuals who are severely dyslexic or who were raised in different cultural and linguistic environments.
3. It is inappropriate for individuals who have severe visual difficulties or who are blind.
4. It should also be administered along with other standardized memory tests, particularly when the examiner suspects that the test taker's motivation is suboptimal.

REY AUDITORY VERBAL LEARNING TEST

Description

This test consists of presenting a list of 15 familiar words to the subject after he or she is instructed to remember as many of these words as possible. After the entire list of words is presented, the subject must recall them in any order. The first list is presented a total of five times. After the subject has completed the fifth trial, the examiner presents a new list of 15 words. Once again, the subject has been instructed to remember as many words as possible. Immediately after this, the subject is instructed to recall as many words as possible from the original list.

Strengths

1. This test has been reported to be effective in discriminating between normal adults and neurologic patients.
2. This test can be administered in 10 to 15 minutes and is relatively easy to score.

Limitations

1. Poor performance on this test can be due to a variety of non-neurological factors.
2. Poor performance on this test should be corroborated by the individual's medical records and other neuropsychological test data.

REY–OSTERRIETH COMPLEX FIGURE TEST

Description

This test consists of instructing the subject to copy a complex geometric figure on a sheet of white paper. The subject's ability to draw this figure from memory is assessed after a delay of approximately 3 minutes and again after a delay of approximately 30 minutes.

Strengths

1. This test can be easily administered and scored.
2. Individuals with predominantly right-hemisphere brain damage tend to perform more poorly on this test than individuals with predominantly left-hemisphere brain damage.

3. Individuals with diffuse brain damage tend to perform more poorly on this test than patients with chronic psychiatric conditions.
4. This test appears to be sensitive to traumatic brain injury and drug use.

Limitations

1. Poor performance on this test can be due to a variety of non-neurological factors.
2. Poor performance on this test should be consistent with the individual's medical records and other neuropsychological test data.

RIVERMEAD BEHAVIORAL MEMORY TEST — SECOND EDITION

Description

This test consists of 12 tests that are based on the study of memory problems frequently experienced in traumatically brain-injured patients. This test can be given in approximately 25 minutes.

Strengths

1. This test appears to be a useful complement to many of the traditional memory assessment tests.
2. It appears to be ecologically valid and predicts everyday memory functioning.
3. It may be helpful in predicting whether patients who have sustained severe traumatic brain injuries can live independently.
4. It does not appear to be significantly affected by the effects of anxiety or depression.

Limitations

1. It is not sensitive to mild traumatic brain injuries.
2. It may not be particularly sensitive to specific types of memory deficits.
3. It should be utilized in conjunction with standardized memory tests.

RUFF-LIGHT LEARNING TEST

Description

This test assesses visuospatial learning and memory in adults. It can be administered to individuals whose ages range from 16 to 70. It can usually be administered to neurologically intact individuals in 30 to 40 minutes. Brain-impaired individuals may take as long as an hour. Long-term recall is assessed after a 60-minute delay.

Strengths

1. The two versions of this test have high test–retest reliability.
2. This test has been found to be effective in distinguishing individuals who have sustained damage to their right hemisphere.

Limitations

1. Clinical uses of this test are limited by the background and expertise of the examiner.
2. Interpretations of the test scores should not be attempted without a clear understanding of brain–behavior relationships.

Wide Range Assessment of Memory and Learning — Second Edition

Description

It was designed to assess memory skills in children and adults. The age range of the second edition was extended to adulthood. It can be administered in just under an hour. The screening battery can be given in 20 minutes.

Strengths

1. The second edition of this test is considerably better than the first edition.
2. The manual is well written and provides an exhaustive review of the psychometric properties of the test.
3. The test allows for continuity between children and adults, which is a necessity in longitudinal studies or for retesting.

Limitations

1. There is no evidence that it can distinguish between different types of memory disorders in children or adults.
2. It is questionable whether this test is capable of monitoring changes in memory functioning over time.
3. No work has been done to determine its ecological validity.

Wechsler Memory Scale — Revised

Description

This test assesses an individual's memory for verbal and nonverbal stimuli, meaningful and abstract material, under conditions of both immediate and delayed recall. It was designed to evaluate memory functioning in individuals ranging in age from 16 to 74 years.

Strengths

1. It has been the most widely used test to assess memory.
2. The administration and scoring of this test is relatively straightforward.
3. This test possesses adequate normative data and reliability.

Limitations

1. This test has been harshly criticized for inadequately assessing memory deficits.
2. Poor scores on this test are frequently made by individuals whose native language is not English or who have low premorbid IQs.
3. This test does not evaluate remote or olfactory memory.
4. Poor performance on this test can reflect factors such as anxiety, depression, psychotic thinking, pain, fatigue, medications, hysteria, or suboptimal motivation.

Wechsler Memory Scale — Third Edition

Description

This test assesses an individual's memory for visual and verbal stimuli under conditions of immediate and delayed recall. It was designed to evaluate the memory functioning of individuals ranging in age from 16 to 89.

Strengths

1. The norms on this test are superior to the norms of its predecessor.
2. It is relatively easy to administer and score.

Limitations

1. Individuals who are retested within a 6-week interval improve considerably in their delayed memory scores.
2. Emotional factors such as depression are likely to affect performance.
3. Because it can take as long as 2 hours to administer to a brain-injured patient, many neuropsychologists are reluctant to administer the full battery.
4. This test may not be appropriate for individuals who are hearing impaired or who have a speech disability.
5. When this test is administered to individuals who are not fluent in English or for whom English is the second language, any attempt to translate the test on an individual basis may render the normative data invalid.

TESTS TO ASSESS ABSTRACT THINKING

PROVERBS TEST

Description

This test presents the individual with 12 proverbs of equivalent difficulty. The individual is required to write out what the proverb means. A 3-point scoring system is used depending on the level of abstract thinking contained in the responses. There is also a multiple-choice version of this test that requires the patient to pick one of four possible answers.

Strengths

1. Individuals who sustain either diffuse or predominantly frontal lobe brain injuries typically do poorly on this test.
2. This test is relatively easy to administer and score.

Limitations

1. Individuals who have been raised in a different cultural background or whose native language is not English will often have difficulty interpreting the proverbs.
2. Individuals who are psychotic may provide bizarre interpretations.
3. Individuals with low premorbid intellectual functioning or limited educational backgrounds may not fully understand what a proverb is.

SIMILARITIES TEST

Description

This test presents the individual with words that represent common objects (e.g., table and chair) or concepts (e.g., democracy and monarchy). The subject is asked how the objects are alike. Scoring is based on a 3-point scale.

Strengths

1. This test appears to possess high test–retest reliability.
2. Poor scores on this test tend to be associated with left temporal and frontal lobe pathology.
3. An individual's score on this test tends to be vulnerable to the effects of dementia.

Limitations

1. This test is inappropriate for individuals who have been raised in a different cultural background or whose native language is not English.
2. It is inappropriate for individuals who are psychotic or severely depressed at the time of testing.
3. A diagnosis of brain damage should not be made solely on the individual's performance on this test.

TESTS TO ASSESS CONCEPTUAL THINKING/PROBLEM-SOLVING SKILLS

CATEGORY TEST

Description

This test assesses the individual's conceptual thinking and problem-solving skills. The individual is shown 208 stimulus cards and must decide whether the card represents the number 1, 2, 3, or 4. The subject is provided immediate feedback as to whether the answers are correct or incorrect. Based on this feedback, the subject must determine the underlying principle on each of the seven subtests.

Strengths

1. This test is considered to be one of the most sensitive tests in the Halstead–Reitan Battery to detect the presence of brain impairment.
2. It possesses high test–retest reliability and good validity.

Limitations

1. It tends to be insensitive to individuals who have sustained predominantly orbitofrontal lobe brain damage.
2. An individual's performance on this test appears to be influenced by age, educational background, and premorbid level of intellectual functioning.
3. It can take as long as 2 hours to administer this test.
4. An individual's performance on this test needs to be corroborated by his or her medical records and other neuropsychological test data.
5. It may not be appropriate for individuals who have significant visual or hearing impairments or are significantly anxious, depressed, or psychotic at the time of testing.

RAVEN PROGRESSIVE MATRICES TEST

Description

This is a test of conceptual thinking and problem solving. Individuals are presented with a rectangle containing a set of designs with one part missing. They must decide which one of the six or eight parts located directly below the figure correctly completes the design. This test consists of 60 items that are broken down into five sets of 12 items of increasing conceptual difficulty.

Strengths

1. It serves as a relatively culture-free test of intellectual functioning.
2. It is relatively easy to administer and score.

3. It possesses adequate test–retest reliability, even when testings occur as long as 6 or 12 months apart.
4. It is well suited for individuals whose native language is not English or who are aphasic or hearing or motorically impaired.

Limitations

1. It should not be administered to individuals who have significant visual impairments or severe visual neglect.
2. An individual's score on this test should be corroborated by preinjury academic records and achievements and other neuropsychological test data.

Ruff Figural Fluency Test

Description

This test requires the patient to generate as many words as possible beginning with specific letters of the alphabet. It examines the individual's capacity for fluid and divergent thinking and ability to shift cognitive sets.

Strengths

1. This test can be easily administered in approximately 10 minutes.
2. Validity studies have demonstrated its sensitivity to individuals who have sustained severe traumatic brain injuries.

Limitations

1. This test does not appear to be appropriate for individuals with significant motor deficits, particularly involving dominant hand, or individuals with significant visual impairments.
2. Individuals with high levels of anxiety or who are significantly depressed at the time of testing may perform poorly on this test.
3. This test has no built-in way of determining whether the individual is performing optimally.

Wisconsin Card Sorting Test

Description

This test evaluates the individual's problem-solving skills, cognitive flexibility, ability to maintain a particular conceptual set, and concept formation. The subject is presented with a maximum of 128 cards that must be matched to one of four cards according to one of three categories (color, form, or number). The subject is informed whether correct or incorrect after each sorting response. The subject must deduce the underlying principle based on this feedback.

Strengths

1. This test has been shown to be sensitive to dorsolateral lesions of the frontal lobe.
2. Validity studies using this test have demonstrated an overall hit rate of 72% in its ability to discriminate between brain-damaged patients and normal controls.

Limitations

1. It appears to be relatively insensitive to orbitofrontal lobe damage.
2. Poor performance on this test can reflect visual impairment, color blindness, visual perceptual difficulties, impaired hearing, psychotic thinking, severe depression or anxiety, histrionic behavior, or suboptimal motivation.

3. An individual's performance on this test should be compared with the results of other neuropsychological tests of problem solving and concept formation.
4. Poor performance on this test is not necessarily indicative of frontal lobe pathology.
5. Bright individuals may do poorly on this task, particularly if they develop a complicated strategy during testing.

TESTS AND MEASURES TO ASSESS THE EXECUTIVE FUNCTIONS OF THE BRAIN

BEHAVIORAL ASSESSMENT OF THE DYSEXECUTIVE SYNDROME

Description

This test consists of a collection of six novel tests that are similar to real world activities that are likely to be problematic for individuals who have impaired executive functions.

Strengths

1. This test appears to be a useful tool to evaluate the executive functions of individuals who have sustained severe traumatic brain injuries.
2. This test has been found to be a better predictor of an individual's executive functions in real-world situations than have other neuropsychological tests.

Limitations

1. This test may not be sensitive to individuals who have sustained mild traumatic brain injuries.
2. Individuals who are depressed, have significant hearing, motor, or visual impairments, or are significantly anxious may perform poorly on this test.

BEHAVIOR RATING INVENTORY OF EXECUTIVE FUNCTION

Description

This test was designed to assess the executive functioning of children. It relies on questionnaires that are completed by teacher and parents. It can be used on children and adolescents ranging in age from 5 to 18. It also has a preschool version that can be given to children from age of 2 to just under 6 years of age. The raters are asked to rate a child or adolescent using a 3-point scale. It usually takes 10 to 15 minutes to complete the test.

Strengths

1. Overall inter-rater reliability coefficients are generally good.
2. It appears to be a psychometrically sound instrument that has been well designed.
3. The manual is well written.

Limitations

1. Clinical studies have only examined the parent form.
2. The normative sample has an uneven number of subjects in each normative age group.

DELIS–KAPLAN EXECUTIVE FUNCTION SYSTEM

Description

This test battery has been designed to detect relatively subtle and mild forms of executive dysfunction utilizing a process-oriented test approach. It can be administered to individuals whose ages range from 8 to 89 years in about 90 minutes.

Strengths

1. It has been designed to assess various dimensions of the executive functions of the brain.
2. Alternative forms of the test are available.

Limitations

1. The test–retest reliability of this test varies from low to high.
2. The test scores are affected by practice effects.
3. It is not clear whether this test can distinguish between different executive dysfunction profiles.

FRONTAL SYSTEMS BEHAVIORAL SCALE

Description

This rating scale was designed to measure behaviors that are commonly seen with damage to the frontal lobes and the executive functions of the brain. It tries to get the patient and family to identify neurobehavioral symptoms that may not be seen on neuropsychological testing. It can be given to individuals whose ages range from 18 to 95.

Strengths

1. It allows multiple observers to rate changes in the patient's behavior in natural settings.
2. It supplements neuropsychological test data that often contain little information about the patient's neurobehavioral functioning in natural settings.
3. It appears sensitive to frontal lobe pathology and executive dysfunction.

Limitations

1. Self ratings by the patient make little sense since patients with frontal lobe damage are usually unaware of any changes in their behavior.
2. The ratings are also sensitive to pathology in nonfrontal areas of the brain.

RUFF NEUROBEHAVIORAL INVENTORY

Description

This self-report questionnaire was designed to measure the current psychological status of individuals whose lives have been altered by a catastrophic event such as traumatic brain injury or spinal cord injury. It can assist the clinician identify specific areas that have been affected and areas that have been preserved. It can be given to individuals of both sexes whose ages range between 18 and 75 years of age.

Strengths

1. It probes deeper into the patient's concerns, functioning, and strengths than traditional psychological tests.

2. This test, unlike most psychological tests, was designed for individuals who have sustained neurological trauma.
3. It can provide clinicians with relevant information about their patients.

Limitations

1. Its correlations with other psychological tests tend to be low since it appears to be measuring different issues and problems.
2. Test–retest reliability coefficients tend to be low.

TESTS TO ASSESS PERSONALITY/EMOTIONAL ADJUSTMENT

BECK ANXIETY INVENTORY

Description

This test consists of 21 descriptive statements of anxiety symptoms that are rated on a 4-point scale. Scoring of this test consists of adding up the numerical scores for each of the 21 symptoms.

Strengths

1. This test can be administered in 5 to 10 minutes.
2. This test appears to have fairly good test–retest reliability.

Limitations

1. An individual's score on this test can be intentionally inflated because of its obvious face validity.
2. An individual's score on this particular test should be consistent with other personality tests, the behavioral observations of the examiner, and medical records.

THE BECK DEPRESSION INVENTORY

Description

This test contains 21 forced-choice statements that assess depressive symptoms. The patient's total score is the sum of the numbers circled for the 21 test items.

Strengths

1. This test can be easily administered to assess an individual's subjective symptoms of depression.
2. This test appears to have excellent test–retest reliability and to have fairly high concurrent validity coefficients with other measures of depression.

Limitations

1. Individuals involved in litigation or being evaluated by the courts may purposely test as severely impaired because of its obvious face validity.
2. Individuals who sustain severe traumatic brain injuries may not test as depressed because of poor awareness of cognitive and emotional problems.
3. This test was not specifically designed to evaluate depression in the elderly.

DETAILED ASSESSMENT OF POSTTRAUMATIC STRESS

Description

This test has been designed to evaluate individuals who have been exposed to a significant psychological stressor or trauma. It has been developed to help identify adults who have an acute or posttraumatic stress disorder. It consists of 104 test items that can be completed in 15 to 20 minutes.

Strengths

1. It provides a very detailed assessment of the various symptoms associated with either an acute or posttraumatic stress disorder.
2. It is relatively easy to administer.
3. Computer software is available for both test administration and scoring.

Limitations

1. Other psychological tests need to be administered since this test does not assess psychiatric symptoms such as anxiety, depression, and psychosis.
2. Clinicians should be careful not to make the diagnosis of a traumatic disorder based entirely on the test result.
3. Individuals who are malingering can obtain profiles that are generally consistent with posttraumatic disorder.

MILLON CLINICAL MULTIAXIAL INVENTORY — III

Description

This personality inventory contains 175 questions that require the individual to respond in a true/false format.

Strengths

1. An individual's scores on this test have been found to be moderately correlated to the diagnostic criteria set forth in the *Diagnostic and Statistical Manual of Mental Disorders*.
2. It is relatively easy to administer and can usually be completed by most individuals in approximately 30 minutes.
3. It attempts to directly assess preexisting personality traits or disorders.
4. Computerized narrative reports are commercially available.
5. Research studies have demonstrated its validity and reliability.

Limitations

1. This test was not designed to diagnose brain damage.
2. It may not accurately assess preexisting personality traits or disorders.
3. An individual's profile on this test should be corroborated by other neuropsychological tests, medical records, and interviews with significant others.
4. It is not suitable for individuals who have limited reading and vocabulary skills since it requires eighth-grade reading comprehension skills.

Minnesota Multiphasic Personality Inventory — II

Description

This test is the most widely used personality inventory to assess an individual's level of psychological adjustment. It contains 567 items that can be answered in a true or false manner. It can be given to individuals whose ages range from 18 to 89 years of age. It usually takes 1 to 2 hours to complete.

Strengths

1. This test has built-in validity scales to determine whether the individual is exaggerating or minimizing his or her psychological problems.
2. It appears to be sensitive to a variety of personality disorders and psychiatric problems.
3. It has adequate reliability and validity.
4. It is the most widely used test to assess an individual's psychological and emotional functioning.

Limitations

1. Clinical interpretations should be made with caution if the patient is brain damaged.
2. It should not be used to diagnose brain damage.
3. The MMPI-1 requires a minimum of a sixth-grade level of reading comprehension.
4. Psychologists should not permit an individual to take the test home since there is no way of determining whether this individual may have consulted with others or textbooks while taking this test, or whether or not the test was actually completed by them.

Minnesota Multiaxial Personality Inventory — Adolescent (MMPI-A)

Description

The MMPI-A was developed for adolescents between the ages 14 and 18 and contains 478 items. It usually takes about 90 minutes to complete.

Strengths

1. It was specifically designed for adolescents.
2. It relies on many of the items contained in the MMPI.

Limitations

1. Clinical interpretations should be made by clinicians who have a background in clinical psychology and clinical measurement.
2. This test should not be used to diagnose individuals with a suspected brain injury.
3. Some of the clinical scales are sensitive to cognitive difficulties and are likely to produce an invalid profile.

Personality Assessment Inventory

Description

This self-administered objective test of personality and psychopathology contains 344 test items that comprise 22 nonoverlapping scales.

Strengths

1. This test appears to be psychometrically superior to the MMPI-2 and possesses a wide range of clinical domains.
2. Individuals who are proficient at reading at only the fourth-grade level can be administered this test.
3. It appears to have good test–retest reliability and good concurrent validity with other widely used personality inventories and measures.
4. Since the test items are straightforward, this test can usually be completed in approximately 45 minutes.
5. A computerized interpretative profile and narrative report is commercially available and can assist the psychologist in scoring and interpreting the test data.

Limitations

1. This test was not designed to determine whether an individual has brain damage and therefore should not be used for this purpose.
2. Caution should be exercised in testing patients whose first and native language is not English.
3. Individuals with impaired cognitive abilities as a result of brain damage, recent drug use, withdrawal from drugs or alcohol, or exposure to toxic chemicals, or who are disoriented due to a neurological disorder or disease should be tested with caution.
4. This test may not be appropriate for patients who are confused, exhibit psychomotor retardation, are easily distracted, or are under extreme emotional distress at the time of testing.
5. This test may not be appropriate for individuals who have visual field cuts or significant visual handicaps.
6. An individual's profile on this test should be compared with other personality measures to determine its validity.

TRAUMA SYMPTOM INVENTORY

Description

This inventory was designed to assess acute and chronic symptoms of psychological trauma. It can be given to individuals who are 18 years and older. It can usually be completed in 20 minutes.

Strengths

1. This test evaluates a patient's psychological response to trauma.
2. Computer software is available to score the test data.

Limitations

1. Other psychological tests should be given since this test does not fully describe the individual's psychiatric symptoms.
2. This test can easily be manipulated by bright individuals in medi-legal cases.
3. A diagnosis of posttraumatic stress disorder should only be made when it is supported by the patient's clinical history, psychiatric records, and other psychological tests.

Index